Baja
California

Wayne Bernhardson

Baja California

4th edition

Published by
Lonely Planet Publications
Head Office: PO Box 617, Hawthorn, Vic 3122, Australia
Branches: 150 Linden St, Oakland, CA 94607, USA
10a Spring Place, London NW5 3BH, UK
1 rue du Dahomey, 75011 Paris, France

Printed by
Colorcraft Ltd, Hong Kong

Photographs by

Ross Barnet	Rick Gerharter	Jennifer Johnsen	Michael Sullivan
Wayne Bernhardson	Robert Holmes	Robert Raburn	Seena Sussman

Front cover: Bahía Concepción, Robert Holmes

First Published
March 1988

This Edition
January 1998

Although the author and publisher have tried to make the information as accurate as possible, they accept no responsibility for any loss, injury or inconvenience sustained by any person using this book.

National Library of Australia Cataloguing in Publication Data

Bernhardson, Wayne.
Baja California.

4th ed.
Includes index.
ISBN 0 86442 445 0.

1. Baja California (Mexico) – Guidebooks. I. Title.

917.2204836

Wayne Bernhardson

Born in Fargo, North Dakota, Wayne Bernhardson grew up in Tacoma, Washington, and earned a PhD in geography at the University of California, Berkeley. He has traveled widely in Latin America and lived for extended periods in Chile, Argentina and the Falkland (Malvinas) Islands.

His other Lonely Planet credits include *Argentina, Uruguay & Paraguay*, *Buenos Aires*, *Chile & Easter Island*, *South America on a shoestring* and *Rocky Mountain States*. Wayne resides in Oakland, California, with his affectionate Alaskan malamute, Gardel.

MARÍA MASSOLO

From the Author

Reynaldo and Marta Ayala of Calexico, California, deserve special mention for their hospitality and for their knowledge of the border area in general and Mexicali in particular. Sergio Gracia Valencia and Carlos Guillén of Secture's Mexicali office promptly and conscientiously replied to numerous supplementary requests for information.

Tom and Margarita Melville contributed several important insights on the San Quintín area, as did Jim and Susie Atkinson. Carolina Shepard of the Museo de la Naturaleza y de la Cultura en Bahía de los Angeles graciously reviewed the section on her adopted home and allowed me to work in the museum after hours. Serge Dedina of The Nature Conservancy in Tucson, Arizona, brought me up to date on conservation issues in the Desierto Central. Lucero Gutiérrez of INAH, now resident in Cabo San Lucas, reviewed the material on Desierto Central rock art and offered several useful comments.

Other notable contributions came from Steve and Linda Sullivan of The People's Gallery in San Felipe, Miguel and Claudia Quintana of Mulegé Divers, Roy Mahoff and Becky Aparicio of Baja Tropicales at Bahía Concepción, Trudi Angell of Las Parras Tour in Loreto, Oscar Padilla of the Coordinación Estatal de Turismo in La Paz, Janet Howey of El Tecolote Libros in Todos Santos, Pepe and Libby Murrieta and Fidencio Romero of Cabo Pulmo and Hugh Kramer of Discover Baja Travel Club.

Robert, Pat and Pasha Raburn once again hosted and entertained Gardel in Oakland during my field research in Baja.

This book is dedicated to the memory of James J Parsons (1912 – 97), always an enthusiastic mentor and valued friend.

From the Publisher

The following individuals helped make this 4th edition possible. Laura Harger edited and indexed the manuscript (with feedback from Kate Hoffman and Carolyn Hubbard), and Kate and Sandra Lopen Barker proofread it. Sacha Pearson proofed maps and helped with indexing. Cyndy Johnsen redrew and corrected the maps (under Alex Guilbert's supervision), and she also designed the book (with help from Scott Summers). Diana Nankin and Henia Miedzinski both assisted on the maps. Lisa Summers, Scott Summers, Hugh D'Andrade and Ann Jeffree drew the illustrations, and Hugh designed the cover.

This Book

Wayne Bernhardson researched and wrote this 4th edition of *Baja California* as well as the previous (3rd) edition. Scott Wayne researched and wrote the first two editions of the book, and some of his observations and suggestions remain in these pages.

Warning & Request

Things change – prices go up, schedules change, good places go bad and bad places go bankrupt – nothing stays the same. If you find things better or worse, recently opened or long since closed, please tell us and help make the next edition even more accurate and useful.

We value all of the feedback we receive from travelers. A small team reads and acknowledges every letter, postcard and email, and ensures that every morsel of information finds its way to the appropriate authors, editors and publishers. All readers who write us will find their names in the next edition of the appropriate guide and will also receive a free subscription to our quarterly newsletter *Planet Talk*. The very best contributions will be rewarded with a free Lonely Planet guide.

Excerpts from your correspondence may appear in new editions of this guide; in *Planet Talk*; or in the Postcards section of our website. Please let us know if you don't want your letter published or your name acknowledged.

Thanks

Many thanks to the travelers who used the last edition and wrote to us with helpful hints, useful advice and interesting anecdotes. Your names follow:

JE Beaulne (M), David Berger (USA), AH & SJ Boon van Ostade (NL), Steve Bowers (USA), Jill Buckingham (NZ), Beat Buehlmann (CH), Luigi Cerri (I), Roberto Concha (USA), Rita Crouch (A), James Curtiss & Andrea Tomba (M), Joanna Degnall & J Richard McGinnis (USA), William J Doris (UK), Víctor García (E), Rick Gerharter (USA), J Wayne Gillman (USA), June Ginger (USA), Wolf Gotthilf (D), Mabel Haourt (C), YM Heng (UK), Elaine Hopper (USA), David Huntsinger (USA), Peter Kalberer (USA), Steven Koenig (USA), Dean Larsen (C), Harvey Lozano (USA), Susan Lynch (USA), Ricardo Martínez (M), Brent Matsuda (C), Mario Menghini Pecci (M), Kevin Okell & Janine Bentley (UK), Sergio & Helle Pacinotti (DK), Myra Rudin (USA), Rebecca Shell (M), Clifford Wallis & Shawn Joynt (A), Nicola Watson (UK), Steve Wilson (USA), Karin & Les Wright (UK), Nancy Wright (C), Nerissa Wu (USA).

A (Australia), C (Canada), CH (Switzerland), D (Germany), DK (Denmark), E (Spain), I (Italy), M (Mexico), NL (Netherlands), NZ (New Zealand), UK (United Kingdom), USA (United States of America)

Contents

INTRODUCTION **9**

FACTS ABOUT BAJA CALIFORNIA **11**

History.................. 11
Geography............... 19
Climate.................. 21
Ecology & Environment 23
Flora & Fauna............ 23

Government & Politics 31
Economy 32
Population & People 33
Education................. 34
Arts 34

Society & Conduct 36
Religion................. 37
Language................ 38

FACTS FOR THE VISITOR **39**

Planning................. 39
Highlights 40
Tourist Offices............ 41
Visas & Documents........ 42
Consulates............... 44
Customs................. 45
Money.................. 46
Post & Communications 48
Books................... 50
Newspapers & Magazines.... 53
Radio & TV.............. 54

Photography 54
Time 55
Electricity 55
Weights & Measures....... 55
Laundry................. 55
Health 55
Women Travelers 64
Dangers & Annoyances...... 64
Legal Matters 67
Business Hours &
Public Holidays........... 67

Special Events............ 68
Language Courses 68
Work 69
Accommodations.......... 69
Food.................... 69
Drinks 72
Entertainment 73
Spectator Sports 74
Things to Buy 76

OUTDOOR ACTIVITIES **78**

On & In the Water......... 78
On Land................. 80

Study Programs &
Expeditions 80

Organized Tours 81

GETTING THERE & AWAY... **87**

Air 87
Land.................... 90

Sea..................... 92
Departure Taxes 93

Warning................. 93

GETTING AROUND **94**

Air 94
Bus..................... 95
Car..................... 95

Motorcycle 100
Bicycle.................. 100
Hitchhiking 100

Walking................. 101
Local Transportation....... 101

LA FRONTERA **102**

Tijuana.................. 102
Tecate.................. 124
Around Tecate........... 129
Tijuana-Ensenada
Corridor................. 130
Playas de Rosarito........ 131
Around Playas de Rosarito . . 137
Ensenada 139
Around Ensenada 152
Guadalupe 154

Parque Nacional
Constitución de 1857....... 155
El Alamo &
Valle de Trinidad.......... 156
Maneadero............... 157
Ejido Uruapán 157
Santo Tomás 157
Ejido Eréndira &
Puerto San Isidro.......... 158
San Vicente 158

Colonet 159
San Telmo & Rancho Meling . 159
Parque Nacional
Sierra San Pedro Mártir..... 160
Around Parque Nacional
Sierra San Pedro Mártir..... 162
Colonia Vicente Guerrero ... 162
San Quintín 163
El Rosario 169
Around El Rosario......... 170

DESIERTO DEL COLORADO 171

Mexicali 171
Around Mexicali 185
Los Algodones 187
San Felipe 188
Puertecitos 196
South of Puertecitos 197

DESIERTO CENTRAL & LLANO DE MAGDALENA 198

Misión San Fernando 198
El Mármol 199
Cataviña 200
Bahía San Luis Gonzaga 201
Bahía de los Angeles 202
Santa Rosalillita 206
Rosarito 206
Misión San Borja 206
Paralelo 28 206
Guerrero Negro 207
Around Guerrero Negro 211
Bahía San Francisquito 212
Isla Cedros 213
Around Isla Cedros 215
Península Vizcaíno 215
San Ignacio 216
Around San Ignacio 217
Santa Rosalía 221
Around Santa Rosalía 227
Mulegé 227
Around Mulegé 232
Bahía Concepción 233
San Isidro-La Purísima 234
Around San Isidro-
La Purísima 235
Loreto 236
Around Loreto 242
Llano de Magdalena 244
Puerto López Mateos 245
Ciudad Constitución 245
Puerto San Carlos 248
Around the Llano
de Magdalena 249
El Cien 250

CAPE REGION 251

La Paz 251
Around La Paz 266
Eastern Cape 267
El Triunfo & San Antonio . . . 268
Los Barriles & Buena Vista . 268
Around Los Barriles &
Buena Vista 271
La Rivera 271
Punta Colorada 272
Cabo Pulmo 272
Bahía Los Fraires 272
Central Cape 273
Santiago 273
Around Santiago 273
Miraflores & Caduaño 274
Southern Cape 275
San José del Cabo 275
Around San José del Cabo . . 284
Los Cabos Corridor 284
Cabo San Lucas 286
Western Cape 298
Todos Santos 298
Around Todos Santos 303

INTERNET DIRECTORY 304

SPANISH FOR TRAVELERS 307

GLOSSARY 312

INDEX 316

Maps 316
Text 316

Map Legend

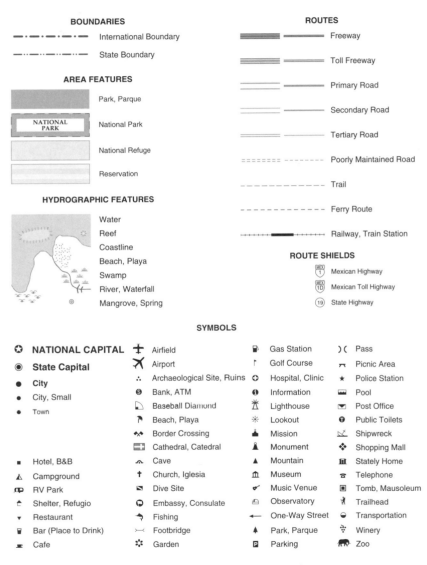

BOUNDARIES

— · — · — · — · — International Boundary

— · · — · · — · · — State Boundary

AREA FEATURES

Park, Parque

NATIONAL PARK — National Park

National Refuge

Reservation

HYDROGRAPHIC FEATURES

Water

Reef

Coastline

Beach, Playa

Swamp

River, Waterfall

Mangrove, Spring

ROUTES

Freeway

Toll Freeway

Primary Road

Secondary Road

Tertiary Road

Poorly Maintained Road

Trail

Ferry Route

Railway, Train Station

ROUTE SHIELDS

MEX 1 — Mexican Highway

MEX 1D — Mexican Toll Highway

19 — State Highway

SYMBOLS

☺ **NATIONAL CAPITAL**
◉ **State Capital**
● **City**
● City, Small
● Town

■ Hotel, B&B
▲ Campground
⬠ RV Park
⛺ Shelter, Refugio
▼ Restaurant
🍺 Bar (Place to Drink)
☕ Cafe

✈ Airfield
✈ Airport
∴ Archaeological Site, Ruins
⊖ Bank, ATM
⚾ Baseball Diamond
⛱ Beach, Playa
✦✦ Border Crossing
⊞ Cathedral, Catedral
⌒ Cave
† Church, Iglesia
⬟ Dive Site
⊙ Embassy, Consulate
🎣 Fishing
⊱⊰ Footbridge
⁂ Garden

⛽ Gas Station
⚑ Golf Course
⊕ Hospital, Clinic
ⓘ Information
⛪ Lighthouse
✳ Lookout
⛪ Mission
🏛 Monument
▲ Mountain
🏛 Museum
♪ Music Venue
⌂ Observatory
← One-Way Street
▲ Park, Parque
P Parking

)(Pass
⊓ Picnic Area
★ Police Station
▭ Pool
✉ Post Office
🚻 Public Toilets
⚓ Shipwreck
❖ Shopping Mall
🏛 Stately Home
☎ Telephone
■ Tomb, Mausoleum
🚶 Trailhead
● Transportation
⚲ Winery
🐗 Zoo

Note: Not all symbols displayed above appear in this book.

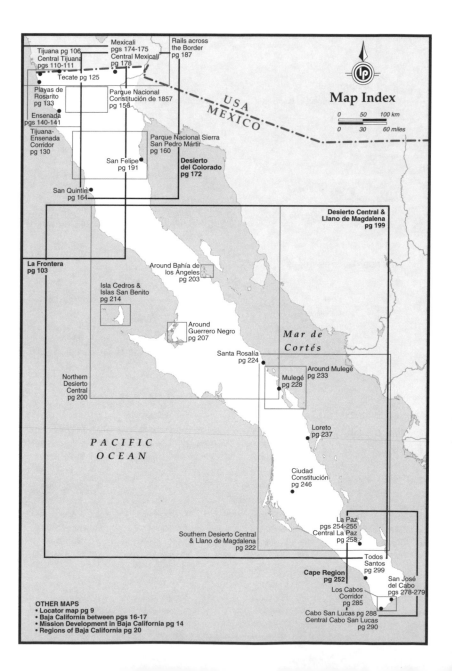

Map Index

0   50   100 km
0   30   60 miles

Tijuana pg 106
Central Tijuana pgs 110-111
Tecate pg 125
Mexicali pgs 174-175
Central Mexicali pg 178
Rails across the Border pg 187
Playas de Rosarito pg 133
Parque Nacional Constitución de 1857 pg 156
Ensenada pgs 140-141
Tijuana-Ensenada Corridor pg 130
Parque Nacional Sierra San Pedro Mártir pg 160
San Felipe pg 191
Desierto del Colorado pg 172
San Quintín pg 164
La Frontera pg 103
Desierto Central & Llano de Magdalena pg 199
Around Bahía de los Ángeles pg 203
Isla Cedros & Islas San Benito pg 214
Around Guerrero Negro pg 207
Santa Rosalía pg 224
Mar de Cortés
Northern Desierto Central pg 200
Mulegé pg 228
Around Mulegé pg 233
Loreto pg 237
PACIFIC OCEAN
Ciudad Constitución pg 246
La Paz pgs 254-255
Central La Paz pg 258
Southern Desierto Central & Llano de Magdalena pg 222
Todos Santos pg 299
Cape Region pg 252
San José del Cabo pgs 278-279
Los Cabos Corridor pg 285
Cabo San Lucas pg 288
Central Cabo San Lucas pg 290

OTHER MAPS
• Locator map pg 9
• Baja California between pgs 16-17
• Mission Development in Baja California pg 14
• Regions of Baja California pg 20

Introduction

Ever since the arrival of the first Spanish explorers in the 1530s, Baja California has been a land of extremes and, later, a land of escapes and escapades. Once thought to be an island, it remains isolated from mainland Mexico, but it now attracts millions of visitors and their dollars to its cities and towns, beaches, mountains and deserts. The Baja Peninsula, however, is much more than a winter amusement park for visitors from north of the border.

Baja California's Cochimí Indians, none of whom survive today, left memorable murals in caves and on canyon walls of the peninsula's central desert. For early European explorers, 'Baja' (its colloquial name among visitors) was both enticing and forbidding, as its coastline of white sandy beaches, tranquil bays and lagoons, and imposing headlands belied its harsh desert interior. Settlement attempts repeatedly failed until the late 17th century, when Jesuit priests succeeded in establishing self-sufficient missions, converting local Indians to Catholicism and teaching them to work the fields and build churches, all in the interest of 'civilizing' them. In less than a century, though, these missions began to collapse as the Indians fell prey to European diseases, and the Spanish crown expelled the Jesuits from the empire.

In the 19th century, ranchers and fishermen from the Mexican mainland settled parts of the peninsula. Prospectors discovered minerals and dug the first mines, prompting foreign companies to establish the first major port facilities and acquire huge tracts of land. Encouraged by major mining discoveries, outsiders poured in to make small fortunes, but most of the peninsula remained largely undeveloped and unaffected. When the mines closed in the early 20th century, many foreigners took the money and ran.

In the 20th century, Baja California became a land of escape. Some of the first to seek refuge were the Magonistas, a splinter group of revolutionaries and

9

mercenaries who briefly 'conquered' northern Baja while fleeing Mexican federal troops. Criminals from mainland Mexico also found remote Baja a good hideout, while Prohibition-era gamblers, drinkers and other 'sinners' from the USA could indulge their habits south of the border. New hotels, restaurants, racetracks, bullrings and casinos lured a new type of escapee – the US tourist.

Today, many of Baja's cities and towns are thriving as more than 50 million people visit some part of the peninsula each year. The popular border towns offer short, inexpensive escapes: shopping sprees in north-of-the-border-style malls and on the streets, sumptuous meals and exotic drinks. The 'escape' continues in bars and nightclubs and at the bullfights, jai alai matches and racetracks. During a fiesta or special event, the pace of celebration becomes frenetic. Visitors exhausted by all this activity can escape to the surrounding mountains, beaches or deserts, where the most popular activity is relaxing in the sun. Outdoor recreation opportunities are nearly limitless: horseback riding in the mountains or on the beach, scuba diving or snorkeling in the Gulf of California (Mar de Cortés), windsurfing, clamming, whale-watching, fishing, sailing, sea kayaking, bicycling, surfing and hiking.

This book describes Baja's most popular attractions but also offers hints on experiencing this exceptional destination beyond stereotypical tourist activities. Detailed, practical information describes everything from octopus tacos to budget accommodations, and the basics are rounded out with essential environmental, cultural and historical background.

A word on terminology: In late Spanish colonial times and under Mexican rule, the general term 'California' meant Baja California (Lower California), and the present US state of California, then a backwater, became known as Alta California (Upper California). Rather than use the latter term, an anachronism except in its historical context, this book will use the more appropriate (if not precisely accurate) term 'mainland California' to refer to areas north of the Mexican border. In many ways, the two form a single California whose political division is misleading – according to one analysis, more than 100,000 jobs in mainland California directly depend on exports to Mexico.

Modern Baja California consists of two separate states: Baja California (capital Mexicali) and Baja California Sur (capital La Paz). When necessary for clarity, this book refers to the individual states as Baja California Norte and Baja California Sur.

Facts about Baja California

HISTORY
First Peoples
At least 12,000 years ago and perhaps much earlier, one of the most significant human migrations occurred when the accumulated ice of the great polar and continental glaciers of the Pleistocene Epoch lowered sea levels around the world, and the ancestors of American Indians crossed from Siberia to Alaska via a land bridge across the Bering Strait. Over millennia, subsequent movements distributed the population southward throughout the Americas.

At least 10,000 years ago, according to radiocarbon dating of artifacts like shell middens, stone tools and arrowheads, descendants of these immigrants reached the Baja Peninsula by way of mainland California. Middens at Punta Minitas in northwestern Baja indicate that shellfish gathering was a key subsistence activity no later than 8000 years ago, but Baja's first peoples also subsisted by hunting, gathering and, later, rudimentary farming. A fluted point used for hunting large animals like mammoths, discovered near San Ignacio in Baja California's Desierto Central, dates from about 12,000 years ago.

Undoubtedly the most spectacular artifacts left by Baja's early inhabitants are their petroglyphs and cave paintings – hundreds or even thousands of rock art sites dot the peninsula from the US border to the tip of Cabo San Lucas. Some of these are abstract designs, while others are representations of humans and animals, reflecting the region's pre-Columbian hunting and gathering economy. The tradition continued even after European contact, as some works include such elements as pack animals and Christian crosses.

European Exploration of 'California'
In 1533 on a voyage commissioned by Hernán Cortés, the conqueror of New Spain (Mexico), mutineer Fortún Jiménez became the first Spaniard to set foot on the Baja Peninsula. Either Jiménez or a later explorer named Francisco de Bolaños applied the name 'California' to the peninsula after a mysterious island mentioned in a romantic narrative called *Las Sergas de Esplandián* (The Exploits of Esplandián), published in Seville by Garcí Ordóñez de Montalvo in 1510.

The precise etymology and meaning of the name 'California' have never been convincingly established, but in Ordóñez de Montalvo's fiction, a queen named Calafia ruled a race of gold-rich black Amazons; there is now consensus that her name eventually became 'California.' Baja's terrain resembled that of Ordóñez de Montalvo's fictional island. Even though a later voyage by Francisco de Ulloa in 1539 proved that it was a peninsula, Europeans did not abandon the idea that Baja was an island until Jesuit missionary Eusebio Kino, in several expeditions between 1699 and 1702 from present-day Arizona and Sonora, proved that it could be reached by land.

After defeating the Aztecs and occupying most of central Mexico, Cortés dispatched several expeditions in search of Calafia's riches. In 1532 Spanish navigator Diego Hurtado de Mendoza sailed north from Acapulco, but his two ships both disappeared shortly after departure. In 1533 the *Concepción* sailed from Tehuantepec in search of Hurtado de Mendoza and Calafia, but soon after leaving Acapulco, the crew mutinied and murdered captain Diego Becerra. Pilot Jiménez took charge, steering the ship into La Paz Bay, but most of the 22 mutineers died at the hands of Pericú Indians. The survivors, however, returned with a sample of black pearls that stimulated Cortés' own interest in Baja, and in 1535 he himself joined an expedition to the area.

With about 400 Spanish settlers, plus black slaves and horses, Cortés founded the colony of Santa Cruz at present-day

Bahía Pichilingue, an inlet of La Paz Bay, and stayed the rest of the year before returning to mainland New Spain. Until late 1536 or early 1537, the rest of the group tried to establish a permanent settlement, but hostile Indians and severe food and water shortages – most of the horses were probably eaten – caused its abandonment. For another century and a half, no Europeans settled in Baja.

In the interim, however, others explored the region. Despite contrary orders from Viceroy Antonio de Mendoza, Cortés sent Ulloa north from Acapulco in 1539. After sailing up the Gulf of California and learning that Baja was a peninsula, Ulloa rounded Cabo San Lucas and sailed up the Pacific coast as far as Bahía Magdalena, Isla Cedros and perhaps Punta Baja (near modern-day El Rosario) before returning south. In 1540 Hernando de Alarcón also reached the mouth of the Colorado River, and in 1542 Portuguese explorer Juan Rodríguez Cabrillo explored the Pacific coast and became the first European to set foot in mainland California. The Spanish crown granted licenses for pearling expeditions to the Gulf, but there were many unauthorized, clandestine voyages as well.

As Spain consolidated its control of New Spain, it also increased trade with the Philippines (which were under the jurisdiction of the Viceroyalty of New Spain). Laden with Asian luxuries like silk, perfumes and spices, as well as gold and silver, Spanish galleons sailing from Manila to Acapulco attracted bounty-hungry buccaneers like Englishman Thomas Cavendish. After Cavendish captured the prize galleon *Santa Ana* near Cabo San Lucas in November 1587, the Spaniards built a fortress there and occasionally dispatched vessels to deter privateers and to explore the coasts.

In 1602 Sebastián Vizcaíno, who had earlier led a pearling expedition to the Gulf, reexplored the Pacific coast as far as Cape Mendocino in mainland California. A major bay and a large desert in central Baja California still bear his name. In 1633 Francisco de Ortega, attracted by the discovery of black pearls near La Paz, sailed north to the mouth of the Colorado and produced one of the first maritime charts of the Gulf, but permanent European settlement awaited the arrival of Jesuit missionaries.

Baja California at Contact

When Europeans first reached the peninsula, upward of 48,000 mobile hunter-gatherers lived in an area comprising most of the modern states of Baja California and Baja California Sur; despite the early introduction of European diseases along the Gulf coast, this population remained fairly stable until the late 17th century. The Río Colorado delta, at the north end of the Gulf, supported a denser population of settled Yuman agriculturalists, perhaps an additional 6000 people.

The peoples of Baja belonged to three major linguistic groups, further subdivided into several tribal entities. North of the 31st parallel were Yuman-speaking peoples closely linked to those of southern mainland California; among them were the Diegueño or Dieguino (now commonly known as Tipai), Kamia or Kumiai (also known as Ipai), Paipai, Cucupah, Ñakipa and Kiliwa. To the south as far as the 26th parallel, the Cochimí were the most numerous of Peninsular Yuman-speaking groups, who also included Cadegomeño, Didiú (Edú), Laymón and Monqui peoples. To their south, non-Yuman speakers included the Guaycura, Cora, Huchití and Pericú.

All these peoples lived in groups that became known as *rancherías*, ranging in size from a few families to upward of 200 people; this term also applied to units linked to Spanish missions but living at a distance from them. Occupying fairly well-defined territories that ranged from the uplands of the central cordillera to the shores of the Gulf and the Pacific, these groups depended on game, wild plant foods (such as pine nuts and the fruit of the pitahaya cactus) and marine resources for their subsistence. In times of stress they even collected pitahaya seeds from their own excrement and toasted them in what Spaniards jokingly called their 'second harvest.'

In Baja's desert environments, Indian peoples usually lived in simple dwellings of local materials near a dependable, permanent water source such as a spring or stream. While groups in the north and south enjoyed a fairly dependable subsistence, by most accounts the Cochimí of central Baja, the peninsula's harshest desert, were often destitute. On the entire peninsula, Indians were too few and too dispersed for effective application of the *encomienda*, a system of forced labor and tribute that the Spanish crown instituted in mainland New Spain and other densely populated parts of the empire. Consequently, missionaries directed the colonization of California and, often unwittingly, brought about the demise of its aboriginal peoples.

Only in the northernmost part of the peninsula do Indian peoples still survive, herding livestock, fishing and building fences. Collecting pine nuts is still an important seasonal activity, and women still produce attractive basketry and pottery.

The Missions

In early 1683 Isidro de Atondo y Antillón, governor of Sinaloa in mainland New Spain, crossed the Gulf of California with Jesuit priest Eusebio Kino to establish a settlement at La Paz, which was soon abandoned because of hostile Indian encounters. Some months later Padre Kino founded Misión San Bruno just north of present-day Loreto, but attempts to catechize local Indians failed and the mission was abandoned within two years.

Twelve years later, in October 1697, Jesuit Padre Juan María Salvatierra arrived with a half-dozen soldiers at present-day Loreto on the Gulf coast of Baja, and soon laid the foundation for Misión Nuestra Señora de Loreto, the first permanent Spanish settlement in the Californias. From Loreto, which became the peninsula's religious and administrative capital, other Jesuits ranged throughout the peninsula to establish similar missions. Over the next 70 years, the Jesuits founded 23 missions and, despite the presence of nominal military authorities, they governed the peninsula.

Misión San Ignacio

The Jesuits meant well, but their altruistic intentions backfired. Along with God, grapes and greener pastures, the missionaries also brought an invisible evil – European microbes to which native peoples had had no exposure and lacked immunological resistance. Epidemics of smallpox, plague, typhus, measles and syphilis (the latter probably of New World origin) decimated the Indian population. The concentration of Indians at missions, as well as regular contact between missions and rancherías, spread the contagion; the Indian population plummeted from approximately 48,000 at contact to barely 3000 by 1820. Of these, fewer than 400 remained in southern and central Baja.

Despite the steady decline of the Indian population, which provided the labor for missionary expansion, the Jesuits continued to seek ideal mission sites in Baja. In the mid-18th century, explorers such as Jesuit Fernando Consag brought more sophisticated knowledge of northern Baja, but the Jesuits' expulsion from the Spanish empire in 1767 precluded the founding of missions there and in mainland California.

Franciscan priests under the authority of Padre Junípero Serra took over the former Jesuit missions, several of which they closed or consolidated. Serra himself traveled northward to establish a chain of missions in Alta California (mainland California), but the Franciscans accomplished little in Baja because they directed most of

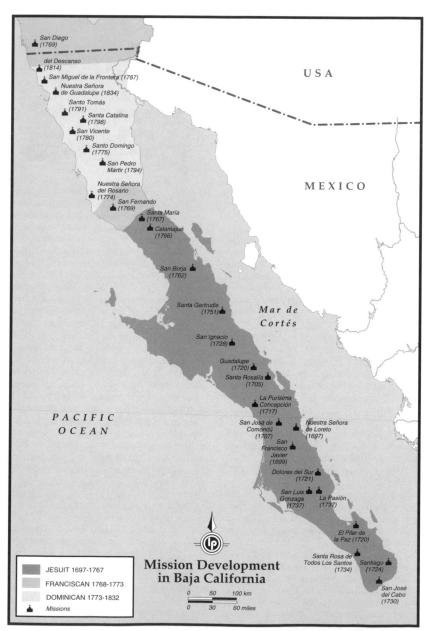

San Diego
(1769)

del Descanso
(1814)

San Miguel de la Frontera (1787)

Nuestra Señora
de Guadalupe (1834)

Santo Tomás
(1791)

Santa Catalina
(1798)

San Vicente
(1780)

Santo Domingo
(1775)

San Pedro
Mártir (1794)

Nuestra Señora
del Rosario
(1774)

San Fernando
(1769)

Santa María
(1767)

Calamajué
(1766)

San Borja
(1762)

Santa Gertrudis
(1751)

San Ignacio
(1728)

Guadalupe
(1720)

Santa Rosalía
(1705)

La Purísima
Concepción
(1717)

San José de
Comondú
(1707)

Nuestra Señora
de Loreto
(1697)

San
Francisco
Javier
(1699)

Dolores del Sur
(1721)

San Luis
Gonzaga
(1737)

La Pasión
(1737)

El Pilar de
la Paz (1720)

Santa Rosa de
Todos Los Santos
(1734)

Santiago
(1724)

San José
del Cabo
(1730)

USA

MEXICO

Mar de
Cortés

PACIFIC
OCEAN

**Mission Development
in Baja California**

JESUIT 1697-1767

FRANCISCAN 1768-1773

DOMINICAN 1773-1832

Missions

| 0 | 50 | 100 km |
| 0 | 30 | 60 miles |

their efforts toward the north. In 1773 Dominican priests replaced them in La Frontera, the region south of present-day San Diego (USA).

Besides establishing seven new missions in Baja, the Dominicans continued to operate the former Jesuit missions until after the Mexican War of Independence in 1821. Three years later, Baja became a federal territory, headed by a governor; by 1832 a newly appointed governor, with support from Mexico City, put an end to the mission system by converting all missions into secular parish churches. In a sense, however, the missions brought about their own demise: declining Indian populations could no longer support them. After the decline of the missions, a mainland *mestizo* (mixed-race) population filled part of the demographic vacuum left by the disappearance of the Indians; the final blow came in 1857 when President Benito Juárez added to the Mexican constitution a clause that required sale of all church properties.

War & Filibustering

For a year during the Mexican-American War (1846 – 48), American troops occupied La Paz, which had become the capital of Baja in 1829. By the Treaty of Guadalupe Hidalgo, signed on February 2, 1848, Mexico officially ceded Alta California to the USA but retained sovereignty over Baja.

Many Americans felt that the troops should have stayed after the war and made Baja part of the new state of California, which was officially accepted into the Union in 1850. American rabble-rousers like the quixotic William Walker (later infamous for proclaiming himself 'President' of Nicaragua) refused to accept the treaty as official policy.

After backing off a plan to occupy the mineral-rich but heavily defended Mexican state of Sonora, Walker took La Paz in 1853 with a group of mercenaries from San Francisco. Raising the flag of the 'Republic of Lower California,' he declared himself president, installed 'cabinet officers' and proclaimed annexation of Sonora. After fleeing La Paz under threat of Mexican retaliation, his forces suffered logistical reverses before their last desperate attempt to take Sonora by marching across Baja and crossing the Colorado River on rafts. They finally surrendered to US authorities.

Foreign Interests & Investment

Establishment of a permanent mestizo population was the key element in consolidating Mexican influence on the peninsula, but by the 1880s, the Mexican government decided to encourage US and European capital investment in Baja and other parts of Mexico. President Porfirio Díaz and his *científicos* (a group of largely Eurocentric, sometimes openly racist advisers), anxious for the Mexican economy to rival those of the USA and Europe, granted major land concessions to foreign investors. The dictatorial Díaz (whose long tenure is known as the *Porfiriato)* and the científicos expected growth in mining, railroads, manufacturing and other sectors.

Since the failure of Walker's invasion, various schemes to develop the peninsula had arisen, such as the Lower California Company's concession to collect orchilla, a lichen used as a dye plant, from San Quintín to La Paz. Under Díaz, who took power in 1876, the main investor in Baja was the International Company of Mexico, based in the US state of Connecticut.

Supposedly the International Company made a US$5 million down payment (total charges were US$16 million) for the right to develop an area that now comprises nearly the entire state of Baja California (northern Baja), as well as offshore islands and some areas on the Mexican mainland. Planning to build railroad lines from San Diego to San Quintín, 200 miles (320 km) south of the US border, and to connect to the state of Sonora, the company also constructed port facilities and flour mills at Ensenada and San Quintín.

The International Company also sought to attract settlers and colonists to Baja but, for three years, had little success. Their 1887 pamphlet *Lower California, the Peninsula, Now Open to Colonists* glorified Baja's fertile land and resources, excellent climate and great agricultural potential. Testimonials from newspapers and farmers supposedly verified these claims with hyperbole typical of mainland California real estate developers to this day:

In conclusion it must be said that all of this beautiful country with its incalculable wealth, sure and rapid development would still have been left bare to the birds and the sky, had it not been for the courage, capital and enterprise of the International Company.

San Diego Sun, March 11, 1887

The great Peninsula of Lower California has been but little known except as an appendage to the Pacific Coast . . . (It) has been purchased outright from the Mexican Government by the International Company. This purchase covers 18,000,000 acres of land, and in it grass grows and water runs . . . Upon these lands are no settlers nor strange social institutions to be displaced or adopted. They are wild, unsubdued, and offer to American enterprise the last frontier . . . The International Company has perfect title to this enormous grant.

Daily Alta California, July 15, 1886

After too many rainless years, however, the International Company surrendered its 'perfect title' to this 'last frontier' and sold out to an English syndicate for US$7 million.

Bringing in several colonist families, the syndicate finished the mills in San Quintín and Ensenada, built part of a railroad and planted wheat, but the rains failed and harvests were nil. Those colonists who did not end up in San Quintín's first cemetery returned to England or moved to other parts of Baja, where Anglo surnames like Jones and Smith are not unusual.

While the International Company and other potential investors were promoting Baja's agricultural development, several important mineral discoveries occurred around the peninsula, including gold and silver strikes. One of the largest projects, operated by the French syndicate Compañía del Boleo at Santa Rosalía, produced

copper until the 1950s. There were also small nickel, mercury, graphite and sulphur mines, and many foreigners flocked to Baja to find their fortune in the mines.

With thousands of foreign miners, engineers, traders and ranchers living and working in Baja, it was not surprising that rumors began to circulate in mainland California that the USA might annex Baja California. In January 1891 the *Evening Bulletin* of San Francisco carried a story entitled 'Lower California, a Belief that it Will Belong to the United States Soon':

'Sooner or later, and it may come very soon, there is going to be trouble between the United States and Mexico over Lower California,' said General Cadwallader of San Diego to a *Post* man. 'Geographically it is a piece of country that fits into our area much more naturally than as a possession of Mexico. The miners from our side are continually going down there prospecting, and if there should be any big gold discoveries, as is quite probable, seeing that it is very rich in minerals, there would be a rush of people into Lower California who would no more pay respect to the Mexican authority or Mexican laws than they would to the Chinese Empire.

'This may not be the origin of the difficulty, but it is only a question of time when trouble will arise, and the best thing to do is to discount such contingency by buying the country from our Mexican friends . . . I don't know what the Mexicans would want for it, or even if they would be willing to sell at all, but they are shrewd people, and doubtless have long ago found out that the strip is of far more value to the United States than to them.'

Although the United States never annexed Baja, US investors acquired or controlled huge tracts of land in southern mainland California and northern Baja. Among them were Harrison Gray Otis, publisher of the *Los Angeles Times*; the Spreckels family of San Francisco, who made fortunes in the US sugar industry; and the powerful Southern Pacific Railroad.

From the turn of the century, following major agricultural development projects in the Imperial Valley just north of Mexicali, the Mexican government promoted commercial agriculture in the

A: RICK GERHARTER

C: SEENA SUSSMAN

D: WAYNE BERNHARDSON

B: SEENA SUSSMAN

A: Granite formations, Desierto Central
B: A peaceful corner

C: 'Cielito Lindo,' anyone?
D: Agave, Desierto Central

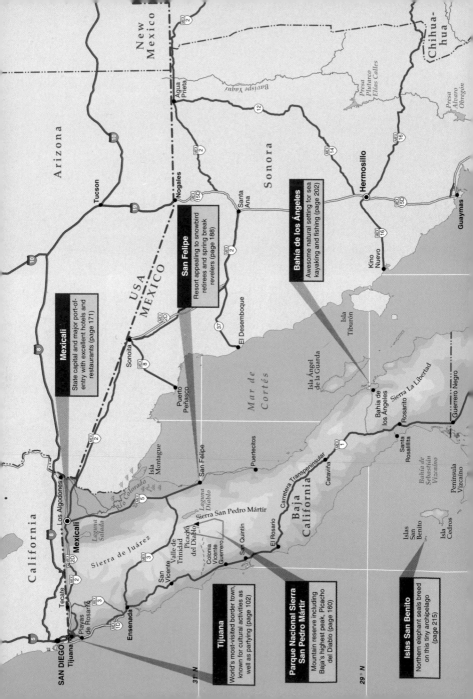

Mexicali

State capital and major port-of-entry with excellent hotels and restaurants (page 171)

San Felipe

Resort appealing to snowbird retirees and spring break revelers (page 188)

Bahía de los Ángeles

Awesome natural setting for sea kayaking and fishing (page 202)

Tijuana

World's most-visited border town, known for cultural activities as well as partying (page 102)

Parque Nacional Sierra San Pedro Mártir

Mountain reserve including Baja's highest peak, Picacho del Diablo (page 160)

Islas San Benito

Northern elephant seals breed on this tiny archipelago (page 215)

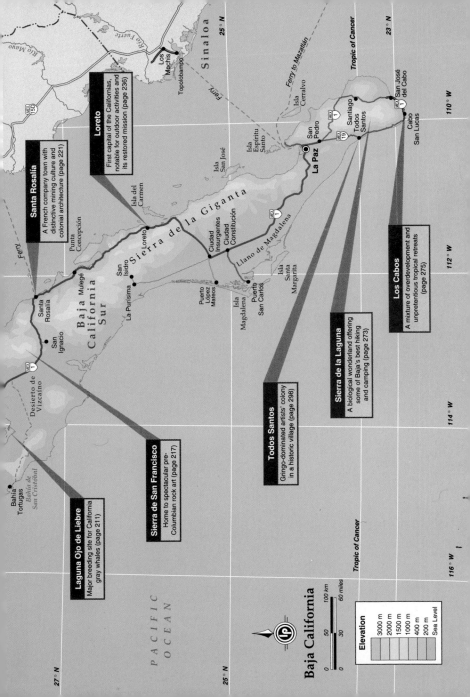

Santa Rosalía
A French company town with distinctive mining culture and colonial architecture (page 221)

Loreto
First capital of the Californias, notable for outdoor activities and its restored mission (page 236)

Laguna Ojo de Liebre
Major breeding site for California gray whales (page 211)

Sierra de San Francisco
Home to spectacular pre-Columbian rock art (page 217)

Todos Santos
Gringo-dominated artists colony in a historic village (page 298)

Sierra de la Laguna
A biological wonderland offering some of Baja's best hiking and camping (page 273)

Los Cabos
A mixture of overdevelopment and unpretentious tropical retreats (page 275)

Los Mochis
Topolobampo

Río Mayo

Río Fuerte

Sinaloa

Ferry to Mazatlán

25° N

Tropic of Cancer

23° N

Isla Cerralvo

MEX 1

San José del Cabo

MEX 1

Cabo San Lucas

Santiago

Todos Santos

San Pedro

MEX 19

MEX 1

La Paz

Isla Espíritu Santo

Isla San José

Isla del Carmen

Punta Concepción

Mulegé

Loreto

San Isidro

La Purísima

San Ignacio

Santa Rosalía

MEX 1

Desierto de Vizcaíno

Sierra de la Giganta

Baja California Sur

Ciudad Insurgentes

Ciudad Constitución

MEX 1

Llano de Magdalena

Puerto López Mateos

Isla Magdalena

Puerto San Carlos

Isla Santa Margarita

Bahía Tortugas

Bahía de San Cristóbal

110° W

112° W

114° W

116° W

Tropic of Cancer

25° N

27° N

PACIFIC OCEAN

Ferry

Baja California

0   50   100 km

0   30   60 miles

Elevation
3000 m
2000 m
1500 m
1000 m
400 m
200 m
Sea Level

A: WAYNE BERNHARDSON

B: ROBERT HOLMES

C: ROBERT HOLMES

A: Whale-watching off Puerto López Mateos
B: Punta Chivato

C: Setting sail in Cabo San Lucas

fields between Mexicali (which replaced Ensenada as the territorial capital) and the Colorado River delta. Water development in this region was the prime factor in Baja California's political and economic emergence.

Revolution & Its Aftermath

The Mexican Revolution of 1910, which lasted a decade, temporarily interrupted development. Warfare had little impact on most of the peninsula, but in 1911 a ragtag army of the Liberal Party, an anarchist force under the influence of exiled Mexican intellectual Ricardo Flores Magón, swept through northern Baja's lightly defended border towns from Mexicali to Tijuana in an attempt to establish a regional power base. Militant labor organizations like the Industrial Workers of the World (IWW or 'Wobblies') from the US side of the border assisted the revolutionaries, many of whom had been imprisoned or exiled in mainland California, with money and weapons.

The Magonistas, as Flores Magón's forces were also known, took Tijuana in a single morning as curious onlookers watched from across the border, but attempts to establish a government failed because many of the Magonistas were foreign mercenaries, soldiers of fortune who were disinterested in government as such. When the Mexican army approached Tijuana, the rebel 'government' crumbled and the Magonistas fled across the border.

After the war Baja continued in isolation, excluded from most of the grandiose political and economic development plans under discussion in Mexico City, but Prohibition in the USA reinvigorated the border economy. After enactment of a US constitutional amendment and passage of legislation outlawing the production, sale and consumption of alcoholic beverages north of the border, mainland Californians flocked to Tijuana, Ensenada and Mexicali for drinking, gambling and sex.

Border towns both prospered and suffered from this North American invasion,

as money flowed in with an assortment of corrupt characters. By the late 1930s, despite the repeal of Prohibition, the situation was so out of control that reformist President Lázaro Cárdenas banned casino gambling, threw the bad guys out of town, instituted various educational and agricultural reforms (such as the *ejido* system of peasant cooperatives) and built the Sonora-Mexicali railroad to reduce the territory's economic dependence on the US and its isolation from mainland Mexico. Despite

closure of the casinos, betting and similar diversions still exist on a reduced scale.

One proposal that might have transformed the peninsula was the establishment of a settlement area for Jewish refugees from Nazi Germany, which was briefly but seriously considered by Jewish leaders in the USA, but nothing came of this. In 1952 Baja's political status improved as its northern half became the Mexican state of Baja California; voters chose a governor and state representatives, but most of the peninsula remained isolated from the rest of the country for another two decades.

By 1973, completion of paved México 1, the 1050-mile (1690-km) Carretera Transpeninsular Benito Juárez, linked the northern borderlands to Baja's southern extremities. Less than a year later, south of the 28th parallel, Baja California Sur became Mexico's 30th state. Countless Americans began to venture across the border and drive the length of the peninsula, and regular ferry services between southern Baja and mainland Mexico also began.

The Ejido & Its Future

Historically, since colonial times, the term *ejidos* referred to communal grazing lands on the outskirts of rural communities in mainland Mexico. In the mid-19th century, a law intended to divest the Catholic Church of its extensive landholdings ironically cost Indian communities their ejidos, but not until the turn of the century, when the Díaz dictatorship weakened, was there agitation for their return.

Potential *ejidatarios* were among the most enthusiastic supporters of the Mexican Revolution of 1910, and the creation of Mexico's present system of cooperative landholdings was a direct if delayed outcome of that war. In the 1930s President Lázaro Cárdenas oversaw the conversion of the great haciendas that once controlled nearly half of Mexico's land into the modern-day ejido system. In central and southern Mexico, ejidos are largely communities of individual small-scale corn farmers, but in Baja California and other parts of northern Mexico, the institution is rather different. Community members work the land collectively.

In the Mexicali area, for example, most ejidos were formed from lands once owned by the Colorado River Land Company, later to benefit returnees from the US Government's *bracero* program, which had allowed Mexican farm laborers to work north of the border. Like the company, some collective ejidos could take advantage of economies of scale to produce commodities like cotton, but others entered activities like fishing, forestry, mining and stock-raising. In Baja they are often involved in tourism – guests in coastal campgrounds frequently rent their spaces from the local ejido and buy their gasoline from ejido-run Pemex stations.

Since the 1930s, the ejido has given a larger segment of the Mexican population a stake in the country's progress. The system's continuing symbolic presence is apparent in the names that ejidos take – names like Revolución, Plan de Ayala, Francisco Villa and Lázaro Cárdenas that refer to key elements or personalities in modern Mexican history.

The ejido is under siege, however, from NAFTA. Legislation sponsored by former Mexican President Carlos Salinas de Gortari made it possible for ejidos to dispose of lands that were theirs to use but not to sell. The government argues that it wishes to make bank credit more easily available to the ejidos by permitting them to use their resources as collateral, so that they will be more competitive under the international trade regime.

Many ejidatarios, however, worry that they could lose their lands to the banks as they did to the haciendas over a century ago. The ruling Partido Institucional Revolucionario still pays lip service to agrarian reform – it went out of its way to purchase advertising in Baja California dailies on a recent anniversary of 1937's famous 'Asalto a las Tierras' (Assault on the Lands) in Mexicali – but there is widespread suspicion of the government's motives.

At the same time, the ejido system causes problems as it grants opportunities. One ejido in Baja California Sur has opposed a management plan to protect pre-Columbian rock art in the Sierra de San Francisco because it wants to build a road into the area. Another, near Mulegé, brought segments of the tourist economy to a near halt for several months in 1996 – 97 by occupying the Hotel Serenidad to publicize its land claims. ∎

Contemporary Baja

In many ways Baja California is still a frontier, as the Transpeninsular has done more to reduce the isolation between northern and southern Baja than it has to link the peninsula to the rest of Mexico. The highway's economic benefits have been fewer than anticipated, partly because economic development has been geared to North American visitors and markets, but development has reduced unemployment and generally lifted the standard of living above that of most of mainland Mexico.

At the same time, the border towns have grown extraordinarily rapidly as desperate Mexicans and Central Americans have flocked north in hopes of crossing to the USA. While the end of Central America's recent civil wars has reduced the number of political refugees headed north, Baja California remains a major destination for immigrants who cross the border, rarely with official documentation, in search of work in mainland California. Another attraction is the manufacturing boom associated with *maquiladoras*, border-town industrial plants that take advantage of cheap Mexican labor to assemble US-made components for duty-free reexportation to the north.

Relatively few visitors appreciate that the fast-growing cities of Tijuana and Mexicali have become major educational centers, preparing highly qualified professionals in the health sciences and other occupations and encouraging intellectual exchange both within Baja California and across the border. The Universidad Autónoma de Baja California, with campuses in both Tijuana and Mexicali, El Colegio del Norte and the Universidad Iberoamericana are all important research and teaching institutions that have also patronized literature and the arts.

This, unfortunately, is not the whole story. Tijuana and other border cities are also home to drug cartels and smugglers who operate with impunity, in part because of official corruption. A particularly unfortunate corollary is Mexico's (and Baja's) increasing militarization, which, while relatively innocuous at present, could become a serious problem should the Mexican armed forces come to see themselves as the country's saviors from disorder. There are ominous parallels with the 1970s, when – partly at the behest of the US – citizens of other Latin American countries suffered coups and state terrorism at the hands of their militaries. Although Mexico's 20th-century history does not suggest that such a development is likely, no one should assume the country is immune to such developments.

GEOGRAPHY

Between the Pacific Ocean to the west and the Gulf of California (popularly called the 'Sea of Cortez') to the east, Baja California is a desolate but scenic peninsula of mountains, plains, headlands and beaches stretching from the mainland California state border, between 32°N and 33°N, to Cabo San Lucas 800 miles (1300 km) south. It also shares short borders with the US state of Arizona and the Mexican state of Sonora, both across the Río Colorado delta at the northeastern corner of peninsula. The peninsula's width ranges from 30 to 145 miles (50 to 230 km), and its total land mass of about 55,000 sq miles (143,000 sq km) is about the size of the US state of Illinois or of England and Wales combined.

Tectonic activity during late Miocene, about 12 million years ago, separated the peninsula from mainland Mexico along the famous San Andreas Fault. Pacific Ocean water invaded the elongated structural trough that is now the Gulf of California, whose extensive coastline, along with Baja's Pacific shores, offers some of world's finest and most isolated beaches. Influenced by the south-flowing California Current, the waters of the Pacific tend to be cooler than those of the Gulf, which enjoy the warmth of the North Equatorial Current for much of the year but also exhibit great spatial and seasonal variation because of the Gulf's great depth and its latitudinal extent. In the Cape Region, cool temperate and warm equatorial waters mix, but in the north, the Gulf waters are very shallow because of sedimentation from the Río Colorado, and thus their temperatures vary with the weather.

North of El Rosario on the Pacific, most beaches are within walking distance of the Transpeninsular or are accessible by ordinary passenger car, but in the Desierto Central (Central Desert) south of El Rosario to the border with Baja California Sur, a tough 4WD vehicle may be necessary to reach isolated coves, beaches and fish camps. The plains near Guerrero Negro merge into the Desierto de Vizcaíno, which

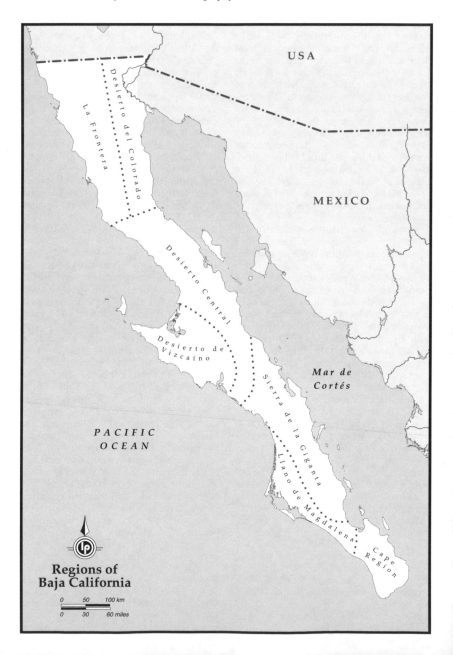

USA

MEXICO

La Frontera

Desierto del Colorado

Desierto Central

Desierto de Vizcaíno

Sierra de la Giganta

Mar de Cortés

PACIFIC OCEAN

Llano de Magdalena

Cape Region

Regions of Baja California

0   50   100 km

0   30   60 miles

extends to San Ignacio and westward into the Península Vizcaíno. Travelers in this area should be cautious when wandering off main thoroughfares without appropriate off-road equipment and supplies. Daytime is often murderously hot, but nights can be frigid.

South of the state border, the Transpeninsular jogs inland beyond Guerrero Negro and eastward to San Ignacio, where an underground spring, utilized by Jesuits in the 18th century to plant thousands of palms and establish a mission, nurtures one of Baja's few substantial oases. Beyond San Ignacio, the highway passes Las Tres Virgenes (Three Virgins), a Quaternary cluster of volcanic peaks and massive lava flows, the towns of Santa Rosalía and Mulegé and several popular Gulf beach areas. It then cuts back west to the Llano de Magdalena (Magdalena Plain) and other beaches farther south. The mountainous Cape Region beyond La Paz, with its rocky headlands, coves and sandy beaches, is an increasingly popular tourist destination.

Dotting Baja's Gulf waters are numerous islands that are undersea extensions of peninsular mountain ranges; isolated since the creation of the Gulf, they support unique plant communities and large breeding colonies of seabirds. The largest island, Isla Angel de la Guarda, is 42 miles (68 km) long and 10 miles (16 km) wide; it reaches an altitude of 4324 feet (1297 meters).

Several mountain ranges together form the backbone of the entire peninsula. The northernmost major range is the granitic Sierra de Juárez, a southern extension of mainland California ranges; its alpine meadows in Parque Nacional Constitución de 1857 are a surprising highlight. East of the mountains, around Mexicali, the Río Hardy meets the Colorado in the extensively irrigated and intensively cultivated delta.

Farther south, in another national park, the Sierra San Pedro Mártir range features Baja's highest peak – 10,126-foot (3038-meter) Picacho del Diablo (Devil's Peak), which is often capped with snow. This range resembles mainland California's Sierra

Nevada, with low foothills gradually leading up into pine forests and steep mountain peaks, but the brutally hot and arid Desierto del Colorado on its eastern slope reaches nearly to the 30th parallel, where the Sierra La Asamblea marks its approximate southern limit. The mountains of central Baja are mostly Tertiary marine sediments, but volcanic peaks and recent lava flows often conceal their bedrock.

Beyond Loreto, the Sierra de la Giganta is southern Baja's most prominent range, stretching nearly to La Paz. Farther south, the granitic peaks of the forested Sierra de la Laguna, reaching up to 7000 feet (2100 meters), divide the Cape Region in half. The tropic of Cancer runs almost precisely through the town of Todos Santos, about midway between La Paz and Cabo San Lucas.

CLIMATE

Thanks to the cool, southward-flowing California Current, which branches off the Subarctic Current at about 45°N latitude, Baja California's Pacific coast is relatively mild throughout the year; average temperatures range from 60°F to 75°F (16°C to 24°C). Summer temperatures often reach 85°F (30°C), but sea breezes and convective fogs like those in mainland California provide natural air-conditioning. Like mainland California, northern Baja experiences a winter rainy season, with perhaps 90% of annual precipitation falling from December to March. At higher elevations, especially in the Sierra de Juárez and the Sierra San Pedro Mártir, precipitation takes the form of snow, which may last well into spring. On winter nights, even at sea level, frosts are not unknown.

Inland from the Pacific, summer temperatures soar upward of 110°F (43°C), humidity is almost nil and rain is rare, especially across the eastern slopes of the sierras in the Río Colorado delta; summers in the area from Mexicali to San Felipe are murderously hot. The Desierto Central between El Rosario and San Ignacio is blistering, and between El Rosario and Cataviña strong winds sometimes make driving

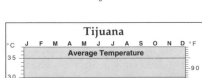

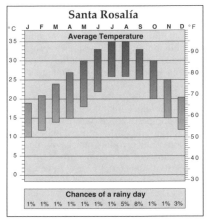

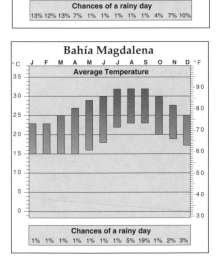

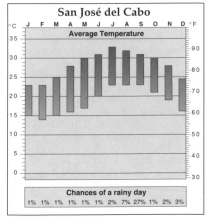

dangerous. The Gulf coast also suffers strong winds, including extended northers in winter, and high summer temperatures.

Temperatures in the Cape Region from La Paz to Cabo San Lucas are also very high, but in summer this area often experiences storms and even violent hurricanes (*chubascos*), because of tropical low-pressure areas in the Pacific. Winter is generally warm and sunny.

The accompanying charts offer a sample of Baja California's climatic conditions. Tijuana represents most of the Pacific coast of northern Baja, while Bahía Magdalena is

more typical of the southern Pacific coast almost to Guerrero Negro. Figures for San José del Cabo illustrate conditions in the Cape Region, while those for Santa Rosalía more closely resemble those along the Gulf of California (the Desierto del Colorado region at the northern end of the Gulf, however, is much cooler in winter, especially at night).

Travelers should remember that temperatures can vary dramatically, especially with altitude, and that low average rainfall figures can disguise infrequent but truly dangerous weather events like hurricanes.

ECOLOGY & ENVIRONMENT

From the international border to Cabo San Lucas, Baja California's fragile desert and maritime environments are facing a variety of challenges. Urban population growth has caused various problems; in Tijuana, for instance, the inability to build adequate housing and sewage facilities has meant serious pollution of the Río Tijuana, which flows across the border into mainland California. The density of luxury hotels for foreign tourists in Cabo San Lucas has had a similar impact on the once pristine tropical waters of the Gulf of California.

Other environmental issues of concern include deforestation and erosion in the Sierra de Juárez of northern Baja, illegal overfishing throughout the length of the Gulf by both sport and commercial interests, potentially deleterious effects of increased salt production on the gray-whale nursery at Laguna San Ignacio and toxic mining residues at sites like Santa Rosalía. The proliferation of off-road races throughout the peninsula has done inestimable damage to its flora and fauna – hardly any place in Baja seems off-limits to noisily polluting and carelessly driven motorcycles, ATVs and 4WD vehicles.

The Programa Golfo de California, operated by Conservation International Mexico (☎ (622) 1-01-94, fax (622) 1-20-30), Miramar 59-A, Colonial Miramar, Guaymas, Sonora 85450, stresses conservation on the islands of the Gulf. Some grassroots conservationists criticize the organization for its top-down approach.

FLORA & FAUNA

For visitors interested in natural history, Baja California offers a wealth of botanical and zoological attractions. A relatively small number are unique to the peninsula, but some, like the migrating gray whales of Scammon's Lagoon, are reason enough to plan a trip to the peninsula.

Plants & Plant Communities

Responding to accusations that Jesuit missionaries engaged in clandestine commerce with the English, German Padre Johann Jakob Baegert wrote that 'there is nothing in California except wacke and other worthless rocks, and it produces nothing but thorns.' If, he added, the English would have accepted these in exchange for wood and water, there could have been a flourishing commerce because 'nothing is so common in California as rocks and thorns, nothing so rare as moisture, wood and cool shade.'

Most of Baja California is conspicuously desert, but there is a greater variety of habitats and species than Padre Baegert knew in his limited experience of the peninsula. The following pages present some of Baja's most prominent and interesting plants, identifying them by Spanish and English common names as well as their biological nomenclature. When more than one species of a genus is present, the abbreviation 'spp' denotes this fact.

In botanical terms the northern coast and foothills, from the US border to El Rosario, are a continuation of mainland California, covered with oaks and chaparral vegetation like manzanita, ceanothus (California lilac) and chamise *(Adenostoma fasciculatum)*. Above the chaparral belt, paralleling the ocean, the Sierras de Juárez and San Pedro Mártir support a longitudinal strip of coniferous forest that also resembles areas north of the border. The dominant species are piñon pine *(Pinus*

Barrel cacti

Endangered Species

The Convention on International Trade in Endangered Species of Wild Fauna and Flora (CITES) is a diplomatic agreement regulating trade in plants and animals that are either in immediate danger of extinction or declining so rapidly that they soon may be in danger of extinction. Regulations are complex, but in general, commercial and noncommercial exploitation of such species is either banned or placed under severe restrictions. In many instances, all commerce in a given species is prohibited; in most other cases, the export of endangered plants and animals from a country is prohibited without express authorization from that country's government.

Most species protected by CITES are assigned either to Appendix I (endangered: under immediate threat of extinction without remedial action) or Appendix II (threatened:

Appendix I

Flora
Otay mesa mint, *Pogogyne nudiuscula*
salt marsh bird's beak,
   Cordylanthus maritimus

Fauna
Baja pronghorn antelope,
   Antilocapra americana peninsularis
caguama (green sea turtle),
   Chelonia mydas agasizii
California least tern, *Sterna antillarum*
Cedros mule deer,
   Odocoileus hemionus cedrosensis
cochito (Gulf harbor porpoise),
   Phocoena sinus*

Guadalupe fur seal,
   Arctocephalus townsendii
hawksbill sea turtle,
   Eretmochelys imbricata
leatherback sea turtle,
   Dermochelys coriacea
light-footed clapper rail,
   Rallus longirostris levipes
loggerhead sea turtle,
   Caretta caretta
olive ridley sea turtle,
   Lepidochelys coriacea
totuava (seatrout or weakfish),
   Cynoscion macdonaldii

---

quadrifolia), whose edible nuts were a key part of the indigenous diet, and Jeffrey pine *(Pinus jeffreyi)*, but other pines, as well as spruce, cypress and fir, are present in smaller numbers.

Below about 3300 feet (1000 meters), east of the sierras and far to the south, the Sonoran Desert botanical region comprises several distinct subregions. From the US border as far as Bahía de los Angeles, it consists of small-leaved shrubs like ocotillo *(Fouquieria splendens)* and the closely related *palo adán (F burragei* and *F diguetti)*, which bloom only at rare times of heavy rainfall, and cacti like *nopal* (prickly pear, *Opuntia* spp). South of Bahía de los Angeles almost to La Paz, a narrow coastal strip on the Gulf of California features imposing cacti like the *cardón (Pachycereus* spp), which reaches a height of 65

feet (20 meters), and many species of *biznaga* (barrel cactus, *Ferocactus* spp). All of these cacti produce edible fruit or seeds, most notably the *tuna*, fruit of the nopal.

Nearly unique to Baja is the *cirio* tree *(Idria columnaris)*, popularly known as a 'boojum' because of its supposed resemblance to the tall, twisted creature in Lewis Carroll's poem *The Hunting of the Snark*. Closely related to ocotillo but the only member of a separate genus, the slow-growing cirio reaches 65 feet (20 meters) in height; its distribution is limited to an area from the southwestern foothills of the Sierra San Pedro Mártir almost to San Ignacio, to Isla Angel de la Guarda and to parts of Sonora. Until it branches, it most closely resembles an inverted carrot in shape.

More characteristic than the boojum, however, are the various species of *Agave*

perhaps regionally endangered). Some recovering species have been reassigned from Appendix I to Appendix II. Appendix III listings cover species that require close monitoring to determine their vulnerability.

Travelers should take special care not to hunt, purchase or collect the following species of plants and animals found in Baja California, nor should they purchase products made from these plants and animals without explicit authorization from authorities in Mexico City. Otherwise, such products may be confiscated by US Customs. The list below is partial, and travelers should consult with US Customs before attempting to import any such products.

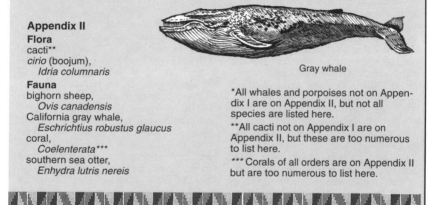

Appendix II
Flora
cacti**
cirio (boojum),
    Idria columnaris

Fauna
bighorn sheep,
    Ovis canadensis
California gray whale,
    Eschrichtius robustus glaucus
coral,
    Coelenterata***
southern sea otter,
    Enhydra lutris nereis

Gray whale

*All whales and porpoises not on Appendix I are on Appendix II, but not all species are listed here.

**All cacti not on Appendix I are on Appendix II, but these are too numerous to list here.

*** Corals of all orders are on Appendix II but are too numerous to list here.

(century plant, a genus that includes *A tequilana*, the source of tequila) and *Yucca*, both of which dot the Desierto de Vizcaíno of central Baja. The abundant agave was a major food source for the Cochimí Indians, but consuming the plant's nutritious heart involved uprooting it and cooking it in a long, laborious process. The root of the yucca, also known as *guacamote*, was roasted on the fire until edible. In certain areas substantial concentrations of fruit-bearing palms *(Washingtonia robusta* and *Erythea armata)* flourished, but the Cochimí used them more as timber.

Farther south, on the Pacific slope, the Desierto de Vizcaíno and the Llano de Magdalena support different species of agave, plus cacti like the cardón and the *pitahaya agria (Machaerocereus gummosus)*, whose slightly acid fruit was consumed by native

peoples; its stems also made a useful fish poison. The *datilillo (Yucca valida*, a treelike form of yucca) bears a fruit resembling a date, while the wild figs of the *zalate (Ficus palmeri)* were more palatable to Indians than to missionaries.

The Sierra de la Giganta, running from Loreto nearly to La Paz, is home to many common trees and shrubs like acacia and mesquite *(Prosopis* spp), a handful of native palms like *Erythea brandegeei* and many cacti, including nopal and the *pitahaya dulce (Lemaireocereus thurberi)*. As far north as San Borja, the *pitahaya dulce*, known to English-speakers as the organ pipe cactus, yields a sweet fruit that was the Cochimí equivalent of candy. The pitahaya dulce was a key food source for native peoples who camped near local concentrations of the plant for the late summer and early autumn harvest, which was a major social and religious occasion.

After gorging themselves on the fruit, they would defecate in a particular spot and, later, collect the dry feces to winnow the undigested seeds, which they milled and ate during winter food shortages. Padre Johann Jakob Baegert, who observed the Guaycura Indians at San Luis Gonzaga, wrote that 'it was difficult for me, indeed, to give credit to such a report until I had repeatedly witnessed this procedure,' which, he added, was accompanied by 'much joking.'

South of the Sierra de la Giganta, most of the Cape Region is an arid tropical zone of acacia and other leguminous trees and shrubs, sumac *(Cyrtocarpa edulis,* whose fruit is edible) and fan palm *(Erythea brandegeei).* Pines and oaks, however, appear side by side with palms and cacti at higher elevations in the well-watered Sierra de la Laguna; the piñon pine produces edible seeds.

In addition to these major zones, other plant associations appear sporadically in much more restricted geographical ranges but are botanically significant and constitute critical wildlife habitat, especially for birds. These areas include coastal dunes, coastal salt marshes, freshwater marshes, mangrove swamps and vernal pools. The dense, salt-tolerant mangroves, present along segments of both the Pacific and Gulf coasts of Baja California Sur, also provide spawning habitat for fish and shellfish.

Many desert plants, including numerous species of cacti, are on Appendix I or II of the Convention on International Trade in Endangered Species of Wild Fauna and Flora (CITES) list. Travelers should not purchase or otherwise obtain living plants, or products made from these plants, for import into the USA. There are restrictions and prohibitions under international law.

Birds

Baja California's bird habitats are strongly correlated with its plant communities but vary with climate, elevation and latitude. The major geographical divisions of the northern Pacific coast, the mountainous Sierra San Pedro Mártir, the Desierto del Colorado, the Desierto de Vizcaíno and the Cape each have characteristic groups of bird species, though the desert species are widespread outside those areas.

The many Gulf islands, in addition, have large colonies of nesting seabirds despite their lack of endemic species. Among the most noteworthy are the black storm-petrel *(Oceanodroma melania)* and the least storm-petrel *(O microsoma),* the brown pelican *(Pelecanus occidentalis),* the cormorants *(Phalacrocorax auritus* and *P penicillatus),* the frigate bird *(Fregata magnificens),* the boobies *(Sula nebouxi* and *S leucogaster),* Craveri's murrelet *(Synthliporamphus craveri),* Heermann's gull *(Larus heermanni),* the yellow-footed gull *(L livens),* the elegant tern *(Sterna elegans)* and the brown noddy *(Anous stolidus).*

Seabirds prosper from the Midriff Islands of the central Gulf south toward Cabo San Lucas because nutrients upwelling from deep submarine canyons feed abundant fish and plankton near the surface. In pre-Columbian times aboriginal peoples collected eggs and captured birds that had established breeding colonies on the islands and on the mainland. Unfortunately, ever since European settlement, practices like egg collecting, degradation of habitat through agricultural development and the unwise introduction of ecologically exotic species like cats and goats have led to indirect (coincidental) extinctions, while uncontrolled shooting has even brought direct (intentional) extinctions. On the Pacific island of Guadalupe, for example, domestic goats so reduced the vegetative cover that endemic races of flickers, wrens and towhees died out, while cats may have eliminated the Guadalupe storm-petrel and shooters destroyed the crested caracara. Massive agricultural development on the Río Colorado has also eliminated native vegetation and reduced bird habitat.

Sanford Wilbur's *Birds of Baja California* is a comprehensive listing of species found on the peninsula and surrounding islands, but its lack of illustrations makes it unsuitable for field use. Field-oriented birders might acquire RT Peterson and EL Chalif's *A Field Guide to Mexican Birds*, which covers the mainland, the peninsula and offshore islands. *The Audubon Society Field Guide to North American Birds, Western Region*, by Miklos Udvardy, focuses on birds of the USA and Canada, but there is considerable overlap with Baja California and the Mexican mainland.

Land Mammals

Baja is home to a variety of unique mammals, including the black jackrabbit *(Lepus insularis)* of Isla Espíritu Santo and the fish-eating bat *(Pizonyx vivesi)* of the Gulf. More characteristic, however, are animals like the mule deer *(Odocoileus hemionus)*, peninsular pronghorn antelope *(Antilocapra americana peninsularis)* and endangered desert bighorn sheep *(Ovis canadensis)*. The Cedros mule deer *(O hemionus cedrosensis)* is an endangered subspecies on its namesake Pacific island.

A Starker Leopold's *Wildlife of Mexico* is a good source of information on Mexican mammals (and some birds), though oriented primarily toward game management. Only a handful of Leopold's game animals are found on the Baja Peninsula.

Marine Mammals

From January to March, visitors flock to the lagoons of central Baja to view the migration and mating of the California gray whale *(Eschrichtius robustus* or *E gibbosus)*, but other species of whales and dolphins also frequent the waters of the Pacific and the Gulf. Among them are the finback whale *(Balaenoptera physalus)* and the humpback whale *(Megaptera novaeangliae)*.

The following readily available books are good sources of information on whales: Richard Ellis' *The Book of Whales*, Steven Leatherwood's *The Sierra Club Handbook of Whales and Dolphins* and Stanley Minasian's *The World's Whales*.

For information on whale-watching, see the Organized Tours entry in the Outdoor Activities chapter and the Guerrero Negro, Laguna San Ignacio and Bahía Magdalena

entries in the Desierto Central & Llano de Magdalena chapter.

Other marine mammals include the endangered Gulf of California harbor porpoise *(Phocoena sinus)*, the recovering but still threatened southern sea otter *(Enhydra lutris)*, the threatened Guadalupe fur seal *(Arctocephalus townsendii)*, and the more common sea lion *(Zalophus californianus)*, northern elephant seal *(Mirounga angustirostis)* and harbor seal *(Phoca vitulina)*. Sea lions and elephant seals can be seen at several offshore Pacific islands, most notably Isla Cedros and the Islas San Benito, about midway down the peninsula.

Fish & Marine Life

The waters of the Pacific support a cool temperate flora and fauna resembling that off the coast of mainland California, with kelp (like *Macrocystis*) and mollusks, sea urchins and barnacles, but shallow areas like Laguna San Ignacio and Bahía Magdalena support more tropical life forms.

Because of the range of temperatures in the Gulf of California, its flora and fauna are relatively limited in numbers of species, especially in the northern half of the Gulf. Total biomass is fairly large, however, because of algal blooms – the term 'Vermillion Sea,' often applied to the Gulf, derives from this phenomenon. In some shallow lagoons, especially toward the south of the peninsula, mangrove swamps are incubators for Gulf fauna such as oysters. Crustaceans like spiny lobsters and rock crabs were common fare in aboriginal Baja. The venomous yellow-bellied sea snake *(Pelamus platyrus)* frequents inshore waters of southern Baja.

Most of today's important marine life, especially that of interest to the tourist, is pelagic (native to open seas) rather than native to inshore waters. Over 800 species of fish, many of them excellent eating, inhabit the Gulf; many of these attract sportfishing enthusiasts who increasingly have adopted a catch-and-release policy in an attempt not to endanger the popular game species like the marlin (the efficacy of catch-and-release is open to question).

The totuava *(Cynoscion macdonaldii)*, known commonly as sea trout or weakfish, is endangered in the Gulf of California.

Souvenir hunters should be aware that all species of black coral, of the order *Antipatharia*, are on Appendix II of the CITES endangered species list; exports of black coral products, such as jewelry, require a permit from Mexico City in order to be allowed into the USA. Black coral is mined with dredge hooks, and substantial reef areas are destroyed in the process of obtaining material for relatively insignificant amounts of these products.

Reptiles
Desert environments support many reptiles, including snakes, lizards and turtles. Baja has an abundant and varied snake population, and rattlesnakes *(Crotalus* spp) are

Tracking the Turtle

The great whales get all the press. Few travelers know as much about the sea turtles that, historically, have been as important to the peoples of the tropics as whales have been to the peoples of the Arctic. Called 'the world's most valuable reptile' by the late geographer James Parsons, the Pacific green turtle *(Chelonia mydas)* is endangered throughout the world, and its conservation should be a major priority in Baja California and the rest of Mexico.

The green turtle *(caguama negra* or *tortuga prieta* in Baja) is a grazing reptile that feeds on marine grasses in tropical and subtropical seas, though wandering individuals have been found as far north as England and as far south as Argentina and Chile. Individuals can weigh up to 800 lbs (360 kg), though most weigh 300 lbs (135 kg) or less. Males rarely leave the sea, but females migrate long distances to haul out on the sandy beaches of isolated tropical islands, where they lay their eggs.

For millennia, the green turtle has provided protein to people in the tropics via its meat and eggs, but the exploration of the globe by Europeans marked the beginning of the species' decline. Northern European sailors netted the abundant turtles of the Caribbean, for example, and kept them aboard ships as sources of fresh meat on their trips around the Horn – feeding them bananas and bathing them in saltwater to keep them alive. By the 18th century, fresh turtle meat and turtle soup were luxuries in London, but by the 19th century, they reached the British capital in cans.

Outside the protein-scarce tropics, turtle has always been a delicacy, and commercial pressures resulted in overhunting in such important areas as the Caribbean coasts of Nicaragua and Costa Rica (where eggs on the nesting beaches at Tortuguero were frequently raided as well). The result was a transfer of protein from the poor countries of the tropics to the rich countries of the midlatitudes.

Baja California's turtles shared this unfortunate history. At Bahía Tortugas on Península Vizcaíno, one 19th-century ship netted almost 200 turtles in a single pass. Many were canned or shipped north to San Francisco or San Diego for sale or further processing. As recently as the 1960s, the Ruffo family's Empacadora Baja California in Ensenada was canning as much as 100 tons of turtle soup in a single season.

In the 1970s increasing concern over the green's declining numbers resulted in its placement (and that of all other sea turtles) on Appendix I of the Convention on International Trade in Endangered Species of Wild Fauna and Flora. Still, it is not unusual to find surreptitious trade in turtle products, even though Mexico outlawed sea-turtle hunting in 1990. A casual inquiry by the author at a taco stand in Guerrero Negro was answered with a description of where to buy turtle products. At some point in the future, the species may recover enough to permit it to resume its historical role in the human ecology of the a serious concern throughout the peninsula. More than half the reptiles on islands in the Gulf of California are endemic species or subspecies.

Isla Santa Catalina, southeast of Loreto, is home to the so-called rattleless rattle-snake; the endemic *C catalinensis* has only a single rattle segment, which by itself is incapable of making any sound. *C ruber lorenzoensis*, a similar species on San Lorenzo Sur, may have either a single rattle segment or a full rattle.

Sea turtles, all of which are endangered species, inhabit the Gulf of California and nest on some of its beaches. Travelers should avoid consuming any turtle products or acquiring souvenirs made from turtle shells, which may not be imported into the USA. The Pacific green turtle *(Chelonia mydas*, colloquially known as the *caguama*

tropics, but as environmental opponents of NAFTA have argued (with some credibility), the Mexican government has done a poor job of enforcing international agreements on turtle conservation.

Baja visitors are unlikely to come across nesting sites, which are usually at remote spots like Isla Socorro in the Revillagigedo group some 280 miles (450 km) south of Cabo San Lucas and on the Michoacán coast. Nevertheless, greens and other turtle species are not unusual in Baja waters; there are recent reports of nesting sites on the Eastern Cape around Bahía Los Frailes and near San José del Cabo. In Baja California (Norte), the green has been spotted at Gulf island sites like Angel de la Guarda, Rasa, Salsipuedes, San Luis and San Lorenzo, as well as at Bahía de los Angeles, Bahía San Luis Gonzaga, Puertecitos, San Felipe and even the mouth of the Río Colorado. On the Pacific coast, turtles have been seen at Isla Cedros, Bahía San Quintín and Ensenada.

The warmer waters of Baja California Sur are better turtle habitat, and turtles appear in many of the same areas frequented by calving gray whales: Laguna Ojo de Liebre (Scammon's Lagoon), Laguna San Ignacio and Bahía Magdalena. The juvenile turtle populations of the Gulf appear to feed more on algae than on sea grasses.

Recent research has indicated that Baja's loggerhead turtles *(Caretta caretta)* undertake even more impressive nesting journeys than do the greens, crossing 6500 miles (10,500 km) of the open Pacific to southern Japan's Kyushu Island. (A handful of Baja loggerheads appear to nest in the Australian state of Queensland.) 'Rosita,' a juvenile loggerhead kept in captivity for seven years after her capture in a net off Bahía de los Angeles, was tagged and released into the Pacific at Santa Rosalillita in mid-1994; 16 months later, she turned up in a fisherman's net off Kyushu.

Recently scientists have been satellite-tracking the migration of another loggerhead, 'Adelita,' released at Santa Rosalillita in 1996. For details on Adelita's progress, check the Sea Turtle News & Information website; its address is listed in the Internet Directory in the back of this book. ∎

negra or *tortuga prieta)* is the most important, but other species include the leatherback *(Dermochelys coriacea,* or *tortuga laúd)*, the western ridley *(Lepidochelys olivacea)*, the loggerhead *(Caretta caretta)* and hawksbill *(Eretmochelys imbricata,* or *tortuga carey)*. The diminutive hawksbill can easily bite off a finger. Mexicans most commonly apply the word *caguama* to the green, but the term can mean any species of turtle.

Turtle-oriented travelers will find a great deal of entertaining and informative literature on the subject, including Archie Carr's *So Excellent a Fishe,* James J Parsons' *The Green Turtle and Man* and Jack Rudloe's *Time of the Turtle.* At Bahía de los Angeles, the Secretaría de Medio Ambiente has a modest turtle conservation project where it's possible to see leatherbacks, hawksbills and greens; for details, see the Bahía de los Angeles entry in the Desierto Central & Llano de Magdalena chapter.

National Parks & Other Reserves

Mexico has established four major *parques nacionales* (national parks) on the Baja Peninsula, and several other units receive varying degrees of juridical protection, but direct protective activities and informational services are limited.

Reserva de la Biosfera Alto Golfo y Delta del Río Colorado Straddling the states of Baja California and Sonora at the northern end of the Gulf of California, this sprawling 3609-sq-mile (9383-sq-km) reserve unites xerophytic (desert) scrub, coastal dunes, estuaries and marine environments in a single unit.

Parque Nacional Constitución de 1857

On the plateau and eastern slope of the Sierra de Juárez, this 19-sq-mile (49-sq-km) park, barely an hour's drive from Ensenada, is a good place for camping and rock climbing. Shallow, sprawling Laguna Hanson, surrounded by shady pine forests, is a major stopover for migratory birds on the Pacific flyway. See the park's entry in the La Frontera chapter for more information.

Parque Nacional Sierra San Pedro Mártir Reaching altitudes above 10,000 feet (3000 meters) in the Sierra San Pedro Mártir, this roughly 236-sq-mile (614-sq-km) park contains some of the peninsula's most varied terrain and vegetation, and it is an excellent choice for backcountry camping and backpacking in the spring. It can be approached either from Colonet/San Telmo on the Pacific side of the peninsula or from San Felipe on the Gulf side, where the 10,126-foot (3038-meter) spire of Picacho del Diablo, also known as Cerro Providencia, is most impressive. See the park's entry in the La Frontera chapter for more information.

Reserva de la Biosfera Islas del Golfo

Created in 1978, this 579-sq-mile (1505-sq-km) reserve includes all the islands in the Gulf of California, comprising parts of the states of Baja California, Baja California Sur and Sonora; the reserve overlaps the borders of the new marine national parks at Loreto and Cabo Pulmo (see below). Three international conservation groups are working to protect its xerophytic scrub and thorn forest: Conservation International de México in the Midriff region and for planning in general, the Mexican branch of the Worldwide Fund for Nature (WWF-México) in the Midriff, and The Nature Conservancy at Isla Espíritu Santo and in the new Loreto marine national park.

Reserva de la Biosfera El Vizcaíno

Stretching across the central peninsula just south of the border between the states of Baja California and Baja California Sur, this 9833-sq-mile (25,566-sq-km) reserve is Latin America's largest single protected area, though some of the terms of protection are ambiguous. It contains the important gray-whale calving sites of Laguna Ojo de Liebre and Laguna San Ignacio, a population of the endangered peninsular pronghorn antelope and pre-Columbian rock art sites together designated a UNESCO World Heritage Site. See the reserve's entry in the Desierto Central & Llano de Magdalena chapter for more information.

Parque Marino Nacional Bahía de Loreto Recently approved by the Mexican congress under grassroots pressure from residents concerned about overexploitation of maritime resources, this 799-sq-mile (2077-sq-km) unit consists of a smattering of offshore islands and their surrounding waters in the vicinity of Baja's historical capital. Among its notable environments are mangroves, coastal dunes and xerophytic and spiny coastal scrub. See the Loreto entry in the Desierto Central & Llano de Magdalena chapter for more information.

Parque Marino Nacional Cabo Pulmo Protecting a unique coral reef (the northernmost in the eastern Pacific) and its surrounding waters off the southern Gulf of California's thinly populated Eastern Cape, this 127-sq-mile (70-sq-km) unit was Mexico's first underwater national park. See the Cabo Pulmo entry in the Cape Region chapter for more information.

Reserva de la Biosfera Sierra de la Laguna In the high mountains of the Cape Region, this 434-sq-mile (1128-sq-km) reserve, established in 1994, protects a truly unique mixture of coniferous, deciduous and palm forests. For more information about the Sierra de la Laguna, see the Cape Region chapter.

GOVERNMENT & POLITICS

The peninsula of Baja California consists of two separate states, Baja California (capital Mexicali) and Baja California Sur (capital La Paz). Each state is further subdivided into *municipios*, roughly equivalent to US counties, each of which is administered by a *cabecera* (county seat). Each municipio in turn consists of several *delegaciones*.

Baja California consists of the municipios of Tijuana, Playas de Rosarito, Tecate, Mexicali and Ensenada; Baja California Sur consists of the municipios of Mulegé, Comondú, La Paz and Los Cabos. The size of municipios can be very disproportionate – the municipio of Tijuana, containing the bulk of Baja California's population, is only 576 sq miles (1498 sq km, about 2.2% of the state's area), while that of Ensenada is 18,900 sq miles (49,140 sq km, over 73% of the state's area).

As elsewhere in Mexico, the official Partido Institucional Revolucionario (PRI) has dominated politics for most of this century, but the Partido de Acción Nacional (PAN) is strong here and elsewhere along Mexico's northern frontier. Many observers have labeled the PAN conservative because of its assertive free-market orientation, but its appeal derives at least as much from widely felt regional antagonism against Mexico City's centralized, bureaucratic authority. The present governor of Baja California is the PAN's Héctor Terán Terán, while the governor of Baja California Sur is the PRI's Guillermo Mercado Romero.

Baja California drew particularly unfavorable attention in 1994 with the assassination of the PRI's highly regarded presidential candidate Luis Donaldo Colosio in Tijuana. Police immediately apprehended the hapless gunman, but there remain serious unanswered questions regarding motivations behind the assassination, among them whether conservative elements in the PRI may have targeted Colosio, who was generally considered a reformist. Colosio's designated PRI replacement was current President Ernesto Zedillo, who spent much of his youth in Mexicali.

Mexican President Ernesto Zedillo

ECONOMY

Agriculture and fishing remain major industries, but tourism has become the motor that drives the economy. Over the past two decades, every major town and city has seen a construction boom in hotels and related infrastructure. Fonatur, Mexico's federal tourism development agency, has promoted major resort complexes at Loreto and Los Cabos (San José del Cabo and Cabo San Lucas) with foreign and Mexican capital, attempting to transform these places into luxury resorts like Cancún in the Yucatán.

Baja's popularity as a tourist destination is undeniable. Tijuana claims to be the world's busiest border city, as over 45,000 people cross the line daily (16 million annually). Both Mexicali and Tijuana have built cultural centers to attract more visitors, and each year more drivers explore the Transpeninsular and its side roads or jet into resorts at Loreto, La Paz or Los Cabos.

Some locals find this interest in Baja ironic because, as more North Americans head south for inexpensive holidays or retirement in Baja, countless Mexicans and Central Americans flock to Tijuana and Mexicali to arrange surreptitious border crossings with smugglers known as *coyotes* or *polleros* for up to US$500 per person. Passage of a tough immigration law in 1986 made it illegal for US businesses to hire undocumented foreigners, but this has not deterred thousands of unauthorized workers from trying to cross the border by any means possible – on foot or hidden in railway boxcars, car trunks or truck trailers. In the attempt, many have died of thirst and heat exhaustion in summer, cold and hypothermia in winter.

Mexicans of all socioeconomic categories bitterly resent the metal fences and stadium lighting that the US government has erected along the border in recent years. Texas newspaper columnist Molly Ivins recalls that when, in the mid-1980s, a US government official proposed a massive barrier along the Texas border, sponsors of a chili cook-off held a fence-climbing contest for a case of Lone Star beer. The winning time was seven seconds.

In fact, such impediments have barely slowed border-crossers; instead they have merely rerouted them to other, more hazardous crossing areas like the mountains around Tecate or the blistering desert near Mexicali. This has also made much of the border area a dangerous no man's land where self-styled US vigilantes carry automatic weapons to control undocumented border-crossers. Until the North American Free Trade Agreement (NAFTA) addresses the one major issue it ignored – the free movement of labor as well as goods – the problem will not go away.

Maquiladoras

One alternative to this massive exodus to 'the other side' is the promotion of long-term foreign investment to create jobs in Mexico. Presently foreign investment has taken the form of *maquiladoras*, which are twin assembly-plant operations owned and run by foreign companies, mostly US or Japanese.

Most Mexican towns along the US-Mexico border, including Tijuana, enjoy limited duty-free status, allowing foreign companies to import parts and raw materials from the USA to their maquiladoras without paying taxes. Mexican workers, whose hourly wage is a fraction of their counterparts' across the border, assemble the components, which are then shipped back to the lucrative US market for sale.

Maquiladora workers, mostly young women, seem generally satisfied because their wages are nearly double the average wage in Mexico (despite higher living costs along the border) and their jobs sometimes provide additional training and other benefits. Mexico is pleased with reduced unemployment and increased foreign exchange, but the maquiladoras' contribution to the country's economy and industrial base is minimal because their scope is so limited, and they provide little prospect of long-term investment. Maquiladora wages, relatively high by Mexican standards, still average only about US$1 per hour.

With the implementation of NAFTA, the border area may lose some of the economic advantages that derive from its duty-free status, but it will still benefit from its geographic proximity to the USA.

The Borderlands Economy & NAFTA

Even some Mexican professionals are poorly paid: a full-time university professor, for instance, may earn less than a minimum-wage laborer north of the border. Nevertheless, border towns make a major contribution to the economies of their US counterparts, as many residents of Tijuana, Mexicali and other settlements have special 'border-crosser' status that allows them to enter the USA for shopping trips and to visit relatives. In 1993, in response to anti-immigrant hysteria in mainland California, political activists in Tijuana organized a two-day boycott of San Diego businesses to accentuate the significance of the Mexican contribution to the borderlands economy.

Mexico's federal government eagerly anticipated the ratification of NAFTA, approved in late 1993 by the US Congress, hoping it would give Mexican goods wider access to US markets and perhaps encourage expansion of the peninsula's (and the country's) industrial base and employment, but Mexico's low wages and spotty environmental record spurred opposition to the agreement north of the border. Opposition forces within Mexico have voiced widespread concern that NAFTA and other recent economic measures mark the return and triumph of the discredited ideas of Porfirio Díaz and his científicos.

The Mexican economy's collapse at the end of disgraced former President Carlos Salinas de Gortari's term in 1994 led to a precipitous devaluation of the Mexican peso and a bailout in the form of massive loans from the US government. The peso has since stabilized and the Mexican government repaid the loans ahead of schedule in early 1997, but the reduction of social spending has meant increased unemployment and exacerbated population movement toward the north.

POPULATION & PEOPLE

Baja's population consists largely of *mestizos*, individuals of mixed Indian and European heritage, mostly immigrants or descendants of immigrants from mainland Mexico. Official results of the 1995 intercensus give Baja's total population as about 2.5 million – 2,112,140 in the state of Baja California (northern Baja) and 375,494 in the state of Baja California Sur (southern Baja). In Baja California Sur, 70% of the population was born in the state; in northern Baja, the figure was 53%, reflecting massive immigration from mainland Mexico. In northern Baja, perhaps 2% of the population is foreign, mostly US citizens residing in Tijuana.

Most *bajacalifornianos* (inhabitants of Baja California) live in cities in the extreme northern and southern parts of the peninsula. Tijuana (official population 966,097) accounts for the bulk of Baja's total population; Mexicali (officially 505,016) is the second-largest city. Ensenada (officially 192,550) is third, while La Paz (officially 154,314) is the fourth-largest city and the largest in Baja California Sur.

Many informed analysts suspect that official figures understate the actual figures, though the intercensus seems more credible than the ostensibly complete census of 1990. Poorly paid official census takers, however, make limited efforts to count areas like Tijuana's burgeoning and dangerous shantytowns with any accuracy. Another common explanation for undercounting is that the state government of Baja California is under control of the PAN, the opposition party, and that the federal government of the PRI, which has ruled Mexico in one form or another for nearly the entire century, intentionally understates the figures in order to limit the disbursement of population-based federal assistance to the states. There is also suspicion that the federal government wishes to downplay the phenomenal growth of border cities because of the sensitivity of the immigration issue across the line.

Indigenous Peoples & Early Settlers

Permanent European settlements, which began in the 17th century as Jesuit missions or small military camps, exposed the indigenous population to deadly epidemics that reduced their numbers from upward of 48,000 at contact to barely 3000 by 1820. Baja's 1500 or so remaining Indians, often known by the generic term Cochimí after the now extinct peoples of the Desierto Central, live mainly in the Sierra San Pedro Mártir, the Sierra de Juárez and the lowlands near the Río Hardy. They belong to tribal groups like the Diegueño (Tipai), Paipai, Kiliwa, Cucupah and Kamia, but few follow the traditional subsistence economy of hunting and gathering. Nearly all speak Spanish, but indigenous language use is still vigorous among the Tipai, Paipai and Cucupah.

The past decade has seen the influx of large numbers of Indians from central Mexico to the city of Tijuana in particular, often as a staging point for crossing the US border. Several thousand Mixtecs from rural Oaxaca have settled in the San Quintín area, driven by poverty in the south and attracted by farming jobs in Baja despite relatively low wages. For this reason, mainland indigenous languages are more common than in the past; bilingual schools have even been established in Tijuana, San Quintín and elsewhere.

In the 19th century, Baja's first fishing villages, *ranchos* (rural settlements) and secular towns appeared, along with mining operations that attracted fortune-seekers from around the world. Many established bajacalifornianos are descendants of settlers whose roots were in mainland Mexico or in other parts of the world – some trace their ancestry to the USA, southern and northern Europe or even China. Thanks to these enclaves, unexpected surnames like Smith, Jones and even Crosthwaite and McLish are not unusual on the peninsula.

EDUCATION

Systematic formal education began with the arrival of the Jesuit missionaries in 1697. Not until 1867 did the first secular school open, in Santo Tomás, soon followed by others in Real del Castillo, San Vicente, Tecate and El Rosario. After the turn of the century, educational facilities improved rapidly, and by the time Baja California became a state, there were over 230 primary schools, nine secondary schools and a university.

School attendance, obligatory throughout Mexico from the ages of six to 14, is increasing but is still low in some rural areas. The state-run Universidad Autónoma de Baja California now has sites in Tijuana and Mexicali, as does the private Centro de Enseñanza Técnica y Superior. El Colegio de la Frontera and the Universidad Iberoamericana have campuses in Tijuana, while the Universidad Autónoma de Baja California Sur has a La Paz campus.

Several of these institutions have exchange programs and research affiliations with institutions north of the border, including San Diego State University, the University of California at San Diego and the Scripps Institute of Oceanography in La Jolla.

ARTS

Though underappreciated by most visitors, Baja California's arts scene has many figures and performers worthy of attention.

Dance

Since the mid-20th century, both traditional and experimental dance have prospered on the peninsula, mostly in association with the universities and the Casa de la Cultura de Baja California, the state-sponsored arts agency. Since 1983, Mexicali's Paralelo 32 dance group, associated with the Universidad Autónoma there, has traveled widely throughout the state and the country to promote their craft.

Music

Live musical performances take place on the streets and plazas, even on the buses, at almost any time. Many people play music for a living, including marimba teams with their big wooden xylophones; mariachi groups with violinists, trumpeters, guitarists and a singer, all dressed as *charros* (Mexican cowboys); *norteña* groups with guitar and accordion performing *corridos* (folk ballads); popular brass bands known as *bandas* and ragged lone buskers.

In Mexico's thriving popular music industry, corridos are still popular alongside rock and even punk music, while styles imported from elsewhere in the Americas include tango, bossa nova, salsa and Andean panpipe music.

Norteña Los Tucanes de Tijuana, a popular northern group, specializes in what can only be called *corridos narcotraficantes*, a contemporary manifestation of the classic outlaw genre of the border folk ballad. Sinaloa-based Tierra Brava, whose musicians hail from La Paz, occasionally play the peninsula as well.

Rock Baja California has a particularly vibrant rock music scene, most evident in Tijuana. Among the popular bands are Staura (a sort of Sonic Youth clone), Solución Mortal (hard-core punk), Tijuana No (Clash-inspired salsa-punk; the group has also toured mainland California), Paradoxa (thrash), Mercado Negro (UK-style punk), Beam (California punk), Crime of the Century (a Kiss clone with members from both sides of the border) and Giovanna (pop). Ensenada's Yeo is a heavy-metal act.

Classical Baja's larger cities, most notably Tijuana and La Paz, support classical music at venues like Tijuana's Centro Cultural; ensembles also tour smaller towns and cities. One of the most interesting groupings is Tijuana's Orquesta Baja California, consisting of immigrant Russian musicians under conductor Eduardo García Barrios, a Mexican who studied at Moscow's Tchaikovsky Conservatory prior to the breakup of the Soviet Union.

Literature
Not much literature is specifically Baja Californian as opposed to Mexican in general, but two short-story collections are worth seeking out. The stories of Daniel

Reveles' *Enchiladas, Rice and Beans* are set in Tecate, while Federico Campbell's *Tijuana* deals with life in Baja's border boomtown. The latter includes a useful introduction by translator Debra A Castillo.

Film
Early Hollywood directors gave such insulting treatment to the Mexican borderlands through depictions of casinos and prostitution that Baja California's first cinematic production, *Raza de Bronce* (Race of Bronze) (1927), was a nationalistic response to what director Guillermo Calles perceived as racist stereotyping. In the 1970s authorities in the municipio of Tecate built a cinema village to attract US directors of westerns, but local talent did not flourish until the video format became an inexpensive alternative.

With support from the Universidad Autónoma de Baja California, bajacalifornianos have produced documentaries on such topics as the Jesuit colonization of the peninsula and the Chinese community of Mexicali, as well as short fictional pieces like Gabriel Trujillo's quasibiography of the French poet Rimbaud. Since the mid-1980s, the city of Tijuana has occasionally sponsored a film and video festival to reward the efforts of emerging talent.

Independent US director Jonathan Sarno's oddball romance *Ramona* (1992), which won several awards and is available on video, was set partly in Tijuana. Hollywood recently went south again, with 20th Century Fox opening a lot on the outskirts of Playas de Rosarito for the filming of director James Cameron's budget-busting *Titanic*, scheduled for release in December 1997. One of the peninsula's most incongruous sights in recent memory was the studio's 880-foot-long replica of the famous ocean liner (which sank in 1912 after striking an iceberg near Newfoundland) on the headlands overlooking the Pacific south of town.

Theater
Tijuana, Mexicali and La Paz, all of which have outstanding stage facilities, are Baja

California's dramatic centers. Like film, dance and painting, peninsular theater grew with the universities and the Casa de la Cultura; numerous theater companies have offered aspiring actors the opportunity to develop their talents. Groups like the well-established Thalía Company of Mexicali and the more experimental Los Desarraigados of Tijuana have performed in Mexico City, the USA and overseas.

Visual Arts
Few visitors appreciate what a fertile environment Baja California has provided for the visual arts. Throughout the peninsula, from Tijuana to Los Cabos, evidence of cultural links with mainland Mexican cultural movements like the muralist tradition are apparent, but sculpture and painting flourished even before the creation of the Instituto de Ciencias y Artes del Estado (ICAE, now part of the Instituto de Bellas Artes) and the Universidad Autónoma in the 1950s. Both institutions supported local artists and others who had relocated from mainland Mexico.

After the Universidad Autónoma abandoned the arts community, individual artists combined to form groups like the Círculo de Escultores y Pintores (Circle of Sculptors and Painters) and the Profesionales de Artes Visuales (Visual Arts Professionals). Since 1977, the Bienal de Artes Plásticas de Baja California has been an important competition for artists from the region.

One recent informal movement in the local scene is *cholismo*, the equivalent of European or North American punk, often expressed in street murals featuring traditional Mexican figures like the Virgin of Guadalupe in unconventional contexts. The binational Taller de Arte Fronterizo (Border Art Workshop), with members in Tijuana and San Diego, often stages performance-art shows and events with borderlands themes.

Rubén Martínez describes Tijuana's thriving independent arts community in great detail in the essay 'Tijuana Burning'

in his collection *The Other Side*. Baja California Sur also has a lively arts community, revolving around the village of Todos Santos, which partly but by no means exclusively derives from expatriate North Americans who have relocated to the area. Their work, however, lacks the urgency of that of artists on the borderlands, and more closely resembles styles and themes of US expatriates from Taos and Santa Fe.

SOCIETY & CONDUCT
Baja California is both a frontier region and an immigrant zone, and both US and Mexican influences are evident. Despite conscious efforts, the Mexican government never succeeded completely in removing the border region from the US economic sphere, and it now actively encourages US participation and investment through NAFTA.

Most bajacalifornianos are city dwellers who live near the US border and work in manufacturing, agriculture and service industries like tourism. While remote from mainland Mexico, the peninsula is demonstrably Mexican even though many of its people feel ambivalent toward north-of-the-border consumerism (apparent in the US-style shopping malls in Tijuana and Mexicali), toward the dominance of US television programs and films and toward the necessity of conducting much of the region's business and commerce in English.

Many residents also feel ambivalent, however, toward what they perceive as an unresponsive state centralized in distant Mexico City; this, in part, explains the electoral success of PAN, a challenger to PRI, which has dominated Mexican politics for the past 70 years.

To reinforce the region's Mexican identity for the benefit of tourists and locals, national authorities have built modern cultural centers emphasizing the country's history and diverse cultural traditions, with conspicuous monuments to Mexican heroes. Such efforts are probably superfluous; despite the pervasiveness of US influence in many spheres, Baja's inhabitants are resolutely Mexican even if they wish to share the wealth – aspiring to own a Toyota doesn't mean the purchaser wants to be Japanese.

Nationalism

Mexican nationalism's historical roots date from a late-18th-century mestizo culture that developed along an axis running from Puebla to Mexico City and Guadalajara, but the protracted War of Independence from Spain and subsequent struggles against Spanish, American and French interlopers intensified nationalistic feelings. Foreign economic influence (by the British and Americans at the turn of the century and, more recently, by the Americans again) has also been an issue of contention, especially among radicals and intellectuals. But while Mexicans present a unified front to foreigners, they also acknowledge their country's shortcomings; the typical Mexican despises corrupt politicians, police and government officials, and resents inefficiency in public organizations.

Many if not most Mexicans assume that light-skinned visitors are citizens of the USA, and some resent *gringo* wealth, privilege and past military interventions in Mexican territory. Fair-skinned visitors who are not US citizens may still find themselves called 'gringo', a term that is often but not always pejorative – much depends on context and it can be purely descriptive or even friendly. Another common term, which seems largely descriptive, is *güero* (blond), often applied to virtually any fair-skinned person, whether Mexican or foreigner.

Machismo

Machismo, a common trait throughout Latin America, is an exaggerated masculinity designed to impress other men more than women; it is usually innocuous if rather unpleasant, but can on occasion turn to violence. Many Mexican women, in turn, exaggerate their femininity and defer to male authority in public, but exceptions

to both these roles are not unusual. Foreign women, often seen as sexually available by Mexican men, may attract unwelcome attention. Most women find such attention more of a nuisance than a danger, but some may feel more comfortable traveling with a male companion.

RELIGION

Mexicans are a religious people and physical manifestations of their faith are evident everywhere. Baja California lacks the monumental religious architecture of mainland Mexico, but many of the original Jesuit, Franciscan and Dominican missions still survive, at least in ruin; some of these, like Misión Santa Gertrudis in central Baja, are important pilgrimage sites despite their remoteness. Roadside shrines bear witness not just to victims of traffic accidents but also to important religious figures like the Virgin of Guadalupe. Some of these shrines are intriguing examples of folk art and are well worth a stop on the highway.

Catholicism

Like other Mexicans, the majority of bajacalifornianos are Roman Catholic. Jesuit missionaries pioneered colonization of the peninsula and, in their domain, exercised more authority than the formal institutions of colonial government until their expulsion from the Spanish empire in 1767. Almost everyone from all social strata and racial groups belonged to the Church because, in addition to salvation, it offered education and other social services.

In the 19th and 20th centuries (until 1940), colonial and republican authorities enacted legislation restricting the wealth and influence of the Church. Anticlerical provisions in the Mexican constitutions of 1857 and 1917 included obligatory civil marriage (a Mexican church marriage has no legal standing), a ban on political activity and property ownership by the clergy and a requirement that all church buildings first be authorized and approved by the government. (To this day, all church buildings of every denomination *belong* to the government.) Most of these provisions remain in the constitution but are rarely enforced.

Despite tensions with the state, the Church remains influential, especially as a symbol and an institution of social cohesion – since 1531 the Virgin of Guadalupe has been the most binding symbol of all. The appearance of the dark-skinned Virgin to a Christian Indian named Juan Diego, which led to construction of a landmark church, has been regarded as a link between the Catholic and non-Catholic Indian worlds and a symbol of Mexican nationalism.

Protestantism

While Roman Catholicism is Mexico's dominant religion, evangelical Protestantism is growing here as elsewhere in Latin America. Protestantism in Mexico dates from the Revolution of 1910, when many Mexicans found it an effective outlet for protesting the influence of the traditional Church, but even the smallest communities now often have evangelical churches competing with the Catholics. In the larger cities, like Tijuana, these churches frequently occupy storefronts.

LANGUAGE

Spanish is Mexico's official language, but English is fairly widely spoken along the border (where there are many hybrid 'Spanglish' usages) and at tourist-oriented businesses throughout the Baja Peninsula. Among the Tipai, Paipai and Cucupah of northern Baja, among the mostly Mixtec immigrants in the San Quintín area and even in Tijuana, indigenous languages are frequently spoken.

See the Spanish for Travelers appendix for a quick plunge into the primary language on the peninsula.

Border Spanish

Spanish-speakers on both sides of the US-Mexico border have unselfconsciously adopted many English words. Perhaps the best marker of the cultural border, as opposed to the political border, might be the geographical point where bathrooms taps start to be marked 'C' and 'F' for *caliente* and *frío* rather than 'H' and 'C' for 'hot' and 'cold.'

The following list shows a few common border terms with their English and standard Spanish equivalents. For purposes of differentiation, some of the border-Spanish (or 'Spanglish') spellings are phoneticized, but this can be misleading because the words themselves are rarely written down. Spanglish is essentially an oral language, though occasionally English words are adopted as written and given a Spanish tone.

English	Spanglish	Standard Spanish
brake	el breque	el freno
clutch	el clutch	el embrague
junk	el yonke	las chacharas
lunch	el lonche	el almuerzo
pickup truck	la pickup	la camioneta
rug/carpet	la carpeta*	la alfombra
six pack	el six pack	n/a
truck	la troca	el camión
vacuum cleaner	la vaquium	la aspiradora
yard (distance)	la yarda	vara
yard (lawn)	la yarda	el jardín

*In standard Spanish, *carpeta* means 'notebook.'

Facts for the Visitor

PLANNING

When to Go

For the most part, Baja California is a winter playground whose tropical and subtropical climates appeal to escapees from the frozen north. Temperatures in excess of 110°F (43°C) discourage summer visitors on the Gulf of California and in the Cape Region, but mild weather on northern Baja's Pacific coast makes it very pleasant at that time. During spring break, US university students jam Pacific and Gulf resorts like Ensenada and San Felipe – making these prime places to avoid unless you're one of the revelers. Since not all universities have identical vacation periods, this congestion can last for weeks in March and April.

However, visitors with special interests, such as wildlife viewing, may find other seasons rewarding. The bird colonies of the Midriff Islands, from Bahía de los Angeles south, are most active in the relatively warm month of May, and the desert bighorn sheep is easiest to spot in the withering summer heat of the eastern escarpment of the Sierra de Juárez and Sierra San Pedro Mártir, where it must frequent the few reliable water sources.

Maps

The *Baja Almanac* (Baja Almanac Publishers, 4535 W Sahara, Suite 105, Las Vegas, NV 89102) contains topographical maps at a scale of 1:100,000. Its two volumes cover Baja California (Norte) and Baja California Sur.

Perhaps the best practical road map of Baja is published by the Automobile Club of Southern California, available free of charge to members of the American Automobile Association (AAA); nonmembers can try asking a member for help in getting a copy or can purchase a copy for US$3.95. Several Baja bookstores and other tourist-oriented enterprises, such as Mulegé Divers, carry the AAA map, which is not totally reliable off main roads.

International Travel Map Productions (PO Box 2290, Vancouver, BC, V6B 3W5 Canada) publishes the finely annotated *Baja California* at a scale of 1:1,000,000, which sells for about US$7.95; while excellent for planning trips and background information, it's a bit cluttered for field use.

Ediciones Corona (☎ (65) 52-88-06, Calle G 175, Mexicali, Baja California, México), publishes the Guías Urbanas series of very detailed maps and directories for Mexican cities, including Tijuana, Mexicali, Tecate, Ensenada, San Felipe and La Paz, as well as the Valle de Mexicali. While these maps are up to date, their gray-and-light-blue color scheme makes some of them difficult to read.

For map orders, try the Map Centre (☎ (619) 291-3830), 2611 University Ave, San Diego, CA 92104, or Maplink (☎ (805) 692-6777), 30 S Lapatera Lane, No 5, Santa Barbara, CA 93117. The latter publishes an extensive mail-order catalog.

What to Bring

Clothing that is worn in Baja resembles clothing worn in southern mainland California – cool and casual. Men can wear jeans, shorts, tennis shoes, sandals, T-shirts or just about anything else, especially on the beach. Ties and jackets are only obligatory in the fanciest restaurants, and often not even in these. Women can dress similarly but may prefer conservative clothing in town or if traveling alone.

Sweaters and lightweight jackets are often necessary in winter but only occasionally in summer. A lightweight rain jacket, preferably a loose-fitting rain poncho, can be very handy; winter storms can hit northwestern Baja hard even though it's rarely cold by north-of-the-border standards, while tropical downpours sometimes happen in southern Baja's Cape Region, south of La Paz.

Toiletries like shampoo, shaving cream, razors, soap, dental floss and toothpaste are readily available, but bring your own contact lens solution, tampons, contraceptives and deodorant. Other desirable items include sunglasses, a flashlight, a baseball cap or wide-brimmed hat, a disposable lighter, a pocketknife, a couple yards of cord, diving or snorkeling equipment, fishing equipment, sunscreen, a small sewing kit, a money belt or pouch, a small Spanish-English dictionary and lip balm. (See the Health entry in this chapter for a list of suggested medical items to bring.)

HIGHLIGHTS

Some of Baja California's finest experiences are not the ones that tourist offices usually promote. This entry highlights some of the best, from north to south.

Unlike the typical border crossing, the modest manufacturing center of **Tecate** more closely resembles a mainland Mexican town than does any other settlement in the entire state of Baja California (Norte).

In dry weather, at least, any vehicle with reasonable clearance and a relatively short wheelbase can re-create the nostalgic feeling of driving the peninsula before the paving of the Transpeninsular – so long as the driver is willing to devote at least one full day to the **Puertecitos-Laguna Chapala Road**, a route that can be hell on tires.

Founded by Jesuits and finished by Dominicans, the remote mission village of **San Borja** occupies a scenic oasis reached by a spectacular road from the Transpeninsular or from the paved lateral to Bahía de los Angeles.

Visitors to Isla Cedros, itself an off-the-beaten-track destination, can sometimes catch a lift on a fishing boat to the elephant seal colony on the westernmost island of the tiny, remote archipelago of the **Islas San Benito**, off central Baja's Península Vizcaíno.

Declared a UNESCO World Heritage Site, the dissected (cut by irregular valleys

Tourist Traps

Like every destination, Baja California has its share of places that are overrated or simply distasteful. Travelers who head to these places should be aware of what they're getting into.

La Bufadora Scads of kitschy souvenir stands overwhelm the modest significance of this seaside blowhole south of Ensenada. Everybody goes here; nobody knows why.

San Felipe On the Gulf side of the peninsula, two hours south of Mexicali, this ear-splitting resort belongs to low-life real estate speculators, roaring ATVs and, during spring break, US university students taking advantage of Mexico's lenient liquor laws. In summer, it's a furnace.

Nopoló South of Loreto, the 'mother of the missions,' orderly paved streets wind among weed-filled lots at this presumptuous resort that owes its existence to the ambitions of Fonatur bureaucrats. Nopoló squanders scarce resources, particularly fresh water (for its golf course), that could be utilized much better elsewhere.

Cabo San Lucas If chugging 28 post-dinner shots of tequila (a noted record at one waterfront bar/restaurant) is your idea of a good time, Cabo San Lucas is for you. On waking from your stupor, you may learn that you've signed a time-share contract on one of Cabo's fungus-like condominiums. ∎

and hills) volcanic plateau of the **Sierra de San Francisco** contains the most extraordinary rock art sites of the many sites that dot the peninsula from the borderlands to the Cape Region. The mule-back descent into the sierra's canyons from the village of San Francisco de la Sierra, north of San Ignacio, is an unforgettable experience.

Aficionados of industrial archaeology will find the former French company town of **Santa Rosalía** worth exploring for the ruins of its massive copper-smeltering operation, as well as its unusual residential architecture and a church designed by the famous Eiffel, of Tower fame.

The drive north along the western side of the Bahía de La Paz to the fish camp of **San Evaristo** is like viewing a cutaway of Arizona's Grand Canyon of the Colorado. Ordinary passenger cars can go as far as Punta El Mechudo, where the route starts to climb, but high-clearance, short-wheelbase vehicles can continue to some of the most secluded camping and fishing areas on the peninsula.

Limited beach access has kept the Cape Region artists' colony of **Todos Santos** from suffering the relentlessly tasteless overdevelopment of the nearby Los Cabos area. The gringo presence, while palpable, is more subdued and refined than almost anywhere else on the peninsula.

The most worthwhile sight in the Cape Region, the interior mountain range known as the **Sierra de la Laguna**, is a botanical wonderland where aspens, cacti, oaks and palms grow in close proximity, refreshing mountain streams rush through granite canyons, and 7000-foot peaks offer relief from the tropical heat of the lowlands. No other place on the peninsula is more deserving of national park status, as it provides what is probably Baja's best hiking and backpacking.

TOURIST OFFICES
Local Tourist Offices
The federal government agency Fonatur runs offices at Nopoló and San José del Cabo, but their sole function is to disseminate information about luxury resorts at Nopoló and Los Cabos (San José del Cabo and Cabo San Lucas) and promote their development.

Offices of the Secretaría de Turismo del Estado (Secture) in Tijuana, Tecate, Mexicali, Playas de Rosarito, San Felipe, Ensenada and La Paz are affiliated with the state governments of either Baja California

(northern Baja) or Baja California Sur (southern Baja). The staff at all these offices are helpful in providing information about those cities and any other place in Baja, and may also help make hotel reservations throughout the peninsula. Secture also sponsors honorary delegations in a few smaller towns, like San Quintín.

Local offices of the Cámara Nacional de Comercio (Canaco, National Chamber of Commerce) and the Comité de Turismo y Convenciones (Cotuco, Committee on Tourism & Conventions) can be found in Tijuana, Ensenada, Tecate and Mexicali. The Ensenada Cotuco office is among the best-organized sources of information in Baja, while those in Tecate and Mexicali are helpful but have more limited resources.

Tourist Offices Abroad
Mexican government tourist offices outside Mexico know little about Baja California, but they do have the latest information on matters like tourist card requirements and can also issue tourist cards and car permits. Mexican government tourist offices abroad include:

Canada
  1 Place Ville Marie, Suite 1526, Montréal, Québec H3B 2B5 (☎ (514) 871-1052)
  2 Bloor St W, Suite 1801, Toronto, Ontario M4W 3E2 (☎ (416) 925-0704)
  999 W Hastings St, Suite 1610, Vancouver, BC V6C 1M3 (☎ (604) 669-2845)
France
  4 Rue Notre Dame des Victoires, 75002 Paris (☎ 01.42.86.56.30)
Germany
  Wiesenhüttenplatz 26, D60329 Frankfurt-Am-Main (☎ (69) 25-34-13)
Italy
  Via Barberini 3, 00187 Rome (☎ (6) 487-2182)
Japan
  2-15-1 Nagata-Cho, Chiyoda-Ku, Tokyo 100 (☎ (3) 580-2962)
Spain
  Velázquez 126, Madrid 28006 (☎ (01) 561-3520)
UK
  60/61 Trafalgar Square, London WC2N 5DS (☎ (0171) 839-3177)

USA
California
1801 Century Park E, Suite 1080, Los
Angeles, CA 90067 (☎ (310) 203-8191)
Florida
2333 Ponce de Leon Blvd, Suite 710, Coral
Gables, FL 33134 (☎ (305) 443-9160)
Illinois
70 E Lake St, Suite 1413, Chicago, IL
60601 (☎ (312) 606-9015)
New York
405 Park Ave, Suite 1401, New York, NY
10022 (☎ (212) 755-7261)
Texas
5075 Westheimer Blvd, Houston, TX 77056
(☎ (713) 829-1611)

In the USA, general tourist information for
Mexico can also be accessed by calling
☎ (800) 446-3942.

Tourist Publications

The *Baja Times* and *Baja Sun* are English-
language publicity rags distributed free at
hotels, restaurants, souvenir stores and
tourist offices throughout the peninsula.
Though both provide information about
events, restaurants and tourist-related news
in northern Baja, they are probably most
useful for their discount coupons for
restaurants and bars. *Baja Visitor* is a *Baja
Sun*-clone newsletter that appears in several different giveaway versions covering
Tijuana, Playas de Rosarito, Mexicali,
Ensenada, San Quintín and San Felipe.

Other sources of current information
include newsletters published by Sanborn's Mexico Club (Sanborn's Insurance,
☎ (210) 686-0711, PO Box 310, McAllen,
TX 78502) and distributed at most of their
border offices; the Mexico West Travel
Club (PO Box 1646, Bonita, CA 92002);
and *Los Cabos News*, a newsletter focusing
on southern Baja published by Vagabundos
del Mar (PO Box 824, Isleton, CA 95641).
The Discover Baja Travel Club (☎ (619)
275-4225, (800) 727-2252, 3089 Claire-
mont Drive, San Diego, CA 92117) publishes the highest-quality newsletter of any
such organization.

In the Los Cabos-La Paz region, several
other publications (wholly or partially in

English) provide information useful to
travelers. These are mostly free and available in restaurants and hotel lobbies;
see the Cabo San Lucas entry in the Cape
Region chapter for more information.

VISAS & DOCUMENTS

Every visitor beyond the immediate border
area should carry a valid passport and a
Mexican government tourist card at all
times; see Tourist Cards, below, for details.
Consular visas may be required for travel
by citizens of some countries. Drivers must
have a valid driver's license, current vehicle
registration and, if planning to travel to
mainland Mexico, a temporary import
permit for each vehicle (including motorcycles and boats), obtainable at the border.
(See the Getting Around chapter for information on the paperwork needed to take a
vehicle into mainland Mexico.) These
requirements are in flux, so verify information before going.

Visas

Anyone planning to live in Mexico or to
own or rent a vacation home there needs
the multiple-entry, nonimmigrant FM-3
visa, valid for one year and renewable for
another five. Retirees over the age of 50
who are eligible for residence require a
variant on this visa.

Tourist Cards

By law, US and Canadian citizens may
cross Mexican land borders for periods of
less than 72 hours with barely a glance
from immigration officials and no inspection of documents (it is advisable to carry
proof of citizenship or residency in order
to return to the USA, however). In practice oversight is so limited that visitors in
the immediate border zone can stay much
longer almost without concern, but all
visitors regardless of age need a tourist
card for travel south beyond Maneadero
on the Pacific coast or south beyond San
Felipe on the Gulf of California, or to
enter Baja by air or sea. A tourist card is
also necessary for travel to mainland
Mexico.

Tourist cards are issued by Mexican government tourist offices, consulates and embassies, by immigration authorities at border crossings, by airlines flying to Mexico from North America, by automobile clubs in the USA and Canada and by some travel agencies. At the border crossing itself, Servicios Migratorios (Immigration) must validate the card.

Requirements for a validated tourist card at the border depend on nationality:

- Travelers born in the United States need proof of citizenship, preferably a passport or birth certificate. A birth certificate must clearly show official certification, such as an embossed seal.
- Naturalized US citizens need a photo and proof of citizenship (a passport or a certificate of naturalization from the Immigration & Naturalization Service). Again, a US passport is preferable.
- Canadian citizens need a passport or birth certificate.
- For latest requirements for citizens of other countries, contact a Mexican consulate or tourist office. As this book went to press, citizens of European Community countries needed only a passport. Brazilians, South Africans, holders of Hong Kong passports and citizens of most other Asian, African and South American countries needed consular visas. Some, but not all, must pay US$29 for the privilege.

Tourist cards are valid for 180 days. Visitors who overstay the time limit may be subject to fines, but few are asked to show their tourist cards at land borders. On the other hand, travelers arriving from southern Baja at Tijuana's Aeropuerto Internacional Abelardo L Rodríguez will probably be asked to show their card before being allowed to claim baggage. Keep in mind that replacing a lost tourist card can mean a tiresome, time-consuming encounter with Mexican bureaucracy.

For short-term visitors, a driver's license or identity card issued by a department of motor vehicles is usually accepted as proof of US citizenship, but citizens of other countries must have their passports and appropriate US visas to return to the USA.

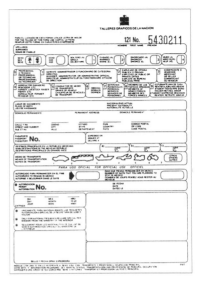

Tourist card

Be certain of the entry and re-entry status of your US visa before departing for Mexico.

Driver's License

To drive in Baja California, you need a valid US or Canadian driver's license or an International Driving Permit. US and Canadian licenses are widely recognized, but the International Driving Permit may require some explanation, since Baja police are unaccustomed to it.

A car permit is only required for mainland Mexico; it also serves as a tourist card for the driver. It is preferable to validate car permits at the border, but it may be possible to do so in Ensenada or at the ferry terminal near La Paz. See the Getting Around chapter for more information on car permits.

Minors

Every year numerous parents run away to Mexico with a child because of legal disputes with the child's other parent in the USA. For this reason, Mexican

Consulates

Mexico has extensive diplomatic representation around the world, though more in the USA than anywhere else. The listings below are consulates rather than embassies (embassies deal with diplomatic matters rather than tourist inquiries), though in some cases the embassy and consulate are at the same site.

Mexican Consulates Abroad

Australia
135-153 New South Head Rd
Level 1, Edgecliff, Sydney
NSW 2027
☎ (02) 9326-1311

Canada
2000 Rue Mansfield
Montréal, Québec H3A 2Z7
☎ (514) 288-2707

199 Bay St W, Suite 4440
Toronto, Ontario M5L 1E9
☎ (416) 368-2875

1130 W Pender St
Vancouver, BC V6E 4A4
☎ (604) 684-3547

France
·4 Rue Notre Dame des
Victoires, 75002 Paris
☎ 01.42.86.56.20
fax 01.42.86.05.80

Germany
Kurfürstendamm 72
10709 Berlin 1
☎ (030) 324-9047

Adenauerallee 100
53113 Bonn
☎ (0228) 914-8634
fax (0228) 914-8619

Neue Mainzerstrasse 57
6000 Frankfurt 1
☎ (069) 230-1514

UK
8 Halkin St
London SW1X 7DW
☎ (0171) 235-6393

USA
Washington, DC
2827 16th St NW
Washington, DC 20009
☎ (202) 736-1000

Arizona
541 10th St
Douglas, AZ 85607
☎ (520) 364-3107

486 Grand Ave
Nogales, AZ 85621
☎ (520) 287-2521

1990 W Camelback Rd
Suite 110, Phoenix, AZ 85015
☎ (602) 242-7398

553 S Stone Ave
Tucson, AZ 85701
☎ (520) 882-5595

California
331 W 2nd St
Calexico, CA 92231
☎ (760) 357-3863

830 Van Ness Ave
Fresno, CA 93721
☎ (209) 233-9770

2401 W 6th St,
Los Angeles, CA 90057
☎ (213) 351-6800

Transportation Center
201 E 4th St, Room 209
Oxnard, CA 93030
☎ (805) 483-4684

1010 8th St
Sacramento, CA 95814
☎ (916) 441-3287

532 North D St
San Bernardino, CA 92401
☎ (909) 889-9836

1549 India St
San Diego, CA 92101
☎ (619) 231-8414

870 Market St, Suite 528
San Francisco, CA 94102
☎ (415) 392-6576

380 N 1st St, Suite 102
San Jose, CA 95113
☎ (408) 294-3414

Colorado
48 Steele St
Denver, CO 80206
☎ (303) 331-1112

Florida
1200 NW 78th Ave
Suite 200, Miami, FL 33126
☎ (305) 716-4977

823 E Colonial Dr
Orlando, FL 32803
☎ (407) 894-0514

---

authorities require a notarized 'Permission for a Minor to Travel in Mexico' form, signed by both parents, permitting children under the age of 18 to enter the country accompanied by one parent (minors traveling with both parents do not require this permission) or a legal guardian. The form is available from Mexican government tourist offices and from the California State Automobile Association (CSAA).

Fishing License
Anglers 16 years or older need a fishing license; those importing boats need a boat license as well. For more information, see the Outdoor Activities chapter.

Pet Permit
Travelers entering Mexico with dogs or cats must have proof of vaccination (issued within three days of crossing the border) against rabies and other conta-

Georgia
3220 Peachtree Rd NE
Atlanta, GA 30305
☎ (404) 266-1913

Illinois
300 N Michigan Ave
2nd Floor, Chicago, IL 60601
☎ (312) 855-0056

Louisiana
World Trade Center
2 Canal St, Suite 840
New Orleans, LA 70130
☎ (504) 522-3596

Massachusetts
20 Park Plaza, Suite 506
Boston, MA 02116
☎ (617) 426-4942

Michigan
600 Renaissance Center
Suite 1510, Detroit, MI 48243
☎ (313) 567-7709

Missouri
1015 Locust St, Suite 922
St Louis, MO 63101
☎ (314) 436-3233

New Mexico
400 Gold SW, Suite 100
Albuquerque, NM 87102
☎ (505) 247-2139

New York
8 E 41st St
New York, NY 10017
☎ (212) 689-0456

Oregon
1234 SW Morrison
Portland, OR 97205
☎ (503) 274-1442

Pennsylvania
Bourse Bldg, 111 S Independence Mall E, Suite 1010
Philadelphia, PA 19106
☎ (215) 922-4262

Puerto Rico
654 Av Muñoz Rivera
Suite 1837, Hato Rey
PR 00918
☎ (809) 764-0258

Texas
200 E 6th St, Suite 200
Austin, TX 78701
☎ (512) 478-2300

724 E Elizabeth St
Brownsville, TX 78520
☎ (210) 542-2051

800 N Shoreline Blvd
Suite 410
Corpus Christi, TX 78401
☎ (512) 882-3375

8855 Stemmons Freeway
Dallas, TX 75247
☎ (214) 630-7341

300 E Losoya
Del Rio, TX 78840
☎ (210) 775-9451

140 Adams St
Eagle Pass, TX 78852
☎ (210) 773-9255

910 E San Antonio St
El Paso, TX 79901
☎ (915) 533-3644

3015 Richmond Ave, Suite 100, Houston, TX 77098
☎ (713) 524-2300

1612 Farragut St
Laredo, TX 78040
☎ (210) 723-6369

600 S Broadway Ave
McAllen, TX 78501
☎ (210) 686-0243

511 W Ohio, Suite 121
Midland, TX 79701
☎ (915) 687-2335

127 Navarro St
San Antonio, TX 78205
☎ (210) 227-9145

Utah
458 East 200 S, Suite 110
Salt Lake City, UT 84111
☎ (801) 521-8502

Washington
2132 3rd Ave
Seattle, WA 98121
☎ (206) 448-3526

Foreign Consulates in Baja California
As might be expected, the USA maintains a greater diplomatic presence in Baja than does any other foreign country, with a large consulate in Tijuana and a smaller one in Cabo San Lucas. A few other countries, most notably Canada, have representation in Tijuana; for details, see individual city entries.

gious diseases; the proof must also be approved by the US Department of Agriculture and a Mexican consulate (which will charge US$16 for the privilege). It is also a good idea to carry an International Health Certificate, obtainable from any veterinarian.

Before taking a pet to Mexico, confirm re-importation requirements for the USA. Unless you have no alternative, it's probably better to leave your pet at home.

CUSTOMS
Mexican Customs inspectors seldom hassle foreign visitors on entry, though firearms are prohibited and will be confiscated. If you are carrying foreign-manufactured items like cameras, computers, radios and TVs into Baja from the USA, it's wise to register them with US Customs before crossing the border, though registration is usually unnecessary if you have the original receipts for the items.

Each US resident returning to the USA from Baja or elsewhere in Mexico may bring in duty-free items with a total retail value up to US$400, for personal use only and not for resale. The exemption may only be used once in any 30-day period, but over 2700 items, including handicrafts, are exempt from these limits.

Limits on the importation of liquor are stricter. Adult US residents (21 years or older) crossing the California border by car or on foot may bring only one liter of hard liquor (spirits), wine or beer into mainland California every 30 days. Residents returning to mainland California by bus, taxi or air may import one liter of alcohol duty free; additional alcoholic beverages are subject to duty, but may enter in any quantity considered reasonable for personal use. Visitors to northeastern Baja California can avoid mainland California's more stringent liquor requirements by returning to the USA at San Luis Río Colorado on the Sonora-Arizona border.

There is a complex list of regulations for agricultural products, but in general, plants, seeds, soil, pork, poultry, live birds and straw are prohibited. Most fruits and vegetables are permitted, except for avocados, sugar cane, potatoes, sweet potatoes and yams. For more detailed information, ask US Customs for the brochure 'Mexican Border: US Agricultural Quarantine Information.'

MONEY

Both Mexican pesos and US dollars are commonly used in Baja, but US dollars may not be accepted in some small towns and villages. The same symbol ($) is used for both currencies; restaurants, hotels, gas stations and other establishments that deal with North Americans will put *Dlls* or *m/n* after prices to indicate whether they are in US dollars or *moneda nacional* (national money), respectively.

Under the currency reform of 1993, the Mexican government slashed three zeros off the hyperinflated peso (M$) of the 1980s to create the new peso (N$), consisting of 100 centavos. Coins exist in values of N$0.05, N$0.10, N$0.20, N$0.50, N$1, N$2, N$5 and N$10. Bank notes, bearing the portraits of historical figures, come in denominations of N$10 (Emiliano Zapata), N$20 (Miguel Hidalgo), N$50 (José María Morales) and N$100 (Nezahualcoyotl).

Costs

All prices listed in this book are in US dollars but are subject to change. While President Ernesto Zedillo's economic policies have achieved a stable exchange rate, prices are in constant flux and rising Mexican inflation has eroded most of the dollar's briefly elevated purchasing power. Several inauspicious political events, including the assassinations of PRI presidential candidate Luis Donaldo Colosio in Tijuana and PRI official Francisco Ruiz Massieu in Mexico City, the continuing Maya Indian uprising in the state of Chiapas and the emergence of guerrilla warfare in the state of Guerrero, have not yet translated into economic instability.

Food and accommodations cost more in Baja California than in the rest of Mexico, and only slightly less than in the USA. Prices are highest near the border and in tourist centers like La Paz and Cabo San Lucas. By buying food from fruit and vegetable markets or corner food stands, it is possible to eat more cheaply, but prices at better restaurants equal or even exceed those north of the border.

Accommodations are relatively costly, and it's hard to find a good double room for less than US$25 per night. Camping is the cheapest way to go – you can camp cheaply in many RV parks and for free on almost any beach.

Traveler's Checks, ATMs & Credit Cards

Traveler's checks are generally accepted in tourist areas and most banks will cash them, but the bureaucracy involved in doing so can be tiresome. Some banks will not cash more than US$200 of checks at a time.

ATMs are common in Baja's larger cities and tourist areas, but are few on the long stretch of the Transpeninsular between Ensenada and Ciudad Constitución.

MasterCard and Visa are the most widely accepted credit cards at tourist establishments; American Express is less widely accepted. Always check to see if there will be a *recargo* (surcharge) for using a credit card. Note that Pemex stations will *not* accept credit cards for payment – gasoline purchases are cash only.

Currency Exchange
Between 1980 and 1993, the peso's value declined from US$1=M$22 to US$1= M$3100, at which point the currency reform struck three zeros from the peso, to the relief of everyone with pocket calculators. The exchange rate remained stable until mid-1994, when outgoing President Carlos Salinas de Gortari, under pressure in a collapsing economy, ordered a precipitous devaluation as part of an economic bailout loan (since repaid) from the United States. The official exchange rate has fallen to about US$1=N$7.80 but has remained stable for some time.

Changing Money
Money can be exchanged at banks, hotels and *casas de cambio* (exchange houses). Banks and cambios offer virtually identical rates and may pay less for cash than traveler's checks. Cambios are usually quicker and less bureaucratic than banks.

Banks rarely charge commissions, but they may only change a certain minimum amount of foreign currency. Some cambios, mostly in the border towns on the US side, may charge a commission; those in San Ysidro (across the border from Tijuana) are notorious for cheap tricks like charging 'no commission' for pesos into dollars, but a substantial commission for dollars into pesos.

Hotels, especially at the top end of the scale, offer poor rates and often charge commissions as well.

Tipping & Bargaining
In restaurants, it is customary to tip about 10% of the bill. In general, waiters are poorly paid, so if you can afford to eat out, you can afford to tip. Even a small *propina* will be appreciated. Taxi drivers do not require tips, although you may round off the fare for convenience.

Bargaining is a way of life in Mexico, but less so in Baja than in other parts of the country. In some instances, artisan's souvenirs are open to negotiation, as are cab fares, but the market-style haggling so common in mainland Mexico is unusual.

Taxes
Hotel taxes in Baja generally run about 10% for luxury lodgings, but generally do not apply to budget accommodations. Before taking a room, ask whether the price includes an IVA *(impuesto de valor agregado*, value-added tax). Unless otherwise noted, accommodations prices listed in this book include any applicable tax.

Student Discounts
Student discounts are almost unknown and, unless you're in Mexico for an extended period, hardly worth pursuing. Baja's few museums offer very small discounts on already low admission fees to students under 26 who hold a card from either the Servicio Educativo de Turismo de los Estudiantes y la Juventud de México (SETEJ) or Consejo Nacional de Recursos para la Atención de la Juventud (CREA). These cards also entitle holders to youth hostel membership and lower hostel rates. Cards can be obtained at the La Paz youth hostel (see the Cape Region chapter for its address).

Both CREA and SETEJ occasionally conduct group tours of Baja and other parts of Mexico. For more information, contact the Asociación Mexicana de Albergues de la Juventud (☎ (5) 525-2548, (5) 525-2974), Glorieta del Metro Insurgentes, Local CC-11, Colonia Juárez, México DF 06600, or SETEJ (☎ (5) 211-0743, (5) 211-6636), Hamburgo 301, Zona Rosa, México DF.

POST & COMMUNICATIONS

The Servicio Postal Mexicano (the formal name for Mexico's national postal service) sells postage stamps and sends and receives mail at every *oficina de correos* (post office) in Baja California. Its snappy logo is no reflection of its efficiency – letters from Tijuana, for instance, arrive in San Diego only after passing through Mexico City. Most northern Baja businesses with dealings north of the border maintain post office boxes in San Ysidro or Calexico.

Sending Mail

Airmail letters to North or Central America cost about US$0.30, to Europe US$0.50 and to Australasia US$0.60. Service is not always dependable – an airmail letter from Cabo San Lucas to Los Angeles, via Mexico City, may take anywhere from four days to a fortnight. Mail to Europe takes one to three weeks.

When sending a parcel or letter via airmail, mark it conspicuously with the phrase *'Por Avión.'* To guarantee that it will arrive, send it registered or, better yet, entrust it to a private service like UPS or Federal Express.

Receiving Mail

Receiving mail can be somewhat tricky. You can send or receive letters and packages care of a post office if they are addressed
as follows:

John SMITH (capitalize surname)
Lista de Correos
Town/City Name
State (Baja California or Baja California Sur)
00000 (postal code if known)
MÉXICO

When a letter arrives at a locale's main post office, the postmaster places it on an alphabetical list that is updated daily. Ask the sender to mark the letter, or package, *'favor de retener hasta llegada'* (please hold until arrival); otherwise, it may be returned to the sender after 15 days.

If expected correspondence does not arrive, ask the clerk to check under every possible combination of your initials, even 'M' (for Mr, Ms, and so on). There may be particular confusion if correspondents use your middle name, since Mexicans use both paternal and maternal surnames for identification, with the former listed first. Thus a letter to Mexican 'Ernesto Zedillo Ponce de León' will be found under 'Z' rather than 'P,' while a letter to North American 'William Jefferson Clinton' may be found under 'J,' even though 'Clinton' is the proper surname.

Telephone

Mexico's privatized telephone system continues to be revamped, with fiber-optic lines replacing copper wire and line-microwave systems. At first, these improvements will affect only long-distance services, but improvements to local lines should take place in the near future.

Local and domestic long-distance calls are moderately priced, starting around US$0.05 for a local call, and easy to place from a *caseta de teléfono*, a telephone office that is usually part of a store or pharmacy, easily identified by its telephone-shaped symbol. There are increasing numbers of public telephones in major cities like Tijuana and Mexicali, as well as resort towns like San Felipe and Playas de Rosarito, but they are often located at the noisiest intersections and are frequently out of order. In addition to coins, the newer Larga Distancia Automática (Automatic Long Distance, or Ladatel) public telephones accept more convenient magnetic phone cards. Phone cards are available in values of N$25, N$35, N$50 and N$100 and are issued by Telnor, the northern Mexican telephone company.

From standard telephones, dial ☎ 02 for domestic long distance, 04 for local information or 09 for international service. From the Ladatel phones, dial ☎ 91 for domestic long distance, 92 for domestic person-to-person, 95 for the USA and Canada, 96 for the USA and Canada collect

Phone Home or Fly Home?

If you're considering a call home from any of the convenient public phones that urge you to charge the call to MasterCard, Visa or American Express, you should be aware of the very high charges imposed by the Texas-based company that owns them. These shockingly expensive devices only require dialing '0' to contact an international operator, but talk for an hour on one and you may spend enough to buy a roundtrip plane ticket – rates are as high as US$23 for the first minute and US$8 per minute thereafter. Many Baja travelers have found unwelcome surprises on their next credit-card bill.

Unless you can afford to skip your next mortgage payment, the best rule is not to use any phone that encourages you to use a bankcard. Note especially that some of these phones resemble Pacific Bell or AT&T phones. ■

or person-to-person, 98 for all other countries or 99 for all other countries person-to-person. After dialing that number, dial the area code and number within the country you're calling.

International calls can still be time-consuming, but services have improved and some formerly isolated locations, such as Bahía de los Angeles, now have telephone service. Standard rates are about US$1 per minute to the USA, US$2 per minute to Western Europe. Collect or credit-card calls are generally cheaper, but not all offices permit collect calls; those that do usually levy a surcharge of up to US$2, so truly destitute travelers may not be able to place a call. The best sites to place long-distance calls are the casetas or *cabinas* at larger bus terminals, like Tijuana's Central Camionera, where bankcards like Visa may be used to charge the call.

Telephone codes for collect and credit-card calls to the USA and Canada appear below (for other countries, dial ☎ 113):

Canada	☎ 95-800-010-1990
USA (AT&T)	☎ 95-800-462-4240
USA (MCI)	☎ 95-800-674-7000
USA (Sprint)	☎ 95-800-877-8000

Discount hours for Ladatel 91 and 92 numbers (50% off) are 8 pm to 8 am weekdays and all day Sunday. Discount hours for Ladatel 95 numbers (one-third off, except Alaska and Hawaii) are 7 pm to 7 am weekdays, all day Saturday and midnight to 5 pm Sunday. Discount hours for Ladatel 98 numbers (one-third off) are all day Saturday and Sunday, but weekday times depend on the region called: South America and the Caribbean, 5 pm to 5 am; Europe, Africa and the Near East, 6 pm to 6 am; Central America, 7 pm to 7 am; and Asia and Oceania, 5 am to 5 pm.

Visitors should beware and avoid the prominent blue telephones, now common throughout the peninsula, that permit bankcard calls (Visa, MasterCard, etc) to the USA and elsewhere. Charges for these operator-assisted calls are very high; if you use one, expect a very unpleasant surprise when the next month's bill arrives. See the sidebar Phone Home or Fly Home? for more information.

Note that many US area codes, including some area codes in mainland California, are scheduled to be changed in coming years. Should you have trouble reaching a mainland California phone number, call US information and inquire whether the area code has changed.

Fax, Telegraph & Email

Most larger post offices offer fax services, as do telegraph offices, major hotels, larger bus terminals and private telephone offices. Telégrafos Nacionales sends cables both within Mexico and overseas; charges depend on whether the telegram is *ordinario*, *urgente* or *extra urgente*.

Email access is available through Internet service providers in Baja's larger cities; see individual city/town entries for recommendations.

BOOKS

The available books on Baja are numerous, so readers can afford to be selective. From the early Jesuit journals to the latest guidebook, quality varies, but for a more enjoyable experience, learn before you go.

Guidebooks & General Interest

Carl Franz's *The People's Guide to Mexico* is the 10th edition of an irreverent classic whose attitude is summarized by the motto 'Wherever you go, there you are.' Really a guide to everyday situations travelers encounter in Mexico, it's an essential complement to books like this one, which deal more with specific destinations. If you are traveling further afield, Lonely Planet also has guidebooks to Mexico; Costa Rica; Guatemala, Belize and Yucatán; a shoestring guide to Central America; and a guide to mainland California and Nevada.

Long out of print but still available from specialist bookstores is Peter Gerhard and Howard Gulick's informed, intelligent *Lower California Guidebook* (Arthur H Clark Company, Glendale, CA, 1962). It's a classic guide to driving the peninsula prior to the completion of the Transpeninsular, and it's still a worthwhile companion on the road.

Intended primarily for drivers, the Automobile Club of Southern California's *Baja California Guidebook* is available free to members of the club and its affiliates, but is also available in commercial bookstores for US$7.95. A more valuable entry, well worth acquiring, is John Minch and Thomas Leslie's *The Baja Highway*, which logs Baja's main roads with exceptionally informative commentary on the geographical, geological and biological features along the way. Its shortcomings are mediocre sketches of landforms and animals,

the absence of a glossary for terms that may be unfamiliar to general audiences and the absence of a bibliography.

Activity Guidebooks

For a variety of outdoor activities, easily the best choice is Walt Peterson's *The Baja Adventure Book*. Covering fishing, boating, kayaking, rock climbing, backpacking, windsurfing and many other possibilities, it also contains many useful maps, but its oversize format is unwieldy for backpackers. It contains almost no information on cities, however.

Bicycling Bonnie Wong's *Bicycling Baja* is the only guidebook to bicycling the peninsula, but its coverage rarely addresses unpaved roads, except in the far north; mountain bikers will in most instances have to be pioneers.

Boating Leland Lewis' well-illustrated *Baja Sea Guide* charts yacht anchorages on Baja's Pacific and Gulf coasts. The 3rd edition of Jack Williams' *Baja Boaters Guide* covers practically every possible mooring along the Pacific coast (Vol I) and the Sea of Cortez (Vol II).

Camping If you're planning to drive extensively, to camp in trailer parks or elsewhere, to backpack in the countryside or to go boating on the Gulf, consider acquiring Carl Franz's *Camping in Mexico* and *RV Camping in Mexico* (John Muir Publications, PO Box 613, Santa Fe, NM 87504). The latter has a lengthy, detailed chapter on many established RV parks and camping areas in Baja. Another good source, though some of the information is sketchy, is Fred and Gloria Jones' *Baja Camping: The Complete Guide*.

Walt Peterson, author of *The Baja Adventure Book* (see above), has joined forces with Michael Peterson to produce *Exploring Baja by RV*.

Diving Michael and Linda Farley's *Baja California Diver's Guide* (Marcor Publishing, Calistoga, CA, 1991) is a detailed guide to diving off the Pacific and Gulf coasts. More recent entries are Susan Speck's *Baja Diving* (Aqua Quest Publications, Locust Valley, NY, 1995) and Pisces Books' Baja dive guide.

Fishing Packed with information on identifying various species and where, when and how to catch them, the 4th edition of Tom Miller's *Angler's Guide to Baja California* includes several maps, drawings and charts. It's available from Baja Trail Publications, PO Box 6088, Huntington Beach, CA 92646.

The 2nd edition of Neil Kelly and Gene Kira's *The Baja Catch* covers both inshore and deep-water fishing. It's available from Apples & Oranges, PO Box 2296, Valley Center, CA 92082.

Flora & Fauna *The Baja California Plant Field Guide* by Norman C Roberts describes over 400 plants on the peninsula. For US$25, it's available from Natural History Publishing Co, PO Box 962, La Jolla, CA 92037. Specialists should consult Ira L Wiggins' voluminous *Flora of Baja California*.

Ann Zwinger's *A Desert Country near the Sea* is an unusual first-person natural history of Baja's Cape Region. Interspersed with descriptions and attractive illustrations of flora and fauna are informative historical vignettes of people and places, but her style is a bit, well, florid.

Roger Tory Peterson's *Field Guide to Mexican Birds* covers both the mainland and Baja California. Sanford Wilbur's *Birds of Baja California* is more specialized, but its handful of illustrations show only those birds unique to the peninsula.

Daniel Gotshall's *Marine Animals of Baja California: A Guide to the Common Fish & Invertebrates* (Western Marine Enterprises, Marina del Rey, CA, 1988) has lavish color photographs of Baja's sea life. Steven Leatherwood and Randall Reaves' *The Sierra Club Handbook of Whales & Dolphins* is useful for whale-

watchers. Ted Case and Martin Cody's *Island Biogeography in the Sea of Cortez* is a collection of essays for specialists or enthusiastic amateurs in the fields of oceanography, geology, botany, mammalogy, ornithology, herpetology (the study of reptiles and amphibians) and ichthyology (the study of fish), as well as those interested in the human impact on the Gulf environment.

Hiking Jim Conrad's *No Frills Guide to Hiking in Mexico* contains a brief chapter on Baja. Parts of Walt Peterson's *The Baja Adventure Book* do a much better job; its size and weight make it unwieldy for hikers, but features like the 1:50,000 contour map of the trail up Picacho del Diablo in Parque Nacional Sierra San Pedro Mártir are very useful.

Sea Kayaking Andromeda Romano-Lax's *Sea Kayaking in Baja* describes a handful of kayaking routes, mostly on the Gulf of California, but some experienced kayakers have found its usefulness limited.

Travel Literature
John Steinbeck's classic combination of travelogue and natural history essay, *The Log from the Sea of Cortez* (available in a 1995 Penguin reprint), was one of the earliest studies of marine life in the Gulf of California. Steinbeck's biologist companion, Ed Ricketts, was the model for Doc in the novelist's famous *Cannery Row*.

Ray Cannon's *The Sea of Cortez* (Lane Books, Menlo Park, CA, 1966) is a coffee-table book, with first-rate photos, published by a lifelong Baja enthusiast. Literary naturalist Joseph Wood Krutch wrote *The Forgotten Peninsula*, recently reissued in paperback, about his own travels in pre-Transpeninsular Baja.

Into a Desert Place is Graham Mackintosh's narrative of his two-year, 3000-mile (5000-km) walk around the Baja coast, which has been called 'one of the most grueling and challenging solo bipedal treks ever taken' (Sierra Club, San Francisco).

Jonathan Waterman's *Kayaking the Vermillion Sea: Eight Hundred Miles Down the Baja* is an account of a two-month kayak trip by the author and his wife from the Río Colorado delta to the tip of the peninsula.

History

Available in paperback, Michael C Meyer and William L Sherman's *The Course of Mexican History* is one of the best general accounts of Mexican history and society. For a general introduction to Baja, see WW Johnson's *Baja California*.

Prehistory California's cave paintings have attracted the attention of both popular and academic writers; a basic overview is Campbell Grant's *Rock Art of Baja California* (Dawson's Bookshop, Los Angeles, CA, 1974), which also reproduces French explorer Léon Diguet's *Notes on the Pictographs of Baja California*, dating from 1895.

Harry Crosby's *Cave Paintings of Baja California* (Copley Books, Acton, MA, 1975) is a more detailed effort by an enthusiastic aficionado that contains excellent color and B&W photographs, plus several fairly general maps. Clement Meighan and VL Pontoni's *Seven Rock Art Sites in Baja California* (Ballena Press, Socorro, NM, 1978) is an edited collection of systematic archaeological assessments of specific sites. Readers who understand Spanish might acquire María del Pilar Casado and Lorena Mirambell's *El Arte Rupestre de México* (Instituto de Antropología y Historia, México DF, 1990), which contains a major chapter on Baja California.

Colonial Baja & the Missions Several classic studies of colonial Baja make fascinating reading and are still available in university libraries and occasionally in specialist bookstores. Among them are Peveril Meigs' *The Dominican Mission Frontier of Lower California* (University of California Press, Berkeley, CA, 1935) and Homer Aschmann's *The Central Desert of Baja California: Demography and Ecology* (University of California Press, Berkeley, CA, 1959), both of which focus on pre-Columbian peoples and their contact with the missions. For the perspective of an early Jesuit father, obtain Johann Jakob Baegert's *Observations in Lower California* (University of California Press, Berkeley, CA, 1952, reprinted 1979), which was originally published in Germany in 1771, only four years after the Jesuits' expulsion from the peninsula. A modern and comprehensive history of early colonial times is Harry Crosby's *Antigua California: Mission and Colony on the Peninsular Frontier, 1697 – 1768*.

On the subject of piracy and the Manila galleons, see Peter Gerhard's succinct and readable *Pirates of the Pacific, 1575 – 1742*.

Postcolonial Baja William Walker's adventures in Baja (and elsewhere) are the subject of *The World of William Walker* by Albert Carr. James Blaisdell's *The Desert Revolution* tells of Ricardo Flores Magón's quixotic attempt to influence the Mexican Revolution from the Baja periphery. James Sandos' *Rebellion in the Borderlands: Anarchism and the Plan of San Diego, 1904 – 1923* provides more detail on the Magonista movement and some of its offshoots.

Norris Hundley's *Dividing the Waters* details the controversy between the US and Mexico over the Colorado River delta. More recent and comprehensive is Hundley's *The Great Thirst: Californians and Water, 1770s – 1990s*.

Contemporary Baja & the Borderlands In recent years, the US-Mexico borderlands have drawn an extraordinary amount of attention from both academic and popular writers. This section presents both general books on the region and others dealing specifically with Baja California.

Ted Conover's *Coyotes* is a compellingly readable account of undocumented immigrants by a writer who befriended Mexican workers while picking fruit with them in the orchards of Arizona and Florida, lived among them in their own country and accompanied them across the desert border despite concerns about his (and their) personal safety at the hands of the police and other unsavory characters. He concludes that 'the majority [of laborers] would make good neighbors; I'd welcome them as mine.' Similar themes appear in Luis Alberto Urrea's grim but fascinating *Across the Wire: Life and Hard Times on the Mexican Border*, which focuses on the problems of immigrants and shantytowns in a Tijuana that very few tourists ever see. Urrea's recent *By the Lake of the Sleeping Children: The Secret Life of the Mexican Border*, a combined effort with photographer John Lueders-Booth, deals with garbage pickers – the ultimate recyclers – in Tijuana.

Rubén Martínez's collected essays on Mexican and Mexican-American culture in *The Other Side* include a lengthy piece on Tijuana. Oscar Martínez's *Troublesome Border* deals with current borderland issues like population growth, economic development and ecology, and international migration.

Mexican Border Cities, by Daniel Arreola and James Curtis, analyzes urban economic and cultural development south of the border with illuminating essays on topics like the infamous *zonas de tolerancia* of sex, drink and gambling. Less rigorously academic, but perhaps more accessible, is Alan Weisman's *La Frontera: The United States Border with Mexico*, which explores all aspects of border life and culture, from the shining skyscrapers of San Diego and Tijuana to poverty-stricken shantytowns and the seedy zona of Nuevo Laredo. Exceptional B&W photos by Jay Dusard further enhance an often eloquent text.

Lawrence Herzog's *Where North Meets South* is a unified account of the border region by a single author with considerable experience. Abraham F Lowenthal and Katrina Burgess' *The California-Mexico Connection*, an edited collection of essays, analyzes many aspects of the intertwined economic, social and cultural relations between mainland California and its southern neighbor.

Bookstores

For out-of-print items on Baja California and Mexico, request a catalog from Howard Karno Books (☎ (619) 749-2304, (800) 345-2766), PO Box 2100, Valley Center, CA 92082. Dawson's Bookshop (☎ (213) 469-2186), 535 N Larchmont Blvd, Los Angeles, CA 90004, no longer publishes the 51-volume Baja California Travel Series, dealing with a variety of topics both historical and contemporary, but full sets are still available for about US$2000, along with the odd individual volume.

Few Baja bookstores *(librerías)* specialize in English-language material, but most major cities and towns have one that stocks some books titles in English. Baja's many trailer parks are full of North Americans who may be willing to swap reading material. Try also trailer park offices, some of which have accumulated many shelves of books that can be traded. Hotels catering to tourists also carry English-language books and publications.

NEWSPAPERS & MAGAZINES

Baja California has a rich journalistic heritage and a thriving local press in addition to national newspapers. Of the nine main dailies in Baja California, those with the highest circulations are Mexicali's *La Voz de la Frontera* and Tijuana's *El Mexicano*. Tijuana's *El Heraldo de Baja California*, the state's first daily, dates from 1941.

Other notable dailies include *ABC* in Mexicali and Ensenada; Tijuana's *El Día*, *Diario de Baja California* and *Ultimas Noticias*; Mexicali's *El Centinela*; and *Novedades de Baja California* in Mexicali, Tijuana and Ensenada.

Though published locally, *Diario 29* is a regional edition of *El Nacional*, a Mexico City paper that generally supports the Partido Institucional Revolucionario (PRI).

In addition to the daily press, there are numerous magazines of varying content, including cultural supplements to the daily papers.

The Tijuana-based *Zeta* – whose editor J Jesús Blancornelas received an International Press Freedom Award from the New York-based Committee to Protect Journalists for his exposés and candid criticisms of political and police corruption, drug lords, and the connections among them – is a crusading weekly alternative to the generally conservative daily press. Every edition includes a full-page appeal for a thorough investigation of the 1988 killing of former *Zeta* columnist Félix Miranda by the bodyguard of Tijuana businessman Jorge Hank Rhon (owner of Caliente racetrack and the many betting venues of the same name). Extensive readers' letters give a good sampling of the state's most articulate public opinion; *Zeta* also publishes a Mexicali edition.

In Baja California Sur, the main dailies are the La Paz-based *Diario Peninsular* and *El Sudcaliforniano*. *La Güicha*, a new satirical magazine whose main targets are political figures in the state capital of La Paz, also publishes arts and music reviews.

Baja California's free English-language papers, Ensenada's *Baja Sun* and its variants, clones and imitators, are thinly disguised publicity rags that promote the peninsula as a tourist destination and an area for real estate investment – or speculation. Articles include occasional topics of interest to travelers; more useful are the papers' coupons for hotel and restaurant discounts and free drinks.

RADIO & TV
Four television stations operate in Baja California (Norte), two in Mexicali and one each in Tijuana and Ensenada, but cable and satellite services are widely available throughout the peninsula. The Mexican multinational TV network Televisa maintains a large studio and production facilities in Tijuana.

Of the 41 radio stations in Baja California

(Norte), 26 are on the AM band and 15 on the FM band. All are commercial except for four FM stations, mostly associated with the Universidad Autónoma de Baja California, that emphasize cultural programming.

Travelers in northern Baja can often hear English-language broadcasts from the US, but mountainous topography often disrupts reception. At night, it's possible to hear them much farther down the peninsula. Cabo San Lucas' FM radio station does an hour of English-language news in the late afternoon.

PHOTOGRAPHY
It is generally better to bring film from the USA or Canada, where it is cheaper. Mexican Customs laws theoretically permit an individual to import a maximum of one camera and 12 rolls of film, but enforcement is so lax as to be nonexistent. Color-print film is plentiful in Baja, but slide film is difficult to find, especially in smaller locales. With all film, beware of out-of-date rolls.

Color-print film tolerates a wide variety of conditions but lacks the resolution of slide film. Kodachrome slide film, which portrays reds and nearby colors of the spectrum exceptionally well, is ideal for desert scenery, but Fujichrome is much cheaper and by no means inferior. For certain subjects, such as cave paintings and the interiors of historic buildings like the missions, carry high-speed (ASA 400) film to avoid using a flash, which is not permitted at these sites.

Always protect camera lenses with an ultraviolet (UV) filter. In tropical light conditions, the UV may not be sufficient to prevent washed-out photos; a polarizing filter can correct this problem and also dramatically emphasize skies and cloud formations, improving results on mountain and shoreline landscapes. If shooting in proximity to saltwater, as for instance on whale-watching excursions, take special precautions to protect your equipment from corrosion; plastic grocery bags are an inexpensive safeguard.

TIME

The northern state of Baja California is on Pacific Standard Time (PST), while Baja California Sur is on Mountain Standard Time (MST), which is one hour ahead of PST. PST is eight hours behind Greenwich Mean Time (GMT), while MST is seven hours behind GMT.

In summer, PST is moved ahead one hour for Pacific Daylight Time (PDT) and thus becomes the same as MST. Northern Baja is always on the same time as the US state of California.

ELECTRICITY

Electrical current, plugs and sockets in Mexico are the same as in the USA and Canada: 110 volts, 60 cycles and flat, two-prong plugs.

WEIGHTS & MEASURES

In Mexico the metric system is official, but the colloquial use of US measures, especially miles and gallons, is widespread in Baja California. Because so many people drive to Baja in cars manufactured north of the border whose odometers read in miles, this book uses both miles and kilometers to indicate distance. Landmarks along the Transpeninsular and other main roads may be indicated by the appropriate roadside kilometer marker (placed by the Mexican highway department).

Temperatures, weights and liquid measures are also given in both US measures and their metric equivalents. See the conversion table at the back of this book for further information.

LAUNDRY

US-style laundromats are becoming more common, at least in larger cities and tourist destinations; travelers can either do the wash themselves or leave it for the staff for a nominal additional charge. Figure about US$3 to US$4 per load.

HEALTH

Travel health depends on your predeparture preparations, your day-to-day health care while traveling and how you handle any medical problem or emergency that does develop. For extended stays in Baja or elsewhere in Mexico, medical insurance is advisable. Many US insurance companies, like Blue Cross, will extend their coverage to travel in Mexico.

While the list of potential dangers may seem frightening, with basic precautions, adequate information and a little luck, few travelers suffer anything worse than upset stomachs.

Travel Health Guidebooks

Compact but very detailed and well-organized, the 4th edition of Dirk Schroeder's *Staying Healthy in Asia, Africa & Latin America* is probably the best all-around guide to travelers' health. The 3rd edition of Dr Richard Dawood's *Travelers' Health: How to Stay Healthy All Over the World* is comprehensive, easy to read, authoritative and highly recommended, but too large to lug around. David Werner's *Where There Is No Doctor: A Village Health Care Handbook* is more suited to those working in rural development than to travelers.

The 2nd edition of Maureen Wheeler's *Travel with Children* (Lonely Planet, 1996) offers basic advice on travel health for younger children.

There are also a number of excellent travel health websites. The Lonely Planet website has links to the World Health Organization and the US Centers for Disease Control & Prevention.

Predeparture Preparations

Health Insurance A travel insurance policy covering theft, loss and medical problems is a wise idea. There is a wide variety of policies; your travel agent will have recommendations. International student travel policies handled by the Student Travel Association (STA) or other similar organizations are usually a good value. Some offer lower and higher medical expense options, but the higher ones are more appropriate for countries where medical costs are extremely high. Check the small print:

- Some policies specifically exclude 'dangerous activities' like scuba diving, motorcycling and even trekking. If these activities are on your agenda, avoid this sort of policy.
- You may prefer a policy that pays doctors or hospitals directly, rather than you having to pay first and file claims later. If you have to file a claim later, keep all documentation. Some policies ask you to call back (reverse charges) to a center in your home country for an immediate assessment of your problem.
- Check whether the policy covers ambulance fees or an emergency flight home. If you have to stretch out, you will need a second seat, and somebody has to pay for it!

Medical Kit It's useful to carry a small, straightforward medical kit. This should include:

- Aspirin or panadol for pain or fever
- Antihistamine (such as Benadryl), which is useful as a decongestant for colds, to ease the itch from allergies, insect bites or stings, and to help prevent motion sickness
- Antibiotics, which are useful for traveling off the beaten track; they must be prescribed, however, and you should carry the prescription with you.
- Kaolin preparation (Pepto-Bismol), Imodium or Lomotil for stomach upsets
- Rehydration mixture to treat severe diarrhea, which is particularly important if traveling with children
- Antiseptic such as Betadine, which comes as impregnated swabs or ointment, and an antibiotic powder or similar 'dry' spray for cuts and grazes
- Calamine lotion to ease irritation from bites or stings
- Bandages for minor injuries
- Scissors, tweezers and a thermometer (airlines prohibit mercury thermometers)
- Insect repellent, sunscreen lotion, lip balm and water purification tablets
- A couple syringes, in case you need injections; ask your doctor for a note explaining why they have been prescribed.

Ideally, antibiotics should be administered only under medical supervision and should never be taken indiscriminately, as they are specific to the infections they treat. Overuse of antibiotics can weaken your body's ability to deal with infections naturally and can reduce the drugs' efficacy. Take only the recommended dose at the prescribed intervals and continue taking it for the prescribed period, even if the illness seems to be cured earlier. Stop taking antibiotics immediately if you have any serious reactions, and don't use them at all if you are not sure that you have the correct one.

In many countries, if a medicine is available at all, it will generally be available over the counter and the price will be much cheaper than in North America or Europe. However, check expiration dates and try to determine whether storage conditions have been adequate. In some cases, drugs that are no longer recommended or have even been banned elsewhere are still being dispensed in Third World countries.

Vaccinations Travelers to Mexico, including Baja California, are not required to get any vaccinations, but it's a good idea to be up to date on your diptheria and tetanus vaccines, at least. If you plan to travel to small towns and villages in mainland Mexico, polio and typhoid shots are recommended.

Infectious hepatitis is the most common travel-acquired illness that can be prevented by vaccination. Protection can be provided in two ways – either with the antibody gammaglobulin or with a new vaccine called Havrix.

Gammaglobulin is not a vaccination but a ready-made antibody that reduces the chances of hepatitis infection. Because it may interfere with the development of immunity, it should not be given until at least 10 days after administration of the last vaccine needed. It should also be given as close as possible to departure because it is most effective in the first few weeks after administration; its effectiveness tapers off gradually between three and six months.

Havrix provides long-term immunity (possibly more than 10 years) after an initial course of two injections and a booster at one year. Though more expensive than gammaglobulin, it has many advantages, including length of protection and ease of administration. It is important to know that, as a vaccine, it takes about three weeks to provide satisfactory protection – hence the need for careful planning prior to travel.

Other Preparations Make sure you're healthy before traveling. If embarking on a long trip, make sure your teeth are OK; there are lots of places where a visit to the dentist would be the last thing you'd want to do. If you wear glasses, take an extra pair and your prescription. Losing your glasses can be a real problem, although in many places you can get new glasses made up quickly, cheaply and competently.

If you require special medication that may not be available locally, carry an adequate supply. Take the prescription, with the generic rather than the brand name, as it will facilitate obtaining replacements. It's a wise idea to have the prescription with you to show you legally use the medication, as over-the-counter drugs may be illegal or even banned without a prescription, depending on where you are.

Food & Water

Many Baja travelers worry about potential health problems from food and water, which can include dysentery, giardiasis, hepatitis A and, in extremely rare instances, typhoid and polio. The common maladies – upset stomach and diarrhea – can be minimized or even avoided by taking a few precautions.

Everyone has heard the infamous warning about Mexico: Don't drink the water. It's often true – the water can be potable, but bacterial differences can still make you sick. Generally, it is best to avoid tap water for drinking, brushing your teeth, washing

fruit and vegetables or making ice cubes. *Agua purificada* (purified water) and *hielo* (ice) are available throughout Baja from supermarkets, *ultramarinos* (small grocery stores) and *licorerías* or *vinos y licores* (liquor stores).

Off the main roads, some sort of water purification system is advisable, unless you carry enough bottled water with you. You can purify water with *yodo* (iodine), which is sold in pharmacies; add about seven drops per quart of water. Otherwise, use *gotas* (water purification drops) or *pastillas para purificar agua* (pills), sold in pharmacies and supermarkets. Hidroclonazone water purification tablets usually are sold in supermarkets.

Another alternative is to boil the water vigorously for at least five minutes or use a portable water filter. Compact water filters are available from major US camping supply stores.

It is generally safe to eat cooked food as long as you don't punish your stomach by consuming large portions immediately upon arrival. Take it easy – you may even want to have your first meal in one of the many restaurants that cater mainly to North Americans. Do not avoid local restaurants, taco stands and street-corner fish and fruit carts – just introduce yourself to them gradually. Eating a clove of raw garlic every day for a week prior to your trip also has been suggested by many travelers, who say that it staves off stomach problems.

Avoid uncooked or unpasteurized dairy products like raw milk and homemade cheeses. Dairy products from supermarkets are usually *pasteurizado*, but in restaurants you can't be sure. *Licuados con leche* (milkshakes) from juice stands are usually safe because the government requires the use of pasteurized milk and purified water.

Avoid most raw fruits and vegetables unless you can wash and/or peel them yourself. In tourist-oriented hotels and restaurants, salads are usually safe. If thoroughly cooked, meat, chicken and most types of seafood are safe.

Basic Rules

A normal body temperature is 98.6°F (37°C); more than 3.5°F (2°C) higher is a 'high' fever. A normal adult pulse rate is 60 to 80 beats per minute (children 80 to 100, babies 100 to 140). You should know how to take a temperature and a pulse. As a general rule, the pulse increases about 20 beats per minute for each 2°F (1°C) rise in body temperature.

Your respiration rate can also be an indicator of illness. Count the number of breaths per minute: from 12 to 20 is normal for adults and older children, up to 30 for younger children and 40 for babies. People with high fever or serious respiratory illnesses like pneumonia (acute lung infection) breathe more quickly than normal. Over 40 shallow breaths a minute usually means pneumonia.

Many health problems can be avoided by basic hygiene. Wash your hands frequently, as it's easy to contaminate your own food. Clean your teeth with purified water rather than tap water. Avoid climatic extremes: stay out of the sun when it's hot, dress warmly when it's cold. It is also important to dress sensibly. You can get worm infections from walking barefoot or dangerous cuts from walking barefoot over coral. Avoid insect bites by covering bare skin when insects are around, by screening windows and beds and by using insect repellents. Seek local advice: If you're told the water is unsafe because of jellyfish or sharks, don't go in. In situations where there is no information, play it safe.

Medical Problems & Treatment

Potential medical problems can be broken down into several areas: extremes of temperature, altitude or motion; insanitation; diseases spread by animal or human contact; simple cuts, bites or scratches; and insect bites or stings. Self-diagnosis and treatment can be risky, so seek qualified help if possible. Treatment dosages indicated in this section are for emergency use only. Seek medical advice before administering any drugs.

Embassies and consulates can usually recommend a good place to go for such advice. So can five-star hotels, which often recommend doctors with five-star prices (this is when medical insurance is really useful).

Hospitals & Clinics Almost every locale in Baja has either a hospital or medical clinic and Cruz Roja (Red Cross) emergency facilities, all of which are indicated by road signs showing a red cross. Hospitals are generally inexpensive and dependable for typical ailments (such as diarrhea or dysentery) and minor surgery (such as stitches). On the other hand, clinics are often understaffed and too overburdened with local problems to be of much help, though they are linked by a government radio network to emergency services.

For serious medical problems needing immediate treatment at more sophisticated facilities, San Diego-based Air-Evac International (☎ 95-800-0100986 toll free in Mexico; (619) 292-5557, (800) 854-2569 in the USA) can arrange flights to the USA at any time of the day or night. They also accept collect calls for evacuations.

Taking the Heat & Cold

Fungal Infections Hot-weather fungal infections are most likely to occur on the scalp, between the toes or fingers (athlete's foot), in the groin (jock itch or crotch rot) and on the body (ringworm). You get ringworm (a fungal infection, not literally a worm) from infected animals or by walking on damp surfaces, like shower floors.

To prevent fungal infections, wear loose, comfortable clothes, avoid artificial fibers, wash frequently and dry carefully. If infected, wash the area daily with a disinfectant or medicated soap and water, rinse and dry well and apply an antifungal cream or powder like tolnifate (Tinaderm). Try to expose the infected area to air or sunlight as much as possible. Wash towels and underwear in hot water and change them often.

Heat Exhaustion Dehydration or salt deficiency can cause heat exhaustion. Take time to acclimatize to high temperatures and make sure that you get enough liquids. Salt deficiency is characterized by fatigue, lethargy, headaches, giddiness and muscle cramps. Salt tablets or adding salt to your food may help. Vomiting or diarrhea can also deplete your liquid and salt levels. Anhydrotic heat exhaustion, caused by an inability to sweat, is rare. Unlike other forms of heat exhaustion, it is likely to strike people who have been in a hot climate for some time rather than newcomers.

Heat Stroke Long, continuous periods of exposure to high temperatures can leave you vulnerable to this serious, sometimes fatal, condition, which occurs when the body's heat-regulating mechanism breaks down and body temperature rises to dangerous levels. On arriving in a hot climate, avoid strenuous activity and excessive alcohol intake, and do drink other liquids well before you desperately need.them.

Symptoms include feeling unwell, lack of perspiration and a high body temperature of 102°F to 105°F (39°C to 41°C). When sweating ceases, the skin becomes flushed and red. Severe, throbbing headaches and lack of coordination also occur, and victims may become confused or aggressive. Eventually they become delirious or go into convulsions. Hospitalization is essential, but meanwhile get victims out of the sun, remove their clothing, cover them with a wet sheet or towel and fan them continually. Give fluids if they are conscious.

Hypothermia At high altitudes, cold and wet can kill. Changeable weather can leave you vulnerable to exposure – after dark, temperatures in the mountains or desert can drop from balmy to below freezing, while a sudden soaking and high winds can lower your own body temperature so rapidly that you may not survive. Disorientation, numb skin, irrationality, physical exhaustion, hunger, shivering and related symptoms are warnings that you should seek warmth, shelter and food. If possible, avoid traveling alone; partners are more likely to avoid hypothermia successfully. If you must travel alone, especially when hiking, be sure someone knows your route and when you expect to return.

Seek shelter when bad weather is unavoidable. Woolen clothing and synthetics, which retain warmth even when wet, are superior to cottons. A quality sleeping bag is a worthwhile investment, although goosedown loses much of its insulating quality when wet. Carry high-energy, easily digestible snacks like chocolate or dried fruit. Get victims out of the wind or rain, remove wet clothing and replace it with dry, warm clothing and give them hot liquids – not alcohol – and high-calorie, easily digestible food.

Prickly Heat Prickly heat, an itchy rash caused by excessive perspiration trapped under the skin, usually strikes people who have just arrived in a hot climate and whose pores have not yet opened sufficiently to cope with greater sweating. Keeping cool, bathing often, using a mild talcum powder and even resorting to air-conditioning may help until you acclimatize.

Sunburn In Baja's desert climate, you can get sunburned very quickly, even on cloudy days. Use a sunscreen and take extra care to cover areas that don't normally see sun – your feet, for example. A hat provides added protection; use zinc cream or some other barrier cream on your nose and lips. Calamine lotion or cold tea are good for mild sunburn. Protect your eyes with good-quality sunglasses.

Remember: The sunshine on the beach and in the water is deceptive and will burn you quickly. Wear a T-shirt while snorkeling or swimming.

Motion Sickness
Eating lightly before and during a trip reduces the chances of motion sickness. If you are prone to motion sickness, try to

find a place that minimizes disturbance: near the wing on aircraft, close to midship on boats or near the center on buses. Fresh air usually helps, while reading or cigarette smoke don't. Commercial antimotion sickness preparations, which can cause drowsiness, have to be taken before the trip commences; when you're feeling sick, it's too late. Ginger, a natural preventative, is available in capsule form.

Diseases of Insanitation

Diarrhea Almost every Baja traveler fears diarrhea, popularly known as Montezuma's Revenge or *turista*. Stomach problems can arise from dietary changes – they don't necessarily mean you've caught something. Introduce yourself gradually to exotic and/ or highly spiced foods.

Avoid rushing to the pharmacy and gulping antibiotics at the first signs. The best things to do are to avoid eating, to rest and to drink plenty of liquids (tea or herbal solutions, without sugar or milk). Many cafés serve chamomile tea *(agua de manzanilla)*; otherwise, try mineral water *(agua mineral)*. About 24 to 48 hours should do the trick, but if symptoms persist, see a doctor. If you must eat, keep to bland foods.

Severe diarrhea or dysentery (as defined below) often cause dehydration and painful cramps. Relieve these with fruit juice or tea, with a tiny bit of dissolved salt. Lomotil or Imodium may bring relief from symptoms, although they do not actually cure the problem. Only use these drugs if absolutely necessary – for example, if you *must* travel. Under all circumstances, fluid replacement is imperative. Do not use these drugs if the person has a high fever or is severely dehydrated. For children under 12 years of age, Lomotil and Imodium are not recommended.

In certain situations, antibiotics may be indicated (avoid gut-paralyzing drugs like Imodium or Lomotil if these symptoms are present):

- Watery diarrhea with blood and mucus
- Watery diarrhea with fever and lethargy

- Persistent diarrhea that does not improve after 48 hours
- Severe diarrhea, if it is logistically difficult to stay in one place

The recommended drugs (adults only) would be either norfloxacin 400 mg twice daily for three days or ciprofloxacin 500 mg twice daily for five days. These drugs are not recommended for children under age 12 or pregnant women.

The drug bismuth subsalicylate has also been used successfully; the adult dosage is two tablets or 30 ml, and for children it is one tablet or 10 ml. This dose can be repeated every 30 minutes to one hour, with no more than eight doses in a 24-hour period.

The drug of choice for children would be co-trimoxazole (Bactrim, Septrin, Resprim), with dosage dependent on weight. A five-day course is given. Ampicillin or amoxycillin may be given in pregnancy, but medical care is necessary.

Dysentery This serious illness, caused by contaminated food or water, results in severe diarrhea, often with blood or mucus in the stool. Fortunately, it is less common in Baja than in the rest of Mexico.

There are two kinds of dysentery. Bacillary dysentery is characterized by a high fever and rapid development; headache, vomiting and stomach pains are also symptoms. Highly contagious, it generally lasts no longer than a week. Amoebic dysentery develops more gradually and causes no fever or vomiting, but persists until treated; it can recur and cause long-term damage.

A stool test is necessary to diagnose which kind of dysentery you have, so seek medical help quickly. In case of emergency, note that norfloxacin or ciprofloxacin can be used as presumptive treatment for bacillary dysentery, and metronidazole (Flagyl) for amoebic dysentery.

For bacillary dysentery, norfloxacin 400 mg twice daily for seven days or ciprofloxacin 500 mg twice daily for seven days are the recommended dosages. If these are unavailable, a useful alternative is co-trimoxazole (Bactrim, Septrin, Resprim) 160/800 mg twice daily for seven days. This is a sulfa drug and must not be used by people with a known sulfa allergy. For children, co-trimoxazole is a reasonable first-line treatment. For amoebic dysentery, the recommended adult dosage of metronidazole (Flagyl) is one 750 mg to 800 mg capsule three times daily for five days. Children between eight and 12 years old should have half the adult dose; the dosage for younger children is one-third the adult dose.

An alternative to Flagyl is Fasigyn, taken as a two-gram daily dose for three days. Avoid alcohol during treatment and for 48 hours afterward.

Giardiasis Present in contaminated water, the intestinal parasite giardia causes stomach cramps, nausea, a bloated stomach, watery, foul-smelling diarrhea and frequent gas. Giardiasis can appear several weeks after exposure to the parasite; symptoms may disappear for a few days and then return, a pattern that may continue. Tinidazole (Fasigyn) or metronidazole (Flagyl) are the recommended drugs, but only under medical supervision. Dosage is a two-gram single dose of Fasigyn or 250 mg of Flagyl three times daily for five to 10 days. Antibiotics are useless.

Hepatitis Spread by contaminated food or water, hepatitis A is a common problem among travelers to areas with poor sanitation. With good water and adequate sewage disposal in most industrialized countries since the 1940s, very few young adults now have any natural immunity and must be protected. Protection is through the new vaccine Havrix or the short-lived antibody gammaglobulin.

Hepatitis A symptoms are fever, chills, headache, fatigue, generalized weakness and aches and pains, followed by loss of appetite, nausea, vomiting, abdominal pain, dark urine, light-colored feces and jaundiced skin; the whites of the eyes may turn yellow. Seek medical advice, though there is not much you can do except rest, drink lots of fluids, eat lightly and avoid fatty foods. People who have had hepatitis must forego alcohol for six months after the illness, as hepatitis attacks the liver, which needs time to recover.

Hepatitis B, formerly called serum hepatitis, spreads through contact with infected blood, blood products or bodily fluids; it may be spread, for example, through sexual contact, unsterilized needles or blood transfusions. Other risky situations could include a shave or tattoo in a local store, or body piercing. Type B symptoms resemble type A's, but are more severe and may lead to irreparable liver damage or even liver cancer.

There is no treatment for hepatitis B, but an effective prophylactic vaccine is readily available. The immunization schedule requires two injections at least a month apart followed by a third dose five months after the second. Persons who should receive a hepatitis B vaccination include anyone who anticipates contact with blood or other bodily secretions, either as a health care worker or through sexual contact with the local population, particularly those who intend to stay in the country for a long period of time.

'Hepatitis non-A non-B' is a blanket term formerly used for several different strains of hepatitis, which now have been separately identified. Hepatitis C resembles B but is less common. Hepatitis D (the 'delta particle') is also similar to B and always occurs in concert with it; its occurrence is currently mainly among IV drug users. Hepatitis E, however, is similar to A and is spread in the same manner, by water or food contamination.

Tests are available for these strains but are very expensive. Travelers shouldn't be too paranoid about this apparent proliferation of hepatitis strains; they are fairly rare (so far) and following the same precautions as for A and B should be sufficient to avoid them.

Worms These parasites are most common in rural, tropical areas, and a stool test when you return home is not a bad idea.

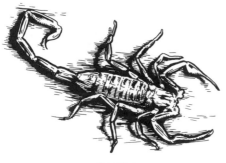

Scorpion

They can be present in unwashed vegetables or in undercooked meat, or you can pick them up through your skin by walking barefoot. Though generally not serious, infestations may not show up for some time and, if left untreated, can cause severe health problems. A stool test is necessary to pinpoint the problem, and medication is often available over the counter.

Diseases Spread by People & Animals

HIV/AIDS HIV, the Human Immunodeficiency Virus, may develop into AIDS *(SIDA)*, Acquired Immune Deficiency Syndrome. Any exposure to blood, blood products or bodily fluids may put an individual at risk. In many developing countries, transmission is primarily through heterosexual sexual activity, unlike industrialized countries, where transmission is mostly through sexual activity between homosexual or bisexual males or IV drug users' contaminated needles. Apart from abstinence (the only sure way to avoid infection), the most effective preventative is always to practice safe sex using condoms. Without a blood test, it is impossible to detect the HIV-positive status of an otherwise healthy-looking person.

HIV/AIDS can also be spread through blood transfusions; many developing countries cannot afford to screen blood for infection. It can also be spread by dirty needles – vaccinations, acupuncture, tattooing and body piercing are potentially as dangerous as IV drug use if the equipment is not clean. If you do need an injection, buy a new syringe from a pharmacy and ask the doctor to use it. You may also want to take a couple syringes with you, in case of emergency.

Rabies Dogs are noted rabies carriers, but a bite, a scratch or even a lick by an infected mammal can cause infection; scrub the spot immediately with soap and running water, then clean it with an alcohol or iodine solution. If there is any possibility of infection, seek medical help immediately. Even if the animal is not rabid, all bites should be treated seriously, as they can become infected or result in tetanus. A rabies vaccination is now available and should be considered if you are in a high-risk category: for example, if you intend to explore caves (bat bites could be dangerous) or work with animals.

Sexually Transmitted Diseases Sexual contact with an infected partner spreads these diseases. While abstinence is the only 100% effective preventative, condoms are a significant deterrent. Gonorrhea, herpes, chlamydia and syphilis are among these diseases; sores, blisters or rashes around the genitals or discharges or pain when urinating are common symptoms. Symptoms may be less marked or absent in women. Syphilis symptoms eventually disappear, but the disease continues and can cause severe problems in later years. Treatment for gonorrhea and syphilis is by antibiotics.

There are numerous other sexually transmitted diseases, for most of which effective treatment is available. However, there are no cures for herpes or AIDS. Abstinence and condoms are the most effective preventatives.

Tetanus Difficult to treat but preventable with immunization, this potentially fatal disease is found in the rural tropics. Tetanus occurs when a wound becomes infected by a germ that lives in soil and in the feces of animals and people, so clean all cuts and animal bites and apply an antiseptic cream or solution. Use antibiotics if the wound becomes hot or throbs or if pus is seen. Tetanus is known as lockjaw; early symptoms may be discomfort in swallowing or stiffening of the jaw and neck, followed by painful convulsions of the jaw and entire body.

Cuts, Bites & Stings
Cuts & Scratches Cuts easily become infected in hot climates and may heal slowly. Treat any cut with an antiseptic solution; when possible, avoid bandages and Band-Aids, which can keep wounds wet. Coral cuts are notoriously slow to heal, as the coral injects a weak venom into wounds; avoid cuts by wearing shoes when walking on reefs, and clean any cut thoroughly with an antiseptic. Coral cuts can result in serious infection.

Bites & Stings Bee *(abeja)* and wasp *(avispa)* stings are more painful than dangerous. People who are allergic to them, however, may suffer breathing difficulties, and require urgent medical care. Use calamine lotion for relief and ice packs to reduce swelling. There are some spiders with dangerous bites, but antivenin is usually available. Scorpions often shelter in shoes or clothing, and their stings are notoriously painful – check your shoes and clothing in the morning. Various sea creatures can sting or bite dangerously or are dangerous to eat. Again, seek local advice about potentially dangerous areas.

Bedbugs, Fleas & Lice Bedbugs *(chinches)* and fleas *(pulgas)* live in various places, but particularly in dirty mattresses and bedding. Spots of blood on linen or on the wall around the bed might suggest staying elsewhere. Bedbugs leave itchy bites in neat rows. Calamine lotion may help.

All lice *(piojos)* cause itching and discomfort. They make themselves at home in your hair (head lice), your clothing (body lice) or your pubic hair (crab lice). You catch lice through direct contact with infected people or by sharing combs, clothing and the like. Powder or shampoo treatment will kill the lice, after which infected clothing should be washed in very hot, soapy water and left in the sun to dry.

Jellyfish Local advice is the best way of avoiding contact with these sea creatures and their stinging tentacles. Stings from most *medusas* are not dangerous, just painful. Dousing in vinegar *(vinagre)* will deactivate any stingers that have not 'fired.' Calamine lotion, antihistamines and analgesics may reduce the reaction and relieve the pain.

Snakes Rattlesnakes *(cascabeles)* are common in the desert. To minimize the odds of being bitten, always wear boots, socks and long trousers when walking through undergrowth where snakes may be present. Keep your hands out of holes and crevices, and be cautious when collecting firewood.

Though painful, rattlesnake bites rarely kill healthy adults; children, elderly people and those in poor physical condition are more at risk. Antivenin is usually available. Keep the victim calm and still, wrap the bitten limb tightly, as you would for a sprained ankle, and then attach a splint to immobilize it. Seek medical help; tourniquets and sucking out the poison are now completely discredited.

Ticks *Garrapatas* may be present in chaparral vegetation, where hikers often get them on their legs or in their boots. Pulling them off increases the likelihood of infection, but an insect repellent may keep them away. Smearing chemicals on the tick is not recommended; instead, press down around the tick's head with tweezers, grab the head and gently pull upward. Avoid pulling the rear of the body, as this may increase the risk of infection and disease.

Women's Health

Gynecological Problems Poor diet, lowered resistance due to the use of antibiotics for stomach upsets and even contraceptive pills can lead to vaginal infections in hot climates. Keeping the genital area clean and wearing cotton underwear and skirts or loose-fitting trousers will help prevent infections.

Yeast infections, characterized by rash, itch and discharge, can be treated with a vinegar or even lemon-juice douche (diluted with water) or with yogurt containing active cultures. Nystatin, miconazole or clotrimazole suppositories are the usual medical prescription.

Trichomonas is a more serious infection with a discharge and a burning sensation when urinating. Male sexual partners must also be treated. If a vinegar-water douche is not effective, seek medical attention. Flagyl is the prescribed drug.

Pregnancy Most miscarriages occur during the first three months of pregnancy, so this is the riskiest time to travel. Miscarriage is not uncommon and can lead to severe bleeding. The last three months should also be spent within reasonable distance of good medical care. A baby born as early as 24 weeks stands a chance of survival, but only in a good modern hospital. Pregnant women should avoid all unnecessary medication, but vaccinations and malarial prophylactics should still be taken when possible. Additional care should be taken to prevent illness, and special attention should be paid to diet and nutrition. Avoid alcohol and nicotine in particular.

Women travelers often find that their periods become irregular or even cease while they're on the road. Remember that a missed period in these circumstances doesn't necessarily indicate pregnancy. There are health posts or family planning clinics in many small and large urban centers, where you can seek advice and have a urine test to determine whether you are pregnant.

WOMEN TRAVELERS

In a land of machismo, women should consider making some concessions to local custom. Mexicans generally believe in the *difference* rather than equality between the sexes, and women on their own may have to put up with unwelcome attention. Mexican men may assume that unaccompanied foreign women are fair game; this can get tiresome, but the best discouragement is a cool but polite initial response and a consistent, firm 'No!'

If you choose to do things an average Mexican woman would not do, such as challenging a man's masculinity, drinking in a cantina or hitchhiking alone, you are likely to be the target of unwanted attention, significant hostility or even violence. Although informal 'dress codes' are more permissive than in the recent past, avoid clothing that Mexican men may interpret as provocative. Wearing beach attire in town is not appropriate.

Tijuana police are known for harassing unaccompanied women on their early morning 'disco patrol'; to avoid one of these unpleasant encounters after a night of dancing, take a taxi back to the border or to your hotel instead of driving. In a serious emergency, seek help at a consulate in Tijuana or Cabo San Lucas.

DANGERS & ANNOYANCES
Safety & Theft

Thanks mainly to stereotyped foreign movies and machismo, Mexico has a reputation as a violent country, but physical safety is rarely a problem unless you somehow get deeply involved in a quarrel – dangerous weapons like handguns are much less common south of the border. More at risk are your possessions – particularly those you carry around with you. Reports of theft from rooms are rare, but there have been instances of thefts from tourist vehicles, usually when left alone for substantial periods in remote areas. Car theft is a serious problem in its own right, especially if your vehicle is conspicuous; take precautions.

Alcoholic Beverages

Drinkers, especially youthful visitors to border towns, should know that public consumption of alcoholic beverages is illegal in Mexico and may lead to confrontations with the police; in any event, it is rude behavior. Legally, alcohol may not be purchased before 10 am, whether in a bar or elsewhere.

Police, Military & Other Officials

Some Mexicans call the Judiciales (state and federal police) a 'mafia with badges' who view their positions as a license to extort money and favors from ordinary citizens or, worse, to torture and even kill those who run afoul of their caprice. See Ted Conover's *Coyotes* for a harrowing story of their treatment of undocumented workers trying to cross the US border.

Immigration officers and similar officials may also subtly (or openly) seek bribes (see the La Mordida entry, below), but the federal government has made genuine efforts to reduce the practice. Nobody, however, expects corruption to disappear very soon.

A more recent and unsettling development is the increasing use of police and military roadblocks throughout the peninsula, ostensibly to control drugs and weapons. For the moment, the police presence

The Militarization of Mexico

Given the undeniable level of corruption in the Mexican police, the enlistment of the generally respected armed forces in the drug war – largely at the urging of the US government – is understandable and even welcome among some sectors of the populace despite nationalistic mistrust of the USA. Nevertheless, the seemingly innocuous incorporation of the Mexican military into daily life may be cause for concern.

The short-term explanation for the military's increasing influence is the Zapatista uprising of New Year's Day 1994, in the southern state of Chiapas. Thanks in part to the drug trafficking problem, the military's presence has become palpable even in remote Baja, what with endless roadside inspections, the routine sight of soldiers armed with M-16s strolling through small towns like Loreto, and (for residents and visitors in remote areas) unexpected visits from the coast guard, soldiers and even generals. The growth of army garrisons in towns like Guerrero Negro, on the border between Baja California and Baja California Sur, could not be more conspicuous.

All this means more power for the military, though its reputation for integrity has suffered with incidents like the arrest of General Jesús Gutiérrez Rebollo, President Ernesto Zedillo's top antidrug official, for apparent links with traffickers. Given the seemingly endless litany of assassinations and corruption and the stubborn unwillingness of the ruling Partido Institucional Revolucionario's more recalcitrant elements to surrender political power, it's conceivable that Mexico might fall prey to serious social and political disorder, like that experienced by Central and South American countries from the mid-1960s through the late 1980s.

With logistical help from north of the border (Gulf War surplus is a conspicuous part of military gear in Baja), the Mexican military might even take power, just as Chilean and Argentine generals proclaimed themselves saviors of their countries in the 1970s – as ludicrous as this idea may seem when baby-faced 18-year-olds naively ask you whether you're carrying drugs or weapons. A recent item in the La Paz daily *El Sudcaliforniano* quoted Mexico's defense minister to the effect that the military plays neither a political nor an economic role in the country but rather, by implication, is the servant of the people. The very necessity of this denial is a pretty good indicator that military influence may not have reached its apogee. ■

is more sinister; the Judiciales have a proven record of serious corruption, while most Mexicans view the military, which has never played the domestic interventionist role that the armed forces in other Latin American countries have, with considerable respect.

Nevertheless, there are signs that the military is vulnerable to the same temptations as the police, what with the recent detention of two generals (General Jesús Gutiérrez Rebollo, ostensible head of the country's antidrug efforts, and Brigadier General Alfredo Navarro Lara) accused of links to drug interests.

If stopped by the Judiciales, travelers should take particular care to watch all of them closely; there are many authenticated cases of their planting drugs on unsuspecting tourists. If they ask to see the trunk or the back of your car, lock the front (as inconspicuously as possible, to avoid angering them).

Dealing with the military is not yet such a problem, at least in Baja. Most soldiers manning the checkpoints are adolescent conscripts who naively ask drivers whether they are carrying guns or drugs, make a cursory inspection and then let them pass. Should conditions in Mexico worsen, however, these checkpoints could become unpleasant.

As of early 1997, the major military checkpoints were south of Playas de Rosarito on the Transpeninsular (México 1, the free highway to Ensenada), south of San Quintín, at the Bahía de los Angeles junction on the Transpeninsular, at the state border just north of Guerrero Negro, on the Eastern Cape road from San José del Cabo to Los Frailes, north of the junction of México 5 (the Mexicali-San Felipe highway) and México 3 (the Ensenada-San Felipe highway), and north of San Felipe on México 5. The sole Judiciales checkpoint was just south of Loreto on the Transpeninsular, just beyond the Nopoló turnoff.

Travelers returning north across the border should not assume that US Customs & Immigration officials are exempt from such dishonesty. Corrupt US officials often traffic in drugs and take advantage of powerless immigrants, but abuses against all classes of border-crossers are well documented.

La Mordida

Historically, Mexico has been notorious for *la mordida* (literally 'the bite,' or bribe). The most frequent opportunity for the mordida is a traffic violation, such as driving the wrong way on a one-way street or running a stop sign. Realists do not expect the mordida to disappear from Mexican life at any time in the near future, but petty harassment of tourists for minor matters seems to be declining.

Tourists should never directly offer money to a police officer, because that is illegal; one strategy is to tell the officer that, if he forgives you, you will be extremely grateful (*'Si me perdona, se lo podría agradecer'*). This is a roundabout but effective way of sounding out the situation, and courteous travelers have escaped awkward situations without paying anything. Alternatively, make a subtle suggestion like offering a few pesos to purchase a *refresco* (soft drink) or *caguama* (large bottle of beer) because you're thirsty and you wonder if the officer is also.

In an unambiguously desperate situation, some drivers hand over a US$20 bill (or more) beneath their driver's license when the officer requests the license. Drivers should know that the Mexican drivers' manual (*reglamento de tránsito*) explicitly limits the offenses for which a driver may be taken into police custody. Each state has its own manual; try obtaining one at bookstores or from street vendors.

Natural Hazards

Baja's Pacific coast is part of the circum-Pacific 'ring of fire,' which stretches from Asia to Alaska to Tierra del Fuego. Active vulcanism is minimal in Baja, but earthquakes can be very serious, since they strike without warning and rustic construction often does not meet seismic safety standards. Travelers staying in budget accommodations should make contingency plans for safety and even evacuation before going to sleep at night. Adobe buildings are especially vulnerable.

While rain is rare in the Baja desert, flash floods are a serious hazard in the backcountry and even on paved highways like the Transpeninsular. If weather is threatening, seek high ground away from watercourses, which can fill instantly with runoff. Wait for low water before attempting to cross any swollen stream – even if you must wait for days. If your vehicle becomes stuck under such conditions, abandon it rather than risk drowning.

Recreational Hazards

Many of Baja's Pacific beach areas have dangerous offshore rip currents, so ask before entering the water and be sure someone on shore knows your whereabouts; surfers and swimmers should also beware of sharks. In wilderness areas like Parque Nacional Sierra San Pedro Mártir, the consequences of an accident can be very serious, so inform someone of your route and expected return.

LEGAL MATTERS

Mexico's judicial system is based on the French Napoleonic Code, which presumes an accused person is guilty until proven innocent. There is no jury trial; if you have problems such as a car accident (and the police arrive on the scene), everyone involved is considered guilty and liable until proven otherwise. Without car insurance, you will be detained until fault has been established. Prior to arriving in Baja, consider purchasing legal or juridical insurance, which covers you against damage caused to federal property (like street signs) and injury to persons. Such insurance allows the insurance adjuster to get you out of jail without having to post a bond.

If you encounter legal hassles with public officials or local businesspeople in Baja, contact La Procuraduría de Protección al Turista (Attorney General for the Protection of the Tourist, ☎ (66) 84-21-38 in Tijuana, (61) 6-36-86 in Ensenada, (65) 2-57-44 in Mexicali and (657) 7-11-55 in San Felipe). Each office has English-speaking aides.

BUSINESS HOURS & PUBLIC HOLIDAYS

Businesses are generally open 9 am to 2 pm and 4 to 7 pm weekdays. Banking hours are 9 am to 1:30 pm weekdays. Siesta, or break time, is between 2 and 4 pm.

Banks, post offices and government offices are closed on most holidays, celebrations and events listed below and may be closed on local holidays as well.

Bajacalifornianos observe all major national and Catholic holidays, but special festivities and fairs like Carnaval and saints' days usually take place only in major towns and cities. See the regional entries for information on local holidays.

Travelers expecting to stay at hotels in Tijuana, Tecate, San Felipe, Ensenada, Mulegé, La Paz, San José del Cabo or Cabo San Lucas during religious holidays, special fairs or US holidays such as Thanksgiving and Memorial Day should make reservations.

January
1st – *Año Nuevo* (New Year's Day)
24th – *Día de la Bandera* (Flag Day)

February
5th – *Día de la Constitución* (Constitution Day)
Late February to early March – *Carnaval* (Carnival). Celebrated in Ensenada, San Felipe and La Paz, usually the week before Lent, with parades, music, food and fireworks

March
19th – *Día del Señor San José* (St Joseph's Day). Bajacalifornianos celebrate the festival of St Joseph, San José del Cabo's patron saint, with street dances, horse races, food fairs and fireworks.
21st – *Natalicio de Juárez* (Birthday of President Benito Juárez)

March/April – *Semana Santa* (Holy Week), starting on Palm Sunday, a week before Easter, is celebrated in every church in Baja California on variable dates in March and April; some areas become so overrun that gasoline may be rationed.

May

1st – *Día del Obrero* (Labor Day)

5th – *Cinco de Mayo*. Marks the anniversary of victory over the French at Puebla (1862)

10th – *Día de la Madre* (Mother's Day)

June

1st – *Día de la Armada* (Navy Day)

September

8th – *Día de Nuestra Señora de Loreto* (Our Lady of Loreto). Festival of founding of Loreto

15th to 16th – *Día de la Independencia*. Commemorates Mexican independence from Spain (1821). The biggest celebrations take place in Tijuana and La Paz, with fireworks, horseraces, folk dances and mariachi bands.

October

12th – *Día de la Raza* (Columbus Day). Celebrates the country's Spanish heritage

November

1st to 2nd – *Todos Santos, Día de los Muertos* (All Saints Day, Day of the Dead). Festivities take place throughout Baja, but are especially colorful in Tijuana and La Paz. Breads and candies made to resemble human skeletons are sold in almost every market and bakery, and papier-mâché skeletons and skulls appear everywhere.

20th – *Día de la Revolución* (Anniversary of the Revolution of 1910)

December

12th – *Día de Nuestra Señora de Guadalupe* (Festival of Our Lady of Guadalupe). Tecate hosts one of the most interesting celebrations of this day. Groups come from all over Baja to display their costumes and dancing, while Mexicali holds colorful nightly processions from the first of the month.

25th – *Navidad* (Christmas Day). Marks the end of a week of *posadas*, parades of costumed children re-enacting the journey of Mary and Joseph to Bethlehem. Children also celebrate by breaking a *piñata* (papier-mâché animal) full of candy.

SPECIAL EVENTS

While not official holidays, events like the Baja 1000 (an annual off-road motor race) are good excuses to celebrate. For details, see individual city entries.

LANGUAGE COURSES

Most of Baja's popular language courses are at schools in Ensenada. Travelers have enthusiastically recommended the Center of Languages & Latin American Studies (☎ (61) 78-60-00, cllas@tnl-online.com), Avenida Riveroll 1287, whose US contact (☎ (619) 279-0996, (800) 834-2256) is at 5666 La Jolla Blvd, No 116, La Jolla, CA 92037. Besides standard language courses, the Center offers specialized instruction for professionals in nursing, teaching or law enforcement. It can also arrange community college or university credit in the USA.

Regular students pay a one-time registration fee of US$100, plus US$125 per week (30 hours instruction) from September to June; in the summer months of June, July and August, the weekly charge is US$145. Weekend courses cost US$75. The center will arrange housing with Mexican families for US$20 to US$25 per day, meals included.

The Colegio de Idiomas de Ensenada (☎ (61) 76-01-09, (61) 76-65-87), Blvd JA Rodríguez 377, also offers intensive instruction in classes of no more than five students for US$125 weekly (30 hours instruction) or US$70 weekends (eight hours both Saturday and Sunday), plus a one-time registration fee of US$125. Classes include one local tour weekly. Accommodations with a Mexican family are available for about US$20 to US$22 per day with meals, but students may also choose hotel accommodations. The school's US contact is the International Spanish Institute (☎ (619) 755-7044), PO Box 2237, Del Mar, CA 92014-1537.

Language instruction is also available in La Paz, the capital of Baja California Sur; see the La Paz entry for details.

WORK

Except for those directly involved in tourist specialties, like natural history tours or diving, work is not an attractive alternative in Baja. Wages are low by US or European standards, and permits are hard to obtain, though this does not seem to deter the slimy real estate speculators of Cabo San Lucas. English tutoring may be feasible in Tijuana or Mexicali, but competition is stiff because of the proximity to the border.

Anyone interested in establishing a business in Baja must establish a Mexican corporation; to do so, consult a Mexican attorney on the proper immigration and business procedures.

ACCOMMODATIONS

Accommodations in Baja range from luxury resorts, vacation hotels, and budget hotels and motels to *casas de huéspedes* (guesthouses). Camping both in and out of RV parks is the most popular alternative for budget travelers. There is a single *villa deportiva juvenil* (youth hostel) in La Paz, Baja California Sur.

Camping

Camping is free on almost any beach, but wherever formal facilities are available, expect to pay from US$3 to US$20 per night; most sites are in the US$8 to US$12 range. Many have full hookups for electricity, water and sewerage.

If you're planning to camp extensively, acquire Carl Franz's *Camping in Mexico* and *RV Camping in Mexico* for suggestions on what to bring, how and where to camp, cooking and many other camping topics. Many of the RV guide's descriptions of Baja RV parks and campgrounds are out of date, but it's still a worthwhile acquisition. For current campground information, check AAA's Baja California guidebook.

Youth Hostels

Aside from camping, the most inexpensive option is the villa deportiva juvenil, but only La Paz now has one. The Consejo Nacional de Recursos para la Atención de la Juventud (CREA), associated with Hostelling International, charges US$4 and up per night for members and non-members. You can obtain a CREA card at the hostel.

Hotels & Motels

By US or European standards, many hotels and motels are in the budget range, with double-room rates starting around US$20 to US$25, but a handful are cheaper and still tolerable. Standards vary, and room rates and external appearance are not always accurate indicators of quality. Go inside, ask to see a room, sniff around and sit on a bed to see how much it sags.

Tourist hotels are often affiliated with chains based in the USA and Mexico, such as Quality Inn, Comfort Inn, Travelodge and Holiday Inn. Their Baja rates tend to be somewhat lower than those for comparable accommodations in the USA, from US$50 to US$100 for a double room. The principal Mexican chains, with standards equivalent to their US counterparts, include La Pinta, El Presidente and Castel. Double rates start around US$55 per night.

Most luxury resort hotels are south of La Paz along the eastern and southern shores of the Cape Region. Double-room rates start around US$80 per night and reach US$250 or even higher.

FOOD

Mexicans generally eat three meals a day: *desayuno* (breakfast), *almuerzo* (lunch) and *cena* (dinner). When eating in a restaurant, note that waiters will not bring the check until you ask for it – to do otherwise would be extremely rude.

All meals usually include one or more of the following staples:

tortillas – thin, round patties of pressed corn or wheat-flour dough cooked on griddles. *Harina* (flour) tortillas are common in northern Mexico and Baja, but *maíz* (corn) tortillas are more traditional. Both can be served under, on or wrapped around just about any type of food.

frijoles – beans; they are served boiled, fried, refried, in soups, on tortillas or with eggs as part of almost every meal.

chiles – come in numerous varieties. Some, such as the *habanero* and *serrano*, are almost always hot, while others, such as the *poblano*, vary in spiciness according to when they were picked. If your tolerance is limited, ask whether the chile is *picante* (spicy hot) or *muy picante* (very spicy hot). If you exceed your tolerance and start to choke, start eating or drinking sugar, beer, milk, bread or anything else that might extinguish the fire. Note, however, that water usually exacerbates the pain.

Breakfast usually consists of *café* (coffee) or *jugo* (juice), a *bolillo* (sweet roll) or *pan tostado* (toast) and *huevos* (eggs) in any of a variety of styles. When ordering eggs, never ask *'¿Tiene huevos?'* ('Do you have eggs?'), because *huevos* is slang for 'testicles' in this context. Instead, ask *'¿Hay huevos?'* ('Are there eggs?')

Huevos fritos are fried eggs, while *huevos rancheros* are also fried, but smothered with tomato sauce and served on a tortilla. *Huevos revueltos* are scrambled, sometimes served with *chorizo* (sausage) or frijoles. *Huevos revueltos estilo Mexicano*, also known as *huevos estrellados*, contain tomato, onion, chile and garlic.

Lunch, the day's biggest meal, is usually served about 2 pm. Dinner, a lighter version of lunch, is served about 7:30 pm. In restaurants that do not cater primarily to tourists, lunch and dinner menus (if available) may change daily, weekly or not at all. Meals may be ordered à la carte or on a fixed-price basis. A fixed-price *comida corrida* (set menu) may cost as little as US$1. Most fixed-price meals include soup, a main dish, one or two side dishes and dessert. Dishes at either lunch or dinner can include the following *antojitos* (traditional dishes):

burrito – any combination of beans, cheese, meat, chicken and seafood, seasoned with salsa or chile and wrapped in a flour tortilla

chilaquiles – scrambled concoction of eggs, chiles and bits of tortillas

chiles rellenos – poblano chiles stuffed with cheese, meat or other foods, dipped in egg whites, fried and baked in salsa

enchilada – ingredients similar to those in tacos and burritos, wrapped in a flour tortilla, dipped in sauce and then baked or fried

machaca – cured, dried and shredded beef or pork mixed with eggs, onions, cilantro and chiles

quesadilla – flour tortilla topped or filled with cheese and occasionally other ingredients, then heated

taco – ingredients similar to the burrito, wrapped in a soft or crisp corn tortilla

tamale – steamed corn dough stuffed with meat, beans or chile and wrapped in corn husks

tostada – flat, crisp tortilla topped with meat or cheese, tomatoes, beans and lettuce

Soups

sopa – soup

gazpacho – chilled vegetable soup spiced with hot chiles

menudo – tripe

pozole – hominy soup with some meat and vegetables

sopa de arroz – rice soup, really more rice than soup, commonly served at lunch

sopa de pollo – chicken soup

Seafood

Available in restaurants most of the year, seafood (both finfish and shellfish) is the best of Baja cuisine. Clams, oysters, shrimp and prawns are also often available as *cocteles* (cocktails) from roadside stands in almost every city and town. Note that fish that is alive in the open water is referred to as *pez*, while fish after it has been caught is called *pescado*.

atún – tuna

cabrilla – sea bass

ceviche – raw seafood marinated in lime and mixed with onion, chile, garlic and tomato

filete de pescado – fish fillet

huachinango or *pargo* – red snapper

jurel – yellowtail

lenguado – flounder or sole

pescado al mojo de ajo – fish fried in butter and garlic

pez espada – swordfish

sierra – mackerel

tiburón – shark

trucha de mar – sea trout

mariscos – shellfish
abulón – abalone
almejas – clams
callos – scallops
camarones – shrimp
camarones gigantes – prawns
cangrejo – large crab
jaiva – small crab
langosta – lobster
ostiones – oysters

Meat & Fowl
asado – roast
barbacoa – barbecued by placing under
    hot coals
biftec – beefsteak
birria – barbecued lamb or goat on a spit
cabra – goat
carne – meat
carne al carbón – charcoal-grilled meat
carne asada – grilled meat
carnitas – deep-fried pork
chicharrones – deep-fried pork rinds
chorizo – pork sausage
chuletas de cerdo – pork chops
conejo – rabbit
cordero – lamb
costillas de puerco – pork ribs or chops
hígado – liver
jamón – ham
milanesa – breaded beefsteak (chicken-fried
    steak)
patas de puerco – pig's feet
pato – duck
pavo or *guajolote* – turkey
pollo – chicken
pollo asado – grilled chicken
pollo con arroz – chicken with rice
pollo frito – fried chicken
puerco – pork
tocino – bacon or salt pork

Fruit
frutas – fruits
coco – coconut
dátil – date
fresa – strawberry; often used to refer to any
    berry
guayaba – guava
higo – fig
limón – lime or lemon
mango – mango
melón – melon
naranja – orange
papaya – papaya
piña – pineapple
plátano or *banana* – banana

tomate – tomato
toronja – grapefruit
uva – grape

Vegetables
Vegetables are rarely served as separate dishes, but rather are mixed into salads, soups and sauces.

verduras or *legumbres* – vegetables
aceituna – olive
aguacate – avocado
calabaza – squash or pumpkin
cebolla – onion
champiñon – mushroom
chícharo – pea
ejote – green bean
elote – corn on the cob
jícama – root crop, resembling potato or
    apple, eaten with a sprinkling of lime, chile
    and salt
lechuga – lettuce
papa – potato
papitas fritas – potato chips
zanahoria – carrot

Desserts
bolillo or *birote* – French-style rolls, sometimes
    sweet
flan – custard
helado – ice cream
nieve – flavored ice, Mexican equivalent of US
    'snow cone'
paleta – flavored ice on a stick, equivalent to US
    popsicle, Australian icy-pole or UK ice-lolly
pan dulce – sweet roll
pastel – cake
postre – dessert

MICHAEL SULLIVAN

Other Food
azúcar – sugar
crema – cream
guacamole – mashed avocado mixed with onion, chile sauce, lemon, tomato and other ingredients
leche – milk
mantequilla – butter
mole – sauce made from unsweetened chocolate, chile and many spices, often served over chicken or turkey
pimienta negra – black pepper
queso – cheese
sal – salt
salsa – sauce made from chile, onion, tomato, lemon or lime juice and spices

At the Table
cuenta – bill
cuchara – spoon
cuchillo – knife
menú – menu
plato – plate
propina – tip, usually 10% to 15% of the bill
servilleta – napkin or serviette
tasa – cup
tenedor – fork
vaso or *copa* – glass

DRINKS
Tea & Coffee
Té and *café* are available throughout Baja California, but *té de manzanilla* (chamomile) is more common in restaurants than standard *té negro* (black tea). Regular coffee is mostly instant Nescafé but is sometimes ground, and will almost always be served heavily sweetened unless you request otherwise. Unless you specifically ask for it, coffee or tea rarely arrives before a meal.

In tourist centers like Playas de Rosarito, Ensenada and Cabo San Lucas, cappuccino and other espresso drinks are becoming more widely available.

café con crema – coffee with cream; cream is usually served separately
café con leche – about half hot milk and half coffee
café negro or *café americano* – black coffee with nothing added except sugar
café sin azúcar – coffee without sugar; ordering this keeps the waiter from adding heaps of sugar but doesn't mean that coffee won't taste sweet – sugar is often added to coffee beans during processing

Juices
Fresh fruit and vegetable *jugos* (juices), *licuados* (shakes) and *aguas frescas* (flavored waters) are all popular. All the fruits and a few of the squeezable vegetables mentioned above are used either individually (as in jugos or aguas frescas) or in some combination (as in licuados). At reputable chains like La Michoacana, these are made with purified water.

A basic licuado is a blend of fruit or juice, water and sugar. Other items can be added or substituted: raw egg, milk, ice and flavorings like vanilla or nutmeg. Delicious combinations are practically limitless.

Aguas frescas are made by mixing fruit juice or syrup (made from mashed grains or seeds) with sugar and water; look for them in big glass jars on the counters of juice stands. Try the delicious *agua fresca de arroz* (rice water), which has a sweet, nutty taste; it is sometimes called *horchata*. *Cebada*, made with barley, is also tasty and refreshing.

Soft Drinks
Almost every *refresco* (soft drink) available in the USA is also available in Baja; two of the better Mexican brands are apple-flavored Sidral and Manzanita. Other flavors, like *fresa* (strawberry), *limón* (lime) and *cereza* (cherry) tend to be too sweet, but Peñafiel is a generally acceptable local brand.

Alcoholic Drinks
Mezcal, Tequila & Pulque Mezcal, tequila and pulque are derived from the sap of the *maguey (Agave* spp), a fiber plant with long, wide, slightly curved spikes that is a Mexican domesticate. Mezcal and tequila are made in similar ways. Mezcal can be made from any species of maguey, but tequila is made only from *A tequilana*, which grows in and around the mainland town of Tequila. The plant's spikes are stripped away to expose the plant's *piña* (core), which is chopped, roasted, shredded and then pressed to remove the juice. Sugar is added to the juice and, after the resulting

mixture has fermented four days, it is twice distilled. Following distillation, the mezcal and tequila are aged in wooden casks for periods ranging from four months to seven years. The final product is a potent, golden-colored liquid, bottled and priced according to its age – the longer the aging, the higher the price.

The traditional manner of drinking mezcal or tequila involves licking the back of your hand and sprinkling salt on it, licking the salt, downing the shot of mezcal or tequila in one gulp and sucking on a lime. When the bottle is empty, you are supposed to eat the worm (preferably fried) that is traditionally added to each bottle before it is filled.

Foreigners unaccustomed to the potency of straight tequila often take it in a mixed drink called a *margarita*. There are more than 100 types of margarita, most of them made by adding lime juice and orange liqueur to tequila in a salt-rimmed glass; fresh fruit, often strawberries or peaches, may be added.

When shopping for tequila, look for the letters 'DGN,' which stand for Dirección General de Normas (Bureau of Standards), certifying that the tequila is made with *A tequilana* rather than other species.

Pulque, a mildly alcoholic, foamy, milky drink, is extracted directly from the sap of the maguey. Because this liquid spoils quickly, it cannot be bottled or easily shipped long distances; since most pulque is produced near Mexico City, it is difficult to find it in Baja bars and homes.

Spirits & Liqueurs Baja is a shopper's paradise for inexpensive spirits and liqueurs made in Mexico: Bacardi Rum, brandy (the Pedro Domecq brand comes from Baja), Controy (Cointreau, an orange liqueur), Kahlua (coffee liqueur) and Oso Negro vodka.

Remember that US Customs permits the importation of only one liter of liquor per person (over 21 years of age) every 30 days into mainland California, unless crossing by common carrier (bus, taxi or airplane). Common-carrier passengers may import any amount of alcohol destined for 'personal use,' a vague term meaning more than a single bottle but much less than a truckload. Duty, payable on quantities in excess of one liter, is higher for hard liquor than for beer and wine.

Beer Late 19th-century German immigrants first established breweries in Mexico, and their techniques and technology have been a major factor in Mexican beer's popularity throughout North America. The landmark Tecate brewery, the only one in Baja, now belongs to Cervecería Cuauhtémoc, Mexico's second-largest brewery conglomerate, and also produces other brands, like Carta Blanca. Tecate is still one of the most popular beers in Baja, but other popular brands include Corona, Carta Blanca, Dos Equis and Sol Especial.

In restaurants and bars unaccustomed to tourists' tastes, beer may be served at room temperature. If you want cold beer, order *'una cerveza helada, por favor.'*

Wine Wine is less popular than beer and tequila, but Baja has several significant wineries in and around Ensenada: Vinícolas Domecq, Formex-Ybarra and Bodegas de Santo Tomás. Domecq is renowned for its Los Reyes table wines, while Formex-Ybarra has over 800 acres (320 hectares) of vineyards in the Valle de Guadalupe and is known for its Terrasola table wine. LA Cetto has opened its Tijuana installation for tours and tasting.

Bodegas de Santo Tomás hopes to produce wines that can compete with the northern product. Having planted several varieties of grape from mainland California, it has begun producing pinot noir, chardonnay and cabernet. In addition, it has teamed with northern mainland California's Wente Vineyards to produce a new premium cabernet known as Duetto, due on the market in late 1997.

ENTERTAINMENT

Historically, Baja California has had a reputation for border-town bawdiness, but this notoriety is largely outdated despite the continued existence of Tijuana's Zona Norte and the tawdrier parts of Mexicali's La Chinesca.

Both Tijuana and Mexicali are increasingly cosmopolitan cities with a variety of nightlife activities, ranging from spectator sports like baseball and horseracing to glitzy nightclubs and pop music concerts to symphony orchestras and serious drama. In tourist resorts like San Felipe and Cabo San Lucas, bars and nightclubs stay open nearly all night for live music and dancing. Sports bars with satellite TV connections, even in very remote places, attract tourists to Monday night football and other athletic events.

The cinema was once a dominant form of entertainment throughout Mexico, but the video revolution has subverted the big screen almost everywhere in Baja; only in Tijuana, Playas de Rosarito, Mexicali, Ensenada and La Paz will moviegoers still find first-run features.

SPECTATOR SPORTS
Baseball
While soccer is more important than *béisbol* in Mexico as a whole, baseball is demonstrably more significant in Baja California: small boys, using broken table legs for bats and balls coming apart at the stitches, play into the twilight on empty sandlots, while nearly every sizable town has a groomed sandlot field or even a stadium. Teams sometimes travel hundreds of miles for weekend games, which are social events as much as athletic competitions. While the winter professional leagues are worth watching, the amateurs are, in their own way, equally interesting, and travelers should not hesitate to stop and watch a Sunday afternoon game.

While Mexican professionals have not matched the success of their Caribbean counterparts in the US major leagues, the Liga Mexicana del Pacífico offers outstanding competition, good facilities and a chance to see young players on the way up. As of the 1996 – 97 season, Baja California's only team was the Aguilas de

Mexicali, where US stars like Mike Piazza of the Los Angeles Dodgers have sharpened their skills. The league's other franchises are Los Mochis (Cañeros), Ciudad Obregón (Yaquis), Navojoa (Mayos), Culiacán (Tomateros), Hermosillo (Naranjeros) and Guasave (Algodoneros).

Boxing
Of all sports, boxing brings out the passion in Mexican audiences, whose identification with individual champions matches their allegiance to their country. When US boxer Frankie Randall won a judges' decision over Mexican super-lightweight champion Julio César Chávez in 1994 for Chávez's first career loss in over 90 matches, one Tijuana daily moaned that 'they robbed us of our hero.'

Horseracing
Especially popular in border towns, horseraces take place at several *hipódromos* (racetracks) around Baja. The peninsula's most famous racetrack, the Agua Caliente complex in Tijuana, has been closed (except for dogracing) for some time because of a labor dispute.

Jai Alai
This is the Basque game *pelota*, brought to Mexico by the Spanish. Played with a hard ball on a very long court, it's a bit like squash or handball; curved baskets attached to the arm are used instead of racquets. Baja's largest jai alai *frontón* (venue) is in Tijuana. For more information, see the sidebar on jai alai in the La Frontera chapter.

Rodeos
Mexican *charreadas*, which frequently take place during fiestas and other special occasions, are particularly popular in northern Mexico but occur throughout the peninsula. Unlike North American rodeo riders, however, *charros* (Mexican cowboys) rely on style and skill rather than speed and strength; rodeos are competitive events, but there are no cash prizes and

Corridas de Toros

To many if not most gringos, bull-fighting hardly qualifies as a sport or even as entertainment, but Mexicans consider it a traditional spectacle that lends itself to a variety of symbolic interpretations – in the circular ring, the bull and the matador may be seen as the center of the universe. Symbolism aside, the bullfight's importance to Mexican society is expressed by the common adage that Mexicans arrive on time for only two events – funerals and bullfights.

The *corrida de toros* (literally, running of the bulls) or *fiesta brava* (wild festival) begins promptly, usually at 4 pm on winter Sundays and at 5 pm in summer. To the sound of music, usually a Spanish *paso doble*, the *matador* in his *traje de luces* (suit of lights) and his *toreros* (assistants) salute local authorities and the crowd in the traditional *paseíllo*. Then the first of six bulls is released from its pen for the first of the ritual's three *suertes* (acts) or *tercios* (thirds).

The cape-waving toreros tire the bull by luring it around the ring. After a few minutes, two *picadores* on elaborately padded horses enter the ring and approach the bull to jab their long *picas* (lances) into its shoulders, weakening the bull without killing it. After the picadores leave the ring, the *suerte de banderillas* begins as the toreros attempt to stab three pairs of elongated darts into the bull's shoulders without being impaled on its horns.

Then comes the *suerte de muleta*, the climax in which the matador has exactly 16 minutes to kill the bull. After fancy capework designed to tire the animal, the matador exchanges his large cape for a smaller one and takes sword in hand, baiting the bull to charge before delivering the *estocada* (lunge) with his sword. The matador must deliver the estocada between the horns from a position directly in front of the animal.

If the matador succeeds, as is usual, the *estoque* (death) is quick and bloody. As the bull collapses, an assistant dashes into the ring to slice its jugular and chop off its ears and tail for the matador – should the crowd decide he is deserving (the tail is given less frequently). The dead bull is usually dragged from the ring and butchered for sale, but in rare instances, a bull that displays *bravura* (that is, shows itself to be a real fighter) may be 'pardoned' to fight another day. ∎

admission fees go to offset the costs of staging the events.

Female riders, known as *escaramuzas*, play an important but different role in the rodeo. While athletic, this role is ambiguous, derived from aristocratic traditions of equestrianism but also, at least symbolically, from female couriers in the Revolution of 1910. In style, escaramuzas ride sidesaddle – a dubious symbol of feminism. Readers particularly interested in the subject should obtain Kathleen Mullen Sands' *Charrería Mexicana: An Equestrian Folk Tradition*.

Soccer

Mexico has twice hosted the World Cup soccer finals, but on neither occasion did the home side advance beyond the quarter-finals. Mexican players lag behind those in other Latin American countries – the best tend to go to Europe for better competition and higher salaries. Although there's a decent professional league and several impressive stadiums, attendance is low, in part because TV coverage is so extensive. América (of Mexico City) and Guadalajara are among the top clubs. A goal is a *gol*, a ball is a *pelota*, a penalty is a *penalty*, a foul is a *falta* and a referee is an *árbitro*.

THINGS TO BUY

Baja's tourist centers – Tijuana, Playas de Rosarito, Mexicali, Ensenada, La Paz and Los Cabos – are full of souvenirs from throughout Mexico, but relatively few crafts come from Baja California itself. A few jewelry stores carry traditional silver jewelry and cutlery from Taxco. Carved doors and other woodwork from Guadalajara can be bought or ordered in Ensenada. A variety of other crafts are also available: woven baskets, colorful *rebozos* (shawls), brightly painted ceramic animals, hand-painted tiles, intricately decorated leather boots and wrought-iron staircases.

Many crafts sold in Baja qualify as junk or kitsch, like wrought-iron cages with stuffed birds, black velvet paintings, over-sized embroidered sombreros, bull horns and onyx chess sets. The exceptions to

this general rule are Paipai, Kumiai and Cucupah Indian basketry, pottery and jewelry, which are available in those communities as well as in major tourist cities like Ensenada.

Travelers should know that the importation into the USA of black coral jewelry, a specialty from Baja's Cape Region, is restricted under Appendix II of the Convention on International Trade in Endangered Species of Wild Fauna and Flora (CITES). (See the sidebar on endangered species in the Facts about Baja California chapter for more information.) Export permits for black coral can be obtained only from Dr Exequiel Ezcurra, Dirección General de Aprovechamiento Ecológico de los Recursos, Río Elba 20, 10° Piso, Co y Delegación Cuauhtémoc, 06500 México DF, México.

It is much better, however, not to encourage the destruction of endangered habitats by purchasing items made of coral, which is dredged from the reefs at great ecological cost. Other products regulated under either Appendix I (absolutely prohibited) or Appendix II (allowed only with formal export permit) include cacti, sea turtles and marine mammal products. These products can be confiscated and those in possession of them can be prosecuted under civil and criminal laws.

Baja's best bargains are medical services such as dentistry and optometry, and prescription pharmaceuticals. Because Mexican prices for such services and products are typically a fraction of their cost north of the border, some US insurance companies have begun to pay claims for medical services on the other side. Remember, of course, to declare to US Customs that porcelain crown fitted in Tijuana or Mexicali!

Pharmaceuticals require caution. Self-medication is a risky business; the Tijuana weekly *Zeta* once reported that only a handful of the 540 pharmacies in Tijuana, Tecate and Playas de Rosarito complied with regulations requiring a qualified doctor or pharmacist on duty, and that some pharmacies had promoted outdated or inappropriate medications as 'impulse' items.

Analgesics, antiparasitics, antibiotics and the like require particular attention. At least one US citizen has gone to jail for purchasing items like Prozac, which do require a prescription, in questionable circumstances. If in doubt, don't buy it.

Border towns like Tijuana and Mexicali do a thriving business in car body repair, painting and upholstery at prices from one-third to one-half of their cost north of the border. Mufflers, brakes and similar repairs are equally inexpensive.

Outdoor Activities

Much of Baja's appeal for visitors from north of the border springs from its outdoor activities, especially when inclement winter weather makes pastimes like camping, hiking and water sports difficult or impossible in most of the US and Canada.

Mexicans are less enamored of camping and hiking than beachgoing and water sports, but visitors will find some mountain areas suitable for the former activities. Tents-only campgrounds are rare, though tent camping is possible at most trailer parks and beaches. In some areas horses are available for rent.

A good general guidebook to outdoor activities in Baja is Walt Peterson's *The Baja Adventure Book*. For sport-specific books, see the Books section in the Facts for the Visitor chapter.

ON & IN THE WATER
Diving
There is an increasing number of quality dive shops on the peninsula, mostly at southern Baja locations like La Paz, Cabo Pulmo, San José del Cabo and Cabo San Lucas, but also at Mulegé and at La Bufadora near Ensenada.

Most resorts and surrounding towns have shops that arrange boats and rent out snorkels, masks, fins and other diving paraphernalia, but serious participants may prefer to bring their own equipment. The best dive sites, with subtropical and tropical conditions, are near Mulegé, Loreto, La Paz, Cabo Pulmo (the eastern Pacific's northernmost coral reef) and Cabo San Lucas.

Fishing
Sportfishing is especially popular off the Pacific coast and in the Gulf of California. Tom Miller's *Angler's Guide to Baja California* is a worthwhile acquisition for fishing enthusiasts. Another is the recently updated *The Baja Catch* by Neil Kelly and Gene Kira (see the Books entry in the Facts for the Visitor chapter for ordering information).

Anyone 16 years or older who plans to do any beach or offshore fishing in Baja will need a fishing license; for an application, contact the Secretaría de Pesca (Mexican Fisheries Department, ☎ (619) 233-6956), 2550 5th Ave, Suite 101, San Diego, CA 92103. Do not fish any species, such as the popular but endangered totuava of the Gulf, which are in *veda* (temporarily or permanently illegal to fish).

According to the California Department of Fish & Game, any fish obtained legally in Mexico may enter California upon submission of form FG901; contact ☎ (619) 467-4201, 4949 Viewridge Ave, San Diego, CA 92123, for information about declaration forms, permits and limits. For requirements of other US states or Canadian provinces, check with the respective authorities.

For seasonal suggestions on fishing, see individual entries for Ensenada, San Quintín, San Felipe, Bahía San Luis Gonzaga, Bahía de los Angeles, Mulegé, Loreto, La Paz, the Eastern Cape, San José del Cabo and Cabo San Lucas.

Sea Kayaking
With its lengthy coastline, Baja California offers limitless opportunities for sea kayaking. The areas most convenient to mainland California are from Ensenada south toward Punta Banda, but the most interesting areas are the Gulf islands of the Midriff from Bahía de los Angeles south to La Paz. These feature abundant wildlife and countless anchorages for well-equipped campers. Sheltered Bahía Concepción, south of Mulegé, is another major hot spot for recreational kayakers.

Hazards to sea kayakers include the large swells of the open Pacific and high winds on the Gulf, both of which can swamp unsuspecting novices; even experts should respect these natural phenomena and inquire about local conditions. Note also that Mexican government regulations prohibit sea kayaking when whales are present in the Pacific coastal lagoons of Baja California Sur.

Surfing

Surfers enjoy Baja's Pacific coast and even parts of the far southern Gulf of California, but be aware that the entire coastline between Tijuana and Ensenada is heavily polluted. Areas farther to the south are more suitable for this sport. Baja's best surf spot, Isla Natividad off the tip of Península Vizcaíno, is almost inaccessible except by boat or small plane.

To reach the best spots, surfers need sturdy vehicles, should carry extra parts and gasoline, plenty of water and all supplies, and should be especially conscientious about carrying out their trash. Those who speak Spanish will find that local fishermen are good sources of information, since they know where to find the *olas* (waves).

Virtually the entire Pacific coast of Baja and areas along the Eastern Cape as far north as Punta Arenas contain a multitude of surf sites. The most popular are easily accessible areas, like those along the northern Pacific coast in and around Ensenada, and Los Cabos sites like Zipper's. Dedicated surfers favor isolated spots with difficult access, such as the Islas de Todos Santos near Ensenada and Isla Natividad near Guerrero Negro. For more details, consult individual geographical entries in this book. *México Surf Spot's Map* (sic) has considerable detail on Baja California; it is available for about US$10 from beach-supply and surf shops in and around Playas de Rosarito.

Some businesses, such as surf shops in Playas de Rosarito and San José del Cabo, cater specifically to surfers, and major surfing sites are less crowded and competitive than in southern mainland California. US periodicals like *Surfer* (☎ (714) 496-5922), PO Box 1028, Dana Point, CA 92629, often contain material on both Baja California and Baja California Sur; by

Angler's Glossary

The following list should help English-speaking fishing enthusiasts avoid confusion when talking with Mexican guides and anglers. Note that in Mexico some terms may be understood differently than they are in other Spanish-speaking countries. *Jurel*, for instance, commonly means 'mackerel' elsewhere.

barracuda	*picuda*
black marlin	*marlín negro*
blue marlin	*marlín azul*
crevalle	*toro*
dolphin fish	*dorado*
grouper	*garropa*
halibut	*lenguado*
mackerel	*macarela*
needlefish	*agulón*
roosterfish	*pez gallo*
sailfish	*pez vela*
shark	*tiburón*
sierra	*sawfish*
skipjack	*barrilete*
snapper	*pargo*
striped marlin	*marlín rayado*
yellowfin tuna	*atún*
yellowtail	*jurel*

calling the above number, surfers can get the most current information.

Whale-Watching

In winter the coastal lagoons of Baja California Sur are a nursery for the California gray whale, and thousands of visitors, both Mexicans and foreigners, gather every year to observe mothers and their calves cavorting in the lagoons' shallow waters. It is possible to arrange informal full- or half-day whale-watching trips on local fishing boats at Guerrero Negro, at Ojo de Liebre and San Ignacio lagoons and at Bahía Magdalena. These are much cheaper than organized trips arranged in the USA but are also less extensive and informative.

Windsurfing

Baja's windsurfing capital is Los Barriles, a fast-growing settlement on the Eastern Cape, but Bahía de la Ventana, southeast of La Paz via a good paved highway, is rapidly gaining popularity. In these areas and around Los Cabos, equipment is easy to come by, but elsewhere windsurfers will have to bring their own. The sheltered waters of Bahía Magdalena, west of Ciudad Constitución, have great potential, but the area's limited infrastructure makes for awkward logistics (whale-watching season is also a problematic time here).

ON LAND
Bicycling

Bicycling is increasingly popular as both bicycles and roads improve – bicycling the length of Baja is now probably more common than driving it was before completion of the Transpeninsular. However, the distance between settlements and lack of water in some areas can be serious drawbacks without logistical support, and cyclists should be adept mechanics. Narrow shoulders on most highways can be hazardous, but Mexican drivers are remarkably respectful and courteous toward cyclists (the same is not always true of north-of-the-border road hogs).

The Baja border areas, particularly the cities of Tecate and Ensenada, host a variety of bicycling events annually; for details, see the respective city entries. Rental bikes are readily available in resort areas like Loreto, La Paz and Los Cabos.

Hiking

Hiking and backpacking are less common in Baja than they are north of the border, but there are many suitable areas for these activities, like Parque Nacional Constitución de 1857 (including canyons on the eastern scarp of the Sierra de Juárez), Parque Nacional Sierra San Pedro Mártir, the Sierra de San Francisco of the Desierto Central, the Sierra de la Giganta west of Loreto and the Sierra de la Laguna in the Los Cabos area. Because most of Baja is desert, hikers must carry large amounts of water and adequate food supplies, and should be aware of hazards like rattlesnakes, flash floods and unanticipated heat (even in winter) that can lead to dehydration.

Riding

In some areas of Baja California, horses, mules and burros are still a significant means of transportation for both humans and cargo. Beach resorts like Playas de Rosarito, Ensenada and Cabo San Lucas are popular for recreational horseback riding, while mules are the prime means of access to areas like the Sierra de San Francisco, with its extraordinary pre-Columbian cave paintings.

Tennis & Golf

These sports are popular among the handful who can afford equipment and fees. Many upscale hotels have tennis courts, and some have golf courses or putting greens that waste inordinate amounts of water in Baja's unrelentingly dry desert environments.

STUDY PROGRAMS & EXPEDITIONS

Many educational institutions and organizations based in mainland California offer programs in and research expeditions and tours to Baja. Tour companies are listed at the end of this chapter.

Colleges and universities often conduct

short research trips to study flora, fauna, gray whales, ancient cave paintings and various other topics. The itineraries and academic-department sponsors change every year; contact the following institutions or individual colleges and universities for current information:

Office of the Chancellor, California Community Colleges, 1107 9th St, Sacramento, CA 95814 (☎ (916) 445-8752)
Extension Division, University of California (Los Angeles), 405 Hilgard Ave, Los Angeles, CA 90024 (☎ (310) 825-9971)
University Research Expedition Program, University of California (Berkeley), Berkeley, CA 94720 (☎ (510) 642-6586)

The Smithsonian Institution also organizes expeditions and study tours to Baja; in mid-February it runs a nine-day whale-watching cruise aboard the *MV Sea Lion* that visits La Paz, Isla Partida, Isla Espíritu Santo, Gordo Banks, Cabo San Lucas and Bahía Magdalena, and returns overland to La Paz. Costs range from US$2690 to US$3990, double occupancy, plus airfare. Contact Smithsonian Study Tours (☎ (202) 357-4700, fax (202) 633-9250), 1100 Jefferson Drive, SW, Suite 3077, MRC 702, Washington, DC 20560.

Glendale Community College runs two-to three-week summer courses for university credit in natural history, marine biology and Spanish at its field station in Bahía de los Angeles; fees range from US$550 to US$650, including transportation and most meals. For further information, contact the Baja California Field Studies Program (☎ (818) 240-1000, ext 5515), Glendale Community College, 1500 N Verdugo Rd, Glendale, CA 91208.

ORGANIZED TOURS

General and special-interest tours are increasingly popular ways to explore Baja California. Whale-watching expeditions, desert bicycling trips, sea kayaking and windsurfing in the Gulf of California, beach camping trips and fishing trips are only a few of the many types of tours available. The following list may help you determine tour operators' specialties (see the Tour Companies entry at the end of this chapter for more information):

Agriculture – Global Exchange, Ol' McConnell's Farm & Fun Tours
Astronomy – Forum Travel International
Bicycling – Baja Expeditions, The Touring Exchange
Bird-Watching – Elderhostel, Nature Expeditions International, Oceanic Society Expeditions, San Diego Natural History Museum
Botany – San Diego Natural History Museum
Diving – Baja Dive Adventures (see Mr Bill's Boardsailing Adventures in the Tour Companies entry, below), Baja Expeditions, Horizon Charters
Fishing – Baja Fishing Resorts, Tony Reyes Sport Fishing, Vela's Baja Highwind Center
Hiking – Baja Discovery, National Outdoor Leadership School
Horseback Riding – Saddling South (see Paddling South in the Tour Companies entry, below), Vela's Baja Highwind Center
Language, History & Culture – Elderhostel, Global Exchange
Mountain Biking – Backroads Bicycle Touring, Baja Expeditions, Kayak Port Townsend, Pedaling South (see Paddling South in the Tour Companies entry, below), Mr Bill's Boardsailing Adventures/Baja Dive Adventures, The Touring Exchange, Vela's Baja Highwind Center
Photography – Baja Discovery
RV Tours – Point South RV Tours
Sea Kayaking – Baja Expeditions, Baja Tropicales, Green Tortoise Alternative Travel, Kayak Port Townsend, Mountain Travel Sobek, National Outdoor Leadership School, Oceanic Society Expeditions, Outdoor Adventure River Specialists, Paddling South, REI Adventures, San Diego Natural History Museum, Southwest Sea Kayaks, The Touring Exchange
Snorkeling – Baja Expeditions, Elderhostel, Oceanic Society Expeditions, Vela's Baja Highwind Center
Surfing – Baja Surf Adventures
Whale-Watching – American Cetacean Society, Baja California Tours, Baja Discovery, Baja Expeditions, Discover Baja Travel Club (see Baja Tropicales in the Tour Companies entry, below), Elderhostel, Forum Travel International, Green Tortoise Alternative Travel, Mountain Travel Sobek, Natural Habitat Adventures, Nature Expeditions International, Oceanic Society Expeditions, Outdoor Adventure River Specialists, Pacific Sea Fari

Tours, San Diego Natural History Museum, Spirit of Adventure Charters

Windsurfing – Mr Bill's Boardsailing Adventures, Vela's Baja Highwind Center

Tour Companies

The following list contains addresses for and additional information about US tour companies operating in Baja California. Some operators can combine several activities, such as sea kayaking, whale-watching, snorkeling and camping, in the same trip. Unless otherwise noted, transportation to the activity site is not included in the prices listed below.

Many of these tour operators maintain websites that provide additional details on their offerings: see the Internet Directory in the back of the book for these addresses.

American Cetacean Society (☎ (310) 548-6279), PO Box 1391, San Pedro, CA 90733, is a nonprofit group that focuses on whale conservation and organizes several whale-watching trips every year to help support its activities. It publishes the quarterly journal *Whalewatcher* and the newsletter *Whale News* for its members and also produces two information kits about whales and dolphins (US$5 each, plus tax and shipping).

Backroads Bicycle Touring (☎ (510) 527-1555, (800) 462-2848 toll free outside California), 801 Cedar St, Berkeley, CA 94710, has five- and six-day 'multisport adventure' trips, emphasizing mountain biking, in southern Baja's Cape Region,

starting in San José del Cabo and ending in Cabo San Lucas. While most routes are not difficult, van shuttle support is available in a pinch. With accommodations in hotels, trip prices start at US$1495 per person; with camping, prices are around US$895.

Baja California Tours (☎ (619) 454-7166, fax (619) 454-2703, BajaTours@aol.com), 7734 Herschel Ave, Suite O, La Jolla, CA 92037, runs four-day overland whale-watching trips to Laguna Ojo de Liebre (US$425), also called Scammon's Lagoon, and weeklong overland trips to La Paz (US$999), including three days of whale-watching and return travel by air. It also maintains a database on whale-watching trips in general.

Baja Discovery (☎ (619) 262-0700, (800) 829-2252, bajadis@aol.com), PO Box 152527, San Diego, CA 92195, runs five- to eight-day whale-watching trips that cost around US$1195 to US$1530 per person. These combine comfortable hotel accommodations (usually the La Pinta chain) with beach camping. Small 22-foot *pangas* (skiffs) allow passengers to get close enough to pet the whales. Baja Discovery also runs seven-day van trips to Bahía de los Angeles on the Gulf of California for about US$1095 per person, and spring and autumn hiking trips lasting from five to eight days for about US$500 to US$1300. For further information, contact Karen Ivey at the San Diego office.

Baja Expeditions (☎ (619) 581-3311, (800) 843-6967, fax (619) 581-6542, travel@bajaex.com), 2625 Garnet Ave, San Diego, CA 92109, is Baja's oldest and largest natural history and adventure travel company, emphasizing whale-watching, diving and sea kayaking. Knowledgeable naturalists and guides accompany every trip to explain the flora, fauna and environment. The cheaper trips start at around US$299 for two-day diving trips from La Paz, US$850 for five-day kayak trips in the Gulf and US$995 for whale-watching camps at San Ignacio. The company's most expensive trip, a nine-day diving expedition to the very remote Socorro

Islands, runs as high as US$2475. Baja Expeditions' vessels include the 50-foot *Río Rita* for short trips out of La Paz and the 80-foot MV *Don José* for longer excursions.

Baja Fishing Resorts (☎ (818) 591-9463, (800) 368-4334, fax (818) 591-1077), PO Box 9016, Calabasas, CA 91372, offers packages of four and five days with lodging, meals and fishing in the Eastern Cape area for US$300 to US$500 per person.

Baja Surf Adventures (☎ (760) 744-5642, (800) 428-7873, fax (760) 727-9868), PO Box 1381, Vista, CA 92085, offers weekend (US$275) and weeklong (US$850) Baja surf camps, weeklong central Baja surf caravans (US$725 to US$950) and six-day fly-in surf trips to Los Cabos (US$700).

Baja Tropicales/Mulegé Kayaks (☎ (115) 3-04-09, fax (115) 3-01-90), Apdo Postal 60, Mulegé, Baja California Sur 23900, México, offers local sea kayak trips from Playa Santispac near Mulegé for US$39 per person, including meals and beverages; a minimum of four people is required. In addition, it offers five- and six-day trips around Bahía Concepción and to spots like Isla San Marcos, Bahía Magdalena and Laguna Ojo de Liebre. Prices start around US$300. Rental equipment is available for experienced kayakers, starting around US$25 per day. The company's mainland California contact is Discover Baja Travel Club (☎ (619) 275-4225, (800) 727-2252, discovbaja@aol.com).

Elderhostel (☎ (617) 426-8056), 75 Federal St, Boston, MA 02110, caters to travelers over 55 years of age. It offers two-week language, history and culture programs based in La Paz from late October through early May (US$1158). Other Elderhostel programs include weeklong whale-watching at Bahía Magdalena in January and February (US$1077) and a weeklong excursion to the southern islands of the Gulf of California (US$924).

Forum Travel International (☎ (510) 671-2900, fax (510) 671-2993), 91 Gregory Lane, Suite 21, Pleasant Hill, CA 94523, offers several trips to Baja, including whale-watching and special astronomy-oriented trips, at very reasonable prices.

Global Exchange (☎ (415) 255-7296, (800) 497-1994, fax (415) 255-7498, lisa@globalexchange.org), 2017 Mission St, Suite 303, San Francisco, CA 94110, runs three-day 'reality tours' of the San Diego/Tijuana border area (US$350), focusing on issues like farm workers' northward immigration and maquiladora labor. While some might dismiss these trips as radical chic, they successfully introduce middle-class visitors to peoples and lives outside their own experiences, one of the goals of meaningful travel.

Green Tortoise Alternative Travel (☎ (415) 956-7500, (800) 867-8647, info@greentortoise.com), 494 Broadway, San Francisco, CA 94133, offers Baja bus trips with one or two weeks of beach camping and sea kayaking, usually between November and April. Nine-day trips cost around US$300 to US$330, meals included, while 14 day trips cost around US$420 to US$470, meals included. Meals are mostly vegetarian.

Horizon Charters (☎ (619) 277-7823, fax (619) 560-6811, divesd@aol.com), 4178 Lochlomond St, San Diego, CA 92111, offers diving cruises along Baja's Pacific coast and also works with other operators like Pacific Sea Fari (see below).

Kayak Port Townsend (☎ (360) 385-6240, fax (360) 385-6062, 102047.3556@compuserve.com), 435 Water St, PO Box 1387, Port Townsend, WA 98368, runs a series of kayak tours at various Gulf of California locations between Loreto and La Paz from November through April (with a hiatus in January, except for custom tours). Prices range from US$645 (seven days) to US$845 (11 days); some trips include a substantial mountain-biking component.

Mountain Travel Sobek (☎ (510) 527-8100, (800) 227-2384 toll free in the USA, (800) 282-8747 toll free in Canada, fax (510) 525-7710, info@mtsobek.com), 6420 Fairmount Ave, El Cerrito, CA 94530, offers seven-day kayak trips in the Gulf of

California and seven-day whale-watching excursions at Bahía Magdalena, both starting at US$995.

Mr Bill's Boardsailing Adventures/Baja Dive Adventures (☎ (541) 386-7610, (800) 533-8452, fax (541) 386-4899, bajabill@balandra.uabcs.mx), 111 Oak St, Hood River, OR 97031, based in Los Barriles, offers weeklong windsurfing vacations but also arranges other activities, most notably diving, sea kayaking and mountain biking. Accommodations are at Los Barriles' hillside Casa Miramar B&B. Off-season rates (early November to mid-December, mid-March to June) are US$475 per person double occupancy, US$575 single, but there's also a bunk rate of US$395. In-season rates (mid-December to mid-March) are US$575 per person double occupancy, US$675 single (US$495 bunk rate). Additional activities are not included, but there's a bargain rate of US$325 per week for nonwindsurfers.

National Outdoor Leadership School (NOLS) (☎ (307) 332-6973, fax (307) 332-1220, admissions@nols.edu), 288 Main St, Lander, WY 82520-3128, though not exactly a tour company, does conduct a number of demanding Baja-based natural history and outdoor skills courses, including sailing, sea kayaking, climbing and hiking. University credit is available; most courses last about three weeks and cost around US$2200, but the 10-week semester courses cost about US$7300.

Natural Habitat Adventures (☎ (303) 449-3711, (800) 543-8917, fax (303) 449-3712), 2945 Center Green Court, Suite H, Boulder, CO 80301, runs 11-day 'Ultimate Baja' whale-watching tours in February and early March. Prices start at US$2895 per person.

Nature Expeditions International (☎ (520) 721-6712, (800) 869-0639, fax (520) 721-6710, NaturExp@aol.com), 6400 E El Dorado Circle, Suite 210, Tucson, AZ 85715, plans to combine trips to mainland Mexico's Barranca del Cobre (Copper Canyon) with sailing trips on the Gulf of California, visiting several hard-to-reach islands to view birds, whales and other wildlife.

Oceanic Society Expeditions (☎ (415) 441-1106, (800) 326-7491, fax (415) 474-3395), Fort Mason Center, Bldg E, San Francisco, CA 94123, is a nonprofit enterprise specializing in natural history trips to Baja's Pacific and Gulf coasts. Led by experienced naturalists, its whale-watching, sea kayaking, snorkeling, bird-watching and camping trips range from seven to 12 days. A few tours use the 88-foot *Spirit of Adventure*. Eight-day kayaking trips departing from Loreto cost US$995, eight-day island cruises in the Gulf of California cost US$1390 and nine-day whale-watching cruises to Laguna San Ignacio cost US$1690. A 12-day cruise down Baja's Pacific coast, visiting the Islas de Todos Santos off Ensenada, Islas San Benito, Laguna San Ignacio, Bahía Magdalena and many sites in the southern Gulf, costs US$2250. A weeklong trip combining Gulf islands and mainland Mexico's Barranca del Cobre starts at US$1930.

Ol' McConnell's Farm & Fun Tours (☎ (760) 352-3688), 23341 McConnell Rd, El Centro, CA 92243, leads conventional excursions to locations like Ensenada and San Felipe but also arranges industrial tours of border maquiladoras and agricultural tours of the Valle de Mexicali as tour director for the Imperial County Farm Bureau (☎ (760) 352-3831), 1000 Broadway, El Centro, CA 92243.

Outdoor Adventure River Specialists (OARS) (☎ (209) 736-4677, (800) 346-6277, fax (209) 736-2902, reservations@oars.com), PO Box 67, Angels Camp, CA 95222, runs weeklong whale-watching excursions to Bahía Magdalena (US$1250 to US$1450, airfare included) and weeklong sea kayak trips in the Gulf of California (US$1225 to US$1450, airfare included).

Pacific Sea Fari Tours (☎ (619) 226-8224, fax (619) 222-0784), 2803 Emerson St, San Diego, CA 92106, runs several sea-based tours, emphasizing whale-watching,

Riding the *olas*

WAYNE BERNHARDSON

along the Pacific coast and Gulf of California. Whale-watching expeditions (the company's specialty) take place from late January to April. Sample itineraries include seven days of island-hopping in the Gulf (US$1390), eight days of cruising islands and whale-watching sites along the Pacific (US$1690) and 11 days of sailing from San Diego to Cabo San Lucas or La Paz, including island-hopping in the Gulf (US$2250).

Paddling South (☎ (113) 5-10-10, fax (113) 5-09-00), Las Parras Tour, Francisco Madero s/n, Loreto, Baja California Sur 23880, México, specializes in sea kayaking around the Loreto area but also arranges mountain-biking tours as Peddling South and horseback tours of the Sierra de la Giganta backcountry as Saddling South. Co-owner Trudi Angell leads a few kayak trips for women only and is also the local operator for REI Adventures (see below). In the US, contact Paddling South at ☎ (707) 942-4550, 4510 Silverado Trail, Calistoga, CA 94515.

Point South RV Tours (☎ (909) 247-1222, (800) 421-1394, fax (909) 924-3838), 11313 Edmondson Ave, Moreno Valley, CA 92555, conducts tours for RV enthusiasts, organizing caravans from San Diego to Cabo San Lucas that can be extended to mainland Mexico. It also offers special insurance policies for assistance during mechanical breakdowns, which

cover towing, parts shipping, hospital costs and other matters not normally covered by Mexican car insurance policies.

REI Adventures (☎ (800) 622-2236, fax (206) 395-4744, travel@rei.com), PO Box 1938, Sumner, WA 98390, runs eight-day sea kayak trips out of Loreto for US$995 per person.

San Diego Natural History Museum (☎ (619) 232-3821, ext 203), PO Box 1390, San Diego, CA 92112, offers whale-watching day trips to the Coronado Islands (US$64); weekend overnights on the *Pacific Queen* to the Islas de Todos Santos (US$285 per person); weekend excursions to Cañón Palomar on the eastern slope of the Sierra de Juárez (US$95), Parque Nacional Constitución de 1857 (US$125) or Parque Nacional Sierra San Pedro Mártir (US$205, museum members only); eight-day overland whale-watching safaris to Laguna San Ignacio for US$985 per person on a car-pool basis; and fly-down whale-watching trips to Laguna San Ignacio for US$1530 per person.

As part of a long-term project on northern Baja California's biogeography, the museum also offers inexpensive overnight and weekend programs to La Rinconada, a private coastal ranch; to the desert around San Felipe in search of wildflowers; and to Punta Banda for sea kayaking. Other excursions include an extended weekend in Cataviña in search of the ostensibly extinct Lindsay's hedgehog cactus and a week's bird-watching tour from San Diego south to La Paz and Cabo San Lucas, returning to Tijuana by air, in conjunction with Baja Discovery. The latter costs US$1695 per person.

Southwest Sea Kayaks (☎ (619) 222-3616, fax (619) 222-3671, kayaked@aol.com), 2590 Ingraham St, San Diego, CA 92109, arranges a wide variety of moderately priced sea kayak excursions in the Ensenada area, the Midriff Islands of the central Gulf of California and southern Baja, including whale-watching trips at Laguna Ojo de Liebre and Bahía de los Angeles. Trips usually involve driving and car-pooling to the put-in point. Southwest also publishes an informative quarterly newsletter.

Spirit of Adventure Charters (☎/fax (619) 226-1729), 1646 Willow St, San Diego, CA 92107, works with Pacific Sea Fari (see above) on whale-watching trips of similar itineraries and duration at comparable prices. It also offers private yacht charters.

Tony Reyes Sport Fishing runs weeklong fishing trips among the Midriff Islands of the Gulf of California aboard the 86-foot *José Andrés*; it also offers trips out of La Paz from January through April. Tony Reyes' US agent is The Longfin Tackle

Store (☎ (714) 538-9300, fax (714) 538-1368), 1333 S Yorba St, Orange, CA 92869.

The Touring Exchange (☎ (360) 385-0667, (800) 853-2252), PO Box 265, Port Townsend, WA 98368, leads one- to two-week bicycle, mountain-bike and kayak excursions of varying difficulty from January to April. Based in La Paz, its 'Endurance Camps,' training rides from Mulegé to Cabo San Lucas, are definitely not for beginners. Prices range from US$550 to US$895. Its intensive six-day language camps, involving 20 hours of instruction, cost US$285.

Vela's Baja Highwind Center (☎ (415) 373-1100, (800) 223-5443, fax (415) 373-1111, info@verlawindsurf.com), 16 E 3rd Ave, Suite 6, San Mateo, CA 94401, is part of Vela Windsurf Resorts, based in northern mainland California. Each winter (November to April) it bases itself at the Hotel Playa del Sol in Los Barriles (south of La Paz), where the season's highlight is an annual windsurfing championship race, usually held in early January. World-class windsurfing instructors hold weekly classes with prototypes of the latest equipment direct from the manufacturers. Mountain biking, snorkeling, horseback riding and fishing are also possible. Weeklong trips start around US$789 per person, double occupancy.

Getting There & Away

Most travel to Baja California, whether by air, land or sea, is from the USA – in fact, it is largely from California. Many visitors, though, travel from other western US states or from Canada's western provinces through California, or fly into Baja from major western airports. A relative handful travel from elsewhere in North America or cross from mainland Mexico.

AIR
Airports & Airlines
Baja California has international airports with extensive flight schedules at Tijuana, Mexicali, Loreto, La Paz and Los Cabos, plus secondary airports at San Felipe (with no commercial flights at present) and Guerrero Negro (with limited flights via airports in northern mainland Mexico).

The USA
From the USA, the main carriers are Aero California, Alaska Airlines and Mexicana de Aviación (Mexicana). Aeroméxico, its subsidiary Aerolitoral, America West, American Airlines, Continental Airlines and Taesa offer limited alternatives. The telephone numbers of these companies (toll free in the USA) are as follows:

Aero California	☎ (800) 237-6225
Aeroméxico/Aerolitoral	☎ (800) 237-6639
Alaska Airlines	☎ (800) 426-0333
America West	☎ (800) 235-9292
American Airlines	☎ (800) 433-7300
Continental Airlines	☎ (800) 231-0856
Horizon Air	☎ (800) 547-9308
Mexicana	☎ (800) 531-7921
Taesa	☎ (800) 328-2372

Travelers with Special Needs
If you have special needs of any sort – a broken leg, dietary restrictions, dependence on a wheelchair, responsibility for a baby, fear of flying – you should let the airline know as soon as possible so that they can make arrangements for you. You should remind them when you confirm your reservation (at least 72 hours before departure) and again when you check in at the airport. You might also call around the airlines before you make your reservation to find out how they can handle your particular needs.

Airports and airlines can be surprisingly helpful, but they do need advance warning. Most international airports can provide escorts from check-in desk to plane when needed, and there should be ramps, lifts, accessible toilets and reachable phones. Aircraft toilets, on the other hand, are likely to present problems; travelers should discuss this with the airline at an early stage and, if necessary, with their doctor.

Guide dogs for the blind will often have to travel in a pressurized luggage compartment with other animals, away from their owner, though smaller guide dogs may be admitted into the cabin. Guide dogs are not subject to quarantine as long as they have proof of vaccination against rabies. Deaf travelers can ask that airport and inflight announcements be written down for them.

Children under age two usually travel for 10% of the standard fare (or free on some airlines) as long as they don't occupy a seat. They don't get a luggage allowance. 'Skycots' should be provided by the airline if requested in advance; these will hold a child weighing up to about 22 lbs (10 kg). Children between ages two and 12 can usually occupy a seat for one-half to two-thirds of the full fare, and they do get a luggage allowance. Strollers often may be taken on as hand luggage. ∎

Fares are almost impossible to pin down because of seasonal variations and advance purchase requirements; those given below should only be taken as very general indicators. When booking flights with Mexicana or Aero California, check special fares and combined airfare and hotel packages. Fares are generally US$20 to US$30 lower on flights that arrive and depart Monday to Thursday. Accommodations at resort-style hotels in Baja are often much cheaper if arranged through an airline or travel agency as part of a package.

To/From Tijuana, Mexicali & Guerrero Negro Taesa flies from Chicago to Tijuana via an awkward Mexico City connection. Mexicana flies from Tijuana to Los Angeles International Airport (US$58 one way) daily but offers no flights in the opposite direction.

Aeroméxico's subsidiary Aerolitoral flies from Tucson and Phoenix to Tijuana and Mexicali via the mainland Mexican city of Hermosillo (Sonora) and to Guerrero Negro via Hermosillo.

To/From Loreto, La Paz & Los Cabos Aero California is the only airline offering direct flights from the USA (Los Angeles only) to Loreto, which cost about US$212 roundtrip.

Twice daily, Aero California flies from Los Angeles to La Paz for about US$200 one way, US$245 roundtrip. Aeroméxico flies daily to La Paz from Los Angeles and Tucson; Aeroméxico and Aero California also have daily flights from Tijuana to La Paz for about US$315 roundtrip (that's right, it's more expensive within Mexico).

Mexicana flies to Los Cabos from Los Angeles (twice daily) and Denver (Tuesday, Thursday, Saturday and Sunday); other routings are possible with connecting airlines or via mainland Mexican cities. Fares can be as low as US$235 roundtrip from Los Angeles and US$280 from Denver; one-way fares are actually higher.

Alaska Airlines flies daily to Los Cabos from Los Angeles (US$285 one way, US$235 roundtrip), from San Francisco (US$315 one way, US$360 roundtrip), from San Diego (US$285 one way, US$298 roundtrip) and from Phoenix (US$275 one way, US$320 roundtrip). Alaska Airlines and its subsidiary Horizon Air serve 79 cities and towns in Alaska, the Pacific Northwest, the northern Rocky Mountain states, California and the Southwest, plus several locales in Canada and Asiatic Russia.

Aeroméxico flies from San Diego to Los Cabos daily (US$165 one way weekdays, US$175 weekends; watch for seasonal variations). Aero California flies to Los Cabos at least daily from Los Angeles, Phoenix and Denver. America West flies twice daily from Phoenix to Los Cabos (US$221 one way, US$378 roundtrip). Continental Airlines flies daily from Houston to Los Cabos (US$406 one way, US$513 roundtrip). American Airlines flies daily except Tuesday from Dallas/Fort Worth to Los Cabos (US$497 roundtrip).

Getaway Packages The above airlines and several California-based travel agencies and tour companies offer bargain packages for short-term visitors. If you're flying to Loreto, La Paz or Los Cabos, check specials offered by Mexicana, Alaska Airlines and various travel agencies for short stays at resort hotels. Often available on short notice, these may cater to specific activities like sportfishing or golfing, and sometimes cost little more than normal airfare. Aero California works with many agencies and tour companies, including the following in southern mainland California:

Barvi Tours offers three-night packages at the Posada Real Los Cabos or Hotel Meliá San Lucas. The staff, mostly born in Mexico and thoroughly familiar with the country, can arrange fishing trips throughout Baja, generally from Los Cabos or La Paz. (☎ (310) 474-4041, (800) 824-7102)

Island Flight Vacations deals with hotels like Cabo San Lucas' Plaza Las Glorias and Hotel Meliá Cabo Real. (☎ (310) 410-0909, (800) 426-4570)

Mexico Travel Experts offers packages such as three nights at San José del Cabo's Hotel Palmilla or Cabo San Lucas' Hotel Finisterra. (☎ (800) 326-2252)

Check Sunday travel sections of major US newspapers for additional listings. Before committing to any package, confirm hotel and airline reservations that the operator supposedly has made for you. Although problems are unlikely, you don't want to show up at the airport or hotel only to find yourself without tickets or reservations.

Australia & New Zealand

The cheapest and most direct route across the Pacific is to fly to the US Pacific coast (Los Angeles or San Francisco) and make the short hop south to Baja from there. The main carriers are Qantas, Air New Zealand and United.

Discount fares from Australia to Los Angeles range from A$1450 to A$1820 roundtrip, depending on season of travel. Airfares from New Zealand range from NZ$1800 to NZ$1950 roundtrip. If you wish to stop over in Hawaii or plan to stay abroad for more than two months, you will generally pay more.

The UK & Continental Europe

There are no direct flights from Europe to Baja California – you must first fly to North America or Mexico City and from there fly to Baja. Usually, the cheapest alternative is to fly to Los Angeles and then head south, rather than fly to Mexico City and travel north.

So-called bucket shops in London can provide the best deals. Check out newspapers and magazines like the Saturday *Independent* for suggestions. One-way fares from London to Los Angeles run from about £187 to £239; roundtrip excursions cost about £297 to £345. One-way fares to Mexico City are around £265 to £290, while roundtrip excursions cost from £380 to £436.

If you're traveling from the UK, you will probably find that the cheapest flights are advertised by obscure bucket shops whose names haven't yet reached the telephone directory. Many such firms are honest and solvent, but there are a few rogues who will take the money and run, reopening elsewhere a month or two later under a new

name. If you're suspicious about a firm, don't give them all the money at once – leave a deposit of 20% or so and pay the balance on receiving the ticket. If they insist on cash in advance, go elsewhere. And once you have the ticket, call the airline to confirm that you are booked on the flight.

Since bucket shops come and go, it's worth inquiring about their affiliation with the Association of British Travel Agents (ABTA), which guarantees a refund or alternative if the agent goes out of business. The following are reputable London bucket shops:

Campus Travel, 52 Grosvenor Gardens, London SW1 (☎ (0171) 730-3402)
Journey Latin America, 16 Devonshire Rd, Chiswick, London W4 2HD (☎ (0181) 747-8315)
Passage to South America, 13 Shepherds Bush Rd, London W6 7LP (☎ (0171) 602-9889)
South American Experience, 47 Causton St, London SW1 (☎ (0171) 976-5511)
STA Travel, 86 Old Brompton Rd, London SW7 3LQ (☎ (0171) 937-9921)
117 Euston Rd, London NW1 2SX (☎ (0171) 937-9921)
Trailfinders, 194 Kensington High St, London W8 7RG (☎ (0171) 938-3366)

To Mexico City, British Airways sometimes offers inexpensive courier flights (around £300) in conjunction with Polo Express (☎ (0181) 564-7009). There is one such seat on each flight; couriers get a full luggage allowance (23 kg plus one piece of hand baggage), have to dress 'smartly' (no jeans) and must be over 18. You can book up to three months in advance, but patience is needed – reaching them by phone takes ages. Call between 9 am and 5 pm weekdays.

In Berlin, check out the magazine *Zitty* for bargain fare advertisements. Throughout Western Europe you can find agencies that provide bargain fares, including the following:

France
Council Travel, 31 Rue Saint Augustine, Paris 2ème (☎ 01.42.66.20.87)
Council Travel, Rue des Pyramides, Paris 1er (☎ 01.44.55.55.44)

Germany
    Alternativ Tours, Wilmersdorferstrasse 94, Berlin (☎ (030) 881-2089)
    SRID Reisen, Bergerstrasse 1178, Frankfurt (☎ (069) 430-191)
    SRS Studentenreise Service, Marienstrasse 23, Berlin (☎ (030) 281-5033)
Ireland
    USIT Travel Office, 19 Aston Quay, Dublin (☎ (01) 679-8833)
Italy
    CTS, Via Genova 16, Rome (☎ (06) 46-791)
Netherlands
    Malibu Travel, Damrak 30, Amsterdam (☎ (020) 623-6814)
    NBBS, Rokin 38, Amsterdam (☎ (020) 642-0989)
Spain
    TIVE, Calle José Ortega y Gasset, Madrid (☎ (01) 401-1300)
Switzerland
    SSR, Leonhardstrasse 5 & 10, Zürich (☎ (01) 261-2956)

Mainland Mexico

Internal Mexican flights are generally a bit cheaper than comparable flights in the USA, though there are exceptions. There are direct daily flights from several mainland Mexican cities to Tijuana, Mexicali, Loreto, La Paz and Los Cabos. Consult Aeroméxico, Aero California or Mexicana for specific route details, and see the Air entry in the Getting Around chapter for more information.

LAND
The USA

Border Crossings From west to east, there are six official border crossings from mainland California to Baja: Tijuana, Mesa de Otay, Tecate, Mexicali, Calexico East and Los Algodones. At any crossing Mexican Customs & Immigration will validate tourist cards and process car permits free of charge.

San Ysidro-Tijuana Open 24 hours a day, this is one of the world's busiest border crossings.
Mesa de Otay Opened to relieve pressure on the San Ysidro-Tijuana crossing, Mesa de Otay is open 6 am to 10 pm daily. East of downtown Tijuana near the airport, it offers a far less congested port of entry for drivers.

Tecate Open 6 am to midnight daily, the Tecate border crossing is about 30 miles (50 km) southeast of San Diego via California State Hwys 94 and 188.
Calexico-Mexicali Open 24 hours a day, this congested crossing is about 8 miles (13 km) south of El Centro via California State Hwy 111. The new border crossing at Calexico East, open 6 am to 10 pm daily, has relieved some of the pressure.
Andrade-Los Algodones This ostensibly remote border is nevertheless bustling. About 7 miles (11 km) west of Yuma, Arizona, via US Interstate 8 and California State Hwy 186, it's open 6 am to 8 pm daily.

Bus & Trolley Travelers can enter Baja California by land at any of the crossings mentioned above. There are frequent buses and trolleys (light rail) to the San Ysidro crossing. Buses also run to Calexico-Mexicali and to Yuma in Arizona (the closest US city to the Andrade-Los Algodones crossing).

Greyhound (☎ (800) 231-2222) is the major bus operator from the USA to the border. If you're planning to travel extensively by bus in the USA, consider Greyhound's Ameripass, which costs US$199 for seven days of unlimited travel, US$299 for 15 days or US$409 for 30 days; it's available at every Greyhound terminal.

To/From Tijuana Many buses run daily from San Diego and Los Angeles to Tijuana. A modern light-rail trolley line also runs from central and suburban San Diego to the border.

The San Diego Trolley (☎ (619) 233-3004), a contemporary version of what once was San Diego's only mass transit system, runs every 15 minutes from 5 am to midnight from downtown San Diego to the border crossing at San Ysidro. The maximum fare is US$1.75.

Greyhound departs frequently from its downtown Los Angeles terminal at 1716 E 7th St en route to its San Diego terminal at 120 W Broadway and to Tijuana's downtown bus terminal at the corner of Avenida Madero and Calle 1a (Comercio) (US$12 one way). There are at least 20 buses daily between about 6 am and 10 pm.

Waiting patiently at one of the world's busiest borders

Mexicoach (☎ (619) 428-9517) runs frequent buses (US$1) from 4570 Camino de la Plaza, San Ysidro, to its new Tijuana terminal on Avenida Revolución between Calle 6a (Flores Magón) and Calle 7a (Galeana).

Every half-hour from 6 am to 9 pm, ATC/Vancom (☎ (619) 427-6438) runs buses from the corner of Broadway and 3rd Ave or Broadway and Front St in downtown San Diego to San Ysidro for only US$1.50. The trip to the border takes 80 minutes.

Five Star Tours (☎ (619) 232-5040, (800) 553-8687), located in downtown San Diego's Amtrak station at 1050 Kettner Blvd, runs day trip transportation to downtown Tijuana (US$14 roundtrip), Tijuana's airport (US$16 roundtrip) and Playas de Rosarito (US$22 roundtrip). The first departure is at 9 am, the last return from Playas de Rosarito at 5 pm; it's possible to return the following day for an additional charge. The downtown Tijuana stop is on Revolución between Calle 6a (Flores Magón) and Calle 7a (Galeana); the Playas de Rosarito stop is at the Rosarito Beach Hotel.

To/From Calexico/Mexicali Greyhound runs buses from Los Angeles (15 daily), San Diego (six daily) and Phoenix (via Yuma, four daily) to El Centro and Calexico for the border crossing to Mexicali. A one-way fare from San Diego to Calexico is US$17, while the fare from Los Angeles to Calexico is US$27. The fare from Phoenix to Calexico is US$29 one way.

Greyhound's Calexico terminal is at 121 1st St, almost directly on the border, while its Phoenix terminal is at 2115 E Buckeye Rd.

Train Amtrak runs 10 to 12 passenger trains daily from its Los Angeles terminal at 800 N Alameda St to its San Diego terminal at 1050 Kettner Blvd near Broadway. From the San Diego terminal, trolleys go directly to the border at San Ysidro. One-way/roundtrip fares are US$25/33. For current fare and schedule information, phone Amtrak (☎ (800) 872-7245).

Car Countless visitors drive their own vehicles into Baja California from the USA. Those traveling no farther south than San Felipe or Ensenada and staying less than 72 hours do not need a tourist card or car permit, but those continuing to mainland Mexico, either by ferry from Baja or overland from Mexicali, will need a car permit/tourist card (for the driver) and a tourist card for each passenger.

Liability insurance, purchased from a Mexican company, is essential for driving in Mexico; Mexican law does not recognize policies from companies based in other countries, though some US policies will pay claims in Mexico. While insurance is not obligatory, it can prevent serious legal problems for anyone involved in an accident.

According to Mexican law, the principals in an accident are guilty until proven innocent. Regardless of details, foreigners are more likely to be considered guilty than locals, especially if they have no insurance, in which case police detention is probable until fault is established. Understandably, it is common for the victims of a nonlethal accident to leave the scene before the police arrive.

Visitors to Baja California are strongly advised to obtain insurance against car theft, which is common in the border region.

For more information about tourist cards, see the Visas & Documents entry in the Facts for the Visitor chapter. For information about car permits and insurance, see the Car entry in the Getting Around chapter.

Taxi Taxis are available on both sides of the border in San Diego-Tijuana and Calexico-Mexicali, and on the Mexican side in Tecate and Los Algodones. There is a singular advantage in taking a taxi across the border from Baja California into mainland California: passengers on common carriers are not subject to import limitations on alcoholic drinks, including beer, wine and spirits, as long as those spirits are for personal use. For more information, see the Customs entry in the Facts for the Visitor chapter.

Mainland Mexico
Bus Buses run regularly from major centers throughout Mexico to Mexicali. From Mexicali, you can continue to other Baja cities and towns (see the Mexicali Getting There & Away entry for details).

Train Ferrocarriles Nacionales de México offers daily service from Mexico City to Mexicali, with intermediate stops in Guadalajara, Mazatlán, Sufragio/Los Mochis, Guaymas and Hermosillo. In some cases, it is necessary to change trains at Benjamín Hill (Sonora). First-class fares are roughly twice the price of 2nd-class fares but are still cheaper than buses (which, however, are faster and more comfortable).

See the Mexicali Getting There & Away entry for train schedules and other details. With the impending privatization of Mexican railroads, services are likely to change and prices may increase dramatically.

SEA
The USA
Cruise ships and private yachts are the only ways to travel by sea from the USA to Baja.

Cruise Ship The cruise ship *Jubilee*, operated by Carnival Cruise Lines (☎ (800) 327-9501) sails every Sunday from Pier No 93-A at the port of San Pedro near Los Angeles. Weeklong cruises visit Cabo San Lucas, Puerto Vallarta and Mazatlán; prices start around US$600 per person but can be much more expensive if demand is high or at certain times of the year.

Private Yacht If you know something about boats and sailing, try looking for a crew position on one of the many boats that sail south from mainland California. Marinas at Dana Point, Newport Beach, Belmont Shores and Marina del Rey are all good places to ask, but one correspondent has offered these detailed suggestions for southbound travelers on the Pacific coast:

From October through February, sailboats converge on San Diego to rest, make repairs and purchase provisions. Crews also frequently change, and it is a perfect place for crew to be added. Crews with experience are in demand, and just about any type of deal they want with regard to costs is possible. There is a place for the novice. A person who is willing to ask questions and learn can also do quite well. Many of the skippers are engaged in their first open-ocean experience and may not be all that relaxed. I would encourage potential crews to have frank discussions about costs, equipment, safety, nudity and expectations. The last is very important for females (crew) and male skippers.

Shelter Island in San Diego is where almost all skippers meet and are available. Throughout the boating communities, we are linked via radio for news and information. The radio networks are referred to as UHF nets or simply local nets. The key is that you do not need to have a radio to participate. Yachties are more than happy to broadcast that potential crew is available. Shyness has no place.

Make inquiries and/or send three-by-five cards for posting on the bulletin board to Downwind Marine (☎ (619) 224-2733, fax (619) 224-7683), 2819 Canon St, San Diego, CA 92106, where 'Radio Mike' operates the local net. For vessels in Baja, Downwind is a supplier of spare parts, and drivers buying parts will often take passengers as far as La Paz to share gas.

Any vessel traveling south along the Baja coast beyond Ensenada or staying more than three days in Ensenada must file a crew list with a Mexican consulate before entering Mexican waters. All registration papers and other relevant documentation must also be on board. For information on boat insurance, see the Getting Around chapter.

Mexico's Secretaría de Pesca (Fisheries Department, ☎ (619) 233-6956) maintains an office at 2550 5th Ave, Suite 101, San Diego, CA 92103, to provide necessary forms and information. It's open 8 am to 2 pm weekdays only.

Mainland Mexico
Ferry One alternative between mainland Mexico and Baja is ferry travel across the Gulf of California. Boats sail between Santa Rosalía and Guaymas, La Paz and Topolobampo (near Los Mochis) and La Paz and Mazatlán at least weekly.

Grupo Sematur de California, a Mexico-based conglomerate, has improved ferry services over the last few years, but fares have risen considerably, especially for vehicles. See the La Paz entry in the Cape Region chapter and the Santa Rosalía entry in the Desierto Central & Llano de Magdalena chapter for specific schedule and fare information for these ferries.

Note that if you bring a vehicle from Baja into mainland Mexico on a ferry, you will need a permit; see the Car Permits entry in the Getting Around chapter for more information.

Ferries between Baja California and mainland Mexico have four passenger classes: *salón* (reclining bus- or airplane-style seats), *turista* (a room with several bunks), *cabina* (a private room with bath) and *especial* (a private suite); the relatively short (eight-hour) Santa Rosalía-Guaymas run offers *salón* and *turista* only.

DEPARTURE TAXES
For Mexican domestic flights, the airport tax is around US$8; for international flights, it is US$13. Both are payable in either local or US currency.

WARNING
The information in this chapter is particularly vulnerable to change: prices for international travel are volatile, routes are introduced and canceled, schedules change, special deals come and go, and rules and visa requirements are amended. Airlines and governments seem to take a perverse pleasure in making price structures and regulations as complicated as possible. Check directly with the airline or a travel agent to make sure you understand how a fare (and any ticket you may buy) works. The travel industry is highly competitive and there are many lurks and perks.

You should get opinions, quotes and advice from as many airlines and travel agents as possible before you pay. The details given in this chapter should be regarded as pointers and are not a substitute for your own careful, up-to-date research.

Getting Around

Joseph Wood Krutch, in his classic *The Forgotten Peninsula*, observed that 'Baja is a splendid example of how much bad roads can do for a country' in preserving it much as it was when Europeans first saw it. In 1973, however, the opening of the 1050-mile (1690-km) Carretera Transpeninsular Benito Juárez (Transpeninsular Highway), also called México 1, eliminated this major obstacle to large-scale tourism. Less than a year later, Baja California Sur (southern Baja California) became a separate, bona fide Mexican state.

Modern Baja has a transpeninsular bus system, six international airports, countless airstrips, taxis and car-rental agencies in major cities and towns, and plenty of donkeys, mules and horses. On or near paved routes, the car is the principal mode of transportation. Off these main roads, travel on gravel roads or corrugated dirt tracks requires caution, but 4WD vehicles are essential only in truly extreme cases. Nevertheless, if you have any doubts, be cautious when heading off the main routes.

AIR

Three major domestic carriers and several smaller ones connect the peninsula's airports at Tijuana, Mexicali, Loreto, La Paz and Los Cabos with the Mexican mainland. In addition, Ensenada, Guerrero Negro, Isla Cedros and Bahía Tortugas have very limited commercial aviation; for information on these destinations, see the appropriate sections. Many towns have air taxi charter services; some resorts, especially in Los Cabos, provide air taxis for their guests.

For the telephone numbers of Aero California, Aeroméxico and Mexicana, which have direct flights to the USA and within Baja California, see the Getting There & Away chapter.

With airfares more volatile than other prices in the travel business, the sample fares in the tables below are approximations based on purchasing a one-way ticket at the airport without a reservation. Most carriers have significantly cheaper fares with advance reservations, even for one-way flights; some routes, such as Tijuana-Guadalajara, also have very inexpensive promotional fares, but available seats may be limited.

From Tijuana

To	Airline	One-Way Fare
Guadalajara	Aero California	US$142
	Aeroméxico	US$150
	Mexicana	US$137
	Taesa	US$184
La Paz	Aero California	US$170
	Aeroméxico	US$156
Los Mochis	Aero California	US$150
	Aeroméxico	US$250
Mexico City	Aero California	US$164
	Aeroméxico	US$164
	Mexicana	US$197
	Taesa	US$200

From La Paz

To	Airline	One-Way Fare
Guadalajara	Aero California	US$104
	Aeroméxico	US$115
Los Mochis	Aero California	US$164
Mazatlán	Aero California	US$80
Mexico City	Aero California	US$181
	Aeroméxico	US$207

Nearly every town and village in Baja California has an airstrip, though most are only large enough for small private aircraft. Private pilots should consult Arnold Senterfitt's self-published *Airports of Baja California* for information about every airstrip and airport on the peninsula; to obtain the book, call or write Baja Bush Pilots (☎ (602) 730-3250), 1255 Baseline, No 138, Mesa, AZ 85202. Another useful resource is Galen Hanselman's *Fly Baja*, available from QEI Publishing, PO Box 1236, Halley, ID 83333.

BUS

Air-conditioned buses operate daily between Tijuana and La Paz for about US$48 one way (22 to 24 hours); they are fairly comfortable but stop in almost every town and city between Tijuana and La Paz to let off and pick up passengers. Since it is impossible to predict how many seats will be available at any given stop, there is no guarantee of a seat at intermediate stops. However, it is rare not to get a seat, except around holidays. See the Tijuana and La Paz Getting There & Away entries for specific departure information. Some *elite* or *especial* services, only slightly more expensive, serve meals and show films.

Buses (some air-conditioned) also run frequently between La Paz and Cabo San Lucas (via San José del Cabo or Todos Santos), Tijuana and Ensenada, Tijuana and Playas de Rosarito, Tijuana and Mexicali (via Tecate), and Ensenada and San Felipe. See the Getting There & Away entries for these cities/towns for schedules, fares and information on other routes.

Tickets can be bought just before departure, but to be assured a seat on long-distance trips, it's a good idea to purchase a ticket in advance. The frequent departures for short trips from Tijuana, Mexicali and Ensenada usually make advance purchase unnecessary.

CAR

Car travel is usually more convenient than bus travel, and it is often the only way to reach isolated towns, villages, mountains and beaches. Many North Americans take RVs, but these gigantic gas guzzlers are dangerous on Baja's narrow paved highways and awkward and almost useless off them.

To drive in Baja California, you need a valid US or Canadian driver's license or an International Driving Permit; see the Visas & Documents entry in the Facts for the Visitor chapter for more information.

Car Permits

A car permit is required for mainland Mexico; for travel in Baja California only,

STOP   ESCUELA   PUENTE   GANADO
       School   ANGOSTO   Cattle
                 Narrow
                 Bridge

CRUCE   YIELD   CURVA   VADO
FFCC   Right   PELIGROSA   Dip
Railroad   of Way   Dangerous
Crossing   Curve

ZONA DE   CAMINO   HOMBRES
DERRUMBES   SINUOSO   TRABAJANDO
Slide Area   Winding Road   Men Working

Mexican road signs

no separate car permit is necessary and no bond or credit-card deposit is required, even for additional vehicles such as a boat/trailer or motorcycle. Regulations covering car permits are subject to change; contact a Mexican consulate or the American Automobile Association (AAA) before going.

Drivers planning to drive to mainland Mexico or to take a ferry from Baja to the mainland will need a permit, and must either post a *fianza* (bond) for approximately half the value of the vehicle or leave a nonrefundable deposit of US$11 on Visa or MasterCard. Mexican Customs authorities instituted this bothersome requirement, transacted at the Banco del Ejército at any border crossing, to prevent the illegal sale of US vehicles in Mexico.

A car permit, which also serves as a tourist card for the driver, can be obtained at the border, in Ensenada or at the ferry terminal in La Paz (Pichilingue). It is preferable to obtain one at the border; if regulations change, it would be a major inconvenience to have to return all the way to the border for a permit. The Tijuana office is on the right-hand side of the border post beyond the crossing, adjacent to the Customs & Immigration office, but the less congested Mesa de Otay office is more expeditious. Permits are valid for 180 days.

You must have a permit for each vehicle that you bring into mainland Mexico. Drivers with a clear title to their car or other vehicle, including boats and motorcycles, will have no difficulty obtaining a vehicle permit, but no individual may enter mainland Mexico with more than one such vehicle, even if the vehicle is in his or her name. However, with the owner's notarized permission, an accompanying passenger may obtain a permit for an additional vehicle. Thus, if you bring a motorcycle as well as a car, a companion will have to obtain a permit for the motorcycle with your authorization.

To obtain a car permit, show proof of citizenship (such as a passport or birth certificate) and the original current registration or notarized bill of sale for each vehicle, including motorcycles and boats. If the vehicle belongs to or is registered to a bank or company (such as a car-rental agency), you will need these documents plus a notarized affidavit of authorization. This affidavit is also required if the vehicle will be driven by someone without the registered owner present. The original current registration is also necessary. Bringing these documents is advisable even for visitors to Baja California, where customs inspections are less stringent.

Drivers leaving a credit-card deposit may exit at any border crossing, but those leaving a bond must exit by the same border crossing that they entered in order to redeem the bond. Do not neglect to check in with Mexican authorities and return your car permit on returning to the USA or your credit card may be charged for the entire value of your car – which is much higher in Mexico than north of the border.

Drivers in mainland Mexico may not leave the country without their vehicle, even if it breaks down, without permission from the Registro Federal de Vehículos in Mexico City or a branch *registro* or *hacienda* (treasury department) in another city or town. This is to reduce vehicle theft and the illegal importation of vehicles for resale in Mexico.

Insurance

Mexican law only recognizes Mexican car insurance – non-Mexican insurance policies are not valid anywhere in the country, though some US policies extend their coverage into northern Mexico. Though not obligatory, insurance is highly recommended because all parties in a car accident are considered guilty until proven innocent. This means that you must prove to the police that you have the means to pay all injuries and damages or wait in jail until the case goes to court. Insurance prevents your detention.

There are many insurance offices at every Baja border crossing, some of them open 24 hours a day. Rates are government-controlled and thus fairly standard on both sides of the border, but policies may also be arranged through representatives in the USA. Most major US insurance companies and automobile clubs (which usually require membership) can arrange coverage. If you're planning to spend more than a few days in Baja, contact representatives offering group coverage, whose rates may be 20% to 30% lower than standard policies' rates. Private clubs, such as Discover Baja, can also arrange insurance coverage.

Below is a list of some US-based companies offering Mexican insurance policies:

Anserv Insurance Services offers home, business and legal services protection in addition to car insurance. 3900 Harney St, Suite 250, San Diego, CA 92110 (☎ (619) 296-4706)

Borderline Insurance Services provides car insurance and tourist information. 2004 Dairy Mart Rd, Suite 103, San Ysidro, CA 92073 (☎ (619) 428-0095, (800) 332-2118)

Instant Mexico Insurance Services is open 24 hours a day for car insurance, tourist information, currency exchange, maps, tourist cards and fishing and boat permits. 223 Via de San Ysidro, San Ysidro, CA 92173 (☎ (619) 428-4714, (800) 345-4701)

A: RICK GERHARTER

B: RICK GERHARTER

A: Abloom in the Desierto Central
B: *Cardón barbón*

C: WAYNE BERNHARDSON

C: Ocotillo, Desierto Central

A: Frigate bird, Gulf of California
B: Tarantula near Santa María Toris, Desierto Central
C: Elephant seals breed on the Islas San Benito in winter
D: Gray whale, Puerto López Mateos

International Gateway Insurance Brokers offers a typical three-day policy for a car worth US$8000 for about US$25; insurance for aircraft, homes, RVs and motorcycles is also available. 3450 Bonita Rd, Suite 103, Chula Vista, CA 92013 (☎ (619) 422-3028, (800) 423-2646 toll free in California)

MacAfee & Edwards Mexican Insurance Specialists offers insurance policies for cars, airplanes and boats. Maps and tourist cards are also available. 260 S Los Robles, Suite 303, Pasadena, CA 91101 (☎ (818) 792-7399, (800) 334-7950, fax (818) 792-7322)

Mexico Services can arrange full boating insurance packages as well as car insurance. 12601 Venice Blvd, Los Angeles, CA 90066 (☎ (310) 398-5797, fax (310) 398-2048)

Mex-Insur arranges car, RV, airplane and boat insurance and also provides information. US Interstate 5 at the Via de San Ysidro exit, San Ysidro, CA 92173 (☎ (619) 428-1121)

Oscar Padilla Mexican Insurance is California's oldest and largest Mexican insurer. 1660 Hotel Circle N, Suite 735, San Diego, CA 92108 (☎ (800) 258-8600)

Another company is Texas-based Sanborn's, which has been in the Mexican insurance business since 1948. Sanborn's has offices at many border crossings, but for Baja-bound travelers, their only mainland alternative (☎ (619) 352-4647, (800) 638-9423) is at 444 S 4th St, El Centro, CA 92243.

Sanborn's represents Seguros Del Centro, a major Mexican insurance company. Rates are competitive with those of other insurance companies and agencies, and claims are promptly processed and settled in the USA.

Unlike most insurance agencies, Sanborn's also provides clients with extremely detailed, mile-by-mile Travelogs, custommade for each traveler's trip. A typical Travelog describes, down to a tenth of a mile, every bump, stoplight and gasoline station, as well as other road-related details. It also offers a listing service for passengers and drivers who want to share a trip through Baja or other parts of Mexico.

Frequent travelers and others planning extensive trips through Mexico might consider joining Sanborn's Mexico Club. Membership includes special annual group insurance rates, a quarterly newsletter, accommodations discounts, health tips and plenty of information about campgrounds and RV parks. If local Sanborn's offices don't have complete information, you can contact Travelog editor 'Mexico Mike' Nelson at Sanborn's main office (☎ (210) 686-0711, sanborns@hiline.net), PO Box 310, McAllen, TX 78502.

For Mexico Club members, a one-year, full-coverage policy on a vehicle valued up to US$25,000 costs about US$650 per year. Shorter periods are available, but are relatively more expensive on a per-day basis; after 30 days, premiums drop considerably.

In general, monthly (or longer-term) policies are much better deals than short-term policies – unless, of course, you plan to visit Baja for only a few days.

Gasoline

The oil industry is still a Mexican government monopoly, and gasoline is officially available only at Petróleos Mexicanos (Pemex) stations throughout the peninsula. In some towns, private individuals sell fuel out of drums, usually at a considerable markup.

Unleaded Magna Sin gasoline is now widely available, but it's still a good idea to carry at least a 5-gallon (23-liter) spare can if you plan to leave the paved roads. Extra fuel is also a good idea because massive caravans of 20 or more RVs can deplete supplies at isolated Transpeninsular stations like the one at Cataviña in the Desierto Central.

Except in the immediate border area, where gasoline prices are lower, Magna Sin costs US$1.36 per gallon (N$2.82 per liter) throughout the peninsula. Leaded Nova, which is not suitable for vehicles with catalytic converters, is cheaper but disappearing rapidly.

Road Conditions

In towns and cities, beware of *alto* (stop) signs, potholes and *topes* (speed bumps). Wide one-way streets in Tijuana, for example, are infamous for stop signs placed on one street corner or the other,

WAYNE BERNHARDSON
Beautiful views and blind curves – Baja roads are a challenge.

but not on both. Consequently, drivers in the far-left lane may not see a stop sign on the right corner until they are already in the intersection. Sometimes stop signs are not posted on corners but painted in bold letters on the street just before the intersection, and drivers looking at the corner can miss the painted letters. Driving slowly and carefully should eliminate the danger of overlooking stop signs.

Speed-bump signs, speed bumps and potholes can also be easy to miss until it's too late, but highway driving has its own set of problems and challenges. The toll portion (México 1D) of the Transpeninsular between Tijuana and Ensenada is the best-maintained highway in Baja – four lanes, wide, smooth and fast, with spectacular coastal views. Baja's other highways offer equally spectacular scenery – multicolored desert landscapes, dark, craggy volcanoes, verdant valleys and vineyards – but the landscape can distract your attention from sharp curves and narrow lanes. Keep your eyes on the road between glances at the landscape, and take all road signs seriously.

If you must leave the road and go onto the shoulder, slow down and ease your car off the pavement; the narrow shoulder is several inches below the pavement and slopes steeply downward.

Driving off the main roads presents special problems. Many unpaved roads are graded and passable even for ordinary passenger vehicles, but sharp stones and other hazards can shred even heavy-duty tires, forcing wise drivers to travel at much slower speeds than on paved roads. In such circumstances, Mexican drivers regularly deflate their tires, to as little as 22 or even 20 lbs per square inch, in order to avoid punctures and smooth out the rough surfaces. This obviously reduces fuel efficiency, but gas is cheaper than a set of new tires.

Anyone planning more than a day trip off paved roads should carry extra food, fuel, water and sleeping bags. Remember that many, if not most, unpaved roads quickly become impassable after rain, and even locals avoid them until they've had a chance to dry out. If you're in doubt, stop the car, get out, check the road and, if not absolutely certain you can continue, turn back.

Help!
Organized to deal with tourists' car problems on the highways, the Mexican government's Angeles Verdes (Green Angels) are teams of bilingual mechanics in bright-green trucks who patrol each stretch of highway in Baja at least twice each day. They can make minor repairs, replace small parts, provide gasoline and oil and arrange towing or other assistance by shortwave and citizen-band radio if it is

needed. Service is free and parts, gasoline and oil are provided at cost. If a telephone is nearby, contact their national 24-hour emergency hot line (☎ 5-250-0123).

Most serious mechanical problems can be fixed efficiently and inexpensively by mechanics in Baja's towns and cities if the parts are available. On the other hand, don't expect miracles if your problems are linked to state-of-the-art computerized systems or other features foreign to Mexican mechanics. Volkswagens (without fuel-injection engines) are the most common cars and thus the easiest to have repaired in Baja.

Because Baja's notoriously bad roads take a heavy toll on tires, *llanteras* (tire repair shops) are ubiquitous, even in many out-of-the-way spots, but they cannot work miracles on a tire that has been shredded by sharp rocks or other hazards, so avoid driving too fast. Ordinary llanteras, especially those in remote areas, may have only a limited selection of spares. Other than major cities like Tijuana, Ensenada, Mexicali and La Paz, the best places to buy tires along the Transpeninsular are Guerrero Negro, Santa Rosalía and Ciudad Constitución.

Off-Highway Driving

Thousands of miles of rough dirt roads and tracks crisscross Baja's backcountry. Many are passable in an ordinary passenger car, but others require a 4WD vehicle with high clearance. You must be well prepared, however, and your vehicle must be in excellent condition; some areas are so isolated that getting stuck can be dangerous. Heat, drought, rain, flash floods and snakes are among the hazards that may bedevil an unprepared driver. Some travelers may prefer to form an informal convoy with other vehicles.

Essentials for excursions off paved highways include water, a first-aid kit, tools, flares, matches and a disposable lighter. For more information, consult the *Baja California Guidebook*, published by the Automobile Club of Southern California, which also publishes a detailed map of Baja

that shows almost every off-road route described in the book. Once available to club members only, the map can be purchased in many Baja stores for about US$4; or at club offices and bookstores in the USA for US$7.95.

Rental

Rental cars are available in Mexicali, Tijuana, Ensenada, La Paz, San José del Cabo and Cabo San Lucas from major agencies like Hertz, Avis, Budget and National. Smaller, independent agencies also operate in these cities.

Daily rates from international rental agencies start around US$45, depending on the agency, when and how long you rent the car, the amount of insurance you want, the number of miles you plan to drive, whether you make your reservation in the USA or in Baja, where you return the car and so on. Note that travelers who wish to rent a car in one location and drop it off in another (for example, to rent in San Diego and drop off in La Paz) will usually pay high drop-off charges, maybe as much as an additional US$20 per day. Since rates and specials change almost daily, call each agency for the latest information:

Avis Rent A Car	☎ (800) 331-2112
Budget Rent A Car	☎ (800) 527-0700
Dollar Rent A Car	☎ (800) 421-6868
Hertz Rent A Car	☎ (800) 654-3131
National Car Rental	☎ (800) 328-4567
Thrifty Car Rental	☎ (800) 367-2277

Local agencies' rates tend to be slightly lower, but, like those of US-based companies, they change frequently. Shop around if you decide to rent a car on arrival.

No agency in Baja allows its cars to be taken to the USA, but some San Diego-based agencies do permit their rental cars to be taken into Mexico. National allows cars as far south as Ensenada, but charges an additional US$16 per day for Mexican insurance. Avis will allow its vehicles to be driven 450 miles (725 km) into Mexico, but drivers must pay US$11 to US$14 per day for supplementary Mexican insurance.

Perhaps the best deal is from Colonial Ford (☎ (619) 477-2711) in National City, California, which rents Ford Escorts for US$162 per week, plus US$11 per day for insurance, and permits its vehicles anywhere in Baja.

Note that Mexican rental contracts usually stipulate a large deductible for collision damage, usually at least US$1000 and/or up to 10% of the vehicle's value.

MOTORCYCLE

Traveling Baja California's paved roads and highways by motorcycle is fast, thrilling and economical, but recommended only for experienced motorcyclists. The challenges of traveling by car in Baja become dangers on a motorcycle. A good helmet and protective clothing are advisable because the graveled, potholed roads can easily cause a spill.

Exercise extreme caution on corners, especially those that are marked *¡Peligro!* (Danger!) – gasoline often sloshes out of Pemex trucks on curves and makes the roads slippery. Livestock on the road can also pose a serious hazard.

Carry extra water and food if traveling alone, because if you have mechanical problems on an isolated stretch of road, you should avoid leaving your bike unattended. An experienced, well-prepared rider can cover the Transpeninsular from Tijuana to La Paz in three days.

Venturing off the paved roads and onto the trails and tracks of the peninsula requires careful preparation and a machine suitable for off-road travel. Many street bikes are not suitable for off-road riding. Parts are scarce, although street mechanics are geniuses at repair and improvisation. For other motorcyclists' perspectives on touring Baja, read Alex Kinglake's 'Biker's Guide to Baja' in the January 1989 issue of *Road Rider* magazine. See the Car entry in this chapter for additional information about driving in Baja.

BICYCLE

Bicycling is an increasingly popular way to tour Baja. In northern Baja, annual summer

races and recreational rides on the paved routes between Tecate and Ensenada, Tijuana and Ensenada and Playas de Rosarito and Ensenada attract more and more people, mostly mainland Californians.

Many others are riding the entire length of the peninsula, occasionally solo, but such a trip requires a tent, sleeping bag, tools, spare tubes and tires, food, several water jugs, a first-aid kit and other supplies. Cyclists should be in top physical shape, have excellent equipment and be prepared to handle their own repairs, even in the middle of nowhere. Small towns and villages often have bicycle mechanics, but they may lack replacement parts for complex repairs.

Racing bicycles are suitable for paved roads like the Transpeninsular, but potholes are numerous and highway shoulders are very steep and narrow; even though most Mexican drivers are courteous to cyclists, there are likely to be anxious moments when that 18-wheeler blows by at 70 mph (112 kph). On the graveled or dirt roads that crisscross much of the peninsula, a mountain bike *(todo terreno)* is a much better choice, but even then thorns are a major hazard to bicycle tires.

Some companies now offer bicycle tours of isolated areas like Península Vizcaíno; see the Organized Tours entry in the Outdoor Activities chapter for details.

HITCHHIKING

Hitchhiking is never entirely safe in any country in the world, and we don't recommend it. Travelers who decide to hitchhike should understand that they are taking a small but serious risk. You may not be able to identify the local rapist/murderer before you get into his vehicle. However, many people do choose to hitchhike, and the advice that follows should help to make their journeys as fast and safe as possible.

For those with no fixed schedule, hitchhiking is possible on Baja's main roads and highways. Displaying your destination on a readable sign is a good idea. The temperature in the desert can plunge at night, and being stranded is no picnic; hitchhikers should anticipate long waits and carry sun protection in addition to warm, windproof clothing. A water bottle and snack food are imperative.

Of course, you should always use your best judgment in deciding whether or not to accept a lift; hitchhiking is definitely not advisable for single women, but anyone can fall into a difficult or unpleasant situation.

WALKING

Anyone contemplating hiking or walking any part of Baja should read Graham Mackintosh's *Into a Desert Place*, the story of his two-year, 3000-mile (5000-km) walk around the coast of Baja California. Mackintosh lived off the sea and desert, eating rattlesnakes, cacti and abalone and drinking distilled seawater. The book is an entertaining read, informative and useful even for much shorter trips.

LOCAL TRANSPORTATION
Bus

Intracity buses exist only in and around Tijuana, Ensenada, San Quintín, Mexicali and La Paz. These buses are cheap (around US$0.40), often dilapidated and not too crowded.

Taxi

Every large town and city in Baja California has taxi service. Most taxis are private, with government-regulated fares, though haggling over fares is still the rule. In Tijuana, Loreto, San José del Cabo and Cabo San Lucas, you will also find bright-yellow, government-run minivans called Aeroterrestre taxis that provide transportation to and from major airports; fares are government-controlled and not subject to bargaining.

In Tijuana and other large cities, route taxis, usually painted in white and another primary color, are only slightly more expensive than local buses and are much faster. Look for the destination painted on the taxi's body.

Donkeys, Mules & Horses

In isolated parts of Baja California, away from paved roads, people still depend on donkeys, mules and horses. But unless you are on an organized backcountry tour, renting a horse at the beach or looking to buy a donkey or mule, you're unlikely to be traveling on these animals. One major exception is the Sierra de San Francisco in the Desierto Central, where the only access is by mule; for details, see the Desierto Central & Llano de Magdalena chapter.

La Frontera

TIJUANA

Fast-growing Tijuana (official population 966,097) suffers from an exaggerated, largely outdated reputation as a tawdry booze-and-sex border town, a gaudy place whose curio stores overflow with kitschy souvenirs like wrought-iron birdcages and ceramic burros. That Tijuana still exists, but the developing cityscape of modernistic office buildings, housing developments and *maquiladoras* marks Baja California's largest border city as a place of increasing sophistication. Certain areas, such as the Zona Río southeast of downtown, may sink under the weight of shopping centers that make them seem like extensions of mainland southern California's mall culture.

Meanwhile, in the 'suburbs,' impoverished immigrants inhabit hillside dwellings of scrapwood and cardboard where retaining walls of worn tires check the soil from washing away during winter storms. These people lack basic services like potable water and trash collection (except for those who actually live at the dump). The city is notorious, of course, for the masses of undocumented immigrants who, at nightfall, intrepidly cross the Río Tijuana and other permeable points along the US border. Most of these desperate, impoverished families and individuals come from regions like the Bajío (in the states of Jalisco, Michoacán, Guanajuato and Querétaro) and the states of Oaxaca, San Luis Potosí, Guerrero and México. The indigenous presence is more conspicuous than ever as Mixtecs from Oaxaca and Mayas from Chiapas and Yucatán line the sidewalks.

Nevertheless, for many inhabitants and immigrants Tijuana is a city of hope, one of Mexico's most prosperous cities, thanks in part to its proximity to southern mainland California's large retail markets and the heavy influx of US tourists (an average of 45,000 people cross the border each day – 16 million annually – and San Diego traffic

reports now include an obligatory mention of rush-hour delays at the border). Local retail activity has also expanded as maquiladora wages circulate in the local retail sector, supporting additional employment. Statistics suggest that nearly 70% of the economic activity derives from 'frontier transactions' (including exports and tourism), about 17% from maquiladoras, 5% from local commerce, 4% from various services, 3% from local industry and 1% from agriculture and fishing.

Tijuana has also become a major educational center, thanks to the growth of institutions like the Universidad Autónoma de Baja California and the Universidad Iberoamericana del Noroeste. The city's cultural importance extends to the arts, an influence deriving in part from official institutions like the Centro Cultural Tijuana, as well as from individuals and groups who lack state sponsorship or encouragement. But at the same time, the city's inability to provide basic infrastructure – demand for Río Colorado water is expected to exceed supply by 2003 if a new aqueduct is not built – threatens to stop its economic and physical growth.

History

In colonial times, the area now known as Tijuana fell under the jurisdiction of Misión San Diego, Alta California, but with the secularization of the missions in 1832, the Kumiai neophytes of Punta Tía Juana became peons. At the end of the Mexican-American War (1848), the newly relocated international border turned the modest *rancho* (rural settlement) of Tijuana into a port of entry overnight, but it remained a backwater even after the government opened a formal customs depot in 1874.

In 1889 the rancho was subdivided and Pueblo Zaragoza (Tijuana's official name until 1929) was created, but the population

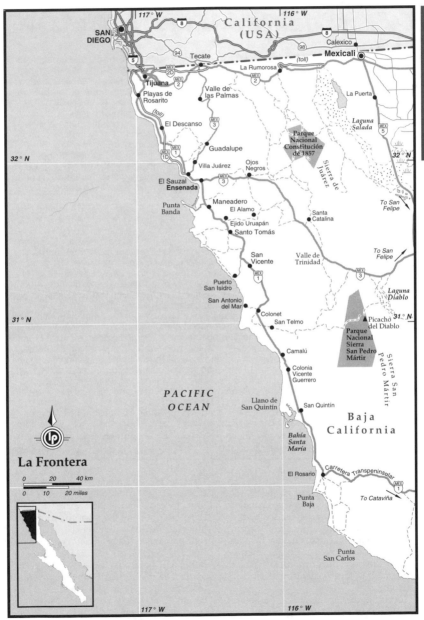

La Frontera

0   20   40 km

0   10   20 miles

La Frontera

La Frontera is that part of the state of Baja California (Norte) that corresponds roughly to the Dominican mission frontier; over two centuries since the establishment of their missions, the main lines of communication still follow El Camino Real, the missionaries' route. It is also the area most heavily frequented by visitors from north of the border. Many if not most visitors view its cities and beaches as enclaves of hedonistic enjoyment, but this superficial image hides a more complex and interesting reality.

Northern Baja undeniably is a playground for mainland Californians. Only a three-hour drive from Los Angeles, it attracts large numbers of US citizens in search of inexpensive vacations south of the border. The Mexican federal government's *fideicomiso*, a 30-year bank trust, eased restrictions on property ownership and promoted the construction of resort complexes and time-share condominiums along the coast. Some US citizens also find Baja's low rents attractive – substantial numbers of them rent Tijuana apartments at a fraction of the cost of comparable housing in San Diego and commute to jobs just across the border.

This approach, however, gives an incomplete picture of the border region's vitality. The conspicuous tourist towns and idyllic beach resorts mask the fact that this is one of Mexico's fastest-growing, most innovative and most prosperous areas, and not only because of US influence. Tijuana and Mexicali are major cities and important manufacturing centers in their own right, while Mexicali's Río Colorado hinterland is, like mainland California's Imperial Valley, a major agricultural producer. Unlike most US cities, whose centers are virtually empty after dark, the border towns enjoy a lively street life in which the tawdry attractions of the *zonas de tolerancia* play only a minimal role. One observer has ironically noted that downtown San Diego, with its strip joints and porn houses, more closely resembles the Tijuana of the past than does the Tijuana of the present.

Many travelers are surprised that Tijuana has a flourishing arts community, officially symbolized by the federal government's Centro Cultural Tijuana, an ambitious project with first-rate facilities that are little visited by foreigners. The Programa Nacional Fronterizo, expressing Mexico City's apprehension that *fronterizos* (inhabitants of the border region) may identify more readily with the nearby USA than with the distant capital, has erected conspicuous monuments to Mexican heroes like Benito Juárez and Miguel Hidalgo to promote nationalism. Richard Rodríguez, a US writer of Mexican ancestry, has remarked that Tijuana's imposing statues 'were set down upon the city like paperweights upon a map. They are reminders from the capital.'

There is also a thriving alternative arts scene here. Rubén Martínez, a Los Angeles-based writer of Mexican and Salvadorean heritage, once wrote that Tijuana's young

---

grew very slowly, to only 242 in 1900 and less than 1000 at the end of WWI. The fledgling city, however, drew upscale tourists from north of the border to facilities like the US-owned Tijuana Hot Springs Hotel and soon became a center for gambling, greyhound racing, boxing matches and cockfights. Other facilities, like bars and bordellos, further 'diversified' the local economy.

Tourist development suffered a setback in 1911, when the forces of anarchist leader Ricardo Flores Magón's Partido Liberal (Liberal Party) tried to use Baja as a territorial foothold during the Mexican Revolution. After holding the town for six weeks, however, the indecisive rebels fled federal reinforcements. Rebel commander Caryl Pryce, a Welshman, was detained for violating US neutrality laws when he fled north. The intellectual Flores Magón, who remained in exile in Los Angeles, where he edited a weekly newspaper, was later tried for espionage in the USA. Convicted

artists are producing work that 'reflects the clashing, the melding, the hybridization of culture that is taking place here, virtually invisible to the Northern eye.'

Commerce is booming as well, due in part to foreign investors (mostly US and Japanese) who underwrite construction of new factories, commercial centers, shopping centers and housing complexes. Baja's duty-free status permits the sale of many imported goods at prices lower than those in the USA and attracts US, European, South Korean and Japanese manufacturers, who have established over 500 *maquiladoras* (twin assembly plants) employing tens of thousands in and around Tijuana. Maquiladoras are equally important to the economies of Mexicali, Tecate and border towns in other Mexican states.

At these plants, raw materials or components for items like TV sets and refrigerators can be imported duty free and then exported back to the USA with duty payable only on the value added to the original materials. Mexico's low labor costs – a fraction of those in the USA – are a major incentive to foreign investors. They are also a matter of controversy: well-paid workers north of the border worry that the North American Free Trade Agreement may drive manufacturing jobs south of the border. It has been noted that the US-Mexico border is the only place where the First World borders the Third.

These new business developments have attracted many immigrants, primarily from Mexico City and the states of Jalisco, Michoacán, Sinaloa and Sonora. For some, the border region is a way station en route to the USA; the US Immigration & Naturalization Service claims that 5000 undocumented people cross the international border every week, with or without the help of *coyotes* or *polleros*. These smugglers' clients are a mix of migrants who traditionally worked part of the year in the US but who now have been barred by restrictive US immigration laws, and novices who have no idea what to expect across the frontier. With the end of the Central American wars of the 1980s and early 1990s, political refugees are now relatively few.

Despite increased surveillance, at least 300 people continue to jump the fence daily and polleros now charge up to US$800 to spirit them from Tijuana to Los Angeles. Documented and undocumented immigrants and even US citizens of Mexican heritage have found themselves targets of opportunistic attacks by mainland California politicians like Governor Pete Wilson and US Senators Barbara Boxer and Dianne Feinstein, and by Proposition 187, an anti-immigrant measure approved by California voters in 1994. Feinstein even proposed a US$1 'admission' charge on legal border-crossers to finance increased police and paramilitary surveillance here. One newspaper columnist ironically observed that 'she forgot to mention the two-drink minimum.' ■

on flimsy evidence, he died years later in prison in Leavenworth, Kansas.

After 1915, despite restrictive US wartime measures, Tijuana's tourist industry recovered; during Prohibition, it positively flourished as thirsty US residents flocked to Tijuana for alcohol, gambling and sex – and displaced US businesses flocked there to offer these services. During these years, the municipal administration paved streets, improved the water system, built schools and attracted industries like breweries, distilleries and even an aircraft factory (headed by the former Mexican President Abelardo Rodríguez, for whom Tijuana's international airport was named). Foreign businesses, though, were slow to employ Mexican workers in responsible posts.

After Prohibition, President Lázaro Cárdenas outlawed casinos and prostitution – Tijuana's main casino became a high school, the Instituto Tecnológico Industrial Agua Caliente – but the Great Depression of the 1930s probably had a greater impact

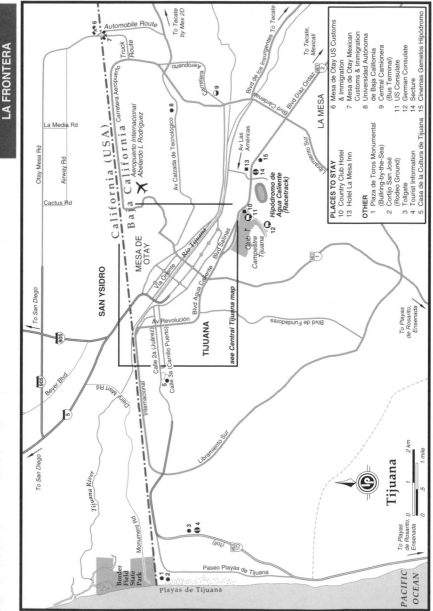

PLACES TO STAY
10 Country Club Hotel
13 Hotel La Mesa Inn

OTHER
1 Plaza de Toros Monumental
   (Bullring-by-the-Sea)
2 Cortijo San José
   (Rodeo Ground)
3 Tollgate
4 Tourist Information
5 Casa de la Cultura de Tijuana
6 Mesa de Otay US Customs
   & Immigration
7 Mesa de Otay Mexican
   Customs & Immigration
8 Universidad Autónoma
   de Baja California
9 Central Camionera
   (Bus Terminal)
11 US Consulate
12 German Consulate
14 Secture
15 Cinemas Gemelos Hipódromo

than executive intervention. As bankrupt US-owned businesses reverted to Mexican control and northern Baja became a customs-free zone, jobless Mexican returnees from the USA remained in Tijuana rather than going back to their hometowns, doubling the city's population (to about 16,500) by 1940. The presently notorious borderside Colonia Libertad dates from this period.

During WWII, with the US Army absorbing nearly all able-bodied American men, the US and Mexican governments established the *bracero* program, allowing Mexican workers north of the border to alleviate serious labor shortages. This program, lasting until 1964, led to major growth in border-area commerce, and by 1960 Tijuana's population had grown tenfold to over 180,000.

In each succeeding decade, the city's population has probably doubled, although truly reliable statistics are hard to find; in all likelihood, it substantially exceeds the official figure of just under one million. Uncontrolled growth has brought serious social and environmental problems, as the municipal administration has failed to provide adequate housing, potable water and public health services for many parts of the city; contamination of the Río Tijuana, which enters the USA west of the San Ysidro border crossing, is one of several major binational environmental issues.

Tijuana has never completely overcome its image as a paradise for sinners. During and immediately after WWII, the city experienced probably its seamiest era as the infamous Avenida Revolución attracted US servicemen from nearby San Diego. In recent years the city has cleaned up its act considerably, though the Zona Norte at the northern end of Avenida Revolución retains some of the style (and substance) of the postwar era.

Most of 'La Revo,' though, now appeals to a younger crowd of US university students and their cohorts, who take advantage of Mexico's permissive drinking laws (18-year-olds may purchase alcohol and frequent bars) to party until dawn. At the same time, families feel more comfortable in the city's streets and stores than they did in sleazier times.

Orientation

Tijuana parallels the US border for about 12 miles (19 km). Flowing northwest across the border before emptying into the Pacific Ocean, the Río Tijuana divides the older part of the city to the south and southwest from the newer Mesa de Otay sector on a broad hilltop to the northeast. Mesa de Otay contains the international airport, most of the city's maquiladoras, newer residential neighborhoods and major shopping areas.

Central Tijuana features a regular grid pattern of north-south *avenidas* (avenues) and east-west *calles* (streets), but it often lacks street signs; most streets have numbers that are more frequently used than their names. The city's intended center was Plaza Zaragoza, now Parque Vicente Guerrero, but Avenida Revolución (formerly called Avenida Olvera), five blocks to the east, soon became the city's commercial heart.

A new numbering system for street addresses has created some confusion. Because some businesses still rely on the old system, this entry generally uses the new system but also locates sites like hotels and restaurants by their cross streets when there is any ambiguity. Another source of confusion is that some streets have more than one name, such as Paseo de Tijuana, also known as Avenida del Centenario.

The San Ysidro-Tijuana border crossing is north of the river, about a 10-minute walk from downtown. Taxis are numerous, but any bus with a 'Central Camionera' placard goes downtown and costs about US$0.30. To reach the commercial center by foot, continue through the Plaza Viva Tijuana shopping mall to the pedestrian bridge over the river, cross the street and proceed to Calle 1a (also called Comercio or, west of Avenida Revolución, Artículo 123). Most of Tijuana's seedier bars and clubs are in the area north of Calle 2a (Juárez) and west of Avenida Revolución.

South of Calle 1a, Avenida Revolución is the city's tourist center, where many visitors crowd its numerous bars and purchase cheap liquor, imported goods and Mexican handicrafts. Its major landmark is the Frontón Palacio Jai Alai (Jai Alai Palace), but the surrounding area also contains many bungalows moved intact from San Diego and other north-of-the-border communities during the construction of US Interstate 5. Unlike most US cities, in Tijuana, commercial, industrial and residential uses exist side by side.

Directly east of the Frontón, the Zona Río, Tijuana's new commercial center, straddles the Río Tijuana. Paseo de los Héroes, Paseo de Tijuana and Via Oriente, the principal streets in this part of town, all parallel the river. Major public buildings, like the Palacio Municipal (City Hall), have relocated here.

West of the Frontón, between downtown and the ocean, lie both spiffy suburbs and hillside shantytowns that are known as *asentamientos irregulares* (literally, irregular settlements). Formally, all Tijuana boroughs or neighborhoods are known as *colonias* (sometimes as *fraccionamientos*), and addresses are much easier to locate if one knows the name of the colonia.

None of Tijuana's tourist offices has a satisfactory city map; the best available are the Guías Urbanas *Tijuana* map, published by Mexicali's Ediciones Corona; the Guía Roji *Ciudad de Tijuana* map; and the commercial Guía T *Tijuana y Playas de Rosarito* street atlas. All of these have shortcomings, but they're good enough for anyone but a cartographic perfectionist.

Information

Visitors to Tijuana will find Bob McPhail's pocket-sized *The Tijuana Handbook & Souvenir Guide* (CF Publishing, Imperial Beach, CA, 1996) a handy guide to the city's tourist and shopping areas, though it's not really suitable for anything out of the ordinary. It's widely available in San Diego and at the Mexicoach bus terminal in Tijuana for about US$3.

Border Crossings One of the world's busiest border crossings, the San Ysidro-Tijuana port of entry is open 24 hours a day. Northbound, two emergency gates (the second gate on the far left and Gate No 1) allow immediate entry to the USA for US and Mexican citizens needing urgent medical attention. From 6 am to 8 pm weekdays, there are carpool lanes for vehicles with at least four passengers.

The alternative crossing at Mesa de Otay, east of downtown near the airport, has relieved some of the pressure by absorbing about 20% of the cross-border traffic in the Tijuana-San Diego area; it's open 6 am to 10 pm. Drivers wishing to avoid the perpetual backup at San Ysidro usually find the Otay crossing quicker, but the time it takes to drive to Otay and return to US Interstate 5 after crossing the border can be a drawback.

Arrange vehicle insurance either before crossing the border or at the border (Otay is much quicker than San Ysidro). See the Insurance entry in the Getting Around chapter for details. For general information about customs and immigration, see the Visas & Documents entry in the Facts for the Visitor chapter; for information about car permits, see the Getting Around chapter.

Tourist Offices Tijuana has several tourist offices downtown, in the Zona Río and in the newer suburbs to the southeast.

The Secretaría de Turismo del Estado de Baja California (Secture, ☎ (66) 81-94-92, fax (66) 81-95-79) is on the 3rd floor of the Edificio Plaza Patria at the corner of Blvd Díaz Ordaz and Avenida Las Américas. The English-speaking staff answer queries relating to northern Baja and have a mediocre tourist map of the state and several important cities and towns. The central office hours are 8 am to 3 pm and 5 to 7 pm weekdays; if you have any legal problem, contact Auxilio Turístico (☎ (66) 81-94-92) in the same offices. Hours are 8 am to 7 pm, but it can be reached 24 hours a day.

For most visitors, the Secture office (☎ (66) 88-05-55) in Plaza Santa Cecilia, alongside Hotel Nelson at the corner of Avenida Revolución and Calle 1a (Artículo 123), will be much more convenient than the Plaza Patria office. It's open 9 am to 7 pm daily and has friendly, capable, English-speaking staff.

The private Cámara Nacional de Comercio, Servicios y Turismo de Tijuana (Canaco, the Tijuana Chamber of Commerce, ☎ (66) 85-84-72, (66) 88-16-85), at the corner of Avenida Revolución and Calle 1a (Comercio) diagonally across from Plaza Santa Cecilia, is open 9 am to 7 pm daily. It has helpful, gregarious, English-speaking staff and a wide selection of printed matter on Baja California and, to some degree, the rest of Mexico.

There is an office of Tijuana's Comité de Turismo y Convenciones (Cotuco, the Committee on Tourism & Conventions, ☎ (66) 84-05-37, fax (66) 84-77-82) at the corner of Paseo de los Héroes and Francisco J Mina in the Zona Río. It also operates a kiosk, open sporadically, on Avenida Revolución between Calle 3a (Carrillo Puerto) and Calle 4a (Díaz Mirón).

Foreign Consulates Befitting its growing commercial importance, Tijuana is home to numerous foreign consulates, no longer just those of its North American Free Trade Agreement (NAFTA) partners but also those of several European countries:

Canada
    German Gedovius 10411, Local 101, Zona Río (☎ (66) 84-04-61, fax (66) 84-03-01)
France
    Avenida Revolución 1651, 3rd Floor (☎ (66) 85-71-72, fax (66) 85-77-35)
Germany
    Avenida Mérida 221, Colonia Hipódromo (☎ (66) 80-25-15, fax (66) 80-18-30)
UK
    Blvd Gustavo Salinas 1500, Colonia Aviación, La Mesa (☎ (66) 86-53-20, fax (66) 81-84-02)
USA
    Tapachula 96, Colonia Hipódromo (☎ (66) 81-74-00)

Money Tijuana's countless *cambios* (currency exchange houses) keep long hours, but almost everyone accepts US dollars, except for bus drivers. Banks, though slower and more bureaucratic, offer slightly better rates; ATMs are numerous. Beware of cambios on the US side, some of which advertise 'no commission' on exchanges of pesos for US dollars but charge up to 8% for converting US-dollar traveler's checks into pesos. Change money on the Mexican side instead.

Travelers heading south into Baja California or east into mainland Mexico will find a convenient cambio at the Central Camionera, Tijuana's long-distance bus terminal.

Post & Communications Tijuana's main post office is at the corner of Avenida Negrete and Calle 11a (Calles). Hours are 8 am to 4 pm weekdays. Because of the city's size, there are many postal codes.

Tijuana has many Ladatel public telephones and long-distance offices both downtown and in the outskirts. The Central Camionera has several booths with an operator in attendance and a public fax machine as well.

Travel Agencies One of Tijuana's oldest travel agencies, Viajes Honold's (☎ (66) 88-11-11, fax (66) 88-15-02), is at Avenida Revolución 828 at the corner of Calle 2a (Juárez). There are many others both downtown and in the Zona Río.

Bookstores Sanborn's (☎ (66) 88-14-62), at the corner of Avenida Revolución and Calle 8a (Hidalgo), is a Mexican institution known for its food and sundries, but it also has a good book department with a large selection of US and Mexican newspapers and magazines.

Librería El Día (☎ (66) 84-09-08), Blvd Sánchez Taboada 10050 in the Zona Río, has a good choice of books on Mexican history and culture, including a section on Baja California, and a handful of books in English. Librolandia (☎ (66) 85-36-58), on

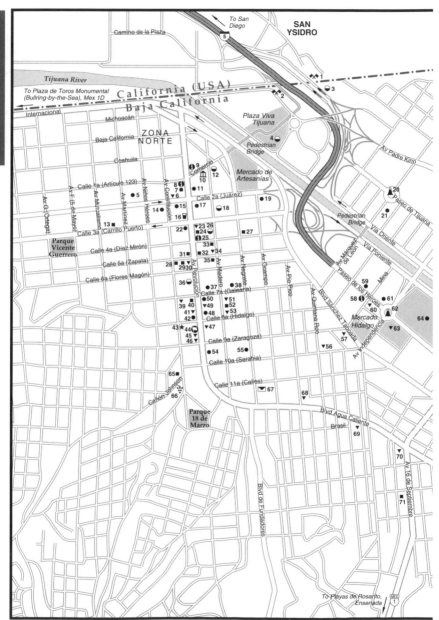

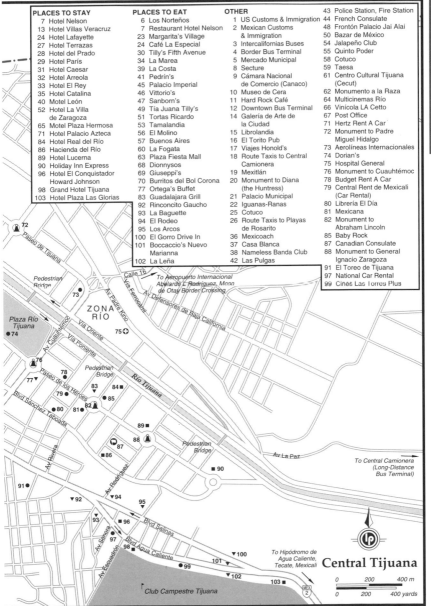

LA FRONTERA

PLACES TO STAY
7 Hotel Nelson
13 Hotel Villas Veracruz
24 Hotel Lafayette
27 Hotel Terrazas
28 Hotel del Prado
29 Hotel París
31 Hotel Caesar
32 Hotel Arreola
33 Hotel El Rey
35 Hotel Catalina
40 Motel León
52 Hotel La Villa
de Zaragoza
65 Motel Plaza Hermosa
71 Hotel Palacio Azteca
84 Hotel Real del Río
86 Hacienda del Río
89 Hotel Lucerna
90 Holiday Inn Express
96 Hotel El Conquistador
Howard Johnson
98 Grand Hotel Tijuana
103 Hotel Plaza Las Glorias

PLACES TO EAT
6 Los Norteños
7 Restaurant Hotel Nelson
23 Margarita's Village
24 Café La Especial
30 Tilly's Fifth Avenue
34 La Marea
39 La Costa
41 Pedrín's
45 Palacio Imperial
46 Vittorio's
47 Sanborn's
49 Tía Juana Tilly's
51 Tortas Ricardo
53 Tamalandia
56 El Molino
57 Buenos Aires
60 La Fogata
63 Plaza Fiesta Mall
68 Dionnysos
69 Giuseppi's
70 Burritos del Bol Corona
77 Ortega's Buffet
83 Guadalajara Grill
92 Rinconcito Gaucho
93 La Baguette
94 El Rodeo
95 Los Arcos
100 El Gorro Drive In
101 Boccaccio's Nuevo
Marianna
102 La Leña

OTHER
1 US Customs & Immigration
2 Mexican Customs
& Immigration
3 Intercalifornias Buses
4 Border Bus Terminal
5 Mercado Municipal
8 Secure
9 Cámara Nacional
de Comercio (Canaco)
10 Museo de Cera
11 Hard Rock Café
12 Downtown Bus Terminal
14 Galería de Arte de
la Ciudad
15 Librolandia
16 El Torito Pub
17 Viajes Honold's
18 Route Taxis to Central
Camionera
19 Mexitlán
20 Monument to Diana
(the Huntress)
21 Palacio Municipal
22 Iguanas-Ranas
25 Cotuco
26 Route Taxis to Playas
de Rosarito
36 Mexicoach
37 Casa Blanca
38 Nameless Banda Club
42 Las Pulgas

43 Police Station, Fire Station
44 French Consulate
48 Frontón Palacio Jai Alai
50 Bazar de México
54 Jalapeño Club
55 Quinto Poder
58 Cotuco
59 Taesa
61 Centro Cultural Tijuana
(Cecut)
62 Monumento a la Raza
64 Multicinemas Río
66 Vinícola LA Cetto
67 Post Office
71 Hertz Rent A Car
72 Monument to Padre
Miguel Hidalgo
73 Aerolíneas Internacionales
74 Dorian's
75 Hospital General
76 Monument to Cuauhtémoc
78 Budget Rent A Car
79 Central Rent de Mexicali
(Car Rental)
80 Librería El Día
81 Mexicana
82 Monument to
Abraham Lincoln
85 Baby Rock
87 Canadian Consulate
88 Monument to General
Ignacio Zaragoza
91 El Toreo de Tijuana
97 National Car Rental
99 Cines Las Torres Plus

Central Tijuana

0   200   400 m
0   200   400 yards

Club Campestre Tijuana

To Hipódromo de
Agua Caliente,
Tecate, Mexicali

To Central Camionera
(Long-Distance
Bus Terminal)

Plaza Río
Tijuana

ZONA
RÍO

To Aeropuerto Internacional
Abelardo L Rodríguez, Mesa
de Otay Border Crossing

Calle 2a (Juárez) between Avenida Revolución and Avenida Constitución, is also worth a visit.

Cultural Centers An imposing neoclassical brick building (formerly the Escuela Alvaro Obregón, dating from 1929) houses the Casa de la Cultura de Tijuana (☎ (66) 87-26-04) on pleasant grounds at Calle Lisboa 5, Colonia Altamira. It presents lectures, art exhibitions and film festivals; its small Café Literario is open 1 to 8 pm weekdays. Take any blue-and-white taxi (marked 'Colonia Altamira') westbound from Calle 3a (Carrillo Puerto) or walk up Calle 4a (Díaz Mirón); instead of the busy street, try the hillside staircase, which offers fine views of the city.

The Instituto de Cultura de Baja California (☎ (66) 83-59-22) holds film festivals and cultural events at its Sala de Usos Múltiples, Paseo de Tijuana 10150 alongside the Palacio Municipal in the Zona Río.

Tijuana's most important cultural center is the Centro Cultural Tijuana (Cecut); see the separate entry in this chapter.

Medical Services The Cruz Roja (Red Cross) (☎ 132) has moved to the Via Oriente in the Zona Río. Tijuana's Hospital General (☎ (66) 84-09-22) is north of the river, on Avenida Padre Kino west of the junction with Avenida Rodríguez, but Tijuana has many other medical facilities catering to visitors from north of the border.

Emergency The central police station (☎ 134) is at Avenida Constitución 1616 at Calle 8a (Hidalgo); the fire station (☎ 136) is next door.

Dangers & Annoyances *Coyotes* and *polleros* (smugglers) and their client *pollos* (undocumented border-crossers) congregate in the Zona Norte and along the Río Tijuana west of the San Ysidro border crossing, especially around twilight. After dark this area can be unsafe and is better avoided. The same is true of Colonia Libertad, east of the San Ysidro border crossing.

Drivers at stoplights may find that street children wash their windshields first and ask questions later. If you don't need a wash, a wagging finger can be an effective deterrent.

La Revo
Virtually every visitor to Tijuana has to experience at least a brief stroll up raucous Avenida Revolución, popularly known as 'La Revo,' between Calle 1a (Artículo 123) and Calle 8a (Hidalgo) – a mishmash of futuristic nightclubs, bellowing hawkers outside seedy strip bars, brash taxi drivers, tacky souvenir stores, street photographers with zebra-striped burros, discount liquor stores and first-rate restaurants. If you need to walk from north to south but find the sensory assault from clashing high-tech sound systems too overwhelming, try the more conventional shopping street of Avenida Constitución, paralleling La Revo one block west.

Frontón Palacio Jai Alai
Oddly Baroque in style, begun in 1926 but not completed until 1947, this striking Tijuana landmark fronts most of an entire block on Avenida Revolución between Calle 7a (Galeana) and Calle 8a (Hidalgo); a connecting door leads to LF Caliente Sports Book, with multiple giant TV screens for watching team sports, horse racing, boxing and other athletic events, mostly played north of the border.

Jai alai matches start at 1 pm Monday and Tuesday, 8 pm Thursday through Sunday; doors open about an hour earlier, and players start warming up around 7:30 pm. The Frontón (☎ (66) 85-25-24) is closed Wednesdays. General admission is US$2.

Zona Norte
West of Avenida Revolución and north of Calle 1a (Artículo 123), this area preserves the unsanitized atmosphere of Tijuana's tawdriest times. Municipal and tourist officials prefer not to dwell on its continued existence, but the area is still of sufficient economic importance that authorities cannot, or will not, eradicate it.

Boasting a lunch counter appropriately known as Aquí Te Espero (I'll Wait for You Here), the Zona Norte is also an infamous haven for coyotes and undocumented border-crossers, and it's not a recommended destination for foreigners lacking street savvy, at least after dark. Most hotels and motels in the area are very cheap and equally disreputable.

Galería de Arte de la Ciudad

With exhibits and events involving the art community from both sides of the border, the municipal art gallery occupies the former Palacio Municipal (City Hall, from 1921 to 1986). At the building's entrance are two modest but interesting murals; the tranquil courtyard also contains a library and a worthwhile bookstore.

The gallery (☎ (66) 85-01-04), at the corner of Avenida Constitución and Calle 2a (Juárez), only a block from the rowdiness of La Revo, is open 9 am to 7 pm weekdays. Admission is free.

Museo de Cera

Strategically placed at the corner of Avenida Madero and Calle 1a (Comercio) to attract foot traffic en route from the border to La Revo, Tijuana's wax museum is a monument to kitsch. Its bizarre combination of figures ranges from Aztec emperor Cuauhtémoc to Emiliano Zapata, Marilyn Monroe, the famed Mexican comedian and film star Cantínflas, Michael Jackson and Bill Clinton. The museum (☎ (66) 88-24-78) is open 10 am to 6 pm daily. Admission costs US$1 but is free for children six years of age or younger.

Mexitlán

It's tempting to suggest that this self-consciously nationalistic tourist attraction, featuring dioramas of many of Mexico's most significant archaeological monuments and distinguished public buildings (plus more than a handful of less distinguished ones), could draw bigger crowds by laying down some Astroturf, drilling a few holes, buying a few putters and reopening as a miniature golf course. It has an upstairs restaurant, but nearly all the street-level stores are vacant, and the impression is one of a clever but costly white elephant. Still, it's a far more appealing spot than the wax museum, especially for visitors interested in Mexico's varied architecture.

Mexitlán (☎ (66) 38-41-01), on top of a parking garage at the corner of Avenida Ocampo and Calle 2a (Juárez), is open 9 am to 5 pm daily except Monday. Admission is US$1.25 for adults; children under 12, who get in free, seem irresistibly tempted to play with (and potentially destroy) everything within their reach, which means nearly all the exhibits.

Vinícola LA Cetto

Still run by descendants of Italian immigrants who arrived in Baja California in 1926, the LA Cetto winery has opened its Tijuana facilities, near the southern end of Avenida Constitución, to tours and tastings. With vineyards in the Valle de Guadalupe between Tecate and Ensenada, Cetto produces a variety of tasty red and white varietals, as well as sparkling wines, at reasonable prices.

Tours take place on demand between 10 am and 5:30 pm Tuesday through Sunday for US$1 without tasting or US$2 with a sampling of four wines. There is no minimum group size; arrange for large groups in advance, however. There is also a boutique with Cetto wines and souvenirs for sale, but remember that pedestrians and drivers may take only one liter of wine across the border into mainland California.

Vinícola LA Cetto (☎ (66) 85-30-31, fax (66) 85-35-52) is at Cañón Johnson 8151, a diagonal in Colonia Hidalgo just southwest of Avenida Constitución; its US mailing address is PO Box 434260, San Ysidro, CA 92143.

Mercado Hidalgo

Bordering Avenida Independencia and Blvd Sánchez Taboada, sprawling Mercado Hidalgo is the city's major market for fruit, vegetables and, to a lesser degree, souvenirs and the like. It also has a handful of decent but inexpensive restaurants and juice bars.

Centro Cultural Tijuana

Mexico's federal government built Tijuana's modern cultural center to reinforce the Mexican identity of its border population with exhibits chronicling mainland Mexican history. Despite this transparently ulterior motive, it has provided the city a cultural resource that would be the pride of any comparably sized city in the world.

Often known by its acronym, Cecut, the center houses the **Museo de las Identidades Mexicanas** (Museum of Mexican Identities), an **art gallery** with rotating exhibitions and a 1000-seat **theater** with frequent major performances, as well as the globular **Cine Planetario**, an Omnimax cinema with all the architectural charm of the Three Mile Island nuclear power plant (it is colloquially known as 'La Bola' – The Ball). The Cine Planetario presents three short films on a 180° screen. *El Pueblo del Sol*, a cinematic tour of Mexico in English, is shown at 2 pm Friday, Saturday and Sunday. The other two films, in Spanish, change periodically. Admission is US$4.50.

The museum offers rotating exhibitions on a variety of themes in regional and national history. The building's basement level contains a photographic gallery of writers and artists who have given presentations here, plus an impressive display of posters of past events. The center also contains a bookstore with a good general selection of works in Spanish on Mexico and Baja California in particular, plus a few coffee-table photo books. Admission to the Museo de las Identidades Mexicanas is US$1, while the art gallery is free of charge.

The center (☎ (66) 84-11-11), at the corner of Paseo de los Héroes and Avenida Independencia in the Zona Río, is open 11 am to 8 pm weekdays and 11 am to 9 pm weekends. From the city center, catch any gold-and-white route taxi on Avenida Constitución at Calle 3a (Carrillo Puerto). From the border bus lot, catch a 'Baja P' bus.

City Monuments

Like other Mexican border cities, Tijuana has a number of *glorietas* (traffic circles) graced by monuments that, in some instances, are reminders from the federal government that the city is indeed part of Mexico. Set mostly among the broad avenues of the Zona Río, these massive statues include the Aztec emperor **Cuauhtémoc** at Avenida Cuauhtémoc and Paseo de los Héroes, Mexican independence martyr **Padre Miguel Hidalgo** at Avenida Independencia and Paseo de Tijuana and an equestrian statue of **General Ignacio Zaragoza** (defender of the city of Puebla from the French invasion of 1862) at Paseo de los Héroes and Avenida Abelardo Rodríguez. The **Monumento a la Raza**, at Paseo de los Héroes and Avenida Independencia, exalts Mexican nationalism.

Other monuments are less clearly nationalistic and even seem misplaced. The monument to **Abraham Lincoln**, at Paseo de los Héroes and Avenida Diego Rivera, honors the US President who emancipated his country's African-American slaves, while **Diana**, at the junction of Avenida Márquez de León and Paseo de Tijuana, honors the huntress of Greek mythology.

Playas de Tijuana

Popular with locals, Tijuana's beaches tend to get crowded, especially during summer bullfights (the Plaza de Toros Monumental

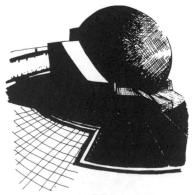
La Bola

is located here). A blue-and-white bus marked 'Playas' runs along Calle 3a (Carrillo Puerto) and goes westward to the beaches.

Organized Tours

San Diego Minitours (☎ (619) 477-8687) offers organized day tours of Tijuana. Tours depart San Diego at 9 and 10 am, noon and 2 pm, returning at 2, 4, 5 and 6 pm. The cost is US$26 for adults, US$14 for children.

For a truly exhaustive (and potentially exhausting) view of the city's history, try to hook up with one of the Centro Cultural's infrequent, six-hour weekend tours of La Antigua Tijuana (Old Tijuana), which are free of charge. For more information and reservations, call ☎ (66) 34-35-80 or (66) 84-11-11, ext 228.

Special Events

Lasting two weeks in early September, the **Feria Viva Tijuana** features a food fair and big-name Mexican entertainment. The climax is September 16, Mexico's independence day.

Places to Stay

Tijuana has a wealth of accommodations in all categories, from the really seedy to the truly luxurious. Tourist authorities try to steer visitors away from less expensive but sometimes very acceptable alternatives.

Places to Stay – budget

Most of Tijuana's cheapest accommodations are in or near the Zona Norte, which is not really an advisable place to stay – partly for safety reasons but also because it can be so deafeningly noisy that it's impossible to sleep.

Probably the cheapest acceptable place is *Hotel del Prado* (☎ (66) 88-23-29), Calle 5a (Zapata) No 8163 between Avenida Revolución and Avenida Constitución, which is clean and comfortable despite graffiti on some interior walls. Rates average about US$10 single or double. One-star *Hotel Catalina* (☎ (66) 85-97-48), Calle 5a (Zapata) at the corner of Avenida

Madero, offers singles/doubles starting around US$12/16; those with TV cost US$20/22. Its US mailing address is PO Box 3544, San Ysidro, CA 92073.

The older *Hotel El Rey* (☎ (66) 85-14-36), Calle 4a (Díaz Mirón) No 8235 between Avenidas Revolución and Madero, has sagging mattresses in rooms that are otherwise acceptable. Singles/doubles cost US$13/16. Perhaps downtown's best budget hotel is *Hotel Lafayette* (☎ (66) 85-39-40), Avenida Revolución 926 above Café La Especial, but it's often full, especially on weekends. Rates are US$16/22 single/double.

Hotel Arreola (☎ (66) 85-90-81), very centrally located at Avenida Revolución 1080 at the corner of Calle 5a (Zapata), has carpeted rooms with B&W television and telephone for US$20/26 single/double. For visitors with vehicles, perhaps a better bargain is *Motel Plaza Hermosa* (☎ (66) 85-33-53), Avenida Constitución 1821 at the corner of Calle 10a (Sarabia). Singles/doubles cost US$20/26 weekdays, US$25/30 weekends, with secure parking.

Much more quiet than its busy location would suggest, friendly *Hotel Villas Veracruz* (☎ (66) 85-90-30), Calle 3a (Carrillo Puerto) No 7856 between Avenida Martínez and Avenida Mutualismo, charges about US$24 single or double for rooms with telephone and color TV, set around an attractive patio.

Hotel Nelson (☎ (66) 85-43-03, fax (66) 85-43-04), Avenida Revolución 721, has long been a travelers' favorite because of its central location and its 92 clean, basic and carpeted rooms, plus its bar and inexpensive coffee shop. Windowless interior singles/doubles with telephone and spotless toilets cost US$19/22 but may be tough on claustrophobics; rooms with a view, a color TV and the less than soothing sounds of La Revo cost US$28/32.

Very friendly *Hotel París* (☎ (66) 85-30-23), Calle 5a (Zapata) No 8181 between Avenidas Revolución and Constitución, has singles/doubles with telephone, color TV and air-conditioning for US$27. *Hotel Caesar* (☎ (66) 85-16-06, fax (66) 85-34-92),

Avenida Revolución 1079 at the corner of Calle 5a (Zapata), exhibits personality, its rooms painted in varied shades of green and hallways lined with posters and photographs of matadors and bullfights; its restaurant created the Caesar salad (whose recipe appears on its business card). Singles/doubles cost US$28/38.

Places to Stay – middle

At *Hotel La Villa de Zaragoza* (☎ (66) 85-18-32, fax (66) 85-18-37), a brown stucco motel at Avenida Madero 1120 directly behind the Frontón Palacio Jai Alai, all rooms include TV, telephone, heat and air-conditioning. Singles/doubles start around US$30/36 plus IVA (value-added tax) at what is probably the best hotel in the immediate downtown area; rooms for nonsmokers and handicapped people are available.

Hotel Terrazas (☎ (66) 88-27-11), Calle 4a (Díaz Mirón) No 8432 between Avenidas Negrete and Ocampo, has rooms with color TV, air-conditioning and room service for US$33/50 single/double. Similarly priced *Motel León* (☎ (66) 85-63-20, fax (66) 85-40-16), Calle 7a (Galeana) No 8151 between Avenidas Revolución and Constitución, is a convenient central motel with telephone, restaurant room service and parking. The inviting *Hotel Palacio Azteca* (☎ (66) 81-81-00, fax (66) 81-81-60), Avenida 16 de Septiembre 213 near the toll-free road to Playas de Rosarito and Ensenada, is a good value for US$35/39 single/double.

At the *Country Club Hotel* (☎ (66) 81-77-33, fax (66) 81-76-92; (800) 303-2684 in the USA), Tapachula 1 across from the Hipódromo de Agua Caliente, most suites and other rooms overlook the golf course and the city. All have full carpeting, aircon, cable TV, telephone and private bath for US$49. Amenities include a swimming pool and a coffee shop/restaurant serving typical Mexican breakfasts.

The 120-room *Hotel La Mesa Inn* (☎ (66) 81-65-22, fax (66) 81-28-71; (800) 303-2684 in the USA) is at Blvd Díaz Ordaz 50, a continuation of Blvd Agua Caliente. Singles/doubles cost US$41/50 plus IVA; all have carpets, satellite TV, telephone and air-conditioning. Facilities include a coffee shop, a Chinese restaurant, a pizza parlor, two bars and a swimming pool. Rooms in the newer section are larger. Its US mailing address is 1181 Broadway, Suite 2, Chula Vista, CA 91911.

The *Hacienda del Río* (☎ (66) 84-86-44, fax (66) 84-86-20; (800) 303-2684 in the USA), Blvd Sánchez Taboada 10606 in the Zona Río, charges US$48/52 plus IVA for singles/doubles; amenities include a restaurant and swimming pool.

Places to Stay – top end

Modern and efficient *Hotel Real del Río* (☎ (66) 34-31-00, fax (66) 34-30-53), José María Velasco 1409 in the Zona Río, charges US$51/56 single/double. The 200-room, high-rise *Hotel Plaza Las Glorias* (☎ (66) 22-66-00, fax (66) 22-66-02), at Blvd Agua Caliente 11553, caters primarily to business clients, with singles/doubles starting at US$56 plus IVA. All rooms have color TV, air-con and telephone. Its US postal address is PO Box 43-1588, San Ysidro, CA 92173.

Hotel El Conquistador Howard Johnson (☎ (66) 81-79-55, (66) 86-22-51, fax (66) 86-13-40; (800) 446-4656 in the USA) is across from the Club Campestre Tijuana at Blvd Agua Caliente 10750 – look for the pseudocolonial architecture. All 110 rooms have air-con, cable TV and telephone; rates start around US$60 single or double.

Modern *Hotel Lucerna* (☎ /fax (66) 34-20-00; (800) 582-3762 in the USA), Paseo de los Héroes 10902 at the corner of Avenida Rodríguez, also caters to business visitors but is starting to show signs of deferred maintenance. Singles/doubles, all with air-con, color TV and telephone, cost US$63/70 plus IVA, continental breakfast included. It has a restaurant, piano bar and swimming pool. Its US mailing address is PO Box 437910, San Ysidro, CA 92143.

At Blvd Agua Caliente 4500, glittery 23-story towers make the *Grand Hotel Tijuana*

(☎ (66) 81-70-00, fax (66) 81-70-16; (800) 647-3146 in the USA) the city's most prominent hotel. The tallest buildings in town, they house a shopping mall and many offices and restaurants. Additional attractions include a swimming pool, a golf course and various convention facilities. Rooms cost US$80, but ask for AAA member discounts.

The new *Holiday Inn Express* (☎ (66) 34-69-01, fax (66) 34-69-12; (800) 465-4329 in the USA) is at Paseo de los Héroes 18818 near the junction with Blvd Sánchez Taboada in the Zona Río. Rooms here are the most expensive in town, costing US$110 plus IVA.

Places to Eat

Tijuana's multitudinous restaurants serve everything from traditional antojitos to Chinese, Italian, Swiss and Greek cuisine. The main areas for dining are La Revo and the surrounding downtown areas, Blvd Agua Caliente and its extensions and the Zona Río.

La Revo & Downtown *Restaurant Hotel Nelson*, at the corner of Avenida Revolución and Calle 1a (Artículo 123), is a sterile, gringo-style coffee shop with cheap meals that are improving in quality. Seats near the window are good for people-watching. On the eastern side of Avenida Constitución between Calle 1a (Artículo 123) and Calle 2a (Juárez), *Los Norteños* is a popular juice bar and taco stand.

On the eastern side of Avenida Revolución, at the foot of the stairs near the corner of Calle 3a (Carrillo Puerto), *Café La Especial* (☎ (66) 88-66-54) has very decent Mexican food at reasonable prices and is far quieter than the average eatery on La Revo.

At the corner of Calle 3a (Carrillo Puerto) and Avenida Revolución, *Margarita's Village* (☎ (66) 85-38-62) is better known for beer and tequila than for its food; it also has a branch at the Plaza Viva Tijuana, a short walk from the San Ysidro border crossing.

One of Tijuana's most popular gringo hangouts, *Tía Juana Tilly's* (☎ (66) 85-60-24) is next to the Frontón Palacio Jai Alai on Avenida Revolución, while the related *Tilly's Fifth Avenue* (☎ (66) 85-90-15) is near the corner of Avenida Revolución and Calle 5a (Zapata). Both food and drinks seem overpriced, but most people come for the booze and party atmosphere.

One of Tijuana's best values is the diner-style *Tortas Ricardo* (☎ (66) 81-86-55), a bright and cheerful place at the corner of Avenida Madero and Calle 7a (Galeana). Breakfasts are excellent, the tortas are among the best in town and it's open 24 hours a day. Tamales are surprisingly scarce in Tijuana, but the exception is reasonably priced *Tamalandia* (☎ (66) 85-75-62), Calle 8a (Hidalgo) No 8374, which offers a variety of fillings, including beef, chicken and shrimp, plus desserts like flan, cheesecake and carrot cake. It's open 9 am to 9 pm daily except Sunday, when it's open 11 am to 7 pm; it also delivers.

At the corner of Avenida Revolución and Calle 8a (Hidalgo), *Sanborn's* (☎ (66) 88-14-62), the local branch of the famous Mexican department store, has both a bar and a good restaurant. For generous portions of good, reasonably priced pizza and pasta, try *Vittorio's*, Avenida Revolución 1269 at the corner of Calle 9a (Zaragoza). *Palacio Imperial*, Avenida Revolución 1659, is the most central of Tijuana's many Chinese restaurants.

Two of downtown's best seafood restaurants are *Pedrín's* (☎ (66) 85-40-62), Avenida Revolución 1115 between Calles 7a (Galeana) and 8a (Hidalgo), and nearby *La Costa* (☎ (66) 85-84-94), at Calle 7a (Galeana) No 8131 between Avenidas Revolución and Constitución. German-run *La Marea* (☎ (66) 85-65-90), Calle 5a (Zapata) No 8170, is another alternative.

For baked goods, *El Molino* (☎ (66) 84-90-40), at Avenida Quintana Roo and Calle 10a (Sarabia), is open 24 hours a day. Since 1928, it has made everything from ordinary bolillos (typical Mexican bread) to elaborate wedding cakes.

Blvd Agua Caliente Although Blvd Agua Caliente is a bit distant for pedestrians, it has many eateries worth trying. Unpretentious *Dionnysos* (☎ (66) 84-85-08), at the corner of Avenida Pío Pico and Blvd Agua Caliente, serves excellent Greek specialties like souvlaki, gyros, spanako-pita and moussaka at moderate prices. Pizza and pasta are available at *Giuseppi's* (☎ (66) 84-10-18), Blvd Agua Caliente 2600 at the corner of Avenida Querétaro. With a variety of inexpensive takeout burritos, *Burritos del Bol Corona*, near the corner of Avenida 16 de Septiembre and Blvd Agua Caliente, is all that remains of Avenida Revolución's now defunct landmark Bol Corona eatery.

Misleadingly named *Rinconcito Gaucho* (☎ (66) 86-55-66), Blvd Agua Caliente 1490, began 30 years ago as an Argentine restaurant, but while it still features very fine beef, the menu is definitely not South American. *El Rodeo* (☎ (66) 86-56-40), Blvd Salinas 10332, is a fine beef restaurant with eccentric decor – antique gas pumps, Coke machines and a shrine to assassinated PRI presidential candidate Luis Donaldo Colosio.

La Leña (☎ (66) 86-29-20), Blvd Agua Caliente 11191 next to the Grand Hotel Tijuana, serves some of Tijuana's best Sonoran beef; its carne asada is particularly good. Lunches and dinners cost from US$10 to US$25. *Boccaccio's Nuevo Marianna* (☎ (66) 86-22-66), supposedly one of the best restaurants in town, serves Italian and seafood dishes, but its neoclassical decor is formal to the point of stodginess and the quality doesn't match the prices. It's at Blvd Agua Caliente 11250 near the Club Campestre Tijuana. *Los Arcos* (☎ (66) 86-47-57), at the corner of Blvd Salinas and Avenida Escuadrón, is the Tijuana branch of a popular Mexican seafood chain.

La Baguette (☎ (66) 23-41-48), Blvd Agua Caliente 9615, a short distance east of El Toreo de Tijuana bullring, is the local branch of a popular Baja chain that offers good croissants and other pastries.

At the junction of Blvd Agua Caliente and Blvd Salinas, the *El Gorro Drive In* (☎ (66) 86-38-26) deserves a look not so much for its ordinary food as for its oddball architecture – it's literally in the shape of a classic Mexican sombrero.

Zona Río For the cheapest restaurants in the Zona Río and perhaps in the city, visit the Mercado Hidalgo, bordering Avenida Independencia and Blvd Sánchez Taboada; one special recommendation is *Rincón del Oso*.

Plaza Fiesta mall, at the corner of Paseo de los Héroes and Avenida Independencia, features several restaurants and cafes serving food and drink from various countries. Well worth a splurge, *Saverio's* (☎ (66) 84-73-72) is an outstanding Italian restaurant with pizza, pasta and seafood (prices are much higher than those of the more modest Vittorio's, above), open 7:30 am to 10 pm daily except Monday. In the same complex, try also *Taberna Española* (☎ (66) 84-75-62), a popular choice for Spanish meals and tapas.

At the corner of Paseo de los Héroes and Mina, *La Fogata* (☎ (66) 84-22-50) is a good choice for Sonoran beef. At Blvd Sánchez Taboada and Calle 9a (Zaragoza), *Buenos Aires* (☎ (66) 84-73-32) offers an Argentine menu centered on beef and pasta.

Ortega's Buffet (☎ (66) 34-36-55), on Paseo de los Héroes near the corner of Avenida Cuauhtémoc, serves seafood and Mexican dishes at modest prices. *Guadalajara Grill* (☎ (66) 34-30-65), at the corner of Paseo de los Héroes and Avenida Rivera, is part of the Carlos 'n' Charlie's chain better known for drinking than for dining, but the food is palatable.

Entertainment
Cinemas In central Tijuana the few remaining cinemas show cheap Mexican porn, but in and around the shopping centers in the Zona Río and on Mesa de Otay, it's still possible to see first-run films from Mexico, Latin America, the USA and

Europe. Admission generally costs US$3 to US$4.

The *Multicinemas Río* (☎ (66) 84-04-01) are in the Plaza Río Tijuana at the corner of Paseo de los Héroes and Avenida Independencia, while the related *Multicinemas Otay* (☎ (66) 23-13-70) are in the Centro Comercial Otay on Carretera Aeropuerto in Mesa de Otay. The two-screen *Cinemas Gemelos Hipódromo* (☎ (66) 81-40-36) are on Blvd Agua Caliente just east of the racetrack. The *Cines Las Torres Plus* are in the same complex as the Grand Hotel Tijuana at Blvd Agua Caliente 4500.

Nightclubs & Bars Rowdy Avenida Revolución is home to numerous venues for ear-splitting live and recorded music at places like the local branch of the *Hard Rock Café* (☎ (66) 85-02-06), Avenida Revolución 750; *Iguanas-Ranas*, at the corner of Avenida Revolución and Calle 3a (Carrillo Puerto); *El Torito Pub* (☎ (66) 85-16-36), upstairs at Avenida Revolución 643; and many others.

Las Pulgas (☎ (66) 88-13-68), Avenida Revolución 1501, has live *banda* music, while the *Jalapeño Club*, Avenida Revolución 1714, offers both banda and *norteña*. The *Casa Blanca* (☎ (66) 85-77-87), on Calle 7a (Galeana) between Avenida Revolución and Avenida Madero, is another banda-norteña venue; one block east is a nameless modern club with similar offerings.

Most of the rest of Tijuana's fancier nightclubs are in the Zona Río, such as the kitschy *Baby Rock* (☎ (66) 34-24-04), Avenida Rivera 1482 (correspondents to the respected Tijuana weekly *Zeta* have complained of its discriminatory admission policies). Single women from north of the border should beware Tijuana's police department's notorious 'disco patrol,' which reportedly hangs around the area at closing time; for the unsavory details, see Luis Alberto Urrea's *Across the Wire*.

Bars in the Plaza Fiesta mall in the Zona Río are the best place to hear Tijuana's thriving alternative music scene – though quality varies among the numerous garage bands that play clubs like *La Peña*, *Ranas* and *Sótano Suizo* (☎ (66) 84-88-34).

Spectator Sports

Bullfights From May to September, *corridas de toros* take place from 4 to 6 pm every Sunday at two bullrings. The larger, more spectacular venue is the Plaza de Toros Monumental, the renowned bullring-by-the-sea in Playas de Tijuana, only a short distance from the border fence; the other is El Toreo de Tijuana on Blvd Agua Caliente between central Tijuana and the Agua Caliente racetrack. Spring bullfights take place in El Toreo de Tijuana bullring, while summer events are scheduled for Playas de Tijuana.

For reservations in Tijuana, visit the Cotuco kiosk (☎ (66) 85-22-10, (66) 85-15-72) on Avenida Revolución between Calles 3a (Carrillo Puerto) and 4a (Díaz Mirón); in San Diego, contact Five Star Tours (☎ (619) 232-5049, fax (619) 232-7035; (800) 553-8687) in the Amtrak station at Broadway and Kettner Blvd. Prices range from US$19 to US$45 (seats in the shade are costlier).

Greyhound Racing Ever since the Hipódromo de Agua Caliente's owner, Tijuana multimillionaire Jorge Hank Rhon, refused to give in during a sustained labor dispute several years ago, the ponies no longer circle this landmark racetrack, so the place has literally gone to the dogs. In fact, it would be more accurate to call it a *galgódromo*, since greyhound races with pari-mutuel wagering take place at 7:45 pm daily and at 2 pm weekends. Just beyond the Club Campestre Tijuana on Blvd Agua Caliente, the track (☎ (66) 81-78-11, ext 637) is open all year; admission and parking are both free.

Rodeos Usually free of charge, *charreadas* take place Sunday afternoons from May to September at one of four venues in the Tijuana area – ask Secure or Canaco (see Tourist Offices in this entry) for the latest details. One popular rodeo ground is the Cortijo San José in Playas de Tijuana, just south of Plaza de Toros Monumental.

Things to Buy

Avenida Revolución and Avenida Constitución are the main shopping streets. As part of a duty-free zone, Tijuana offers good deals on some imported goods, but the implementation of NAFTA may undercut this status. Calvin Klein, Ralph Lauren and several other top-name designers have opened stores in Tijuana, but most of their merchandise is manufactured in Mexico.

Local handicrafts are plentiful, especially jewelry, wrought-iron furniture, baskets, silver, blown glass, pottery and leather goods; bargaining is the rule in smaller stores. A new and very worthwhile attraction is the Bazar de México (Tijuana Arts & Crafts Center, ☎ (66) 86-52-80) at the corner of Avenida Revolución and Calle 7a (Galeana), alongside the Frontón Palacio Jai Alai, with a particularly good selection of handcrafted furniture. Try also the Mercado Municipal (municipal market) on Avenida Niños Héroes between Calle 1a (Artículo 123) and Calle 2a (Juárez), or the sprawling Mercado de Artesanías (Artisans' Market) at Calle 1a (Comercio) and Avenida Ocampo just south of the northernmost pedestrian bridge over the Río Tijuana.

Mexican liquor and beer are popular buys, though prices are higher than in other border cities. Remember that US Customs regulations allow only one liter of liquor and six bottles of beer per adult (21 years or older) to be taken into mainland California, unless you arrive by common carrier (air, bus or taxi).

Many visitors take advantage of Tijuana's low-priced car body and upholstery

---

Jai Alai

Fast-moving jai alai, played in a long, walled *frontón* in either a singles or doubles format, originated in the Basque borderlands of France and Spain. The very agile and highly skilled *pelotaris* wear an elongated wicker basket on one arm to catch and throw a hard rubber ball with a tightly woven goatskin casing – a skill roughly akin to an outfielder catching a rocketing line drive with his gloved hand and throwing it in the same motion.

WAYNE BERNHARDSON
Pelotaris take the court

However, the game is more similar to a hybrid of tennis and handball, as pelotaris alternatively serve and then play the caroming ball off the court's very high front and rear walls. Six or eight individual pelotaris or two-man teams play to win, place or show for the benefit of spectators who bet on each game; some spectators find doubles more interesting, as the volleys last much longer.

The individual or team remains on court until losing a point, and then the next in the rotation takes the court. The first to score six points wins; if there is no winner after the first round (as is usually the case), each point counts double. The next two highest scorers play for second and third place. Frontón staff are on hand to explain details to neophytes, and the bilingual narration is very helpful in elucidating the game's intricacies. ■

repair shops along Avenida Ocampo, where prices are typically less than half of those north of the border. Most of these shops have English-speaking staff and do good work, but clarify your expectations beforehand and get a written estimate before committing yourself to repairs.

Other visitors frequent Tijuana's equally low-priced dentists for fillings, crowns, bridges and dentures. Cut-rate pharmaceuticals and physicians also attract refugees from the avaricious drug companies, insurers and doctors of the USA.

Tijuana has a wide selection of department stores, such as Dorian's in the Plaza Río Tijuana at the corner of Paseo de los Héroes and Avenida Independencia. For a selection of Mexican music, check out Quinto Poder (☎ (66) 88-39-48), Avenida Negrete 1781, which is particularly strong in alternative rock.

Getting There & Away

Air Mexico's fourth-busiest airport, Aeropuerto Internacional Abelardo L Rodríguez (☎ (66) 83-20-21, (66) 83-21-18), is on Mesa de Otay east of downtown; it has become a popular departure and arrival point, but except for occasional promotions, fares are only slightly cheaper than similar US-based fares.

Aeroméxico (☎ (66) 85-22-30, (66) 82-41-69 at the airport), along with its commuter subsidiary Aerolitoral, has moved to Plaza Río Tijuana, Paseo de los Héroes, Local A 12-1. Aerolitoral flies to Tucson and Phoenix from Tijuana via the mainland Mexican city of Hermosillo (Sonora) and to Guerrero Negro via Hermosillo. Besides serving many mainland Mexican destinations, Aeroméxico has a daily nonstop flight to La Paz and a daily flight to La Paz via Mazatlán.

Mexicana (☎ (66) 34-65-66, (66) 82-41-83 at the airport), Avenida Rivera 1511 in the Zona Río, flies daily to Los Angeles (but not *from* Los Angeles) and also serves many mainland Mexican cities.

Taesa (☎ /fax (66) 34-15-03, (66) 83-55-93 at the airport), Paseo de los Héroes 9288, flies to mainland Mexican destinations,

with Sunday connections to Chicago via Mexico City.

Aero California (☎ (66) 84-21-00), in the Plaza Río Tijuana at the corner of Paseo de los Héroes and Avenida Independencia, flies daily to La Paz and also serves many mainland destinations from Mexico City northward.

Aerolíneas Internacionales (☎ (66) 83-61-31), a recent startup at Avenida Cuauhtémoc 1209, Local 105, in the Zona Río, flies to Hermosillo, Culiacán, Guadalajara, Aguascalientes, Cuernavaca and Mexico City.

Bus Tijuana has three bus terminals. Only Autotransportes de Baja California (ABC, local services, ☎ (66) 86-90-10) and US-based Greyhound (☎ (800) 231-2222 north of the border) use the handy downtown terminal at the corner of Avenida Madero and Calle 1a (Comercio). Both ABC and Greyhound also use the less convenient Central Camionera, the departure point for nearly all long-distance buses. From the Plaza Viva Tijuana, just south of the San Ysidro border crossing, ABC and Autotransportes Aragón offer convenient services to Ensenada; in Ensenada, Aragón makes easy connections to points south as far as San Quintín. Between 9 am and 10 pm on Friday, Saturday and Sunday, ABC goes directly from San Ysidro's Border Station Parking to Playas de Rosarito.

The cavernous and flagrantly misnamed Central Camionera (☎ (66) 26-17-01) is on Tijuana's outskirts, about 3 miles (5 km) southeast of the city center at Blvd Lázaro Cárdenas and Río Alamar, where Blvd Cárdenas becomes the airport road. To reach the Camionera, take any 'Buena Vista,' 'Centro' or 'Central Camionera' bus (US$0.30) from Calle 2a (Juárez) east of Avenida Constitución; these buses also stop at the border bus lot. For US$0.50, quicker and more convenient gold-and-white route taxis (marked 'Mesa de Otay') stop on Avenida Madero between Calle 2a (Juárez) and Calle 3a (Carrillo Puerto).

To/From the USA Several companies, including ATC/Vancom, Greyhound, Intercalifornias and Mexicoach offer services between Los Angeles, San Diego, San Ysidro and Tijuana. Greyhound and Intercalifornias also offer long-distance bus services.

Greyhound has terminals in San Diego (☎ (619) 239-3266) at 120 W Broadway and in San Ysidro (☎ (619) 428-1194) at 799 E San Ysidro Blvd. Buses from San Diego and San Ysidro depart almost every hour between about 5:30 am and 12:30 am, charging US$5 to Tijuana's downtown terminal and US$7 to the Central Camionera; check with Greyhound for the latest schedules, however.

Greyhound also runs at least 20 buses daily from its Los Angeles terminal at 1716 E 7th St en route to San Diego and Tijuana's downtown bus terminal. Buses to Los Angeles (3½ hours) run at least hourly from 6:30 am to 12:30 pm from the Central Camionera and make connections to cities and towns in mainland California's Central Valley. The fare to San Diego is US$7, to Los Angeles US$18 and to Fresno US$30.

Intercalifornias (☎ (66) 83-62-81), on the eastern side of the road just south of the San Ysidro border crossing, goes to Los Angeles and points in the Central Valley; its fares are comparable to Greyhound's.

Mexicoach (☎ (66) 85-14-70; (619) 428-9517 in San Ysidro) runs frequent buses from its San Ysidro terminal at 4570 Camino de la Plaza to its new Tijuana terminal on Avenida Revolución between Calle 6a (Flores Magón) and Calle 7a (Galeana). It's also possible to catch these buses just north of the border. One-way fares are US$1.

ATC/Vancom (☎ (619) 427-6438 in San Diego) runs buses from the corner of Broadway and 3rd Ave or Broadway and Front St in downtown San Diego to the US side of the border (80 minutes, US$1.50).

A variety of minivans operate between the border and San Ysidro-area communities. Most vans terminate next to the end of the trolley line; fares average US$1 to US$2.

To/From Elsewhere in Mexico Transportes Norte de Sonora/Elite (☎ (66) 21-29-48) offers 1st-class buses throughout the country that have air-conditioning and toilets. Autotransportes del Pacífico (☎ (66) 21-26-06) and ABC (☎ (66) 21-26-68) operate mostly 2nd-class services to numerous destinations on mainland Mexico's Pacific coast (Autotransportes del Pacífico) and in Baja California (ABC). ABC's Servicio Plus is comparable to Norte de Sonora's Servicio Elite (both offer luxury buses).

Buses leave Tijuana's downtown bus terminal en route to:

Playas de Rosarito – 30 minutes, US$1; about every 40 minutes from 6 am to 8 pm. Rosarito-bound passengers can also catch route taxis on Avenida Madero between Calle 3a (Carrillo Puerto) and Calle 4a (Díaz Mirón).
Ensenada – 1½ hours, US$5.50; at least hourly from 5 am to 6 pm
Tecate – one hour, US$1.25; half-hourly from 5:30 am to 8 pm

From the Central Camionera (☎ (66) 21-29-82, ask for the appropriate extension), there are services to:

Tecate – 1½ hours, US$1.25; at least hourly from 5:30 am to 10 pm
Ensenada – 1½ hours, US$5.50; at least hourly from 5 am to midnight with ABC
Mexicali – four hours, US$7; at least hourly from 5:30 am to 10 pm
San Quintín – six hours, US$11; daily at 12:30 and 4 pm with ABC
San Felipe – six hours, US$15; daily at 8 am with ABC; buses run more frequently from Ensenada
Guerrero Negro – 10 hours, US$12; daily at 7 pm with ABC
Santa Rosalía – 12 hours, US$30; daily at 4:30 and 7:30 pm with ABC
La Paz – 22 to 24 hours, US$48; daily at 8 am, noon and 6 and 9 pm with ABC
Express to Guadalajara/Mexico City – 36 to 46 hours, US$85; several times daily with Elite and Crucero. Autotransportes del Pacífico and Transportes Norte de Sonora are a few dollars cheaper but less comfortable than Elite. All three lines stop en route at most major towns and cities, including San Luís

Río Colorado (US$10), Sonoita (US$15), Nogales (US$30), Hermosillo (US$30), Guaymas (US$32), Ciudad Obregón (US$40), Los Mochis (US$44), Culiacán (US$50), Mazatlán (US$54), Tepic (US$60) and Guadalajara (US$65).

Norte de Sonora also runs three buses daily to Puerto Peñasco (Sonora) on the mainland coast of the Gulf of California.

From the Plaza Viva Tijuana, only a few minutes' walk south of the border, Autotransportes Aragón and ABC (☎ (66) 83-56-81) offer convenient and inexpensive service to Ensenada. Aragón leaves hourly between 8 am and 9 pm and charges US$5 one way, US$7.50 roundtrip, with connections to points south as far as San Quintín.

Train Amtrak (☎ (800) 872-7245 in the USA) runs daily trains between Los Angeles and San Diego. For schedule and fare information, see the Train entry in the Getting There & Away chapter. The San Diego Trolley (see below) runs from San Diego's Amtrak station directly to San Ysidro.

Trolley For US$1.75, the San Diego Trolley (☎ (619) 233-3004) is one of the cheapest ways from San Diego's Amtrak station in the Center City to the San Ysidro border. Two lines converge on Center City: the North-South Line runs from Mission Valley through Center City and on to the border at San Ysidro, stopping near the pedestrian bridge into Mexico; the East Line runs from Santee and El Cajon to the transfer station at 12th St and Imperial in downtown San Diego.

Trolleys depart every 15 minutes or so from about 5 am to midnight. A leaflet with full schedule and fare information can be obtained at each station.

From San Diego International Airport (Lindbergh Field), San Diego Transit bus No 2 goes directly to the trolley stop at Plaza America in San Diego, across from the Amtrak station; it runs from 5:34 am to 1:10 am weekdays, 5:34 am to 1:03 am weekends and holidays. If you're making the bus-trolley connection, be sure to request a free transfer.

Getting Around

To/From the Airport The government-regulated taxi service (☎ (66) 83-10-20) runs airport cabs from central Tijuana. Cabs can also be caught on the street; fares are about US$8 after bargaining. Sharing the ride can reduce the cost to about US$2 per person for up to five people.

From the border, take any bus marked 'Aeropuerto' from the street just past the taxi stand, for about US$0.30; from downtown, catch the airport bus or a blue-and-white route taxi on Calle 5a (Zapata) between Avenida Constitución and Paseo de los Héroes.

Bus From the border, just about any bus from the taxi stand will drop passengers downtown near the Frontón Palacio Jai Alai on Avenida Revolución. At the bus stop, there is usually a man with a notebook who directs people toward the right bus to any destination in town.

The 'Baja P' bus goes to the Centro Cultural de Tijuana and the Plaza Río and Plaza Fiesta shopping malls. Standard fares are about US$0.30.

Car Rental Rental cars are cheaper in San Diego, where some companies permit their cars to be taken across the border; for information on these companies, see the Getting Around chapter. Locally, however, try Central Rent de Mexicali (☎ (66) 84-22-57), Paseo de los Héroes 10001 in the Zona Río.

Other companies include:

Avis
    Avenida Cuauhtémoc 406, Colonia Aeropuerto (☎ (66) 83-06-03, (66) 83-23-10 at the airport)
Budget
    Av Paseo de los Héroes 9988 in the Zona Río, one block east of Avenida Cuauhtémoc (☎ (66) 84-02-53)
Hertz
    Hotel Palacio Azteca, Avenida 16 de Septiembre 213 (☎ (66) 86-43-71)

National
  Blvd Agua Caliente 10598 (☎ (66) 86-21-
  03) Aeropuerto Internacional Abelardo L
  Rodríguez (☎ (66) 82-44-33)

Taxi Tijuana taxis lack meters, and cabbies
sometimes overcharge gringos, especially
for the five-minute trip from the border to
central Tijuana – they may charge about
US$5 per person for a trip that should only
cost about US$3. Try out your bargaining
skills; in general, expect to pay from US$2
to US$5 for most city taxi rides. A ride to
the Central Camionera costs about US$6
from the border.

Route taxis (about US$0.40) are only
slightly dearer and much quicker than city
buses. From Avenida Madero and Calle 3a
(Carrillo Puerto), gold-and-white station-
wagon cabs (marked 'Mesa de Otay') go
frequently to the Central Camionera.

TECATE

Far enough from Tijuana to be off the
main tourist route, the somnolent but
fast-growing border settlement of Tecate
(official population 47,005) more closely
resembles a mainland Mexican *pueblo*
(town) than does any other locality in
northern Baja California. Known for its
family life, Tecate lacks even the dubious
attractions of a *zona de tolerancia* – an
apparent arson fire once destroyed a nearly
completed casino.

Most mainland Mexican cities and towns
have a *zócalo*, a central plaza decreed by
the Spanish colonial Laws of the Indies,
around which the major public buildings
are clustered. Even postcolonial cities
like Tijuana, Ensenada and Mexicali have
similarly picturesque plazas, but they are
often remote from the centers of activity.
Tecate's Parque Hidalgo, though, remains
the town's social center for both visitors
and locals. On weekends mariachi bands
play here, and fiestas take place throughout
the year.

Across the US border, Tecate's mainland California namesake is still barely a
wide spot in the road, but US discount
retailers have begun to take advantage

of the growing Mexican market. Under
NAFTA, this trend is likely to continue.
Another event that may change the city's
character is a proposed railroad linking
the US border at Tecate to the port of
Ensenada.

About 1.4 million people cross the border legally here every year, a small fraction
of the numbers at Tijuana, but increasing
numbers of illegal border-crossers have
spawned an ugly armed vigilantism on the
US side of the border. Between 1994 and
1996, the number of undocumented Mexicans apprehended by the US Border Patrol
at Tecate rose from just 2300 to more than
78,000, proving that increased controls
along the San Diego-Tijuana crossing have
merely displaced northbound migrants.

History

Tecate's origins derive from an 1831 land
grant to a Peruvian named Juan Bandini
(who became the mayor of San Diego
immediately before the US takeover of Alta
California), but the establishment of early
businesses and the development of agriculture in the 1880s really put the town on
the map. The surrounding countryside
yielded both grains and fruit crops like
grapes and olives.

In 1911 Ricardo Flores Magón's Liberal
Party army occupied Tecate before marching west to Tijuana, but the Mexican federal government regained control after six
weeks. After 1915 the railroad linked Tijuana, Tecate and Tucson (Arizona); it is
now exclusively a freight line except for the
occasional tourist jaunt from Jacumba
(mainland California) to Tecate (Baja California). Completion of México 2, the last
link on the Tijuana-Mexico City highway,
was a further boost to the economy.

Tecate's onetime whiskey factory, a
major employer, folded with the repeal
of US Prohibition; businessman Alberto
Aldrete's malt factory, founded in 1928,
expanded into a major brewery by 1944
but soon went bankrupt. Acquired by a
Mexican conglomerate after several years'
management by the Banco de México, it is
still an important employer, producing up

LA FRONTERA

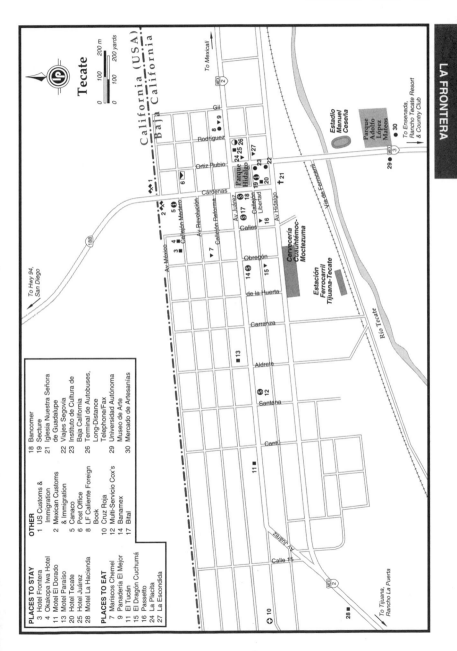

Tecate

PLACES TO STAY
3 Hotel Frontera
4 Okakopa Iwa Hotel
11 Motel El Dorado
13 Motel Paraíso
20 Hotel Tecate
25 Hotel Juárez
28 Motel La Hacienda

PLACES TO EAT
7 Mariscos Chemel
9 Panadería El Mejor
11 El Tucán
15 El Dragón Cuchumá
16 Passetto
24 La Placita
27 La Escondida

OTHER
1 US Customs &
   Immigration
2 Mexican Customs
   & Immigration
5 Canaco
6 Post Office
8 LF Caliente Foreign
   Book
10 Cruz Roja
12 Multi-Servicio Cox's
14 Banamex
17 Bital

18 Bancomer
19 Secture
21 Iglesia Nuestra Señora
   de Guadalupe
22 Viajes Segovia
23 Instituto de Cultura de
   Baja California
26 Terminal de Autobuses,
   Long-Distance
   Telephone/Fax
29 Universidad Autónoma
   Museo de Arte
30 Mercado de Artesanías

to 1200 cans per minute of two of Mexico's best-known beers, Tecate and Carta Blanca. Maquiladoras, however, are the major employers; the largest is Schlage Locks, employing about 3000 people. Opened in 1986, the Universidad Autónoma de Baja California's extension center has enhanced the town's cultural environment.

Like other Baja border towns, Tecate has sprawled dramatically over the past decade, in part because presumptive border-crossers have remained in the area; some claim the actual population is at least double the official figure. This seems too high, but growing numbers have clearly stressed local resources and accentuated social problems that barely existed in past decades – town residents now lock their doors against thieves, for example. Still, by border-town standards, Tecate is an atypically placid and appealing destination.

Orientation

Tecate is about 34 miles (55 km) east of Tijuana and 90 miles (145 km) west of Mexicali. México 2, the east-west route linking Tijuana and Mexicali, divides into Avenida Benito Juárez to the north and Avenida Hidalgo two blocks south. Avenida Juárez runs past Parque Hidalgo (Tecate's main square) and the bus terminal, while Avenida Hidalgo runs parallel to it and past the brewery.

Lázaro Cárdenas runs north from Avenida Hidalgo past the western side of Parque Hidalgo and straight to the border crossing. Ortiz Rubio runs parallel to and one block east of Cárdenas, passes the eastern edge of Parque Hidalgo and heads south to become México 3 to Ensenada. Just south of the river are Estadio Manuel Ceseña, the city's baseball park, the Universidad Autónoma's extension center and the larger square of Parque Adolfo López Mateos.

Information

Border Crossing The Customs & Immigration posts on both sides of the border are open 6 am to midnight daily, but Mexican officials issue car permits only from 8 am to

4 pm. Saturday is the busiest day; Sunday, surprisingly, is relatively quiet.

Tourist Offices Secture's cramped offices (☎ (665) 4-10-95) on the southern side of Parque Hidalgo have abundant printed matter; though English-speaking staff are not always available, they make an effort to be helpful. Office hours are 8 am to 7 pm weekdays, 10 am to 3 pm weekends.

At the border proper, Canaco has a small information kiosk with adequate town maps and additional printed matter, open 8 am to 8 pm weekdays, 9 am to 4 pm Saturday and 9 am to 2 pm Sunday. Its staff usually speak English, and car insurance is also available here.

Money Most businesses readily accept US dollars, but Tecate also has several banks on Avenida Juárez and around Parque Hidalgo. These include Banamex, Bancomer and Banco Internacional (Bital).

Multi-Servicio Cox's operates an exchange service on Avenida Juárez between Aldrete and Santana; it's open 9 am to 7 pm daily except Sunday.

Post & Communications Tecate's post office is at the corner of Ortiz Rubio and Callejón Madero, three short blocks north of Parque Hidalgo. The postal code is 21400.

Tecate has plenty of public telephones, but the best place to make a long-distance call is the bus terminal, which has several phone booths and a fax machine.

Travel Agency Viajes Segovia (☎ (665) 4-27-55, fax (665) 4-27-56) is at Ortiz Rubio 260-2, south of Parque Hidalgo.

Cultural Centers The Instituto de Cultura de Baja California (☎ (665) 4-14-83) is newly relocated on the southern side of Parque Hidalgo. It offers art exhibits, films (usually in video format) and other cultural events. The Universidad Autónoma's Centro de Extensión, just south of the bridge over the Río Tecate, hosts occasional traveling exhibitions of *bajacaliforniano* art.

Medical Services The Cruz Roja (☎ 132) is at the western end of Avenida Juárez. Tecate has numerous medical clinics, dentists and pharmacies that serve visitors from north of the border.

Things to See & Do

Tecate's street life centers on **Parque Hidalgo**, the main plaza, which features a bandshell surrounded by well-tended gardens and a statue of independence hero Miguel Hidalgo. Unlike most Mexican cities, Tecate's main ecclesiastical landmark, the **Iglesia Nuestra Señora de Guadalupe**, is not on the plaza but one block south, at the corner of Cárdenas and Avenida Hidalgo.

Tecate's main secular landmark, the **Cervecería Cuauhtémoc-Moctezuma** (☎ (665) 4-11-11), on Avenida Hidalgo between Cárdenas and Obregón, offers brewery tours at 10 am daily by reservation only, preferably for at least 10 people. It's best to call no less than two weeks in advance for reservations, but it's worth trying to hook up with another tour or to persuade the publicity people to offer one on the spot. The brewery, Tecate's largest building, produces some of Mexico's best-known beers, including Carta Blanca and the town's namesake Tecate; after the tour, guests sample the results in its **Jardín Cerveza**.

Behind the brewery, the now deserted **Estación Ferrocarril Tijuana-Tecate** (railway station, dating from 1915) served the San Diego & Arizona Eastern line that ran along and across the border for over 60 years; for historical details, see the Rails Across the Border sidebar in the Desierto del Colorado chapter.

Every fortnight or so, the San Diego Railroad Museum (☎ (619) 595-3030, (888) 228-9246, fax (619) 595-3034) runs 'Ticket to Tecate' Saturday excursions from its headquarters in Campo, across the border in eastern San Diego County. For US$35, excursions include a brewery tour and lunch in Tecate; special wine-tasting excursions in July and August cost US$65.

Special Events

While less extroverted than Tijuana and Ensenada, Tecate holds several festivals that are more frequented by locals than by foreigners.

Those below are in addition to regular Mexican holidays like Cinco de Mayo and mid-September's Día de la Independencia (Independence Day). Double-check with the tourist offices, since events often change from year to year.

May

Midmonth – *Paseo Ciclista Tecate-Ensenada* (Tecate-Ensenada Bicycle Race). Up to 15,000 cyclists participate in one of Tecate's biggest annual events, usually held in mid-May but sometimes held at a later date. For more information, contact the Tecate offices of Secture or Canaco.

Midmonth – *Carrera de Relevos* (Tecate-Ensenada Relay Marathon). Competitors in this 66-mile (106-km) footrace consist of teams of five people, at least one of whom must belong to the opposite sex. For more information, contact the same parties as for the Paseo Ciclista.

June

Late June – *Nacional de Bicicleta de Montaña* (National Mountain-Biking Championships). For more information, contact the Club de Ciclismo de Montaña Los Traviesos (☎ (665) 4-22-46).

July

Midmonth – *Feria Tecate en Marcha* (Tecate in Progress). Celebrated with parades and rodeos; it is sometimes held in September. Takes place in Parque Adolfo López Mateos. For more information, contact the Desarollo Social y Promoción Económica del Honorable Ayuntamiento (☎ (665) 4-13-19, (665) 4-15-22).

August

Early August – *Romería de Verano* (Summer Festival). Popular local festival in Parque Hidalgo, including food stalls, artisanal goods and regional music and dance

October

Early October – *Fundación de Tecate*. The city celebrates its anniversary for nearly two weeks.

December

12th – *Día de Nuestra Señora de Guadalupe* (Festival of Our Lady of Guadalupe). In one of the peninsula's most interesting celebrations of this holiday, groups from all over Baja visit Tecate to display their costumes and dancing.

Midmonth – *Posadas de Tecate* (Annual Pre-Christmas Parades)

Places to Stay

Reportedly frequented by smugglers who help undocumented Mexicans across the border, *Hotel Juárez* is at Avenida Juárez 230, almost next door to the bus terminal. Dark, gloomy singles/doubles with private bath cost about US$9/12. *Motel Paraíso* (☎ (665) 4-17-16), Aldrete 83 just north of Avenida Juárez, is ragged around the edges but very hospitable for US$10 single or double.

Friendly *Hotel Frontera* (☎ (665) 4-13-42), Callejón Madero 131, offers basic but tidy rooms for US$10 with shared bath, US$18 with private bath. The spartan, unheated singles/doubles at *Hotel Tecate* (☎ (665) 4-11-16), on Cárdenas a half-block south of Parque Hidalgo, are a poorer value for US$15/20, slightly more with color TV (the hot showers are dependable and the toilets are very clean, however).

Motel La Hacienda (☎ (665) 4-12-50, (665) 4-09-53), Avenida Juárez 861, west of the town center, offers clean, carpeted, air-conditioned doubles with TV and a swimming pool for US$18, an outstanding value.

Tecate's newest accommodations are at the very fine *Okakopa Iwa Hotel* (☎ (665) 4-11-44), Callejón Madero 141, just one block west of the border post. Singles/doubles with air-con, color TV, telephone and secure parking cost US$33.

The 41-room *Motel El Dorado* (☎ (665) 4-11-02, fax (665) 4-13-33), at Avenida Juárez 1100, has comfortable singles/doubles with air-con, cable TV, telephone and carpeting for US$41/44. Its US postal address is PO Box 160, Tecate, CA 91980.

Places to Eat

Despite its modest size, Tecate has a number of good eateries. *La Placita*, a sidewalk taco stand on the eastern side of Parque Hidalgo, serves some of Tecate's juiciest tacos. The southern side of Avenida Juárez between the bus terminal and Parque Hidalgo has wall-to-wall taco stands of good to excellent quality, but the prize is *Mariscos Chemel* (☎ (665) 4-41-12), on Obregón between Avenida Revolución and Callejón Reforma, where locals swarm for succulent, inexpensive fish and shrimp tacos.

Inconspicuous *La Escondida* (☎ (665) 4-21-64) almost lives up to its name – 'the hidden' – but offers good antojitos in a pleasant environment, if you can locate the entrance at Callejón Libertad 174 between Ortiz Rubio and Rodríguez. It's open 7 am to 5 pm daily except Sunday. *Passetto* (☎ (665) 4-13-61), Callejón Libertad 200, less than a block west of Parque Hidalgo, serves moderately priced Italian dishes like spaghetti and ravioli. *El Dragón Cuchumá* (☎ (665) 4-05-40), on Obregón between Avenida Hidalgo and Callejón Libertad, is a Chinese restaurant named after the mountain that straddles the nearby border. Motel El Dorado's *El Tucán* (☎ (665) 4-11-02) serves various continental and Mexican dishes at above-average prices.

Locals swear that *Panadería El Mejor* (☎ (665) 4-00-40), Avenida Juárez 331, a half-block west of the bus terminal, bakes the best bread and pastries in Baja. It's open 24 hours a day (with free coffee).

Entertainment

LF Caliente Foreign Book (☎ (665) 4-05-13) runs a betting salon with big-screen TVs at the corner of Avenida Juárez and Rodríguez.

Things to Buy

Hand-painted clay tiles and Tecate beer are the town's specialties; both are much cheaper than in the USA, but ask US Customs about tiles before purchasing any quantity. There's a small Mercado de Artesanías (☎ (665) 4-17-50) just south of

A: WAYNE BERNHARDSON

C: WAYNE BERNHARDSON

B: MICHAEL SULLIVAN

A: Street photographers and their striped friend, Tijuana

B: Food stand, Ensenada

D: ROBERT RABURN

E: WAYNE BERNHARDSON

C: Seafood market, Ensenada

D: Produce packers and tomatillos, Tijuana

E: Mercado Hidalgo, Tijuana

A: WAYNE BERNHARDSON

B: WAYNE BERNHARDSON

C: WAYNE BERNHARDSON

D: WAYNE BERNHARDSON

A: Laguna Hanson, Parque Nacional
Constitución de 1857

B: *Tierra y Libertad*, mural by Juan Zuñiga
Padilla, Playas de Rosarito

C: Santo Tomás Vineyards in winter

D: Mural, Galería de Arte de la Ciudad,
Tijuana

Parque Adolfo López Mateos, across from the Universidad Autónoma's Centro de Extensión.

Many US citizens also cross the border for groceries and pharmaceuticals because prices are lower here.

Getting There & Away
Tecate's Terminal de Autobuses is at the corner of Avenida Juárez and Rodríguez, one block east of Parque Hidalgo. ABC buses to Tijuana (US$1.25) leave almost every half-hour, while ABC and Transportes Norte de Sonora go to Mexicali (US$5.50) at least hourly between about 6 am and midnight. There are also at least five buses daily to Ensenada (US$5). ABC runs three buses daily to Puerto Peñasco (Sonora) and goes to Santa Rosalía (US$30) at 2:30 pm and to La Paz (US$47) at 7 pm daily.

México 2 is a key route for every major bus company in Baja California and northwestern Mexico; for an idea of services passing through Tecate, see the Tijuana Getting There & Away entry.

AROUND TECATE
Rancho Tecate Resort & Country Club
On México 3, about 6 miles (10 km) south of Tecate in the Tanama valley, Rancho Tecate Resort & Country Club (☎ (665) 4-00-11, fax (665) 4-02-41) features a hotel, a partially completed nine-hole golf course, tennis courts, a restaurant, two artificial lakes and a swimming pool. Rooms range from US$40 to US$80 per night. Its US Customer Relations Office (☎ (619) 234-7951) is at 2550 5th Ave, Suite 111, San Diego, CA 92103, but it usually refers potential customers to the Tecate number.

Rancho La Puerta
On México 2, 3 miles (5 km) west of Tecate, luxuriously landscaped Rancho La Puerta (☎ (665) 4-11-55; (760) 744-4222, (800) 443-7565, fax (760) 744-5007 in mainland California) is a health spa and resort for patrons who can afford at least US$1315 per person, double occupancy, for the minimum one-week stay – only slightly less than a year's wages for a maquiladora laborer. Founded in 1940 by self-improvement gurus Deborah and Edmund Szekely, the resort boasts that its location at the foot of border-straddling Mt Cuchumá is 'the south rim of the last surviving Southern California "safe zone" for the environmentally sensitive.' It features two staff members for each guest.

According to its brochure, the resort does not cater to those 'guests who weigh 35% more than the accepted norms, or guests who have difficulty in walking, or seeing, or those with serious health problems.' Vacancies are booked as far as a year in advance; for reservations in the USA, contact Rancho La Puerta at the numbers above or write PO Box 463057, Escondido, CA 92046-3057. The Rancho provides free transportation to and from San Diego International Airport (Lindbergh Field), Saturday only, and handles immigration formalities on the spot.

Budget-conscious travelers with hunger pangs can probably afford the antojitos at *Café Sierra Bonita* next to Rancho La Puerta's entrance.

Hacienda Santa Verónica
Climbing to a high plateau, México 2 passes through a zone of small farms and ranches where Hacienda Santa Verónica (☎ (66) 85-97-93, (66) 38-40-71 in Tijuana), about 15 miles (24 km) southeast of Tecate via a lateral off the main highway, offers rooms with fireplace and patio, a swimming pool, six tennis courts and an RV park/campground. Visitors seeking peace and quiet should know that 5000-acre Santa Verónica simultaneously boasts the 'first all-purpose off-road and dirt-racing facility in the world,' intended to showcase 'Gran Prixs, ATVs, sprint cars and super modifieds.'

Rooms cost US$50 per night for a double. Seasonal packages are available. RV spaces cost US$15 per night with full hookups, access to restrooms, showers, laundry, and sports and fossil-fuel facilities.

LA FRONTERA

La Rumorosa

East of Tecate for about 40 miles (64 km), México 2 passes through an imposing panorama of immense granite boulders to La Rumorosa, where it descends the precipitous Cantú Grade, with extraordinary views of the shimmering Desierto del Colorado. Mexico's federal government built a new limited-access highway eastbound with the intention of making the old highway one-way westbound and instituting a heavy toll along the route, but the vigorous objections of Baja California's state government and many citizens have forced it to keep the older highway open in both directions. The only other nontoll alternative, the parallel US Interstate 8, is limited to those with border-crosser passports.

TIJUANA-ENSENADA CORRIDOR

México 1D, a divided toll road that is the fastest way to Ensenada, can be reached directly from the international border at Tijuana by following the euphemistically incomplete 'Ensenada Scenic Road' signs (which say nothing of the hefty toll) along Calle Internacional. Running along the border fence almost to the ocean (see the

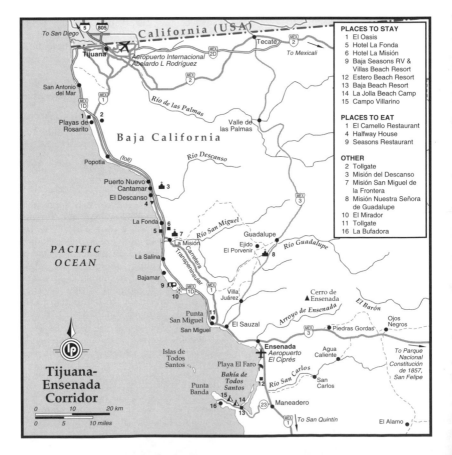

PLACES TO STAY
1 El Oasis
5 Hotel La Fonda
6 Hotel La Misión
9 Baja Seasons RV & Villas Beach Resort
12 Estero Beach Resort
13 Baja Beach Resort
14 La Jolla Beach Camp
15 Campo Villarino

PLACES TO EAT
1 El Camello Restaurant
4 Halfway House
9 Seasons Restaurant

OTHER
2 Tollgate
3 Misión del Descanso
7 Misión San Miguel de la Frontera
8 Misión Nuestra Señora de Guadalupe
10 El Mirador
11 Tollgate
16 La Bufadora

Tijuana-Ensenada Corridor

Tijuana map), the road turns south just before the Playas de Tijuana exit and passes through the first of three tollgates.

Tolls for the entire 68-mile (110-km) stretch from Tijuana to Ensenada, which takes about 1½ hours, are about US$4 for an ordinary passenger vehicle or motorcycle, twice that for a motor home and about US$12 for vehicles with trailers. One-third of the toll is charged at each of three gates – Playas de Tijuana, Playas de Rosarito and San Miguel – though there are several other exits along the route. Note that, although vehicle access is limited, the livestock that jump the fences to graze on the irrigated median strip are a serious traffic hazard.

Two-lane, toll-free México 1 (the Transpeninsular) passes through equally spectacular scenery, but heavier traffic makes it slower. From the Tijuana border crossing, follow the signs to central Tijuana and continue straight (west) along Calle 3a (Carrillo Puerto), turning left (south) at Avenida Revolución. Follow Avenida Revolución to the end, where it veers left (east) and becomes Blvd Agua Caliente. Turn right just before the twin towers of the Grand Hotel Tijuana and head south.

At Playas de Rosarito on the coast, the roads run parallel for several miles. Just past La Fonda, the Transpeninsular turns inland and zigzags through the countryside for 21 miles (34 km) before crossing the toll road again.

Information

Just beyond the Playas de Tijuana tollgate, there's a tourist information booth with a few brochures and maps of Tijuana and Playas de Rosarito.

El Oasis

Pleasingly landscaped El Oasis (☎ (66) 31-32-50, fax (66) 31-32-52; (888) 709-9985 toll free in mainland California), a beachfront hotel/RV-park resort at Km 25 south of Tijuana on México 1D, has 55 paved sites with small patios, brick barbecues and full hookups, including cable TV. Facilities include a nine-hole golf course, tennis courts, swimming pool, spa and grocery, as well as a clubhouse with bathrooms, sauna, TV, laundry and weight room. RV rates are US$31 per night weekdays, US$37 Friday and Saturday, plus tax. Hotel rates start at US$79 double weekdays, US$89 Friday and Saturday.

El Camello, an ocean-view restaurant that is also part of the resort, has a good but pricey menu of items like crab hors d'oeuvres, Manhattan clam 'showder' and shrimp in garlic sauce. Most entrées include soup or salad and garlic bread.

PLAYAS DE ROSARITO

In 1827 José Manuel Machado obtained a grant of 11 leagues of land south of Rancho Tijuana that, now divided into several ranchos, also includes the city of Rosarito, officially founded in 1885. The valley of Rosarito marks the original boundary between Alta and Baja California, which after the Mexican-American War was moved north to Tijuana.

In 1916 the Compañía Explotadora de Baja California purchased 14,000 acres (5600 hectares) of the Machado concession; in 1927 this became Moreno & Compañía, which began the Hotel Rosarito. Completed by Manuel Barbachano, it became the landmark Rosarito Beach Hotel.

A few years ago, Rosarito (official population 37,121) was a modest fishing village with its single posh resort hotel (known mainly to Hollywood stars and hangers-on), long sandy beaches (frequented only by a handful of surfers) and a few taco stands, but its 'discovery' has fostered a noisy commercial strip with numerous resort-style hotels and fine restaurants. Signs are now as likely to be in English as in Spanish. Its beaches, fishing, organized bicycle rides and races and horseback riding are the main attractions. Beachgoers who fall asleep in the sun, though, may awaken with treadmarks on their backs or chests from the three-wheelers that speed up and down the hard-packed sand.

Acknowledging the town's growth and growing importance, the state government

LA FRONTERA

granted Rosarito *municipio* status in mid-1995; both the municipio and the town are known formally as Playas de Rosarito. Hollywood has also rediscovered Rosarito, using a site a few kilometers south of town to build a full-scale model of the *Titanic* for director James Cameron's mega-overbudget film of the same name.

Orientation

Rosarito's main street, Blvd Benito Juárez, is a segment of the Transpeninsular. On weekends, it becomes a two-way traffic jam, due mostly to traffic from southern mainland California. Nearly all its hotels and restaurants are on the western side of this boulevard, some of them directly fronting the beach. While many places do have street addresses, the numbering system is confusingly erratic and most people use landmarks like the Rosarito Beach Hotel as points of reference. Since most east-west streets crossing the central segment of Blvd Juárez are named, this entry uses those cross streets to indicate directions whenever possible.

Information

Several tourist-oriented publications focus on Rosarito, most notably the *Baja Sun* and the *Tourist Guide*, both giveaway publicity rags loaded with advertising, promos and the occasional useful and interesting article. *Baja Visitor* also provides Rosarito information.

Tourist Office Secture (☎ /fax (661) 2-02-00), the local representative of the state-run tourist agency, occupies an office in the Plaza Villa Floresta, a minimall at Blvd Juárez 20000, on the western side near the second stop sign as you approach town from the north. It has a modest selection of English-language brochures and leaflets, along with recent issues of *Baja Sun* and other giveaways; English-speaking staff will deal with tourist hassles and may help find accommodations in Rosarito or Ensenada. It's open 9 am to 7 pm weekdays, 10 am to 4 pm weekends.

Immigration Rosarito's Servicios Migratorios (☎ (661) 3-02-34) is on Las Acacias directly behind the police station. If you haven't obtained a tourist card to travel south beyond Ensenada, you can do so here, but Ensenada officials are more accustomed to the process.

Money Nearly all merchants accept US dollars in payment or will exchange them for pesos. Banks include Bital on Blvd Juárez between Cedro and Abeto, Banamex at the corner of Blvd Juárez and Ciprés and Banca Serfin on Blvd Juárez between Roble and Encino.

Post & Communications Rosarito's post office is on Las Acacias east of the police station; the postal code is 22710. Several pharmacies and other stores along Blvd Juárez have private phone facilities.

Travel Agency Expediciones Ecotur (☎ (66) 31-11-83), north of town at Km 18 on the Transpeninsular, organizes backcountry excursions, including hiking, mountain biking, climbing and similar activities. Its US address is 482 W Border Village Rd, Suite 244, San Ysidro, CA 92173.

Laundry There's a Lavamática at the Quinta Plaza shopping center at the northern end of town, and another on the eastern side of Blvd Juárez between Las Acacias and Roble.

Medical Services Hospital Santa Lucía (☎ (661) 2-04-40), open 24 hours a day, is at Avenida Mar del Norte 557 behind the police station. Clínica Santa Verónica, on Nogal just west of Blvd Juárez, is also open 24 hours a day.

Emergency The police station (☎ (661) 2-11-10/1) is at Blvd Juárez and Las Acacias. For the Cruz Roja, dial ☎ 132.

Museo Wa Cuatay

Rosarito's small historical and anthropological museum, near the Rosarito Beach

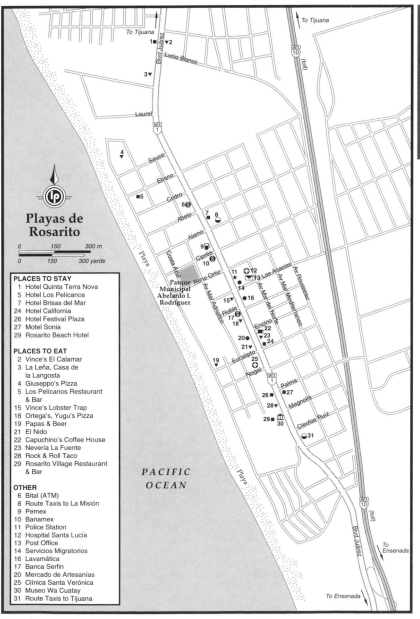

Playas de Rosarito

0 ____ 150 ____ 300 m
0 ____ 150 ____ 300 yards

PLACES TO STAY
1 Hotel Quinta Terra Nova
5 Hotel Los Pelicanos
7 Hotel Brisas del Mar
24 Hotel California
26 Hotel Festival Plaza
27 Motel Sonia
29 Rosarito Beach Hotel

PLACES TO EAT
2 Vince's El Calamar
3 La Leña, Casa de
   la Langosta
4 Giuseppo's Pizza
5 Los Pelícanos Restaurant
   & Bar
15 Vince's Lobster Trap
18 Ortega's, Yugu's Pizza
19 Papas & Beer
21 El Nido
22 Capuchino's Coffee House
23 Nevería La Fuente
28 Rock & Roll Taco
29 Rosarito Village Restaurant
   & Bar

OTHER
6 Bital (ATM)
8 Route Taxis to La Misión
9 Pemex
10 Banamex
11 Police Station
12 Hospital Santa Lucía
13 Post Office
14 Servicios Migratorios
16 Lavamática
17 Banca Serfin
20 Mercado de Artesanías
25 Clínica Santa Verónica
30 Museo Wa Cuatay
31 Route Taxis to Tijuana

PACIFIC
OCEAN

Hotel, offers a good introduction to the area from pre-Columbian times to the present, dealing with subjects like the missions, creation of the *ejidos* and the beginnings of tourism. With a selection of indigenous artifacts and good historical photographs, plus occasional traveling exhibitions from mainland Mexico, it's open 10 am to 4 pm daily except Tuesday. Admission is free.

Parque Municipal Abelardo L Rodríguez

The amphitheater at Rosarito's beachfront plaza contains the impressive 1987 mural *Tierra y Libertad* (Land and Liberty) by Juan Zuñiga Padilla, proof that Mexico's celebrated muralist tradition is still alive and well. Traditional motifs include the eagle and plumed serpent and Emiliano Zapata and his followers.

Horseback Riding

Horses can be hired at several locations on the western side of the Transpeninsular in Rosarito. From the highway, most people gallop toward the beach and, when appropriate, off into the sunset. Rates average about US$5 to US$10 per hour.

Water Sports

Both swimmers and surfers should be aware that Rosarito's beaches and the entire coastline between Tijuana and Ensenada are heavily polluted, and that neither activity is advisable in the area.

Tony E Surf Shop (☎ (661) 2-11-92) is in the northern end of town on Blvd Juárez opposite Ortega's Place (see Places to Eat in this entry); it and many other places sell a useful surfer's map of Mexico (US$10) that includes many Baja breaks.

Places to Stay

Because it's a resort town and so close to the border, Rosarito lacks consistent budget accommodations; rates vary both seasonally and between weekdays and weekends, making it difficult to categorize hotels and motels by price.

Places to Stay – budget

Camping There's no camping in Rosarito proper, but there are quite a few sites both north and south of town.

On the coast, the *KOA Trailer Park/ Campground* (☎ (66) 86-14-12), 7 miles (11 km) north of Rosarito and 12 miles (19 km) south of Tijuana, has all the typical facilities and RV hookups common at KOA campgrounds in the USA; sites cost about US$16 per night for two people, US$1 for each additional person. Take the San Antonio del Mar exit off México 1D (the Ensenada toll road).

Popotla Trailer Park (☎ (661) 2-15-02), about 5 miles (8 km) south of town on the Transpeninsular, caters to long-term campers; about 30 spaces are available to short-termers for US$14 a night. The park has an ocean-view restaurant, a clubhouse, showers, toilets and easy beach access.

South of Popotla at Km 38, *Surfpoint Camping* welcomes surfers for US$5 per person. Showers are only tepid, but the toilets are well kept.

Hotels & Motels The financially challenged can try *Motel Sonia* (☎ (661) 2-12-60), on the eastern side of Blvd Juárez at Palma, for US$20 single or double. Among Rosarito's budget favorites is the 24-room *Marsella's Motel* (☎ (661) 2-04-68), at newly paved Calle del Mar 75, a few blocks west of Blvd Juárez and a few blocks north of the ballpark at the northern end of town. Though it's become a bit rundown, clean, carpeted and spacious rooms with wood paneling, large beds and cable TV cost only US$20 weekdays, US$35 weekends. *Motel Don Luis* (☎ (661) 2-11-66), Blvd Juárez near Calle Rosarito, also in the northern end of town, has singles/doubles for US$25; some rooms lacking TV go for only US$20.

Motel Colonial (☎ (661) 2-15-75), about a half-mile west of Blvd Juárez at Primero de Mayo 71 in the northern end of town, is an aging, pseudocolonial building whose lobby fixtures give it some character – lots of wrought iron, pastel paintings and a giant antique jukebox. Most rooms are suites with separate living/dining areas, kitchenette, double bed and enough space for cots and sleeping bags. Prices start around US$20, but rooms with ocean views cost US$25 and up.

The still sparkling *Hotel California* (☎ (661) 2-25-50; (800) 944-9275 toll free in mainland California), at Blvd Juárez and Eucalipto, has found a niche among college students during spring break, when its US owner/manager more or less gives them the run of the place; the rest of the year it's more sedate. Single/double rates are US$25/35.

Places to Stay – middle

At Km 35.5 of the Transpeninsular, about 6 miles (10 km) south of town, *Hotel Calafia* (☎ (661) 2-15-81, fax (661) 2-15-80; (800) 225-2342 north of the border) bills itself as a cultural-historical center, in part due to tenuous links with Misión del Descanso (see the Around Playas de Rosarito entry in this chapter), but it has an attractive oceanfront setting. Rates start around US$22 double off-season, US$36 in-season; its US postal address is PO Box 433857, San Diego, CA 92143.

Closer to town, about half a mile (1 km) south of the Rosarito Beach Hotel, the friendly *Paraíso Ortiz Motel* (☎ (661) 2-10-20) has cabin-style rooms for US$25 single/double during the week, but rates rise to US$35 on weekends and US$45 in summer. It's a bit quieter than accommodations in Rosarito proper. Its US mailing address is PO Box 435349, San Ysidro, CA 92143.

Motel El Portal de Rosarito (☎ (661) 2-00-50), at the corner of Vía de las Olas and Blvd Juárez, has singles/doubles from US$31 to US$49, but winter rates can be as low as US$25. Its US mailing address is PO Box 309, San Ysidro, CA 92143.

One of Rosarito's better values is the increasingly sprawling *Hotel Los Pelícanos* (☎ (661) 2-04-45) at the beach end of Ebano adjacent to Restaurant Los Pelícanos. Basic singles or doubles cost US$35 to US$45, plus US$7.50 for each additional person. Rooms with ocean-view balconies cost US$55. The US mailing address is PO Box 433871, San Diego, CA 92143.

The *Hotel Quinta Terra Nova* (☎ (661) 2-16-42/44/48/50), part of a tourist complex at Blvd Juárez 25500 in the center of town, contains three restaurants and bars and a commercial center. Motel rooms, all with showers, color TV and telephone, cost US$35/55 single/double for a very fine place.

Hotel Brisas del Mar (☎ (661) 2-25-47, fax (661) 2-26-15; (800) 697-5223 in the USA), Blvd Juárez 22 between Alamo and Abeto, has off-season doubles from US$43, but rooms with ocean views start at US$53, plus US$15 for each additional person. Summer and weekend rates are US$16 more per room. Special rooms with jacuzzi are available at premium prices. The US mailing address is PO Box 189003, Coronado, CA 91912.

Places to Stay – top end

Facing the ocean on Blvd Juárez, the *Rosarito Beach Hotel* (☎ (661) 2-11-06, fax (661) 2-11-76; (619) 498-8230, (800) 343-8582 in the USA) opened in the late 1920s during Prohibition in the USA and quickly became a popular watering hole and gambling haven for Hollywood stars like Orson Welles and Mickey Rooney. Larry Hagman of *Dallas* fame, Vincent Price and Mexican presidents Miguel Alemán, Adolfo López Mateos and Adolfo Ruiz Cortines have also been guests.

The best rooms are suites in the new building closest to the beach. Despite its popularity and prestige, room rates remain surprisingly modest – US$59 for doubles on weekends, with an occasional special rate of US$39 for doubles during the week, plus 10% tax. Prices include access to all facilities: restaurant, swimming pool, racquetball courts and gymnasium. In the USA write to PO Box 430145, San Ysidro, CA 92143 for more information.

The high-rise *Hotel Festival Plaza* (☎ (661) 2-29-50; (800) 453-8606 in the

USA), on Blvd Juárez a short distance north of the Rosarito Beach Hotel, has standard doubles for US$49 weekdays and US$59 weekends, plus more expensive penthouses, suites and villas. At Km 37 on the Transpeninsular is the *Hotel Las Rocas* (☎ /fax (661) 2-21-40; (800) 733-6394 toll free in mainland California), whose balconied suites and rooms overlook the ocean; all have fireplace, kitchenette and satellite TV. Double rates start at US$70 Friday and Saturday night and in summer, and start at US$49 the rest of the week and off-season; more expensive suites are also available. Its postal address is PO Box 8851, Chula Vista, CA 91912-8851.

Places to Eat
At Blvd Juárez 2884 at the northern end of town, upscale *La Fachada* (☎ (661) 2-17-85) gets rave reviews from almost everyone for specialties like steak and lobster. *Ortega's Place* (☎ (661) 2-00-22), just south of La Fachada, serves tasty lobster dinners; its weekly Sunday champagne brunch is also a big attraction for US$9. Another *Ortega's* (☎ (661) 2-27-91) is in the Plaza Oceana, Blvd Juárez at Roble; next door is *Yugu's Pizza* (☎ (661) 2-08-20). *El Jardín* (☎ (661) 2-11-16), alongside Motel Don Luis toward the northern end of town, serves Mexican seafood dishes.

At the Centro Comercial Ejido Mazatlán about one block north of the Hotel Quinta Terra Nova, *Palacio Royal* (☎ (661) 2-14-12) is a huge, conspicuous Chinese restaurant. *La Leña* (☎ (661) 2-08-26), just south of the Terra Nova, specializes in beef; at the same location is *Casa de la Langosta* (☎ (661) 2-09-24), a seafood restaurant specializing in lobster. A short walk from the beach is *Giuseppo's Pizza* (☎ (661) 2-16-08), a pleasant Italian place just off Sauce, offering shrimp pizza and pasta entrées at moderate prices.

Near the beach on Ebano, just south of Giuseppo's, *Los Pelícanos Restaurant & Bar* (☎ (661) 2-17-37) serves a variety of excellent seafood and steak specials at higher prices; also try its quail in garlic sauce. *El Nido* (☎ (661) 2-10-30), on Blvd Juárez at the corner of Eucalipto, is part of a popular Baja chain.

Vince's Lobster Trap (☎ (661) 2-12-53), Blvd Juárez 39 near the corner of Las Acacias, has been highly recommended for lobster dinners; the same owner runs *Vince's El Calamar* (☎ (661) 2-00-37), opposite the Centro Comercial Quinta del Mar in the northern part of town. On the beach a few blocks southwest of the Lobster Trap, *Papas & Beer* (☎ (661) 2-04-44) is one of a chain of brightly decorated watering holes better known for partying than dining – there's a small cover charge, and a hefty bouncer keeps rowdies, minors (under 18) and other undesirables from entering this outdoor bar and its sandlot volleyball court. A similar crowd hangs out at *Rock & Roll Taco* (☎ (661) 2-29-50) on Blvd Juárez just north of the Rosarito Beach Hotel.

The *Rosarito Village Restaurant & Bar* (☎ (661) 2-01-44), part of the Rosarito Beach Hotel, is known for massive margaritas and weekend mariachis. The weekend brunch is an excellent value for US$9. For espresso drinks and pastries, a good choice is *Capuchino's Coffee House* (☎ (661) 2-29-79), Blvd Juárez 890-3 between Encino and Eucalipto. Next-door *Nevería La Fuente* offers an excellent selection of fruit-flavored juices and ices.

Entertainment
Every Friday night, the *Rosarito Beach Hotel* presents performances by mariachis, singers and gaudy cowboys (who do rope tricks). Performances take place from 7 pm to 2 am, but the main show starts at 9 pm.

The Hotel Festival Plaza's bar, the *Lobby*, sometimes offers live jazz. Both *Papas & Beer* and *Rock & Roll Taco* have live, less subdued music as well.

Cines Río (☎ (661) 2-11-05), on Blvd Juárez kitty-corner from Motel El Portal de Rosarito at the northern end of town, is a two-screen cinema showing recent movies, usually Hollywood fare.

Things to Buy

At Blvd Juárez 306 near the intersection with Encino, the Mercado de Artesanías is a 200-stall handicraft market where you can haggle for serapes, wind chimes, hats, T-shirts, dresses, Batman piñatas, ceramic Buddhas and clay pots. It's open 9 am to 6 pm daily.

Getting There & Away

Route taxis leaving from a stand near the Rosarito Beach Hotel connect Rosarito with Tijuana (US$1); taxis running to points south as far as La Misión leave from the southern side of Hotel Brisas del Mar at Alamo and Blvd Juárez.

ABC buses between Tijuana and Ensenada stop at the tollgate at the southern end of Rosarito but do not enter the town itself. Southbound travelers may find it more convenient to take a route taxi to La Misión and flag down the bus there.

AROUND PLAYAS DE ROSARITO
Puerto Nuevo

If tectonic uplift were not raising this section of the coastline from the sea, the village of Puerto Nuevo, about 13 miles (21 km) south of Playas de Rosarito on the Transpeninsular, might sink beneath the weight of its 30 or so seafood restaurants. (See the Tijuana-Ensenada Corridor map.) All of them specialize in lobster, usually cooked in one of two manners: *ranchera* (simmered in salsa) or *frito* (buttered and grilled or fried). All have similar prices, about US$15 for a full lobster dinner and US$10 for a grilled fish dinner. Garlic shrimp is also popular.

Ortega's is one of the largest and best known in town – look for the shiny, modern building that towers over every other. (Ortega's owns five restaurants in Puerto Nuevo and two in Playas de Rosarito.) Don't judge Puerto Nuevo restaurants by decor, though; the *Miramar*, for instance, looks ordinary, but its food, particularly lobster, is exceptional.

South of Puerto Nuevo, the *Grand Baja Resort* (☎ (661) 4-14-93; (619) 685-1260,

(800) 275-3280 toll free in mainland California) offers junior suites, sleeping four people, from US$55 off-season (October through March), US$65 the rest of the year. Studios with kitchenette are slightly more expensive. One- and two-bedroom apartments start at US$95 and US$140, respectively. Its US postal address is 2630 E Beyer Blvd, No 44, San Ysidro, CA 92143.

At Km 45 on the Transpeninsular just south of Puerto Nuevo, the sprawling *New Port Beach Hotel* (☎ (661) 4-11-88, fax (661) 4-41-74; (800) 582-1018 toll free in mainland California), has single/double rooms for US$55 except on weekends, when rates climb to US$65. Its US postal address is 482 W San Ysidro Blvd, No 2599, San Ysidro, CA 92173-2410.

Misión del Descanso

Just south of Puerto Nuevo at **Cantamar**, ATV assaults on the Valle de los Médanos (Valley of the Dunes) have nearly destroyed this delicate coastal environment. About 1½ miles (3 km) south of Cantamar, a gravel road off the Transpeninsular passes east beneath the toll road to the site of the Dominican Misión del Descanso, one of the last missions founded in California; to find the road, look for the greenhouses at Vivero La Central on the northern side of the Río Descanso.

When Misión San Miguel, about 5 miles (8 km) south, lost its irrigable lands to floods, Fray Tomás de Ahumada moved part of its operations north to this site around 1817. The two missions operated simultaneously for some time, but Descanso was also known as San Miguel Nuevo. As of the historian Peveril Meigs' visit in 1927, adobe ruins still existed; an apparent guardhouse overlooked the mission from a 150-foot (45-meter) slope on the southern side of the valley.

The present church, dating from the turn of the century, occupies the mission site, now commemorated by a large marker. Fridays a priest opens the church and may have more detailed information. An abandoned adobe house on a knoll to the east was part of the 1827 Machado grant that assumed control of the mission lands.

The original boundary between the Dominican and Franciscan mission provinces, and thus between Baja and Alta California prior to the Treaty of Guadalupe Hidalgo, was just north of here but was later moved to Tijuana.

Well known among mainland Californians who surf the reef breaks at nearby Punta Mesquite, about 3 miles (5 km) south of Puerto Nuevo on the Transpeninsular, the *Halfway House* is a small but popular restaurant serving typical antojitos, steak-and-eggs specials, hamburgers and hot dogs. The garden on the northern side of the house is a great viewpoint for afternoon photographs.

La Misión

The village of La Misión, on the Transpeninsular's inland turn south of the Halfway House, is most notable as the site of the Dominican **Misión San Miguel de la Frontera**, also known as San Miguel Encino and San Miguel Arcángel. Founded in 1787 at a site unknown today, the mission moved up the valley of the Río San Miguel when the spring it depended on dried up. This valley dissects a broad fault surface known locally as a mesa, which is surrounded by higher lava flows.

Fishing from balsa rafts, local Indians relied mostly on seafood for their subsistence, but the mission also grew wheat, maize, barley and beans, and it grazed over 1600 cattle and 2100 sheep at its peak. The highest Indian population, about 400, occurred in 1824 – a fairly large number at this late date. In the late 19th century, Russian immigrants moved into the area.

The few remaining ruins are protected under a tiled roof behind the Escuela Primaria La Misión (the elementary school), at Km 65.5 about one mile (1.6 km) south of the bridge over the Río San Miguel. They include the foundations and some adobe walls of the church and adjacent buildings.

Places to Stay & Eat Overlooking a broad sandy beach at Km 59 on the Transpeninsular, *Hotel La Misión* (☎ (615) 5-02-05, fax (661) 2-24-24; (562) 420-8500 in mainland California) has bargain doubles for US$29 weekdays, US$45 weekends, plus 10% tax. Suites with jacuzzi cost US$56 weekdays, US$75 weekends, plus tax. Its restaurant/bar has cheap dinner specials, plus live music on weekends. The US postal address is PO Box 439060, San Ysidro, CA 92143.

Hotel La Fonda (☎ (66) 48-17-40, (66) 28-73-53 in Tijuana), an oceanfront resort motel and restaurant at Km 59 on the Transpeninsular, 19 miles (31 km) south of Rosarito, also resembles a mission with its tiled roof, banana trees and flower-lined paths. The restaurant's specialties include prime rib, lobster, shrimp and scallops. It has live music several nights weekly.

Detached from the bar and restaurant, the hotel is quiet, but its security is very suspect – the night watchman saw nothing odd in the arrival of a rickety station wagon at 3:30 am and the subsequent hot-wiring and high-speed departure of the author's own 4WD pickup.

Rates average about US$50 per night for oceanfront rooms and US$70 for an apartment (which sleeps four), but there are off-season bargains as low as US$15 single. Make reservations at least two weeks in advance by sending a deposit for one or more nights to PO Box 430268, San Ysidro, CA 92143.

Bajamar

On a headland just north of Punta Salsipuedes and about 7½ miles (12 km) south of the village of La Fonda, at Km 77.5 on México 1D, Bajamar is a Mediterranean-style resort complex focusing on an older but renovated 18-hole golf course and a newer nine-holer, and also featuring swimming pools, tennis courts, a clubhouse and bicycle rentals.

The resort contains 100 privately owned villas but has also opened *Hotel Hacienda Las Glorias* (☎ (615) 5-01-51/2) for short-term visitors. Daily rates, not including taxes, range from US$65 weekdays to US$85 weekends and holidays for standard guest rooms; suites cost US$120 weekdays, US$130 weekends and holidays. Weekday and weekend golf packages are also available, and the course is open to both regular hotel guests and the public. For more information and reservations in mainland California, contact Bajamar reservations (☎ (800) 522-1516), Tours Etc (☎ (619) 232-4653) or Best Golf (☎ (888) 817-4653).

Free *camping* is possible on an attractive beach at Km 71 on México 1D.

At Km 72, *Baja Seasons RV & Villas Beach Resort* (☎ (66) 28-61-28, fax (66) 48-71-06; (619) 422-2777, (800) 754-4190 in the USA) has 134 landscaped spaces with full hookups on an attractive stretch of beach 17 miles (27 km) north of Ensenada. Facilities include the *Seasons* restaurant, a swimming pool, tennis courts and a laundry. There is also a small grocery and a clubhouse with big-screen TV. Rates range from US$25 to US$30, depending on beach access. For more information, contact Baja Seasons at 1177 Broadway, Suite 2, Chula Vista, CA 91911.

El Mirador

El Mirador, a roadside viewpoint about 17 miles (27 km) north of Ensenada and about 11 miles (18 km) south of La Fonda on México 1D, is spectacularly situated above the ocean. A few small stands sell soft drinks and occasionally coconuts.

San Miguel

San Miguel is a small beach community about 5 miles (8 km) north of Ensenada that consists mostly of US retirees in mobile homes; it also offers surfers a good right break. Down by the beach, *Villa de San Miguel RV Park* (☎ (61) 74-62-25) offers camping, full hookups, showers and rustic toilets from US$5 per night. There's a small *seafood restaurant* at the entrance to the RV park.

El Sauzal

The seafood cannery at sedate El Sauzal,

about 2 miles (3 km) north of Ensenada, gives off a powerful fishy odor, but several *trailer parks* and *campgrounds* charge about US$4 to US$10 a night, though it's difficult to find one that doesn't cater mostly to long-term RVers. Try camping for free on any unclaimed stretch of beach, but these are not easy to find; for hotels, check the Places to Stay entry for Ensenada.

ENSENADA

In the daytime hundreds of aging Americans stroll the tranquil streets of Baja's erstwhile territorial capital with shopping lists of prescription pharmaceuticals, but by night the state's third-largest city (official population of 192,550) becomes its biggest party town, where mariachis stroll from bar to bar, norteña bands play for local audiences and rock groups attract mixed crowds of gringos and Mexicans. The city's main attractions remain food (some of Baja's best restaurants are here), drink (it's also the locus of Baja's growing wine industry) and fiestas (there are dozens of special events yearly), but outdoor activities like fishing, surfing and whale-watching are also popular.

Because of the large number of US visitors from mainland California, Ensenada is a reluctant host for spontaneous Fourth

WAYNE BERNHARDSON
Former Mexican President Benito Juárez, Plaza de Las Tres Cabezas, Ensenada

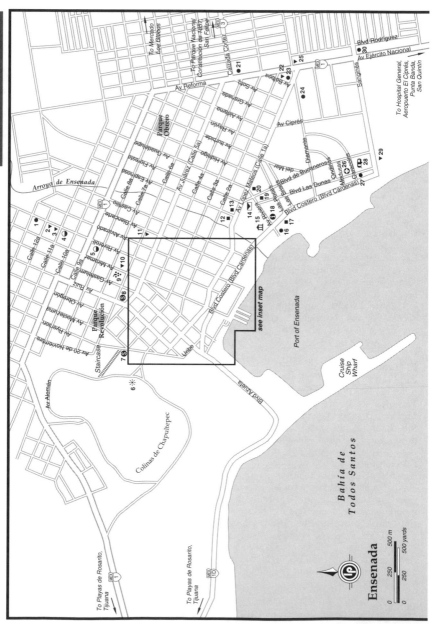

Ensenada

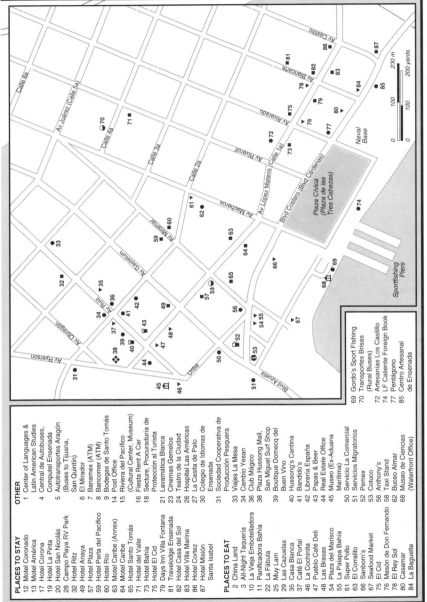

PLACES TO STAY
12 Motel Coronado
13 Motel América
17 Hotel Corona
19 Hotel La Pinta
20 Hotel San Nicolas
28 Campo Playa RV Park
32 Hotel Ritz
49 Hotel Anaya
57 Hotel Plaza
59 Hotel Perla del Pacífico
60 Hotel Río
63 Motel Caribe (Annex)
64 Motel Caribe
65 Hotel Casa del Sol
71 Hotel Santo Tomás
73 Hotel del Valle
75 Hotel Bahía
75 Hotel El Cid
79 Days Inn Villa Fontana
81 Travelodge Ensenada
82 Hotel Casa del Sol
83 Hotel Villa Marina
86 Hotel Cortez
87 Hotel Misión
Santa Isabel

PLACES TO EAT
2 China Land
3 All-Night Taquería
10 La Vieja Embotelladora
11 Panificadora Bahía
22 La Fábula
25 Muy Lam
29 Las Cazuelas
35 Casa Blanca
37 Café El Portal
46 La Cochinita
47 Pueblo Café Deli
48 Las Brasas
54 Plaza del Marisco
55 La Palapa Bahía
61 Super Pollo
63 El Corralito
66 Seafood Market
67 Sanborn's
75 El Cid
76 Mesón de Don Fernando
78 El Rey Sol
80 Casamar
84 La Baguette

OTHER
1 Center of Languages &
Latin American Studies
4 Central de Autobuses,
Computel Ensenada
5 Autotransportes Aragón
(Buses to Tijuana,
San Quintín)
6 El Mirador
7 Banamex (ATM)
8 Bancomer (ATM)
9 Bodegas de Santo Tomás
14 Post Office
15 Riviera del Pacífico
(Cultural Center, Museum)
16 Fiesta Rent A Car
18 Secture, Procuraduría de
Protección al Turista
21 Lavamática Blanca
23 Cinemas Gemelos
24 Teatro de la Ciudad
26 Hospital Las Américas
27 La Casita de Palo
30 Colegio de Idiomas de
Ensenada
31 Sociedad Cooperativa de
Producción Pesquera
33 Viajes La Mesa
34 Cambio Yesan
36 Club Mágico
38 Plaza Hussong Mall,
San Miguel Surf Shop
39 Boutique Domecq del
Buen Vino
40 Hussong's Cantina
41 Bandido's
42 Librería España
43 Papas & Beer
44 Real Estate Office
45 Museo (Ex-Aduana
Marítima)
50 Servicio La Comercial
51 Servicios Migratorios
52 Pemex
53 Cotuco
56 Anthony's
58 Taxi Stand
62 Buceo Almar
68 Museo de Ciencias
(Waterfront Office)
69 Gordo's Sport Fishing
70 Transportes Brisas
(Rural Buses)
72 Artesanías Los Castillo
74 LF Caliente Foreign Book
77 Pentágono
85 Centro Artesanal
de Ensenada

of July celebrations, a fact resented by many local residents. At this time of year in particular, visitors from north of the border should take special care to refrain from offensive behavior. Many fireworks now illegal in mainland California can be obtained in Mexico, but this does not imply permission to use them indiscriminately.

History

Located on the harbor of Bahía de Todos Santos, Ensenada has sheltered explorers, freighters and fishing boats for over four centuries. Juan Rodríguez Cabrillo, searching for the Strait of Anián (the mythical Northwest Passage) with his caravels *San Salvador* and *Victoria*, entered the bay to replenish his water supply in September 1542, encountering a small group of Indian hunter-gatherers.

In 1602 Sebastián Vizcaíno named Ensenada de Todos los Santos after All Saints Day, November 1. During colonial times, the harbor was an occasional refuge for Spanish *naos* (galleons) returning to Acapulco from Manila. Naos usually passed the area once or twice yearly, loaded with Oriental treasures like silks, spices, Japanese artwork and jewels; the last one sailed through in 1815.

Ricardo Flores Magón, leader of the Partido Liberal and the Magonista rebels

Far northern Baja was the last part of the peninsula to be missionized; Dominican Padre Juan Crespí passed through Ensenada on his Expedición Sagrada (Sacred Expedition) of 1769, but a shortage of irrigation water prevented the establishment of any mission on the site. The nearest missions were San Miguel de la Frontera (founded 1787) some 30 miles (48 km) north, Nuestra Señora de Guadalupe (founded 1834) about 25 miles (40 km) northeast, and Santo Tomás de Aquino (founded 1791) around 30 miles (48 km) south.

Ensenada's first permanent settlement was established in 1804, when the Viceroy of New Spain granted the surrounding area to José Manuel Ruiz, whose Rancho Ensenada became a prosperous cattle ranch. It was purchased in 1824 by Francisco Gastelum, whose family consolidated farming and ranching interests in the area.

In 1869 discovery of gold at Real del Castillo, 22 miles (35 km) inland, transformed a sleepy backwater. Bahía de Todos Santos was the closest harbor, the ranchos the closest food suppliers, and Ensenada boomed with an influx of miners, merchants and hangers-on. After this initial prosperity attracted investors, the Mexican government designated Ensenada the capital of Baja territory from 1882 to 1915.

In the 1880s the US-owned International Company of Mexico attempted to attract agricultural colonists to the region but failed to live up to its contract (fraud was apparent) and sold out to a British concern, the Mexican Land & Colonization Company. Around this time, Ensenada had five general stores, three hotels, two dress stores, two hardware stores, a mattress factory, a tannery, a fruit cannery, a brewery and several miscellaneous industries (as well as Hussong's renowned cantina, which opened in 1892), but closure of the mines and failure of agricultural colonization ended the boom.

Ensenada briefly revived in the spring of 1911, when a splinter group of anarchist Magonistas occupied the mining hamlet of

El Alamo, 40 miles (64 km) southeast. Their presence so alarmed the hysterical US consul in Ensenada, George Schmucker, that he cabled the State Department with exaggerations of the rebels' importance and sophistication, linking them to an international conspiracy and calling for warships to protect US citizens. State Department officials ignored most of his communications, and Schmucker, who fantasized a biblical Armageddon in Baja California, suffered a nervous breakdown.

Ensenada lost its political primacy during the Revolution, when Colonel Estéban Cantú, concerned over the anarchist Magonistas and an increasing US influence in the border region, shifted the territorial capital to Mexicali. After the Revolution, Ensenada, like Tijuana, began to cater to the 'sin' industries of drinking, gambling and sex during US Prohibition. The Playa Ensenada Hotel & Casino opened in the early 1930s but closed when Mexico's federal government outlawed casino gambling only a few years later. Renamed the Riviera del Pacífico, the Spanish-style hotel tried to function as a resort for another decade; today it's a cultural center that also offers facilities for wedding receptions and similar social occasions.

As more visitors came to Ensenada, entrepreneurs built more hotels and restaurants and the town became a tourist resort and weekend retreat for more than four million visitors annually – mostly southern mainland Californians.

Orientation

Ensenada, 68 miles (110 km) south of Tijuana and 119 miles (192 km) north of San Quintín, is a major fishing and commercial port on sheltered Bahía de Todos Santos. Many of the city's best hotels and restaurants line the waterfront Blvd Costero, also known as Blvd Lázaro Cárdenas. Blvd Costero is also the site of the Plaza Cívica, known colloquially as 'Plaza de Las Tres Cabezas' (Three Heads Plaza) for its massive busts of historical icons Benito Juárez, Miguel Hidalgo and Venustiano Carranza. Avenida López Mateos (also known as Calle 1a), which parallels Blvd Costero for a short distance one block inland (north), also contains many visitor services.

A few blocks further inland is the business center along Avenida Benito Juárez and side streets, an area that includes Ensenada's 'party district' – Avenida Gastelum and Avenida Ruiz (the Ruiz and Gastelum families founded Ensenada). Several bars and cantinas, including the legendary Hussong's, are located on Avenida Ruiz. At the northern end of town, the hills of Colinas de Chapultepec are an exclusive residential zone that usurped the name of an even more exclusive residential zone in Mexico City.

Just north of town, México 3 heads east and then north through the Valle de Guadalupe to the pleasant border town of Tecate. At the southern end of town, Calzada Cortez leads east toward Ojos Negros and Laguna Hanson in Parque Nacional Constitución de 1857 and south to the Valle de Trinidad before descending the eastern scarp of the Sierra de Juárez and connecting with México 5, the north-south route between Mexicali and San Felipe. The southbound Transpeninsular leads to the military checkpoint at Maneadero, beyond which foreigners must have a tourist card.

Information

Several local publications, free from the tourist offices listed below, provide information on the city. The English-language monthly *Baja Sun* is primarily promotional propaganda, but read critically it's still a good source of information about the Tijuana-Ensenada corridor and the rest of Baja. Another freebie is *Ensenada Happenings*.

Published by the Centro Empresarial de Ensenada (☎ (61) 78-18-33, fax (61) 74-09-92), *Enlace* has useful information for business visitors who speak Spanish. Its postal address is Apdo Postal 760, Ensenada, Baja California 22800, México.

Tourist Offices Ensenada's Cotuco office (☎ (61) 78-24-11, fax (61) 78-85-88) is at Blvd Costero 540 at the corner of Avenida

Gastelum, across from the Pemex station. The staff are usually helpful, offering a wide selection of maps and brochures, but their hotel data used to be more thorough. Hours are 9 am to 7 pm weekdays, 9 am to 3 pm weekends.

Secure (☎ (61) 72-30-22, (61) 72-30-00, ext 3081/2/3/4) is at Blvd Costero 1477 at the corner of Las Rocas, just south of the Riviera del Pacífico. The staff are friendly, obliging and well informed. It's open from 9 am to 7 pm weekdays, 9 am to 3 pm weekends.

Immigration At Blvd Azueta 101, around the corner from the Cotuco tourist office, Servicios Migratorios (☎ (61) 74-01-64) is open 8 am to 8 pm daily. Travelers and drivers who have failed to obtain or validate their tourist cards or vehicle permits must do so here if they wish to continue south of Maneadero. Note that this address is directly across the street from the former office.

Money Weekend visitors don't usually bother changing money, but visitors continuing south will find plenty of banks and cambios on or around Avenida Ruiz. ATMs are now common at banks like Bancomer at Avenida Ruiz 500 and Banamex on Avenida Ryerson at the corner of Calle 3a.

Servicio La Comercial, on Uribe north of Avenida Gastelum, cashes traveler's checks with a 1% commission. Cambio Yesan, Avenida Ruiz 201, charges 2%.

Post & Communications Ensenada's main post office, at the corner of Avenida López Mateos and Avenida Riviera, is open 8 am to 7 pm weekdays, 9 am to 1 pm Saturday. The postal code is 22800.

Telnor public telephones are widespread in Ensenada, but the Computel Ensenada office at the bus terminal conveniently allows payment by Visa or MasterCard; avoid the shockingly high-priced, non-Telnor street phones when calling the USA or Canada.

Travel Agency Viajes La Mesa (☎ (61) 78-14-33, fax (61) 78-84-35), Calle 4a No 440-B, will arrange plane, train and bus tickets, and can also assist with hotels, car rentals and tours.

Bookstores Librería España (☎ (61) 74-09-66), Calle 2a No 447-C, sells a small selection of books on the Baja Peninsula in both English and Spanish. An anonymous real estate office on the western side of Avenida Ruiz, just south of Avenida López Mateos, also sells Baja books and souvenirs.

Laundry Lavamática Blanca, in the mall at the corner of Avenida Reforma and Calzada Cortez, offers self-service washers and dryers.

Medical Services Ensenada's Hospital General (☎ (61) 76-76-00) is at Km 111 on the Transpeninsular south of the city. Striking workers closed Hospital Las Américas (☎ (61) 76-03-01), Blvd Las Dunas 130, in early 1997, but it will likely reopen.

Like other large Baja cities, Ensenada also has numerous private doctors and dentists.

Emergency Ensenada's Procuraduría de Protección al Turista (☎ (61) 72-30-22), sharing offices with Secture (see Tourist Offices, above), helps tourists with legal problems.

Other emergency contacts are the Cruz Roja (☎ 132), the Policía (Police, ☎ 134) and the Bomberos (Fire Department, ☎ 136).

El Mirador

Atop the Colinas de Chapultepec, El Mirador offers panoramic views of the city and Bahía de Todos Santos. Climb or drive up Avenida Alemán from the western end of Calle 2a in central Ensenada to the highest point in town. There also is a pedestrian staircase from the western end of Calle 3a.

Bodegas de Santo Tomás

Founded in 1888 near the vineyards of the Valle de Santo Tomás south of Ensenada, Santo Tomás is one of Baja's premier vintners. After purchasing the winery in 1937, former Mexican president Abelardo Rodríguez moved its facilities to Ensenada to expedite shipping; today it is owned and operated by the Mexico-based multinational Corporación Elías Pando.

Varieties include pinot noir, chardonnay and cabernet; up to 120,000 cases are shipped annually throughout Mexico and to Western Europe but not yet to the USA. Santo Tomás is returning its processing operations to new facilities in the valley, but the distribution center will remain in Ensenada.

At Avenida Miramar 666, Santo Tomás (☎ (61) 78-33-33, (61) 78-25-09) offers daily tours including tastings at 11 am and 1 and 3 pm (US$2). It also organizes occasional classical music concerts for US$20 (US$30 with dinner).

Cavas Valmar

This smaller but still respectable winery (☎ (61) 78-64-05, (61) 74-24-69), Calle 19 (also known as Calle Ambar) No 810 at the northern end of Avenida Miramar, offers free tours and tastings by appointment.

Riviera del Pacífico

In an extravagant but still distinguished Mudéjar-style building on the waterfront, the Riviera del Pacífico opened in the early 1930s as the Playa Ensenada Hotel & Casino. Once frequented by Hollywood figures like ex-Olympic swimmer Johnny Weissmuller ('Tarzan'), Myrna Loy, Lana Turner, Ali Khan and Dolores del Río, and briefly managed by US boxer Jack Dempsey, the facility closed in 1938 when President Lázaro Cárdenas outlawed casino gambling.

Open to the public and well worth exploring, the building, now the Centro Social, Cívico y Cultural de Ensenada, offers cultural events such as art exhibitions and film retrospectives and hosts weddings, conventions and meetings. In the lobby there is an impressive three-dimensional mural of the Californias, emphasizing the mission sites of both Baja and Alta California. A museum at the northern end of the building, open 10 am to 4 pm daily except Sunday, charges US$0.75 admission.

With its long wooden bar, an oddball mural by Alfredo Ramos Martínez, magnificent tilework and outstanding historical photos, the Riviera's Bar Andaluz is a great place for a quiet drink. Contrast its subdued elegance with gaudy Las Vegas to sense the decline (or democratization) of the casino as an institution since Prohibition days.

Museo

Built in 1887 by the US-owned International Company of Mexico, Ensenada's oldest public building passed into the hands of the British-owned Mexican Land & Colonization Company before coming under control of Mexican Customs in 1922. Exactly 70 years later, the federal government transferred the building (then called the Aduana Marítima de Ensenada) to the Instituto Nacional de Historia y Antropología (INAH) for renovation as a museum.

Offering rotating exhibitions under INAH's auspices, the museum (☎ (61) 78-25-31) is at Avenida Ryerson 99 at the corner of Uribe. It's open 10 am to 5 pm daily except Monday; admission is free.

Museo de Ciencias de Ensenada

More school-oriented than a general interest facility, Ensenada's modest science museum contains exhibits on both the natural and physical sciences, stressing marine ecology along with endangered species and habitats. Its winter whale-watching cruises (US$15 per person), however, are of interest to the public at large. At Avenida Obregón 1463, the museum (☎ (61) 78-71-92, fax (61) 78-63-35) is open 9 am to 5 pm Tuesday to Friday, noon to 5 pm weekends; admission costs US$0.75.

Mercado Los Globos

Antique collectors may want to explore Ensenada's largest outdoor market at Los Globos, an area of eight square blocks on Calle 9a east of Avenida Reforma, where vendors sell everything from old radios and typewriters to fruit and vegetables. It's open daily, but vendors are more numerous on weekends.

Diving

Buceo Almar (☎ (61) 78-30-13), Avenida Macheros 149, is the local dive shop, but the newest in town is the Diver's Corner Ensenada (☎ (61) 75-00-00, ext 8055; (562) 869-7702 in the USA) at the Hotel Coral & Marina in the Zona Playitas, at Km 103 on the Transpeninsular just north of town. There's another at Punta Banda, the most popular diving spot near Ensenada (see the Around Ensenada entry in this chapter).

Fishing

Among the popular species in the area are albacore, barracuda, bonito, halibut, white sea bass and yellowtail, depending on the season. Many places on Avenida López Mateos offer fishing trips, and there are also charter-boat offices next to the port and seafood market. You can join an organized group for about US$35 a person per day or charter an entire boat (charter rates and vessels vary dramatically, so shop around).

Gordo's Sport Fishing (☎ (61) 78-35-15, fax (61) 74-04-81), near the seafood market behind Sanborn's, runs trips on the 36-foot, 12-passenger *Linda*, the 45-foot, 29-passenger *Gordo I*, the 65-foot, 40-passenger *Gordo II* and the 62-foot *Constellation's Gordo III*; the *Gordo III* is the company's only vessel with a galley. Trips usually leave around 7 am.

Whale-Watching

Between December and March, California gray whales pass through Bahía de Todos Santos on their way to southern Baja calving sites at Laguna Ojo de Liebre (Scammon's Lagoon), Laguna San Ignacio and Bahía Magdalena. Although Ensenada's deep-sea sportfishing fleet can't provide the same intimate experience as southern Baja skiffs in the lagoons, these trips are still a good opportunity to see whales swimming, breaching and diving between the port and the offshore Islas de Todos Santos, as well as to view pelicans, gulls, cormorants and other seabirds skimming the ocean's surface. Sea lions and harbor seals dot the buoys and guano-covered rocks in the harbor and around the islands.

The Museo de Ciencias de Ensenada's waterfront office (☎ (61) 78-71-92, fax (61) 78-63-35) arranges three- to four-hour whale-watching cruises (US$15) between Ensenada and the offshore islands with its own Spanish-speaking guide on local sportfishing vessels. The waterfront office is near Gordo's Sport Fishing, near the seafood market behind Sanborn's.

Language Courses

The Colegio de Idiomas de Ensenada (☎ (61) 76-01-09, (61) 76-65-87), Blvd JA Rodríguez 377, offers intensive Spanish instruction, as does the highly regarded Center of Languages & Latin American Studies (☎ (61) 78-60-00, cllas@ tnl-online.com), Avenida Riveroll 1287. For more details and their US contacts, see the Language Courses entry in the Facts for the Visitor chapter.

Special Events

Over 70 sporting, tourist and cultural events take place in Ensenada each year; the ones listed below are only a sample. Dates are subject to change, so contact one of the tourist offices or event organizers for specific details.

February
Variable dates – *Carnaval* (Carnival or Mardi Gras). Ensenada's biggest truly Mexican celebration

April
Midmonth – *Paseo Ciclista Rosarito-Ensenada*. Bicycle ride; for details, contact Bicycling West (☎ (619) 583-3001 in mainland California)

Midmonth – *Muestra Gastronómica* (Canirac Food Fair)

Late April – *Regata Newport Beach-Ensenada*. Yacht race

May
Midmonth – *Fiesta de los Viñedos en Flor*. Celebrates the beginning of the vintners' season; for details, contact the Asociación de Vitivincultores de Baja California (☎ (61) 74-08-36)

Midmonth – *Paseo Ciclista Tecate-Ensenada* (Tecate-Ensenada Bicycle Race). For more information, contact the Tecate offices of Secture or Canaco.

Midmonth – *Carrera de Relevos* (Tecate-Ensenada Relay Marathon). Competitors in this 66-mile (106-km) footrace consist of teams of five people, at least one of whom must belong to the opposite sex.

June
Early June – *Carrera Fuera de Carretera Baja 500*. Off-highway race

July
Midmonth – *Baja Open*. Beach volleyball tournament at El Faro Beach; for details, contact Ensenada Sports Promotions (☎ (61) 77-66-00)

August
1st or 2nd week – *Fiesta de la Vendimia* (Wine Harvest)

Midmonth – *Clásico de Verano Surf Fiesta*. Surfing competition at Playa San Miguel

September
Midmonth – *Feria Internacional del Pescado y del Marisco*. Seafood cooking competition judged by chefs from San Diego; for details, contact Canirac (☎ (61) 74-04-48)

Midmonth – *Fiestas Patrias*. Mexican independence days

Midmonth – *Annual Juan Hussong International Chili Cook-Off*. Takes place at Hotel Quintas Papagayo, north of town

Midmonth – *Paseo Ciclista de Otoño Rosarito-Ensenada*. Bike ride

Midmonth – *Muestra Gastronómica* (Food Fair)

October
Midmonth – *Aniversario de El Real del Castillo*. Anniversary of gold strike in the mountains east of Ensenada, with period costumes; takes place in the village itself, with music, dance and prizes for costumes

Midmonth – *Exposición Fiesta Viva*. A commercial event promoting Ensenada's economic development

November
Midmonth – *Tecate Baja SCORE 1000*. Baja's classic off-highway race from Ensenada to Cabo San Lucas; in theory, it now keeps to established routes instead of tearing up virgin desert

December
Midmonth – *Desfile Navideño Club Amigos de Ensenada* (Annual Christmas Parade)

Places to Stay
Although Ensenada has many hotels, demand can exceed supply at times – on weekends and in summer, reservations are advisable. Unless there's a special event, weekday accommodations are not a problem, but as in Playas de Rosarito, rates vary both seasonally and between weekdays and weekends, making it difficult to categorize hotels by price.

Don't expect to sleep at any motel on Avenida López Mateos on Friday or Saturday nights – it's the local cruising strip.

Places to Stay – budget
Camping At the southern end of central Ensenada, barely a block off Blvd Costero at the corner of Blvd Las Dunas and Sanginés, *Campo Playa RV Park* (☎ (61) 76-29-18) has dozens of small, grassy sites with shade trees for pitching a tent or parking a camper or motor home. Fees are US$10 for camping, US$12 with hookups, both including access to hot showers. Light sleepers should know that a new cantina has opened nearby with excellent live norteña music on weekends – but you may not want to hear it at 4 am.

Hotels & Motels Several cheap hotels dot a seedy area of Avenida Miramar just north of Avenida López Mateos, where rooms cost US$7 or even less, but don't expect to get much sleep among the rowdy bars and strip joints. A conspicuous placard at the *Hotel Perla del Pacífico* (☎ (61) 78-30-51), Avenida Miramar 229, warns guests that it will tolerate 'no bad behavior, no alcohol' – which may be an idea of what to expect. The *Hotel Río* (☎ (61) 78-37-33), Avenida Miramar 230, may be the best of this dubious bunch, but Avenida Macheros has similar accommodations.

Central Ensenada's best bargain is *Motel Caribe* (☎ (61) 78-34-81), Avenida López Mateos 628, which has singles/doubles with private bath as cheap as US$10/15 (these are across the street at Avenida López Mateos 627; rooms at the main building are better and slightly more expensive). *Hotel Anaya* (☎ (61) 78-27-21), Avenida Gastelum 127, is worth a look for US$15 single or double. Dark, gloomy and spartan but reasonably clean, *Hotel Plaza* (☎ (61) 78-27-15), Avenida López Mateos 540, costs about US$17/20 single/double. Rooms away from the street are much quieter.

A bit farther out Avenida López Mateos, two reasonable places are better bets for a good night's sleep. *Motel América* (☎ (61) 76-13-33), at Avenida López Mateos and Avenida Espinosa, south of the dry bed of the Arroyo de Ensenada, has clean, simple singles/doubles with kitchenette for US$18/20, though it's not anything special. Nearby, the older, slightly cheaper *Motel Coronado* (☎ (61) 76-14-16), at Avenida López Mateos 1275, resembles the América and has firm beds but lacks kitchenettes.

Places to Stay – middle

The renovated and upgraded *Days Inn Villa Fontana* (☎ (61) 78-38-37), Avenida López Mateos 1050, has a bar, coffee shop, swimming pool with sun deck, jacuzzi and parking. Comfortable rooms with full carpeting, air-con, cable TV and balcony cost from US$30/36. Weekend prices are 10% higher.

Popular *Hotel Bahía* (☎ (61) 78-21-03, fax (61) 78-14-55) covers an entire block on Avenida López Mateos and Blvd Costero between Avenidas Riveroll and Alvarado. Clean, carpeted singles/doubles with balcony, heater and small refrigerator start around US$31/42.

Modern, well-kept *Hotel del Valle* (☎ (61) 78-22-24), Avenida Riveroll 367 between Calle 3a and Calle 4a, is really a motel, with 21 carpeted singles/doubles

with cable TV for US$35/40. At Avenida Ruiz 379 at Calle 3a, the older *Hotel Ritz* (☎ (61) 74-05-01, fax (61) 78-32-62) is a remodeled downtown hostelry that's managed to retain some character; rates are US$35/45 for carpeted rooms with cable TV and telephone.

At Blvd Costero 1442, facing the harbor near the Riviera del Pacífico, the tile-roofed *Hotel Corona* (☎ (61) 76-09-01, fax (61) 76-40-23) has 100 rooms, all with balcony, color TV and air-conditioning, at US$38/46. The high-rise *Hotel Villa Marina* (☎ (61) 78-33-21, (61) 78-33-51), at the corner of Avenida López Mateos and Avenida Blancarte, offers a swimming pool and restaurant, as well as harbor views from many of its rooms. Doubles start at US$39 weekdays and off-season, but prices climb rapidly at other times.

Hotel Casa del Sol (☎ (61) 78-15-70), Avenida López Mateos 1001 at the corner of Avenida Blancarte, and *Hotel Cortez* (☎ (61) 78-23-07, fax (61) 78-39-04; (800) 303-2684 in the USA), Avenida López Mateos 1089 at the corner of Avenida Castillo, offer similar amenities. Rooms with air-conditioning, TV and pool access start at US$48/58 at the Casa del Sol; they're slightly less (about US$40) at the popular Cortez, which is often booked solid on summer weekends.

Hotel La Pinta (☎ (61) 76-26-01, fax (61) 76-36-88), at the corner of Blvd de Bucaneros and Avenida Riviera across from the post office, belongs to a variable but mostly mediocre chain of hotels on the peninsula. Singles/doubles cost US$40/45 weekdays, US$60/65 weekends; facilities include a swimming pool and restaurant.

Places to Stay – top end

Half a block from Hotel La Pinta at Avenida López Mateos 1534, *Hotel San Nicolás* (☎ (61) 76-19-01, fax (61) 76-49-30) caters mostly to groups and has a coffee shop, restaurant and swimming pool with a waterfall and Aztec-style decor. Singles/doubles start around US$52 plus IVA. Its US postal address is PO Box 437060, San Diego, CA 92143.

Hotel Santo Tomás (☎ (61) 78-15-03, fax (61) 78-15-04; (800) 303-2684 in the USA), conveniently central at Blvd Costero 609 between Avenidas Miramar and Macheros, charges around US$50/54 weekdays; weekend rates rise by about 10%. At Avenida López Mateos 993 across from the Days Inn Villa Fontana, *Hotel El Cid* (☎ (61) 78-24-01, fax (61) 78-36-71) offers singles/doubles from US$52/72; it has a swimming pool, an outstanding restaurant and a nightclub.

At Avenida Blancarte 130 near Avenida López Mateos, the *Travelodge Ensenada* (☎ (61) 78-16-01; (800) 255-3050 in the USA) has a swimming pool, jacuzzi, restaurant and bar – upon arrival, every guest receives one hour of free margaritas. For US$60, comfortable rooms with air-con, cable TV, shower bath and telephone are overpriced in comparison with its competition.

At the corner of Blvd Costero and Avenida Castillo, the 52-room, colonial-style *Hotel Misión Santa Isabel* (☎ (61) 78-36-16, fax (61) 78-33-45) features a restaurant, swimming pool and convention facilities. Rooms with telephone, TV and spotless bath cost US$60/65. Some travelers, however, have complained of cramped rooms here.

Probably the area's finest accommodations are at *Hotel Las Rosas* (☎ (61) 74-43-10, fax (61) 74-45-95), on an oceanside bluff at Km 105 of the Transpeninsular, 4 miles (6.5 km) north of Ensenada. All rooms have balcony, minibar, cable TV, cushy beds and telephones; there are also exercise rooms and a racquetball court. Singles/doubles start at US$115/132 plus 10% tax.

Places to Eat

As a popular tourist spot, Ensenada has eateries ranging from corner taco stands and basic restaurants offering antojitos to places featuring varied seafood, Chinese and sophisticated French cuisine.

At the *seafood market* just off Blvd Costero, near the sportfishing piers, try the deep-fried fish or shrimp tacos. *Plaza del Marisco*, on Blvd Costero across from the Pemex station, is a similar cluster of seafood taco stands of good quality. For carnitas (pork) or carne asada (beef) tacos, the all-night stand at the corner of Avenida Riveroll and Calle 11a, near the bus terminal, is very popular.

The Franco-Mexican chain *La Baguette*, near the corner of Avenida Blancarte and Blvd Costero, is a good spot to sample typical pan dulce (pastry), croissants or two-foot baguettes. One of Ensenada's largest and most popular bakeries is *Panificadora Bahía* (☎ (61) 78-19-66) at the corner of Calle 6a and Avenida Blancarte. Over three dozen types of pan dulce are baked here daily, as well as bolillos.

Modest *El Corralito* (☎ (61) 78-23-70), alongside the Motel Caribe annex at Avenida López Mateos 627, is a good breakfast spot, as is *Casa Blanca* (☎ (61) 74-03-16), Avenida Ruiz 254, which also offers decent fixed-price lunches for about US$2. *Mesón de Don Fernando*, on Avenida López Mateos at the corner of Avenida Alvarado, has comparable breakfasts; for lunch and dinner, it serves lobster tacos and burritos, plus several other seafood dishes.

Up the block from Hussong's Cantina, *Café El Portal* is a quiet sidewalk cafe at Avenida Ruiz 153, luring caffeine junkies with satisfying cappuccinos, mochas and lattes, along with tasty desserts, at north-of-the-border prices despite its largely Mexican clientele. It opens late, so don't expect to get your early morning fix here. *Pueblo Café Deli* (☎ (61) 78-80-55), Avenida Ruiz 96, has sophisticated ambiance, espresso and good snack food; hours are 8 am to midnight daily. *Sanborn's*, on Blvd Costero between Avenidas Miramar and Macheros, has a 24-hour coffee shop.

For marinated Mexican-style chicken, grilled or roasted over an open flame, try *Las Brasas* (☎ (61) 78-11-95), Avenida López Mateos 486 near Avenida Gastelum, or *Super Pollo* on Calle 2a at the corner of Avenida Macheros. At either place, a half (US$3) or whole (US$6) chicken comes with salsa, tortillas and condiments. Super Pollo serves greasy fries, but the tortillas are good.

Pizza is relatively uncommon in Ensenada, except for the chain restaurant *La Fábula* (☎ (61) 77-15-15), Avenida Balboa 169 near the movie theater. *La Cochinita* (☎ (61) 78-34-43), at the corner of Avenida Ryerson and Uribe, serves inexpensive, quasi-Japanese fast food.

Of Ensenada's dozen or more Chinese restaurants, *Muy Lam* (☎ (61) 76-11-18), Avenida Ejército Nacional 1001 at the corner of Diamante, and *China Land* (☎ (61) 78-66-44), Avenida Riveroll 1149, are established favorites.

La Palapa Bahía, alongside the Plaza del Marisco on Blvd Costero, is a moderately priced seafood restaurant. On the northern side of Blvd Costero near Avenida Alvarado, *Casamar* (☎ (61) 74-04-17) is a costlier alternative specializing in items like lobster salad, Filet Manila (a broiled fish fillet smothered in mango sauce), a variety of shrimp dishes, fried frogs' legs and octopus. At Avenida López Mateos 993, part of its namesake hotel, *El Cid* has first-rate seafood and excellent service at reasonable, though not inexpensive, prices.

Las Cazuelas (☎ (61) 76-10-44), on Sanginés opposite Campo Playa RV Park, has an appealing but expensive menu of seafood dishes like abalone and lobster. Prices for breakfasts and antojitos are more reasonable, but service can be erratic; there's lots of movement but not much gets done.

One of Baja's finest dining experiences, *El Rey Sol* (☎ (61) 78-17-33), Avenida López Mateos 1000, is an elegant and venerable but far from stodgy French-Mexican restaurant specializing in seafood, chicken and vegetable dishes, plus breakfast omelets. Full dinners can run US$20 or above, but selective diners can find equally appealing but lower-priced items; drinks are excellent and reasonably priced, the service attentive but unobtrusive.

Across the street from the Santo Tomás winery at the corner of Avenida Miramar and Calle 7a, *La Vieja Embotelladora* (☎ (61) 74-08-07) was never really a bottling plant, despite its name. Modernized

for upscale dining but with its huge wooden wine casks and other unique features intact, the cavernous building provides great atmosphere; the cheapest lunches or dinners cost about US$10, while lobster dishes run about US$25.

La Cueva de los Tigres (☎ (61) 76-64-50) is a popular seafood restaurant on Playa Hermosa about a mile south of the intersection of Avenida Reforma and Sanginés; a sign on the Transpeninsular points the way. An abalone-steak dinner costs upward of US$20 but is not a great value.

One mile (1.6 km) north of Ensenada on the Transpeninsular, *Hussong's El Pelícano Restaurant & Oyster Bar* (☎ (61) 74-45-75) serves seafood (including abalone) and reasonably priced Mexican combinations, and it's the only restaurant in town serving chili con carne – owner Juan Hussong organizes the annual International Chili Cook-Off. All meals include soup or salad, fresh vegetables and bread or tortillas.

Entertainment

Cinemas The *Cinemas Gemelos* (☎ (61) 76-36-16), at the corner of Avenidas López Mateos and Balboa, show recent Hollywood fare.

Theater Ensenada's *Teatro de la Ciudad* (☎ (61) 77-03-92), on Diamante between Avenidas Ciprés and Ejército Nacional, hosts plays, film cycles and other cultural events.

Bars & Cantinas Potent, tasty and inexpensive beer, margaritas and other liquors are prime attractions for gringos, especially those who have not yet reached the mainland California drinking age of 21. On weekends most bars and cantinas along Avenida Ruiz, which might more accurately be called 'Avenida Ruido' (Avenue Noise), are packed from early afternoon to early morning.

Thanks in part to bumper stickers and T-shirts widely disseminated on the Pacific coast, *Hussong's* (☎ (61) 78-32-10),

Avenida Ruiz 113, is probably the best-known cantina in the Californias – though its namesake beer now comes from Mazatlán. After arriving from Germany in the late 19th century, the Hussong family used their knowledge of traditional German brewing to establish one of Ensenada's first cantinas. Their early customers were miners and ranchers, now replaced by a more distinctly diverse crowd of college students, mariachi bands, tattooed bikers and retirees. Hours are between 10 am and 2 am, but tables and even spots at the bar are at a premium after midafternoon.

Nearby *Papas & Beer* (☎ (61) 74-01-45), at the corner of Avenidas López Mateos and Ruiz, caters mostly to college students on vacation; a small army of bouncers keeps things under control. Roaring music drowns out conversations, but the margaritas are sweet and fruity; hours are 10 am to 3 am.

Anthony's (☎ (61) 74-03-49), at the corner of Uribe and Avenida Miramar just north of Blvd Costero, is a rowdy place that attracts a broader clientele for retrograde disco-style music. *Pentágono*, at the corner of Blvd Costero and Avenida Alvarado, specializes in salsa music.

Bandido's, at the corner of Avenida Ruiz and Calle 2a, is an excellent norteña venue frequented mostly by Mexicans. Across the street, bands at *Club Mágico* rely on three chords and an attitude. *La Casita de Palo*, at the corner of Caracoles and Blvd Las Dunas, has great norteña music until the early hours on weekends.

Betting *LF Caliente Foreign Book* is directly behind the Plaza Cívica on the nameless waterfront street running parallel to Blvd Costero.

Things to Buy
Many items sold in Tijuana stores are available here at slightly lower prices (see the Tijuana Things to Buy entry), but the selection is smaller. Liquors and beers from all over Mexico are also available at discount prices. Wine prices are fairly reasonable because of the nearby wineries in the Guadalupe and Santo Tomás valleys – try the Boutique Domecq del Buen Vino (☎ (61) 78-37-25), Avenida Ruiz 149 between Hussong's Cantina and Café El Portal.

Stores along Avenida López Mateos overflow with colorful serapes, wrought-iron birdcages, silver jewelry (and cheap imitations), wood carvings, leather goods and other crafts from throughout Mexico; very few items actually come from Baja itself. Artesanías Los Castillo (☎ (61) 78-29-61), Avenida López Mateos 815, sells Taxco silverwork.

Galería de Pérez Meillon (☎ (61) 74-03-94), in the Centro Artesanal de Ensenada, Blvd Costero 1094, Local 39, sells first-rate indigenous pottery and other crafts from Baja California's Paipai, Kumiai and Cucupah peoples, as well as from the Tarahumara of mainland Mexico.

For quality surfing gear, try San Miguel Surf Shop in the Plaza Hussong mall on Avenida Ryerson.

Getting There & Away
Air The Sociedad Cooperativa de Producción Pesquera (☎ (61) 78-11-66), Avenida Ryerson 117, has information on flights to Isla Cedros, near the border between Baja California and Baja California Sur. These flights usually leave Tuesday and Friday mornings and cost US$65 one way, but tickets must be purchased from Aerocedros (☎ (61) 76-60-76) at the military Aeropuerto El Ciprés south of town. Cheaper and more frequent flights to Isla Cedros are available from Guerrero Negro (see the Desierto Central & Llano de Magdalena chapter).

Bus Ensenada's Central de Autobuses (☎ (61) 78-65-50) is at Avenida Riveroll 1075 at the corner of Calle 11a, 10 blocks north of Avenida López Mateos.

ABC (☎ (61) 78-66-80) is the main peninsular carrier, with numerous buses from Ensenada to Playas de Rosarito and Tijuana as well as points south:

Playas de Rosarito/Tijuana – 1½ hours, US$5; almost every hour from 5 am to 11 pm

Tecate – 1½ hours, US$6; at least five times daily

Mexicali – 3½ hours, US$11; at least four times daily

San Felipe – five hours, US$10; daily at 8 am and 6 pm

Loreto – 16 hours, US$30; five times daily from 10 am to 11 pm

La Paz – 23 hours, US$43; four times daily from 10 am to 11 pm

Note that Tijuana-bound buses drop Rosarito passengers at the tollgate rather than in Rosarito proper.

Between 6 am and 7 pm, Autotransportes Aragón (☎ (61) 78-85-21), Avenida Riveroll 861 at Calle 8a just south of the main bus terminal, goes hourly to Tijuana (US$5) and to San Quintín (US$7). Aragón also links up with Intercalifornias buses to Los Angeles (US$20) and several towns in mainland California's Central Valley.

Transportes Brisas (☎ (61) 78-38-88), at Calle 4a No 771, serves nearby rural destinations like Maneadero (US$2), El Sauzal and Ejido Uruapán.

Elite/Tres Estrellas de Oro (☎ (61) 78-67-70) and Transportes Norte de Sonora (☎ (61) 78-66-77) operate from the same counter at the bus terminal, with buses to mainland Mexican destinations like Guaymas (US$32), Mazatlán (US$54), Guadalajara (US$68) and Mexico City (US$79). Norte de Sonora fares on 2nd-class buses are up to 15% cheaper.

Getting Around
Car Rental Renting a car is much cheaper in Tijuana or in San Diego, even with additional daily charges for Mexican insurance, than it is in Ensenada. The only local agency is Fiesta Rent A Car (☎ (61) 76-33-44), Avenida Club Rotario s/n, Local 11.

Taxi Taxis are available 24 hours a day at several corner stands along Avenida López Mateos – one major stand is at the corner of Avenida Miramar.

AROUND ENSENADA
Islas de Todos Santos
Professional surfers frequent these two islands, about 12 miles (19 km) west of Ensenada, especially when winter storms bring towering surf to the smaller Isla Norte. (See the Tijuana-Ensenada Corridor map.) In early 1997 the islands hosted the Torneo Mundial de Surfing, the world surfing championships. A Japanese-sponsored mariculture project on the larger Isla Sur is cultivating abalone for the Asian market. While there's no scheduled transportation to the islands, it's possible to hire a launch; to do so, ask around the Ensenada sport-fishing piers.

Playa El Faro
Playa El Faro, about 2 miles (3 km) north of Estero Beach's turnoff on the Trans-peninsular (follow the signs), has the small *El Faro Beach Motel* (☎ (61) 77-46-30, fax (61) 77-46-20) as well as a *trailer park/campground*. The motel has eight clean, simple rooms with bath and shower for US$40, but proximity to the beach is its only attraction.

Camping is possible on a sandy lot next to the beach, with electricity, water, showers and toilets for US$12; sites without hookups cost US$7. The mailing address for both campground and motel is Apdo Postal 1008, Ensenada, Baja California 22800, México.

Estero Beach Resort
So sprawling that it issues its own map, Estero Beach Resort (☎ (61) 76-62-30, fax (61) 76-69-25) is a antiseptic gringo enclave immediately south of Playa El Faro, about 6 miles (10 km) south of Ensenada. It includes, besides a luxury hotel and RV park, tennis courts, a recreation hall and a restaurant; theoretically, this is Mexico, but *all* road signs are in English only. The resort's sole redeeming feature is the **Museo de la Naturaleza y de las Culturas Precolombinas** (☎ (61) 76-62-35), displaying quality replicas of ceramics and statuary from various Mexican

cultures, including Olmec, Maya, Aztec and Teotihuacán; it also contains a well-arranged seashell collection that, unfortunately, lacks any explanation of their biological or ecological context.

Estero Beach Resort charges US$12 to US$16 for RV sites for two people, plus US$3 for each extra person. Most sites have full hookups, with hot showers and clean toilets also available. Horses can be hired nearby.

Hotel doubles range from US$28 to US$72 off-season (mid-September through March) and rise to US$48 to US$82 the rest of the year. Suites run from US$110 to US$180. For information and reservations, write Apdo Postal 86, Ensenada, Baja California 22800, México.

San Diego's Southwest Sea Kayaks offers introductory weekend sea kayak classes here for US$125, including kayak rental; three-day courses cost US$200. For contact information, see the Outdoor Activities chapter.

Baja Beach Resort

About 10 miles (16 km) south of Ensenada and 1 mile (1.6 km) before La Jolla Beach Camp (see the La Bufadora entry, below), the Baja Beach Resort (☎ (615) 4-02-20; (800) 842-3118 toll free in southern California only) is a major hotel/resort complex with 100 hotel rooms, four tennis courts, two swimming pools, a marina, sailboat rentals, a charter fishing boat, two bars, a restaurant and a coffee shop.

Nonmembers pay US$40 for doubles weekdays, US$55 weekends. The US mailing address is PO Box 905, Chula Vista, CA 91912.

La Bufadora

Perhaps the single most overrated sight in all of Mexico, La Bufadora is a tidal blowhole that spews water and foam through a V-shaped notch in the headlands of the Punta Banda peninsula, but unless the sea is really rough, it hardly merits a detour from Ensenada or the Transpeninsular. Nevertheless, it remains the area's most popular weekend destination for tourists and locals alike.

La Bufadora has undergone recent improvements, however, so that the endless souvenir stands are tidier than before, there's regular trash collection and the public toilets (US$0.30) at the otherwise empty exhibition center (now boasting a small cactus garden) are clean enough to use without gagging. A less fortunate if understandable development is the array of Indian beggars at the approach to the souvenir stands.

BCN-23, the paved road to Punta Banda, leaves the Transpeninsular at Maneadero and passes several campgrounds and roadside stands that sell chile peppers and olives. Beyond the Baja Beach Resort are a few isolated campsites and, at the end of the road past a gaggle of taco stands and dozens of souvenir stalls, the unimpressive La Bufadora. Sandy lots sporadically collect US$1 for parking.

Diving Probably the best reason to visit the area, Dale Erwin's La Bufadora Dive Center (☎ (615) 3-20-92) offers underwater excursions to view sea anemones, sea urchins and other underwater life. The Canadian operator has three boats, two compressors, complete sets of diving gear and many wet suits for rent at reasonable prices. If the shop is closed, try contacting Erwin at his house behind the art gallery in the village of Cantú, 5 miles (8 km) east of La Bufadora. For more information, write La Bufadora Dive Center at Apdo Postal 102, Maneadero, Baja California 22790, México.

Places to Stay Camping at *Rancho La Bufadora*, with a view, outhouse access and use of a few fire rings, costs US$5 per night for two people. Bring water, which is trucked into the settlement from time to time. Electricity has recently been introduced. Local ejidos rent slightly cheaper sites above La Bufadora.

Most houses on the hill above belong to gringos who favor the spectacular view and inexpensive lot rents (from about US$50 per month). For further information about the lots and the campground, contact José León Toscano (☎ (61) 78-71-72) at Apdo Postal 300, Ensenada, Baja California 22800, México.

The other two main campgrounds on Punta Banda, *La Jolla Beach Camp* (US$6 per site) and next-door *Campo Villarino* (☎ (615) 4-20-45, (61) 76-42-46, fax (615) 4-20-44, (61) 76-13-09), US$10 per site, have attracted many permanent mobile-home residents. Villarino is markedly shadier, but both campgrounds have electricity, clean bathrooms with hot showers, and small grocery stores with canned goods, milk and purified water. Villarino's US postal address is PO Box 2746, Chula Vista, CA 91912.

Places to Eat Many *stalls* at La Bufadora serve fish tacos, shrimp cocktails and churros (deep-fried dough dipped in sugar). There are also seafood restaurants with lower prices and better ocean views than Ensenada. *Los Panchos* serves up specialties like mesquite-grilled fish, breaded shrimp, Pacific lobster and a savory 'Siete Mares' (Seven Seas) soup loaded with shrimp, octopus, fish, crab claws and other fresh seafood. It's open 9 am to sunset and is closed Thursday.

Near the entrance to Rancho La Bufadora is *Los Gordos*, where photographs, memorabilia and graffiti cover the walls and over 400 baseball caps hang from the rafters. Specialties include a Mexican combo, deep-fried calamari, lobster and shrimp in garlic butter. The bar is a favorite watering hole for US expatriates.

Restaurant La Bufadora, up the hill from Los Gordos, specializes in full lobster dinners but also serves fish dinners and lobster burritos.

Getting There & Away Transportes Brisas (☎ (61) 78-38-88), at Calle 4a No 771 in

Nuestra Señora de Guadalupe

Ensenada, offers regular bus service as far as Maneadero; supposedly another bus runs from the Ensenada terminal to Punta Banda every Sunday. Several Ensenada travel agencies offer package tours by van or bus on weekends, when tour buses pack the lots. Ensenada's Las Dunas Tours is the main perpetrator.

GUADALUPE
Settled by turn-of-the-century Russian immigrants, the village of Guadalupe is at Km 78 of México 3 (the Ensenada-Tecate highway), about 18 miles (29 km) northeast of the junction with the Transpeninsular. The village contains ruins of the Dominican **Misión Nuestra Señora de Guadalupe**, the last mission built in the Californias (founded 1834 and destroyed by Indians only six years later). Set in a fertile zone for grain farming and grazing, it was a powerful and important mission during its brief existence. There are Indian

pictographs on a huge granite boulder known as **Ojá Cuñúrr**, where the canyon of the Río Guadalupe narrows, but almost nothing remains of the mission.

The Russians, pacifist refugees from the area of present-day Turkey, first arrived in Los Angeles, but found the lands not to their liking and chose to head south across the border in 1905. They first lived in Indian dwellings known by their Kumiai name of *wa*, but soon built adobe houses that the Kumiai later emulated; the present museum is a Russian adobe. Across from the site of the former Dominican mission are the arches of the former Russian school, unfortunately demolished some years ago. The nearby Russian cemetery still contains headstones with Cyrillic inscriptions.

The surrounding valley is now one of Mexico's major vineyard regions, but grapes arrive at Domecq (the huge winery at the edge of town) from vineyards throughout thc peninsula. Both Domecq and nearby Vinícola LA Cetto are open for visits 9 am to 4 pm daily except Sunday, and their products are available at most liquor stores throughout the peninsula. In August the **Fiesta de La Vendimia** (wine harvest festival) takes place at several of the valley's wineries.

Museo Comunitario de Guadalupe

Only a handful of families of demonstrably Russian descent remain in the area, but INAH's Museo Comunitario documents community history with photographs and Russian artifacts like samovars, a Russian bible and traditional clothing. In addition to the interior exhibits, antique farming machinery decorates the museum grounds.

To reach the museum, follow the dirt road at the end of the paved lateral off México 3. Hours are 9 am to 4 pm Wednesday through Saturday, 9 am to 3 pm Sunday; admission is free.

Getting There & Away

Buses from Ensenada to Tecate will drop passengers at the paved lateral to the village on México 3.

PARQUE NACIONAL CONSTITUCIÓN DE 1857

In the Sierra de Juárez southeast of Ensenada and north of the highway to San Felipe, a striking plateau of ponderosa pines comprises most of Parque Nacional Constitución de 1857, a 12,000-acre (4800-hectare) park whose shallow and marshy but pleasant and solitary **Laguna Hanson** abounds with migratory birds – ducks, coots, grebes and many others – in autumn. Hunting is fortunately prohibited, so birdwatchers will find the park an exceptional destination at this time of the year. Check the dying pines for woodpeckers; anglers may hook catfish, bluegills and largemouth bass.

Lakeside camping, at about 4000 feet (1200 meters) elevation, is ideal except in winter. Because livestock is plentiful, the water is only suitable for dousing your campfire; bring your own. Fuel wood is scarce in the shoreline campgrounds but more abundant in the surrounding hills; dry and not-so-dry cow patties are an easily acquired addition in a pinch. Only pit toilets are available. Camp robbers like gray squirrels and even coyotes will abscond with any food left in the open, but the coyotes' howling at least seems to quiet the cattle. Expect hordes of mosquitoes in late spring.

The low granite outcrops north and west of Laguna Hanson offer stupendous views but require difficult ascents through dense brush and over and beneath massive rockfalls – watch for ticks and rattlesnakes. The easiest view route is to take the abandoned road northwest from near the ruined cabins and pit toilets to the first dry watercourse, and then follow it toward the peaks; expect dead ends that are too steep to climb, but follow tunnels through the rockfalls before emerging on a saddle below the two main peaks. This short climb, which should take only about an hour, is nevertheless very tiring.

Technical climbers will find challenging routes up the open granite despite the limited relief – most pitches do not exceed 200 to 300 feet (60 to 90 meters). The

LA FRONTERA

terrain resembles mainland California's Joshua Tree National Park.

On the eastern side of the park at the base of the Sierra de Juárez are several beautiful desert palm canyons, the most accessible of which is **Cañón Guadalupe**; for more information, see the Around Mexicali entry in the Desierto del Colorado chapter.

Getting There & Away

There is no public transport to the park; visitors must drive. Southeast of Ensenada at Km 39 on México 3 toward San Felipe, a paved lateral reaches the village of Ojos Negros, whose decent Restaurant Oasis has an English-speaking owner who's happy to provide tourist information. From Ojos Negros, a 27-mile (43-km) dirt road, passable for almost any passenger car despite its frequent washboard surface, climbs eastward onto the plateau and into the park.

Parque Nacional Constitución de 1857 is also accessible from México 3 by a steeper road just east of Km 55, about 10 miles (16 km) southeast of the Ojos Negros junction, and by dirt roads leading south from México 2 (the Tijuana-Tecate-

Mexicali highway). Drivers with low-clearance vehicles will undoubtedly prefer the Ojos Negros road, although the road from Km 55 should be passable for most, especially after the first 4.4 miles (7 km); the total distance is about 20 miles (32 km).

EL ALAMO & VALLE DE TRINIDAD

From Ojos Negros, México 3 continues south to a marked junction with a dirt road leading west to the once-bustling mining town of El Alamo. After the discovery of gold here in 1888, El Alamo boomed with thousands of gold-seekers, but the ore gave out quickly and it's now almost deserted.

From the junction, the highway leads south into the verdant Valle de Trinidad – a prosperous agricultural development and, in the late 19th century, a mining zone – before crossing the San Matías pass toward San Felipe. Just south of the junction, but 5 miles (8 km) east of the highway, is the site of the former **Misión Santa Catalina de los Paipais**, one of two Dominican missions in the peninsula's northern interior.

Founded in 1798, with a population over 600 at its peak in 1824, Santa Catalina de los Paipais was the Dominicans' largest mission but also one of the most precarious. Its altitude (about 3500 feet, or 1050 meters) and cool climate meant the mission was not agriculturally self-sufficient, and neophytes continued to collect wild foods, like piñon nuts, in the surrounding countryside. Indian hostility was widespread, and an uprising in 1840 destroyed the mission. Unfortunately, parts of the adobe walls are the only remaining ruins, on a hillock above the present village cemetery. An easily identifiable circular mound marks the remains of the mission watchtower.

Now known officially as Santa Catalina, the village is a sprawling hodgepodge of wrecked cars, a few adobe houses and trailers and abandoned greenhouses – remnants of a federal government scheme to raise jojoba. Competing Catholic and Pentecostal churches, both emphasizing the term *indígena* in their formal titles, compete for the souls of the remaining Paipai, who still speak their native language in addition to Spanish and continue to collect piñon nuts in the fall.

MANEADERO

The farm settlement of Maneadero, on the Transpeninsular about 10 miles (16 km) south of Ensenada and just beyond the turnoff to Punta Banda, contains little of note except a military guns-and-drugs checkpoint south of town that sporadically checks immigration papers; if yours are not in order, you'll have to return to Ensenada. Some travelers without proper ID have used *la mordida* (a bribe) to get past the police in the past, but the military are a different matter.

EJIDO URUAPÁN

On the eastern side of the Transpeninsular 10 miles (16 km) south of Maneadero, Ejido Uruapán (population about 650) is known for sea urchins, strawberries and quail – which draw hunters from north of the border. The sea-urchin processing plant, established with Japanese aid, exports countless *erizos* across the Pacific.

The Japanese have also built greenhouses for cultivating strawberries, mostly for export to California. The well-shaded and well-maintained *campground* at the junction with the Transpeninsular has brick barbecue pits and is a fine site for camping or picnicking.

SANTO TOMÁS

The Dominican mission village of Santo Tomás, 6½ miles (10.5 km) south of Ejido Uruapán, takes its name from the surrounding Valle de Santo Tomás, one of Baja's key wine-producing areas. Founded in 1791 as the last link in the chain connecting Alta and Baja California, **Misión Santo Tomás de Aquino** soon moved upstream from its original site to escape infestations of gnats and mosquitoes that made it both uncomfortable and unhealthy. Winter rains bring forth hordes of harmless toads, who stage Darwinian sprint trials across the Transpeninsular in reckless defiance of the thundering 18-wheelers passing north and south.

The wine industry is a legacy of the Dominicans, who planted thousands of vines and other fruit crops, most notably olives. At its peak, in 1824, neophytes may have exceeded 400 – more than today's population of 350. Abandoned in 1849, it was the last Dominican mission to maintain a priest. A few crumbling ruins of the original mission remain on an alluvial fan

Sea urchin

where the river canyon narrows west of the Transpeninsular, but only a few faint foundations denote the upstream site, just north of El Palomar's campground/RV park (see below).

For modern visitors, Santo Tomás' key institution is venerable **El Palomar**, a cluster of businesses including a general store, a restaurant, a motel, an RV park/campground and a picnic area at Km 51. El Palomar's *campground* sits among a grove of olive trees and bamboo; the olives are harvested, bottled and sold in the general store. In summer the park's two tennis courts, volleyball court, children's playground, swimming pool and 100 barbecue pits attract up to 2000 visitors daily, sometimes including rowdy and unpleasant groups of middle-aged off-roaders from southern mainland California. There are only 30 spaces with full RV hookups, at US$12.50 for two people.

On the slope behind the restaurant, *Motel El Palomar* (☎ (615) 3-80-02) offers clean, simple singles/doubles with hot water and heating starting at US$25.

Portions at El Palomar's *restaurant* are huge and prices fairly high, so some visitors may wish to share a platter. The specialty is lobster tacos, accompanied by small but potent margaritas, but other specials include breaded shrimp, rib steak, abalone chowder, beef tacos and cheese enchiladas.

For more basic but cheaper meals, try the *Mi Refugio* truckstop about half a mile (1 km) down the road, where passing truckers hang their personal coffee mugs on the wall.

EJIDO ERÉNDIRA & PUERTO SAN ISIDRO

Near the coast south of Santo Tomás, Ejido Eréndira is a small farm community where you can stock up on bread, milk, gasoline and other basic supplies for a beach trip to Puerto San Isidro, an appealing fishing cove.

Puerto San Isidro is home to *Castro's Fishing Place*, where Fernando Castro Ríos rents several rustic *cabañas* (cabins) next to

his home, facing the ocean, for US$25 per night; camping is free. Toilets are outside; refrigerator, sink, stove and six bunks are inside. Jorge Arballo leads all-day (7 am to 2 pm) fishing trips for US$25 per person. For more information, contact Fernando Castro Ríos (☎ (61) 76-28-97), Apdo Postal 974, Ensenada, Baja California 22800, México.

South of Puerto San Isidro via a dirt road, pretentiously named *Malibu Beach Sur* has an RV park offering camping, fishing and surfing; there are plans for an airstrip and a marina with launching facilities.

To reach Ejido Eréndira and Puerto San Isidro, take the paved lateral off the Transpeninsular about 10 miles (16 km) south of Santo Tomás (look for the 'Ejido Eréndira' sign) for about 6½ miles (10.5 km).

SAN VICENTE

The bustling agricultural community of San Vicente (population 3126), on its namesake arroyo 7 miles (11 km) south of the Ejido Eréndira junction, was the site of **Misión San Vicente Ferrer** (founded 1780), one of the few Dominican missions that never moved from its original site. In some ways, it was the most important of them both for its centrality – convenient to the other Pacific coast missions – and its strategic location, exposed to Indian attacks from the east. The largest and most heavily fortified Dominican mission, it never enjoyed the protection of more than 31 soldiers, but it controlled over 300 Indian neophytes.

These neophytes cultivated maize, wheat and beans and tended the mission's livestock, which numbered up to 750 cattle and 1150 sheep, plus horses, burros and goats. After Yuman Indians destroyed most of the mission, it closed in 1833, but for another 16 years the Mexican army maintained its garrison here. Substantial foundations and some walls of the fort and mission are still visible northwest of town, as is the stonelined *acequia* (irrigation canal); follow the dirt road west across from the *llantera* (tire repair shop) half a mile (1 km) north of town, near the northbound sign that says 'Santo Tomás 37, Ensenada 80.'

Information

English-speaking Henriqueta McFarland runs a state-sponsored tourist information post, conspicuously signed and with a decent selection of maps and brochures, at her house at Km 89 on the eastern side of the Transpeninsular – ring the bell at any reasonable hour.

San Vicente has a post office and Telnor long-distance service at the bus terminal. The postal code is 22900. Buses running between Ensenada and points south stop here.

Museo Comunitario

San Vicente boasts a new community museum, half a block west of the Transpeninsular on the northern side of the plaza. It contains the usual information on the missions as well as agricultural development – note the vintage machinery outside the building. Hours are 9 am to 3 pm weekdays; admission is free.

Places to Stay & Eat

Café Alexsy's (☎ (616) 5-66-76), at Km 90 on the eastern side of the Transpeninsular, has good, reasonably priced meals and rooms with shared baths and hot showers starting at US$6 per person. Very basic *Motel El Camino* (☎ (616) 5-66-11), at Km 91 at the southern edge of town, has spartan, unheated but fairly clean rooms, most with private bath (about US$15 to US$17), and a few doubles with shared bath (about US$10 to US$12).

COLONET

Colonet, a major farming community 23 miles (37 km) south of San Vicente, is a good place to replenish supplies and fill your gas tank or backpack if you're heading to the beach at San Antonio del Mar or inland to Rancho Meling and Parque Nacional Sierra San Pedro Mártir. There are no accommodations in the town itself, but *Nuevo Hotel Sonora*, north of town at Km 121, has basic singles/doubles for US$10. The beach at San Antonio del Mar, 4 miles (6.5 km) northwest, has good camping and clamming.

SAN TELMO & RANCHO MELING

The village of San Telmo is 4 miles (6.5 km) east of the Transpeninsular on the graded dirt road to Rancho Meling, Parque Nacional Sierra San Pedro Mártir, Picacho del Diablo and the observatory. A clinic operated by the Flying Samaritans (a team of volunteer doctors and nurses from California) operates in the village, which is subdivided into San Telmo de Abajo (lower San Telmo) and San Telmo de Arriba (upper San Telmo).

San Telmo's most notable cultural feature is the very faint remains of a **Dominican chapel**, built between 1798 and 1800; this was part of an *asistencia* (way station) under the jurisdiction of the mission at Santo Domingo near present-day Colonia Vicente Guerrero to the south. Look for its foundations behind a small, much newer chapel at the entrance to San Telmo de Arriba.

Rancho Meling (☎ (61) 76-98-85, (61) 77-62-23; (619) 758-2719 in mainland California), some 27 miles (43 km) east of San Telmo, is a Baja institution. After arriving from Norway in the early 1900s, Soren Meling and his family established the 10,000-acre (4000-hectare) ranch still

Yucca

run by their descendants, who also offer accommodations, meals, horseback riding and pack trips into Parque Nacional Sierra San Pedro Mártir. Rates are US$65/115 single/double with full board; for more details, contact Rancho Meling at Apdo Postal 1326, Ensenada, Baja California 22800, México, or PO Box 189003, No 73, Coronado, CA 92178.

PARQUE NACIONAL SIERRA SAN PEDRO MÁRTIR

Baja California's most notable national park comprises 236 sq miles (614 sq km) of coniferous forests and granitic peaks reaching above 10,000 feet (3000 meters), plus deep canyons leading down into their steep eastern scarp. Major native tree types include several species of pines, plus incense cedar, Douglas fir and quaking aspen, while the most conspicuous fauna includes raccoon, fox, coyote and mule deer. The rare desert bighorn sheep inhabits some remote canyon areas.

Unlike Parque Nacional Constitución de 1857, the park has no major bodies of water. Westward-flowing streams like the Río San Rafael, Arroyo Los Pinos and Arroyo San Antonio support the endemic San Pedro Mártir rainbow trout, but wildfowl no longer breed here, as they did a century ago, because of a history of grazing and timber cutting. On the plus side, the absence of north-of-the-border, Smokey-the-Bear fire suppression policies has meant the preservation of natural open meadows in some areas.

Among the typical breeding land birds are the mountain quail, pinyon jay, mountain chickadee, pygmy nuthatch, western bluebird, Cassin's finch, pine siskin, red crossbill and dark-eyed junco. The park is also a potential site for reintroduction of the endangered California condor.

To help protect and preserve the sierra's unique attributes from inappropriate development and recreation, as well as thoughtless fire suppression policies, Mexican scientists are hoping to obtain international biosphere reserve status for the park. For more information on the subject, contact Forests of the Californias/Bosques de las Californias, 482 W San Ysidro Blvd, Suite 250, San Diego, CA 92173-2410.

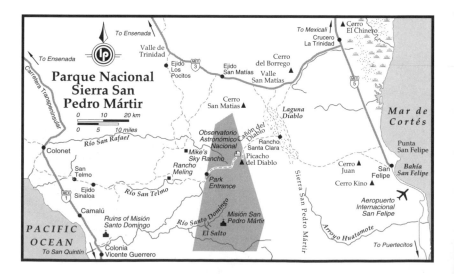

Climate

The Sierra San Pedro Mártir has a temperate climate similar to the mountains of southern mainland California; most precipitation falls in winter, when the snow depth at higher altitudes can be 3 feet (1 meter) or more, but the area also gets summer rainfall in the form of thunderstorms. The average annual temperature is around 59°F (16°C), with highs approaching 68°F (22°C), but winter temperatures can drop well below freezing. At higher elevations, even in summer, changeable weather is a potential hazard.

Things to See & Do

The Sierra San Pedro Mártir is an under-appreciated area for hiking, camping and backpacking, in part because access is awkward and it's a little far for weekend trips from mainland California. Still, for anyone seeking relief from overcrowded recreational areas north of the border, it's well worth exploring, especially in the spring, when snow keeps more northerly areas inaccessible.

Within the park are many suitable car camping areas and hiking trails, though trail maintenance is limited and hikers should carry a compass along with the usual cold- and wet-weather supplies, canteens and water purification tablets. Below about 6000 feet (1800 meters) or even a bit higher, beware of rattlesnakes. A detailed topographic map (see below) is essential.

The **Observatorio Astronómico Nacional**, Mexico's national observatory, features an 84-inch diameter telescope and a permanent staff of about a dozen. About 1¼ miles (2 km) from the locked gate at the parking area at the end of the public road from San Telmo, it's open to the public 11 am to 1 pm, Saturday only.

The 10,126-foot (3038-meter) summit of **Picacho del Diablo**, also known as Cerro Providencia, draws climbers from throughout the Californias, but only a handful actually reach the summit because route-finding is so difficult. Determined climbers should obtain the 2nd edition of

Walt Peterson's *The Baja Adventure Book*, which includes a good map and describes several routes up the peak.

An even better choice to carry is Centra Publications' *Parque Nacional San Pedro Mártir*, with an area map at a scale of 1:100,000 (5/8 inch=1 mile or 1 cm=1 km) and details at a scale of 1:31,680 (1 inch=1/2 mile or 1 km=3.2 cm).

Norman Clyde, perhaps the most famous mountaineer ever in mainland California's Sierra Nevada, wrote *El Picacho del Diablo, the Conquest of Lower California's Highest Peak, 1932 & 1937* (Dawson's Bookshop, Los Angeles, CA, 1975).

Getting There & Away

There is no public transport to Sierra San Pedro Mártir. Visitors will have to drive their own vehicles; high clearance and a short wheelbase are advisable, though 4WD is not essential.

To/From San Telmo From San Telmo de Abajo, south of Km 140 on the Transpeninsular, a graded dirt road climbs eastward through San Telmo de Arriba past Rancho Meling to the park entrance, about 50 miles (80 km) from the highway. Abounding with quail, rabbits, chipmunks and road-runners, the road is passable for most passenger vehicles despite two major fords of the Río San Telmo. Spring runoff may cause problems for cars with low clearance, and drivers should probably avoid the road immediately after a snowfall in the high country, when the warm sun can melt the snow very quickly.

To/From San Felipe The summit of Picacho del Diablo, visible from the desert floor near San Felipe, is snowbound from late October to early March. The rest of the year, it is reached via a difficult climb that begins in Cañón del Diablo (Devil's Canyon), accessed by a sandy road northwest of San Felipe. The road is reportedly safe and the surface mostly hard and dry, but ask for up-to-date information in San Felipe before attempting it.

Northwest of San Felipe, the road leads to Laguna Diablo, a usually dry salt lake, and Rancho Santa Clara, which marks the eastern approach to the park. From Rancho Santa Clara, follow tracks west of the dry lake bed, keeping Cañón del Diablo in sight.

An alternative route to Rancho Santa Clara is a good graded road that leaves México 3, the Ensenada-San Felipe highway, just east of Km 164; rather than going down the middle of Laguna Diablo, the road keeps to high ground along its eastern shoreline. A conspicuous roadside tire marks the turnoff to Rancho Santa Clara, which itself is marked by a similar tire.

About 1¼ miles (2 km) up the canyon, there's a striking waterfall. At about the 8-mile (13-km) point, you reach Campo Noche, a good campsite before starting an ascent the next day. For more details, consult *The Baja Adventure Book* (see above), the Mexican government topographic maps *San Rafael H11B45* and *Santa Cruz H11B55* and/or the Centra Publications map.

AROUND PARQUE NACIONAL SIERRA SAN PEDRO MÁRTIR
Mike's Sky Rancho
Thirty-seven miles (60 km) west along México 3 from the junction with Highway 5 is a 22-mile (35-km) road to Mike's Sky Rancho (☎ (66) 81-55-14 in Tijuana), situated in a small valley surrounded by the pine-covered foothills of the Sierra San Pedro Mártir. The graded dirt road makes it accessible to most passenger vehicles, but those seeking quiet and solitude should know that it's popular with fossil-fuel fanatics on motorcycles. At a few points, the road is steep and tricky for ordinary passenger cars.

The rancho offers worn but tidy motel-style rooms with kerosene stove and private bath, plain but hearty meals and a large swimming pool. Rooms cost around US$22 per person, breakfast and lunch US$6 each, dinner US$12, full board US$45. For more information, contact Mike's Sky Rancho at the number above or write PO Box 5376, San Ysidro, CA 92073.

Misión San Pedro Mártir
Founded in 1794 in the mountains east of San Quintín, Misión San Pedro Mártir de Verona was the most isolated Dominican mission. The initial site at Casilepe proved inadequate, wrote founder Fray Cayetano Pallás, when the crops froze. The new site at Ajantequedo, at an altitude of 5500 feet (1650 meters), was marginal but adequate for a neophyte population that never exceeded about 100.

Established as a possible link to *rancherías* (groups of Indians) on the Gulf and on the Río Colorado delta, the mission lasted only until 1824 because of its insecure location and the area's relatively small number of Indians. After its demise, San Pedro's neophytes relocated to Misión Santo Domingo. Ruins still exist and may be reached either from Rancho Santa Cruz or from La Grulla, north of the mission in Parque Nacional Sierra San Pedro Mártir.

COLONIA VICENTE GUERRERO
Colonia Vicente Guerrero is a booming agricultural center (population 9062) straddling the Transpeninsular, which is the town's main street. It now has a single traffic light, a bank and a casa de cambio, but has little else of interest to visitors except its shady plaza Parque General Vicente Guerrero, a small community museum and nearby Misión Santo Domingo. The long sandy beaches west of town, however, are well worth a visit; in the summer months, surf fishing is excellent.

The bus terminal is in the center of town on the Pacific side of the highway.

Misión Santo Domingo
Founded in 1775 by Manuel García and Miguel Hidalgo at the mouth of the canyon of the Río Santo Domingo, Misión Santo Domingo de la Frontera was the second of nine Dominican missions in Baja California; it soon moved to a verdant upstream confluence about 5 miles (8 km) east of the present-day Transpeninsular. At first the mission was chaotic and undisciplined, with many Indians deserting, but by 1796 more than 350 neophytes tended livestock

and harvested grain here. By 1839 measles and smallpox had wiped out most of them, and the mission was abandoned.

To reach the ruins, the best-preserved of any Dominican frontier mission, go east on the dirt road on the northern side of the Río Santo Domingo, at the northern entrance to town. Note the massive landmark **Peñón Colorado**, the reddish bluff that rises out of the sediments at the entrance to the canyon.

Though many walls are standing, the ruins are truly ruins; historian Peveril Meigs remarked in 1939 that the mission church then served as a pigpen. Parts of the system of irrigation canals from mission times are still in use, though, and the ruins are now fenced off from animals.

Every year in the first week of August at the site of the ruins, the **Fiesta de Santo Domingo** features horse racing, rodeos, dancing and food stalls. A short distance west of the ruins is a pleasant private park with a swimming pool and a cafe – a good spot for a picnic, accessible for a very modest admission.

Places to Stay & Eat

Colonia Vicente Guerrero has only two motels, but there are also two RV parks/campgrounds at the southwestern end of town. The turnoff for both campgrounds is at Km 176 on the western side of the highway just before the butane-gas station.

Mesón de Don Pepe RV Park & Restaurant (☎ (616) 6-22-16, fax (616) 6-22-68), which suffers from the noise of passing trucks on the highway, charges US$8.50 per night for RV sites with full hookups for two people, plus US$1 for each extra person; sites without hookups cost US$7. Tent campsites on a pleasant grassy area cost only US$5. Hot showers are available and the restaurant serves reasonably priced seafood and typical Mexican meals. Barbecued lamb is a weekend special.

Follow the dirt road on the southern side of Mesón de Don Pepe west to *Posada Don Diego RV Park* (☎ (616) 6-21-81); note that crafty Don Pepe built a conspicuous

entrance road to ensnare potential Don Diego customers. Proclaiming itself 'one of the finest RV parks in Baja,' Don Diego has spacious sites with full hookups for US$11, attracting southbound caravans. Only a few sites command shade, but there are also hot showers, a laundry room, a restaurant and a bar. The restaurant deserves a visit even for travelers with no intention of staying in town – it has outstanding antojitos and seafood, gigantic margaritas at moderate prices (perhaps a sneaky method of inducing diners to spend the night) and world-class flan for dessert.

Don Diego is closer to the beach, but the muddy road beyond the RV park can be difficult for ordinary passenger vehicles. Hiking to the beach, which offers great clamming (respect size limits), takes 30 to 45 minutes.

Conspicuously signed at Km 174 on the western side of the Transpeninsular, *Motel Sánchez* (☎ (616) 6-22-01) has large, fairly clean rooms for US$10/13 single/double. Also on the western side, at Km 170, *Motel Ortiz* has rooms with double bed and hot water for US$10; rooms with two beds cost US$17.

El Vaquero, a steakhouse at the northern end of town, is easy to miss at 50 mph (80 kph) because of its inconspicuous rustic decor. There are also numerous *taco stands* and a few *groceries*, such as Conasupo, selling fruit, vegetables, bread and other staples.

SAN QUINTÍN

San Quintín is the focus of an increasingly important agricultural region on the Llano de San Quintín (San Quintín Plain), but attractive Pacific beaches at the foot of a group of cinder cones also make it an ideal area for camping, clamming, beachcombing and fishing. Offshore Isla San Martín is part of the volcanic cordon that protects the plain from the ocean's erosive power. San Quintín's permanent population, including other communities straddling the Transpeninsular for about 12 miles (19 km) to the south, numbers upward of 20,000.

LA FRONTERA

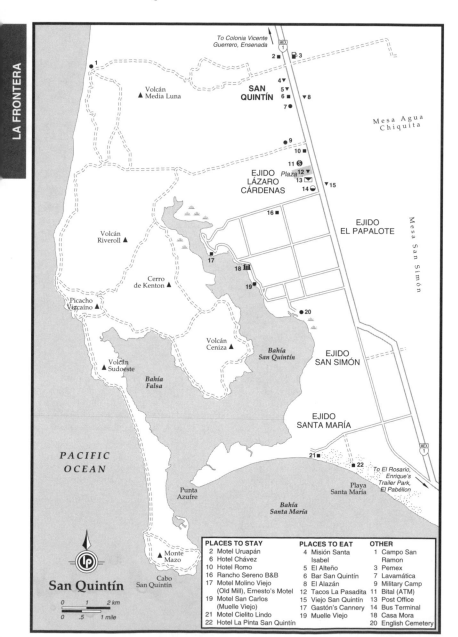

To Colonia Vicente
Guerrero, Ensenada

MEX 1

SAN
QUINTÍN

Volcán
▲ Media Luna

Mesa Agua
Chiquita

EJIDO
LÁZARO
CÁRDENAS

Plaza

EJIDO
EL PAPALOTE

Mesa San Simón

Volcán
Riveroll ▲

Cerro
de Kenton ▲

Picacho
Vizcaíno ▲

Volcán
Ceniza ▲

Bahía
San Quintín

EJIDO
SAN SIMÓN

Volcán
▲ Sudoeste

Bahía
Falsa

EJIDO
SANTA MARÍA

PACIFIC
OCEAN

To El Rosario,
Enrique's
Trailer Park,
El Pabéllon

MEX 1

Punta
Azufre

Playa
Santa María

Bahía
Santa María

▲ Monte
Mazo

Cabo
San Quintín

San Quintín

0   1   2 km
0   .5   1 mile

PLACES TO STAY
2 Motel Uruapán
6 Hotel Chávez
10 Hotel Romo
16 Rancho Sereno B&B
17 Motel Molino Viejo
   (Old Mill), Ernesto's Motel
19 Motel San Carlos
   (Muelle Viejo)
21 Motel Cielito Lindo
22 Hotel La Pinta San Quintín

PLACES TO EAT
4 Misión Santa
   Isabel
5 El Alteño
6 Bar San Quintín
8 El Alazán
12 Tacos La Pasadita
15 Viejo San Quintín
17 Gastón's Cannery
19 Muelle Viejo

OTHER
1 Campo San
   Ramon
3 Pemex
7 Lavamática
9 Military Camp
11 Bital (ATM)
13 Post Office
14 Bus Terminal
18 Casa Mora
20 English Cemetery

History

Several briny coastal lagoons near San Quintín provided salt for the nearby Dominican missions in colonial times; 19th-century Russian settlements north of San Francisco Bay (USA) also acquired their salt here. The Russians and Americans hunted sea otters nearly to extinction, bringing Northwest Indians and their canoes along for the venture.

In the late 19th century, San Quintín was the focus of settlement schemes by the English-based Mexican Land & Colonization Company, which bought the concession of the International Company of Mexico – a US-based corporation that had obtained land rights to most of northern Baja for a massive colonization effort during the Porfiriato. The International Company attracted few settlers, but the Land & Colonization Company introduced English colonists and established a steam-powered flour mill, a customs house, a pier, schoolhouses, fertilizer plants and, after a few years, a cemetery.

The company also laid about 19 miles (31 km) of track, hoping to link up with the Southern Pacific Railroad in San Diego, but insufficient rainfall prevented the sustained cultivation of the wheat they had hoped to market north of the border. Today, only the Molino Viejo (Old Mill), the Muelle Viejo (Old Pier) and the cemetery testify to the English presence.

High-tech irrigation has at least temporarily overcome some of the problems encountered by early colonists, but fields west of the Transpeninsular are suffering because growers have extracted so much fresh water that brackish seawater has contaminated the aquifers on which they rely. Cultivation has largely moved east of the highway, but some observers believe that this strategy may only provide a short reprieve for an unsustainable system.

Recent years have seen an influx of Mixtec Indians from impoverished rural Oaxaca, many of whom previously worked for mainland Sinaloa growers and labor contractors who have expanded operations into the San Quintín area. The 1995 intercensus recorded about 12,000 Mixtec speakers in the state of Baja California, but this figure may rise as high as 20,000 or more during the spring harvest. Some unscrupulous contractors pay these Indians, poorly educated and with large families, US$4 or less per day for harvesting tomatoes and other off-season crops for the US market.

In addition to these wages, low even by Mexican standards, farm laborers suffer serious health problems because local agriculture relies heavily on chemical fertilizers and pesticides, with almost no protective equipment or instruction for those who apply them. Angus Wright's *The Death of Ramón González* deals with the theme of pesticide poisoning in a different part of Mexico.

Groups from north of the border occasionally offer health clinics in the area, but their efforts are largely ineffectual because itinerant workers following the harvest do not receive regular medical attention for their ailments.

Orientation

San Quintín sits on a sheltered harbor 116 miles (187 km) south of Ensenada on the Transpeninsular. The name San Quintín commonly refers to an area that includes not only San Quintín proper but also ejidos to the south – Lázaro Cárdenas, San Simón and Santa María. San Quintín and Lázaro Cárdenas stretch out along the Transpeninsular for about 3 miles (5 km), while the hamlet of San Simón is about 4 miles (6.5 km) south of Lázaro Cárdenas and adjacent to the highway. Santa María, a farming area west of the Transpeninsular, surrounds Hotel La Pinta San Quintín and Motel Cielito Lindo.

Because there aren't any named streets except for the highway and no street addresses whatsoever, it can be difficult to actually find anything in the San Quintín area – refer to the map, but trust your own eyes as well. Because San Quintín is so spread out, it's much better to drive than to rely on public transportation – off the highway, transportation is negligible. The best beaches are south near Santa María and north toward Colonia Vicente Guerrero.

Information

Between Colonia Vicente Guerrero and San Quintín at approximately Km 178, the local Promotora Turística de San Quintín (☎ (616) 6-24-98) has built a sparkling new tourist office in cooperation with Secture and stocked it with a wealth of printed material, but it might be an exaggeration to say they've actually *opened* it. Theoretically, hours are 8 am to 7 pm daily.

Opposite the plaza in Lázaro Cárdenas, half a block off the highway, Bital cashes traveler's checks with no commission and has a convenient ATM.

There's a post office (postal code 22930) in Lázaro Cárdenas, as well as pharmacies, Pemex stations and groceries along the Transpeninsular in both Lázaro Cárdenas and San Quintín. Check the pharmacies for phone and fax services. If your clothes are dirty, there's a Lavamática in San Quintín on the western side of the highway.

Dangers & Annoyances There have been an increasing number of vehicle break-ins and the occasional robbery in the San Quintín area; especially vulnerable are those camping in remote areas. It's not cause for paranoia, but visitors should take precautions.

Things to See

San Quintín's most interesting cultural landmarks are the remains of the early English settlement. The **Molino Viejo** has undergone substantial renovation and now features a restaurant that's the center of local nightlife, a good hotel and an attractive waterfront area for hanging out.

Midway between the Molino Viejo and the old pier, the wood-framed **Casa Mora** is the only remaining residence from the English period. An Ensenada businessman moved it from a site near the Molino Viejo a few years back, saving it from demolition, but hasn't yet followed up on plans to make it a museum.

Pilings alone now remain of the **Muelle Viejo**, but it's a good place to watch wildlife, particularly the tens of thousands of Brant geese that winter on and around Bahía San Quintín. The motel restaurant here has good bay views.

At the **English Cemetery** south of the Muelle Viejo, the single identifiably English headstone is a recent construction memorializing Francis Barthemelon Henslowe of Wermigley, Norfolk and Santa María, who died July 24, 1896.

Beaches

Activities in the region center around the beaches and the ocean; the best easily accessible beaches are near Hotel La Pinta San Quintín in the Santa María area. Some people drive onto the beaches at low tide, a very bad idea not just because it tears up the beaches and disturbs other people, but also because the tide rises very quickly and can strand unsuspecting drivers, at least temporarily. Saltwater doesn't do car bodies any favors either.

Fishing

Fishing licenses are necessary for both clamming and fishing; the tourist office and sportfishing guides are both authorized to issue them to anyone over 16 years of age. Do not take undersized clams (those smaller than your hand) or you'll risk a hefty fine.

Daily rates for fishing, including guide and *panga* (skiff), start at around US$150 for up to three people. The day starts early, around 6 or 6:30 am, and ends before 2 pm because the winds make the water too choppy after this hour. Surf fishing is also a favorite here.

The main fishing operators are Tiburón's Pangas (☎ /fax (616) 5-27-68, (61) 71-47-30) at the Molino Viejo complex and Ron and Judy Baker's San Quintín Sportfishing (☎ (619) 222-8955 in mainland California, (619) 593-2252 voicemail only), based at Motel Cielito Lindo. The latter's mailing address is Apdo Postal 7, Cielito Lindo, San Quintín, Baja California 22930, México.

The following list indicates which fish are most common each month in the vicinity of San Quintín:

January – cabrilla, corvina, white sea bass
February – corvina, white sea bass
March – cabrilla, corvina, white sea bass
April – cabrilla, corvina, sea trout, white sea bass
May – cabrilla, corvina, sea trout, sierra
June – cabrilla, corvina, croaker, grouper, sea trout, sierra
July – cabrilla, corvina, croaker, grouper, sea trout, sierra
August – cabrilla, corvina, croaker, grouper, sea trout, sierra
September – cabrilla, corvina, grouper, sea trout, sierra
October – cabrilla, grouper, sea trout
November – white sea bass
December – white sea bass

Surfing
Surfers will find good breaks at the southern end of Cabo San Quintín, southwest of town, but getting there presents a problem without a 4WD vehicle or a boat.

Places to Stay
The cheapest lodgings are right on the Transpeninsular, but heavy truck and car traffic makes them the noisiest as well. If you're planning to stay at any place off the main highway, try to arrive in daylight because the maze of dirt roads west of the Transpeninsular is poorly signed and difficult to negotiate in the dark. The exception is the paved road to Hotel La Pinta San Quintín and Motel Cielito Lindo.

Camping Free camping is feasible at the beach near *Hotel La Pinta San Quintín*, but stay well above the water line. Formal campsites with pleasant *palapas* (palm-leaf shelters) – tents, vans and pickups only – and access to hot showers are available at *Motel Cielito Lindo* (see below) for US$5. *Motel San Carlos* (see below) has eight modest but shady campsites with fireplaces, hot showers and toilets for US$8 per night. *Motel Molino Viejo* (see also below) charges US$11 per site without

hookups, US$16 with hookups; it's hooked into the local grid for reliable electricity, but it's still windy, barren and close to breeding skeeters in summer.

About 10 miles (16 km) south of San Quintín and half a mile (1 km) west of the Transpeninsular, beachfront *Enrique's RV Park* and adjacent *El Pabellón* both have basic facilities for tents and RVs for US$5 per night. Backpackers without vehicles have complained about the shortage of nearby supplies, but a grocery that is only about a 20-minute walk away has just opened, and clamming and surf fishing are superb.

Hotels & Motels Several travelers have applauded the economical *Hotel Romo* (☎ (616) 5-23-98), on the highway just south of the Mexican Army's 67th Batallón de Infantería, which has bargain singles for US$9. Basic *Motel Uruapán* (☎ (616) 5 20 58), at Km 190, is a bed and a roof over your head, with hot water and overhead fans; singles/doubles cost just US$9/11.

Rooms at the well-kept *Hotel Chávez* (☎ (616) 5-20-05), at Km 194 just before the bridge, have tiled shower with hot water, filtered drinking water and, in some units, full kitchen with utensils and cookware; singles/doubles starting at US$17 are an excellent value.

Perhaps the most unique choice is Susie Atkinson's *Rancho Sereno* (☎ (61) 71-44-75), an American-run B&B on 11 quiet, wooded acres between the Transpeninsular and Bahía San Quintín; take the signed turnoff at Km 196 opposite the Policía Federal de Caminos. Reservations are preferable for the three available rooms, which range from US$50 to US$65 for doubles, but she can sometimes handle drop-in guests. Rates include a pitcher of margaritas on arrival, a large American-style breakfast with local touches, most notably homemade tortillas, and use of a spacious recreation room. The US contact is Marcía Beltrán (☎ (909) 982-7087), 1442 Hildita Ct, Upland, CA 91786.

Signs on the Transpeninsular also point to the upgraded *Motel Molino Viejo* (☎ (61) 71-33-53, (616) 1-33-53 cellular in Mexico, fax (616) 5-33-76), on the site of the former flour mill 3 miles (5 km) west of the highway. Some of the old machinery still remains, while the motel has several attractive rooms, a few with kitchenette, starting about US$32/38, ranging up to US$90 for comfortable two-bedroom suites sleeping four people. Its US representative is Baja Outfitter (☎ (619) 428-2779, (800) 479-7962, fax (619) 428-6269), 223 Via de San Ysidro, Suite 2, San Ysidro, CA 92173.

Just north of the Molino Viejo, basic *Ernesto's Motel* caters almost exclusively to hunters who come to blow away Brant geese in winter. Neither appealing nor welcoming, it costs about US$20 per night but gives discounts for longer stays.

Southwest of town in Ejido El Papalote, a wooden sign on the Transpeninsular points to a dirt road that crosses a field for about 1¼ miles (2 km) to friendly *Motel San Carlos* (no phone) on Bahía San Quintín, part of the Muelle Viejo complex just north of the English cemetery and about 1¼ miles (2 km) southeast of Motel Molino Viejo. Simple rooms, each with bathroom, hot shower and bay views, start around US$20 single/double. Its mailing address is Apdo Postal 111, Bahía San Quintín 22930, Baja California, México.

Presently undergoing badly needed repairs, *Hotel La Pinta San Quintín* (☎ (616) 5-28-78), south of town in Ejido Santa María, falls short of the standards of its sister hotels, but its beachfront location is suitable for clamming, surf fishing and other beach activities. Each room has two double beds and a shower/bath, plus balconies facing a wide sandy beach. Rates are about US$55/60 single/double. In the USA contact La Pinta Hotels (☎ (800) 336-5454) or write PO Box 120637, Chula Vista, CA 91912, for information and reservations.

Motel Cielito Lindo, south of town near Hotel La Pinta San Quintín, occupies attractive grounds near the beach, offering rooms with two queen-size beds each and a shower/bath for US$35 single/double; it also has a bar, a restaurant and a taco stand.

Places to Eat

Tacos La Pasadita, a popular stand at the northeastern corner of Lázaro Cárdenas' plaza, on the western side of the Transpeninsular, has exceptional fish tacos. It closes whenever the proprietor runs out of fish, so get there early. Across from the plaza, try *Viejo San Quintín* for a more substantial meal.

Bar San Quintín, alongside Hotel Chávez in San Quintín proper, has good breakfasts, but the service can be sluggish. *El Alteño*, just to the north, is an excellent seafood restaurant with specials for all budgets. *El Alazán*, across the highway, is a highly regarded steakhouse. North of Hotel Chávez, *Misión Santa Isabel* (☎ (616) 5-23-09) has a good reputation for steak and seafood.

Gastón's Cannery, at the Molino Viejo, is the area's most expensive restaurant. You're paying for the atmosphere of a adapted sardine cannery as much as for the food, but good live entertainment in the bar is a plus. The *Muelle Viejo*, part of Motel San Carlos, offers good lunches and dinners at moderate to expensive prices, with good bay views.

Getting There & Away

The long-distance bus terminal (☎ (616) 5-30-50) is in Lázaro Cárdenas on the western side of the Transpeninsular, half a mile (1 km) south of the plaza. ABC, Autotransportes Aragón and Autotransportes Aguila keep somewhat erratic schedules but run direct buses from San Quintín to the following locations:

El Rosario – one hour, US$2; at least three times daily
Ensenada – two hours, US$6.50; hourly from 6 am to 7 pm
Tijuana – 3½ hours, US$11; hourly from 6 am to 7 pm
Guerrero Negro – six hours, US$12; at least three times daily
Mexicali – six hours, US$16; at least twice daily

San Ignacio – 7½ hours, US$16; at least three times daily

Santa Rosalía – nine hours, US$18; at least three times daily

Mulegé – 10 hours, US$21; at least three times daily

Loreto – 12 hours, US$26; at least three times daily

Ciudad Constitución – 15 hours, US$32; at least three times daily

La Paz – 18 hours, US$36; at least three times daily

Getting Around

Transportes Ejidales vans regularly shuttle between San Quintín and Camalú to the north and between San Quintín and Santa María to the south; you can flag down the vans anywhere en route. Their primary clientele is farm workers; an average trip costs about US$0.50.

EL ROSARIO

El Rosario marks the southern border of the Dominican mission frontier; known in pre-Spanish times as the Cochimí Indian ranchería of Viñadaco, it was officially founded in 1774 as Misión Nuestra Señora del Rosario Viñadaco. An abundant water supply permitted cultivation of wheat, corn and deciduous fruit, including almonds and peaches, while missionaries also directed the harvesting of lobster, abalone and clams. After relocating once when the major spring dried up, the mission closed in 1832 because epidemics had so ravaged the Cochimí population that no laborers remained for the mission fields.

After the mission closed, El Rosario was the seat of military government for northern Baja but remained thinly populated until the late 1840s, when retired soldier Carlos Espinosa received a grant of 4000 acres (1600 hectares) from Governor José Castro. The Espinosa family is still prominent in the area.

Orientation & Information

El Rosario, about 36 miles (58 km) south of San Quintín, consists of two parts: Rosario de Arriba (population 1809), along the Transpeninsular north of the Arroyo de Rosario, and Rosario de Abajo (population 386), 1½ miles (2.5 km) downstream. The few tourist services are in Rosario de Arriba, except for Rosario de Abajo's large billiard hall, which is about the only entertainment in town.

El Rosario's postal code is 22960.

Museo

El Rosario's nameless museum, on the southern side of the highway, is a disorganized collection of objects of little antiquity and even less interest, but it's been spiffed up a bit recently. If it's not open and you really want to see it, ask for the key at Casa Espinosa (see Places to Stay & Eat, below).

Misión Nuestra Señora del Rosario

Only limited remains of the mission's two sites are still standing. The initial mission site is at the end of a short dirt road above the highway, about 150 yards (137 meters) west of Motel Sinai, but only the outlines of the foundations are still visible. At Rosario de Abajo, across the Río del Rosario, several standing walls make up the ruins of the later mission.

Places to Stay & Eat

Next to the Pemex station at the northern end of town, *Motel Rosario* (☎ (616) 5-88-50) is a low building with a satellite dish in front. Rooms with double beds, costing only US$10, are clean but very basic and plain. At Km 56.5 at the eastern end of town, the newer *Motel Sinai* (☎ (616) 5-88-18) has singles/doubles for US$22, plus an RV park that charges US$10 for full-size RVs and US$7 for smaller vehicles. Electricity and water are available, and campers may use the shower in the motel office, but only a rustic pit toilet is available. The laundromat next door is now part of the motel and can wash clothes for guests or campers.

With the completion of the Transpeninsular in late 1973, *Casa Espinosa*, between the two motels, became a favorite stop for a variety of travelers. In the early days of Baja road races, celebrities like Steve McQueen, James Garner and Parnelli Jones sampled Doña Anita Espinosa's lobster burritos here. Elderly Doña Anita no longer actively participates in its daily operations, but the restaurant has modernized and expanded into souvenirs and accommodations, offering very clean and pleasant rooms with two beds for US$20.

Yiyo's, at the eastern end of town beyond Motel Sinai, has palatable breakfasts. *El Grullense*, at the bus terminal, serves basic cheap antojitos. There are also several good *taco stands*.

Getting There & Away

Buses stop at El Rosario's terminal on a schedule similar to that of San Quintín's terminal (see above). Southbound buses depart about an hour later than those leaving San Quintín; northbound buses depart about an hour earlier.

AROUND EL ROSARIO
Punta Baja

At the end of a good but sometimes rough road that leads west 10½ miles (17 km) from El Rosario, the fish camp of Punta Baja also attracts surfers and sea kayakers to a good right-point break in the winter, but no tourist services are available.

From the hill overlooking the camp, arriving tourists and local goatherds can see the five volcanoes of the San Quintín area to the north, as well as the camp's satellite dish and school basketball courts.

Punta San Carlos

Some 46 miles (74 km) south of El Rosario by a series of decent graded and not-so-decent dirt roads, Punta San Carlos is one of the best windsurfing spots on the Pacific side of the peninsula.

Desierto del Colorado

At the foot of the Sierra de Juárez and the Sierra San Pedro Mártir, the lowlands of the Río Colorado delta and the region south to the Gulf port of San Felipe are, at least in summer, a roaring furnace where temperatures often exceed 110°F (45°C). Initially slow to be settled by Europeans, the agricultural Valle de Mexicali area grew rapidly in the 20th century as irrigation allowed farmers to take advantage of rich soils and a long, productive growing season.

San Felipe's beaches and sportfishing draw more visitors than any other regional attraction, but the eastern canyons of the sierras attract increasing numbers of campers and hikers. South of San Felipe, the village of Puertecitos is the starting point for a rugged but rewarding alternative southbound connection to the Transpeninsular for drivers, motorcyclists and even cyclists. Odds are that this route will be paved in the next few years.

MEXICALI

Bustling Mexicali (official population 505,016), capital of the state of Baja California and also the northwestern terminus of Mexico's passenger rail system, is a prosperous agricultural and industrial center that relies on Río Colorado irrigation water to grow vegetables, wheat and cotton in the delta's silt-laden soil.

Of all Mexico's northern border cities, Mexicali most impressively dwarfs its US counterpart, with a population at least 10 times that of neighboring Calexico and the Imperial Valley. Making an enormous economic contribution to the US border cities, at least three times as many Mexicans cross the line into mainland California than do foreigners southbound into Baja – it's a popular saying that when Mexicali gets a cold, Calexico gets pneumonia. Many visitors pass through Mexicali on their way south to San Felipe or east to Sonora and mainland Mexico, but only a handful stop for more than gasoline, cheap liquor, brief shopping sprees or visits to tawdry bars.

However, Mexicali, like Tijuana, is shedding its stereotypical border-town image; in the southern part of the city, the Centro Cívico-Comercial (Civic & Commercial Center) includes local, state and federal government offices, a medical school, a bullring, cinemas, a bus terminal, hospitals and restaurants. Mexicali, unlike San Felipe or Cabo San Lucas, is reluctant to pander to tourists and is thus all the more interesting; its historic core along the border makes for a rewarding excursion that reveals as much about mainland California as it does about Baja.

History

In pre-Columbian times, relatively dense populations of sedentary Yuman farmers inhabited the Río Colorado delta, an area that the early Spaniards failed to colonize because of its remoteness, hostile climate and determined peoples who resented missionary intrusions. Conditions changed in the early 20th century, when entrepreneurs from north of the border realized the agricultural potential of the deep river-borne sediments, if only they could be irrigated.

Events north of the border both contributed to and detracted from Mexicali's development. Since the mid-19th century, ambitious speculators and their engineers had sought to convey water from the Colorado to the Imperial Valley in California, but the sprawling Algodones Dunes were an insuperable obstacle with the available technology. Charles Rockwood's California Development Company circumvented this problem by diverting water from the Colorado's main channel into its westward-flowing Alamo channel, south of the border, and hence to the Imperial Valley. In return for permission to cross Mexican territory, Rockwood promised Mexico half the diverted water.

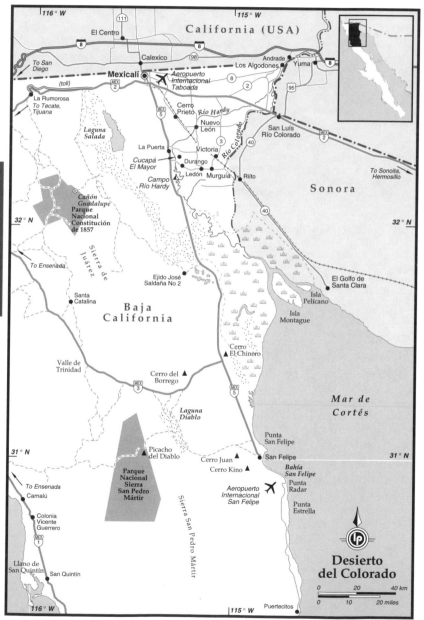

Desierto del Colorado

0   20   40 km

0   10   20 miles

With completion of the Alamo Canal in 1902, the site known as Laguna del Alamo began to prosper and the following year was formally founded as the city of Mexicali. In succeeding years, however, floodwaters silted up the canal's Hanlon Headgate and several bypasses near Andrade in mainland California, so the company excavated a newer, more direct channel between the river and the canal. It did not, however, build a headgate that could accommodate the major floods of 1905. These floods poured water into the dry channel of the Río Nuevo for months, obliterating parts of the fledgling settlement of Mexicali as it swept north into mainland California's Salton Sink – which soon became the Salton Sea. Not until early 1907 did massive efforts by the Southern Pacific Railroad, which acquired the California Development Company shortly after the 1905 fiasco, succeed in returning the Colorado to its main channel.

After this reprieve Mexicali rebounded, only to falter and then benefit from the Revolution of 1910, when it was briefly occupied by anarchist Magonistas. The Mexican government grew alarmed at the Magonistas' internationalist membership and at agricultural developments north of the border – especially since Mexico had lost so much territory by the 1848 Treaty of Guadalupe Hidalgo. In 1915 these concerns led Colonel Estéban Cantú, a military political appointee, to relocate the territorial capital from Ensenada to Mexicali, though he governed more or less independently of either the revolutionaries or the established government. In 1952 Mexicali became capital of the new state of Baja California.

In Mexicali's early decades, nearly all the land was under control of the Colorado River Land Company, a US concern that engaged in large-scale cotton cultivation with imported Chinese laborers, who were later replaced by Mexicans from the mainland states. In the 1920s US Prohibition fostered drinking, gambling and prostitution south of the border.

In 1937, after the famous 'Asalto a las Tierras' (Assault on the Lands) by laborers in the Mexicali valley, the government of President Lázaro Cárdenas forced the Colorado River Land Company to sell most of its land to Mexican farmers and *ejidos* (peasant cooperatives). Around the same time, however, the Colorado River Compact among the US states in the great river's watershed led to the construction of the All-American Canal, north of the border, which bypassed Mexico and reduced the amount of water available to Mexican growers.

The company's imprint on the cityscape is still apparent – its historic headquarters is now an office building, while the open spaces along the railway line, now giving way to shopping malls, are reminders of the numerous cotton mills that employed many city residents.

In 1947 the Ferrocarril Sonora-Baja California linked Mexicali to mainland Mexico via the rail junction of Benjamín Hill (Sonora); highways and airline and communication links followed in short order. The city enjoys excellent cultural and educational facilities, thanks largely to institutions of higher education like the Universidad Autónoma de Baja California, the Universidad Pedagógica Nacional, the Instituto Tecnológico Regional and the Centro de Enseñanza Técnica y Superior.

Orientation
On the eastern bank of the intermittent Río Nuevo, most of Mexicali's main streets run east-west, paralleling the border. From Mexican Customs & Immigration, Avenida Francisco Madero heads east past Parque Niños Héroes de Chapultepec, running through Mexicali's central business district of modest restaurants, stores, bars and budget hotels. The other streets that run parallel to Avenida Madero are also key shopping areas; better hotels and restaurants begin to appear a few blocks east of the border crossing. The largely residential area west of the Río Nuevo is known as Pueblo Nuevo.

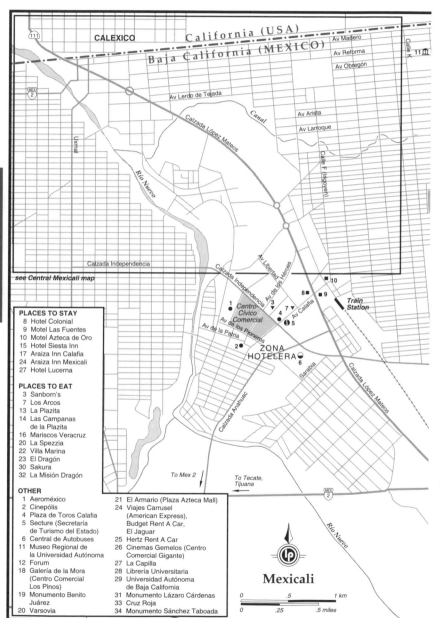

DESIERTO DEL COLORADO

CALEXICO

California (USA)
Baja California (MEXICO)

Av Madero
Av Reforma
Av Obregón

Av Lerdo de Tejada

Canal

Av Arista
Av Lartoque

Calzada López Mateos

Río Nuevo

Uxmal

Calle F (Ingoyen)

Calle K
11

Calzada Independencia

see Central Mexicali map

Calzada Independencia

Av Libertad

Av de los Heroes

Train
Station

8
10
9

1 Centro
Cívico
Comercial

Av de los Pioneros

Av Calafia
3
7
4
5

2

Av de la Patria

ZONA
HOTELERA
6

Calzada Anahuac

Sarabia

Calzada López Mateos

To Mex 2

To Tecate,
Tijuana

Río Nuevo

MEX 2

Mexicali

0   .5   1 km
0   .25   .5 miles

PLACES TO STAY
8 Hotel Colonial
9 Motel Las Fuentes
10 Motel Azteca de Oro
15 Hotel Siesta Inn
17 Araiza Inn Calafia
24 Araiza Inn Mexicali
27 Hotel Lucerna

PLACES TO EAT
3 Sanborn's
7 Los Arcos
13 La Plazita
14 Las Campanas
   de la Plazita
16 Mariscos Veracruz
20 La Spezzia
22 Villa Marina
23 El Dragón
30 Sakura
32 La Misión Dragón

OTHER
1 Aeroméxico
2 Cinepólis
4 Plaza de Toros Calafia
5 Secture (Secretaría
   de Turismo del Estado)
6 Central de Autobuses
11 Museo Regional de
   la Universidad Autónoma
12 Forum
18 Galería de la Mora
   (Centro Comercial
   Los Pinos)
19 Monumento Benito
   Juárez
20 Varsovia

21 El Armario (Plaza Azteca Mall)
24 Viajes Carrusel
   (American Express),
   Budget Rent A Car,
   El Jaguar
25 Hertz Rent A Car
26 Cinemas Gemelos (Centro
   Comercial Gigante)
27 La Capilla
28 Librería Universitaria
29 Universidad Autónoma
   de Baja California
31 Monumento Lázaro Cárdenas
33 Cruz Roja
34 Monumento Sánchez Taboada

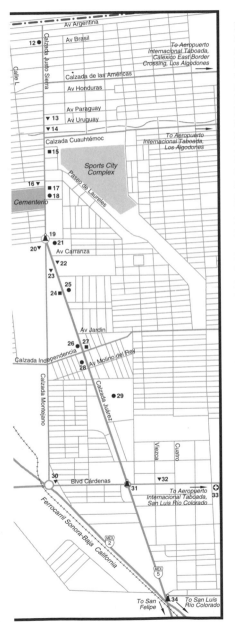

Unfortunately, much of Mexicali is no longer pedestrian-friendly, because local, state and federal authorities have consciously shifted government services to the new Centro Cívico-Comercial and discouraged commercial development near the border zone. From the border, the broad diagonal Calzada López Mateos heads southeast through Mexicali's relatively new industrial and commercial section, where cotton and flour mills once lined the rail route. For pedestrians, this new decentralization isn't so bad when the weather is cool, but the lack of trees or any other shade is almost lethal in summer's heat. Drivers are mostly courteous, but the busy boulevards have their own momentum – even Olympic sprinters may find crossing them difficult.

The Zona Hotelera, an area of posh lodgings and restaurants just beyond the Centro Cívico-Comercial, is about 2¼ miles (3.5 km) southeast of the border post. Calzada López Mateos continues south another 3 miles (5 km) before dividing into México 5 (to San Felipe) and México 2 (to Sonora).

Information
Border Crossings Calexico-Mexicali's border crossing in downtown is open 24 hours a day, but drivers should avoid the northbound afternoon rush hour. US and Mexican authorities have opened a new border complex, Calexico East, in the industrial-park area east of downtown, at the junction of Avenida República Argentina and Blvd Abelardo L Rodríguez. This has relieved the heavy congestion of the main crossing, much as Mesa de Otay has in Tijuana. Hours here are 6 am to 10 pm daily.

If you're traveling east to mainland Mexico or south beyond Ensenada or San Felipe, obtain a tourist card; if you're driving to the mainland, get a combined car permit and tourist card. Both are available from Mexican Customs & Immigration at either crossing. A tourist card is no longer necessary for travel south to San Felipe, at least for trips of 72 hours or less, but beyond this area a tourist card is essential.

DESIERTO DEL COLORADO

US Customs & Immigration officials at Calexico sometimes x-ray the luggage of pedestrians crossing the border, so it is wise to remove photographic film from bags and backpacks.

Tourist Offices The Secretaría de Turismo del Estado (Secture, ☎ (65) 55-49-50/1, fax (65) 55-49-52) is in the Plaza Baja California mall on Avenida Calafia, opposite the Plaza de Toros Calafia. It's open 8 am to 7 pm weekdays, 9 am to 3 pm Saturday and 9 am to 1 pm Sunday. An English-speaker is always on duty.

The Comité de Turismo y Convenciones (Cotuco, Mexicali's Committee on Tourism & Conventions, ☎ (65) 57-23-76, (65) 57-25-61) is at the corner of Calzada López Mateos and Camelias about 1¾ miles (3 km) southeast of the downtown border crossing. The staff usually include an English-speaker, and Cotuco's city map is very useful. Hours are 8 am to 7 pm weekdays. Its US postal address is PO Box 7901, Calexico, CA 92231.

Across the border, Calexico's Chamber of Commerce (☎ (760) 357-1166), 1100 Imperial Ave (Hwy 111), is also a good source of information; it's open 8 am to 5 pm weekdays. The US-Mexico Visitor Information Center (☎ (760) 357-4883), 747 Imperial Ave in Calexico, is really the Oscar Padilla Automobile Insurance Agency, but the staff are helpful. Hours are 6 am to 9 pm Monday to Thursday, 6 am Friday to 9 pm Saturday and 7 am to 6 pm Sunday. Look for discount-coupon books for Mexicali's better restaurants.

Money *Cambios* (currency exchange offices) are so abundant, especially in the immediate border area, that it's hardly worth visiting banks, which offer exchange services 9 am to 1:30 pm on weekdays only. Downtown banks with ATMs include Bancomer at Azueta and Avenida Madero, Banco Internacional (Bital) at the corner of Avenida Madero and Morelos, and Banamex across the street to the south, but many other banks in both Mexicali and Calexico have 24-hour ATMs.

Travelers passing through Calexico can change money (cambios in Calexico usually offer slightly better rates than their Mexicali competitors) and buy car insurance along Imperial Ave (Hwy 111), which leads straight to the border. There are also several cambios just across the border in Mexicali; these do not charge any commission on exchanges.

Post & Communications Mexicali's central post office is on Avenida Madero at the corner of Morelos. Downtown Mexicali's postal code is 21000, but the city is so large that there are many others.

Phone booths are common in pharmacies and similar businesses, but public telephones are numerous.

Online addicts can surf the Web and read their email at Café Internet Mexicali (☎ (65) 54-12-49) at the corner of Avenida Reforma and Calle D (Salazar).

Travel Agencies Mexicali has many downtown travel agencies, among them Aero Olímpico Tours (☎ (65) 52-50-25), Avenida Madero 641, and Viajes Ana Sol (☎ (65) 53-47-87), Avenida Madero 1324-A near the rectory of the university. The American Express representative is Viajes Carrusel (☎ (65) 66-05-09) in the Araiza Inn Mexicali at Calzada Juárez 2220.

Bookstores Librería Universitaria, across from the Universidad Autónoma on Calzada Juárez just south of Calzada Independencia, has a good selection of books (mostly in Spanish) on Mexican history, archaeology, anthropology and literature. It also carries the excellent Guías Urbanas series of city maps, including maps of Mexicali, Tijuana, Tecate, Ensenada, San Felipe and La Paz, as well as others of mainland Mexico.

Closer to the border, on Avenida Madero between Altamirano and Morelos, Librería Madero has a smaller but still respectable selection of books on similar subjects. Another store with a small selection of high-quality books is Librería INAH (☎ (65) 52-35-91), Avenida Reforma 1310, Local 3.

Cultural Centers The Instituto de Cultura de Baja California (☎ (65) 53-58-74) presents film series at the Teatro del Estado's Café Literario on Calzada López Mateos.

The main campus of the Universidad Autónoma de Baja California, on Calzada Juárez just south of Calzada Independencia, has a theater that hosts numerous cultural events, including live drama and lectures.

Medical Services For emergencies, the Cruz Roja (Red Cross, ☎ 132, (65) 61-81-01) is at Blvd Cárdenas 1492. The Hospital Civil (☎ (65) 56-11-28) is at the corner of Calle del Hospital and Avenida Libertad near the Centro Cívico-Comercial.

In the grid of streets near the border are many clinics, laboratories, pharmacies and hospitals catering to US visitors, such as the Hospital México-Americano (☎ (65) 52-27-49), Avenida Reforma 1000 at the corner of Calle B. Dentists trained at the Mexicali campus of the Universidad Autónoma offer quality work at a fraction of the cost north of the border.

La Chinesca

Near Mexicali's main border crossing, a pagoda gracing the **Plaza de la Amistad** (Friendship Plaza) is the first visitors see of La Chinesca, Mexico's largest Chinatown. Mostly centered along Avenida Juárez and Altamirano south of Calzada López Mateos, it was established shortly after the city's founding at the turn of the century, when the Colorado River Land Company and other landowners sought Chinese lessees who then imported 'coolie' labor to raise cotton on surrounding farmland. It's not what it once was, but the sector still contains many Chinese restaurants, other businesses and typically Sino-Mexican architecture.

From its beginnings La Chinesca was a center of commerce and social interaction for the immigrant community, peaking around the 1920s. When President Lázaro Cárdenas ordered the confiscation of large landholdings in 1937 in order to create ejidos, many Chinese landholders and their laborers swelled the population by relocating to the city. Perhaps 10,000 Mexicans of Chinese ancestry remain in Mexicali, supporting institutions like a Chinese language school, a cultural institute and the 600-member Asociación Chung Shan.

Recently, near the corner of La Chinesca's Altamirano and Avenida Zuazua, a concentration of rehearsal halls for banda groups has developed. The groups proclaim their presence by displaying their names and telephone numbers on bass drums on the sidewalk. In late afternoon, after band members finish their day jobs, it's possible to hear them practice – or hire them for a gig.

For a detailed account of the establishment of La Chinesca, including a fascinating building-by-building Sanborn's fire insurance map of 1925, see James R Curtis's article 'Mexicali's Chinatown' in the *Geographical Review* (Vol 85, No 3, July 1995).

Galería de la Ciudad

Local artists display their paintings, sculptures and photographs for sale at reasonable prices at this private gallery (☎ (65) 53-50-44) at Avenida Obregón 1209 just east of Calle D (Salazar). It's open 9 am to 8 pm weekdays and 9 am to 1 pm Saturday.

Museo Regional de la Universidad Autónoma

Permanent displays at this modest eight-room museum – also known as El Museo Hombre, Naturaleza y Cultura (Museum of Man, Nature & Culture) – cover subjects like geology, paleontology, human evolution, colonial history and photography, but there are also traveling exhibitions on topics such as indigenous textiles from mainland Mexico.

At the corner of Avenida Reforma and Calle L, the museum (☎ (65) 54-19-77) is open 9 am to 6 pm weekdays, 9 am to 4 pm weekends. Admission costs about US$0.60.

Teatro del Estado

A variety of theatrical and musical performers, like Cuba's La Tropicana dance

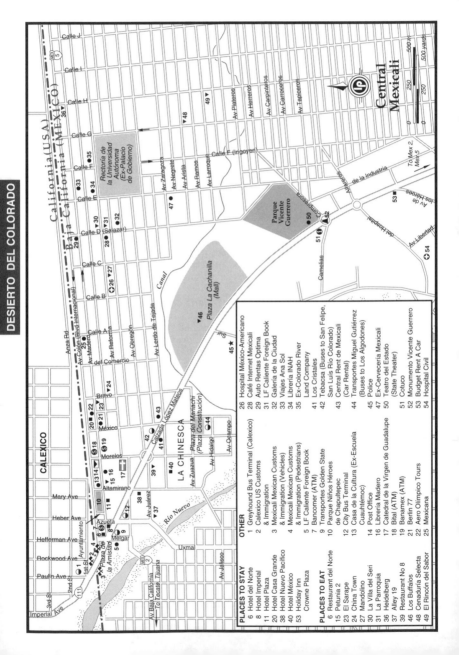

DESIERTO DEL COLORADO

PLACES TO STAY
6 Hotel del Norte
8 Hotel Imperial
11 Hotel Plaza
20 Hotel Casa Grande
38 Hotel Nuevo Pacífico
40 Hotel México
53 Holiday Inn
   Crowne Plaza

PLACES TO EAT
15 Restaurant del Norte
15 Petunia 2
23 El Sarape
24 China Town
27 Mandolino
30 La Villa del Serí
31 La Parroquia
36 Heidelberg
37 Alley 19
39 Restaurant No 8
46 Los Buffalos
48 Cenaduría Selecta
49 El Rincón del Sabor

OTHER
1 Greyhound Bus Terminal (Calexico)
2 Calexico US Customs
3 Mexicali Mexican Customs
   & Immigration (Vehicles)
4 Mexicali Mexican Customs
   & Immigration (Pedestrians)
5 LF Caliente Foreign Book
7 Bancomer (ATM)
9 Transportes Golden State
10 Parque Niños Héroes
   de Chapultepec
12 City Bus Terminal
13 Casa de la Cultura (Ex-Escuela
   Cuauhtémoc)
14 Post Office
16 Librería Madero
17 Catedral de la Virgen de Guadalupe
18 Bital (ATM)
19 Banamex (ATM)
21 Berlín 77
22 Aero Olímpico Tours
25 Mexicana

26 Hospital México-Americano
28 Café Internet Mexicali
29 Auto Rentas Optima
31 LF Caliente Foreign Book
33 Galería de la Ciudad
34 Librería INAH
35 Ex-Colorado River
   Land Company
41 Los Cristales
42 Tebacsa (Buses to San Felipe,
   San Luis Río Colorado)
43 Central Rent de Mexicali
   (Car Rental)
44 Transportes Miguel Gutiérrez
   (Buses to Los Algodones)
45 Police
47 Ex-Cervecería Mexicali
50 Teatro del Estado
   (State Theater)
51 Cotuco
52 Monumento Vicente Guerrero
53 Budget Rent A Car
54 Hospital Civil

troupe, appears throughout the year at the state theater, an ultramodern building seating 1100 spectators and equipped with the 'latest acoustical technology'; its Instituto de Cultura de Baja California also presents retrospective film series in the Café Literario. The theater (☎ (65) 54-64-18) is on the eastern side of Calzada López Mateos, just north of Avenida Tapiceros, opposite the Cotuco tourist office.

Centro Cívico-Comercial
The highlights of Mexicali's modern civic center, located along Calzada Independencia just north of the Zona Hotelera, are the state government's **Poder Ejecutivo** (Governor's Office), **Cámara de Diputados** (Legislature) and **Poder Judicial** (Supreme Court). The plaque on the monument between them describes Mexicali as 'La Ciudad Cuyo Cielo Capturó Al Sol' (The City Whose Sky Captured the Sun).

Historic Buildings
The **Catedral de la Virgen de Guadalupe**, at the corner of Avenida Reforma and Morelos, is Mexicali's major religious landmark. One block north, on Avenida Madero between Altamirano and Morelos, the former Escuela Cuauhtémoc is a neoclassical building that now serves as the city's **Casa de la Cultura** (☎ (65) 52-96-30), which hosts rotating art exhibitions.

Now housing the rectory of the Universidad Autónoma, the grounds of the former **Palacio de Gobierno** (Government Palace, built between 1919 and 1922) interrupt Avenida Obregón just east of Calle E. Just north of this imposing building, at the intersection of Avenida Reforma and Calle F (Irigoyen), the former headquarters of the **Colorado River Land Company** (1924) is now used for offices, but its attractive patio fountain and restored balcony murals merit a visit.

At the corner of Avenida Zaragoza and Calle E, two blocks southwest of the rectory, the former **Cervecería Mexicali** (Mexicali Brewery) sits vacant but in a good state of preservation despite fire damage in 1986. Opened in 1923 under a German

master brewer, it satisfied local demand for half a century and even managed to export some of its production.

City Monuments
Mexicali's monuments, which appear on its *glorietas* (traffic circles), are dedicated to past presidents, peasants, the fishermen of San Felipe and various other luminaries. Some notable figures honored in stone and steel are **Benito Juárez** on Calzada Justo Sierra, **Lázaro Cárdenas** at the intersection of Blvd Cárdenas and Calzada Juárez, **Vicente Guerrero** on Calzada López Mateos and **Rodolfo Sánchez Taboada** (also on Calzada López Mateos).

Special Events
Mexicali hosts a multitude of annual festivals and events, ranging from dog shows and golf tournaments to off-highway races; most are less gringo-oriented than those in other parts of the peninsula. The list below is a sample of the more important ones (for detailed information, contact Secture, the state tourist information office):

March
14th – *Aniversario de Mexicali.* Celebration of the city's founding in 1903

May
18th – *Triatlón Campo Mosqueda.* Mexicali's triathlon

September
16th – *Festejos de Independencia.* Celebrates Mexico's Independence Day
Late September – *Feria del Libro* (Annual Book Fair)
Late September to mid-October – *Fiesta del Sol* (Festival of the Sun). Also commemorating the city's founding, the Fiesta del Sol events include pop music concerts, cockfights, art exhibits, theatrical performances and parades. A crafts exposition, local industrial products and agriculture are also highlighted.

October
Late October – *Paseo Ciclista Mexicali-San Felipe* (Mexicali-San Felipe Bicycle Race)

November
Early November – *Feria de Muestra Gastronómica* (Gastronomic Fair). Cooking competition among Mexicali chefs

Places to Stay – budget

In and around La Chinesca are several places like *Hotel Nuevo Pacífico* (☎ (65) 52-94-30), Avenida Juárez 95 near the corner of Altamirano, offering cheap but noisy accommodations in dubious surroundings from about US$8 double. Central Mexicali's best bargain may be family-oriented *Hotel México* (☎ /fax (65) 54-06-09), Avenida Lerdo de Tejada 476 between Altamirano and Morelos, where some rooms cost as little as US$10 single, though those with amenities like air-conditioning, TV, private bath and parking are a bit dearer. *Hotel Plaza* (☎ (65) 52-97-57), Avenida Madero 366, charges US$15/18 single/double, reasonable prices for a respectable downtown hotel.

Closer to the border, the *Hotel Imperial* (☎ /fax (65) 53-63-33), Avenida Madero 222 (with an additional entrance on Calzada López Mateos), is fairly clean, but the plaster is chipping and the bedspreads are worn; for US$18/25, there are better values. Near the railroad station, the one-star, 37-room *Motel Las Fuentes* (☎ (65) 57-15-25), Calzada López Mateos 1655, has singles/doubles with TV for US$18/26. *Motel Azteca de Oro* (☎ /fax (65) 57-14-33), de la Industria 600 across from the train station, falls short of its self-proclaimed *elegancia*, but each room has telephone, TV and air-con for US$19 single or double.

Places to Stay – middle

Conveniently close to the border crossing, at Melgar 205, the landmark Deco-style *Hotel del Norte* (☎ (65) 52-81-01) has 52 rooms, some with color TV and air-con, for US$23/33. Its downstairs restaurant serves moderately priced Mexican dishes, lunch and dinner specials and huge margaritas. *Hotel Casa Grande* (☎ (65) 53-57-51) faces the border fence at Avenida Cristóbal Colón 612. It offers rooms with air-con and TV for US$24/26, and it has a swimming pool.

At the 173-room *Araiza Inn Calafia* (☎ (65) 68-33-11), Calzada Justo Sierra 1495 about 1½ miles (2.5 km) southeast of central Mexicali, rates start around US$35/37, plus IVA (value-added tax), for simple but comfortable and air-conditioned rooms with cable TV; secure parking is available. *Hotel Siesta Inn* (☎ (65) 68-20-01, fax (65) 68-23-05; (800) 426-5093 in the USA), Calzada Justo Sierra 899, has carpeted singles/doubles starting around US$38, but better rooms cost only a little more. There's a coffee shop next to the lobby.

Ordinary accommodations are better and no more expensive in Calexico, just across the border; most motels on 4th St are in the US$20 to US$30 range.

Places to Stay – top end

Many, though not all, of Mexicali's upscale hotels are in the Zona Hotelera, a designated hotel area of Calzada Juárez about 2¼ miles (3.5 km) southeast of the border crossing and north of Calzada Independencia.

At Calzada Juárez 2220, rooms at the *Araiza Inn Mexicali* (☎ (65) 66-13-00, fax (65) 66-49-01), formerly the Holiday Inn Mexicali, start around US$49/52, IVA included.

Highly regarded *Hotel Colonial* (☎ (65) 56-13-12, fax (65) 56-11-41; (800) 437-2438 in the USA), Calzada López Mateos 1048, charges US$52 single/double plus IVA.

Hotel Lucerna (☎ (65) 66-10-00, fax (65) 66-47-06), Calzada Juárez 2151, is known among Mexicali's yuppies and business community for its nightclubs. In an idyllic setting of fountains and pseudo-colonial courtyards, its 192 rooms have color TV and air-conditioning; those overlooking the pool usually have balconies. Rates are US$63/66 plus IVA. Its US postal address is PO Box 2300, Calexico, CA 92231.

The Araiza Inn Mexicali's erstwhile sister, the *Holiday Inn Crowne Plaza* (☎ (65) 57-36-00, fax (65) 57-05-55; (800) 227-6963 in the USA), at the junction of Calzada López Mateos and Avenida de los Héroes, is the most expensive in town at US$91 single or double, plus IVA.

Places to Eat
Mexicali has a variety of quality restaurants in a number of districts throughout the city. Buses are available from the city center.

Mexican Family-run *Cenaduría Selecta* (☎ (65) 52-40-47), a Mexicali institution at Avenida Arista 1510 at Calle G, specializes in antojitos like beef tacos and burritos, but they're not cheap. It's open 8 am to 11 pm. *El Rincón del Sabor* (☎ (65) 54-08-88), nearby at Avenida Larroque 1500 at Calle H, is another good choice for Mexican food.

Part of the Hotel del Norte (see Places to Stay, above), *Restaurant del Norte* is a US-style coffee shop that offers large and inexpensive but rather ordinary specials for breakfast, lunch and dinner. Another good and very inexpensive breakfast place is *Petunia 2*, a friendly no-smoking oasis on Avenida Madero between Altamirano and Morelos.

La Plazita (☎ (65) 68-10-51), Calzada Justo Sierra 377, offers Mexican and international dishes in a pleasant atmosphere at moderate prices (especially with discount coupons). *Las Campanas de la Plazita* (☎ (65) 68-12-13), which is almost next door on Calzada Justo Sierra and under the same management, is very comparable.

El Sarape (☎ (65) 54-22-87), Nicolás Bravo 140 between Avenidas Madero and Reforma, is a popular, even raucous spot with live music; the food is good, but it's not the place for a quiet romantic dinner.

La Villa del Seri (☎ (65) 53-55-03), at the corner of Avenida Reforma and Calle D (Salazar), specializes in Sonoran beef but also has excellent seafood and antojitos. Prices are on the high side, but portions are large, so it's a good value. Across the street is *La Parroquia* (☎ (65) 54-23-13), Avenida Reforma 1200, which doubles as a sports book. *Los Buffalos* (☎ (65) 66-31-16), in the Plaza La Cachanilla mall on Calzada López Mateos, also specializes in beef and seafood.

The Mexican institution *Sanborn's* (☎ (65) 57-03-31) maintains a branch at the corner of Calzada Independencia and Avenida de los Héroes.

Chinese Mexicali's 150-plus Chinese restaurants offer the opportunity to dine well and relatively cheaply – less than US$10 for two in some cases. Opened in 1928, *Alley 19*, Avenida Juárez 8 near the corner of Azueta in La Chinesca, is Mexicali's oldest continuously operating Chinese restaurant; it's well worth a visit for budget travelers. At the corner of Avenida Juárez and Morelos, *Restaurant No 8* is open 24 hours a day. Another downtown choice is *China Town* (☎ (65) 54-02-120), Avenida Reforma 701 at the corner of Bravo.

The pricier but highly regarded *El Dragón* (☎ (65) 66-20-20) occupies a huge pagoda at Calzada Juárez 1830; it's open 11 am to 11:30 pm. The same proprietors operate *La Misión Dragón* (☎ (65) 66-43-20), set among lovely gardens at Blvd Cárdenas 555, a quarter-mile (0.5 km) east of Calzada Juárez. This scenic restaurant is also known for its appealing food.

German *Heidelberg* (☎ (65) 54-20-22), at the corner of Avenida Madero and Calle H, serves hearty Middle European-style food, in addition to Mexican specialties, in a very Germanic setting.

Italian Like every other Italian restaurant in Mexico, *Mandolino* (☎ (65) 52-95-44), Avenida Reforma 1070 between Calle B and Calle C, features the obligatory *Godfather* photograph of Marlon Brando, but its food is excellent and the ambiance is otherwise congenial. *La Spezzia* (☎ (65) 56-10-88), at Calzada Francisco L Montejano 1058 in the Zona Hotelera, is another outstanding choice.

Japanese *Sakura* (☎ (65) 66-48-48), Blvd Cárdenas 200 at the corner of Calzada López Mateos, serves sushi and other Japanese dishes.

Seafood Perhaps Mexicali's most popular seafood restaurant is *Los Arcos* (☎ (65) 56-09-03), Avenida Calafia 454 near the Plaza de Toros in the Centro Cívico-Comercial. *Mariscos Veracruz* (☎ (65) 54-46-90) is at Carroceros Sur 2014 near Calzada Justo Sierra. Another possibility is *Villa Marina* (☎ (65) 68-29-67), Avenida Venustiano Carranza 1199 at the corner of Calzada Juárez in the Zona Hotelera.

Entertainment
Cinemas Mexicali has three major movie complexes showing first-run films: *Cinemas Gemelos La Cachanilla* (☎ (65) 55-67-27) on Calzada López Mateos in the Plaza La Cachanilla; *Cinépolis* (☎ (65) 57-19-85) at Avenida de los Héroes and Avenida de la Patria in the Centro Cívico-Comercial; and *Cinemas Gemelos* (☎ (65) 66-07-48) in the Centro Comercial Gigante at the junction of Calzada Independencia and Calzada Juárez.

Nightclubs *El Jaguar* (☎ (65) 66-13-00), at the Araiza Inn Mexicali on Calzada Juárez, has a dance floor, live music and various floor shows; it's open 9 pm to 3 am Tuesday through Saturday. *La Capilla* (☎ (65) 66-11-00), at Hotel Lucerna, Calzada Juárez 2151, is a music and dance club that is especially popular with university students; hours are 8 pm to 2 am. *Los Cristales*, Calzada López Mateos 570, is renowned for performances by nationally known musicians; hours are 6 pm to 3 am.

Other nightspots include *Varsovia* (☎ (65) 56-10-88) at Calzada Montejano 1058 in the Zona Hotelera; *Forum* (☎ (65) 52-40-91) at the corner of Avenida Reforma and Calzada Justo Sierra; and *Time Out* on Calzada Independencia in the Centro Cívico-Comercial.

Calle México, north of Calzada López Mateos, has most of Mexicali's remaining seedy strip joints; others are scattered throughout La Chinesca. *Berlin 77* (☎ (65) 52-53-33), at the corner of Calle México and Avenida Madero, is a step above most of these. It's open 11 am to 3 am.

Betting At Melgar 166 less than a block from the border, *LF Caliente Foreign Book* (☎ (65) 54-23-13, (65) 54-19-73) accepts bets for almost every major racetrack, as well as other sporting events, in the USA. A second location is within the restaurant La Parroquia at the corner of Avenida Reforma and Calle D (Salazar) opposite La Villa del Seri.

Spectator Sports
Baseball Mexicali's professional baseball team, Las Aguilas (The Eagles), plays in the Liga Mexicana del Pacífico, which begins its official season in October shortly after the World Series in the US. The regular season ends in early January, when a series of playoffs determines the league's

WAYNE BERNHARDSON

representative to the Caribbean Series, which rotates among Mexico, Puerto Rico, the Dominican Republic and Venezuela.

Mexicali's stadium, nicknamed 'El Nido de las Aguilas' (Eagles' Nest), is on Calzada Cuauhtémoc (also known as Avenida Cuauhtémoc) about 3 miles (5 km) east of the border post. Weeknight games begin under the lights at 7 pm; Sunday starting time is 1 pm in the sunshine. Ticket prices range from US$1 (in the remote bleachers) to US$6 (front row behind home plate).

Bullfights On alternate Sundays from October to May, *corridas de toros* take place in the Plaza de Toros Calafia (☎ (65) 57-06-81) at the corner of Avenida Calafia and Calzada Independencia next to the Centro Cívico-Comercial. Tickets are available at the gate; prices range from US$6 to US$19.

Things to Buy

Curio stores selling cheap leather goods and kitschy souvenirs are concentrated on Melgar and Avenida Reforma within easy walking distance of the border. For a more sophisticated selection, try El Armario, Calzada Justo Sierra 1700, Suite 1-A, in the Plaza Azteca mall, or Galería de la Mora (☎ (65) 68-12-55), Calzada Justo Sierra 1515, Locales 2 & 3, in the Centro Comercial Los Pinos.

Mexican beer and hard liquors are cheaper than in the USA, but remember that US Customs regulations allow each adult to bring only one liter of liquor into the USA if arriving on foot or by car. Travelers on common carriers, like airplanes, buses or taxis, can carry any amount as long as it's for personal use, but duty is payable on anything above one liter.

Pharmaceuticals and medical services, including dentistry and optometry, are much cheaper on the Mexican side of the border. Many clinics and hospitals are located on the streets that parallel the US border, including Avenida Reforma and Avenida Obregón.

Getting There & Away

Air Aeropuerto Internacional General Rodolfo Sánchez Taboada (☎ (65) 53-67-42, (65) 53-67-41) is about 7 miles (11 km) east of town via BCN-8.

Aeroméxico (☎ (65) 57-25-51) is at Pasaje Alamos 1008-D in the Centro Cívico-Comercial. Its subsidiary Aerolitoral flies to Tucson and Phoenix from Mexicali via the mainland Mexican city of Hermosillo (Sonora).

Mexicana (☎ (65) 53-54-01, (65) 52-93-91 at the airport), Avenida Madero 833 just west of Calle A, flies daily to Guadalajara (some of these flights continue on to Mexico City) and daily to Hermosillo.

Bus Major intercity bus companies have offices at the Central de Autobuses (☎ (65) 57-24-20, (65) 57-24-50) on Calzada Independencia near Calzada López Mateos. Long-distance services now commonly feature services like video and onboard meals.

The main companies and their telephone numbers are as follows:

Autotransportes de Baja California (ABC) operates exclusively on the peninsula as far south as La Paz, via Tijuana. (☎ (65) 52-65-48)

Autotransportes Estrellas del Pacífico is alongside the main terminal at Calzada Anahuac 553. It goes to Guadalajara and intermediate points four times daily and to Tijuana and Los Angeles four times daily. (☎ (65) 57-18-30)

Transportes del Pacífico goes to mainland destinations along the Gulf of California before turning inland at Tepic and continuing to Mexico City. (☎ (65) 57-24-61)

Transportes Norte de Sonora/Elite competes with Transportes del Pacífico and also serves northern Mexican destinations such as Ciudad Juárez, Chihuahua, Monterrey and San Luis Potosí. Elite offers slightly more expensive 1st-class services. There are about 10 departures daily to Guadalajara and another nine to Mexico City. (☎ (65) 56-01-10)

To/From the USA Across the line in Calexico, Greyhound (☎ (760) 357-1895, (800) 231-2222) is at 121 1st St directly

DESIERTO DEL COLORADO

opposite the pedestrian border-crossing entrance. It has 10 buses daily to Los Angeles (six to seven hours, US$27/47 one way/roundtrip) between 12:20 am and 6:45 pm; from the Los Angeles terminal (☎ (213) 629-8400), there are 15 buses daily to Calexico between 12:35 am and 11:45 pm.

There are frequent daily buses between Calexico and El Centro, Indio, El Cajon, San Diego, Riverside, San Bernardino, Phoenix, Yuma and a few other cities. Schedules and fares change monthly, so call Greyhound for the latest information.

From a stop at Calzada López Mateos 234 at the corner of Melgar near the border, Transportes Golden State (☎ (65) 53-61-59) has services to the mainland California destinations of Indio and Mecca (US$20), Palm Springs (US$22) and El Monte and Los Angeles (US$27) at 8 am and 2:30 and 10:30 pm. It also maintains offices at the Central de Autobuses and, on the Calexico side, picks up passengers at Church's Fried Chicken, 344 Imperial Ave (Hwy 111).

To/From Elsewhere in Mexico ABC fares to destinations within Baja California are as follows:

Destination	Fare
Tecate	US$5.50
Tijuana	US$7
Ensenada	US$11
San Quintín	US$16
Guerrero Negro	US$30
Vizcaíno	US$33
San Ignacio	US$35
Santa Rosalía	US$36
Mulegé	US$38
Loreto	US$42
Ciudad Constitución	US$48
La Paz	US$55

ABC buses to San Felipe (about US$7) depart at 8 am, noon and 4 and 8 pm. The bus to La Paz (a trip of about 24 hours) leaves at 4:30 pm daily. ABC offers almost hourly service to San Luís Río Colorado (1½ hours, US$3.50) on the Sonora/Arizona border, and three buses daily to Sonora's Gulf resort of Puerto Peñasco

(five hours). Tebacsa, on Calzada López Mateos between Morelos and Calle México, has one bus daily to San Felipe at 6 am and many to San Luís Río Colorado.

Transportes Miguel Gutiérrez (☎ (65) 54-68-22, (65) 57-76-50) runs hourly buses to Los Algodones, in the northeastern corner of Baja California across from Andrade, California (only 8 miles – 13 km – from Yuma, Arizona). These leave from Avenida Hidalgo between Aldana and Morelos at the southern end of Plaza Constitución (Plaza del Mariachi).

Typical times and fares to other mainland Mexican destinations include:

Destination	Duration	Fare
Hermosillo	10 hours	US$23
Ciudad Obregón	14 hours	US$31
Los Mochis	17 hours	US$40
Ciudad Juárez	18 hours	US$39
Chihuahua	19 hours	US$44
Culiacán	21 hours	US$48
Mazatlán	24 hours	US$53
Monterrey	29 hours	US$85
Guadalajara	33 hours	US$66
San Luis Potosí	37 hours	US$85
Mexico City	41 hours	US$81

Train The Ferrocarril Sonora-Baja California train station (☎ (65) 57-23-86, (65) 57-21-01, phone between 6:30 am and 1 pm daily for information and reservations) is on Calle F (Irigoyen) near Calzada López Mateos. Passenger services go from Mexicali to Mexico City via Hermosillo, Guaymas (Empalme), Sufragio/Los Mochis (the Barranca del Cobre – 'Copper Canyon' – rail junction), Mazatlán and Guadalajara.

The 1st-class train departs at 9 am and the 2nd-class train at 8:50 pm daily. First-class tickets are available at the station from 9:30 to 11:30 am daily; 2nd-class tickets are sold from 4:30 to 6 pm and 6:45 to 8:30 pm daily. Dining facilities are available on the 1st-class train, but only snack-bar service is available on the 2nd-class train. For mail reservations, write the Jefe de Estación, Estación de Ferrocarril, Box 3-182, Mexicali, Baja California, México, or PO Box 231, Calexico, CA 92231.

Trains heading south stop at Empalme,

6 miles (10 km) east of Guaymas, and at Sufragio, 30 miles (48 km) northeast of Los Mochis, connecting with the eastbound Chihuahua al Pacífico, popularly known to travelers as the Copper Canyon train.

The accompanying table illustrates current fares from Mexicali; sleepers are available at premium prices.

Destination (Km)	2nd	1st
Puerto Peñasco (250)	US$3.50	US$6.50
Caborca (410)	US$5.75	US$10
Benjamín Hill (534)	US$7	US$13.50
Hermosillo (660)	US$7.50	US$16.50
Empalme (Guaymas) (801)	US$11	US$20
Ciudad Obregón (919)	US$13	US$23
Navojoa (987)	US$14	US$25
Culiacán (1340)	US$19	US$34
Mazatlán (1559)	US$22	US$39
Tepic (1875)	US$27	US$47
Guadalajara (2149)	US$30	US$54

Getting Around

To/From the Airport Cabs are the only alternative to the airport, and they're expensive at US$10 but may be shared.

Bus Most city bus routes start from Avenida Reforma just west of Calzada López Mateos, two blocks from the border crossing. The 'Justo Sierra' bus goes to the museum. Any 'Centro Cívico' bus goes to the tourist offices, the Plaza de Toros and the train station. The 'Central Camionera' bus goes to the Centro Cívico-Comercial and the bus terminal. Local bus fares are about US$0.30.

Car Rental International agencies include:
Budget
    Araiza Inn Mexicali, Calzada Juárez 2220 (☎ (65) 66-48-40)
    Holiday Inn Crowne Plaza, Calzada López Mateos and Avenida de los Héroes (☎ (65) 57-36-00, ext 824)
Hertz
    Calzada Juárez 1223 (☎ (65) 68-19-73)

Local independents include Central Rent de Mexicali (☎ (65) 52-22-06), Calzada López Mateos 655, and Auto Rentas Optima (☎ (65) 52-36-17), Avenida Madero 1183.

Taxi A taxi ride from the border to the ballpark, train station or Centro Cívico-Comercial costs about US$6 to US$7; try bargaining, but agree on the fare before accepting the ride. An alternative is to arrange a cab in advance with Ecotaxi (☎ (65) 62-65-65).

AROUND MEXICALI

South of Mexicali, México 5 proceeds through a prosperous farming region en route to the Gulf resort of San Felipe, 120 miles (193 km) south. Most of the area between Mexicali and the border with the mainland Mexican state of Sonora became irrigated farmland at the turn of the century, thanks to Río Colorado irrigation projects and the intrigues of *Los Angeles Times* publisher Harrison Chandler, the Southern Pacific Railroad and the Colorado River Land Company. In the 1930s, Mexican President Lázaro Cárdenas' land-reform measures gave land to laborers and peasants through the creation of many ejidos.

Seventeen miles (27 km) south of Mexicali and 2 miles (3 km) east of the highway, rising clouds of steam mark the **Cerro Prieto** geothermal electrical plant, whose 620-megawatt capacity makes it the largest of its kind in North America. It is not open to the public.

At Km 56, 35 miles (56 km) south of Mexicali, **Cucapá El Mayor** is an Indian village whose **Museo Comunitario** has exhibits on subsistence life and others featuring indigenous artifacts; outside are examples of traditional Cucupah nomadic dwellings. A small store within sells a selection of crafts, including very attractive bead necklaces. Both museum and store are theoretically open 10 am to 1 pm daily, but the hours can be erratic, depending on the availability of clerks.

Another 23 miles (37 km) south along México 5, around Km 79, is the edge of the vast, desolate **Laguna Salada** – 500 sq miles (1300 sq km) of salt flats when dry (as is usual). Although these flats were part of the Gulf of California four centuries ago, today they constitute one of Baja's most arid regions. Unusually heavy rains in the

DESIERTO DEL COLORADO

DESIERTO DEL COLORADO

Rails across the Border

There is no better metaphor for the artificiality of the US-Mexico border than the rail lines that once ran from Tucson to San Diego through Mexican territory. The San Diego & Arizona Eastern Railway, a subsidiary of the powerful Southern Pacific Railroad, consisted of several quasi-independent lines that crossed and recrossed the border en route from the desert to the ocean.

At one time, San Diego expected to be the terminus of a transcontinental railroad, but Southern Pacific's decision to make Los Angeles the end of its Sunset Route passenger line from New Orleans left the border city with only limited service via a spur of the Atchison, Topeka & Santa Fe. Shortly after the turn of the century, however, Southern Pacific built a spur from Niland, California, on its transcontinental route. The spur headed south into the Imperial Valley, crossed the border at Mexicali and headed east to Los Algodones before re-entering the USA and rejoining the Sunset Route near Yuma, Arizona. By passing through Mexican territory, it avoided the obstacle of the Algodones Dunes, which also impeded early irrigation projects on the US portion of the Colorado River.

This Inter-California Railway line was the first link in the border chain. Southern Pacific planned a similar line from San Diego to El Centro on the Inter-California line, but company intrigues and disagreements with outside partners delayed its completion until 1919. The line actually began in Lakeside, a northeastern suburb of San Diego, linked up just south of Chula Vista with a spur from Coronado and entered Mexico at Tijuana. From Tijuana to Tecate, it was known as the Ferrocarril Tijuana-Tecate (Tijuana & Tecate Railway).

At Tecate, the line re-entered the USA as the San Diego & Arizona Eastern line before descending the rugged eastern scarp of the Jacumba Mountains, including the difficult Carrizo Gorge, via a series of switchbacks and tunnels. At El Centro, it joined the Inter-California line, recrossed the border at Mexicali and re-entered the US just beyond Los Algodones.

The San Diego & Arizona Eastern line continued to operate (carrying freight in its later years) until 1970, when Southern Pacific sold the Tijuana & Tecate segment to the Mexican government's Ferrocarril Sonora-Baja California. In 1976 Hurricane Kathleen demolished several trestles on the route, ending operations between San Diego and El Centro. Southern Pacific's former Inter-California line continued to link Niland with

mid-1980s, however, swelled the nearby Colorado and Bravo rivers, turning the landscape into an ephemeral marsh. Southeast of the lake is the Río Colorado delta, a 60-mile (97-km) expanse of alluvium (soil deposited by floodwaters).

Cerro El Chinero (Chinese Hill), just east of México 5 and north of the junction with México 3, memorializes a group of Chinese immigrants who died of thirst in the area.

Cañón Guadalupe

Southwest of Mexicali, and descending the eastern scarp of Parque Nacional

Constitución de 1857 (see the La Frontera chapter), palm-studded Cañón Guadalupe is a delightful hot-springs area superb for hiking, swimming and car camping. Since it's in the rain shadow of the coast range, the weather is dry and pleasant most of the year, but in summer it's brutally hot. In addition to the cold canyon pools and small waterfalls, there are rock art sites in the vicinity.

On México 2 about 22 miles (35 km) west of Mexicali, a smooth graded road that is passable for passenger vehicles in dry weather leads 27 miles (43 km) south to a junction that leads another 8 miles

Calexico, Mexicali and the Sonora-Baja California line, but the segment between Mexicali and Los Algodones, acquired by Mexico in 1964, soon ceased operations.

Recent years, though, have seen a resurrection of service and promises of more to come. San Diego Metropolitan Transit's popular trolley covers the old San Diego & Arizona Eastern route from El Cajón to the border. An eastbound tourist service on the scenic portion of the San Diego & Arizona Eastern route from the mainland California town of Campo is unlikely, however, because of the prohibitive expense of restoring bridges and tunnels.

More likely is the resurrection of the segment from San Diego and Tijuana to Tecate and back across the border to Campo in eastern San Diego County. A tourist service has begun between Campo and Tecate, but the real impetus behind the project is the massive, controversial landfill at the Campo Indian Reservation. Should San Diego decide to dump its trash at Campo, the Tijuana & Tecate line could once again flourish, though the Mexican government has reservations about hauling US waste through its territory and El Cajón's Republican Congressman Duncan Hunter has made hysterical comments about the highly improbable threat of train robberies. Still, the remaining track on this historic line is a continuing symbol of the interdependence of the two Californias. ■

(13 km) west to Cañón Guadalupe. For northbound travelers from San Felipe, the canyon is also accessible by a difficult sandy road (4WD recommended, though not essential) leading northwest from the southern end of Laguna Salada, at the turnoff from México 5 to Ejido José Saldaña No 2. This road is slow, tiresome, sometimes difficult to follow and not really worth doing unless there's no alternative.

The *Guadalupe Canyon Hot Springs & Campground* (☎ (714) 673-2670 in mainland California) has comfortable camping facilities starting around US$10 per site, including hot tubs with water temperatures

up to 110°F (43°C), but most sites are rather more expensive. The restaurant has plain but very good Mexican food, and there is also a large heated swimming pool. The campground is very crowded on weekends, less so during the week; for reservations, mail inquiries to Rob's Baja Tours, PO Box 4003, Balboa, CA 92661. Visa and MasterCard are accepted for reservations but not in the canyon itself.

LOS ALGODONES

First settled by ranchers from Sonora in the mid-19th century, the border town of Los Algodones (estimated population 12,000),

next to Andrade, California, was a stage-coach stop on the route from Yuma (Arizona) to San Diego in the days when the Río Colorado was navigable. Named for the surrounding cotton fields, it is about 40 miles (64 km) east of Mexicali, but only about 8 miles (13 km) west of Yuma across the Río Colorado.

Nearly deserted in the brutally hot summer, Los Algodones bustles in winter, when over a million foreigners cross the border. Many of these are retirees from Yuma who find prescription drugs, eyeglasses and dental work much cheaper here than in the US. So many 'snowbirds' frequent the town that Mexican professionals organize bus charters from Yuma for their benefit.

The border is open 6 am to 8 pm daily, but Mexican authorities will only process car permits from 8 am to 3 pm. There's a tourist information office (☎ (651) 7-76-35) at Avenida B No 261. There are many cambios, but changing money is unnecessary unless you're continuing much farther into Mexico.

Besides its pharmacies, dentists and opticians, Los Algodones is virtually a wall-to-wall assemblage of kitschy souvenirs, but resolute shoppers may find attractive textiles from mainland Mexico.

Things to See
Just north of the border, the **Hanlon Headgate** was part of the Alamo Canal, built by the California Development Company to carry Colorado River water through Mexican territory en route to mainland California's Imperial Valley. In the wet winter of 1905, the headgate burst and water flowed west through Mexico and then north, creating mainland California's Salton Sea and obliterating whatever benefits Mexican farmers had gained from water development. It was two years before the Southern Pacific Railroad, which acquired the California Development Company, halted the flow to the north.

Places to Stay & Eat
Misnamed *Motel Olímpico*, really a hotel in the middle of the block opposite the Delegación Municipal, charges US$10 single or double and, perhaps as a public service, offers condoms for US$1 at the front desk. In Andrade on the US side of the border, the Quechan Indians of Fort Yuma Reservation operate the spacious but hardly luxurious *Sleepy Hollow RV Park* (☎ (760) 572-5101); rates are US$15 without hookups, US$25 with hookups. Its mailing address is 369 Algodones Rd, Winterhaven, CA 92283.

Los Algodones' most popular eateries are *Carlota's Bakery*, mobbed by snowbirds at breakfast, and the adjacent courtyard restaurant *El Paraíso* in the Real Plaza del Sol. *Restaurant Tucán*, just off the main street, has more elaborate meals at reasonable prices, with live music at lunchtime.

Getting There & Away
There is no public transportation across the border at Los Algodones. There is hourly public transportation from Los Algodones to Mexicali, but none from Andrade to Yuma. California State Route 186 is now paved to US Interstate 8, which leads east to Yuma.

SAN FELIPE
Once a tranquil fishing community on Bahía San Felipe, an inlet of the Gulf of California, San Felipe has become 'Noise City,' northern Baja's low-life retort to Cabo San Lucas. A particularly crass form of tourism has transformed it into a haven for roaring ATVs, firecrackers, property speculators and aggressive restaurateurs

who almost yank potential patrons off the sidewalk. The official population is 11,310 but may seem many times that during US holidays and especially during spring break for students from north of the border. 'Lauderdale West' is roughly a six-hour drive from large university populations in Los Angeles, Phoenix and Tucson, and even closer for students from San Diego.

Unlike Cabo San Lucas, however, San Felipe is more amusing than pretentiously insufferable. Local real estate speculators and time-share sellers may be less devious than those in the Cape Region, if only because their clients seem to expect to be bamboozled into buying cactus-covered shoreline tracts whose only source of water is the briny Gulf, and appear to relish it. San Felipe's US sister city is the equally undistinguished San Francisco Bay Area suburb of Hayward. Visit between November and April – after April, temperatures soar as high as 120°F (49°C).

History

In 1721 Jesuit missionary Juan de Ugarte landed at the port of San Felipe de Jesús, which appears in Fernando Consag's map of 1746. In 1797 Fray Felipe Neri, a Dominican priest from Misión San Pedro Mártir, established a small supply depot and settlement here in the hope of replenishing his struggling mission, located in an isolated, mile-high valley about 45 miles (72 km) to the west. Both the depot and the mission failed in the early 1800s, in part because of water shortages. Mission ruins can still be seen, but access is difficult; see the Misión San Pedro Mártir entry in the La Frontera chapter for more information.

Bahía San Felipe remained almost undeveloped until 1876, when speculator Guillermo Andrade decided to exploit a grant of approximately 117 sq miles (304 sq km) from the Mexican government. Andrade, who had obtained the concession almost two decades earlier, built a road to the gold mines at Real del Castillo, 120 miles (193 km) to the northwest, but his attempt to attract business from the

mines was largely unsuccessful because well-established Ensenada was much closer to them.

After establishing control over Mexicali in 1915, Colonel Estéban Cantú opened a rough road south to San Felipe and even planned a railroad, but it was shrimpers from Guaymas, Loreto and Santa Rosalía who really turned San Felipe into a town. In 1925 its population was only about 100, but by 1948, when the improved highway made travel from Mexicali much easier, it had reached nearly 1000.

Half a dozen fishing cooperatives operate out of San Felipe, exporting quantities of shrimp and various fish species to the USA, Canada and elsewhere. The San Felipe fleet has 41 boats, several of which can remain at sea for as long as 40 days.

Sportfishing and warm winters have attracted hundreds of North American retirees, while large hotels and sprawling trailer parks have sprung up to accommodate growing numbers of visitors. Many houses, subdivisions and condominiums are under construction.

Orientation

San Felipe hugs the shoreline of its namesake bay, a curving inlet of the northern Gulf of California, 120 miles (193 km) south of Mexicali. North-south *avenidas* (avenues) bear the names of seas around the world, while east-west *calles* (streets) bear the names of Mexican ports. Avenida Mar de Cortez is the main north-south drag, while Calzada Chetumal leads west to a junction with México 5, the highway north to Mexicali. Downtown along the beach is San Felipe's attractive *malecón* (waterfront promenade).

Northwest of San Felipe is the eastern approach to Parque Nacional Sierra San Pedro Mártir and the famous peak of Picacho del Diablo, via a turnoff from México 3. For more details, see the park's entry in the La Frontera chapter.

Information

One source of information is the English-language monthly *San Felipe Newsletter*, available free around town. Although its main audience is US residents, it contains some useful travel information. Its local postal address is Apdo Postal 105, San Felipe, Baja California 21850, México; the US mailing address is PO Box 5259, Heber, CA 92249.

Tourist Offices Secture (☎ (657) 7-11-55) is at the corner of Avenida Mar de Cortez and Manzanillo across from Motel El Capitán. It's open 8 am to 7 pm weekdays, 9 am to 3 pm Saturday and 10 am to 1 pm Sunday; the staff are helpful and someone usually speaks English. The People's Gallery, on Avenida Mar de Cortez Sur just north of Motel El Cortez, welcomes tourist inquiries as well; it also offers Internet and email services (see the Post & Communications entry, below).

Money Nearly all merchants accept dollars as readily as pesos. Bancomer, San Felipe's only remaining bank, is on Avenida Mar de Cortez just north of Calzada Chetumal. It changes US dollars and traveler's checks from 9 am to 1:30 pm weekdays and also has an ATM. Curios Mitla, at Calzada Chetumal and Avenida Mar de Cortez, operates a cambio.

Post & Communications San Felipe's post office is on Avenida Mar Blanco between Calzada Chetumal and Ensenada. It's open 8 am to 1 pm and 4 to 6 pm weekdays. The postal code is 21850.

Increasing numbers of public telephones are available on the street, in addition to private phone booths.

The People's Gallery, on Avenida Mar de Cortez Sur just north of Motel El Cortez, offers Internet and email services (visitor@canela.sanfelipe.com.mx). Fees are US$12 per hour for using their computers (both Macintoshes and PCs are available), US$7 with your own.

Laundry Lavamática Burbujas is at Avenida Mar Bermejo 212 between Ensenada and Topolobampo; detergent is available and English is spoken. Hours are 8 am to

8 pm Monday to Saturday, 10 am to 2 pm Sunday.

Medical Services San Felipe's Centro de Salud (☎ (657) 7-15-21) is on Avenida Mar Bermejo between Calzada Chetumal and Ensenada; for 24-hour emergency service, however, the Cruz Roja (☎ 132, (657) 7-15-44) is at the corner of Avenida Mar Bermejo and Puerto Peñasco.

Capilla de la Virgen de Guadalupe
The local shrine of the Virgen de Guadalupe, Mexico's great national symbol, is a small monument atop a hill north of the malecón. The climb to the top offers panoramic views of town and bay.

Clamming
Clamming is popular, particularly when very low tides reveal wide expanses of firm, wet sand. The best beaches for clamming are south of town beyond Playa El Faro and north of town beyond Campo Los Amigos. Small, tasty butter clams can be found around rocks, while the larger, meatier white clams are just beneath the wet sand. Check with locals about minimum acceptable sizes – clammers caught with undersized specimens are subject to hefty fines.

Fishing
Fishing draws many visitors to San Felipe, and Bahía San Felipe has become a parking lot of *pangas* (skiffs), shrimpers, trawlers and tuna clippers. Fishing licenses are obligatory for any type of fishing, including surf fishing.

A six-hour excursion on local boats costs US$60 per person for up to four people. Bait is usually provided. Most fishermen use wood or fiberglass pangas ranging in length from about 18 to 22 feet (5.5 to 6.5 meters). Travelers with their own boats will find several launching ramps, including a convenient one at Motel El Cortez, where San Felipe Sport Fishing (☎ (657) 7-10-55) is located. Tony Reyes Sport Fishing (☎ (657) 7-11-20) is at Avenida Mar Bermejo 130.

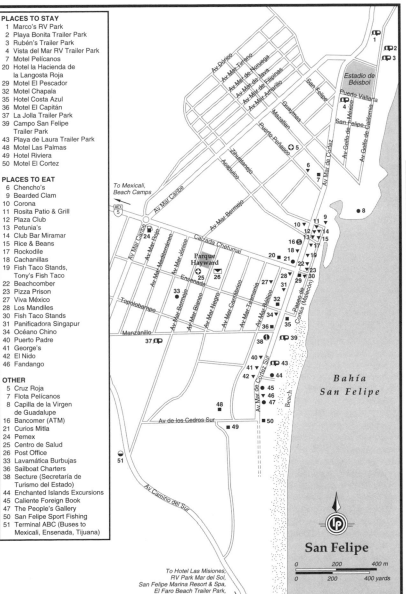

PLACES TO STAY
1 Marco's RV Park
2 Playa Bonita Trailer Park
3 Rubén's Trailer Park
4 Vista del Mar RV Trailer Park
7 Motel Pelícanos
20 Hotel la Hacienda de
la Langosta Roja
29 Motel El Pescador
32 Motel Chapala
35 Hotel Costa Azul
36 Motel El Capitán
37 La Jolla Trailer Park
39 Campo San Felipe
Trailer Park
43 Playa de Laura Trailer Park
48 Motel Las Palmas
49 Hotel Riviera
50 Motel El Cortez

PLACES TO EAT
6 Chencho's
9 Bearded Clam
10 Corona
11 Rosita Patio & Grill
12 Plaza Club
13 Petunia's
14 Club Bar Miramar
15 Rice & Beans
17 Rockodile
18 Cachanillas
19 Fish Taco Stands,
Tony's Fish Taco
22 Beachcomber
23 Pizza Prison
27 Viva México
28 Los Mandiles
30 Fish Taco Stands
31 Panificadora Singapur
34 Océano Chino
40 Puerto Padre
41 George's
42 El Nido
46 Fandango

OTHER
5 Cruz Roja
7 Flota Pelícanos
8 Capilla de la Virgen
de Guadalupe
16 Bancomer (ATM)
21 Curios Mitla
24 Pemex
25 Centro de Salud
26 Post Office
33 Lavamática Burbujas
36 Sailboat Charters
38 Secture (Secretaría de
Turismo del Estado)
44 Enchanted Islands Excursions
45 Caliente Foreign Book
47 The People's Gallery
50 San Felipe Sport Fishing
51 Terminal ABC (Buses to
Mexicali, Ensenada, Tijuana)

To Mexicali,
Beach Camps

Estadio de
Béisbol

*Bahía
San Felipe*

Beach

San Felipe

To Hotel Las Misiones,
RV Park Mar del Sol,
San Felipe Marina Resort & Spa,
El Faro Beach Trailer Park,
Aeropuerto Internacional
San Felipe, Puertecitos

0   200   400 m
0   200   400 yards

Enchanted Island Excursions (☎ (657) 7-14-31), located on a small, nameless private street just south of Playa de Laura Trailer Park, runs overnight excursions on the 37-foot *Viento Loco* for about US$100 per person but also has somewhat cheaper tours to Roca Consag for US$240 (for a maximum of eight people), as well as other Gulf destinations. Its Mexican mailing address is Apdo Postal 50, San Felipe, Baja California 21850, México; its US postal address is 233 Paulin Ave, PO Box 8512, Calexico, CA 92232. Flota Pelícanos (☎ (657) 7-11-88), Avenida Mar de Cortez 122, has similar offerings.

The following list indicates the types of fish that are most common throughout the year in the vicinity of San Felipe:

January – cabrilla, halibut, rockfish
February – cabrilla, halibut, rockfish
March – cabrilla, halibut, rockfish, yellowtail
April – cabrilla, halibut, rockfish
May – barracuda, cabrilla, sea bass, yellowtail
June – barracuda, bonefish, cabrilla, corvina, marlin, rockfish, sea trout, yellowtail
July – albacore, barracuda, bonefish, cabrilla, corvina, marlin, rockfish, sea trout, yellowtail
August – albacore, bonefish, cabrilla, corvina, marlin, rockfish, sea trout, yellowtail
September – barracuda, cabrilla, corvina, marlin, rockfish, sea trout, yellowtail
October – barracuda, cabrilla, corvina, rockfish, sea trout, yellowtail
November – cabrilla, corvina, rockfish, yellowtail
December – cabrilla, rockfish

The totuava, which weighs up to 200 pounds (90 kg) and once attracted countless sportfishermen to the area, was overfished in the 1980s; it is now an endangered species and fishing for it is prohibited.

Water Sports
Sailboat Charters, at Motel El Capitán, also rents paddleboats, kayaks, sailboards and Hobie Cats.

Special Events
On holidays like Thanksgiving, Christmas and New Year's, San Felipe becomes a mechanical zoo of ear-splitting motorcycles, dune buggies and other ATVs that could easily prod otherwise nonviolent pedestrians into carrying a bucket of nails or a spool of piano wire in self-defense.

San Felipe also hosts an abundance of special events, though the hot summer months of June, July and August are usually quiet. The party year starts with early February's **Carnaval San Felipe**, and accelerates in the second half of March with **spring break** for university students from north of the border. Mid-April sees the **Triatlón San Felipe**, drawing competitive cross-trainers in swimming, running and cycling. Street dances and a carnival mark **Día de la Marina Nacional** (National Navy Day), celebrated on June 1.

In late October the **Mexicali-San Felipe Sports Weekend** includes cycling, running and mountain-biking events. The **Feria del Camarón** (Shrimp Festival) in November has become a tourist and gastronomic success despite the decreasing shrimp population in the Gulf. December's **Bienvenida a los Pájaros de la Nieve** – perhaps the antithesis of spring break – acknowledges the annual arrival of snowbird retirees from the frozen north.

Long a preferred destination for fossil-fuel fanatics, San Felipe boasts Mexico's only racing stadium, which serves as both the start and finish of some off-highway races, though most start and finish at the arches on the approach to town. The stadium is about 5 miles (8 km) south of town; the main annual events are the **SCORE San Felipe 250** in early March, mid-September's **Carrera San Felipe 200** and November's **Baja 1000**, the most famous (or infamous) of such races.

Places to Stay

Accommodations in San Felipe, as in Playas de Rosarito, Ensenada and other Baja beach towns, can be hard to categorize because rates vary so much both seasonally and between weekdays and weekends. A budget hotel during the week may well be a midrange place on the weekend or during spring break.

Places to Stay – budget

Camping Campgrounds and RV parks are abundant in San Felipe itself and also dot the beaches to the north and south. In-town sites have better facilities and are generally more expensive, ranging from US$9 to US$20 per night, but there are exceptions. Others cost from US$2 to US$5 for two people. Most places have potable water, electricity and hot showers.

Pete's Camp, 6 miles (10 km) north of San Felipe at the Km 177 marker of México 5, has basic campsites (only a few with shade), but showers, toilets and cold beer are available. *Campo Peewee* near Km 182 is popular with the ATV mob – not a place for quiet relaxation. Rustic *Playa Blanca* at Km 183 has 70 spaces, some with full hookups; toilets and showers are available.

At the northern end of town, *Marco's RV Park* (☎ (657) 7-18-75), Avenida Golfo de California 868, has small but well-equipped campsites and RV sites (full hookups) for US$9. Across the street, *Playa Bonita Trailer Park* (☎ (657) 7-12-15; (909) 595-4250 in mainland California) has 35 sites with hookups, as well as toilets, showers and a restaurant. The cost is US$17 per site, plus US$2 per additional person; prices rise slightly on holidays. The US reservation address is 529 S Alvarado St, Los Angeles, CA 90057.

Rubén's Trailer Park (☎ (657) 7-10-91),

just south of Playa Bonita Trailer Park at Avenida Golfo de California 703, has 54 sites (some shaded) with full hookups. A boat launch, a restaurant, toilets, showers and a patio are also available. Rates are US$15 per night for two and US$2 for each additional person. The postal address is Apdo Postal 196, San Felipe, Baja California 21850, México.

Misleadingly named *Vista del Mar RV Trailer Park*, Avenida Mar de Cortez 631 at the southern end of San Felipe's ballpark, has better views of a vacant lot than of the sea, but it's quiet, immaculately maintained and within easy walking distance of central San Felipe. Rates are US$12 per site without electricity, US$15 with electricity.

La Jolla Trailer Park (☎ (657) 7-12-22), near the center of town at the corner of Avenida Mar Bermejo and Manzanillo, offers 50 fully equipped sites, toilets, showers and laundry facilities. A site costs US$15 per night for two people and US$2 for each additional person. Write PO Box 978, El Centro, CA 92243 for more information.

Playa de Laura Trailer Park (☎ (657) 7-11-28), in San Felipe between Avenida Mar de Cortez and the beach, has 50 sites, half with full hookups and the rest with water and electricity only. Hot showers and rental boats are also available. Costs are US$13 and up per night for two people and US$2 for each additional person. Its US postal address is PO Box 130, Calexico, CA 92231.

Also in town and on the beach is the *Campo San Felipe Trailer Park* (☎ (657) 7-10-12), with showers, toilets and 34 fully equipped sites for US$12 to US$16 for two people (rates depend on beach proximity), plus US$2 for each additional person (children under age six are free). The registration office keeps a selection of trashy novels in English.

San Felipe's cushiest trailer park is *RV Park Mar del Sol* (☎ (657) 7-10-88; (800) 336-5454 in the USA), in the southern end of town at Avenida Misión de Loreto 149 next to Hotel Las Misiones. It offers 85 RV sites with full hookups and 17 tent sites at US$20 per night for two people and US$3 for each additional person. Amenities include access to hotel facilities, showers, toilets, a small grocery, a laundry room, a boat ramp and a restaurant.

El Faro Beach Trailer Park (☎ (657) 7-11-06), 12 miles (19 km) south of Bahía San Felipe at Punta Estrella, charges US$25 per night for sites with full hookups, plus showers, a tennis court and a swimming pool. Follow the airport road south and watch for signs.

Hotels & Motels One-star *Motel El Pescador* (☎ (657) 7-10-44), at the corner of Calzada Chetumal and Avenida Mar de Cortez, has 24 rooms with air-conditioning for US$25/30 single/double weeknights, US$28/32 weekends. Comparable *Motel Pelícanos* (☎ (657) 7-15-71), on Avenida Mar de Cortez north of Puerto Peñasco, costs US$25 weekdays, US$35 Fridays and Saturdays.

Friendly *Motel Chapala* (☎ (657) 7-12-40), Avenida Mar de Cortez 142, offers clean, decent singles/doubles for US$28/30; most rooms have air-con and others have a kitchenette. Its US postal address is PO Box 8082, Calexico, CA 92231.

Places to Stay – middle

Overlooking the town from Avenida de los Cedros Sur near Avenida Mar Báltico, *Hotel Riviera* (☎ (657) 7-11-85) has air-conditioned rooms with private bath and shower, all smelling of disinfectant; its two bars and the murky swimming pool are shelters from the summer heat. Rooms cost about US$31 double (including breakfast) during the week, US$42 weekends. The postal address is Apdo Postal 102, San Felipe, Baja California 21850, México.

Hotel la Hacienda de la Langosta Roja (☎ (657) 7-15-71), Calzada Chetumal 125, adjoins a music store with a deafening sound system aimed toward the street for the pleasure of everyone from Mexicali to Puertecitos (and maybe even Puerto

Peñasco across the Gulf). Rates are US$35/49.

The two-star, 36-room *Motel El Capitán* (☎ (657) 7-13-03), Avenida Mar de Cortez 298 across from the state tourism office, has 40 basic rooms with air-con, satellite TV and swimming pool for US$36 single or double weeknights, US$40 weekends, but there are occasional discounts as low as US$24/28. Its US postal address is PO Box 1916, Calexico, CA 92232.

Across from the Hotel Riviera on Avenida Mar Báltico, three-star *Motel Las Palmas* (☎ (657) 7-13-33, fax (657) 7-13-82) has 45 clean, air-conditioned rooms for about US$40 weeknights, US$50 weekends. It has a pleasant pool area with plenty of lounge chairs, a poolside bar and a view of the Gulf of California.

Motel El Cortez (☎ (657) 7-10-55) is a 90-room beachfront place on Avenida Mar de Cortez Sur near the center of town. Singles/doubles with sea views, air-conditioning, TV and private bath with shower begin at about US$49 single or double, with discounts for AAA members; a few smaller rooms have beachfront patios. Amenities include a restaurant/bar (with satellite TV dish), a swimming pool and a boat ramp. The US postal address is PO Box 1227, Calexico, CA 92232.

Dwarfing others in its category in size (140 rooms) and amenities (pool, satellite TV, bar, restaurant, coffee shop, phones and the like), the extravagantly landscaped *Hotel Costa Azul* (☎ (657) 7-15-48, fax (657) 7-15-49), at Avenida Mar de Cortez and Ensenada, charges US$45 from November through February, US$58 most of the rest of the year. Holiday and weekend rates are higher. Its US postal address is 233 Paulin Ave, PO Box 6252, Calexico, CA 92231. Visitors in search of quiet should know that its owner buses in spring-break revelers from north of the border.

Places to Stay – top end

Two miles (3 km) south of San Felipe at Avenida Misión de Loreto 148, the 190-room *Hotel Las Misiones* (☎ (657) 7-12-80;

(619) 472-6767, (800) 336-5454 in the USA) has extensive facilities including a trailer park, two tennis courts, restaurants, bars, cafeterias and swim-up bars in two of its three swimming pools. Rooms cost about US$75 single or double; all have air-conditioning, color TV, telephone and shower bath. There's a 20% AAA discount. The US mailing address is 233 Paulin Ave, PO Box 7544, Calexico, CA 92231.

San Felipe Marina Resort & Spa (☎ (657) 7-14-55, fax (657) 7-15-66; (619) 558-0295, (800) 291-5397 north of the border) is a new and luxurious facility at Km 4.5 on the road to the airport. Rates normally start around US$105 double, but substantial weekday and off-season discounts are possible.

Places to Eat

As a popular tourist destination, San Felipe has a good selection of restaurants serving the usual antojitos as well as outstanding seafood specialties. For excellent but inexpensive tacos, try the numerous *stands* along the malecón, most of which specialize in fish and shrimp. *Tony's Fish Taco*, at the corner of Calzada Chetumal, is a dependable and inexpensive choice, but many others nearby are worth a try.

George's (☎ (657) 7-10-57), a US-style coffee shop at Avenida Mar de Cortez Sur 336, is a breakfast favorite among local expatriates; hours are 6 am to 9 pm. *Chencho's* (☎ (657) 7-10-58), Puerto Peñasco 233, is a recommended breakfast choice, but the antojitos are ordinary.

Petunia's, Avenida Mar de Cortez 241, specializes in pizza, as does the newly popular *Pizza Prison*, upstairs on Calzada Chetumal between Avenida Mar de Cortez and the malecón.

Despite its coffee-shop appearance, the *Corona* (☎ (657) 7-11-21), at Avenida Mar de Cortez 300, serves a good variety of seafood and Mexican dishes at modest prices. *Cachanillas* (☎ (657) 7-10-39), on Avenida Mar de Cortez just north of Calzada Chetumal, also serves moderately priced seafood. Also on Avenida Mar de Cortez, just south of the tourist office, *Puerto Padre* (☎ (657) 7-13-35) is open 6 am to 9 pm for seafood and antojitos. Nestled between Caliente Foreign Book and The People's Gallery on Avenida Mar de Cortez Sur, *Fandango* (☎ (657) 7-12-90) is an overlooked bargain for Mexican specials like chilaquiles.

On the street side at the northern end of the malecón, *Rosita Patio & Grill* (☎ (657) 7-17-70) has a large and varied menu, emphasizing seafood, at moderate prices. Around the corner on the malecón, *Rice & Beans* (☎ (657) 7-17-70), run by the same owners, has similar fare, with an especially notable fish stew.

Open 6 am to 9 pm, *Los Mandiles* (☎ (657) 7-11-68), at the corner of Calzada Chetumal and Avenida Mar de Cortez, serves seafood and steak, with free appetizers. *Viva México*, on Avenida Mar Báltico just south of Calzada Chetumal, serves steak and seafood at upscale prices. *Océano Chino* (☎ (657) 7-18-66), Avenida Mar de Cortez 146, is a conveniently central Chinese restaurant.

El Nido (☎ (657) 7-10-28), Avenida Mar de Cortez Sur 348, serves various seafood dishes and charbroiled steaks cooked over mesquite charcoal for about US$6 to US$10 for a full meal; hours are 2 to 9 pm (closed Wednesday). El Nido also serves breakfast on Friday, Saturday and Sunday.

For freshly squeezed juice, paletas, aguas, ice cream, milkshakes and similar treats, try *La Michoacana*, with several locations on and around Avenida Mar de Cortez. *Panadería El Buen Gusto* offers a selection of sugary Mexican pastries, as does *Panificadora Singapur*, on Avenida Mar de Cortez just south of Calzada Chetumal.

Entertainment

Several clubs on and around the malecón are primarily nightspots but also serve food. The *Rockodile* (☎ (657) 7-12-19) patio and grill on Avenida Mar de Cortez caters to a mostly younger crowd; a fenced-in sandlot with a volleyball net segregates the grill side from the bar. Specialties include the 'tacodile' (a big, meaty taco) and 'rockodile' (an alcoholic concoction based on tequila).

Just south of the Rockodile at the corner of Calzada Chetumal, the *Beachcomber* (☎ (657) 7-10-44) is a combination sports bar and grill. *Club Bar Miramar* (☎ (657) 7-11-92), with entrances both on the malecón and at Avenida Mar de Cortez 315, is similar in concept. Another is the *Plaza Club*, on Avenida Mar de Cortez just north of Acapulco.

For bettors, *Caliente Foreign Book* (☎ (657) 7-12-90) has a convenient venue on Avenida Mar de Cortez Sur just north of Motel El Cortez.

Things to Buy
San Felipe's biggest source for souvenirs from around Mexico is Curios Mitla, at the corner of Avenida Mar de Cortez and Calzada Chetumal, but the entire street is lined with stores. For arts and crafts by local and expatriate artists, as well as crafts classes, visit The People's Gallery at Avenida Mar de Cortez Sur 5 just north of Motel El Cortez. Open seven days a week, it also serves as an informal tourist information service; the mailing address is Apdo Postal 154, San Felipe, Baja California 21850, México. It sometimes closes in the heat of summer.

Getting There & Away
Air Aeropuerto Internacional San Felipe (☎ (657) 7-13-68) is 8 miles (13 km) south of town via a spur off México 5, but there are presently no commercial flights. The Mexicana subsidiary Aerolitoral may begin commuter services.

Bus Terminal ABC (☎ (657) 7-15-16) is on Avenida Mar Caribe, just south of Avenida de los Cedros Sur. Buses to Mexicali (two hours, about US$7) leave at 7:30 am, noon and 4 and 8 pm.

Buses leave for Ensenada (four hours, US$10) at 8 am and 6 pm daily; some continue to Tijuana (US$15). Service to Puertecitos, south of San Felipe, has been discontinued.

Getting Around
Taxis alone serve the international airport. Fares should be around US$10.

PUERTECITOS
As paved México 5 gradually extends southward, access to the once-isolated string of communities stretching to Puertecitos and beyond is becoming easier; the road to Puertecitos is very good despite numerous *vados* (fords), which require slowing down, and potholes the last few miles. Puertecitos itself (population around 100), 52 miles (84 km) south of San Felipe, is popular with north-of-the-border retirees who festoon their driveways with street signs pilfered from their hometowns.

There is a Pemex station (only rarely open), public telephone service and decent sportfishing in the area. Charters Mar de Cortez, Avenida Mar Caribe 325 in San Felipe, operates diving trips in the area; its US mailing address is 355 W 2nd St, Calexico, CA 92331. Several warm, spring-fed pools near the point just south of town make for good bathing.

Fishing
The following list indicates which fish species are most common each month near Puertecitos:

January – cabrilla, corvina, grouper, white sea bass
February – cabrilla, corvina, grouper, white sea bass
March – cabrilla, corvina, grouper, white sea bass
April – cabrilla, corvina, grouper
May – cabrilla, corvina, grouper, sierra, yellowtail
June – corvina, grouper, marlin, rockfish, sierra, yellowtail
July – corvina, grouper, marlin, roosterfish, sierra, yellowtail
August – corvina, grouper, marlin, roosterfish, sierra, yellowtail
September – grouper, marlin, rockfish, sierra, yellowtail
October – cabrilla, grouper, sierra, yellowtail
November – cabrilla, grouper, white sea bass
December – cabrilla, grouper, white sea bass

Places to Stay & Eat

Playa Escondida Trailer Park charges US$7 per site. Remodeled *Puertecitos Motel & Restaurant* has double rooms for US$35, plus half a dozen RV sites with cold water and occasional electricity for US$8; the restaurant may be closed in the early part of the week.

SOUTH OF PUERTECITOS

Within a few years, the road south of Puertecitos is likely to be paved to its intersection with the Transpeninsular south of Cataviña. For the time being, however, ask about conditions, because much of the road is very rough and subject to washouts as far as Bahía San Luis Gonzaga, about 50 miles (80 km) south. While vehicles with high clearance and short wheelbase are desirable, they are not absolutely essential, and 4WD is not necessary. Allow at least four

hours to Bahía San Luis Gonzaga, and drive slowly to avoid punctures of tires or oil pan.

Trailers and large RVs, with luck and skill, can go as far as La Costilla, about 5 miles (8 km) south of Puertecitos. About 25 miles (40 km) south of Puertecitos, *Campo Turístico Las Paredes* is typical of the many fish camps that dot the mountainous coastline and wait patiently and optimistically for a better road. Camping costs US$3 per night.

Eighteen miles (29 km) south of Las Paredes, the fishing camp at *Punta Bufeo* has tidy, upgraded stone rooms for US$20 double, now with hot showers, and a good restaurant. Beyond Punta Bufeo, the road becomes easier but still requires caution as far as Rancho Grande. For further details on the highway, see the Bahía San Luis Gonzaga entry in the Desierto Central & Llano de Magdalena chapter.

Desierto Central & Llano de Magdalena

One of the least frequented parts of the peninsula, Baja's Desierto Central (Central Desert) extends roughly from El Rosario, where the Transpeninsular turns inland, to Loreto, at the northern end of the Sierra de la Giganta. In pre-Columbian times Cochimí Indians foraged its vast deserts and fished its extensive coastlines. The area is still more rural than other parts of the peninsula, with few resort-style hotels or restaurants with English-language menus. Many of its small farming towns, fishing villages and century-old *ranchos* (rural settlements) are accessible only by dirt and gravel roads.

Most visitors come to central Baja to fish its hidden coves or explore isolated beaches – ideal for camping, clamming and lounging in the sun. Verdant valleys of grapes and tomatoes, extinct volcanoes and massive granite boulders on high plateaus are all accessible to well-outfitted travelers, and Baja's historical heritage is more palpable here than it is farther north. Well-preserved or restored mission churches and modest plazas in San Ignacio, Loreto and elsewhere reveal close links to mainland Mexican life and culture. In Santa Rosalía, French colonial clapboard buildings and a prefabricated Eiffel church recall a 19th-century copper boom that drew miners from around the world.

The region's terrain is diverse and alluring. The sinuous 76-mile (122-km) stretch of the Transpeninsular between El Rosario and Cataviña traverses a surrealistic landscape of huge boulders among stands of the *cardón* cactus (resembling the saguaro of the southwestern USA) and the twisted, drooping *cirio* (nicknamed 'boojum' for its supposed resemblance to an imaginary creature in Lewis Carroll's *The Hunting of the Snark*). The cirio grows only here and in parts of the mainland Mexican state of Sonora.

Beyond Guerrero Negro, the Desierto de Vizcaíno is a harsh, desolate expanse, but the oasis of San Ignacio augurs the semi-tropical environment of the Gulf coast between Mulegé and Cabo San Lucas. The Sierra de la Giganta parallels the Gulf, dividing the region into an eastern semi-tropical zone and a western region of arid lowlands and high plateaus. South of Loreto, the Transpeninsular turns west to the Llano de Magdalena (Magdalena Plain), a major agricultural zone that offers visitors activities like whale-watching, fishing, surfing and windsurfing.

MISIÓN SAN FERNANDO

About 35 miles (56 km) southeast of El Rosario, near the site of the Franciscan mission of San Fernando Velicatá, the roadside settlement of Rancho El Progreso offers simple food and cold drinks. *La Misión RV Park*, across the highway, was chained and out of service at last pass, but campers and RVers can still spend the night nearby. From Km 114 on the Transpeninsular, just west of the rancho, a dirt spur leads west about 3 miles (5 km) to the mission ruins. Despite a couple sandy spots, the road is passable for anything but a low rider.

The famed Franciscan Padre Junípero Serra founded the mission in 1769, but the Dominicans assumed control four years later when Serra decided to concentrate his efforts in Alta California. A few years later, epidemics nearly obliterated the native population, and the mission closed in 1818.

Some of the mission church's adobe walls are still standing, but of greater interest are the **petroglyphs** on a conspicuous granite outcrop a few hundred yards down the arroyo. Dating from about 1000 to 1500 AD, these include both abstract (curvilinear and geometric) and representational (human and animal) designs. Some of the latter appear to be shaman

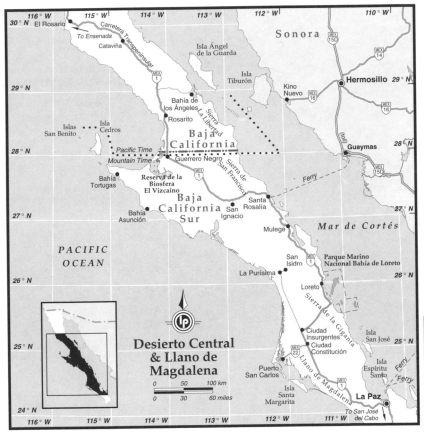

PACIFIC OCEAN

Desierto Central & Llano de Magdalena

0   50   100 km
0   30   60 miles

figures. These resemble sites in mainland California's Imperial, Inyo, Mono and San Bernardino counties more closely than they do Cochimí designs to the south. Unfortunately, vandals have damaged some paintings and others have weathered poorly, but together with the mission ruins they make the trip worthwhile.

EL MÁRMOL

At Km 143, an excellent graded lateral off the Transpeninsular leads to a major onyx quarry presently worked by nearby Ejido Revolución. Once trucked to the Pacific and shipped north to San Diego's Southwest Onyx and Marble Company, the decorative stone now takes the modern highway north to Tijuana, where it's turned into tabletops and similar items. Some still reaches the USA, as it did at the turn of the century.

Well worth seeing are the ruins of the **onyx schoolhouse**, which sheltered the children of the quarry workers when North Americans still ran the operation. The school closed around 1967, but its huge buttresses and unpolished, yard-thick walls are still an imposing sight.

At Km 144 of the Transpeninsular just beyond the El Mármol turnoff, *Rancho Sonora* has basic tourist facilities, including RV parking and a restaurant.

CATAVIÑA

Set in a landscape of massive granite boulders, the isolated oasis of Cataviña, roughly midway between El Rosario and Bahía de los Angeles, is a good place to fill the tank – the next Pemex station on the Transpeninsular is at Villa Jesús María, 123 miles (198 km) south – and stock up on supplies.

For great *free camping*, follow any of the sandy tracks off into the desert north of the arroyo, which runs to the north of Cataviña and west of the Transpeninsular among the boulders and towering cardones. Firewood is plentiful (keep it small, though), but bring food and water. A bonus is a series of Cochimí **cave paintings** east of the highway, just beyond the arroyo.

Those who prefer to stay in Cataviña proper can use the barren *Parque Natural RV Park*, which has hot showers but no electricity, for about US$5 per site. Economical rooms are available at *Cabañas*

Linda on the eastern side of the highway; fatigued visitors with a bigger budget can stay at *Hotel La Pinta*, perhaps the best kept of any of the La Pinta chain. At US$55/60 single/double, it features an attractive cactus garden, a swimming pool and a children's playground.

On the eastern side of the highway is reasonably priced *Café La Enramada*, successful enough to have built a pleasant new *palapa* (palm-leaf shelter) with cardón walls and glass windows to keep out the wind. The cafe offers quality antojitos, seafood specialties and traditional Mexican chocolate (ask for 'chocolate Ibarra' or you may get instant Quik, however). A much better value than the more elaborate restaurant at Hotel La Pinta, it also has a small grocery.

Rancho Santa Inés, at the end of a paved spur half a mile (1 km) south of Cataviña, permits camping, offering toilets and hot showers, for US$3 per site. It also has very clean dormitory accommodations for US$10 per person; a restaurant provides good meals, and its proprietors can arrange excursions to the isolated ruins of **Misión Santa María**, which Walt Peterson's *The Baja Adventure Book* called 'Mission Impossible.' The ruins are 17 miles (27 km) east of the highway by a road difficult even for 4WD vehicles, though ace Baja hiker Graham Mackintosh has walked the trail.

BAHÍA SAN LUIS GONZAGA

About 32 miles (52 km) south of Cataviña, near Laguna Chapala and across from *Lonchería Los Cirios* (a basic restaurant between Km 229 and Km 230 of the Transpeninsular), a graded but rough road, passable even for large RVs, cuts northeast to Bahía San Luis Gonzaga, Puertecitos and the popular Gulf resort of San Felipe. Bahía San Luis Gonzaga is a quiet, beautiful area now experiencing increased but not overwhelming tourist development, primarily attracting fishing enthusiasts. Except for a few large vacation homes, accommodations are fairly basic, though good food is available.

Before taking this road, ask about current conditions at the *llantera* (tire repair shop) next to Lonchería Los Cirios and deflate your tires – the road's sharp rocks can shred even heavy-duty tires that are fully inflated. Driving at speeds higher than 15 mph (24 kph) is not advisable.

About 13 miles (21 km) east of the junction is **Coco's Corner**, a wild assemblage of ready-made objets d'art, including beer-can ornaments, a cactus garden, ocotillo 'street trees,' hubcaps, fan belts and other odds and ends. Radiator water, motor oil and automatic transmission fluid are all available here, as are cold drinks and modest meals. *Camping* is encouraged (free of charge, with pit toilets).

From Coco's Corner, another dirt road leads east to little-visited Bahía de Calamajué; a branch off this road leads to the site of the short-lived **Misión Calamajué** and ruins of a **gold mill** on the Arroyo de Calamajué. The same road continues south toward Bahía de los Angeles but is only suitable for high-clearance vehicles with short wheelbases.

The main road continues about 4 miles (6 km) north to Rancho Las Arrastras de Arriola, which has water, a mechanic, a llantera and cold drinks. The sandy parallel tracks sometimes offer better driving than the main roadway on the 20-mile (32-km) stretch to Rancho Grande on Bahía San Luis Gonzaga itself. The entire stretch from the Transpeninsular to Rancho Grande, where Magna Sin gasoline is available for US$3 per gallon, takes about three hours.

Beyond Bahía San Luis Gonzaga, storms have damaged sections of the roadway to Puertecitos and San Felipe. For more details on this route, which is now very difficult for vehicles with low clearance and impossible for those without a short wheelbase (in other words, no RVs), see the South of Puertecitos entry in the Desierto del Colorado chapter. While 4WD is not necessary, the road is often steep, narrow, washboarded and difficult for any vehicle larger than a camper van. Construction of a Pemex station at Bahía San Luis Gonzaga, however, is a good indicator that this highway will soon be improved and paved (Pemex does not make gasoline deliveries on unpaved roads), so the RV assault cannot be far behind.

Fishing
Anglers usually bring their own boats to Bahía San Luis Gonzaga, though boats and guides may be locally available. The following list indicates which game-fish species are most common each month in and around the area:

January – white sea bass
February – white sea bass
March – corvina, white sea bass
April – bass, corvina, grouper
May – bass, corvina, grouper, yellowtail
June – bass, corvina, grouper, yellowtail
July – cabrilla, corvina, grouper, sierra,
    yellowtail
August – corvina, grouper, sierra, yellowtail
September – corvina, grouper, sierra, yellowtail
October – grouper, yellowtail
November – white sea bass
December – white sea bass

Places to Stay & Eat
RV Park Villas Mar de Cortez rents beachfront RV campsites for US$5 per car plus US$5 per palapa; facilities are limited to pit toilets, and gringo morons sometimes use the nearby airstrip for nighttime drag races. Potable water and cold showers are both available at Rancho Grande's Minimarket San Luis across the highway.

Just to the north, *Alfonsina's* also has its own airstrip, much improved and expanded motel-style accommodations (US$40 for rooms with two double beds and private bath) and a fine seafood restaurant. There's also a single beachfront palapa for car campers for US$5 per night, but how long it will last is open to question.

Two and a half miles (4 km) north is the turnoff for *Papá Fernández*, a popular fish camp with basic accommodations (around $10 per site) and an excellent restaurant; service is a little slow, but the shrimp omelet and the fresh tortillas are worth the wait.

BAHÍA DE LOS ANGELES
In colonial times, Bahía de los Angeles was a supply port for the interior mission of San Borja. About 107 miles (172 km) southeast of Cataviña via a paved spur off the Transpeninsular, it is now a popular fishing village (population 520) on the shore of its sparkling namesake bay, an inlet of the Gulf of California. The surface of the 42-mile (68-km) spur, which meets the Transpeninsular at a junction 65 miles (105 km) south of Cataviña, sometimes resembles the grooved and ridged shell of a leatherback turtle, but parts were recently resurfaced and more improvements are in store.

Many people come here to fish the offshore islands and nearby isolated beaches and to kayak among the Midriff Islands as far south as Loreto, rather than to see Bahía de los Angeles itself. Some have complained that the inshore waters have been fished out, but there is still a yellowtail season from May to October (also one of the hottest periods of the year).

Information
The best source of information on Bahía de los Angeles and the surrounding area is the Museo de la Naturaleza y de la Cultura (see below).

Bahía has a Telnor long-distance office (☎ (66) 50-32-06/7); unfortunately, this office does not permit collect calls.

As of early 1997, the local Pemex station was closed, but Magna Sin was available from Igor, at the northern edge of town, for about US$2 per gallon (roughly a 50% markup).

Dangers & Annoyances Theft, though not epidemic, is increasing. Keep an eye on your belongings, even the large and conspicuous – a small plane recently disappeared from the airfield north of town, and because it was out of reach of radar at Ensenada (to the north) and Loreto (to the south), authorities were unable to track it down.

Museo de la Naturaleza
y de la Cultura

The self-supporting museum of nature and culture features well-organized displays of shells, sea turtles, whale skeletons and other local marine life, and exhibits on native cultures (including Cochimí artifacts and rock art displays), mining, and horsegear and *vaquero* (cowboy) culture. Also on the grounds are a desert botanical garden and a good reconstruction of a mining site. Director Carolina Shepard has undertaken creative projects such as oral histories of local residents.

Just uphill from the central plaza, it is open 9 am to noon and 2 to 4 pm daily. Admission is free, but the museum enjoys volunteer labor and depends on donations and sales of books and T-shirts for support. The volunteers, mostly resident gringos, are a good source of information.

Programa Tortuga Marina

Bahía de los Angeles was once the center of the turtle fishery on the Gulf and, unfortunately, the now illegal practice has not completely disappeared. In a modest facility at the unused Brisa Marina RV

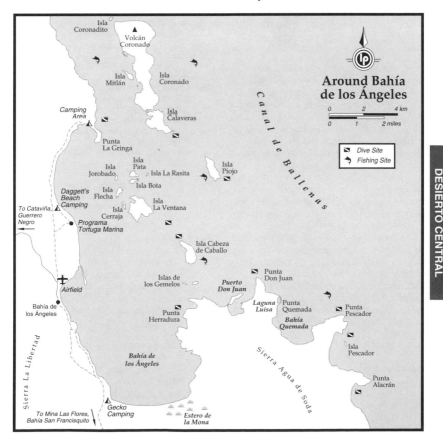

DESIERTO CENTRAL

Fishing

Casa Díaz (see Places to Stay & Eat, below) and a couple other outfitters arrange full-day (6 am to 1 pm) *panga* (skiff) excursions for US$80 to US$90. Those with their own boats can use the launch ramps at Villa Vitta Trailer Park or Guillermo's for about US$6 per day (use is free, however, if you're staying at either place).

The following list indicates which game-fish species are seasonally abundant in the vicinity of Bahía de los Angeles:

January – cabrilla, grouper, roosterfish, yellowtail
February – corvina, grouper, roosterfish, yellowtail
March – corvina, sierra, yellowtail
April – cabrilla, corvina, grouper, halibut, roosterfish
May – cabrilla, corvina, dolphin, grouper, sailfish, yellowtail
June – cabrilla, corvina, dolphin, grouper, marlin, sailfish, yellowtail
July – cabrilla, grouper, marlin, roosterfish, sailfish, yellowtail
August – cabrilla, grouper, marlin, roosterfish, sailfish, yellowtail
September – cabrilla, grouper, sailfish, yellowtail
October – cabrilla, grouper, yellowtail
November – cabrilla, grouper, roosterfish, yellowtail
December – cabrilla, grouper, roosterfish, yellowtail

Park, the Secretaría de Medio Ambiente, Recursos Naturales y Pesca (Semarnap) Sea Turtle Program conducts research on sea turtle biology, ecology, morphometry and conservation. In 1996 the program released a loggerhead turtle named 'Adelita' at Santa Rosalillita on the Pacific side of the peninsula, and tracked it by radio transmitter across the ocean to Japan.

The modest program's tanks offer the opportunity to see endangered sea turtle species like the *tortuga laúd* (leatherback, *Dermochelys* spp), the *tortuga prieta* (green, *Chelonia mydas agasizii*) and the *tortuga carey* (hawksbill, *Eretmochelys imbricata*). At last pass, greens and hawksbills were the only live specimens, but there were impressive leatherback shells.

Parents should keep close watch on their children – despite its innocuous appearance the smallish hawksbill will quickly (but not painlessly) amputate a dangling finger. The Programa Tortuga Marina is north of town on the coast.

Mina Las Flores

About 6 miles (10 km) south of town on the road to Bahía San Francisquito, all that's left of a once prosperous gold mine are the remains of an adobe house and a sturdy, virtually intact smelter.

Sea Kayaking

According to San Diego-based kayaker Ed Gillet, kayaking from Bahía de los Angeles is one of the best and most challenging adventures in the Gulf of California. Northeasterly winds of up to 35 knots can suddenly appear and churn the water into a nasty mess, so expect some exciting paddling.

Isla Coronado, northeast of town, is the most popular local destination for kayakers. To get there, follow the dirt road north out of town for about 5 miles (8 km) to Punta La Gringa; in winter there are usually plenty of campers around to watch your vehicle while you paddle. On Isla Coronado, Gillet recommends camping on the western side (near the islet of **Mitlán**) and fishing on the eastern side. Many kayakers continue north from Punta La Gringa to Punta Remedios and **Isla Angel de la Guarda.**

Those exploring offshore islands should take care to avoid disturbing wildlife; careless visitors have scared many birds, most notably pelicans, from their nests, exposing eggs and chicks to predators and the hot sun.

Gillet has written extensively about kayaking in this area, most notably in the Fall 1989 edition of *Baja Traveler*, and publishes a quarterly newsletter on the activity. For more information, see the Southwest Sea Kayaks listing in the Outdoor Activities chapter.

Gecko Camping, south of town, and a couple other places have rental kayaks at reasonable prices.

Places to Stay & Eat

Bahía de los Angeles has several motels, RV parks and other campsites north and south of town, plus a handful of decent restaurants. *Punta La Gringa*, a beautiful beach area to the north, has several rugged campsites with choice views of offshore islands, but the road is a bit hard to follow, the trash cans are overflowing and toilet facilities are nil.

Daggett's Beach Camping, just north of the Programa Tortuga Marina, charges US$6 per site with access to hot showers and very clean baths; in general, it's much cleaner and tidier than most other area campgrounds.

Congenial *Gecko Camping*, in a quiet shoreline location 3½ miles (6 km) south of town on the Bahía San Francisquito road, has ramshackle cabins for US$10 double with shared flush toilets, newly built bathrooms with hot showers, firewood, regular trash collection and furnishings that appear to have been liberated from a Salvation Army warehouse sealed up since the 1950s. It also offers camping for US$8 per night with access to the same limited amenities.

In town, *Hotel La Hamacas* (☎ (61) 76-87-15 in Ensenada) has clean and spacious doubles for US$20, plus US$10 for each additional person. Its restaurant is a good choice and a bit cheaper than others in town.

Hotel Villa Vitta (☎ (760) 741-9583 in the USA for information and reservations) offers very clean, comfortable, air-conditioned rooms ranging from US$23 to US$60, depending on the number and size of beds. Its restaurant specializes in moderately priced seafood. Across the road, the shabby, shadeless *Villa Vitta Trailer Park* has suspect toilets and a few beachfront spaces with full hookups for about US$5 per vehicle, plus US$2 for hot showers at the hotel (US$3 for nonguests).

Next door, separated from the beach by an unsightly row of trailers and fishing shanties, *Guillermo's Trailer Park & Restaurant* has about 40 spaces for tents and RVs, some with limited shade and a few with full hookups, for only US$4 per night. The baths are less than immaculate, but the hot water supply is reliable, at least at the shower stall alongside the restaurant. Its motel annex has singles/doubles with private bath for US$35/45, while meals at the restaurant cost about US$7 to US$10. The restaurant food is good, the margaritas large but watery and expensive; only during the 4 to 5 pm happy hour are they a good value.

Casa Díaz is a family-run trailer park/campground that includes a grocery and motel, plus a restaurant that may or may not reopen. The motel, consisting of 15 cozy stone cabins with hot showers, charges about US$25/30 for singles/doubles. Camping is possible on the motel grounds for about US$5 for two or three people, but Guillermo's is probably a better choice.

Flor del Mar, at the northern approach to town, is a very good seafood restaurant – try the tasty scallops in particular, but note the price difference (about 30%) between the peso and dollar menus. It pays to pay in pesos.

SANTA ROSALILLITA

Twenty-four miles (39 km) south of the Bahía de los Angeles junction on the Transpeninsular, a road leads 10 miles (16 km) west to Santa Rosalillita, an overgrown fish camp on the Pacific coast. The road is graded but unrelentingly washboarded, and resembles nothing so much as an eternal progression of speed bumps. The exit off the Transpeninsular is signed southbound but not northbound. Across Bahía de Sebastián Vizcaíno from Rosalillita, the twin peaks of Isla Cedros are visible in the distance.

eaches north of **Punta Santa Rosalillita**, reachable by a difficult 7½-mile (12-km) dirt road that requires high clearance, are renowned among surfers for exceptional breaks, while **Punta Rosarito** to the south, known among surfers as 'The Wall,' may be the most consistent break on the entire peninsula.

ROSARITO

Rosarito is a small truck stop 8½ miles (14 km) south of the Santa Rosalillita junction and 32 miles (52 km) south of the Bahía de los Angeles junction. For surprisingly good food, try *Restaurant Mauricio*, whose striking onyx counter comes not from the massive quarry at El Mármol (see the El Mármol entry in this chapter), but from a smaller, local quarry known as El Marmolito. Rosarito (impossible to mistake for the Playas de Rosarito resort between Tijuana and Ensenada) offers the most convenient approach to Misión San Borja, one of the most significant and best preserved on the peninsula.

MISIÓN SAN BORJA

At Rosarito, a lateral off the Transpeninsular leads 21 miles (34 km) east to the extensive ruins of Misión San Borja de Adac, founded here in 1762 by Jesuit Fray Wenceslao Linck because of the area's abundant water supply – the few remaining nearby families still cultivate grapes, olives and other crops. Of all the Jesuit adobes in Baja California, these are the best preserved.

Dominicans built the now restored landmark church, made of locally quarried volcanic stone with many outstanding details, well after the Jesuits' expulsion. See the custodian to climb the spiral staircase to the chorus, and leave a small (or large) donation. Other notable remains include the old mill and wine vats. On October 10, the local saint's day, devotees from throughout the region converge on the tiny *ranchería* (settlement) to pray and party.

The well-signed road from Rosarito is rough in spots, but any vehicle with a short wheelbase and the clearance of a small pickup can handle it. The route passes through a spectacular Wild West valley landscape of cirio, cardón, *torote* (elephant tree), *datilillo* (yucca) and cholla beneath broad volcanic mesas. The road forks about 2 miles (3 km) before San Borja; a sign indicates that both forks go to the mission, but the left (northern) fork is easier on both car and driver.

An alternative route to San Borja leaves the paved road to Bahía de los Angeles at Km 44. By reputation, this is a 4WD route, but some locals profess to have taken ordinary passenger vehicles on the road. Along this route are some pre-Columbian **rock paintings**.

PARALELO 28

Marked by a 140-foot (42-meter) steel monument ostensibly resembling an eagle (but more accurately described by veteran travel writer Joe Cummings as 'the world's largest tuning fork'), the 28th parallel marks the border between the states of Baja California (northern Baja) and Baja California Sur (southern Baja). The time zone changes here: Pacific Time (to the north) is one hour behind Mountain Standard Time (to the south).

The monument also symbolizes the completion of the Transpeninsular, and during celebrations of the highway's completion, thousands jammed the amphitheater at its base. For years the facilities were neglected and trashed almost beyond salvation, but the Mexican army has rehabilitated them and installed a new guns-and-drugs checkpoint.

Hotel La Pinta Guerrero Negro, one of several La Pinta hotels in Baja, sits precisely on the 28th parallel. It has a restaurant, a bar and 28 comfortable singles/doubles for US$55/60, but some of its details show wear and tear. *Trailer Park Benito Juárez*, alongside the hotel, has a few palapas and spacious pull-through sites (but no electricity or hot water) for US$3 per night.

GUERRERO NEGRO

Guerrero Negro (population 10,220), the first settlement south of the 28th parallel,

is a company town that owes its existence to the world's largest evaporative saltworks. Most travelers, however, come here to visit famous Laguna Ojo de Liebre (better known in English as Scammon's Lagoon), the mating and birthing site for California gray whales. The Exportadora de Sal (ESSA) dominates the local economy, but the tourist trade is an important supplement, especially during the winter whale-watching season. A more recent economic factor is the Mexican army, which has a new camp at the Paralelo 28 monument north of town.

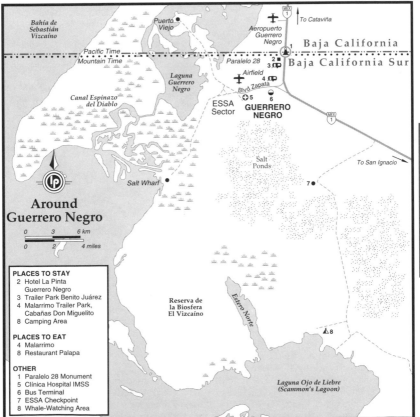

Around Guerrero Negro

| 0 | 3 | 6 km |
| 0 | 2 | 4 miles |

PLACES TO STAY
2 Hotel La Pinta
   Guerrero Negro
3 Trailer Park Benito Juárez
4 Malarrimo Trailer Park,
   Cabañas Don Miguelito
8 Camping Area

PLACES TO EAT
4 Malarrimo
8 Restaurant Palapa

OTHER
1 Paralelo 28 Monument
5 Clínica Hospital IMSS
6 Bus Terminal
7 ESSA Checkpoint
8 Whale-Watching Area

DESIERTO CENTRAL

Scammon & the Whales

Laguna Ojo de Liebre takes its English name, Scammon's Lagoon, from Captain Charles Melville Scammon, an American whaler who frequented the area in the 1850s. Born in Maine, Scammon yearned to captain a trading ship but had to settle for command of less lucrative whalers, like the *Boston* out of San Francisco. In 1857, upon learning from some Mexicans that an estuary near Bahía de Sebastián Vizcaíno was the breeding ground of the gray whale, he headed south.

Each year, gray whales migrate 6000 miles (9700 km) from the Bering Sea to the warmer lagoons of Ojo de Liebre, San Ignacio and Bahía Magdalena, where they stay from January to March. The lagoons offer an ideal, protected place for sexually mature whales (five years or older) to mate, give birth and nurture their offspring. By late March, most have begun the long journey back to the Arctic.

For whalers, the density of whales in constricted, shallow lagoons meant almost literally shooting fish in a barrel, but Scammon's first attempts were disastrous: whales crushed two of his small whaleboats and seriously injured half the crew. Resorting to 'bomb lances' – bombs fired into a whale from a hand-held gun – instead of harpoons, Scammon and his crew managed to get 740 barrels of oil, filling virtually every container on board, which was later sold in San Francisco as lubricant.

By the end of 1859, Scammon and other whalers had nearly eliminated the gray whale from the lagoons. Whaling did not cease until 1935, and it took many decades for the population to recover. Today the US and Mexican governments have effective laws, in addition to international agreements, that protect the gray whale and its habitat.

Informally designated as Parque Natural de la Ballena Gris (Gray Whale Natural Park), Laguna Ojo de Liebre is formally part of the massive Reserva de la Biosfera El Vizcaíno, as is Laguna San Ignacio. The breeding areas of Bahía Magdalena have no formal legal protection beyond wildlife conservation statutes, a situation that has caused conflict among government officials, development interests and local residents, and may cause problems for the whales themselves.

For a detailed account of historical interactions of humans and cetaceans in the area, see David Henderson's *Men and Whales at Scammon's Lagoon* (Dawson's Bookshop, Los Angeles, CA, 1972). Emily Young and Serge Dedina's 'Conservation and Development in the Gray Whale Lagoons of Baja California Sur, Mexico' is an academic report that can be obtained from a website; see the Internet Directory at the end of this book for the website address. ■

Named for the *Black Warrior*, a Massachusetts whaler wrecked nearby in the mid-19th century, Guerrero Negro capitalizes on tourism through its annual **Festival Cultural de la Ballena Gris** (Gray Whale Cultural Festival), lasting three weeks in early February. It includes events as varied as environmental talks, films, bicycle races and a book fair. Other indicators of progress are continuing street improvements, a construction boom and establishment of an FM radio station, but it's still probably the least appealing of any of the whale-watching bases.

Orientation

Guerrero Negro comprises two very distinct sectors: a disorderly strip along Blvd Emiliano Zapata west of the Transpeninsular, and ESSA's orderly company town, with a standard grid pattern that begins shortly after Blvd Zapata curves southwest near the airfield. Most of the town's accommodations and restaurants are in the former area on Blvd Zapata.

Information

Money Banamex, on Blvd Zapata at the entrance to the ESSA sector, will change US dollars and traveler's checks at reasonable rates, with a minimum of bureaucracy, 8:30 to 11 am weekdays. It also has the only ATM between San Quintín and Santa Rosalía. Supermercado La Ballena no longer changes traveler's checks, but accepts US dollars in payment for purchases, giving change in pesos.

Post & Communications The town's post office is in the ESSA sector; the postal code is 23940.

Public telephones are few and poorly maintained, so the several pharmacies with long-distance phone booths are the best alternative. Unfortunately, they do not permit collect calls.

Laundry Lavamática Express, across the street from Motel Las Ballenas (see Places to Stay, below), is open 8 am to 9 pm Monday through Saturday, 9 am to 5 pm Sunday.

Medical Services The town's Clínica Hospital IMSS (☎ (115) 7-04-33) is on the southern side of Blvd Zapata at the point where the road curves southwest.

Water Campers and RVers can obtain purified drinking water at a reasonable cost at Fresk-Pura on the southern side of Blvd Zapata.

Saltworks

ESSA's saltworks consists of about 70 sq miles (182 sq km) of evaporative ponds, each about 110 sq yards (100 sq meters) in area and about a yard deep, just south of Guerrero Negro. In the intense desert sunlight and high winds, water evaporates quickly, leaving a saline residue that is dredged from the pools, hauled to nearby quays and barged to Isla Cedros for transshipment by freighter. The works produces over five million tons of salt annually.

To visit the saltworks, contact Sr Leonardo Villavicencio (☎ (115) 7-00-13), Exportadora de Sal, Guerrero Negro, Baja California Sur 23940, México.

Whale-Watching

Guerrero Negro is the northernmost of Baja's whale-watching locales and has the most abundant accommodations of any of them. Tours from Guerrero Negro, however, are usually briefer than tours elsewhere because they require traveling some distance to the whale-watching sites.

Three-hour tours usually start at 8 and 11 am and cost around US$35. Local operators include Mario's (☎ (115) 7-08-88, fax (115) 7-07-88) and Ecotour Malarrimo (☎ (115) 7-02-50, fax (115) 7-01-00), both at their namesake restaurants (see Places to Eat, below).

Note that whale-watching excursions at Guerrero Negro and more southerly points conform to Mountain Standard Time; southbound visitors who forget to change their watches at the state border will literally miss the bus.

Places to Stay

Guerrero Negro has fairly abundant and reasonably priced accommodations, but the winter whale-watching season can put a strain on these resources. For this reason, reservations are advisable from January through March.

Camping Camping is free at most beaches outside town. In town, the rather barren *Malarrimo Trailer Park* (☎ (115) 7-02-50, fax (115) 7-08-53) charges from US$5 per site for tent camping, US$10 for RVs; not all the electrical outlets work, so check before setting up. Hot water is plentiful and the toilets are clean, but one of the showerheads emits a stream thinner than a pencil lead. The largest RVs, especially those with trailers, may have trouble maneuvering into a site.

Hotels & Motels Well-worn *Dunas Motel* (☎ /fax (115) 7-06-66), at Blvd Zapata and División del Norte, has 28 drab but clean rooms with firm beds and hot showers. Singles cost US$9 plus a refundable key deposit of US$3. *Motel Brisa Salina* (☎ (115) 7-01-15), on the northern side of Blvd Zapata, is comparably priced.

Motel Gamez (☎ (115) 7-03-70), on the northern side of Blvd Zapata toward the airfield, has slightly shabby but adequate rooms for US$12 double; nonguests may use the hot showers for US$2. About 200 yards (182 meters) south across Blvd Zapata, family-run *Mini Hotel Asunción* is simple but very clean and friendly, with hot showers and TV for US$12 single or double. Probably the best value in town is five-room *Motel Las Ballenas* (☎ (115) 7-01-16), just north of Hotel El Morro (see below); clean and tidy, it has hot water and color TV in every room for US$12/16 single/double.

Hotel El Morro (☎ (115) 7-04-14), on the northern side of Blvd Zapata, has clean, pleasant singles/doubles for US$19/21. All rooms have cable TV and hot showers. The upgraded *Motel San José* (☎ (115) 7-14-20), opposite the bus terminal, has singles/doubles with TV and hot showers for US$19/24. Guerrero Negro's newest accommodations are at *Motel Don Gus* (☎ (115) 7-16-11) around the corner from the bus terminal, just off Blvd Zapata, where singles/doubles go for US$21/25; it also has a decent restaurant and a bar. *Motel San Ignacio* (☎ (115) 7-02-70), on the northern side of Blvd Zapata, has clean, spacious singles/doubles with TV for US$22. *Cabañas Don Miguelito* (☎ (115) 7-02-50, fax (115) 7-01-00), part of the Malarrimo restaurant-RV park complex, has pleasant detached singles/doubles for US$22/25.

Places to Eat
Guerrero Negro's best bargains are the numerous *taco stands* along Blvd Zapata, which keep erratic hours but maintain high standards. *Supermercado La Ballena* (☎ (115) 7-06-66) has reasonably priced takeout food at its cafeteria and a wide selection of groceries and produce for campers who plan to go into the backcountry. Its landmark sign depicts a sperm whale rather than the gray whale that draws tourists to the area.

For good breakfasts, try *Cocina Económica Letty* on the southern side of Blvd Zapata, which also serves very fine antojitos and seafood at prices a fraction of those at Malarrimo (see below). *Mario's* (☎ (115) 7-08-08), next door to Hotel El Morro on the northern side of Blvd Zapata, serves excellent, moderately priced seafood.

Highly regarded *Malarrimo* (☎ (115) 7-02-50), on the northern side of Blvd Zapata as you enter town, specializes in seafood ranging from fish and shrimp to clams and abalone, in both traditional antojitos and more sophisticated international dishes. While it's not cheap, portions are abundant and it's still a good value; the margaritas are small but strong.

For paletas and aguas, there's a branch of *La Michoacana* on the southern side of Blvd Zapata.

Getting There & Away
Air Aeropuerto Guerrero Negro is 1.2 miles (2 km) north of the state border, just west of the Transpeninsular. Guerrero Negro also has an airfield near the ESSA sector in town.

The Aeroméxico connector airline Aerolitoral (☎ (115) 7-17-33) flies daily except Sunday to Hermosillo, with connections to Ciudad Juárez, Ciudad Obregón, Chihuahua, Mexico City, Phoenix and Culiacán (weekdays only). Its offices are on the northern side of Blvd Zapata near the Pemex station, but it leaves from Aeropuerto Guerrero Negro.

Aerolíneas California Pacífico (☎ (115) 7-10-00) flies rickety DC-3s (bring your own seat belt – seriously!) to nearby Isla Cedros for US$25 one way. While these flights are the quickest option to the island, they inspire little confidence in their safety. Flights are often booked early, so it's best to reserve at least a day in advance and arrive at 8 am for the 10 am

(Mountain Standard Time) flights, daily except Sunday. Three days a week, these flights continue from Cedros to Bahía Tortugas (US$20), near the tip of Península Vizcaíno. Return flights from Cedros ostensibly leave at 1 pm (Pacific Time), but you should arrive at least an hour ahead of time in case of early departure.

The airline's offices are on the northern side of Blvd Zapata, but flights leave from the airfield near the ESSA sector; look for the yellow shed with blue trim and doors. It's better to make reservations and purchase a return ticket in Guerrero Negro than to do so on Isla Cedros.

You can also fly north to Isla Cedros or Ensenada with Aerocedros (☎ (115) 7-13-35), which now has offices on the northern side of Blvd Zapata in Guerrero Negro. Aerocedros flies Tuesday and Friday at 1 pm to Cedros (US$34) and Ensenada (US$63) from Aeropuerto Guerrero Negro.

Bus From Guerrero Negro's bus terminal on the southern side of Blvd Zapata, Autotransportes de Baja California (ABC) offers services throughout the peninsula, while Autotransportes Aguila operates in Baja California Sur only. Northbound buses depart daily at 2:30 am for Mexicali and for other destinations at 6:30 and 8:30 am and 7:30, 8:30 and 10 pm. Southbound buses to Santa Rosalía and intermediate stops depart daily at 5 and 7:30 am; buses to La Paz and intermediate stops depart at 6 and 8 am, 4:30 and 9 pm and midnight. Approximate fares northbound from Guerrero Negro are as follows:

Destination	Fare
San Quintín	US$13
Ensenada	US$19
Tijuana	US$23
Mexicali	US$31

Sample southbound fares include:

Destination	Fare
Vizcaíno	US$3
San Ignacio	US$6
Santa Rosalía	US$7.50
Mulegé	US$9
Loreto	US$15
Ciudad Constitución	US$19
La Paz	US$25

AROUND GUERRERO NEGRO
Reserva de la Biosfera El Vizcaíno & Laguna Ojo de Liebre

Also known in part as Parque Natural de la Ballena Gris (Gray Whale Natural Park), the 9833-sq-mile (25,566-sq-km) Vizcaíno Biosphere Reserve sprawls from Laguna San Ignacio, Guerrero Negro, Isla Natividad and Isla Cedros across to the Gulf of California, taking in part of the Sierra de San Francisco. It is the joint responsibility of Semarnap (☎ (115) 7-17-77 in Guerrero Negro) and Ejido Benito Juárez (☎ (115) 7-17-33), whose lands the reserve occupies.

Laguna Ojo de Liebre (Scammon's Lagoon) has the greatest number of whales of any of Baja's four main whale-watching sites. Local *pangueros* (fishermen with skiffs) take visitors for 1½-hour excursions on its shallow waters for US$15 for adults (including a postexcursion beer or soft drink at the ejido restaurant), US$10 for children. Whale-watching now officially begins December 15 and lasts until April 15, but whales are few at the earliest dates. Late-season trips, from mid-February on, are likelier to encounter friendly whales.

Five miles (8 km) southeast of the Guerrero Negro junction, at Km 208 of the Transpeninsular, a smooth, graded road leads 15 miles (24 km) southwest to Laguna Ojo de Liebre; all vehicles must register with the guard at ESSA's checkpoint, which controls the access road. (The reason the road is so smooth is that it's almost solid salt, so be sure to get your car washed soon after leaving.)

Camping is possible at the lagoon, where savvy visitors choose sites above the sometimes flooded tidal flats; the more remote sites are also closer to the maternity channel, so that you can hear the whales up close and personal. The ejido charges US$3 per vehicle for camping or day use; its *Restaurant Palapa* has superb food at very reasonable prices – don't miss the tasty almejas rancheras (clams with salsa).

El Arco & Pozo Alemán

About 17 miles (27 km) south of Guerrero Negro, a once paved but now graveled

26-mile (42-km) lateral leads eastward to El Arco, a 19th-century gold-mining town that now serves as a supply center for surrounding ranchos. The replacement of the road's miserably broken pavement by gravel is a godsend, as it's now possible to drive the route without arranging a chiropractor's appointment in advance.

El Arco, which retains a smattering of rusting machinery from its mining heyday, is presently undergoing a minor renaissance due to renewed interest in its ores. The area's real highlight is the nearby ghost town of Pozo Alemán, a few kilometers east on a sometimes rugged dirt road. Its ruins include several residences, the smelter, a blacksmith's shop, a still-functioning windmill and water system and a company store with items still on the counter. Note especially the caves – actually excavations in the steep banks of the arroyo – where the peons resided. A caretaker oversees the ruins and shows visitors around; a small tip is appropriate.

The dirt road continues west to Bahía San Francisquito on the Gulf of California; just west of Bahía San Francisquito, a graded road leads north to Bahía de los Angeles.

Misión Santa Gertrudis

About 23 miles (37 km) east of El Arco via an unpaved road, the isolated Misión Santa Gertrudis La Magna was the focus of the Jesuits' northward missionary efforts. Initially founded as a result of explorations by the famous Jesuit Fernando Consag in 1751, its original adobe church, with a stone foundation, was built under the direction of Fray Sebastián Sisteaga and an extraordinary blind Cochimí Indian named Andrés Comanjí. The German Jesuit Georg Retz took charge of the 600 Cochimí here, digging a well, building *acequias* (irrigation canals) and planting wheat, maize, olives, grapes, dates, pomegranates and figs. The mission also maintained livestock, such as cattle, horses, mules, goats and sheep.

After the Spanish government expelled the Jesuits in 1767, Dominicans took over and finished the small stone church, now undergoing restoration, which bears a ceiling date of 1796. Labor and water shortages forced the mission's abandonment in 1822.

The church museum contains a selection of Guaycura, Cora and Cochimí artifacts, as well as *ofrendas* (offerings) left by pilgrims whose wishes have been granted by Santa Gertrudis – common among the offerings are the lengthy tresses of young women who have visited this popular pilgrimage site. Every November 16, pilgrims jam the village for the **Fiesta de Santa Gertrudis**.

Another landmark is **El Camino Real**, the royal road (really a trail) that still leads 29 leagues (100 miles or 161 km) from San Ignacio to San Borja via Santa Gertrudis. Most travelers prefer the improved road from El Arco, passable for any passenger vehicle and even small RVs (though one van with California plates now stands on blocks behind the church). The entire trip from Guerrero Negro takes 2½ to 3 hours.

BAHÍA SAN FRANCISQUITO

About 52 miles (84 km) east of El Arco and 80 miles (129 km) south of Bahía de los Angeles, Bahía San Francisquito contains the remote, rustic fishing resort *Punta San Francisquito*, most of whose guests arrive by private plane. The road from Bahía de los Angeles is passable for just about any passenger vehicle. The road from El Arco requires high clearance and, at least on the way out, considerable skill and high clearance to climb the short but steep and winding Cuesta de la Ley (4WD is helpful but not essential). At the top of the Cuesta, a sturdy concrete shrine to the Virgin of Guadalupe has all the devotional charm of a public housing project.

Beachfront camping is possible at the resort for just US$5 per site with access to hot showers, while *cabaña* (cabin) accommodations cost US$15 per person, US$30 with full board. Reservations are essential for cabañas but not for camping; the US contact is Armando Tiznado (☎ (619) 690-1000).

A short distance north of the resort, *Puerto San Francisquito* has equally attractive beachfront camping for US$2.50 per person with a saltwater flush toilet, but there's no fresh water available. Outstanding meals, mostly freshly caught seafood, are available by special request from Deborah Wayne-Lucero, a US expatriate resident here for many years. There is no telephone, but there is radio contact from 7:30 to 8:30 am daily at 7.294 on the 40-meter band; the call sign is XE2/KC6UEJ. The resort's mailing address is Apdo Postal 7, San Ignacio, Baja California Sur 23930, México.

ISLA CEDROS

Isla Cedros is a mountainous northward extension of Península Vizcaíno, separated from the mainland by Canal de Kellet, the much smaller Isla Natividad and Canal de Dewey. Reaching altitudes of nearly 4000 feet (1200 meters) above sea level, this desert island is a rewarding, off-the-beaten-track destination for adventurous travelers.

Early Spanish explorers found surprisingly large numbers of Cochimí Indians on the island, whose intransigence led to their forcible relocation to the mainland mission of San Ignacio by the Jesuits. Manila galleons later used Isla Cedros as a port of refuge on their return across the Pacific. The island supports unusual vegetation, including native tree species, and coastal wildlife such as elephant seals and sea lions; Cedros mule deer *(Odocoileus hemionus cedrosensis*, an endangered subspecies) still inhabit the rugged backcountry.

Most of the island's 1465 inhabitants live in the tiny port of Cedros on the sheltered eastern shore, but many also live at ESSA's company town at Punta Morro Redondo at the southern tip of the island, which is the site of the airfield and the transshipment point for salt barged over from Guerrero Negro. The Sociedad Cooperativa de Producción Pesquera, the local fishing cooperative, is the other main employer, but commercial pressure has reduced the offshore abalone, just as earlier hunters vastly depleted the numbers of fur seals and sea otters (otters may have returned to the area). The first abalone divers were Japanese, but the Mexican cooperative took over the business after WWII.

Isla Cedros' commercial abalone season runs from December to June at three different locations: Cabo San Agustín, Cabo Norte and Islas San Benito. Divers work in groups of three and gather up to 100 abalone per day; there is also a lobster season from October to April.

The ramshackle village of Cedros faces Bahía de Sebastián Vizcaíno from the slopes beneath towering Cerro Vargas, also called Cerro Cenizo, whose summit (3950 feet or 1185 meters) is usually hidden by clouds. Your initial impression of dilapidation will soon fade as you discover its good points, but it's definitely not a stereotypical tourist destination. Cedros has no bank or any other place to change money, and you can't even get a margarita, but there is phone service, an IMSS hospital/clinic and a Capitanía del Puerto (port authority).

Several two-story buildings with porches or balconies facing the bay add a touch of vernacular architectural interest. Electricity is only available 6 am to noon and 5 to 11 pm; running water is available mornings only, though most houses have storage tanks. Prices are high because nearly everything is imported – including salt, despite the mountains of it at Punta Morro Redondo.

Things to See

In Cedros' tidy hillside church, murals in the curious **Capilla de la Reconciliación** (Chapel of Reconciliation) depict events in Mexican and Baja Californian history, such as the expulsion of the Jesuits, in a comic-book style. According to local residents, the hilltop **Panteón** (cemetery) harbors the remains of early Japanese divers, but only a single headstone bears a conspicuous Japanese inscription.

Places to Stay & Eat

Accommodations in Cedros are very basic. *Casa de Huéspedes Elsa García*, up the hill

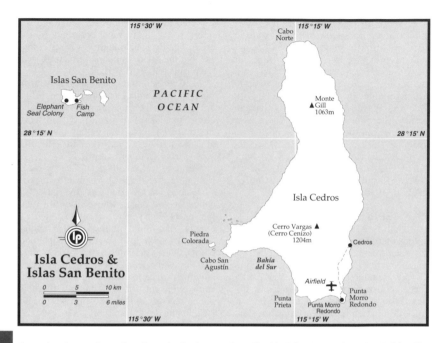

from the dusty triangular plaza, is the best in town, with clean singles/doubles for US$10. Its only competition is shabby, overpriced *Casa de Huésped Aguilar* on the waterfront, which charges US$10 for gloomy singles/doubles with shared bath (no hot water) or US$15 with private bath. To find the unmarked building, walk straight downhill from the church; before entering the grounds of the fishing cooperative, look for the two-story house on your left. If no one is on duty, you'll have to hike up the hill to Manuel Aguilar's house, a brown stucco next to the elementary school and the power plant, to check in.

Cedros has only a few places to eat and, surprisingly enough, prices for abalone are double or triple those on the mainland – few locals or visitors will want to pay US$35 to sample this delicacy at *El Marino*, whose antojitos, fish and shrimp are good and also much more reasonably priced. *La Pacenita* is a bit cheaper, but heavily fried foods are the rule. A friendly *taco stand* up the main drag from El Marino serves only carne asada.

Getting There & Away

Isla Cedros' airfield is at Punta Morro Redondo, about 5 miles (8 km) south of the village. Taxis charge about US$5 per person, but locals will sometimes offer you a ride there. Flights from Guerrero Negro and Ensenada serve Isla Cedros.

Purchase Aerolíneas California Pacífico tickets at Licores La Panga, up the hill from the northern point of Cedros' triangular plaza. Return flights from Isla Cedros to Guerrero Negro (US$25) ostensibly leave at 1 pm (Pacific Time), but travelers should arrive at least an hour ahead of time to avoid being left at the airstrip. Three days a week, these flights return to Guerrero Negro via Bahía Tortugas (US$20), near the tip of Península Vizcaíno.

Flights from Ensenada arrive regularly.

Tickets to Ensenada from Isla Cedros are available at the Sociedad Cooperativa de Producción Pesquera (☎ (115) 8-53-01) in the village of Cedros. The office closes to the public at 1 pm.

AROUND ISLA CEDROS
Islas San Benito

This tiny archipelago consists of three small islands 30 nautical miles (55 km) west of Isla Cedros; the westernmost island, the largest of the three, supports a large winter camp of abalone divers and their families, as well as a substantial breeding colony of northern elephant seals *(Mirounga angustirostis).* The seals begin to arrive in December, but are most numerous in January and February. Another notable animal is the black storm-petrel *(Oceanodroma melania),* locally known as the *nocturno* because it leaves its nesting burrows only at night. Sea turtles and whales are visible offshore (the islands are just off the gray-whale migration route).

Unless you bring camping equipment and enough food and water to stay overnight, expect to spend no more than an hour on shore. Avoid getting too close to the elephant seals, especially the enormous bulls; not only are they potentially dangerous, but frightened bulls may accidentally crush or injure newborn pups, which cannot get out of their way.

Passing yachts often anchor here and sailors come ashore to see the seals, but budget travelers can catch a lift on the *Tito I,* which carries daily supplies to the abalone divers and returns to Isla Cedros with the day's catch. For a passage on the *Tito I,* which is free of charge, visit the Sociedad Cooperativa de Producción Pesquera in the village of Cedros before 1 pm, when it closes to the public. On request, with routine approval by the chief, the secretary will issue a letter to present to the captain that evening for the following day's voyage.

The crew of the *Tito I* are exceptionally friendly and will probably offer breakfast to passengers, but travelers prone to seasickness should refrain from eating too

heavily. The four-hour voyage to the San Benitos, against the wind and the northwestern swell, is generally rougher than the voyage back.

PENÍNSULA VIZCAÍNO

One of Baja's most thinly populated areas, Península Vizcaíno is a sparsely vegetated, mountainous extension of the Desierto de Vizcaíno. For detailed information about driving and road conditions in this area, consult the guidebook published by the Automobile Club of Southern California. While you may not need a rugged 4WD vehicle everywhere – roads are generally passable – conditions are terrible in certain areas.

About 40 miles (64 km) south of Guerrero Negro, the crossroads town of **Vizcaíno** is the gateway to the peninsula; good accommodations are available at *Motel Kadakamán* (☎ (115) 4-00-24, ext 212) for US$15 double. Its rather barren RV park charges US$7; improvements are supposedly underway. Across the road, *Motel Olivia* (☎ (115) 4-00-24, ext 124, fax (115) 4-03-04) charges US$13/16 single/double for rooms with air-con and TV (with a limited selection of channels).

From Vizcaíno's bus terminal at *Restaurant Rosita,* Estado Treinta runs morning buses Monday, Tuesday, Wednesday and Saturday to **Bahía Tortugas** (three hours, US$13) near the western tip of the peninsula, on a partly paved but mostly graded surface negotiable for any vehicle. Passing yachts usually anchor at Bahía Tortugas because it's the only port between San Diego and Cabo San Lucas that has direct refueling facilities, making it a good spot for lifts south despite its remoteness; hang out on the pier near the tuna cannery. Anglers cruise the offshore kelp beds for bass, mackerel and barracuda, while farther offshore they find bonito and yellowtail.

Bahía Asunción, reached by a graded road at the southern end of the Sierra Santa María (no public transport), is a prime site for barracuda, bonito, dorado, yellowfin and yellowtail, but the area is very windy and offshore waters are rough.

Both Bahía Tortugas and Bahía Asunción have Pemex stations, but carry extra fuel in any event.

SAN IGNACIO

After the scrub and cacti forests of the Desierto de Vizcaíno, the palm oasis of San Ignacio (population 761) is a soothing sight. In 1728 the Mexican Jesuit Juan Bautista Luyando located Misión San Ignacio de Kadakaamán here, planting dense groves of date palms and citrus in the Arroyo El Carrizal surrounding the town. After the Jesuits' expulsion, Dominican missionaries supervised construction of the landmark lava-block church (finished in 1786) that still dominates San Ignacio's laurel-shaded plaza.

San Ignacio has become the jumping-off point for whale-watching excursions to Laguna San Ignacio – probably the best spot for contact with so-called friendly whales – and trips to the spectacular pre-Columbian rock art sites in the Sierra de San Francisco.

Surrounding ranchos and fish camps rely on the town for supplies – San Ignacio has several groceries, a handful of restaurants, a hotel, a motel and several modest trailer parks. Its lingering colonial atmosphere offers a pleasant respite from the bustling overdevelopment of some other Baja towns.

Orientation

San Ignacio is 88 miles (142 km) south of Guerrero Negro; the town proper is about 1 mile (1.6 km) south of the Transpeninsular – a paved lateral leads from the highway junction (known as San Lino) past a small lagoon and through groves of date palms into the town. Parking is easy and the town invites walking.

Information

Most services are found around the plaza, including the post office; the postal code is 23930. International collect calls are quick and easy from public telephones on the plaza (remember, however, to avoid the abundant but overpriced blue phones). There's also a private phone office on Hidalgo just east of the plaza, but it charges US$1.50 for the privilege of making a collect call.

Misión San Ignacio

With lava-block walls nearly 4 feet (1.2 meters) thick, the former Jesuit Misión San Ignacio de Kadakaamán is one of Baja's most beautiful churches, in continuous use since its founding in 1728. Opposite the plaza, occupying the site of a former Cochimí ranchería and initiated by the famous Jesuit Fernando Consag, it was completed in 1786 under the direction of Dominican Juan Crisóstomo Gómez. Epidemics reduced the Cochimí population from about 5000 at contact to only 120 by the late 18th century, but the mission lasted until 1840.

Museo San Ignacio

Just south of the mission church, the Instituto Nacional de Historia y Antropología (INAH) has built an impressive new museum that has elaborate displays on the Desierto Central's rock art, including a replica cave-mural site that's the next best thing to descending into Cañón San Pablo (see below). It's open 8 am to 6 pm daily except Sunday; visitors intending to visit any rock art site must request permission here.

Organized Tours

Kuyima (☎/fax (115) 4-00-70), a local cooperative on the plaza, arranges whale-watching trips in season, as well as visits to rock art sites in the surrounding area; its mailing address is Apdo Postal 53, San Ignacio, Baja California Sur 23930, México. Oscar Fischer, at Motel La Posada (see below), charges about US$20 per person to take visitors without vehicles to view the easily reached rock art site at Cueva del Ratón, but mule trips can be arranged more cheaply at San Francisco de la Sierra, with approval from INAH in San Ignacio. For details, see the separate entries on the Sierra de San Francisco and Laguna San Ignacio in this chapter.

Special Events

San Ignacio's **Fiesta Patronal** takes place the last week of July.

Places to Stay

San Ignacio has several basic RV parks at San Lino on the approach to town. On the eastern side of the lateral into San Ignacio, just north of the Hotel La Pinta San Ignacio, the very basic *Martín Quesada RV Park* charges just US$2 per site. On the western side, *Camping La Muralla* lacks shade but has clean new toilets; sites cost US$5 per night. Across the road, *Don Chon* has plenty of shade and a nice riverside location, but no amenities whatsoever.

Just south of Hotel La Pinta on the western side of the road, *El Padrino RV Park* (☎ /fax (115) 4-00-89) has undergone a major cleanup, but lacks shade in some areas despite handsome stands of date palms. There's only a single toilet, plus one in the restaurant, for more than 25 sites, only a few of which have full hookups, but four good showers have a dependable hot water supply. Fees are US$7 per site for camping, US$9 with full hookups; there are also four simple rooms available for US$9, with access to the shared toilets and showers.

Chalita, a restaurant facing the southern side of the plaza, has a few rooms with private bath for US$10. *Motel La Posada* (☎ (115) 4-03-13), the next closest thing to budget accommodations, has comfortable but spartan doubles with hot showers for about US$20. Conspicuously located at Carranza 22 on a rise southeast of the plaza, it often fills up early.

Hotel La Pinta San Ignacio (☎ /fax (115) 4-03-00; (800) 336-5454 in the USA) is on the main road into town, northwest of the plaza. For about US$55 single/double, its pseudocolonial architecture, tiled courtyard, swimming pool and groves of date palms and citrus cater more to affluent vacationers than to shoestring travelers.

Places to Eat

On the southern side of the plaza, *Chalita* serves the usual antojitos at very low prices in a family atmosphere (literally – it's a living room), but service is painfully slow and the food is only so-so. *Taquería Los Arcos*, just east of the plaza on Hidalgo, rarely keeps to its ostensible 5 pm opening time. Next-door *Rene's*, serving ordinary antojitos that taste as if they've been reheated in the microwave, occupies a site once held by the popular *Tota's*. Tota's itself has moved two blocks east, but still serves very good, reasonably priced antojitos and seafood dishes 7 am to 10 pm daily.

Hotel La Pinta San Ignacio also serves typical Mexican food, but at much higher prices, specializing in beef from nearby ranches. *Flojos*, at El Padrino RV Park, serves good, fresh seafood; its lobster is notably cheaper than Tota's and the margaritas are strong and fairly priced, but the live music is stereotypical stuff like 'Cielito Lindo.' On the Transpeninsular west of the San Lino junction, *Quichule* serves good antojitos at moderate prices.

Getting There & Away

Transpeninsular buses no longer enter the town, but instead pick up passengers opposite the Pemex station at the San Lino junction. There are at least five northbound buses daily between 6 am and 3 pm and as many southbound between 6 am and 10:30 pm.

AROUND SAN IGNACIO
Sierra de San Francisco

To date, researchers have located about 500 pre-Columbian rock art sites in an area of roughly 4300 sq miles (11,200 sq km) in the Sierra de San Francisco north of San Ignacio. Reached by a graded road from a conspicuously signed junction at Km 118 of the Transpeninsular, 28 miles (45 km) north of San Ignacio, the village of San Francisco de la Sierra is the gateway to the Desierto Central's most spectacular manifestations of Baja's unique cultural heritage.

About 1½ miles (2.5 km) west of San Francisco de la Sierra, **Cueva del Ratón**

Rock Art of the Desierto Central

WAYNE BERNHARDSON

When Jesuit missionaries inquired about the creators and meaning of the giant rock paintings of the Sierra de San Francisco, the Cochimí Indians responded with a bewilderment that was, in all likelihood, utterly feigned. The Cochimí claimed ignorance of both symbols and techniques, but it was not unusual, when missionaries came calling, to deny knowledge of the profound religious beliefs that those missionaries wanted to eradicate.

At sites like Cueva Pintada, Cochimí painters and their predecessors decorated high rock overhangs with vivid red-and-black representations of *monos* (human figures), *borregos* (bighorn sheep), pumas and deer, as well as more abstract designs. It is speculated that the painters built scaffolds of palm logs to reach the ceilings. Postcontact motifs do include Christian crosses, but these are few and small in contrast to the dazzling pre-Columbian figures surrounding them.

Cueva de las Flechas, across Cañón San Pablo, has similar paintings, but the uncommon feature of arrows through some of the figures here is the subject of serious speculation. One interpretation is that these depict a period of warfare. Similar opinions suggest that they record a raid or a trespass upon tribal territory, or perhaps constitute a warning against such trespass. One researcher, however, has hypothesized that the arrows represent a shaman's metaphor for death in the course of a vision quest. If this is the case, it is no wonder that the Cochimí would claim ignorance of the paintings and their significance in the face of missionaries unrelentingly hostile to such beliefs.

Such speculation is impossible to prove, since the Cochimí no longer exist. However, the Instituto Nacional de Historia y Antropología (INAH) has undertaken a survey of the Cochimí, the largest systematic archaeological survey of a hunter-gatherer people yet attempted in Mexico, and it has discovered that, in addition to rock art and grinding stones, the Cochimí left evidence of permanent dwellings. In recognition of its cultural importance, the Sierra de San Francisco will soon be declared a UNESCO World Heritage Site. It is part of the Reserva de la Biosfera El Vizcaíno, which includes the major gray-whale calving areas of Laguna San Ignacio and Laguna Ojo de Liebre.

Unfortunately, this means more publicity than protection. The Sierra de San Francisco will remain an INAH-protected archaeological zone, which means that foreigners will need entry permits to conduct research (not everyone has been scrupulous in this regard). INAH has already instituted regulations for tourists (for details, see the Sierra de San Francisco entry in this chapter) and probably will impose a modest admission fee to support basic infrastructure and services like an interpretive guidebook to the paintings. INAH will also face the challenge of giving area residents a stake in management of the sites, without which long-term protection of the sites is unlikely to be successful. ■

is the most accessible site, featuring typical representations of *monos* (human figures), *borregos* (desert bighorn sheep) and deer, but they are not as well preserved as paintings elsewhere in the area. The site is well worth seeing for day visitors, however, who must obtain INAH permission at San Ignacio and a guide at San Francisco de la Sierra in order to see the paintings, which are protected by a chain-link fence and locked gate. Visiting hours are 7 am to 5 pm daily.

The area's most rewarding excursion is a descent into the dramatic Cañón San Pablo to see its famous **Cueva Pintada, Cueva de las Flechas** and other magnificent sites. Cueva Pintada, really an extensive rock overhang rather than a cave, is the single most imposing site. Among English-speakers, it is known as Gardner's Cave; the popular American novelist Earle Stanley Gardner wrote several well-known books about his own adventures in the area. Mexicans, however, intensely resent the identification with Gardner and strongly prefer the Spanish term.

Exploring Cañón San Pablo requires a minimum of two days and preferably three. Visitors must obtain permission from INAH in San Ignacio, contract guides through Cuco Arce (☎ (115) 4-02-15, ext 229), the INAH representative at San Francisco de la Sierra, and agree to a series of INAH guidelines and other restrictions in the interest of preserving the paintings. Visitors may not touch the paintings, smoke at the site or take flash photographs – 400 ASA film easily suffices even in dim light. Campfires and alcoholic beverages are prohibited.

Local guides to Cueva del Ratón require only a modest tip, around US$1, but excursions to Cañón San Pablo involve hiring a guide and mule for US$12 per day, a mule for each individual in the party for US$7 per day and additional pack animals, either mules or burros, for US$6, to carry supplies such as tents and food. Visitors must also provide food for the guide; San Francisco de la Sierra has a Conasupo and another small market, but it's better to bring food from Guerrero Negro or San Ignacio.

Backpacking is permitted, but backpackers still must hire a guide and mule; most visitors will find the steep volcanic terrain much easier to manage on muleback, which leaves more time to explore the canyon and enjoy the scenery. The precipitous muleback descent into the canyon takes about five or six hours, and the ascent slightly less; in winter this means almost an entire day devoted to transportation alone. Perhaps the best time of the year is early spring, in late March or April, when days are fairly long but temperatures have not become unpleasantly hot.

San Francisco's residents, descendants of the early vaqueros who settled the peninsula along with the missionaries, still maintain a distinctive pastoral culture, herding mostly goats in the surrounding countryside. They also retain a unique vocabulary with many terms surviving from the 18th century, and produce some remarkable crafts – look at the guides' *polainas* (leather leggings) for riding in the bush, for instance. Such items are generally made to order, but occasionally villagers will have a pair of men's *teguas* (leather shoes) or women's open-toed *huaraches* (sandals) for about US$25.

At the turnoff to San Francisco de la Sierra, INAH has posted conspicuous signs that also warn against attempting to visit the rock art sites without its permission. The road from the Transpeninsular is regularly graded but, because parts of its surface are poorly consolidated at times, there are spots that are difficult for vehicles with poor traction and low clearance (4WD is not necessary, however). It can be very difficult after a rain.

Cuesta Palmarito

At a signed junction at Km 59 of the Transpeninsular, about 9 miles (15 km) east of San Ignacio, a decent road leads 24 miles (39 km) north from Ejido Alfredo

Principal mode of transportation in the Sierra de San Francisco

Bonfil to Rancho Santa Martha, the starting point for excursions to rock art sites at Cuesta Palmarito. Following approval from the office in San Ignacio, the local INAH representative will arrange guides and mules at prices comparable to those at San Francisco de la Sierra.

Punta Abreojos

Reached by a 45-mile (73-km) graded road that leaves the Transpeninsular about 16 miles (26 km) west of San Ignacio, Punta Abreojos is one of the prime fishing spots on Baja's Pacific coast. Cabaña accommodations are available at *Campo René* (☎ (115) 7-00-72, fax (115) 7-04-77).

Laguna San Ignacio

Along with Laguna Ojo de Liebre and Bahía Magdalena, Laguna San Ignacio is one of the major winter whale-watching sites on Baja's Pacific coast, with probably the highest concentration of 'friendly' whales of any location.

Pass the Salt, Please

Despite surviving and recovering from the brutality of commercial whaling, the California gray whale faces contemporary challenges in Baja California. At present, it has become an innocent bystander in a tug of war between Mexican government agencies with dramatically different visions for Laguna San Ignacio, one of the whale's key breeding sites.

The point of contention is a proposed 200-sq-mile (518-sq-km), US$100 million saltworks, to be operated by Exportadora de Sal (ESSA) at the 170-sq-mile (440-sq-km) lagoon. Ancillary works would directly affect 820 sq miles (2124 sq km) and indirectly impact up to 5800 sq miles (15,000 sq km) of the El Vizcaíno biosphere reserve, which contains Laguna San Ignacio. The Guerrero Negro-based ESSA, a state-owned enterprise with a large minority holding (49%) by the Japanese multinational Mitsubishi Corporation, plans a mile-long canal that would pump water continuously from Laguna San Ignacio to clay-lined evaporation beds to produce six million tons of salt annually – a figure that would double ESSA's current production. A 15-mile (24-km) conveyor belt would carry the salt to a 1½ mile (2.5 km) pier near Punta Abreojos, west of the lagoon.

Mexico's powerful Secretaría de Comercio y Fomento Industrial (Secretary of Commerce & Industrial Development) backs the project, but the resolute Instituto Nacional de Ecología (National Ecology Institute) vigorously objects to its potential impact on the area's whales and endangered peninsular pronghorn antelope and on its mangrove wetlands, which serve as incubators for fish and shellfish. The impact on the whales, though, is literally and figuratively the biggest and most controversial issue.

Nobody really knows how much disruption whales can tolerate during courtship and during the birth and raising of their young. ESSA claims that whale numbers have doubled in its three decades of operation at Laguna Ojo de Liebre near Guerrero Negro, but conservationists are skeptical of its data. Less than half of the narrower and shallower Laguna San Ignacio is suitable for whales; it might also suffer from turbulence caused by pumping, which could reduce salinity and temperature in areas frequented by newborn calves. Whales have adapted to human activities at Ojo de Liebre, but studies have shown that noises (like oil drilling and killer-whale sounds) seriously disturb them.

For these reasons, ESSA's project is on hold until the Universidad Autónoma de Baja California Sur completes a new Environmental Impact Assessment; there will be increased pressure on the project's opponents to accede if that assessment upholds ESSA's contentions. Meanwhile, organizations like the US-based Natural Resources Defense Council and the Mexican branch of the Worldwide Fund for Nature have made stopping the project their top priority. ■

Whale-watching excursions take place from mid-December to mid-April, but whales are most abundant in January, February and March. In other seasons the area is an outstanding site for bird-watching in the stunted mangroves and at offshore **Isla Pelícanos**, where about 150 ospreys and as many as 5000 cormorants nest (landing on the island is prohibited, but pangas may approach it). This is not Baja's best fishing area, but cabrilla, corvina, grouper, halibut and sierra are found here, and boats can be hired. Sea kayaking is prohibited when whales are present in the lagoon.

At the La Laguna and La Fridera fish camps on the southern shore of the lagoon, whale-watching excursions of about three hours cost around US$25 per person with José María Aguilar (known by his nickname, 'El Chema'), Francisco Mayoral (nicknamed 'Pachico') and Antonio Aguilar Osuña. Aguilar Osuña has a *house* that he rents for about US$20 to tourists who go out in his boat; knowledgeable visitors claim that his wife cooks the best meals in Baja. Maldo Fischer, at La Base, is another possibility for whale trips; his wife will also prepare meals. *Camping* is another alternative.

Kuyima (☎ /fax (115) 4-00-70), a cooperative with offices on the plaza in San Ignacio, operates a whale-watching camp consisting of 13 spacious tents, each with two cots and sleeping bags, though its intention is to replace the tents with sturdier thatched-roof *palafitos* (walled palapas). Tents equipped with lamps cost US$25 per night, while full board costs an additional US$20 per day. Kuyima also permits free camping nearby for those who take its whale-watching trips (about US$25 per person for three hours).

Camp guests have access to solar shower bags and very clean flush toilets using seawater; the camp itself is spotless and the English-speaking staff are friendly. Meals may be available for drop-ins – the food is excellent and abundant – but mealtimes are fixed (8 am for breakfast, 1 pm for lunch and 7:30 pm for dinner) and camp guests have priority. Kuyima's cozy

solar-powered dining room, out of the prevailing winds, has whale and natural history videos, as well as a library of natural history books.

The road from San Ignacio has deteriorated in recent years and most passenger cars need at least two hours to cover the 38 miles (61 km) to the La Fridera fish camp (assuming no rain has fallen recently) without wrecking their suspension. The first half of the road from the village is spine-wrenching washboard, but the second half is notably better.

The village of San Juanico, known for good surfing, is about 60 miles south of La Fridera via a graded but potentially hazardous road. The village is more safely reached from La Purísima; for details on the roads to San Juanico, see the Around San Isidro & La Purísima entry in this chapter.

SANTA ROSALÍA

Despite the nearby discovery of copper as early as the 1860s, the erstwhile company town of Santa Rosalía (population 10,451) really dates from the 1880s, when the French-owned Compañía del Boleo (one of the Rothschild family's many worldwide ventures) built it under a 99-year concession from the government of Mexican President Porfirio Díaz. Imported timber from Oregon and British Columbia frames the clapboard houses and French-style colonial homes that still stand along the main streets. The Compañía also assembled a prefabricated, galvanized-iron church designed by Alexandre Gustave Eiffel (the same!) for the 1889 World Fair in Paris. The church is still in use, while balconies and porches along the tree-lined streets encourage a spirited street life contrasting with the residential segregation of the mining era.

The French left by 1954, but a palpable legacy remains in the town's atypical architecture, a bakery that sells Baja's best baguettes and building codes decreeing that new construction must conform to the town's unique heritage. Most of the original ore-processing plant is intact; the

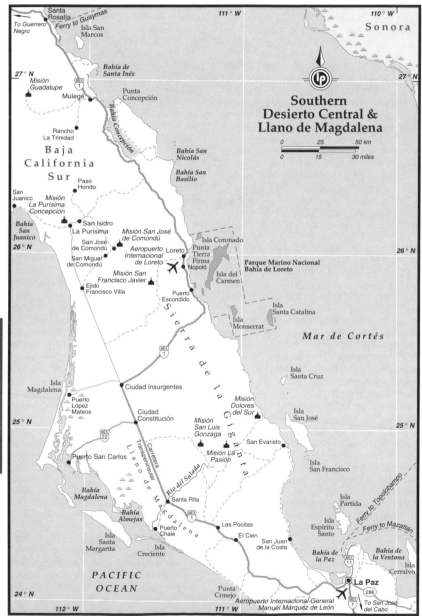

DESIERTO CENTRAL

Eiffel beyond the Tower

Few know that French engineer Alexandre Gustave Eiffel, so renowned for his controversial tower in Paris, also played a significant role in the New World. New York's Statue of Liberty is his most prominent transatlantic landmark, but his constructions also dot the Latin American landscape from Mexico to Chile. Santa Rosalía's Iglesia Santa Bárbara is only one of many examples.

In 1868, in partnership with the engineer Théophile Seyrig, Eiffel formed G Eiffel et Compagnie, which later became the Compagnie des Etablissements Eiffel. While the bulk of its metal construction work took place in France and its colonies, an aggressive agent in Buenos Aires obtained many contracts for public buildings in South America. Among his notable creations were the Aduana de Arica (Customs House, 1872; Arica was part of Peru and is now part of Chile), Arica's Iglesia San Marcos, the gasworks of La Paz (Bolivia) and the railroad bridges of Oroya (Peru). Most of these were designed and built in Eiffel's workshops in the Parisian suburb of Levallois-Perret and then shipped abroad for assembly.

What might have been his greatest Latin American monument effectively ended his career. In the late 19th century, Eiffel had argued strongly in favor of building a transoceanic canal across Nicaragua, but a few years later, he obtained the contract to build the locks for Ferdinand de Lesseps' corruption-plagued French canal across Panama. Implicated in irregular contracts, Eiffel was sentenced to two years in prison and fined a substantial amount; though his conviction was overturned, he never returned to his career as a builder. ∎

Transpeninsular passes beneath its old conveyor belt north of the turnoff into town.

After the mines closed, the federal government took charge of the facilities in order to preserve jobs, but the Compañía Minera de Santa Rosalía closed in 1985, on the eve of the town's centenary, because of a high incidence of arsenic poisoning among miners and their families. There are rumors of renewed mining, but as yet these are just rumors.

Public health problems were not the only adverse impact of mining: from the turn of the century, commercial egg collectors raided the gull colonies of the Midriff Islands to supply miners and their families.

Orientation

Santa Rosalía is on the Gulf coast 45 miles (73 km) east of San Ignacio and 38 miles (61 km) north of Mulegé. Most of central Santa Rosalía nestles in its namesake arroyo west of the Transpeninsular, while residential areas occupy plateaus north and south of the canyon. French administrators built their houses on the northern Mesa Francia, now home to municipal authorities, the museum and many historic buildings, while Mexican officials occupied the southern Mesa México.

The town's narrow *avenidas* (avenues) run northeast-southwest, while its short *calles* (streets) run northwest-southeast. One-way traffic is the rule. Large RVs will find it difficult to navigate around town and should park along or near the Transpeninsular.

Plaza Benito Juárez, about four blocks west of the highway, is the focus of the town. The Andador Costero, overlooking the harbor south of downtown, is an attractive *malecón* (pedestrian walk) with good views of offshore Isla Tortuga.

Information

Most tourist-oriented services are on or near Avenida Obregón, but there is no information office per se.

DESIERTO CENTRAL

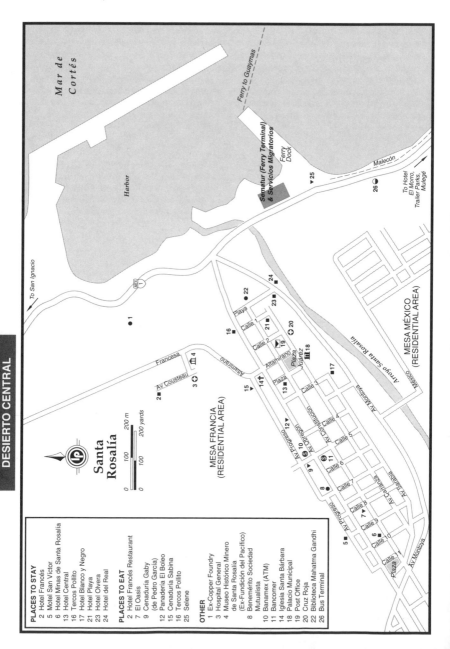

Santa Rosalía

Mar de Cortés

Harbor

Sematur (Ferry Terminal) & Servicios Migratorios

Ferry to Guaymas

Ferry Dock

Malecón

To Hotel El Morro, Trailer Parks, Mulegé

To San Ignacio

MESA FRANCIA (RESIDENTIAL AREA)

MESA MÉXICO (RESIDENTIAL AREA)

Arroyo Santa Rosalía

PLACES TO STAY
2   Hotel Francés
5   Motel San Víctor
6   Hotel Minas de Santa Rosalía
13 Hotel Central
16 Tercos Pollito
17 Hotel Blanco y Negro
21 Hotel Playa
23 Hotel Olvera
24 Hotel del Real

PLACES TO EAT
2   Hotel Francés Restaurant
7   El Oasis
9   Cenaduría Gaby
    (de Pedro García)
12 Panadería El Boleo
15 Cenaduría Sabina
16 Tercos Pollito
25 Selene

OTHER
1   Ex-Copper Foundry
3   Hospital General
4   Museo Histórico Minero
    de Santa Rosalía
    (Ex-Fundición del Pacífico)
8   Benemérito Sociedad
    Mutualista
10 Banamex (ATM)
11 Bancomer
14 Iglesia Santa Bárbara
18 Palacio Municipal
19 Post Office
20 Cruz Roja
22 Biblioteca Mahatma Gandhi
26 Bus Terminal

A: WAYNE BERNHARDSON

B: WAYNE BERNHARDSON

C: WAYNE BERNHARDSON

D: WAYNE BERNHARDSON

A: Palm canyon at Cañón Guadalupe, near Mexicali

B: Swimming hole, Cañón Guadalupe

C: Functional architecture, Valle de Mexicali

D: Puertecitos-Laguna Chapala road near Bahía San Luis Gonzaga

A: Volcanic plug
B: Rancher, Santa María de Toris
C: Only the brave sit out of the shade in the Desierto Central

D: Desert road, Bahía Concepción
E: The grand mountainscape of the Sierra de San Francisco

Immigration Travelers can find the Servicios Migratorios (☎ (115) 2-03-13) in the ferry terminal.

Money Santa Rosalía has the only banks between Guerrero Negro and Loreto; Mulegé-bound travelers should change US dollars or traveler's checks here. Banamex, which has an ATM, and Bancomer are on opposite corners of Avenida Obregón and Calle 5.

Post & Communications The post office is at the corner of Avenida Constitución and Calle 2. The postal code is 23920.

The Hotel del Real, on Avenida Manuel Montoya near the Transpeninsular, has long-distance services, but there are many Telmex public phones.

Medical Services Santa Rosalía's Hospital General (☎ (115) 2-07-89) overlooks the town from a hilltop site on Mesa Francia opposite the historic Fundición del Pacífico (now the town museum). The Cruz Roja (Red Cross) (☎ (115) 2-06-40) is on Avenida Carranza near Calle 2.

Town Landmarks
Due to its origins as a 19th-century company town, Santa Rosalía's architecture is fascinatingly atypical for a Mexican town. Its most famous landmark, at the corner of Avenida Obregón and Altamirano, is the **Iglesia Santa Bárbara**. Designed and erected in Paris, disassembled and stored in Brussels, intended for West Africa and finally shipped to Mexico, where a director of the Compañía del Boleo stumbled upon it by chance, Alexandre Gustave Eiffel's prefabricated church reached Santa Rosalía in 1895 and was reassembled by 1897. It has attractive stained-glass windows.

On the eastern side of Playa near the Transpeninsular, the **Biblioteca Mahatma Gandhi** was another Compañía del Boleo project. The **Benemérito Sociedad Mutualista** (1916), at the corner of Avenida Obregón and Calle 7, features an interesting clock tower.

Many buildings on Mesa Francia also deserve a visit, most notably the **Fundición del Pacífico** (now the local mining museum) and the **Hotel Francés**, as well as the ruins of the **copper foundry** along the Transpeninsular.

Lined with numerous French colonial houses, Avenida Cousteau runs between the Fundición and the hotel; it also displays a wealth of antique mining equipment, including steam locomotives, mine cars, cranes and the like.

Museo Histórico Minero de Santa Rosalía
Once the business offices (Fundición del Pacífico) of the Compañía del Boleo, the museum includes accountants' offices (now filled with scale models of historic buildings like the Benemérito Sociedad Mutualista, the Panadería El Boleo and the Cine Trianon, destroyed by fire some years ago), the purchasing office (filled with maritime memorabilia), the pay office (complete with safe) and the boardroom. Presently undergoing restoration, this new INAH project is off to an excellent start and well worth a visit.

Overlooking the downtown area from Mesa Francia at the southern end of Avenida Cousteau, the museum is open 8 am to 7 pm daily except Sunday. Admission costs US$1.25.

Special Events
Celebrations of Santa Rosalía's **Fundación de la Ciudad** (Founding of the City) last four days in mid-October.

Places to Stay
Camping Just south of town at Km 193 on the Transpeninsular, *Las Palmas RV Park* (☎ (115) 2-01-09, fax (115) 2-00-21) has grassy but shadeless campsites, hot showers, clean toilets and a laundromat, right on Bahía de San Lucas. A space costs about US$6 (with no hookups) to US$10 (full hookups). The small palapa restaurant serves seafood and standard antojitos.

A bit farther south, about half a mile (1 km) west of the Transpeninsular between

DESIERTO CENTRAL

Km 181 and Km 182, spacious *San Lucas RV Park* has a good beach and boat launch sites, and bird-watching is good in the area, but the park lacks amenities other than hot showers. Sites cost US$6 per night.

Hotels & Motels Travelers have recommended 'very quaint' *Hotel Blanco y Negro* (☎ (115) 2-00-80), at the top of a spiral staircase on the 2nd floor of a small building at Avenida Sarabia 1, which has 12 clean, basic rooms for about US$7 with shared bath, US$9 with private bath.

At the corner of Calle 1 and Avenida Carranza, the shabby *Hotel Playa* (☎ (115) 2-23-50) has rooms for US$7 with shared bath, US$10 with private bath. The rooms tend to be noisy and it's not advisable for women traveling on their own.

North of Plaza Juárez, *Hotel Central* (☎ (115) 2-01-76) looks all of its 112 years, but it's passable for US$10 single with shared bath despite creaky wooden floors, peeling wallpaper and bare light bulbs hanging from the ceilings. Its ample 2nd-floor balconies offer good views of Santa Rosalía's lively (but noisy) Avenida Obregón. *Hotel Olvera* (☎ (115) 2-00-57), near the corner of Avenida Montoya and Playa, is one of the best deals in town for budget travelers. Spotless wood-paneled single/double rooms, most with carpets and fans, cost US$11.

Hotel del Real (☎ (115) 2-00-68), on Avenida Montoya, has small, clean and air-conditioned singles/doubles for US$12. Tidy *Motel San Víctor* (☎ (115) 2-01-77), Avenida Progreso 36 at Calle 9, is a pleasant, family-run operation on a shady, quiet street. Its 12 rooms, all with overhead fans, air-conditioning and tiled bath, cost US$13 single or double. *Tercos Pollito* (☎ (115) 2-00-75), part of the restaurant at the entrance to town, has clean but dark singles/doubles for US$16/20. Trying awkwardly to capitalize on the town's historic past, the modern but drab *Hotel Minas de Santa Rosalía* (☎ (115) 2-10-60, (115) 2-01-42), a seemingly half-finished project at the corner of Avenida Constitución and Calle 10, is comparably priced.

Partly restored and otherwise improved *Hotel Francés* (☎ (115) 2-20-52), Avenida Cousteau 15 on Mesa Francia, once catered to French idiosyncrasies but now offers an atmospheric bar/restaurant (open 6 am to 11 pm daily), a small swimming pool, wonderful views of the rusting copper foundry and air-conditioned singles/doubles for US$26/29. Santa Rosalía's best accommodations are at the cliffside *Hotel El Morro* (☎ (115) 2-23-90, fax (115) 2-04-14), about 1 mile (1.6 km) south of town, just off the Transpeninsular. Along with sea views and a relaxed atmosphere, it offers a swimming pool, restaurant and bar for just US$25/31 single/double.

Places to Eat

Taco stands are numerous along Avenida Obregón, but most of them serve nothing but beef. For standard antojitos at good prices, try *Cenaduría Gaby (de Pedro García)* on Calle 5 just north of Avenida Obregón, *Cenaduría Sabina* at the corner of Altamirano and Avenida Progreso, or *El Oasis* at the corner of Avenida Constitución and Calle 8.

Tercos Pollito (☎ (115) 2-00-75), on Avenida Obregón near Calle 1, specializes in chicken but also serves meat and lobster lunches and dinners. South of downtown, the waterfront *Selene* (☎ (115) 2-06-85) serves sumptuous seafood dishes at upscale prices. The restaurant at *Hotel Francés*, enjoying the same resurgent popularity as the hotel itself, is well worth a stop, though the service can be slow.

Started by the French when mining operations were in full swing at the turn of the century, *Panadería El Boleo* (☎ (115) 2-03-10) is on Avenida Obregón between Calle 3 and Calle 4. For many travelers, it's an obligatory stop for delicious Mexican and French breads and pastries. Baking begins at 4 am daily, but baguettes usually sell out by 10 am. Occasionally there's an afternoon batch as well.

Getting There & Away
Bus Autotransportes Aguila and ABC buses between Tijuana and La Paz stop at

Santa Rosalía's Terminal de Autobuses
(☎ (115) 2-01-50) on the western side of
the Transpeninsular opposite the malecón.
Northbound buses go to Guerrero Negro
at 2 am and 3 pm, to Tijuana and intermediate stops at 4 and 5 am and 5 and 6 pm
and to Mexicali and intermediate stops at
midnight. Sample fares are as follows:

San Ignacio	US$2.50
Vizcaíno	US$5.50
Guerrero Negro	US$7.50
San Quintín	US$18
Colonia Vicente Guerrero	US$20
Ensenada	US$25
Tijuana	US$28
Mexicali	US$35

Southbound buses to La Paz and intermediate stops pass at 3, 9:30, 11 and 11:30
am, 8 and 9:30 pm and midnight. Approximate fares are Mulegé, US$3; Loreto,
US$5.50; Ciudad Constitución, US$10;
and La Paz, US$17.

Ferry The Sematur ferry terminal (☎ (115)
2-00-13) is just south of Arroyo Santa
Rosalía, right along the Transpeninsulaı.
Ferries sail to the mainland Mexican town
ot Guaymas (an eight-hour journey when
there are no delays) at 8 am Wednesday and
Sunday; strong winter winds can cause
long delays. Ferries return from Guaymas
to Santa Rosalía at 11 am Tuesday and
Friday.

Ticket windows are open 8 am to 1 pm
and 3 to 6 pm Tuesday and Friday, 6 am to
7:30 am Sunday and Wednesday and 8 am
to 3 pm Thursday and Saturday. Drunks
and pregnant women are not allowed on
the ferry; draw your own conclusions.
Make reservations at least three days in
advance and, even if you have reservations,
arrive early at the ticket office.

Passenger fares each way are US$14 in
salón class (with reclining seats), US$27 in
turista (three-person roomettes). Vehicle
rates start at US$133 for those up to 16
feet, 5 inches (5 meters). Vehicles up to 21
feet, 4 inches (6½ meters) cost US$174; to
29 feet, 6 inches (9 meters) US$240; and to
55 feet, 9 inches (17 meters) US$453.

Buses and motor homes pay US$227, and
motorcycles pay US$20.

It is not possible to obtain a mainland
vehicle permit at Santa Rosalía, so get one
at the US border or Ensenada beforehand;
otherwise it will be necessary to go to La
Paz. For more information about permits,
see the Car Permits entry in the Getting
Around chapter.

Private Yacht Santa Rosalía's small
marina offers some possibilities for catching a ride north or south along the Gulf
coast or across to mainland Mexico.

AROUND SANTA ROSALÍA
Isla San Marcos
At 6 am every Friday, a free boat carries
residents of the magnesium mining settlement on this offshore island to their weekly
shopping spree in Santa Rosalía. Travelers
interested in hiking the island are welcome
to hop aboard the return voyage at 10:30
am (ask around the harbor for the exact
docking site), but they will either have to
wait a week or contact a launch to return to
the mainland. It's also possible to hire a
boat in the tiny fish camp of San Bruno,
about midway between Santa Rosalía and
Mulegé, and visit an offshore sea lion
colony.

MULEGÉ
South of Santa Rosalía, the Transpeninsular tracks the base of the eastern scarp
of the northern edge of the Sierra de la
Giganta, passing the peninsula of Punta
Chivato before winding through the Sierra
Azteca and then dropping into the subtropical oasis of Mulegé (population 3169).
Beaches to the south along Bahía Concepción attract more conventional vacationers
than do areas to the north, but the Mulegé
area is especially popular with divers.

The *ejidatarios* (ejido members) of
Mulegé have a running feud with local
landowners over property rights to some
of the town's most highly developed tourist areas, but nothing is likely to change
despite suits and countersuits and accusations and counteraccusations.

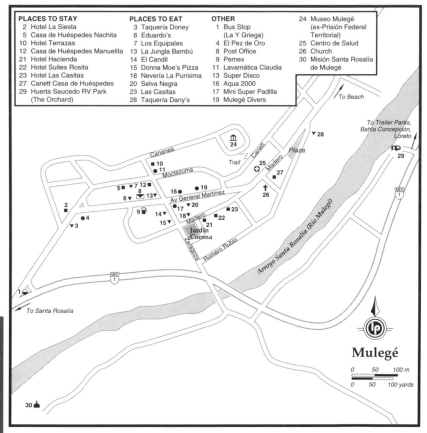

PLACES TO STAY
2 Hotel La Siesta
5 Casa de Huéspedes Nachita
10 Hotel Terrazas
12 Casa de Huéspedes Manuelita
21 Hotel Hacienda
22 Hotel Suites Rosita
23 Hotel Las Casitas
27 Canett Casa de Huéspedes
29 Huerta Saucedo RV Park
    (The Orchard)

PLACES TO EAT
3 Taquería Doney
6 Eduardo's
7 Los Equipales
13 La Jungla Bambú
14 El Candil
15 Donna Moe's Pizza
18 Nevería La Purísima
20 Selva Negra
23 Las Casitas
28 Taquería Dany's

OTHER
1 Bus Stop
   (La Y Griega)
4 El Pez de Oro
8 Post Office
9 Pemex
11 Lavamática Claudia
13 Super Disco
16 Aqua 2000
17 Mini Super Padilla
19 Mulegé Divers
24 Museo Mulegé
   (ex-Prisión Federal
   Territorial)
25 Centro de Salud
26 Church
30 Misión Santa Rosalía
   de Mulegé

Mulegé

Orientation

Mulegé straddles the verdant Arroyo Santa Rosalía (also known as Río Mulegé) about 2 miles (3 km) inland from the Gulf of California; the bulk of visitor services are on the northern side of the river, on or near Jardín Corona, the town plaza. Scrawny mangroves extend along the lower reaches of the river's estuary, frequented by large numbers of birds, while date palms line its banks farther inland. Avoid swimming at the mouth of the estuary, which is badly polluted.

Information

Mulegé has no formal tourist office, but businesses like Mulegé Divers are a good source of information. Visitors intending to spend quite a bit of time in the area might consider acquiring Kerry Otterstrom's self-published guidebook, *Mulegé*, available from several places around town or from the writer himself, who works at the popular bar/restaurant El Candil. From December through April, the biweekly English-language paper *The Mulegé Post* is another useful source of information, including data like tide tables.

Money Travelers needing to change traveler's checks or obtain cash advances on credit cards should do so in Santa Rosalía or Loreto, the closest towns with banks, before arriving in Mulegé.

Mulegé's only *cambio* (currency exchange house), El Pez de Oro at the western end of Avenida General Martínez, keeps erratic hours and does not change traveler's checks, though many Mulegé merchants will change US dollars or accept them in payment for services.

Post & Communications Mulegé's post office has moved to Avenida General Martínez, almost across from the Pemex station. The postal code is 23900.

Long-distance telephone and fax services are available at the Mini Super Padilla grocery on Zaragoza at Avenida General Martínez; its fax line is (115) 3-01-90.

Laundry Efficient Lavamática Claudia (☎ (115) 3-00-57), at the corner of Zaragoza and Moctezuma, is open 8 am to 6 pm daily except Sunday. A full load costs about US$3, washed, dried and folded. The laundromat is also a community meeting place with a useful bulletin board, worth checking for rides and the like.

Medical Services Mulegé's Centro de Salud is on Madero opposite the Canett Casa de Huéspedes.

Dangers & Annoyances Drivers of large RVs (or anything bigger than a van conversion) should not even consider entering downtown Mulegé's narrow, irregular and sometimes steep streets. Besides risking scrapes and dents to your vehicle, you're likely to cause serious and potentially hazardous congestion. Visitors who park downtown should pay special attention to red zones – parking in one can tie up traffic for hours.

Nearby trailer parks are within easy walking distance of downtown, but the riverside road to Huerta Saucedo RV Park is utterly impassable for RVs – use the highway instead.

Water Aqua 2000, on Avenida General Martínez east of Zaragoza, sells purified water and ice at reasonable prices.

Misión Santa Rosalía

Across the Transpeninsular and near the southern bank of the river, restored Misión Santa Rosalía de Mulegé stands atop a hill above the town. Founded in 1705 and completed in 1766, the mission functioned until 1828, when the declining Indian population led to its abandonment. Remodeled several times, the church is less architecturally distinguished – it is imposing but utilitarian, with fewer enticing details – than its counterparts at San Ignacio and San Borja. The exterior is still faithful to the original, but the succeeding centuries have greatly altered the interior.

Behind the church, a short footpath climbs a volcanic outcrop to an overlook with soothing views of the palm-lined Arroyo Santa Rosalía and its surroundings. This is one of the visual highlights of the area, well worth a detour even for travelers not intending to stay in town.

Museo Mulegé

Federal inmates from Mulegé's 'prison without doors,' a strikingly whitewashed neocolonial building on Cananea, overlooking the town, traditionally enjoyed a great deal of liberty. Except for the most serious felons, who were confined in its inner compound, prisoners at the Prisión Federal Territorial usually left at 6 am for jobs in town, returning at 6 pm; in some cases they could even attend town dances and a number of them married locally.

Now the town museum, the building was to undergo a major restoration after decades of neglect, but there's been little progress since the peso crisis of 1994. Its interesting but eclectic artifacts – archaeological and religious materials, cotton gins,

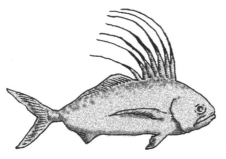

Roosterfish

antique diving equipment and firearms – are more coherently organized than in the past, but pigeons perch in and soil nearly every room in the building. The museum is open 9 am to 1 pm weekdays; admission is free.

Diving
Mulegé's best dive spots are around the Santa Inés Islands (north of town) and just north of Punta Concepción. There is excellent beach diving and snorkeling at Punta Prieta, near the lighthouse at the mouth of Arroyo Santa Rosalía.

Specializing in diving instruction and excursions, Mulegé Divers (☎ /fax (115) 3-00-59) occupies spacious quarters on Avenida General Martínez. A four-hour scuba course costs US$70, including all equipment and a guided underwater dive tour, while a diving excursion involving a boat, a dive-master guide, two tanks and a weight belt is US$40; there is a minimum charge of US$80. Snorkeling excursions cost US$25 to US$30 per person, with a US$70 minimum. Owners Miguel and Claudia Quintana both speak English (Claudia is American).

Rental equipment is also available on a daily basis, including buoyancy compensators (US$8 each), weight belts (US$3), tanks with air (US$6), regulators with pressure gauge and depth gauge (US$8) and wet-suit jackets (US$5). Discounts are available after the first day.

The store also sells snorkeling fins and masks, fishing equipment such as lures and lines, T-shirts, miscellaneous supplies, a good selection of books on the Baja Peninsula and the AAA road map of Baja California. Open 9 am to 1 pm and 3 to 6 pm daily except Sunday, it's also a good and friendly source of information on the Mulegé area.

Fishing
Game-fish species available all year in the Mulegé area include bonito, cabrilla, corvina, crevallo, grouper, pargo, sierra and skipjack. Seasonal species include dorado (May to November), needlefish (June to November), roosterfish (April to October), sailfish (July to October), striped marlin (June to October) and the especially popular yellowtail (November to May). Wahoo make rare appearances.

El Candil restaurant (☎ (115) 3-01-85) has five pangas for rent to sportfishing parties.

Mountain Biking
Mulegé Divers rents mountain bikes for US$2 per hour, US$18 per day, but the per-day rate drops to US$10 for longer rentals. El Candil also rents mountain bikes.

Sea Kayaking
Bahía Concepción, south of Mulegé, is the main destination for kayakers. El Candil also rents kayaks for US$29 per day.

Places to Stay
Since the closing of Hotel Serenidad due to the dispute with the ejido, Mulegé lacks any upscale accommodations. Visitors seeking luxury will have to lower their sights, but the general quality of lodging is good.

Camping Eastbound Madero and Romero Rubio merge into a single dirt road leading to *beach camping* areas near the lighthouse, 2 miles (3 km) northeast of town. This is also a popular party spot for local youth, however, so there's no guarantee of any sleep, at least on weekends.

Abounding with palms, mangoes and citrus, friendly *Huerta Saucedo RV Park* (popularly known as 'The Orchard,' ☎ (115) 3-03-00) is half a mile (1 km) east of town on the river side of the Transpeninsular. RVs driving from central Mulegé should take the highway or the road that passes beneath the Transpeninsular bridge; only small vehicles should take the road on the river's south bank. Spaces with full hookups cost US$10 to US$12 each, while spaces without hookups cost US$5 to US$6 for two people, plus US$1.50 for each additional person. Members of AAA and some other travel clubs get a 10% discount with full hookups. Hot (sometimes lukewarm) showers, improved toilets and a boat ramp are available. The park also offers frequent Mexican buffets and other special meals at bargain prices.

Just beyond Huerta Saucedo, *Villa María Isabel RV Park* (☎ /fax (115) 3-02-46) charges US$4.50 per person for sites without hookups, US$13 with full hookups, but the real reasons to stop here are the fabulous bread and cinnamon rolls at its first-rate bakery – well worth a stop even for those with no intention of staying here.

Guesthouses Cheapest of Mulegé's several guesthouses is the plain, eight-room *Canett Casa de Huéspedes* (☎ (115) 3-02-72) on Madero. It's not a bad place, but late sleepers should know that the church bells across the street chime loudly every quarter-hour from 6 am; singles with private bath cost just US$4.

Casa de Huéspedes Manuelita (☎ (115) 3-01-75), kitty-corner from Lavamática Claudia on Moctezuma, and *Casa de Huéspedes Nachita*, half a block to the west, are comparable if slightly more expensive. Nachita offers hot showers for nonguests for US$2.

Hotels & Motels *Hotel Suites Rosita* (☎ (115) 3-02-70), on Madero just a short walk from the plaza, is a pleasant, family-oriented, budget-style hotel. Each plain room has air-conditioning, a kitchenette and a sitting room with a table. Rooms cost US$16 single or double. Friendly, modern *Hotel La Siesta* (☎ (115) 3-00-47, fax (115) 3-01-90), near the Y-intersection at the entrance to town, has singles/doubles for US$16, but the TV is stuck on a single channel.

Sharing a courtyard with its namesake restaurant, *Hotel Las Casitas* (☎ (115) 3-00-19, fax (115) 3-01-90), on Madero near the junction with Avenida General Martínez, was once home to poet Alán Gorosave. All rooms have hot showers, air-conditioning and plenty of shade trees in front. Singles/doubles are US$20. Improving *Hotel Terrazas* (☎ (115) 3-00-09), on Zaragoza just north of Lavamática Claudia, has several fine rooms with views for US$20/23 single/double.

Suffering from frequent management changes, *Hotel Hacienda* (☎ (115) 3-00-21), Madero 3 at the northeastern corner of the plaza, seems to be an ongoing construction project. Despite the disorder, prices are rising consistently - rooms with twin beds, fridge, air-conditioning and hot showers now cost US$35 single/double. There's a small pool, a bar and a shady patio.

Places to Eat
At the western end of Mulegé just before the Transpeninsular, *Taquería Doney* serves up some of the region's best tacos. *Donna Moe's Pizza*, at the northwestern corner of the plaza, draws steady crowds as well.

At the intersection of Romero Rubio and Madero, *Taquería Dany's* may be the closest the humble taco ever gets to haute cuisine. With a variety of fillings, from carne asada to carnitas to chicken to shrimp, and a cornucopia of tasty condiments, this may be the peninsula's best taco stand. Prices are more than reasonable. *La Almeja*, on the beach near the road to the lighthouse, serves low-priced beer, fish tacos and other seafood.

La Jungla Bambú, beneath Super Disco at the corner of Avenida General Martínez and Zaragoza, is a sports bar with ordinary food except for the midday specials, which are an excellent value. Local expatriates suggest *Eduardo's* (☎ (115) 3-02-58), across from the Pemex station on Avenida General Martínez, which has transcended its fast-food origins to offer varied cuisine, including Friday ribs and a Sunday Chinese special. Remodeled *El Candil* (☎ (115) 3-01-85), on Zaragoza near the plaza, has filling meat and seafood dishes at moderate prices. Its bar is a popular gringo meeting place, with international sports on satellite TV, but later in the evening it draws a more Mexican crowd. The alternate-Sunday pig roast attracts big crowds.

Try *Las Casitas* (☎ (115) 3-00-19) on Madero, one of Mulegé's more upscale places, for typical antojitos (with daily specials) and a few seafood dishes, plus unusual drinks like mango daiquiris. A good breakfast value is the generous combination fruit plate.

Specializing in Sonoran beef, *Los Equipales* (☎ (115) 3-03-30), on Moctezuma just west of Zaragoza, serves outstanding meals that, if dearer than most in town, are worth the money.

Selva Negra, on Avenida General Martínez east of Zaragoza, is worth a stop for desserts and coffee. *Nevería La Purísima*, on the northern side of the plaza, serves homemade Mexican-style ice cream.

Entertainment

Friday, Saturday and Sunday, *Super Disco*, upstairs from La Jungla Bambú at the corner of Zaragoza and Avenida General Martínez, offers live (or sometimes canned) music for dancing.

Getting There & Away

Mulegé has no formal bus terminal, but buses running from Tijuana to La Paz stop daily at the Y-junction (known locally as 'La Y Griega') on the Transpeninsular at the western edge of town.

Northbound buses go to Ensenada (US$27) and Tijuana (US$31) at 4:30 and 10:30 am, to Santa Rosalía (US$2.50) at 4 and 7 pm and to Mexicali (US$38) at 10:30 pm.

Southbound buses go to Loreto (US$4), Ciudad Constitución (US$8) and La Paz (US$13) at 11 am and 9 and 10:30 pm.

AROUND MULEGÉ
Cañón La Trinidad

In Cañón La Trinidad, 18 miles (29 km) southwest of Mulegé via a bumpy dirt road passable for most vehicles with high clearance, visitors can take a hike-and-swim excursion to view several pre-Columbian rock art sites in impressive volcanic overhangs. Another route involves hiking only, but it's longer and less interesting than passing through the canyon's deep pools, especially when the weather's hot. The drive to the canyon from Mulegé involves taking several unmarked junctions from the westbound (San Estanislao) road and can be difficult for a first-timer.

The rock paintings themselves are multicolored Cochimí depictions of human figures and wildlife, including fish and sea turtles. Those at the lower site, visited prior to the swim up the canyon, are more vivid and better preserved, thanks to their more sheltered location. All visitors must check in with the INAH caretakers at Rancho La Trinidad, who lead hikes up the canyon for a very modest fee.

Kerry Otterstrom, bartender at El Candil (see the Places to Eat entry for Mulegé) and a longtime Mulegé resident, leads day trips to Cochimí rock art sites at Cañón La Trinidad for US$35 per person and overnight trips for US$50. The day hikes include a hot meal – all-you-can-eat bean burritos with fresh vegetables and cold beer or soda at Rancho La Trinidad at the end of the hike. Another bilingual guide is Salvador Castro (☎ (115) 3-02-32). Both have dry bags for carrying camera equipment through the canyon; Otterstrom provides wet suits for winter trips, when the air temperature is generally pleasant but the water in the shady canyon can be chilly.

Misión Guadalupe

The dirt road leading from Mulegé to the Rancho La Trinidad junction continues onward to San Estanislao. There, a marked branch leads to the ruins of remote Misión Nuestra Señora de Guadalupe de Huasinapi (established 1720), of which only foundations remain.

Around Mulegé

BAHÍA CONCEPCIÓN

Along Bahía Concepción, south of Mulegé, are more than 50 miles (80 km) of beaches; the most accessible (and most crowded) run along the western edge of the bay, but few people travel the dirt road to Punta Concepción at the peninsula's northern tip. Camping is possible on almost every beach in the area, but most of the best sites charge for the privilege.

EcoMundo

Established under an agreement with Se-marnap (the Mexican government fish-eries agency), the EcoMundo kayaking and natural history center is an extension of Roy Mahoff and Becky Aparicio's long-running Baja Tropicales company. Baja Tropicales continues to offer local kayak trips from its new facilities, south of Mulegé at Km 112 of the Transpeninsular, between Posada Concepción and Playa Escondido. In addition to accommodations (see Places to Stay & Eat, below), the appropriate-technology Eco-Mundo project includes a natural history museum and educational center. It also has a recycling site.

Baja Tropicales kayak trips on Bahía Concepción cost US$39 per person, including meals and beverages, for a minimum of four people. Snorkeling gear can be rented for US$5. In addition, they offer longer five- and six-day trips around Bahía Concepción and to spots like Isla San Marcos, Bahía Magdalena and Laguna Ojo de Liebre (Scammon's Lagoon). Rental equipment is also available for experienced kayakers. For more detailed information, inquire at Hotel Las Casitas in Mulegé or contact Baja Tropicales (☎ (115) 3-04-09, fax (115) 3-01-90), Apdo Postal 60, Mulegé, Baja California Sur 23900, México.

Places to Stay & Eat

At *Playa Santispac*, 13 miles (21 km) south of Mulegé, 35 campsites with palapas at water's edge are available for US$5 apiece. Amenities are limited, but there are cold showers; bring drinking water. *Ana's* has served meals, freshly baked bread and desserts for over a decade here, and also sells groceries. Large RVs can't use the narrow beachside road south of the main area, which leads to less crowded spots.

Posada Concepción RV Park, just over the hill from Playa Santispac, is a grossly overdeveloped gringo enclave with full hookups, hot showers, tennis courts and electricity from 10 am to 10 pm. Permanent and semipermanent residents occupy most of the spots, which cost US$10 per vehicle and US$1 for each additional person. There's a natural hot spring on the beach behind the mill.

EcoMundo (see its entry, above, for contact information) has new accommodations, including bungalows, a youth hostel and tent campsites, at Km 112 on the Transpeninsular, south of Posada Concepción. The cafeteria offers three meals a day.

RV Park El Coyote, 18 miles (29 km) south of Mulegé, is a fine area for beach camping, with flush toilets, drinking water and showers. Rates are about US$5 per vehicle, but it's often unpleasantly crowded. Just south of RV Park El Coyote, at Km 94.5 of the Transpeninsular, the area's best accommodations are at *Resort*

Hotel San Buenaventura (☎ (115) 3-04-08), an attractive stone building where singles/doubles, each with their own shaded patio, start at US$45/50. Also onsite is *George's Olé Sports Bar & Grill*. The Buenaventura's US postal address is PO Box 90139, San Diego, CA 92169.

El Requesón, 28 miles (45 km) south of Mulegé, once made a *Condé Nast Traveler* list of Mexico's top 10 beaches, but its scanty services keep it suitable for short-term camping only. One attractive feature is the *tombolo* (sandspit beach) that connects it to offshore Isla El Requesón except during very high tides. Despite its proximity to the highway, it's relatively quiet; camping here is free.

Free camping is also possible at *Playa Armenta*, a short distance south of El Requesón. It has a short but sandy beach and the narrow access road keeps out larger RVs, but it's more exposed to the highway than El Requesón.

SAN ISIDRO-LA PURÍSIMA

South of Bahía Concepción, the paved Transpeninsular continues to Loreto, but at Km 60 a graded alternative route crosses the Sierra de la Giganta to the twin villages of San Isidro and La Purísima, both also accessible by a very good paved highway from Ciudad Insurgentes (see the Around San Isidro-La Purísima entry, below). Travelers who prefer not to retrace their steps may wish to take the graded road either north- or southbound. Drivers with high-clearance vehicles will find it more enjoyable, while those with RVs or trailers will find it difficult; 4WD is unnecessary, however.

This area was the site of **Misión La Purísima Concepción**, founded in 1717 by Jesuit Nicolás Tamaral, but only foundations remain. The major landmark is the steep-sided volcanic plug of **El Pilón**, a challenge for technical climbers, which lies between the two villages. From La Purísima, a graded road goes northwest to San Juanico, one of the Pacific coast's prime surf spots, and to Laguna San Ignacio, a major whale-watching area. For more information, see the Around San Isidro-La Purísima entry, below.

Neither San Isidro nor La Purísima has a Pemex station, but private gasoline sellers offer both Nova and Magna Sin at about a 25% markup – look for hand-painted signs.

Places to Stay & Eat
San Isidro's very simple *Motel Nelva*, behind the church and conveniently adjacent to the bus terminal, charges US$5 per person; the shared baths have hot water. The only other accommodations are at an unsigned place next door to La Purísima's gas seller that charges US$8 single.

San Isidro has a basic *lonchería* and a *taco stand*, while La Purísima has a *taco stand* and the ordinary *Restaurant Claudia*, with basic antojitos and a few seafood dishes.

Getting There & Away
San Isidro and La Purísima enjoy bus service to La Paz (US$11) at 7 am and at 3 pm daily with Autotransportes Aguila, which picks up most of its passengers in Ciudad Constitución. Buses leave from San Isidro and pass through La Purísima.

AROUND SAN ISIDRO-LA PURÍSIMA
Paso Hondo
Paso Hondo, 19 miles (31 km) north of San Isidro by a dirt road (inquire as to condition), features Cochimí rock art sites.

San José de Comondú
South of San Isidro, a bumpy, rocky, undulating road (which is never really difficult, at least for high-clearance vehicles) crosses a volcanic upland before dropping steeply into San José de Comondú, site of the Jesuit **Templo Misional de San José de Comondú**. The temple dates from the 1750s, although the mission proper began in 1707.

San José de Comondú, midway between the Pacific Ocean and the Gulf of California, was a promising site for a mission because of its perennial spring, where several groups of Indians lived. The Jesuit Franz Inama, an Austrian, oversaw the

construction of the church, abandoned in 1827 and demolished in part at the turn of this century. Harry Crosby's *Antigua California*, working from probably the most elaborate records available for any Jesuit mission in Baja, re-creates daily life at San José de Comondú in considerable detail.

Only part of the mission temple remains intact, but there are extensive walls surrounding it. Restoration is lagging, but the building contains good examples of traditional religious art, though the canvases are deteriorating badly. Note the historic photos, dated 1901, when a major *recova* (colonnade) and two short *campanarios* (bell towers) still existed. Ask for the key to the temple at the bright-green house 30 yards to the east.

West of San José de Comondú is its almost equally picturesque ʼtwin, **San Miguel de Comondú**. Most inhabitants of the area are fair-skinned descendants of early Spanish pioneers, in contrast to later *mestizo* arrivals from mainland Mexico.

For vehicles without high clearance, access to San José de Comondú is easier by a graded lateral from Ejido Francisco Villa that leaves the paved highway about 40 miles (64 km) north of Ciudad Insurgentes. One tricky stream ford may present problems for vehicles with low clearance.

Driving north from San José de Comondú to San Isidro, the steep climb over loose rock may cause some problems. At the crest of the hill, take the left fork to San Isidro.

San Juanico
About 30 miles (48 km) northwest of La Purísima and 60 miles (97 km) south of Laguna San Ignacio, the village of San Juanico is well known among surfers for nearby **Punta Pequeña** at the northern end of Bahía San Juanico. Its right-point breaks, some believe, provide the highest-quality surf on the peninsula in a southern swell between April and October. Other possible activities in the area include windsurfing, sea kayaking, diving and sportfishing for corvina, halibut and especially roosterfish.

DESIERTO CENTRAL

Camping at San Juanico costs US$3 per person per day at a well-run site operated by an American in cooperation with the local ejido, and there's an excellent palapa *restaurant*.

San Juanico is most easily accessed by a good graded dirt road heading north from La Purísima. Unfortunately, the high road south to San Juanico from Laguna San Ignacio, despite its depiction as a graded surface on the AAA map, is potentially hazardous, according to Serge Dedina and Emily Young, who know the area well:

The high road is the worst of all of them, only recommended for high-clearance vehicles (or sturdy little trucks). I wouldn't recommend it to anyone. Locals avoid it always – so there is little traffic to help out if you break down.

The lower road veers off from the graded road approximately 8 miles south of Laguna San Ignacio. This is the Baja 1000 road – and passable by most trucks – granted drivers know how to drive dirt roads. The road passes through a few sand dunes between La Laguna and El Dátil. It is also easy to get lost and very stuck there. In short, avoid the route unless you have a great vehicle and lots of experience driving unmarked roads (with lots of detours), and unless you speak good enough Spanish to understand directions. Given the general lack of topographic features to fix on (only endless dunes and salt flats), I would say this is the easiest place to get lost in the entire peninsula.

LORETO

In 1697 Jesuit priest and explorer Juan María Salvatierra established Misión Nuestra Señora de Loreto on the Gulf coast as the first permanent Spanish settlement in the Californias. In concentrating local Indians at mission settlements instead of dispersed rancherías and converting them to Catholicism, the Jesuits directly extended the influence and control of the Spanish crown in one of the empire's most remote areas.

It was a convenient staging point for missionary expansion even after the official expulsion of the Jesuits in 1767 – in 1769 Franciscan Padre Junípero Serra trekked northward to found the now famous chain of missions in mainland California. Also

the first capital of the Californias, Loreto served that role until its near-destruction by a hurricane in 1829.

Loreto's spectacularly restored mission underscores its role in the history of the Californias. The town remains a modest fishing port (population 8299) with cobblestone streets, though some of its historic past has now fallen beneath developers' onslaughts – the latest incident was the unauthorized demolition of a 200-year-old adobe on the southeastern corner of the Plaza Cívica.

Mexico's tourist promotion agency Fonatur has wisely if reluctantly retreated from plans to turn Loreto into 'Cabo San Lucas Norte' through massive development efforts at Nopoló, a few kilometers south of town. On the other hand, Fonatur's last-gasp promotion of Nopoló's adults-only Diamond Eden Resort has, by some accounts, undercut Loreto proper by monopolizing the area's transportation and publicity resources; few potential visitors may be aware that the area has attractions other than Diamond Eden.

A more positive development, due largely to activism by the grassroots environmental organization Grupo Ecologista Antares, is the Mexican congress' recent creation of Parque Marino Nacional Bahía de Loreto. Comprising 799 sq miles (2077 sq km) of shoreline and offshore islands, Baja's second offshore national park protects the areas north, south and east of town from pollution and uncontrolled fishing.

Orientation

Between the Transpeninsular and the shores of the Gulf of California, Loreto is 210 miles (338 km) north of La Paz and 84 miles (135 km) south of Mulegé. It has a slightly irregular street plan, but the colonial mission church on Salvatierra is a major landmark; most hotels and services are within easy walking distance of it.

The Plaza Cívica, as the *zócalo* (central plaza) is known, is just north of Salvatierra between Madero and Davis. Salvatierra itself is a de facto pedestrian mall (vehicle access is limited and inconvenient), lined

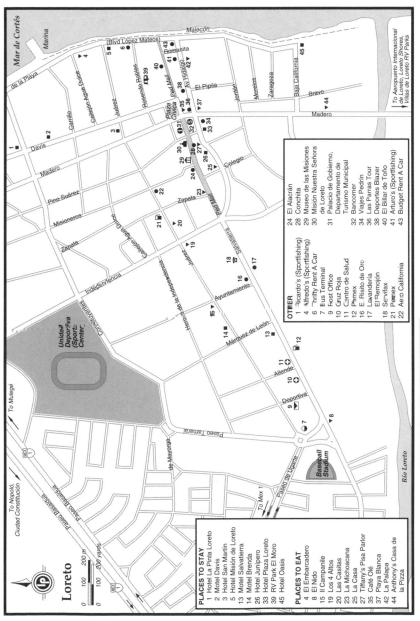

Loreto

0   100   200 m
0   100   200 yards

To Mulegé

To Nopoló,
Ciudad Constitución

Mar de Cortés

DESIERTO CENTRAL

PLACES TO STAY
1   Hotel La Pinta Loreto
2   Motel Davis
3   Hotel San Martín
5   Hotel Misión de Loreto
13 Motel Salvatierra
14 Motel Brenda
26 Hotel Junípero
33 Hotel Plaza Loreto
39 RV Park El Moro
45 Hotel Oasis

PLACES TO EAT
4   El Embarcadero
8   El Nido
15 Il Campanile
19 Los 4 Altos
20 Las Casitas
23 La Michoacana
25 La Casa
27 Tiffany's Pisa Parlor
35 Café Olé
37 Playa Blanca
42 La Palapa
44 Anthony's Casa de
    la Pizza

OTHER
1   Ricardo's (Sportfishing)
4   Alfredo's (Sportfishing)
6   Thrifty Rent A Car
7   Bus Terminal
9   Post Office
10 Cruz Roja
11 Centro de Salud
12 Pemex
16 El Risito de Oro
17 Lavandería
18 El Remojón
18 Servitax
21 Pemex
22 Aero California
24 El Alacrán
28 Conchita
29 Museo de las Misiones
30 Misión Nuestra Señora
    de Loreto
31 Palacio de Gobierno,
    Departamento de
    Turismo Municipal
32 Bancomer
34 Viajes Pedrín
36 Las Parras Tour
38 Deportes Blazer
40 El Billar de Toño
41 Arturo's (Sportfishing)
43 Budget Rent A Car

To Aeropuerto Internacional
de Loreto, Loreto Shores,
Villas de Loreto RV Parks

with topiary laurels, between Independencia and the beach. The beach's attractive malecón is ideal for sunset strolls along the Gulf.

Information

Tourist Office Loreto's Departamento de Turismo Municipal (☎ (113) 5-04-11, fax (113) 5-07-88), in the Palacio de Gobierno on the western side of the Plaza Cívica at Madero and Salvatierra, is open 8:30 am to 3 pm weekdays. Helpful English-speaking staff are usually on duty, and they have a good selection of brochures and fliers.

Customs & Immigration Loreto's Oficina de Migración y Aduana (☎ (113) 5-04-54) is at the airport, south of town.

Money Bancomer, at the corner of Salvatierra and Madero, changes US dollars and traveler's checks from 8:30 to 11:30 am with a minimum of bureaucracy, but has no ATM and does not make cash advances. It also sometimes runs short of cash, so it's better to get there early; the next closest full-service banks are in Santa Rosalía and Ciudad Constitución.

Misión Nuestra Señora de Loreto

Post & Communications Loreto's post office has moved to new quarters on Deportiva just north of Salvatierra. The postal code is 23880.

Servifax, Salvatierra 75 opposite the laundromat, is the best phone office, but closes as early as 7 pm. Several other businesses along Salvatierra offer long-distance services, but add surcharges for collect calls.

Travel & Tour Agencies Viajes Pedrín (☎ (113) 5-02-04, fax (113) 5-07-88) is on the southern side of Avenida Miguel Hidalgo next to Hotel Plaza Loreto.

For the widest selection of activity-oriented tours, including hiking, cycling, horseback riding and sea kayaking, contact the US-Mexican partnership Las Parras Tour (☎ (113) 5-10-10, fax (113) 5-09-00) on Madero just north of Avenida Hidalgo. Its prices are a little higher than other operators', but it also makes a special effort to involve local people in its business, hiring them as drivers, for example.

Laundry Lavandería El Remojón is on Salvatierra between Independencia and Ayuntamiento.

Medical Services Loreto's Centro de Salud (☎ (113) 5-00-39) is at Salvatierra 68 near the corner of Allende. The Cruz Roja (☎ (113) 5-11-11) is also on Salvatierra, just west of Allende.

Dangers & Annoyances The notoriously corrupt Judiciales maintain a guns-and-drugs checkpoint south of Loreto, just beyond the entrance road to Nopoló and the Diamond Eden Resort. Inspections can be thorough and unpleasant; for more information on dealing with the Judiciales, see the Facts for the Visitor chapter.

Misión Nuestra Señora de Loreto

Above the entrance to Misión Nuestra Señora de Loreto, the inscription 'Cabeza y Madre de las Misiones de Baja y Alta California' (Head and Mother of the Missions of Upper and Lower California) aptly describes its role in the history of the Californias. Featuring a floor plan in the shape of a Greek cross, it suffered serious damage when the ceiling and bell tower collapsed during the 1829 hurricane; it has been restored only over the last twenty-five years. The mission is downtown on Salvatierra.

Museo de las Misiones

Alongside the mission church, INAH's greatly improved mission museum recounts the European settlement of Baja California in a generally chronological manner. It now pays more attention to the peninsula's indigenous population, honoring the accomplishments of the Jesuits and their successors without ignoring or denying the native demographic collapse caused by the missions. It also displays a fine selection of the implements of daily life, such as horsegear and household tools, from the early days of European settlement.

Other noteworthy features include an early mission bell, a room of religious art, antique weapons like swords and cannon, a horse-powered *noria* (mill) in the interior courtyard and a kettle big enough to boil a Jesuit in oil. Of particular note is a 15th-century French astronomical globe. The museum bookstore sells a variety of Spanish-language books about the archaeology, anthropology and history of Mexico and Baja California.

Open 9 am to 4 pm weekdays, the Museo de las Misiones (☎ (113) 5-04-41) charges US$1.25 admission.

Diving, Snorkeling & Sea Kayaking

Reefs around Isla del Carmen, Isla Coronado and other sites are superb for water sports. From April to November, the water temperature averages from 75°F to 85°F (24°C to 29°C) and visibility is about 60 to 80 feet (18 to 24 meters). From December to March, the water temperature averages from 60°F to 70°F (15°C to 21°C); visibility is about 30 to 50 feet (9 to 15 meters).

Diving and snorkeling excursions can be arranged at Deportes Blazer (☎ (113) 5-09-11) on Avenida Hidalgo east of

Madero, which also rents scuba gear. Las Parras Tour (see Travel & Tour Agencies, above) rents open-top kayaks and arranges kayak tours ranging from 2½ hours (US$15) to all day (US$30).

Fishing

Many guides are available for all-day fishing trips, but fishing near Loreto is poorer than it once was, as professional shrimpers' gill nets snag and kill up to 10 tons of fish for each ton of shrimp caught. Measures to curtail the depletion of fisheries in the Gulf of California have been largely ineffective, but the creation of the new offshore national park may have a positive impact.

Bonito, cabrilla, corvina, crevalle, grouper, pargo, sierra and skipjack are all-year game species. Dorado swarm offshore from April through October, but striped marlin, needlefish, roosterfish and sailfish also inhabit these waters. From November to May, yellowtail are the main attraction.

Several operators arrange all-day fishing trips, including Alfredo's Sportfishing (☎ (113) 5-01-32, fax (113) 5-05-90) on de la Playa (also known as Blvd López Mateos) between Juárez and Callejón Agua Dulce, Arturo's (☎ (113) 5-04-09, (113) 5-00-22) on Avenida Hidalgo near the intersection with Romanita (an inconspicuous block-long street near the waterfront) and Ricardo's (☎ (113) 5-00-25) at Hotel La Pinta Loreto (see Places to Stay, below).

Special Events

Loreto's main fiestas are early September's **Día de Nuestra Señora de Loreto** and mid-October's **Fundación de la Ciudad**, which celebrates the city's founding in 1699.

Places to Stay – budget

Camping At Rosendo Robles 8, only half a block from the beach and a few blocks from the mission, *RV Park El Moro* (☎ (113) 5-05-42) has about 20 sites with full hookups for US$6 to US$10 apiece, depending on the size of the vehicle. It's very friendly and tidy, with clean baths and hot showers, but has limited shade. It also 'enjoys' a cacophony of roosters and barking dogs for much of the night, and there's a new rock 'n' roll club around the corner.

Spacious *Loreto Shores* (☎ (113) 5-06-29, fax (113) 5-07-11), on the beach across the Río Loreto, has full hookups, clean bathrooms, hot showers and a laundry room, but very little shade. Office hours are 8 am to 1 pm and 2 to 9 pm. Rates are US$5 for camping without hookups, US$12 with hookups; nonguests can use the showers for US$1. The mailing address is Apdo Postal 219, Loreto, Baja California Sur 23880, México.

Nearby *Villas de Loreto* (☎ /fax (113) 5-05-86) has full-hookup sites for US$13.50 and eight double rooms for US$50, including breakfast and plenty of fresh air – it's a completely nonsmoking resort.

Hotels & Motels Very basic *Hotel San Martín* (☎ (113) 5-04-42), Juárez 14, is among the cheapest in town for US$9 single or double, but it's often full. The cheaper and even more basic *Motel Davis*, on Davis between Constituyentes and Carrillo, lacks hot showers but is otherwise passable.

Motel Salvatierra (☎ (113) 5-00-21), at Salvatierra 123 between Allende and Márquez de León, has clean but worn rooms with air-conditioning and hot showers for US$13/18 single/double. The best choice is this category is probably *Motel Brenda* (☎ (113) 5-07-07) on Juárez between Márquez de León and Ayuntamiento, where clean and comfortable rooms with air-con, TV and hot water cost US$15.

Places to Stay – middle
Loreto generally lacks midrange accommodations, but the newly opened *Hotel Junípero* (☎ (113) 5-00-28), on Avenida Hidalgo near the mission plaza, has become popular in part for its reasonable prices (US$20/25) and balconies overlook-

ing the avenue. Attractive *Hotel Plaza Loreto* (☎ (113) 5-02-80, fax (113) 5-08-55), across from the mission at Avenida Hidalgo 2, has singles/doubles for US$35/43.

At the height of the 1996 – 97 tourist season, tax problems closed the 32-room waterfront *Hotel Misión de Loreto* (☎ (113) 5-00-48, fax (113) 5-06-48) on de la Playa (Blvd López Mateos) between Rosendo Robles and Juárez, but odds are that it will eventually reopen with prices slightly higher than the Hotel Plaza Loreto's. Besides air-conditioned rooms, it features a swimming pool and two restaurants.

Places to Stay – top end
On the beachfront at the corner of de la Playa (Blvd López Mateos) and Baja California, the 35-room *Hotel Oasis* (☎ (113) 5-01-12, fax (113) 5-07-95) offers subtropical gardens and rooms with private bath, hot water, air-conditioning and all meals for about US$79/110 single/double.

Hotel La Pinta Loreto (☎ (113) 5-00-25, fax (113) 5-00-26; (800) 336-5454 in the USA), on Davis about 1 mile (1.6 km) north of the plaza, has a swimming pool (not always filled), a restaurant and bar and easy beach access. Its 48 air-conditioned rooms have TV, shower and private balconies facing the Gulf, but some guests have complained that the lack of heating makes winter nights chilly. Singles/doubles cost around US$60/65 plus 10% tax.

Places to Eat
Café Olé (☎ (113) 5-04-95), Madero 14 just south of the Plaza Cívica, serves good, inexpensive breakfasts (with especially tasty hotcakes) and antojitos. *Anthony's Casa de la Pizza* (☎ (113) 5-07-33), on Madero south of Avenida Hidalgo near the Río Loreto, brags of 'the world's worst pizza.' American-owned *Tiffany's Pisa Parlor* (☎ (113) 5-00-04), at the corner of Avenida Hidalgo and Pino Suárez, appeals to an exclusively gringo clientele, in part because of its high prices, but quality is also high, and it's completely tobacco-free.

El Nido (☎ (113) 5-02-84), Salvatierra 154 across from the bus terminal, is the local branch of the widespread Baja steakhouse chain. *Los 4 Altos* (☎ (113) 5-02-84), at the corner of Juárez and Independencia, is a respectable upstairs bar and grill.

El Embarcadero (☎ (113) 5-01-65), on the malecón just south of Callejón Agua Dulce, specializes in seafood, as do the excellent *Playa Blanca* (☎ (113) 5-04-28) on Avenida Hidalgo at the corner of Madero, and the almost equally good *Las Casitas* (☎ (113) 5-11-04) on Juárez between Independencia and Zapata. Las Casitas sells its own sourdough bread (the apple pie is mediocre, however).

La Palapa, a very good seafood restaurant on Avenida Hidalgo just half a block from the beach, is a direct descendant of the popular but now defunct Caesar's, nearly a Loreto institution. *La Casa*, at the corner of Avenida Hidalgo and Colegio, has appealingly upscale ambiance, but there are some moderately priced items on the menu. It has a 4 to 6 pm happy hour.

Il Campanile, at the corner of Ayuntamiento and Juárez, is a new and fairly expensive Italian place that hasn't yet caught on with Mexicans, but local expatriates recommend it highly. Its 'small' pizzas are more than enough to fill two adults. Hours are 5 to 10:30 pm only.

La Michoacana, on Salvatierra near the corner of Zapata, has decent ice cream but much better paletas and aguas.

Entertainment
El Billar de Toño, a rustically appointed club at Salvatierra and Romanita just a stone's throw from the beach, features live rock by local bands. Overnighters at the nearby RV Park El Moro will hear everything clearly enough at no charge, but weeknight rehearsals end fairly early.

Things to Buy
For the best selection of specifically Baja handicrafts, browse the selection at Las Parras Tour on Madero just north of Avenida Hidalgo. For items from throughout the rest of Mexico, try El Alacrán (☎ (113) 5-00-29) at the corner of Salvatierra and Misioneros.

Conchita (☎ (113) 5-06-81), at the corner of Salvatierra and Pino Suárez, has a good selection of jewelry, a decent selection of Baja books, high prices (even postage stamps get marked up) and products made from endangered species like sea turtles that may not be imported into the USA. El Risito de Oro, on Salvatierra next to the Servifax office, carries fine handcrafted jewelry, but also unfortunately deals in suspect items like tortoiseshell and black coral.

Getting There & Away
Air Aeropuerto Internacional de Loreto (☎ (113) 5-04-54) is reached by a lateral off the Transpeninsular, just across the Río Loreto. Aero California (☎ (113) 5-05-00, (113) 5-05-55 at the airport, fax (113) 5-05-66), on Juárez between Misioneros and Zapata, is open 8:30 am to 6 pm daily. It flies twice daily to and from Los Angeles.

Aerolitoral, represented by Viajes Pedrín (see Travel & Tour Agencies in this entry), flies daily to and from La Paz. Connections to many mainland Mexican cities can be made in La Paz; see the La Paz Getting There & Away entry for details.

Bus Loreto's bus terminal (☎ (113) 5-07-67), near the traffic circle where Salvatierra, Paseo de Ugarte and Paseo Tamaral converge, is open 6:30 am to 11 pm.

Northbound buses go to Tijuana (US$35) at 1 am, to Santa Rosalía (US$5.50) at 2 pm and 5 pm, to Tijuana at 3 pm, to Mexicali (US$40) at 9 pm and to Guerrero Negro (US$15) at 11 pm.

Southbound buses for La Paz (US$10) and intermediate stops depart at 8 am, 1, 2 and 11 pm and midnight.

Getting Around
To/From the Airport Taxis to or from the airport cost US$5 for one person, plus US$2 for each additional person.

Car Rental There are two car-rental agencies in town:

Budget
    de la Playa at Avenida Hidalgo
    (☎ (113) 5-10-90)
Thrifty
    de la Playa (Blvd López Mateos)
    at Rosendo Robles
    (☎ (113) 5-08-15, fax (113) 5-08-16)

Bicycle Las Parras Tour rents mountain bikes for US$5 per hour, US$15 per half-day and US$25 per full day (eight hours). Mountain-bike tours are also available.

AROUND LORETO
Isla Coronado

About 3 miles (5 km) northeast of Loreto, opposite Punta Tierra Firma, Isla Coronado is one of the Gulf's most accessible islands and the northernmost island in the Parque Marino Nacional Bahía de Loreto. The turquoise waters along its sparkling sandy beach, facing the mainland, are ideal for snorkeling; there are also many seabirds, mostly pelicans, and the rocky eastern shore has a small sea lion colony.

Many kayakers make the trip to Coronado, where it's possible to camp and there are several palapas for shade, but it's also possible to arrange a panga circumnavigation and beach stop with Las Parras Tour in Loreto (see the Loreto entry in this chapter).

Misión San Francisco Javier

Built from blocks of volcanic stone in the Sierra de la Giganta west of Loreto, San Francisco Javier de Viggé-Biaundó is one of the Californias' best-preserved mission churches, in perhaps the most spectacular setting of any of them. Founded in 1699 at nearby Rancho Viejo by the famous Jesuit Francisco María Piccolo, the Californias' second mission moved to its present site in 1720 but was not completed until 1758.

The church itself is in very fine condition, with its original walls, floors and venerable religious artworks, but visitors may no longer climb the spiral staircase to the chorus. Irrigation canals of Jesuit vintage, the first on the peninsula, still water the

local fields. Every December 3, hundreds of pilgrims celebrate the saint's fiesta here.

Just over a mile (1.6 km) south of Loreto is the junction for the spectacular 22-mile (35-km) mountain road to the village of San Javier, which takes about 1½ hours, not counting photo stops. The dirt surface is graded only to Rancho Viejo but is passable for most passenger cars despite a few bumpy spots and arroyo crossings. Rancho Las Parras, in a verdant canyon halfway to San Javier, grows figs, dates, olives and citrus, but livestock have contaminated most of the water along the route – do not drink without treating it. A spring just before Km 20 westbound should be potable, and there are a couple potential swimming holes.

With an early start, this would be a good day trip on a mountain bike, but parts of the road are steep enough that even the strongest cyclist will probably have to walk for short stretches. The village's only tourist facility is *Restaurant Palapa San Javier* near the mission church, which serves simple meals, cold beer and sodas under a shady palapa. Ask about camping, and there may even be rustic accommodations available.

The road leading southwest from San Javier, passing a series of remote ranchos before reaching the intersection with the paved Ciudad Insurgentes-San Isidro highway just north of Colonia Purísima, is much improved and passable for any vehicle with good clearance. While this interesting road is slower than the paved Transpeninsular, it allows drivers to avoid the unpleasant Judiciales checkpoint south of Nopoló.

Nopoló

In the 1980s Fonatur, the federal tourist development agency also responsible for mainland Mexican debacles like Cancún and Ixtapa, plopped this incongruous resort complex onto an erstwhile goat ranch 4 miles (6.5 km) south of Loreto. Despite construction of an international airport and an elaborate street plan off a single palm-lined avenue, it remains a cluster of largely vacant and weedy lots except for its single upscale hotel, lighted tennis courts, sprawling 18-hole golf course and a handful of private houses. Nopoló also has its own clinic and fire department.

The Campo de Golf Loreto (☎ (113) 3-04-08), which probably uses more water than the entire town of Loreto, features a cart bridge that many isolated rural communities might start a revolution to get. Greens fees are US$30, while cart rentals cost US$30 and club rentals US$15.

In an apparently desperate move to salvage something from Nopoló, Fonatur reached an agreement with the Italian company Allegro Resorts to turn the former Loreto Inn, a 250-room luxury hotel, into the *Diamond Eden Resort* (☎ (113) 3-07-00, fax (113) 3-03-77), an adults-only facility featuring two swimming pools (sometimes heated), tennis courts (sometimes with nets) with a stadium for competitive matches, a nightclub, a bar, two restaurants and a nude beach. Diamond Eden guests are conspicuous in Loreto because of their green wristbands (perhaps the modern equivalents of scarlet letters).

The Diamond Eden's daily rates for all-inclusive packages (including unlimited drinks) range from US$125/190 to US$135/210 single/double; nonguests can use the hotel facilities for US$35 per day. Most packages last four to seven days.

Puerto Escondido

Puerto Escondido, an ostensibly Mediterranean-style marina in a scenic natural port 16 miles (26 km) south of Loreto, was the site of yet another ambitious Fonatur scheme, a joint venture with a French investment company to build a resort complex with five-star hotels, luxurious private homes, condominiums, stores, a fitness center and moorings for 300 yachts. The paved but potholed access road off the Transpeninsular beyond Tripui Resort RV Park aptly symbolizes the ragged results.

Budget travelers can try catching a lift on a yacht at the marina; there's a radio net on channel 68 between 8 and 8:30 am. Ask at the yacht dock near the seawall for permission to use a radio, and state your business.

Tripui Resort RV Park (☎ (113) 3-08-18, fax (113) 3-08-28), a short distance east of the Transpeninsular, is a depressingly

DESIERTO CENTRAL

JENNIFER JOHNSEN

Mountainscape inland from Puerto Escondido

Cascabel, a desert resident

antiseptic RV park/campground/fortress in a noisy location remote from the bay. Full hookups, a swimming pool, lighted tennis courts, a laundry room, a restaurant and a grocery store are available. Rates are US$16 for a vehicle and US$10 for a tent. RV-club members should ask for discounts. Tripui's mailing address is Apdo Postal 100, Loreto, Baja California Sur 23880, México.

Llano de Magdalena

Beyond Puerto Escondido, the Transpeninsular twists and climbs through the Sierra de la Giganta before turning westward into the Llano de Magdalena (Magdalena Plain). A new bronze monument to pioneer agriculturalists graces the road north from the highway junction at Ciudad Insurgentes, an increasingly prosperous town with restaurants, groceries and a Pemex station, but still no accommodations. If you're planning to continue west to Puerto López Mateos or north to San José de Comondú, stock up on supplies here.

One of the key whale-breeding sites on the coast, popularly known as 'Mag Bay' among English-speakers, Bahía Magdalena has had a colorful history despite (or perhaps because of) its thinly populated coastline. In colonial times Sebastián Vizcaíno anchored nearby but, finding no surface water, soon departed. Some years later, missionary Clemente Guillén found no suitable harbor and, though the Jesuits built a lowland chapel under the jurisdiction of Misión San Luis Gonzaga, they never really colonized the area.

Both before and after Mexican independence, the area attracted smugglers; foreign whalers worked the area from 1836 to 1846, assisted by laborers from San José de Comondú. During the Mexican-American War, the US Navy promised local residents US citizenship in return for their support. These residents were forced to leave after the signing of the Treaty of Guadalupe Hidalgo and the failure of secret negotiations that would have kept Baja California under US control in exchange for a cash indemnity.

There have been several other US attempts to acquire the Baja Peninsula. Though the government of Benito Juárez was willing to sell, it set too high a price, but still encouraged foreign projects like Jacob Leese's Lower California Colonization & Mining Company, later known as the Lower California Company. In 1866 this company gained title to all Baja lands between 24°20'N and 31°N (roughly from La Paz to San Quintín) in a transparently fraudulent colonization attempt.

The San Francisco-based company went so far as to issue bogus paper money under the name 'The Bank of Lower California Trust and Loan Association' for the proposed city of Cortez. After an exploration in 1867, one disillusioned member warned that 'to send a party of colonists here, without previous preparation of the land at great expense, would be criminal,' but the company responded with a propaganda barrage in favor of the plan.

As an agricultural colonization project, the company failed scandalously, but its concession to collect orchilla, a valuable dye plant, employed about 500 gatherers in the Llano de Magdalena. This spurred the opening of a customs house and a brief boom until the development of alternative aniline dyes reduced the market. Another attempt at agricultural colonization, under the successor Chartered Company of California, also failed.

In the late 19th century the government of Porfirio Díaz allowed the US Navy to establish a coaling station in Bahía Magdalena and, after the turn of the century, to hold target practice and maneuvers in the area. In the latter years of the Díaz dictatorship, however, a request by the US State Department to extend these agreements aroused nationalist sentiments; one newspaper editor in Mazatlán even thundered that 'the history of Texas and California will be repeated.'

Despite displays of force and fears of Baja's annexation by the US, the Navy departed when the agreements expired. The subsequent sale of the Chartered Company, the spread of the Mexican Revolution and a Mexican fishing agreement with Japan served as pretexts for annexationists in the US Congress and the press (most notably the jingoistic Hearst newspapers) to urge a US takeover, but President Woodrow Wilson resisted the pressure.

Accelerating agricultural development in the latter half of the 20th century finally consolidated Mexican control of the area, and today the region, particularly around Ciudad Constitución, is booming. Its main lure for travelers, whale-watching, brings visitors from around the globe to its small but very appealing port towns. Bahía Magdalena is also one of the largest remaining wetlands on the Pacific coast of North America.

PUERTO LÓPEZ MATEOS

Protected by the barrier island of Isla Magdalena, Puerto Adolfo López Mateos (population 2391), 20 miles (32 km) west of Ciudad Insurgentes by a good paved road, is one of Baja's best whale-watching sites. Boca de Soledad, only a short distance north of the port, boasts the highest density of whales anywhere along the peninsula. The annual **Festival del Ballenato**, celebrating the birth of gray-whale calves, takes place in early February.

The cooperative Unión de Lancheros (☎ (113) 1-51-71) and the Sociedad Cooperativa Aquendi (☎ (113) 1-51-98) run whale-watching pangas from the new pier near their headquarters near the lighthouse; other authorized pangueros include Sergio Tapia García (☎ (113) 1-01-39) and Modesto Camacho Beltrán (☎ (113) 1-51-23). Trips cost US$45 per hour for up to six persons; since people begin to arrive the night before for early-morning departures, camping at nearby Playa Soledad, it's easy to form groups to share expenses. Pangueros stay out as long as their clients wish.

Places to Stay & Eat

Free camping, with pit toilets only (bring water), is possible at *Playa Soledad*. López Mateos' only other accommodations are at the small and simple but new and tidy *Posada Ballena López*, within easy walking distance of the whale-watching pier, for US$10/15 single/double.

Besides a couple so-so *taco stands*, López Mateos has several decent restaurants. *El Palomar*, directly opposite the plaza, serves good and moderately priced seafood specialties, including perhaps the most reasonable lobster in Baja, in a homey environment; across the street, *Cabaña Brisa* is also pretty good. Stick with the seafood at *El Ballenato* (☎ (113) 1-50-29) at the eastern approach to town, where other dishes may lack freshness.

Getting There & Away

Autotransportes Aguila provides daily buses from Ciudad Constitución (US$2) at 11:30 am and 7 pm; return service to Constitución leaves at 6:30 am and 12:30 pm.

CIUDAD CONSTITUCIÓN

Having grown dramatically with the Llano de Magdalena's rapid expansion of commercial agriculture, Ciudad Constitución (population 35,447) bears all the marks of a 'progressive' city: clean, broad paved streets (at least in the center), several banks and even high culture – state and national cultural organizations visit the local Teatro de la Ciudad (City Theater) on their tours.

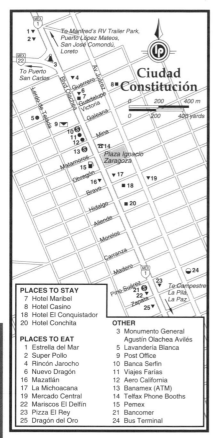

Ciudad Constitución

PLACES TO STAY
7 Hotel Maribel
8 Hotel Casino
18 Hotel El Conquistador
20 Hotel Conchita

PLACES TO EAT
1 Estrella del Mar
2 Super Pollo
4 Rincón Jarocho
6 Nuevo Dragón
16 Mazatlán
17 La Michoacana
19 Mercado Central
22 Mariscos El Delfín
23 Pizza El Rey
25 Dragón del Oro

OTHER
3 Monumento General
   Agustín Olachea Avilés
5 Lavandería Blanca
9 Post Office
10 Banca Serfin
11 Viajes Farías
12 Aero California
13 Banamex (ATM)
14 Telfax Phone Booths
15 Pemex
21 Bancomer
24 Bus Terminal

At the northern entrance to town, at the turnoff to Puerto San Carlos, is a monument to General Agustín Olachea Avilés, a Todos Santos native who participated in the famous Cananea copper strike in Sonora. Olachea Avilés joined the revolutionary forces in 1913, became a general in 1920 at the age of only 28 and put down a Yaqui Indian rebellion in Sonora in 1926. Later, as governor of Baja California's Territorio Sur, he promoted agricultural development in Ciudad Constitución.

Fresh water for cultivation was a serious problem before the exploitation of huge aquifers beneath the plain; Israeli technicians have since advised farmers on water conservation and crop substitution to take advantage of newly drilled wells. Water-efficient crops like garbanzos (chickpeas) and citrus are superseding thirsty, pesticide-dependent cotton.

Because Constitución is primarily an agricultural service center, most travelers find little of interest here, but the city is very convenient to the major whale-watching centers of Puerto San Carlos and Puerto López Mateos, which have only limited accommodations. It is also the *cabecera* (administrative center) of the *municipio* of Comondú.

Orientation
Ciudad Constitución is 134 miles (216 km) northwest of La Paz, 89 miles (143 km) southwest of Loreto and 36 miles (58 km) east of Puerto San Carlos on Bahía Magdalena. The north-south Transpeninsular is the main street, known formally as Blvd General Agustín Olachea Avilés and more commonly as Blvd Olachea, but the city has matured beyond the strip-development phase (unlike such northern Baja towns as San Quintín). Still, most important services are within a block or two of Blvd Olachea, where passing delivery trucks have clipped, bent and twisted the city's once shiny Banamex street signs so that through traffic seems to cross Olachea at every corner. The other major street is the parallel Avenida Juárez, one block east.

Information
Money Constitución has no cambios, but several banks on Blvd Olachea change US dollars or traveler's checks: Banca Serfin at the corner of Galeana, Banamex (with an ATM) at the southwestern corner of Mina and Bancomer on Pino Suárez just west of Blvd Olachea.

Post & Communications The post office is on Galeana just west of Blvd Olachea; the postal code is 23600. Besides Telmex public phones, try the private Telfax phone booths on the eastern side of Blvd Olachea between Matamoros and Mina.

Travel Agency Viajes Farías (☎ (113) 2-00-00, fax (113) 2-12-28), Blvd Olachea 907, is Constitución's only full-service travel agency.

Laundry Lavandería Blanca (☎ (113) 2-07-69) is at the corner of Avenida Lerdo de Tejada and Guadalupe Victoria.

Places to Stay

Camping *Campestre La Pila* (☎ (113) 2-05-62, fax (113) 2-02-29) is an RV park at the end of a dirt road just south of town that leads west for about half a mile (1 km); turn right at the large *maquiladora*. There are now hot showers in addition to electrical outlets, toilets and a swimming pool. On weekends, the park proper is a popular picnic ground, a pleasant, grassy area surrounded by a farm (with accompanying animal sounds) and a few shade trees. At harvest times, freshly picked vegetables are available from the farm. The rate for two people is about US$8; an extra person is US$2.

At the northern end of town near the junction with the highway to Puerto López Mateos, Austrian-run *Manfred's RV Trailer Park* (☎ (113) 2-11-03) has spacious pull-through sites for US$12/14 single/double, but also gives a break to cyclists and motorcyclists (US$6 per site) and car campers (US$9 per site). Thanks to an elaborate drip-irrigation system, the park is increasingly shady; it also has hot showers, a swimming pool, an Austrian restaurant and a spacious apartment with private bath available for US$28 per night.

Hotels *Hotel Casino* (☎ (113) 2-07-57), on Guadalupe Victoria about one block east of Hotel Maribel, has very spartan rooms for about US$13 single or double; the go-cart track across the street can play hell with your afternoon siesta, and the improbable transvestite bar next door could also be a distraction. The much better *Hotel Conchita* (☎ (113) 2-02-66, fax (113) 2-09-73), Blvd Olachea 180, charges US$10/17 single (US$12/19 with

TV). *Hotel Oasis* (☎ /fax (113) 2-44-58), Guerrero 284, is a very good choice for US$15 double.

Hotel El Conquistador (☎ (113) 2-27-45, fax (113) 2-14-43), Bravo 161, is a three-star place charging US$13/15 single/double downstairs, US$15/18 upstairs; it's a bit dark and formal, but its restaurant has decent meals. *Hotel Maribel* (☎ (113) 2-01-55), Guadalupe Victoria 156 near Blvd Olachea, has rooms comfortable enough for a night – each with telephone and TV – for about US$14 single/double upstairs, US$19 downstairs. The attached restaurant offers basic Mexican dishes.

Other choices include *Hotel Reforma* (☎ (113) 2-09-88), Obregón 125, and *Hotel Julia* (☎ (113) 2-23-69), Galeana 219 (both with economical rates), plus moderately priced *Hotel Lizajú* (☎ (113) 2-05-32), Guerrero 251.

Places to Eat

For Constitución's cheapest eats, try the many *taquerías* on Blvd Olachea (which have finally caught up with the fish taco craze) or the *Mercado Central*, on Avenida Juárez between Hidalgo and Bravo. *Pizza El Rey*, on Blvd Olachea between Pino Suárez and Zapata, serves a different sort of fast food.

Super Pollo (☎ (113) 2-09-55), just north of the Olachea monument, specializes in grilled chicken, Sinaloa-style. Next-door *Estrella del Mar* (☎ (113) 2-09-55) is a good seafood restaurant, as is *Rincón Jarocho* (☎ (113) 2-25-25) on the eastern side of Blvd Olachea just south of the monument. Other seafood choices include *Mariscos El Delfín* at Blvd Olachea and Zapata, and *Mazatlán* on Blvd Olachea between Bravo and Obregón.

Constitución has two Chinese restaurants: *Nuevo Dragón* (☎ (113) 2-29-52) on Blvd Olachea between Guerrero and Guadalupe Victoria, and *Dragón del Oro* (☎ (113) 2-53-43) on Blvd Olachea just south of Zapata. Hotel Maribel's *Sancho Panza* is worth a try for Mexican food.

La Michoacana, on Blvd Olachea half a block south of Plaza Ignacio Zaragoza, has dependably good ice cream, paletas and aguas.

Getting There & Away

Air Constitución has no commercial air services, but Aero California (☎ (113) 2-12-11) has an office on Blvd Olachea at the corner of Mina, where it's possible to make or reconfirm reservations for flights from Loreto or La Paz.

Bus North-south ABC and Autotransportes Aguila buses on the Transpeninsular stop at Constitución's terminal (☎ (113) 2-03-76) at the corner of Avenida Juárez and Pino Suárez, one block east of Blvd Olachea.

Buses depart for the nearby whale-watching centers of Puerto San Carlos (US$1.50), at 10:45 am and 3:15 pm, and Puerto López Mateos (US$2), at 11:30 am and 7 pm. Buses to San Isidro (US$4.50) depart at 9:45 am and 6 pm daily.

Northbound long-distance buses go daily to Loreto (US$5), to Santa Rosalía (US$11), to Guerrero Negro (US$18), to Tijuana (US$41) and to Mexicali (US$48). There are 10 southbound buses daily to La Paz (US$5.50), one of which (at 3 pm) continues to Los Cabos.

PUERTO SAN CARLOS

Increasingly popular for some of southern Baja's best whale-watching, Puerto San Carlos (population 3644) is a dusty, windy but friendly deep-water port on Bahía Magdalena about 36 miles (58 km) west of Ciudad Constitución (watch for livestock, including cattle and even pigs, on the paved highway). Puerto San Carlos ships cotton and alfalfa from the fields of the Llano de Magdalena, and a minor building boom has given it the best accommodations of any of Baja's whale-watching destinations. Nearby beaches on Bahía Magdalena are fine for camping, clamming and sportfishing.

In the late 19th century, a US Navy coaling station in the area became a major political controversy in mainland Mexico. A recent Japanese concession of 5000 acres (2000 hectares) for a tourist development south of Puerto San Carlos is on hold; the offshore Isla Magdalena, a barrier island, is under control of the Mexican navy and off-limits to this enterprise.

All Puerto San Carlos' streets are named for Mexican port cities. Gasoline, including Magna Sin and diesel, is available at the Pemex station. The new **Museo Ballena Sudcaliforniana** (Southern Baja Whale Museum) is very rudimentary, displaying only a single gray-whale skeleton and a few rusting artifacts from 19th-century whaling days, but mid-February's **Festival de la Ballena Gris** (Gray Whale Festival) is becoming a big-time event.

Information

Puerto San Carlos lacks a tourist office, but has a post office (postal code 23740), long-distance telephone service and an IMSS clinic.

Whale-Watching

In season (from mid-January through March), local pangueros take up to five or six passengers to view friendly whales in Bahía Magdalena for US$35 per hour (with a two-hour minimum). Some people come for the day from Loreto or La Paz (both about 2½ hours away by car) or even fly in from Cabo San Lucas, but early morning is the best time to see whales. Among the local operators are Ulysturs (☎ (113) 6-00-30), Puerto Mazatlán s/n, and Mar y Arena (☎ (113) 6-02-32, fax (113) 6-00-76) at the corner of Blvd Puerto La Paz and Puerto Loreto.

Places to Stay & Eat

Puerto San Carlos has no formal RV parks; it's possible to camp on the fairly clean *public beach* north of town without charge, but the aging palapas are falling into disrepair and there are no toilets. South of town, people camp among the *mangroves* near the whale-watching launch sites; it's messier, but there's a good selection of bird life – suggesting that aesthetics are more important to humans than to wildlife.

Hotel accommodations are more abundant than in the past, but whale-watching season still puts a strain on local capacity, and reservations are a good idea. Friendly, family-oriented *Motel Las Brisas* (☎ (113) 6-01-52), on Puerto Madero, has basic but clean singles/doubles from US$11/13. The indifferent *Hotel Palmar* (☎ (113) 6-00-35), on Puerto Morelos, charges US$13/16 single/double, while the attractive *Hotel Alcatraz* (☎ (113) 6-00-17, fax (113) 6-00-86) has singles/doubles with TV for US$30/40; its shady *Restaurant Bar El Patio* is unquestionably the best in town. The newest accommodations are found at *Brennan Hotel* (☎ (113) 6-02-88, fax (113) 6-00-19; (510) 428-5464 in the USA), whose well-appointed rooms are also in the US$30/40 range.

A nameless but neatly landscaped *taco stand* at Puerto La Paz and Puerto Madero, around the corner from Motel Las Brisas, has tasty shrimp tacos at very low prices. Unfortunately, it also keeps erratic hours.

Getting There & Away
Based in a small house on Puerto Morelos, Autotransportes Aguila runs buses to Ciudad Constitución (US$3) and La Paz (US$10) at 7:30 am and 1:45 pm daily. This is the only public transportation.

AROUND THE LLANO DE MAGDALENA
Misión San Luis Gonzaga
Founded in 1737 by German Jesuit Lambert Hostell, the date-palm oasis of Misión San Luis Gonzaga, southeast of Ciudad Constitución, closed with the Jesuits' departure in 1768, after an original Indian population of 2000 had fallen to only 300. The Alsatian Jesuit Johann Jakob Baegert left a detailed record of the mission's last two decades.

San Luis' well-preserved church, dating from the 1750s but lacking the embellishments of the San Borja and San Francisco Javier churches, is not one of the mission system's gems, but its twin bell towers are unusual. Besides the church, there are ruins of more recent vintage with elaborate neoclassical columns. The village's only facilities are a school and a Conasupo.

At Km 195, about 9 miles (14 km) south of Ciudad Constitución on the Transpeninsular, a graded lateral good enough even for low riders or mammoth RVs leads 25 miles (40 km) east to the edge of the Sierra de la Giganta and San Luis Gonzaga. Keep watching for the sign reading 'Presa Iguajil.'

Just across the arroyo from the mission, a road suitable for high-clearance, short-wheelbase vehicles only (4WD is not essential) leads 16 miles (26 km) south past Ranchos Iraquí, La Palmilla (Conasupo and cold drinks), El Caporal and Pozo de Iritú to Rancho Las Tinajitas. There it meets another lateral from Santa Rita that climbs east into the sierra to the extensive but poorly preserved ruins of Misión La Pasión (see below). This route is more difficult but much more interesting than the corresponding segment of the Transpeninsular.

WAYNE BERNHARDSON

Misión La Pasión

From Km 128 on the Transpeninsular, a graded dirt road climbs east to Rancho Las Tinajitas (see the entry for Misión San Luis Gonzaga, above) and Rancho Los Ciruelos, beyond which the ungraded surface to the Jesuit Misión La Pasión becomes difficult for vehicles without high clearance. The ruins themselves are just west of Santa María Toris, a friendly rancho beyond which a 4WD route continues toward **Misión Dolores del Sur**, but stops just short of those ruins – they're an hour's hike or five minutes by panga from the end of the route. Santa María Toris itself has a Conasupo market and an *internado* (boarding school) but has no other facilities. There are cave paintings in the canyon below Toris, among its numerous volcanic plugs and mesas, but these are difficult to locate without a guide.

Only foundations remain of Misión La Pasión, which lasted from 1737 until the Jesuits' expulsion in 1767, when its Indians were transferred to Todos Santos. Those foundations are very extensive, however; barely a decade ago, according to local residents, the last standing wall fell. Note that the usually reliable AAA road map places the ruins on the wrong (northern) side of the road and has several other inaccuracies.

At the junction 3 miles (5 km) west of Toris, the right fork leads south to Rancho Las Animas, beyond which a dangerously exciting road, sloping and riddled with gullies (4WD only, with great caution), leads to Rancho Soledad and the Gulf coast fish camp of San Evaristo, where another, less difficult road leads south to La Paz. (See the Cape Region chapter for details of these latter roads.) The road from Las Animas to Soledad offers truly awesome panoramas of the Sierra de la Giganta, but don't take your eyes off the road unless you stop the car.

Puerto Chale

About 36 miles (58 km) south of Ciudad Constitución, a 15-mile (24-km) graded dirt road leads west from the village of Santa Rita on the Transpeninsular to Puerto Chale, a tiny Pacific coast fish camp popular with windsurfers.

EL CIEN

So called because it lies exactly 100 km northwest of La Paz on the Transpeninsular, El Cien has a Pemex station and a decent restaurant; it is 35 miles (56 km) south of Santa Rita. Twelve miles (19 km) farther south, at Km 80 just beyond a microwave station, is a junction with a 12-mile (19-km) dirt road to **Punta Conejo** (some smaller RVs have successfully navigated this route, but not without cosmetic damage).

Countless tiny crabs scurry over Punta Conejo's firm, sandy beach to the safety of their burrows, wary of the gulls overhead; apparent bicycle tracks disappear under a rock overhang where hermit crabs hide from their pursuers. The area attracts many surfers to its right break, mostly in southerly swells, but it's far from crowded; surf fishing is also popular.

At the southeastern end of the beach, a jutting headland consists of a marine conglomerate composed almost entirely of fossils – follow the informal trail at the base of the cliff to some smaller, more secluded beaches, but be prepared to scramble over the rocks. Remember that Mexican law prohibits fossil hunting; in any event, all these fossils are comparatively recent.

There are oyster beds 5 miles (8 km) south of Punta Conejo, but drifting sand makes the road difficult beyond that point even for 4WD vehicles. Surfers headed for **Punta Márquez** might find it easier to approach via the graded road from the Transpeninsular to Ejido Conquista, between Km 55 and 54.

Cape Region

This chapter covers the Cape Region, comprising the modern southern city of La Paz and areas to its south along the Transpeninsular and México 19, including the popular resorts of Los Cabos (San José del Cabo and Cabo San Lucas). This is the costliest and most self-consciously (sometimes aggressively) tourist-oriented part of the peninsula, but it still offers unconventional opportunities for determined travelers.

LA PAZ

Kaleidoscopic sunsets over the bay, a palm-studded *malecón* (waterfront promenade), neocolonial architecture and nearby Península Pichilingue's sandy beaches and warm bays are the main attractions of La Paz (population 154,314), the capital of Baja California Sur. Although undercut by NAFTA tariff reductions, La Paz remains a notable port and has become a resort city as well, despite official opinion (resented by local authorities) that it's more a point of arrival than a destination in its own right.

Most activities in the area are beach-oriented, but authorities acknowledge that Bahía de La Paz proper is badly polluted. Areas beyond the Pemex shore facilities and ferry terminal, toward Playa Tecolote at the tip of Península Pichilingue, are cleaner, pleasanter and safer.

Thanks to its university, several good museums and an important theater and cultural center, La Paz is also a locus for cultural activities. Pichilingue, on the peninsula north of town, is the port for ferries between La Paz and the mainland Mexican ports of Topolobampo and Mazatlán.

History

In 1535 on Península Pichilingue, Hernán Cortés himself established Baja's first European settlement; despite the discovery of pearls in the Gulf of California, it was soon abandoned due to Indian hostility and food and water shortages.

By the late 16th century, England and Holland were disputing Spain's maritime hegemony and buccaneers were raiding Spanish ships throughout the world; the treasure-laden galleons that sailed from Manila to Acapulco were especially popular targets. After the turn of the century, in response to incursions by northern Europeans, Viceroy Gaspar de Zuñiga y Acevedo of New Spain granted Sebastián Vizcaíno a license to exploit the pearl fisheries of the Cape Region and establish settlements to discourage privateers.

Though Vizcaíno renamed Bahía de la Santa Cruz as Bahía de La Paz (Bay of Peace), he abandoned the idea of a settlement there because of the shortage of supplies and the area's limited agricultural potential. In 1720 the Jesuits established a mission, but epidemics and Indian uprisings led to its abandonment only 29 years later. La Paz was briefly occupied by US Marines during the Mexican-American War, then attacked by William Walker during his preposterously incompetent attempt to annex Baja California to the USA.

Mining at nearby El Triunfo, along with pearling and fishing in the Gulf, contributed to the city's postindependence growth. Its political status advanced with the grant of statehood to Baja California Sur in 1974.

Orientation

As the Transpeninsular approaches the city, it runs parallel to Bahía de La Paz and becomes Calzada (Calle) Abasolo; to continue to Cabo San Lucas without visiting downtown La Paz, turn right (south) on 5 de Febrero and follow the signs to 'Carretera al Sur' (the southbound Transpeninsular) and 'Cabo San Lucas.'

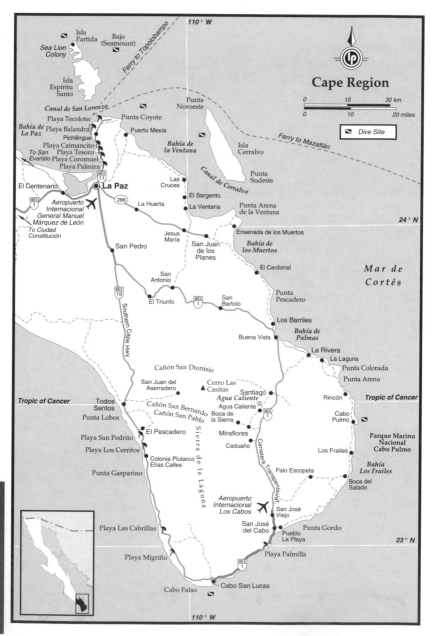

Cape Region

| 0 | 15 | 30 km |
| 0 | 10 | 20 miles |

Dive Site

The Dutch in the Pacific

New World piracy was largely the province of the English, but other Northern European countries eagerly joined in the battle against Spanish wealth and hegemony in the Americas. The French and especially the Dutch were most active in the Caribbean and on the coast of Brazil, but the Dutch had Pacific ambitions as well.

Since the late-16th-century voyage of Sir Francis Drake, British buccaneers had frequented the Pacific coasts of North and South America, despite the distances between their homes and their convenient, well-watered island bases in the Caribbean. Thomas Cavendish's capture of the *Santa Ana* off Cabo San Lucas in 1587 attracted privateers' interest to New Spain (Mexico) and Baja California; British pirates lay in wait for treasure-laden galleons returning from Manila and sometimes took other major prizes.

The Netherlands, having rebelled against Spanish domination in 1566, was eager to make its mark on the seas. The Dutch became rivals of the Spaniards in the Caribbean and the Portuguese in Brazil, and they soon rounded the Horn to the Pacific. Though they lurked at Cabo San Lucas in hopes of emulating Cavendish's windfall, their earliest voyages had limited success. Profit was not the only motive that spurred the Dutch; they were fanatical Protestants who resented the reactionary Catholicism the Spaniards had imposed on them in Europe.

In 1615 the surprisingly genteel occupation of Acapulco by the Dutch privateer Joris van Speilbergen induced the Spaniards to build the famous port's landmark castle, the Fuerte de San Diego. For decades, though, the menace of Dutch privateers forced the Spaniards to send patrols from the mainland to the Cape Region. Península Pichilingue, north of La Paz, even takes its name from the Dutch privateers whom the Spaniards called 'Flexolingas,' after their home port of Vlissingen just north of the modern Belgian border. ■

Four blocks east of 5 de Febrero, Abasolo becomes Paseo Alvaro Obregón, running along the malecón and eventually to Península Pichilingue. On weekend nights, Paseo Obregón is a mile-long traffic jam, while the malecón attracts hordes of teenyboppers.

Most of La Paz has a regular grid pattern that makes orientation easy, although the city center's crooked streets and alleys change their names almost every block. In this area locals occasionally use different street names as well – the official name of block-long Lerdo de Tejada, for instance, is usually ignored in favor of Santos Degollado, the name of its longer extension. Note also that the numbering system along Paseo Obregón is so irregular that it seems completely improvised.

On Avenida Independencia, four blocks from the Muelle Turístico (tourist pier) on the malecón, Plaza Constitución is the traditional heart of the city. Both Plaza Constitución, known officially as Jardín Velasco, and the Muelle Turístico have attractive bandshells. Many tourist activities take place on the Muelle Turístico on weekends.

Information

Tourist Offices The Coordinación Estatal de Turismo, allied with the Secretaría de Turismo del Estado (Secture), maintains an Oficina de Información Turística (☎ (112) 2-59-39) on the waterfront at the corner of Paseo Obregón and 16 de Septiembre. The well-organized, English-speaking staff distribute a variety of leaflets and keep a current list of hotel rates. It's open 8 am to 8 pm weekdays, 9 am to 1 pm Saturday.

The Coordinación Estatal de Turismo has two other offices: the first (☎ (112) 4-01-00, fax (112) 4-07-22, turismo@ lapaz.cromwell.com.mx) is in the Fidepaz

CAPE REGION

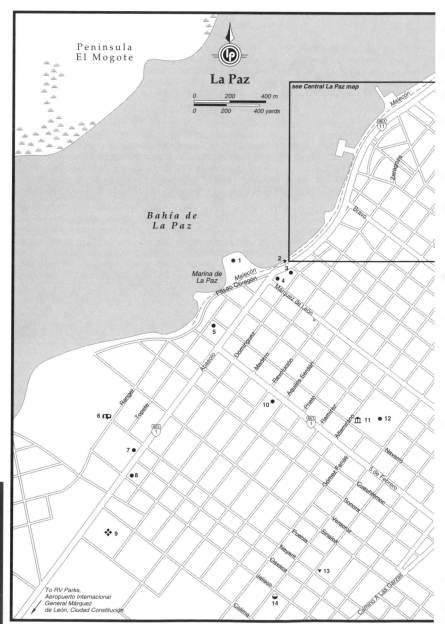

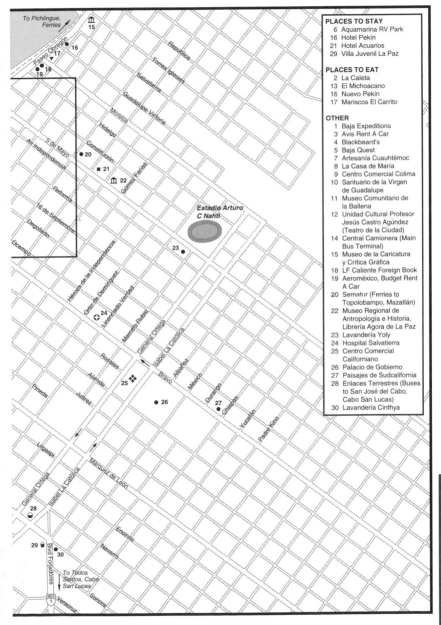

PLACES TO STAY
6 Aquamarina RV Park
16 Hotel Pekín
21 Hotel Acuarios
29 Villa Juvenil La Paz

PLACES TO EAT
2 La Caleta
13 El Michoacano
16 Nuevo Pekín
17 Mariscos El Carrito

OTHER
1 Baja Expeditions
3 Avis Rent A Car
4 Blackbeard's
5 Baja Quest
7 Artesanía Cuauhtémoc
8 La Casa de María
9 Centro Comercial Colima
10 Santuario de la Virgen
   de Guadalupe
11 Museo Comunitario de
   la Ballena
12 Unidad Cultural Profesor
   Jesús Castro Agúndez
   (Teatro de la Ciudad)
14 Central Camionera (Main
   Bus Terminal)
15 Museo de la Caricatura
   y Crítica Gráfica
18 LF Caliente Foreign Book
19 Aeroméxico, Budget Rent
   A Car
20 Sematur (Ferries to
   Topolobampo, Mazatlán)
22 Museo Regional de
   Antropología e Historia,
   Librería Agora de La Paz
23 Lavandería Yoly
24 Hospital Salvatierra
25 Centro Comercial
   Californiano
26 Palacio de Gobierno
27 Paisajes de Sudcalifornia
28 Enlaces Terrestres (Buses
   to San José del Cabo,
   Cabo San Lucas)
30 Lavandería Cinthya

building at Km 5 of the Transpeninsular, southwest of downtown, and is open 8 am to 4 pm weekdays. The other is at Aeropuerto Internacional General Manuel Márquez de León and is open 8 am to 8 pm Monday, Thursday and Friday and 3 pm to 8 pm Tuesday and Wednesday.

Immigration   Servicios   Migratorios (☎ (112) 5-34-93, fax (112) 2-04-29), on the 2nd floor of the Edificio Milhe at Paseo Obregón 2140 between Allende and Juárez, is open 8 am to 8 pm weekdays. Travelers bound for mainland Mexico must have their tourist cards validated before purchasing a ticket; bring a passport or birth certificate. On weekends, immigration officials staff the ferry terminal at Pichilingue and the airport (☎ (112) 2-18-29), but tourist card extensions are available only at the Paseo Obregón office.

Money Most banks and *cambios* (currency exchange houses) are on or around 16 de Septiembre. Banks keep longer hours than formerly, and several also have ATMs.

Bancomer and Banoro are at the intersection of 16 de Septiembre and Esquerro. Banco Santander and Banamex (the latter is probably the most efficient bank in town) are across the street from each other at the junction of Agustín Arreola and Esquerro. Banco Internacional (Bital) is at the corner of 5 de Mayo and Madero.

Shopping centers like the Centro Comercial Californiano, across from the Palacio de Gobierno, and the Centro Comercial Colima, near the corner of Abasolo and Colima, change traveler's checks if the holders make purchases of at least 10% of the face value of the checks. There are also ATMs here.

Post & Communications The post and telegraph office is at the corner of Constitución and Revolución, one block east of Jardín Velasco (Plaza Constitución). The downtown postal code is 23000.

Ladatel phones are now abundant, so it's easy to make long-distance calls with magnetic phone cards, with credit cards or by

reversing charges (remember to avoid the predatory blue phones).

At private phone booths on Paseo Obregón and elsewhere, verify charges before calling, as rates can vary up to 50% between offices. One reasonable place is Jazahel, a small boutique at the corner of 16 de Septiembre and Belisario Domínguez.

Travel Agencies Turismo La Paz (☎ (112) 2-83-00, (112) 2-76-76, fax (112) 5-52-72), Esquerro 1679 near Calle La Paz, is the American Express representative. Turismo Express (☎ /fax (112) 5-63-10) is alongside the tourist office on the Muelle Turístico, while Viajes Coromuel (☎ (112) 2-80-06, fax (112) 5-43-13) is at the corner of Paseo Obregón and Rosales. Viajes Palmira (☎ / fax (112) 2-40-30), on the malecón across from Hotel Los Arcos, also offers all the usual travel services.

Viajes Lybsa (☎ (112) 2-60-01, fax (112) 5-99-77), at the corner of Obregón and Lerdo de Tejada, is a full-service travel agency. Viajes Baja (☎ (112) 2-36-60, (112) 2-41-30) is at Obregón 2110.

Bookstores Librería Contiempo (☎ (112) 2-78-75), Agustín Arreola 25-A near Paseo Obregón, keeps a selection of more or less outdated US newspapers and magazines, but usually carries the most recent issue of the English-language Mexico City *News*.

The Museo Regional de Antropología e Historia (☎ (112) 2-01-62), at the corner of 5 de Mayo and Altamirano, has a good selection of Spanish-language books on Baja California and mainland Mexico; next door, Librería Agora de La Paz (☎ (112) 2-62-04) is even better, offering many of the same items for more reasonable prices.

Laundry Lavandería Yoly is on 5 de Mayo between Licenciado Verdad and Marcelo Rubio, opposite the baseball park. Lavandería Cinthya (☎ (112) 2-96-88) is at the corner of 5 de Febrero and Blvd Forjadores, the highway to Cabo San Lucas.

Medical Services La Paz's Hospital Salvatierra (☎ (112) 2-14-96, (112) 2-15-96)

A: Misión San Ignacio
B: Cuesta El Mechudo, north of La Paz

C: Cueva de las Flechas, Sierra de San Francisco
D: Misión San Ignacio
E: Misión San Francisco Javier, west of Loreto

A: ROSS BARNET

B: WAYNE BERNHARDSON

C: WAYNE BERNHARDSON

D: WAYNE BERNHARDSON

A: Land's End, Cabo San Lucas
B: Kayakers, Bahía Los Frailes

C: Playa del Amor, Cabo San Lucas
D: Fishermen, Western Cape

is on Bravo between Licenciado Verdad and Ortiz de Domínguez. For the Cruz Roja (Red Cross), dial ☎ (112) 2-11-11 or (112) 2-12-22.

Dangers & Annoyances La Paz's uneven sidewalks, many with steps of varying sizes, are virtual minefields for tipsy pedestrians.

Museo Regional de Antropología e Historia

This first-rate anthropological and historical museum, run by the Instituto Nacional de Historia y Antropología (INAH), chronicles the peninsula's past from prehistory to the Revolution of 1910 and its aftermath. Exhibits cover pre-Columbian rock art, native peoples, the mission era, various mining booms, the arrival of independence, the US-Mexican War and William Walker's invasion (note the replica of Walker's flag and the bonds used to finance his adventures). A small gallery contains rotating exhibits by local artists and photographers or seasonal displays on topics like November's Day of the Dead, Mexico's most famous informal holiday. The museum also contains a bookstore with a good selection on both Baja California and Mexico in general.

Set behind an attractive cactus garden at the corner of 5 de Mayo and Altamirano, the museum (☎ (112) 2-01-62) is open 9 am to 6 pm weekdays, 9 am to 1 pm Saturday. Admission is free.

Catedral de Nuestra Señora de La Paz

Nothing remains of La Paz's first cathedral, built in 1720 under the direction of Jesuit missionaries Jaime Bravo and Juan de Ugarte near the site of present-day Jardín Velasco. The present structure dates from 1861, but mimics the style of California mission architecture.

Biblioteca de la Historia de las Californias

La Paz's former Casa de Gobierno (Government House), now a history library, contains a small but valuable collection of books and newspapers in both Spanish and English about the Californias. It also displays thematically appropriate artwork ranging from ghastly (a kitschy representation of Calafia, the mythical Amazon whose name presumably survives in the word 'California') to mediocre (privateer Thomas Cavendish's crew boarding the Manila galleon *Santa Ana)* to respectable (a replica mural of Desierto Central rock art). The library (☎ (112) 5-37-67), on the northwestern side of Jardín Velasco, is open 9 am to 8 pm weekdays.

Teatro de la Ciudad

At the entrance to La Paz's city theater, the **Rotonda de los Hombres Ilustres** (Rotunda of Distinguished Men) is a sculptural tribute to figures who fought against filibuster William Walker's invasion of La Paz in 1853 and the French mainland intervention of 1861. The theater proper offers performances by musical and theatrical groups such as Guadalajara's Ballet Folklórico, as well as occasional film series.

A sprawling concrete edifice, the theater (☎ (112) 5-00-04) is the most conspicuous element of the **Unidad Cultural Profesor Jesús Castro Agúndez** (☎ (112) 5-19-17), a cultural center that takes up most of the area bounded by Altamirano, Navarro, Héroes de la Independencia and Legaspi. Other units within the center include the **Galería Maestro José Carlos Olachea**, exhibiting works by contemporary Mexican artists; the **Archivo Histórico Pablo L Martínez**, a research archive named in honor of a famous Baja historian; and the **Biblioteca Central Filemón C Piñeda**, a general library.

A new feature on the periphery of the grounds at Navarro and Altamirano is the **Museo Comunitario de la Ballena** (Community Whale Museum), which seems to ignore totally its advertised hours of 9 am to 2 pm daily except Monday. If it's open, the admission charge is nominal.

Museo de la Caricatura y Crítica Gráfica

Founded by local caricaturist Jorge Loy, this unusual museum uses illustrations

CAPE REGION

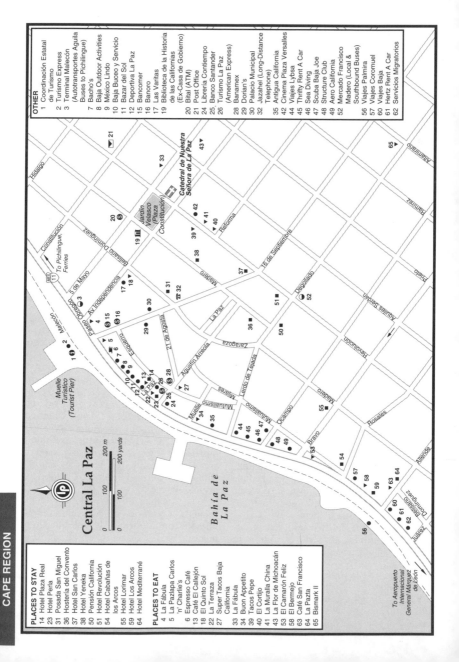

Central La Paz

PLACES TO STAY
14 Hotel Plaza Real
23 Hotel Perla
31 Posada San Miguel
36 Hostería del Convento
37 Hotel San Carlos
38 Hotel Yeneka
50 Pensión California
51 Hotel Revolución
54 Hotel Cabañas de
   los Arcos
55 Hotel Lorimar
59 Hotel Los Arcos
64 Hotel Mediterrané

PLACES TO EAT
4 La Fábula
5 La Pazlapa Carlos
   'n Charlie's
6 Espresso Café
13 Café El Callejón
18 El Quinto Sol
22 La Terraza
27 Super Tacos Baja
   California
33 La Fábula
34 Buon Appetito
39 Tacos Pepe
40 El Cortijo
41 La Muralla China
43 La Flor de Michoacán
53 El Camarón Feliz
58 El Bermejo
63 Café San Francisco
64 La Pazta
65 Bismark II

OTHER
1 Coordinación Estatal
   de Turismo
2 Turismo Express
3 Terminal Malecón
   (Autotransportes Aguila
   Buses to Pichilingue)
7 Bacho's
8 Baja Outdoor Activities
9 México Lindo
10 Baja Buceo y Servicio
11 Bazar del Sol
12 Deportiva La Paz
15 Bancomer
16 Banoro
17 Las Varitas
19 Biblioteca de la Historia
   de las Californias
   (Ex-Casa de Gobierno)
20 Bital (ATM)
21 Post Office
24 Librería Contiempo
25 Banco Santander
26 Turismo La Paz
   (American Express)
28 Banamex
29 Dorian's
30 Palacio Municipal
32 Jazahel (Long-Distance
   Telephone)
35 Antigua California
42 Cinema Plaza Versalles
44 Viajes Lybsa
45 Thrifty Rent A Car
46 Sea Diving
47 Scuba Baja Joe
48 Structure Club
49 Aero California
52 Mercado Francisco
   Madero (Local &
   Southbound Buses)
56 Viajes Palmira
57 Viajes Coromuel
60 Viajes Baja
61 Hertz Rent A Car
62 Servicios Migratorios

from the 19th-century magazine *Orquesta*, along with information on its writers and artists, to place modern Mexican political satire and humor in historical context. Loy's own map-mural of Baja California is a minor masterpiece, depicting Cabo San Lucas with a 'For Sale' sign and a waiter serving time-shares.

One of few museums of its kind in the world and only the second in Mexico, the museum (☎/fax (112) 2-96-61) justifies a stop in La Paz. At Paseo Obregón 755 between Salvatierra and Torres Iglesias, it's open 10 am to 8 pm daily except Monday; admission costs US$0.75 for adults, US$0.40 for children. A cafe/restaurant is in the works.

Santuario de la Virgen de Guadalupe

Paying homage to Mexico's greatest religious icon, the Santuario is La Paz's biggest religious monument, built partly in a mission style with various modernistic touches. It's on 5 de Febrero between Revolución and Aquiles Serdán.

Boat Trips

Hotel Marina (☎ (112) 1-62-54), at Km 2.5 on the highway to Pichilingue, runs sunset booze cruises for US$25 per person, including up to three drinks. Children pay half-price.

Diving & Snorkeling

The main diving and snorkeling destinations in Bahía de La Paz (beware contaminated water) and the Gulf are **Isla de las Focas**, an island just north of Península Pichilingue's Punta Coyote that is renowned for its beaches and sea lion colony; **Los Islotes**, a group of islets just north of Isla Partida with various shipwrecks, underwater caves and reefs and sea lion colonies; and **Isla Cerralvo**, east of Península Pichilingue. Snorkeling trips to Isla de las Focas cost about US$45, while two-tank scuba trips to Los Islotes run around US$85. Prices usually include food and drinks, but try to clarify what's included before booking a trip.

Probably La Paz's best-established dive shop is Baja Buceo y Servicio (☎ (112) 2-18-26, fax (112) 2-86-44), Paseo Obregón 1663, Local 2. Baja Expeditions (☎ (112) 5-38-28, fax (112) 5-38-29), at the Marina de La Paz, gets enthusiastic recommendations but does not rent equipment; it's possible to arrange trips through its San Diego office (for contact information for that office, see the Organized Tours entry in the Outdoor Activities chapter).

Deportiva La Paz (☎ (112) 2-73-33), on Paseo Obregón at the corner of the Calle La Paz *peatonal* (pedestrian walk), arranges dive trips and rents equipment, as does Sea Diving (☎ (112) 3-52-53), at the corner of Paseo Obregón and Ocampo. Scuba Baja Joe (☎ (112) 2-40-06, fax (112) 2-40-00) is around the corner on Ocampo; its mailing address is Apdo Postal 361, La Paz, Baja California Sur 23000, México. Its rates are US$77 per day (9 am to 4 pm) for trips to sites in the immediate La Paz area, US$87 for trips to El Bajo (a seamount near Isla Partida) and Isla Cerralvo.

Baja Quest (☎ (112) 3-53-20, fax (112) 3-53-21), Navarro 55 between Abasolo and Topete, is a newcomer that specializes in diving but also offers sea kayaking and whale-watching. Its snorkeling trips cost US$45 per person, while two-tank dives cost US$85 and three-tank dives US$95. The Cortez Club (☎ (112) 1-61-20, fax (112) 1-61-23, atomba@cortezclub.com; (800) 999-2242 in the USA and Canada), at La Concha Beach Resort (see Places to Stay in this entry), specializes in diving but also rents kayaks, windsurfing equipment, Hobie cats and the like. The US postal address is 7860 Mission Centre Court, No 202, San Diego, CA 92108-1331.

Fishing

Game-fish species available all year in the vicinity of La Paz include bonito, corvina, crevalle, grouper, needlefish, pargo, rock bass, sierra and skipjack. Seasonal species include black and blue marlin (both July to October), dorado (April to December), roosterfish (November to May), sailfish (June to October), snook (December to June, but rare), striped marlin (May to

Sailfish

October), yellowfin tuna (July to November, sporadically) and yellowtail (December to April).

The Hotel Los Arcos lobby (see Places to Stay, below) contains an information desk for the Dorado Vélez Fleet (☎ (112) 2-00-38, (112) 2-27-44, ext 608, fax (112) 5-53-13), which offers trips on boats ranging from 25 to 32 feet (7.5 to 9.5 meters) and provides all equipment, licenses and transportation. Its mailing address is Apdo Postal 402, La Paz, Baja California Sur, México. Most of La Paz's other major hotels and travel agencies can also arrange trips.

Jonathan Roldan's Sportfishing Services at the Cortez Club (see Diving & Snorkeling, above) offers four-night packages, including two days of *panga* (skiff) fishing, at La Concha Beach Resort for US$285 per person, double occupancy.

Sea Kayaking
Baja Outdoor Activities (☎ (112) 5-56-36, fax (112) 5-36-25, boa@cibnor.mx), an Anglo-Mexican company on Paseo Obregón a few doors west of La Pazlapa Carlos 'n' Charlie's, offers kayak trips ranging from half a day (US$30) to a full day (US$80) on and around Isla Espíritu Santo, as well as overnight excursions. Rental kayaks cost US$25 to US$45 per day, with weekly rentals at a slight discount. Its mailing address is Apdo Postal 792, La Paz, Baja California Sur 23000, México.

Baja Quest and the Cortez Club (see Diving & Snorkeling, above) also rent kayaks.

Whale-Watching
The Asociación Nacional de Guías de Ecoturismo y Turismo de Aventura (☎ (112) 5-22-77, fax (112) 5-85-99), at Paseo Obregón and 16 de Septiembre, runs daily tours to Puerto San Carlos on Bahía Magdalena for US$90 per person, including transportation, breakfast, lunch and three hours on the water.

Language Courses
Baja Expeditions (☎ (112) 5-38-28, fax (112) 5-38-29), at the Marina de La Paz, arranges introductory, intermediate and advanced Spanish lessons.

Special Events
February/March
Variable dates – *Carnaval*. La Paz's pre-Lenten celebrations are probably the peninsula's best and among the country's best.

May
3rd – *Fundación de la Ciudad*. *Paceños* take the first five days of the month to celebrate the founding of La Paz in 1535. Events include a dramatization of Hernán Cortés' landing, sports events like a half-marathon and a commercial exhibition.

June
1st – *Día de la Marina* (Navy Day)

November
Late November – *Festival de las Artes* (Arts Festival)

Places to Stay – budget
Camping At Km 4 on the Transpeninsular, west of downtown in a partly shaded area distant from the beach, well-organized *El Cardón Trailer Park* (☎ (112) 4-00-78, fax (112) 4-02-61) has 90 spaces, each with full hookups, electric light and a small *palapa* (palm-leaf shelter). Facilities include a laundry room, a swimming pool, hot showers, clean toilets, a small paperback book exchange and a travel agency. Tent spaces cost US$6, while vehicle spaces cost from US$8 upward. The postal address is Apdo Postal 104, La Paz, Baja California Sur, México.

Just west of El Cardón, shady, secure and

well-kept *RV Park Casa Blanca* (☎ (112) 4-00-09, fax (112) 5-11-42) has a pool, a restaurant and sites with full hookups from US$15 per night.

La Paz Trailer Park (☎ (112) 4-87-87, fax (112) 2-99-38) is a deluxe facility at Brecha California 120, about 1 mile (1.6 km) south of downtown. Facilities include very clean bathrooms and showers, a fine restaurant, a jacuzzi, a swimming pool and a book exchange. Rates are about US$14 for a vehicle site, half that for a tent site.

The bayside fortress of *Aquamarina RV Park* (☎ (112) 2-37-61, fax (112) 5-62-28), at the foot of Nayarit, is highly regarded, but its heavy-duty security gives it an intimidating feeling. Sites cost about US$14.

Hostels, Pensions & Hotels Affiliated with Hostelling International, the *Villa Juvenil La Paz* (☎ (112) 2-46-15) is about 20 blocks southwest of downtown, near the junction of 5 de Febrero, Camino A Las Garzas and Blvd Forjadores (the southbound Transpeninsular). At US$4 per night, a bunk in one of the single-sex, dorm-style rooms is a good value; very cheap meals are also available. The hostel is open 6 am to 11 pm. From downtown, catch any 'Universidad' bus from Mercado Francisco Madero, the city market at the corner of Degollado and Revolución.

Longtime budget favorite *Pensión California* (☎ (112) 2-28-96), Degollado 209, features a patio surrounded by tropical foliage; its walls are lined with quirky artwork. For US$7/11 single/double, each basic room has a ceiling fan, fluorescent light, adjustable blinds and a shower. Under the same management, with identical prices, basic *Hostería del Convento* (☎ (112) 2-35-08), Madero 85, is dark and dilapidated, with tidy but less than spotless toilets.

Hotel San Carlos (☎ (112) 2-04-44), at the noisy corner of Revolución and 16 de Septiembre, charges US$8 single or double. Built around a central patio, the 14-room *Posada San Miguel* (☎ (112) 2-18-02), Belisario Domínguez 1510, is a pleasant, pseudocolonial place whose dark but clean rooms each have a private bath, but the hot water can be erratic. Rates are US$8/11.

Motel-style *Hotel Yeneka* (☎ (112) 5-46-88, fax (112) 2-41-06), Madero 1520, has 20 rooms and a quasicafe with eclectic automotive decor like hub caps and countless bumpers with mud-splattered license plates. Clean singles/doubles with firm beds (mattresses set over concrete) cost US$13/18.

Hotel Revolución (formerly the María Cristina I, ☎ /fax (112) 5-80-22), Revolución 85 near Degollado, has singles/doubles with air-con and pool for US$16. Rooms at *Hotel Pekín* (☎ (112) 5-53-35), Paseo Obregón 875 near Guadalupe Victoria, cost US$17/20. For an excellent value, try *Hotel Lorimar* (☎ (112) 5-38-22, fax (112) 5-63-87), Bravo 110 near Madero, with an attractive courtyard. Bright rooms with air-con and tiled shower with hot water cost US$19/23; there is also good laundry service.

Places to Stay – middle
Hotel Plaza Real (☎ (112) 2-93-33, fax (112) 2-44-24), at the corner of Calle La Paz and Esquerro, charges US$24 double. Recommended *Hotel Acuarios* (☎ (112) 2-92-66, fax (112) 5-57-13), Ramírez 1665 near 5 de Mayo, has a restaurant and a swimming pool. Rates are US$25/27 for rooms with air-con, full carpeting, TV and telephone.

Just out of town on the road to Pichilingue, *Club El Moro* (☎ (112) 2-40-84, fax (112) 5-28-28) charges US$41 double. The mailing address is Apdo Postal 357, La Paz, Baja California Sur, México. The more central *Hotel Mediterrané* (☎ (112) 5-11-95), Allende 36-B, charges US$44.

Historic *Hotel Perla* (☎ (112) 2-07-77, fax (112) 5-53-63), on the malecón at Paseo Obregón 1570, has a swimming pool, a restaurant, a bar and a nightclub. Some rooms offer bay views, while others overlook the pool; all have air-con, TV and private bath. Rates run around US$50 double.

Places to Stay – top end

Rates at bayside *Hotel Marina* (☎ (112) 1-62-54, fax (112) 1-61-77), at Km 2.5 on the Pichilingue road, start at US$51 double. Suites cost more than twice as much.

On Avenida Reforma, the Spanish-style *Hotel La Posada de Engelbert* (☎ (112) 2-40-11, fax (112) 2-06-63), owned by crooner Engelbert Humperdinck, has 25 bungalow-type rooms with brick fireplace; facilities include a swimming pool, tennis courts, a restaurant and a bar. Rates are US$55/75.

Under new management, the *Araiza Inn Palmira* (☎ (112) 1-62-00, fax (112) 1-62-27), about 1½ miles (2.5 km) north of downtown on the Pichilingue road, is a modern hotel appealing to vacationing families and small conventions, with a swimming pool, tennis courts, a restaurant and a nightclub. Its rates range from about US$60 to US$80.

Set among lush tropical gardens on Mutualismo near Paseo Obregón, highly regarded *Hotel Cabañas de los Arcos* (☎ (112) 2-27-44, fax (112) 5-43-13) offers *cabaña*-style rooms with fireplace, tiled floor, thatched roof, TV, air-conditioning and minibar. Rates are about US$83, plus tax, single or double. Its US representative is Baja Hotels (☎ (714) 450-9000, (800) 347-2252, fax (714) 450-9010), 6 Jenner, Suite 120, Irvine, CA 92618.

Its larger but rather less appealing sister, *Hotel Los Arcos* (see contact information above), Paseo Obregón 498 near Rosales, has two swimming pools, a sauna, a restaurant and a coffee shop. All rooms have air-con, telephone, color TV and showers; ask for a bay view. Its rates are identical to those of its sister hotel.

At Km 5 on the road to Pichilingue, the 107-room *La Concha Beach Resort* (☎ (112) 1-61-20/1; (800) 999-2252, fax (619) 294-7366 in the USA) is a beachfront hotel with palm trees, a swimming pool (with poolside bar), a fine Mexican restaurant and a water-sports center (though the water is very shallow here). It charges around US$95 for comfortable, air-conditioned rooms, all with balconies overlooking the bay.

Places to Eat

Super Tacos Baja California, a stall at the corner of Agustín Arreola and Mutualismo, thrives on both local and tourist trade. It's a bit dearer than most taco stands, but the quality of its fish, shrimp, clam and scallop tacos, plus outstanding condiments, more than justifies the extra peso – what other *taquería* offers sweet-and-sour shrimp tacos? It's open 8 am to 6 pm only.

Mariscos El Carrito, at the corner of Paseo Obregón and Morelos, is a palm-shaded seafood stand with tables for taco lovers weary of standing while eating. *Tacos Pepe*, on Revolución between Reforma and Avenida Independencia, has outstanding carnitas.

El Quinto Sol (☎ (112) 2-16-92) is a popular vegetarian landmark and health-food market at the corner of Avenida Independencia and Belisario Domínguez. Besides its bean specialties, it offers large breakfast servings of yogurt (plain, with fruit or with granola or muesli). Licuados, fresh-baked breads and pastries are other specialties. Another good, reasonably priced breakfast choice is *Café San Francisco* (☎ (112) 2-74-79), just south of the malecón at Allende 36-A.

One of downtown's best values, *Café El Callejón*, on the Calle La Paz peatonal, has cheap and very good antojitos; try the chicken mole. *El Cortijo* (☎ (112) 2-25-32), Revolución 1460, is a popular Mexican place that's been around since 1960. Though *El Michoacano* is a little out of the way at the corner of Nayarit and Ortiz de Domínguez, its carnitas are well worth a trip for lunch.

Bismark II (☎ (112) 2-48-54), at the corner of Degollado and Altamirano, is popular with locals for generous helpings of excellent, reasonably priced seafood. *El Camarón Feliz* (☎ (112) 2-90-11), an outdoor restaurant on Paseo Obregón near Mutualismo, specializes in shrimp. *La Caleta* (☎ (112) 3-02-87), right on the malecón at the corner of Pineda, is very popular for its reasonably priced meals and drinks; live music tending toward jazz and ballads is another feature.

For pizza, try *La Fábula* (☎ (112) 2-41-53), across the malecón from the tourist office; there's a branch (☎ (112) 2-18-95) on 5 de Mayo between Revolución and Aquiles Serdán. Both locales are open 1 to 11 pm daily. *La Pazta* (☎ (112) 5-11-95), at Allende 36-B just south of the malecón, has good Italian specials at reasonable prices, but the drinks are small, weak and relatively expensive. Also serving Italian food, upscale *El Bermejo*, at the corner of Paseo Obregón and Rosales, is part of Hotel Los Arcos. *Buon Appetito* (☎ (112) 5-15-00), near the corner of Obregón and Calle Muelle, is an appealing, upscale Italian restaurant.

Serving a predominantly Mexican crowd, *La Pazlapa Carlos 'n' Charlie's* (☎ (112) 2-92-90), on Paseo Obregón near 16 de Septiembre, is part of the extensive chain more noted for drinking than for dining. Down the block at the corner of Paseo Obregón and Calle La Paz, *La Terraza* has good food in attractive, open seating marred by tacky mariachi music.

Nuevo Pekín (☎ (112) 5-09-95), Paseo Obregón 875 near Guadalupe Victoria, is a so-so Chinese restaurant very popular with locals. *La Muralla China* (☎ (112) 2-06-06), Revolución 1440, is comparable. *Restaurant/Bar El Moro* (☎ (112) 2-70-10), near the Araiza Inn Palmira on the Pichilingue road, features Sonoran beef, salad, pasta and a few Cantonese dishes.

Two blocks southeast of Jardín Velasco, on 5 de Mayo between Prieto and Aquiles Serdán, *La Flor de Michoacán* sells delicious aguas, paletas, licuados, ice cream and sandwiches. Frequented more by Mexicans than gringos, the *Espresso Café* (☎ (112) 3-43-73), Paseo Obregón 10 near 16 de Septiembre, is a popular coffee bar that also offers drinks and light meals.

Entertainment
Most of La Paz's nightlife is concentrated on and around Paseo Obregón, but it never reaches the chaos of Cabo San Lucas.

Cinemas *Cinema Plaza Versalles* (☎ (112) 2-95-55), on Revolución near the corner of Avenida Independencia, offers first-run international films on four screens. Admission costs about US$2.

Nightclubs Longtime favorite *Las Varitas* (☎ (112) 5-20-25), Avenida Independencia 111 near Belisario Domínguez, regularly offers live music and dancing; there's a US$2 cover charge. The current hot nightspot is the *Structure Club*, at Paseo Obregón and Ocampo.

Bars *Bacho's* (☎ (112) 3-02-00), Paseo Obregón 1670 between Calle La Paz and 16 de Septiembre, is a popular bar with cheap (but small) drinks and passable food. *Blackbeard's*, at the corner of Paseo Obregón and Márquez de León, is a major gringo hangout for drinks and dancing, offering mostly Santana-style rock 'n' roll. Food is also available.

Betting There is an *LF Caliente Foreign Book* (☎ (112) 5-76-00) venue at the corner of Paseo Obregón and Morelos.

Things to Buy
Peter Gerhard, in his classic *Lower California Guidebook* of the 1960s, tells of a tourist who bought a black pearl in La Paz only to learn that it was an exquisitely burnished ball bearing! Few visitors are so credulous, but local stores have plenty of junk alongside the good stuff.

México Lindo (☎ (112) 2-18-90), Paseo Obregón 10 near the tourist office, has good mainland Mexican items in addition to postcards and T-shirts. Bazar del Sol (☎ (112) 2-36-26), Paseo Obregón 1165 near Calle La Paz, is loaded with kitsch. Antigua California, on Paseo Obregón between Lerdo de Tejada and Muelle, features a wide selection of crafts from throughout the country.

A bit west of downtown, La Casa de María (☎ (112) 2-56-06), on Abasolo between Jalisco and Oaxaca, is a good choice for handicrafts and especially furniture. Artesanía Cuauhtémoc (☎ (112) 2-45-75), across the street at Abasolo 3315, is a weavers' cooperative. Paisajes de Sudcalifornia (☎ (112) 3-37-00), Bravo 1890, specializes in southern Baja art and crafts.

Dorian's, on 16 de Septiembre between Esquerro and 21 de Agosto, is one of the city's major department stores.

On weekends during the Christmas season, countless baubles change hands at the Mercado Navideño, which turns downtown Madero and Avenida Independencia, at right angles to each other, into pedestrian malls.

Getting There & Away

Air Aeropuerto Internacional General Manuel Márquez de León (☎ (112) 2-14-86/7) is just 6½ miles (10 km) southwest of downtown, at the end of a short lateral off the Transpeninsular.

Aeroméxico (☎ (112) 2-00-91), at Paseo Obregón between Hidalgo and Morelos, flies daily between La Paz and Los Angeles, Tucson, Tijuana, Culiacán, Durango, Guadalajara, Guaymas, Mazatlán and Mexico City. Its subsidiary Aerolitoral, at the same address, flies daily to and from Loreto.

Aero California (☎ (112) 5-10-23; (800) 258-3311 in the USA) has offices at the airport and at Paseo Obregón 550 near the corner of Bravo. Hours are 8 am to 6 pm daily. It operates two daily nonstop flights between La Paz and Los Angeles, daily flights to Tucson via Hermosillo and one daily nonstop to Tijuana. It also offers many flights to mainland Mexican destinations, including Los Mochis (for the Barranca del Cobre train), Mazatlán and Mexico City. Most flights have onward national and international connections.

Bus Autotransportes de Baja California (ABC, ☎ (112) 2-30-63), Autotransportes Aguila (☎ (112) 2-42-70), Autotransportes de La Paz (☎ (112) 2-21-57) and Enlaces Terrestres (☎ (112) 3-53-38) operate intercity buses. ABC and Aguila use the Central Camionera (main bus terminal) at the corner of Jalisco and Héroes de la Independencia, while Enlaces Terrestres has its own terminal at the corner of Isabel La Católica and 5 de Febrero.

Northbound ABC/Aguila buses go to:

Ciudad Constitución – three hours, US$5.50; at least five times daily between 7 am and 9:30 pm
Puerto San Carlos – four hours, US$6.50; at 8 am and 2:30 pm daily
Puerto López Mateos – 4½ hours, US$7.50; at 9:30 am and 4:30 pm daily
Loreto – 5½ hours, US$10; at least five times daily between 9 am and 10 pm
La Purísima-San Isidro – six hours, US$10; at 7 am and 3:30 pm daily
Mulegé – eight hours, US$13; at least three times daily between 9 am and 10 pm
Santa Rosalía – nine hours, US$16; at least twice daily, usually morning and afternoon
San Ignacio – 10 hours, US$20; at least four times daily between 10 am and 10 pm
Guerrero Negro – 12 hours, US$25; at least four times daily between 10 am and 10 pm
San Quintín – 18 hours, US$35; at least three times daily between 10 am and 10 pm
Ensenada – 22 hours, US$42; at least three times daily between 10 am and 10 pm
Tijuana – 22 to 24 hours, US$47; at least three times daily between 10 am and 10 pm
Mexicali – 28 hours, US$54; at 4 pm daily

Southbound ABC/Aguila buses depart several times daily for El Triunfo (30 minutes, US$1.50), San Antonio (40 minutes, US$2), Buena Vista (1½ hours, US$4), Miraflores (2½ hours, US$5.50) and San José del Cabo via the Transpeninsular (four hours, US$8).

Aguila buses take the Southern Cape Highway (México 19) from La Paz to Cabo San Lucas (US$6) at least five times daily between 7 am and 7 pm, and to Todos Santos (US$3) at least five times daily between 7 am and 7 pm.

Autotransportes de La Paz buses leave from the front of Mercado Francisco Madero, at the corner of Revolución and Degollado, for Todos Santos (US$3), Cabo San Lucas (US$6) and San José del Cabo (US$7) five times daily between 8:45 am and 5:45 pm. Enlaces Terrestres buses serve Cabo San Lucas, San José del Cabo and intermediate points.

Ferry The major terminal for Sematur ferries to the mainland towns of Topolobampo and Mazatlán is in Pichilingue, about 14 miles (22 km) north of central La Paz. Sematur (☎ (112) 5-38-33, (112) 5-46-66) maintains La Paz offices at the corner of Prieto and 5 de Mayo.

Before they will ship your vehicle, ferry officials require you to show a vehicle permit. To obtain one, you must:

- show an ownership certificate (pink slip) or a valid vehicle-registration certificate and tourist card (Form FMT)
- make a deposit of US$11 on Visa or MasterCard at the Banco del Ejército (Banjército) in Pichilingue as a bond ensuring the vehicle's eventual return to the USA

You can do this 8 am to 3 pm weekdays, 9 am to 1 pm weekends. For more information on vehicle permits, see the Getting Around chapter.

To leave your vehicle in La Paz while returning to the USA or crossing to mainland Mexico, you theoretically will need authorization from Mexican Customs, which may require that you leave the vehicle in a *recinto fiscal* (official impound lot).

Ferry tickets must be confirmed by 2 pm on the day before departure. At 3 pm, seats that have not been confirmed are sold on a first-come, first-served basis, which sometimes results in shoving matches to see who gets to the head of the line.

Weather permitting (high winds often delay winter sailings), the Topolobampo ferry (eight hours) leaves at 11 am daily, but the Tuesday sailing does not permit women or children under age 18 because it carries *carga negra* (hazardous materials). The return ferry from Topolobampo departs at 10 pm daily.

The ferry to Mazatlán (18 hours) departs at 3 pm daily except Saturday, arriving at 9 am the following morning. The return ferry leaves Topolobampo at 3 pm, arriving at 9 am in La Paz.

Approximate one-way fares from La Paz are as follows:

Class	To Topolobampo	To Mazatlán
Salón	US$14	US$21
Turista	US$27	US$41
Cabina	US$41	US$61
Especial	US$54	US$81

Vehicle rates are as follows:

Length	To Topolobampo	To Mazatlán
Up to 5 meters*	US$116	US$190
5.01 to 6.5 meters	US$151	US$247
With trailer up to 9 meters	US$209	US$342
9.01 to 17 meters	US$393	US$646
Bus/motor home	US$198	US$322
Motorcycle	US$15	US$25

*1 meter=3 feet 3 inches

Private Yacht Between November and March, according to one Lonely Planet correspondent, La Paz is a good place to catch a lift on a yacht to mainland Mexico:

The Marina de La Paz, which houses the Dock restaurant, and the Club Cruceros are the best places to hang out. There is a radio at Club Cruceros, and plenty of people to show you how to use it. Also ask Mort, the owner of the Dock – he is always glad to help. The most frequent passage is La Paz to Puerto Vallarta with stops at Bahía de los Muertos, Los Frailes (great coral snorkeling), then Isla Isabél and Puerto Vallarta. Allow about one week, with two to three nights at sea.

Getting Around
To/From the Airport The government-regulated Transporte Terrestre (☎ (112) 5-32-74, (112) 5-62-29) minivan service charges US$7 per person to or from the airport, while private taxis cost about US$13 but may be shared.

To/From the Ferry Terminal Autotransportes Aguila buses leave downtown La Paz for Península Pichilingue and the ferry terminal from the Terminal Malecón (☎ (112) 2-78-98) at the corner of Paseo

Obregón and Avenida Independencia hourly between 7 am and 6 pm. The fare is about US$1.

Bus Most local buses leave from the front of the Mercado Francisco Madero at the corner of Degollado and Revolución.

Car Rental Rates start around US$45 per day, including 300 km of travel; taxes and insurance are extra. The least expensive rental agency is probably Félix (☎ (112) 1-62-54, ext 112, fax (112) 1-63-69) at the Hotel Marina, at Km 2.5 on the Pichilingue road.

International rental agencies include:

Avis
    Paseo Obregón 820 near Márquez de León
    (☎ (112) 2-26-51, (112) 2-18-13 at the
    airport)
Budget
    Paseo Obregón 582 between Morelos and
    Hidalgo (☎ (112) 2-76-55,
    fax (112) 3-36-22)
Hertz
    Paseo Obregón between Juárez and Allende
    (☎ (112) 2-53-00, (112) 4-10-11 at the air-
    port, fax (112) 2-09-19)
Thrifty
    Paseo Obregón at the corner of Lerdo de
    Tejada (☎ (112) 5-96-96, (112) 2-09-65 at
    the airport)
    La Concha Beach Resort, Km 5 on the
    Pichilingue road (☎ (112) 2-65-44)
    Hotel Los Arcos, Paseo Obregón 498
    (☎ (112) 2-27-44)

AROUND LA PAZ
Beaches
There are several small but pleasant beaches north and west of La Paz. To the west are the bayside **Playa El Comitán** and **Playa Las Hamacas**, but no public transportation serves them. El Comitán has deteriorated in recent years and swimming is no longer advisable there.

On Península Pichilingue to the north, the beaches nearest to La Paz are **Playa Palmira**, **Playa Coromuel** and **Playa Caimancito**. Playa Palmira has the *Araiza Inn Palmira*, a marina and a couple

condominium complexes with restaurant and bar, while the latter two have restaurants and bars, toilets and shady palapas. Playa Coromuel also has a big Plexiglas water slide, and its seafood restaurant is good. **Playa Tesoro**, the next beach north, also has a restaurant and shade.

Camping is possible at **Playa Pichilingue**, 110 yards (100 meters) north of the ferry terminal; it has a restaurant and bar, toilets and shade. The road north of Pichilingue is paved to the exceptional beaches of **Playa Balandra** (whose sheltered location is not good for camping because of skeeters in its mangroves) and **Playa Tecolote** (where, across the Canal de San Lorenzo, Isla Espíritu Santo looks like a chunk of southern Utah's canyon country floating on the sea). **Playa Coyote**, on the Gulf side of the peninsula, is more isolated.

Surprisingly uncrowded even in ideal winter weather, Tecolote's wide, sandy beach lacks potable water and other amenities. It does have the nearby steak-and-seafood *Restaurant El Tecolote*, where the fish is excellent but the drinks are watery. Club de Playa El Tecolote (☎ /fax (112) 2-88-85), on the beach and in La Paz on Belisario Domínguez between Avenida Independencia and 5 de Mayo, offers tours from La Paz, arranges kayak trips to Espíritu Santo and rents water-sports equipment. Unfortunately, one of its specialties is deafening, obnoxious Jet Skis.

Local expatriates warn that stealthy and skillful thieves break into campers' cars at Tecolote and other isolated beaches – even while the campers are sleeping.

San Evaristo
West of La Paz, just beyond the village of El Centenario, a paved but potholed spur off the Transpeninsular leads north along the western shore of Bahía de La Paz to **San Juan de la Costa**, a phosphate-mining port with a passable restaurant and a detachment of Mexican marines. The road continues to its northern terminus at San Evaristo, a small fish camp opposite Isla San José on a sparkling inlet of the Gulf of California.

North of San Juan, the graded coastal road skirts the eastern scarp of the Sierra de la Giganta, a multicolored mountain range the layered sediments of which resemble nothing so much as a cutaway of Arizona's Grand Canyon. Most impressive in the morning sun, which accentuates the mountains' vivid colors, the road is badly washboarded in spots but passable even for low-clearance vehicles until a difficult climb at Punta El Mechudo, around Km 54.

The **Cuesta El Mechudo** consists of four crests. The first and last are fairly easy, but the second and third are abrupt climbs on narrow roadways with many loose rocks – meeting another vehicle en route could be disastrous. A 4WD vehicle is preferable but not essential; high clearance and close attention to the roadway are imperative. According to residents at San Evaristo, a Volkswagen Beetle once made the trip, but no one can confirm that it returned successfully to La Paz. One fisherman claims to drive the route at night so he needn't look down.

In April and May, San Evaristo swarms with boaters and campers who enjoy bountiful fishing for snapper and cochinito. Most of the beaches along the San Juan-San Evaristo route are rocky or gravelly, but determined campers will find a few pleasant, sandy and isolated spots.

Just south of San Evaristo, an occasionally graded dirt road leads to the date-palm oasis of El Bosque and to Rancho Soledad, where a dangerously exciting 4WD road (with awesome panoramas of the Sierra de la Giganta's volcanic plateau) continues north to Rancho Las Animas, the ruins of Misión La Pasión and well-preserved Misión San Luis Gonzaga. Two-wheel-drive vehicles with good clearance can probably make it to El Bosque and Rancho Soledad, where a presumably more passable road leads southwest to intersect the Transpeninsular at Las Pocitas, at Km 110. The San Evaristo-Soledad road is easier west-to-east (downhill) than east-to-west (uphill).

La Ventana & Ensenada de los Muertos

Southeast of La Paz, just before the village of San Juan de los Planes, a paved spur off highway BCS-286 turns north toward La Ventana, on its namesake bay opposite Isla Cerralvo. Likely to become Baja's next windsurfing mecca, La Ventana has a large *campground/RV park* with basic services and a nearby restaurant.

About 32 miles (51 km) southeast of La Paz, BCS-286 turns northeast just beyond San Juan de los Planes, where the paved road surface ends, and continues to Ensenada de los Muertos, on its own namesake bay. A popular camping area, Ensenada de los Muertos also has a dive shop.

From a junction just southeast of San Juan de los Planes, an unpaved lateral climbs the Cuesta de los Muertos (Crest of the Dead) and continues south to Los Barriles. Though unsuitable for RVs of any sort, this route is an interesting alternative for visitors with high-clearance vehicles; for more details, see the Around Los Barriles & Buena Vista entry in this chapter.

Eastern Cape

South of La Paz, the Cape Region is defined by the loop formed by the Transpeninsular (México 1) and the Southern Cape Highway (México 19) beyond their junction just south of San Pedro, as well as the unpaved roads south of La Rivera.

On the Eastern Cape south of San Antonio, the Transpeninsular brushes the Gulf at Los Barriles; a short distance farther south, a series of fairly decent dirt roads follows the coastline toward San José del Cabo. South of the junction with the Palo Escopeta road to San José's international airport, however, the frequently gullied coastal road is difficult for vehicles without a narrow body and short wheelbase. RVs should avoid this stretch of the road altogether, as it would be hazardous.

South of Los Barriles, most of the Eastern Cape resembles what overdeveloped Cabo San Lucas and San José del Cabo were decades ago, though roads are improving and the inevitable sprawl is proceeding. The area nevertheless remains in a relatively natural state, its numerous broad, sandy beaches open for placid camping.

Along the southern part of the Eastern Cape, a grassroots alliance of locals and resort operators has created the Grupo Ecológico Cabo Pulmo Los Frailes in the interest of protecting the newly designated Parque Marino Nacional Cabo Pulmo, the area's extraordinary tropical reef environment, from poaching and other threats.

EL TRIUNFO & SAN ANTONIO

El Triunfo, on the Transpeninsular, is the first town beyond the junction of the two highways. Founded after gold and silver strikes in the mid-18th century, it had swelled a century later to a population of more than 4000, mostly *mestizo* miners and Yaqui Indian laborers from the state of Sonora.

Today it might more accurately be called 'El Fracaso' (Failure). After the mines closed in 1912, the population dwindled to just a few hundred, and only a conspicuous brick smokestack, an old mill and some vintage houses remain from its heyday. There are no accommodations, and *Restaurant Las Glorias* seems an ironic name in a virtual ghost town. INAH, however, has recently proposed designating El Triunfo a national historical site, and local artisans produce a few crafts, such as leather toys and colorful handwoven baskets.

Nearby silver strikes spurred the founding of the village of San Antonio in the mid-18th century; it was briefly the capital of the Californias in 1829. Since the failure of the mines in the late 19th century, it has remained a modest farming center in a picturesque canyon. Its cobbled streets and restored buildings give it a more prosperous appearance than El Triunfo, only 4½ miles (7 km) to the west.

Opposite San Antonio's Pemex station, a graded 14-mile (22-km) road follows Arroyo San Antonio to a junction with BCS-286, the paved highway to San Juan de los Planes (southbound) and La Paz (northbound). This is a particularly good mountain-bike route, winding gradually downhill through the arroyo.

LOS BARRILES & BUENA VISTA

The Transpeninsular skirts the northern edge of the Sierra de la Laguna before touching the coast at the small resort of Los Barriles, Baja's windsurfing capital, on Bahía de Palmas. Fishing always attracted visitors between May and October, but since 1981, Vela's Baja Highwind Center has organized group trips and windsurfing competitions here.

Fast-growing Los Barriles has a post office (postal code 23501), telephone service, a laundry, a Cruz Roja station and two supermarkets, but no information office. Baja Money Exchange, in the minimall at the junction of the Transpeninsular and the paved spur into Los Barriles, changes traveler's checks for a 1% commission. The twin community of Buena Vista, with numerous additional services, is only a short distance south along the Transpeninsular.

Windsurfing

Brisk winds averaging 20 to 25 knots descend the 6000-foot (1800-meter) cordillera toward the midmorning launch site at Playa Norte, about 2 miles (3 km) north of Los Barriles; the wind picks up later at more southerly locations. Theoretically, the wind direction and the curving shoreline, running south and then east into the Gulf, make it possible to sail 20 miles (32 km) out to sea without losing sight of the shore, but high wind conditions make the area most suitable for experienced windsurfers.

Based in the San Francisco Bay Area, Vela Windsurf Resorts operates its Baja Highwind Center out of Los Barriles' Hotel Playa del Sol every year from November to April. The season's highlight is an annual championship race, usually held the second week of January.

The center offers various weeklong packages including accommodations at

either the Playa del Sol or Hotel Palmas de Cortez (see Places to Stay, below), all meals, unlimited use of equipment, daily instructional seminars, mountain-bike trips, snorkeling excursions and horseback riding. At the seminars, world-class instructors use the latest prototypes of Mistral, Seatrend, Naish and North equipment direct from the manufacturers.

A slightly cheaper alternative is Mr Bill's Boardsailing Adventures, which offers one-week packages with B&B lodging at Casa Miramar (see Places to Stay, below) and unlimited use of windsurfing equipment, mountain bikes, snorkeling equipment, sea kayaks, fishing gear and sailboats.

For contact information and details on these packages, see the Organized Tours entry in the Outdoor Activities chapter.

Other Water Sports

Vista Sea Sport (☎ (114) 1-00-31), at Hotel Palmas de Cortez and Hotel Playa del Sol, offers dive tours to Cabo Pulmo (US$100), Los Frailes (US$100), Punta Pescadero (US$75), Isla Cerralvo (US$120) and the

Gordo Banks (US$140), and snorkeling tours (US$25 to US$50) in the immediate Los Barriles area. Taxes are additional. The local mailing address is Apdo Postal 42, Buena Vista, Baja California Sur 23580, México; the US contact is Baja Fishing & Resorts (☎ (818) 591-9463, (800) 368-4334), PO Box 9016, Calabasas, CA 91372.

Baja Dive Adventures (☎ (114) 1-02-71), a division of Mr Bill's Boardsailing Adventures at Casa Miramar (see Places to Stay, below), runs similar excursions and also rents equipment, including kayaks, Hobie cats and mountain bikes.

Places to Stay

Camping Most of the area's formal RV parks are just north of Rancho Buena Vista Hotel. *La Capilla Trailer Park*, about 2 miles (3 km) south of town and right on the beach, charges US$7 per day. Facilities include full hookups and well-kept bathrooms with hot showers. Since the wind blows later in the day here, it's more popular with sportfishing parties than with windsurfers.

Martín Verdugo's Trailer Park (☎ (114) 1-00-54) charges US$8 per night for a small vehicle, US$10 for a larger one and US$5 per night for tent sites, but can be very crowded. Facilities include hot showers, full hookups, a laundry room and a sizable paperback book exchange.

Well-organized, Chilean-run *Juanito's Garden* (☎ (114) 1-00-24, fax (114) 1-00-63) charges US$10 per night or US$180 per month for sites with full hookups, though there are only a handful of spaces for transients. It's not on the beach, but it's not far away, either; nonresidents can use the showers (US$2) or the washer and dryers (US$1 each). The mailing address is Apdo Postal 50, Los Barriles, Baja California Sur 23501, México.

Many visitors have commended *Playa de Oro RV Resort* (☎ (114) 1-00-44, fax (114) 1-00-46), perched above the ocean, which is popular with windsurfers for its access to the offshore zephyrs. Facilities include hot showers, a laundry room, clean toilets and full hookups. Site rates start at US$11, depending on proximity to the beach.

Hotels Other than campsites, Los Barriles and Buena Vista generally lack budget accommodations. Just below the minimall on the lateral into town, however, Martín Penuelas has simple *rooms* with hot showers for US$20 and plans to add air-conditioning. The mailing address is Apdo Postal 6, Los Barriles, Baja California Sur 23501, México.

Casa Miramar (☎ (114) 1-02-71), at Km 109 opposite the Pemex station on the Transpeninsular, is a B&B catering mostly to windsurfers, but it also arranges fishing excursions. Rates are US$40/60 single/ double, and there are also bunkroom accommodations for US$25 per person and a family suite for US$95.

In Los Barriles, *Hotel Playa del Sol* (☎ (114) 1-00-44, fax (114) 1-00-46) offers clean, comfortable singles/doubles with full board for US$60/90 plus tax. The 42-room *Hotel Palmas de Cortez* (☎ (114) 1-00-44; (818) 222-7144 in the USA) resembles other hotels in the area. Singles/ doubles with full board cost US$70/110; two-bedroom condominiums cost US$185 for up to five people. Rates do not include 10% in gratuities and another 10% in tax. For further information on either hotel, contact Baja Fishing & Resorts in mainland California (☎ (818) 591-9463, (800) 368-4334, fax (818) 591-1077), PO Box 9016, Calabasas, CA 91372.

Popular with anglers and their families, the 50-room *Rancho Buena Vista Hotel* (☎ (114) 1-01-77, fax (114) 1-00-55; (805) 928-1719, (800) 258-8200, fax (805) 925-2990 in the USA) is southeast of Los Barriles and half a mile (1 km) east of the Transpeninsular. Facilities include a swimming pool, a bar, a restaurant, tennis courts and 20 inboard cruisers for fishing trips. Family-style meals are all-you-can-eat; most of the beef, poultry and vegetables are raised on the hotel's farm. Rooms with screened windows, tiled bathroom, ceiling fans and/or air-conditioning cost US$80/140/180 single/double/triple with full board, excluding 10% gratuity and 10% tax. The hotel closes from mid-August to early October because of heat, humidity and hurricane risk. For more information, contact Rancho Buena Vista at the numbers above; its US mailing address is PO Box 1408, Santa Maria, CA 93456.

At *Hotel Buena Vista Beach Resort* (☎ (114) 1-00-33, fax (114) 1-01-33), a quarter-mile (0.5 km) south of the Rancho Buena Vista, standard singles/doubles cost US$75/125, while premium rooms are US$100/150 plus 10% tax and 10% service; rates include full board. The resort also has a hot mineral spa, a swimming pool and tennis courts. Various accommodations/fishing packages are also available. For more information, write Apdo Postal 574, La Paz, Baja California Sur, México, or contact the US sales office (☎ (619) 425-1551, (800) 752-3555, fax (619) 425-1832, hotelbvbr@aol.com), 100 W 35th St, Suite U, National City, CA 91950.

Rancho Leonero (☎ (114) 5-36-36, fax (114) 1-02-16; (714) 524-5502, (800) 646-2252, fax (714) 524-1856 in the USA) is an isolated resort southeast of La Capilla Trailer Park; follow the dirt road leading south from La Capilla or the signed road off the Transpeninsular. The resort includes an airstrip, cozy rooms, a restaurant and a bar at a spectacular beachfront location. With a reputation for some of Baja's best food, the restaurant sometimes serves up to 120 guests. It also has extensive water-sports facilities, including a dive center complete with rental equipment, and boats for fishing.

Its spotless, spacious rooms have thatched roofs, stone walls, tiled floors and patios overlooking the sea. Singles/doubles with full board start around US$100/175 plus 10% each for service and taxes. For more details, call Rancho Leonero at the numbers above or write PO Box 698, Placentia, CA 92871.

Places to Eat
The *Sunrise Café* in the minimall at the Transpeninsular junction serves US-style

breakfasts and lunches from 6 am to 2 pm. Almost next door, *Thrifty* has passable US-style ice cream.

All the other restaurants are along the main drag in Los Barriles proper. *Paralelo 28*, a small taco stand, is very good but lacks the varied condiments of some peninsular taquerías. *El Sinaloense* serves the usual antojitos.

Longtime gringo favorite *Tío Pablo* (☎ (114) 1-03-30) has a good pizza menu as well as massive portions of Mexican specialties like chicken fajitas – with rice, beans, salad and tortillas, one dish easily feeds two or more people. Despite raucous decor and satellite TV connections for international sports, it's surprisingly sedate, and the margaritas are a bit weak.

Otra Vez (☎ (114) 1-02-49) and *Mañanas* are recent entries in the dining scene. Otra Vez offers a more elaborate menu including Chinese and Thai dishes along with the usual seafood, pasta and beef; it's open 11:30 am to 10 pm. Mañanas tends more toward pizza and pasta; hours are 4:30 to 9:30 pm only.

Other eateries worth trying are *El Corral* and *Calafia*, both in Buena Vista, and *Tía Licha* at the Hotel Buena Vista Beach Resort (see Places to Stay, above).

AROUND LOS BARRILES & BUENA VISTA

North of Los Barriles, a mostly graded but rough and potentially dangerous road, not suitable for large RVs, hugs the coast to Punta Pescadero and El Cardonal, and even crosses the very difficult Cuesta de los Muertos en route to San Juan de los Planes and La Paz. Anyone doing this route with 2WD will find driving from north to south easier. It's more appropriate for mountain biking: the triangular circuit from Los Barriles up the Transpeninsular to San Antonio, down the arroyo to San Juan de los Planes and down the coast to Los Barriles is some 72 miles (115 km) in length. It's somewhat more difficult in the opposite direction.

Recently taken over by a bank after its former owner's creative financing made him a fugitive, *Hotel Punta Pescadero* (☎ (114) 1-01-01, fax (114) 1-00-69; (800) 426-2252 in the USA) is a small, elite resort also accessible by air (it has a paved private landing strip). About 10 miles (16 km) north of Los Barriles, all of its 21 rooms have ocean views from private tiled terraces and patios; several also have fireplaces. Singles/doubles cost US$90, while a one-bedroom villa is US$150; 10% tax and 15% service are added to these prices. Meals are additional but reasonably priced. The mailing address is Apdo Postal 362, La Paz, Baja California Sur 23000, México; the US mailing address is 24831 Alicia Parkway, Suite C-320, Laguna Hills, CA 92653.

The hotel offers full-day sportfishing cruises at Punta Pescadero for US$120 on a panga, US$175 on a super-panga and US$300 on a cruiser. Scuba rentals, surf-fishing equipment and horses are also available.

While most beaches north of Los Barriles are rocky or gravelly, some are suitable for *free camping*. El Cardonal, to the north, is more hospitable than snobbish Punta Pescadero in this regard, but Quebecois-run *El Cardonal Resort* (☎ (114) 1-00-40; (514) 467-4700, fax (514) 467-4668 in Montreal) is also a good choice. Tent sites cost US$4 (US$119 monthly), RV sites with full hookups US$8 (US$199 monthly) and kitchenette apartments with private bath US$44 daily, US$279 weekly, US$499 fortnightly and US$650 monthly. There are hot showers, purified tap water and good meals. The owner also leads rock art excursions at Rancho Boca del Alamo to the north (weekends only) and rents kayaks, fishing pangas (US$149 per day) and fishing cruisers (US$450 per day).

LA RIVERA

At a junction about 12 miles (19 km) south of Los Barriles, a paved lateral off the Transpeninsular leads to the farming village of La Rivera, which lacks hotels but has one quiet Gulfside campground, the shady *Trailer Park La Rivera* (☎ (115) 5-39-00), charging US$8 with hookups. La

Rivera is the last point for supplies south-bound on the Eastern Cape road, so stock up if you're going to Cabo Pulmo, Los Frailes or other points as far south as San José del Cabo.

PUNTA COLORADA

About 4 miles (6 km) from the end of the paved road to La Rivera and just over 11 miles (18 km) from the Transpeninsular, *Hotel Punta Colorada* (☎ (115) 1-00-50, fax (115) 1-00-46) is an anglers' favorite for the abundant roosterfish offshore. Singles/doubles/triples/quadruples cost US$55/90/130/160 with full board, while day rates for fishing trips range from US$195 to US$300.

The US contact is Baja Fishing & Resorts (☎ (818) 222-5066, (800) 368-4334, fax (818) 591-1077), PO Box 9016, Calabasas, CA 91372.

CABO PULMO

Thanks in large part to Cabo Pulmo's road, which remains difficult for larger RVs, the eastern Pacific's northernmost coral reef, on the cusp between tropical and temperate waters, continues to harbor 220 species of colorful tropical fish and a dozen species of petrified coral. Estimated to be 25,000 years old, the reef and 127 sq miles (70 sq km) surrounding it constitute **Parque Marino Nacional Cabo Pulmo**, a legally protected area where no fishing is permitted but diving, snorkeling, sea kayaking and other water sports are extraordinary. Green turtles nest at Playa Las Barracas, about 15 minutes north of Cabo Pulmo, in August and September.

Divers will find the maximum depth of 70 feet (22 meters) in the offshore waters here ideal for optimum air time. Pepe and Chicago-born Libby Murrieta run Pepe's Dive Center (☎ /fax (114) 1-01-01), which organizes guided dives for US$45 (one tank) to US$65 (two tanks); it also rents kayaks (US$25 per half-day) and dive equipment, fills air tanks and offers four-day PADI courses with full certification for US$350. Taxes are additional.

Nondivers can take snorkeling and sightseeing tours with Pepe's, including trips to the Sierra de la Laguna. Rock climbers will find challenging seaview routes on nearby granite (there is also some basalt and other volcanic rock). Fishing is possible in areas away from the reef proper.

Places to Stay & Eat

Free camping is abundant, though infrastructure is almost nil and campers should take special care in disposing of their refuse. The only formal accommodations are at US-owned *Cabo Pulmo Beach Resort* (☎ (114) 1-02-44; (888) 997-8566 in the USA; (208) 788-8823 outside USA), perhaps a model for resort development – it's decentralized but not sprawling, solar-powered and well landscaped but not water-hungry (thanks to a drip-irrigation system). Unlike hotels on the Southern Cape, its comforts aren't extravagant and do not overwhelm its natural environment.

Bungalows with double beds cost US$45 nightly, *casitas* (cottages) US$60 and full houses US$75; all have kitchen or kitchenette. Monthly rentals are available. The resort also offers sea kayaking, climbing, hiking, snorkeling and tennis.

Cabo Pulmo has three places to eat, the relatively basic *Tito's*, the somewhat more elaborate *El Caballero* (associated with Cabo Pulmo Beach Resort, it has excellent and friendly service) and American-run *Nancy's*, offering a casually informal but memorable outdoor dining experience – special mention for the sea scallops, homemade bread and tasty margaritas.

BAHÍA LOS FRAILES

Beyond Cabo Pulmo, the Eastern Cape highway is inadvisable for large RVs, and many of the diners at *Hotel Bahía Los Frailes* (☎ (114) 1-01-22; (800) 934-0295 in the USA) come from yachts anchored offshore. Despite its small size, the place employs a fulltime cook and kitchen staff.

Room rates, including full board, are US$100 per person for a distinctive room with two queen-size beds, US$120 per person in a one-bedroom suite and US$440 for up to four guests in a two-bedroom cabaña. Taxes and gratuities are extra, and there are additional charges for children under 10; children under five generally may stay free of charge. Fishing pangas, with skipper but no tackle, cost from US$150 to US$195 per day; rental kayaks cost US$15 per hour, US$40 per half-day. The local mailing address is Apdo Postal 230, San José del Cabo, Baja California Sur 23400, México; the US mailing address is 2443 Fillmore St, No 367, San Francisco, CA 94115-0295.

Beyond Bahía Los Frailes, the road becomes increasingly rough but still passable for vehicles with good clearance and a short wheelbase. South of the junction with the road to the village of Palo Escopeta and San José del Cabo's international airport, however, the Eastern Cape road is impassable for anything larger than a pickup truck. For more information on this road, see the Around San José del Cabo entry, below.

At Rancho La Vinorama, near the junction of the Palo Escopeta road, some extravagant development has already occurred. Despite a climb through a sandy arroyo from the airport, the Palo Escopeta road is passable for almost any vehicle – an old Volkswagen squareback, with almost no clearance, easily made the trip from the airport to La Vinorama.

Central Cape

Even travelers who deplore the unrestrained development in the Cape Region's coastal areas will enjoy the Central Cape's scenic Sierra de la Laguna, an ecological wonderland that deserves explicit national park status. Several foothill villages provide access to these unique mountains of the interior, which are also accessible from Todos Santos on their Pacific slope. Hikers should plan on spending several days crossing the sierra; the best season is autumn, after the *chubasco* rains have

filled the canyons with fresh water. Days are short, however, at this time of year, and the weather can be very cool at higher altitudes.

SANTIAGO

Tranquil Santiago, a charming village about 6 miles (10 km) south of La Rivera junction and 1½ miles (2.5 km) west of the Transpeninsular, was the site of one of the bloodiest episodes in Baja's history. Pericú Indians revolted and murdered the Jesuit Lorenzo Carranco and several other Spaniards here before being subdued by Spanish soldiers and European epidemics; no trace remains of the mission, which closed in 1795.

The tidy **Zoológico Santiago** contains a variety of animals, including a Bengal tiger, an African lion, a black bear, badgers, bobcats, coatimundi, deer, monkeys, native reptiles (mostly rattlesnakes), peccaries and a collection of colorful macaws. Unfortunately, almost none of the animals are named, so most visitors have to guess at everything other than the big draws. There are swing sets, and many families enjoy a Sunday barbecue here; admission is free.

Places to Stay & Eat

Modest but friendly *Hotel Palomar* (☎ (114) 2-21-65, ext 128, fax (114) 2-21-90), downhill from the plaza, is more notable for its restaurant, serving fine seafood at moderate prices, than for its accommodations. A single/double with hot shower costs about US$20/25; tent camping is possible on the spacious and pleasant grounds. English-speaking owner Sergio Gómez is a good source of information on the Sierra de la Laguna.

AROUND SANTIAGO
Tropic of Cancer

Precisely at latitude 23.5°N, just south of Santiago, a concrete sphere on the Transpeninsular marks the tropic of Cancer, which also passes through Hawaii, Taiwan, central India, Saudi Arabia and the Sahara Desert.

Cañón San Dionisio

Cañón San Dionisio, in the Sierra de la Laguna about 15 miles (24 km) west of Santiago, is one of Baja California's real highlights, a scenic area with a unique ecology where cacti, palms, oaks, aspens and pines grow virtually side by side. The deciduous *huerivo* (aspen, *Populus brandegeei glabra*), whose mainland California counterpart is dormant for up to six months, does not lose its leaves until December and sprouts out again by January. The trail up Cañón San Dionisio is easy to follow, but in some areas hikers must scramble over large granite boulders; if it has rained, there are pools suitable for swimming.

This is the northernmost of three major east-west routes across the Sierra de la Laguna; the others are Cañón San Bernardo, west of Miraflores, and Cañón San Pablo, west of Caduaño. The best guide for hiking these routes is Walt Peterson's *The Baja Adventure Book* (see the Books entry in the Facts for the Visitor chapter).

To reach Cañón San Dionisio from Santiago, take the dirt road off Santiago's plaza to the video store; at the next junction, where the road divides into three, take the middle (uphill) fork. From this point, Cañón San Dionisio is a straight shot. The road is passable for any passenger vehicle driven with caution. Taxi drivers from Santiago will drop hikers at the trailhead for about US$30, not an unreasonable price if two or three can share the expense.

From the western side of the sierra, Cañón San Dionisio is most easily reached from San Juan del Aserradero, a rancho roughly 15 miles (24 km) from Todos Santos that is reached by a complex series of back roads.

Agua Caliente

Five miles (8 km) southwest of Santiago by a good dirt road, Agua Caliente is a nondescript village whose hot spring attracts campers and hikers to the canyon of the Arroyo de Agua Caliente. The spring itself, at the foot of the Sierra de la Laguna, is 2½ miles (4 km) farther west by another dirt road that requires fording a stream. Alongside a dam at the end of the road, the spring is tepid rather than hot (old-timers claim it has cooled considerably in recent years). In theory, Ejido Agua Caliente charges US$5 for camping or day use, but rarely does anyone show up to collect.

MIRAFLORES & CADUAÑO

Miraflores is 5½ miles (9 km) south of Agua Caliente by a dirt road, but also is accessible by a road from the paved Transpeninsular at Km 71, 8½ miles (14 km) south of Santiago. The town itself offers little of interest, but a good 4-mile (6-km) road leads to the village of Boca de la Sierra and **Cañón San Bernardo**, one of the major routes across the Sierra de la Laguna. Ask for guides to view nearby rock art sites.

Only two minutes from the trailhead, at the point where the irrigation canal enters the village, the route crosses the Arroyo Boca de la Sierra and passes an unfortunately trashy campsite. However, it soon ascends into a wonderland of native vegetation and wildlife, including hairy tarantulas and other spiders, peculiar insects that look like walking twigs, and colorful tree frogs, along a series of attractive granite pools. Many of these pools are suitable for swimming.

From the Todos Santos side of the sierra, the trail begins at Rancho Santo Domingo, most easily reached by a series of signed dirt roads leading east from the town of El Pescadero on the Southern Cape Highway (México 19).

The southernmost route across the Sierra de la Laguna goes from the village of Caduaño, a few kilometers south of Miraflores, through **Cañón San Pablo**. The dirt road from Miraflores to Caduaño that appears on both the AAA and ITM road maps no longer exists. It is necessary to return to the Transpeninsular in order to travel between the two villages. To get to Cañón San Pablo from the Todos Santos side, take the dirt road eastbound from El Pescadero and follow the signs past the San Andrés turnoff to Rancho El Güerigo.

Southern Cape

Aggressively vulgar tourist development, especially along the luxury hotel corridor between San José del Cabo and Cabo San Lucas, has turned the Southern Cape into the most expensive and least appealing part of the entire Baja Peninsula. Only central San José del Cabo has retained integrity, and it remains by far the best base of operations for anyone visiting the area.

Baja's southern tip has been, in succession, a sleepy haven for Pericú Indians, a sheltered hideaway for pirates and a string of sedate fishing communities. The Pericú inhabited the foothills of the Sierra de la Laguna to the north, never settling around the Cape proper because fresh water was scarce here, but the majority died soon after arriving Europeans brought deadly diseases.

When Europeans first saw the peninsula in the 16th century, water shortages made the Southern Cape an unappealing place for permanent settlement, but its secluded anchorages offered privateers an ideal base for raiding Spain's Manila galleons. One of the earliest English pirates in the area was Sir Francis Drake, who stopped briefly in 1578 or 1579 to take on water before continuing north to present-day San Francisco. In 1587 Thomas Cavendish commanded three ships that attacked and captured the treasure-laden *Santa Ana* – a galleon that weighed about 700 tons, more than twice the total weight of Cavendish's fleet. Cavendish could take only a fraction of the gold, silver and other booty, abandoning the rest.

By the early 17th century, the Spanish had lost enough gold and silver to prompt the establishment of a small *presidio* (military outpost) at Cabo San Lucas. Around 1730, the Jesuits established Misión San José del Cabo, which became a more permanent settlement. The presidio deterred the pirates and, eventually, both towns became villages whose inhabitants relied on fishing and fish-canning for their live-

lihood. During the Mexican-American War, US troops occupied the area, as did William Walker's forces a few years later.

After WWII, US private pilots brought tales of the area's big game fish and magnificent beaches to listeners north of the border. As more North Americans arrived, upscale hotels and restaurants sprouted like weeds and the federal government built an international airport near San José del Cabo. Cruise ships soon included Cabo San Lucas on their itineraries, and a ferry service (since discontinued) began to operate to and from the mainland city of Puerto Vallarta. In recent years hordes of North American tourists and retirees have frequented the area, central Cabo San Lucas has lost its village ambiance and a string of multistory luxury resort hotels has disfigured the coastline between Cabo San Lucas and San José del Cabo.

SAN JOSÉ DEL CABO

Attacks by developers have not yet succeeded in transforming San José del Cabo (population 21,737), a quaint town of narrow streets, Spanish-style buildings and shady plazas, into a major tourist resort. Grandiose plans for a yacht marina at the outlet of ecologically sensitive Arroyo San José fizzled because of local opposition. Having maintained its open space, San José is a far more pleasant destination than congested, overdeveloped Cabo San Lucas.

The arroyo's dependable fresh-water supply once attracted both the Manila galleons that carried treasure across the Pacific to Acapulco and the buccaneers who preyed on them. Established in 1730 as a mission village, San José suffered Indian rebellions, floods, military attacks (by Spanish loyalists in the War of Independence) and foreign occupation (by US Marines and, later, William Walker), but since the mid-19th century, it has settled into a more placid existence.

Orientation

On the peninsula's southern coast, San José del Cabo is 20 miles (32 km) east of Cabo San Lucas and 112 miles (179 km) south of

William Walker & the Cape

William Walker, the infamously quixotic American adventurer who spent and lost his life trying to build an Anglo empire in Mexico and Central America, was the first to try to bring the sleepy Cape Region into the modern world. In 1853, planning to establish a self-styled 'Republic of Sonora and Lower California,' he sailed south from San Francisco, touching at Cabo San Lucas before anchoring at the territorial capital of La Paz.

Misrepresenting themselves as commercial voyagers to gain permission to land, Walker's forces arrested the governor, took possession of public buildings and raised the flag of the new republic under the legal code of Louisiana – which permitted slavery. Walker, a Tennessee native, later made slavery a cornerstone of his proposed Central American empire in an apparent attempt to gain political support from the slave states of the US South.

Improvised Mexican resistance failed to dislodge Walker from La Paz, but the threat of a more organized Todos Santos force and the failure of his own reinforcements to arrive drove him back to Cabo San Lucas. Concerned that a Mexican warship was trailing him, he abandoned plans to establish a new capital at Bahía Magdalena and returned to Ensenada, where he led a heroically foolish attempt to cross to Sonora. Eventually he straggled across the US border to hatch the Central American schemes that led to his death in Honduras in 1860.

Despite Walker's failures in Baja California, some have argued that his adventures brought territorial gains to the United States – the Gadsden Purchase of southern Arizona and New Mexico brought the USA part of what Walker tried to obtain by force. Today, given the overwhelming Americanization of Cabo San Lucas, concerned Mexicans might well wonder if, in the long run, Walker has triumphed despite his self-imposed disasters. ■

La Paz. It consists of two distinct parts: central San José, atop a hill about 1 mile (1.6 km) inland, remains an authentic Mexican town, while the beachfront *zona hotelera* of resort complexes, condominiums and time-shares is primarily the fault of Fonatur, Mexico's quasigovernmental tourist development agency. Manicured Blvd José Antonio Mijares, named for a Mexican naval officer who distinguished himself for bravery during San José's occupation by US Marines in 1847 – 48, links the two areas.

The northernmost blocks of Blvd Mijares are a miniature gringoland of restaurants and souvenir stores, but compared to Cabo San Lucas the area is tasteful and tranquil. Shady Plaza Mijares is a pleasant place for relaxing with an ice cream.

Zaragoza and Doblado, San José's other major streets, cross Blvd Mijares and lead to the Transpeninsular. If you're walking toward town from the beach, turn left on either street to cross the heart of San José – small, red-tiled buildings, the colonial-style Iglesia San José and Plaza Mijares. The town's few budget hotels and restaurants are on or near these streets.

Across Arroyo San José, Pueblo La

Playa is a tranquil fishing village with limited accommodations and several good restaurants. The unpaved Eastern Cape road to Bahía Los Frailes and Los Barriles is passable for small, narrow vehicles only, and very dangerous for RVs.

Information

Tourist Office The staff at the Dirección General de Turismo Municipal (☎ (114) 2-04-46) on Plaza Mijares are not particularly helpful, but their supply of printed matter is increasing. Hours are 8 am to 3 pm weekdays.

Money The cambio at Aeropuerto Internacional Los Cabos offers very poor rates, so try to avoid changing money until you get to town, where several cambios keep long hours.

Banks pay better rates but keep shorter hours. Bancomer, at the corner of Zaragoza and Morelos, and Banca Serfin, at the corner of Zaragoza and Degollado, both cash traveler's checks and have ATMs; Bancomer has longer lines, but Serfin will not cash more than US$200.

Post & Communications The post office is at the intersection of Blvd Mijares and Valerio González. The postal code is 23400.

Direct and collect calls to the USA are fairly simple from the public telephone office on Doblado across from the hospital, but Ladatel public phones are more common than in the past.

Travel Agencies In the Hotel Fiesta Inn, Contactours (☎ (114) 2-31-00) arranges local tours and offers the usual services. Viajes Damiana (☎ (114) 2-07-52, (114) 2-37-52) is at the corner of Zaragoza and Morelos.

Cultural Center San José's Casa de la Cultura (☎ (114) 2-09-14), on Obregón just north of Plaza Mijares, is more an educational resource for locals than a sightseeing attraction for tourists, but a few interesting historical photographs line the walls.

Laundry Lavandería Vera, on Valerio González about 2½ blocks west of Blvd Mijares, is efficient and reasonably priced. Lavamática San José (☎ (114) 2-41-50), on Valerio González just east of the main bus terminal, is open 8 am to 8 pm daily except Sunday, when it's open 9 am to 5 pm.

Medical Services San José's Hospital Municipal (☎ (114) 2-16-80) is at Doblado and Márquez de León. The Cruz Roja (☎ (114) 2-03-16) is on Blvd Mijares just north of the post office.

Los Cabos Centro Cultural

Off to a good start, San José's new museum features small but meaningful exhibits on pre-Columbian peoples, their rock art and subsistence, and the natural history of whales, plus a collection of historical photographs that could use more narration. At the eastern end of Paseo San José alongside the estuary, it's open 9 am to 5 pm daily except Monday; admission is US$0.75.

Arroyo San José

In colonial times, between raids on Spanish galleons, pirates took refuge at the freshwater Arroyo San José, now a protected wildlife area replenished by a subterranean spring. From the corner of Juárez, a newly constructed, palm-lined pedestrian trail along the estuary parallels Blvd Mijares all the way to the zona hotelera – a delightful alternative to the busy boulevard. Among the common bird species are coots, pelicans, herons, egrets and plovers.

Beaches

San José's white sandy beach areas, **Playa del Nuevo Sol/Playa de California** and **Pueblo La Playa**, are major attractions for visitors. Playa del Nuevo Sol and its eastward extension, Playa de California, are at the southern end of Blvd Mijares, but Pueblo La Playa is really a separate beachside fishing community about 1½ miles (2.5 km) east of the junction of Juárez and Blvd Mijares. It has excellent surf fishing.

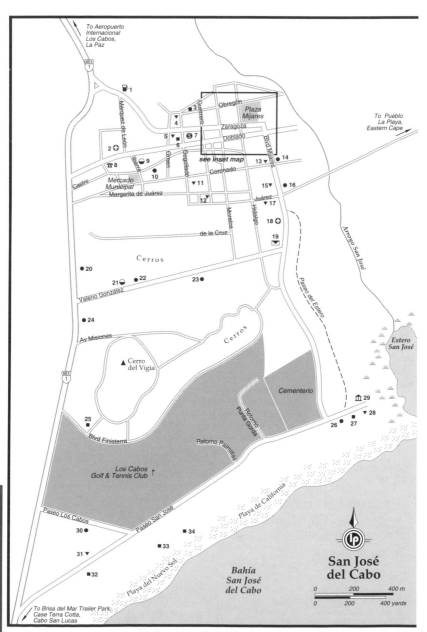

San José del Cabo

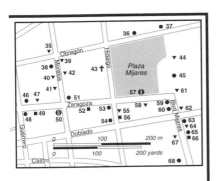

PLACES TO STAY
3   San José Inn
6   Posada Terranova
25 Howard Johnson Plaza
    Suite Resort
27 Forum Resort Presidente
    Los Cabos
32 Hotel Fiesta Inn
33 Hotel Aguamarina
    Los Cabos
34 Hotel Posada Real
37 Posada Señor Mañana
49 Hotel Diana
52 Hotel Ceci
56 Hotel Colli
66 Hotel Tropicana

PLACES TO EAT
4   Barra La Navidad
5   Nuevo Imperial
6   Posada Terranova
11 Pizza Fiesta
12 El Paraje (The Tree House)
13 Just Desserts
15 La Fogata
17 Plaza San José
28 Les Ambassadeurs
31 Pizzería Tropicana
35 La Provence
39 Kokopelli's
40 Los Raspados
41 La Michoacana
42 Jazmín's
44 Damiana
47 Pietro
55 La Bombilla
58 La Cenaduría
61 Café Fiesta
62 Almacenes Goncanseco
64 Helados Bing
66 Tropicana Bar & Grill
67 Iguana Bar

OTHER
1   Pemex
2   Hospital Municipal
7   Banca Serfin (ATM)
8   Telephone Office
9   Enlaces Terrestres
    (Buses to La Paz)
10 Deportiva Piscis
14 Eclipse
16 Crafts Stalls
18 Cruz Roja
19 Post Office
20 Dollar Rent A Car
21 Bus Terminal
22 Lavamática San José
23 Lavandería Vera
24 Thrifty Rent A Car
26 Bones
29 Los Cabos Centro
    Cultural
30 Mexicana
32 Contactours
34 Thrifty Rent A Car
36 Casa de la
    Cultura
38 Galería de Arte
    Da Vinci
43 Iglesia San José
45 Copal
46 Piso 2
48 Casa de Cambio
50 Bancomer (ATM)
51 Viajes Damiana
53 Antigua Los Cabos
54 Killer Hook Surf Shop
57 Dirección General de
    Turismo Municipal
59 Huichol Collection
60 Palacio Municipal
63 Thrifty Rent A Car
65 Victor's Aquatics
68 La Mina

Fishing

Game fish species available all year around Los Cabos include blue marlin, bonito, corvina, crevalle, dorado, grouper, needlefish, pargo, rock bass, roosterfish, sierra, skipjack, striped marlin, wahoo and yellowtail. Seasonal fisheries include black marlin (June to December), sailfish (May to November) and yellowfin tuna (June to November).

In San José proper, Victor's Aquatics (☎ (114) 2-10-92, (114) 2-01-55), based at the corner of Blvd Mijares and Doblado but also reached through major hotels, organizes six-hour panga trips from Playa Palmilla for US$180 (maximum three people) and eight-hour cabin-cruiser trips from US$325 (maximum four) to US$395 (maximum six). Its US contact is Jig Stop Tours (☎ (714) 496-0960, (800) 521-2281, fax (714) 496-1384), 34186 Pacific Coast Hwy, Dana Point, CA 92629. Deportiva Piscis (☎ (114) 2-03-32), on Castro near Ibarra, arranges fishing excursions and also sells and rents tackle.

Beyond the lagoon, the unpaved Eastern Cape road leads to the popular fishing beach at Pueblo La Playa. Local fishermen will arrange fishing excursions at this beach; you can usually find them here in the late afternoon, cutting up their day's catch. La Playa Sport Fishing (☎ (114) 2-11-95 from 6 to 8 pm) in Pueblo La Playa arranges excursions with the local cooperative to the offshore Gordo Banks for marlin, dorado, roosterfish, wahoo, tuna and sailfish. Trips last from 6 am to noon, and cost around US$160 for up to three people. Another possibility is Miguel's Pangas (☎ (114) 2-20-47).

Golf & Tennis

The nine-hole, par-35 course at Los Cabos Golf & Tennis Club (☎ (114) 2-09-05) charges around US$15 for nine holes, US$23 for 18 holes – at these prices it's by far the cheapest course in the entire Los Cabos area.

Tennis courts rent for US$10 per hour during the day, double that per hour at night.

Sea Kayaking

At Brisa del Mar Trailer Park (see Places to Stay, below), Los Lobos del Mar (☎ /fax (114) 2-29-83) arranges guided kayak tours in the vicinity of San José for around US$50 and also does a full-day excursion to Cabo Pulmo for US$99; 10% tax is added to these prices.

Surfing

Mexican-run Killer Hook Surf Shop (☎ (114) 2-24-30), on Hidalgo between Zaragoza and Doblado, is the best source of surfing information in the Los Cabos area. Available rentals include surfboards, boogie boards, surfing videos, snorkeling gear, surf-casting poles, beach umbrellas and mountain bikes. Its mailing address is Apdo Postal 346, San José del Cabo, Baja California Sur 23400, México.

Brisa del Mar Trailer Park also rents surfboards.

Special Events

March 19 marks the **Fiesta de San José**, a celebration of the town's patron saint; festivities last four or five days.

Places to Stay – budget & middle

San José's budget and midrange accommodations are decent and reasonably priced, but there's not much of either, and demand is high. If possible, make reservations in peak season.

Camping Free unofficial beach camping is possible at *Pueblo La Playa*, about 1½ miles (2.5 km) east of town. The best fee site, also near the beach at Pueblo La Playa, is Swedish-run *El Delfín Blanco* (☎ /fax (114) 2-11-99), too small for large RVs but excellent for tent campers (US$9). It also has neatly decorated, twin-bedded cabañas starting at US$26/32 single/double. Non-guests can shower for US$2.50. The mailing address is Apdo Postal 147, San José del Cabo, Baja California Sur 23400, México.

About 2 miles (3 km) southwest of San José, at Km 28 on the Transpeninsular, *Brisa del Mar Trailer Park* has tent and RV spaces (with full hookups) from about US$9 to US$15 for two people, plus US$2 for each additional person. There are hot showers, toilets, a restaurant/bar and a laundromat, plus a few motel-style rooms, but it's very crowded with North Americans from mid-November through February.

Hotels Though urgently in need of a plasterer and a painter, the homely but friendly *San José Inn* (☎ (114) 2-24-64), on Obregón between Degollado and Guerrero, has spacious singles/doubles with private bath, ceiling fans and hot water for US$10/13. It also offers (unofficial) hostel accommodations for as little as US$5 per person. Comparably priced *Hotel Ceci* (☎ (114) 2-00-51), Zaragoza 22, has 20 clean, redecorated rooms with private shower and air-con, but gets very crowded in-season.

Popular *Hotel Diana* (☎ (114) 2-04-90), upstairs at Zaragoza 30, has triples with private bath and TV for US$20. *Hotel Colli* (☎ (114) 2-00-52), on Hidalgo half a block south of Zaragoza, has clean, carpeted rooms for about US$20 single or double.

Its popular and gregarious manager has moved back to mainland Mexico, but

Posada Señor Mañana (☎ /fax (114) 2-04-62), Obregón 1 just north of Plaza Mijares, continues to improve. Prices also continue to increase, however; singles/doubles now start at US$25/30 and range up to US$38 plus 10% tax. With congenial English-speaking staff, it's still one of San José's best values.

Modernized but inviting *Posada Terranova* (☎ (114) 2-05-34, fax (114) 2-09-02), on Degollado between Doblado and Zaragoza, has singles/doubles for US$40/45 and an outstanding restaurant.

Places to Stay – top end

Nearly all the top-end hotels are in the zona hotelera along the beach. In peak season it's worth checking with airlines and travel agencies for special packages.

Casa Terra Cotta (fax (114) 8-05-37), at Km 29 of the San José-Cabo San Lucas highway, 1½ miles (2.5 km) west of San José, is a comfortable, Canadian-run B&B. It charges US$55 double, including vegetarian or traditional Mexican breakfasts.

Best Western's *Hotel Posada Real* (☎ (114) 2-01-55; (800) 528-1234 in the USA) sometimes fails to meet the chain's standards; when guests are few, the jacuzzi and pool go unheated and the hot showers can be sporadic. Singles/doubles cost US$55 in the winter peak season, slightly less the rest of the year.

Reached by a passage through its namesake restaurant, with a verdant tropical garden around its swimming pool, the surprisingly inconspicuous *Hotel Tropicana* (☎ (114) 2-09-07, fax (114) 2-15-90; (510) 939-2725 in mainland California), Blvd Mijares 30 between Doblado and Coronado, has 40 doubles with satellite TV for US$65, breakfast and taxes included. It's probably the best hotel in San José proper (as opposed to the luxury beachfront accommodations).

At Pueblo La Playa, *La Playita Resort* (☎ /fax (114) 2-41-66; (818) 962-2805, (888) 242-4166 toll free in mainland California) is a new, mission-style hotel/restaurant with a pool and other amenities; it charges US$66 single or double. The

postal address is Apdo 437, San José del Cabo, Baja California Sur 23400, México.

The 99-room *Hotel Aguamarina Los Cabos* (☎ (114) 2-00-77, fax (114) 2-02-87; (800) 897-5700 in the USA) is 1½ miles (2.5 km) south of the town center, right on the beach. It has the standard amenities of the US-based Quality Inn chain: a swimming pool, air-con and clean, comfortable, carpeted rooms. Singles/doubles cost US$70, but the off-season (April to mid-December) rate is US$60.

The beachfront *Hotel Fiesta Inn* (☎ (114) 2-07-93, fax (114) 2-04-80), also in the hotel zone, has a restaurant, a bar, golf-club facilities, a swimming pool and around 160 air-conditioned rooms. Singles/doubles cost about US$99 and slightly less in the off-season.

Overlooking Los Cabos Golf & Tennis Club (where its guests get discount rates), the *Howard Johnson Plaza Suite Resort* (☎ (114) 2-09-09, fax (114) 2-08-06; (800) 446-4656 in the USA) is at Paseo Finisterra 1. All rooms have telephone, TV, air-con and purified drinking water, and the hotel also has a minigym, a minimarket, a laundry, a travel agency, two restaurants and a bar. Rates start at US$90 single or double, rising to US$130 for a one-bedroom suite and US$180 for a two-bedroom suite. Taxes are additional.

With ocean views, high standards and even higher prices, the sprawling 250-room *Forum Resort Presidente Los Cabos* (☎ (114) 2-00-38, fax (114) 2-02-32; (800) 327-0200 in the USA), alongside the estuary, has become an all-inclusive resort generally closed to anyone not lodged at the hotel (though day passes are available). Rates start around US$260 and reach up to US$480 double, and include meals (with fixed mealtimes), use of the tennis courts and pool, horseback riding and nightclub admission (including most drinks).

Places to Eat

The very cleanly *Mercado Municipal* (municipal market), on Ibarra between

Coronado and Castro, has numerous stalls offering simple and inexpensive but good and filling meals. *La Bombilla*, on Hidalgo between Zaragoza and Doblado, specializes in antojitos.

Kokopelli's, on Obregón near Morelos, serves superb breakfast burritos in pleasant surroundings, but may soon change hands. *Café Fiesta* (☎ (114) 2-28-08), on the eastern side of Plaza Mijares, has good breakfasts, light meals and desserts, with pleasant outdoor seating, but prices are on the high side; it's open 7 am to 10:30 pm.

The same owners run *Pizza Fiesta* (☎ (114) 2-18-16) at the corner of Degollado and Coronado, which also delivers; hours are 1 to 10 pm, but it's closed Monday. *Pizzería Tropicana* is at the Plaza Los Cabos mall, opposite the Hotel Fiesta Inn in the zona hotelera.

Jazmín's (☎ (114) 2-17-60), on Morelos between Obregón and Zaragoza, offers a wide variety of tasty breakfasts, lunches and dinners at midrange prices, with excellent but unobtrusive service and, incongruously, a paperback book exchange. *Barra La Navidad*, a bit out of the way on Degollado near Obregón, has outstanding beef but also prepares vegetarian brochettes; it also has outdoor seating.

The *Tropicana Bar & Grill* (☎ (114) 2-09-07), on the streetside face of Hotel Tropicana, is a noisy place with a big, open bar and satellite TV coverage of US sports; the restaurant behind the bar serves a variety of Mexican-American fish and meat dishes, including baby-back ribs and a lobster-steak combination.

Iguana Bar (☎ (114) 2-02-66), across the street from the Tropicana at Blvd Mijares 24, is a popular gathering place for expatriates, with good, moderately priced meals and drinks – but its prices aren't always so moderate as its streetside barkers proclaim. *Nuevo Imperial*, at the corner of Green and Zaragoza, specializes in Cantonese cuisine.

La Fogata, at the corner of Blvd Mijares and Juárez, specializes in beef dishes. *Plaza San José*, on Juárez between Hidalgo and Blvd Mijares, specializes in carnitas.

In a restored 18th-century house facing the plaza, *Damiana* (☎ (114) 2-04-99) is a romantic seafood restaurant with wood-beam ceilings and walls decorated with traditional weavings and painted clay vessels. Cloth napkins, tablecloths and candles decorate the tables for mid- to upper-range meals. Reservations are a good idea at this very highly regarded eatery, open 10:30 am to 10 pm.

El Paraje (☎ (114) 2-12-44), in an attractive adobe with a palapa roof at the corner of Guerrero and Margarita de Juárez, serves outstanding fish, fowl, meat and antojitos. Known as 'The Tree House' to English-speakers, it provides outdoor seating for warm nights, and for fleeing the live entertainment from local Neil Diamond wannabes.

La Cenaduría, on Zaragoza between Hidalgo and Blvd Mijares, is an upscale Mexican restaurant with attractive decor. Equally upscale *Pietro* (☎ (114) 2-05-58), on Zaragoza between Guerrero and Morelos, features Italian cuisine. *La Provence* (☎ (114) 2-33-7), at the corner of Obregón and Morelos, is a spiffy, atmospheric and expensive French restaurant. *Les Ambassadeurs* (☎ (114) 2-38-08), part of the Forum Resort Presidente Los Cabos, is open to the public.

Just Desserts (☎ (114) 2-24-06), Coronado 3 just off Blvd Mijares, has a variety of baked goods, including pies, cookies, muffins and cheesecake, along with espresso. It's closed Sunday.

Helados Bing, on Blvd Mijares at the corner of Doblado, has tasty ice cream, paletas, milkshakes and other cold concoctions. *La Michoacana*, on Morelos between Obregón and Zaragoza, serves the usual excellent aguas and paletas. Almost alongside it, *Los Raspados* is a worthy competitor with outstanding juices and ice cream.

Campers and travelers tired of restaurants can obtain staple items – including North American junk food like Twinkies and M&Ms – at *Almacenes Goncanseco* (☎ (114) 2-00-29), a sizable grocery on Blvd Mijares just north of Doblado.

Entertainment

Noisy nightlife doesn't dominate San José the way it does Cabo San Lucas, but clubs like *Eclipse* (☎ (114) 2-16-94), on Blvd Mijares north of Coronado, satisfy most partygoers. *Piso 2*, on Zaragoza between Guerrero and Morelos, is mostly a sports bar, with a late-afternoon happy hour.

Bones (☎ (114) 2-02-11) is the night-club of the Forum Resort Presidente Los Cabos, but is open to the public (for a cover charge). *La Playita* (☎ (114) 2-37-34), part of its namesake hotel in Pueblo La Playa, offers live jazz several nights weekly.

Things to Buy

From 10 am to 2 pm every Sunday, San José's artists and artisans display and sell their paintings, photographs, sculptures, jewelry and other crafts at the Jardín del Arte in Plaza Mijares.

On Blvd Mijares south of Coronado, market stalls sell souvenirs of generally good quality from throughout Mexico; hammocks are an especially good choice.

Antigua Los Cabos (☎ (114) 2-18-10), in a mission-style building on Zaragoza between Morelos and Hidalgo, offers a nicely displayed selection of handcrafted household items like sturdy glassware, plates, mugs and wall hangings. Copal (☎ (114) 2-30-70), on the eastern side of Plaza Mijares, has a very interesting assortment of crafts, especially masks.

Galería de Arte Da Vinci (☎ (114) 2-12-40), an attractive space at Morelos 11, displays and sells works by local, national and international artists. At the corner of Blvd Mijares and Zaragoza, the Huichol Collection has a virtually museum-quality collection of artifacts from mainland Mexico's indigenous peoples. La Mina, in an imaginative setting on Blvd Mijares between Doblado and Coronado, sells gold and silver jewelry.

Getting There & Away

Air Serving both San José del Cabo and Cabo San Lucas, Aeropuerto Internacional Los Cabos (☎ (114) 2-03-41, (114) 2-21-11) is 6½ miles (10 km) north of town. Mexicana (☎ (114) 2-15-30, (114) 2-06-06 at the airport) is at Plaza Los Cabos between the beachfront Paseo San José and Paseo Los Cabos; most of the other airlines have their offices at the airport itself.

Alaska Airlines (☎ (114) 2-10-15, fax (114) 2-10-16) flies daily to San Diego, three times daily to Los Angeles, daily to San Francisco and daily to Phoenix; there are onward connections to Seattle and Anchorage.

Aero California (☎ (114) 2-09-43, fax (114) 2-09-42) flies at least daily to Los Angeles (twice daily Monday, Thursday, Saturday and Sunday), Phoenix and Denver. Mexicana flies twice daily to Los Angeles and daily to Mexico City, both nonstop and via other mainland Mexican cities; it also flies to Denver Tuesday, Thursday, Saturday and Sunday.

Continental Airlines (☎ (114) 2-38-40) flies daily between Houston and Los Cabos, while America West (☎ (114) 2-28-80) serves Phoenix daily. Aeroméxico (☎ (114) 2-03-41) flies daily to San Diego and also serves many mainland Mexican destinations, with international connections via Mexico City.

American Airlines (☎ (114) 2-27-35) flies to and from Dallas/Fort Worth daily except Tuesday.

Aerolitoral, in the same offices as Mexicana, flies Saturday to La Paz and to Culiacán. Aero California flies to Tijuana via Guadalajara and Culiacán daily except Tuesday and Saturday.

Bus From San José's main bus terminal (☎ (114) 2-11-00), on Valerio González just east of the Transpeninsular, Autobuses San José del Cabo goes to Cabo San Lucas (30 minutes, US$1.25) at least hourly between 6:45 am and 10 pm daily. Autotransportes Aguila goes to La Paz (two hours, US$7) at least seven times daily between 6 am and 7 pm. There are direct buses to Loreto (10 hours, US$11) at 9:30 am and to Tijuana (24 to 26 hours, US$54) at 4 pm daily.

Enlaces Terrestres, on Ibarra between Doblado and Castro, runs buses to and from La Paz only.

Getting Around
San José is small enough to be pedestrian-friendly; even from the zona hotelera, the walk into town takes only a half-hour or so. Outside town, buses, taxis or bicycles may be necessary. The largest taxi stand is on Hidalgo between the church (Iglesia San José) and Plaza Mijares.

To/From the Airport From San José, the government-run company Aeroterrestre (☎ (114) 2-05-55) runs bright-yellow taxis and minibuses to Aeropuerto Internacional Los Cabos for about US$12, divisible by the number of passengers. Top-end hotels often arrange transportation for their guests.

Other options for getting to and from the airport include walking 1½ miles (2.5 km) from the airport terminal to the highway and then flagging down a bus, or taking a local bus from the San José terminal to the airport turnoff (the trip costs less than US$1).

Car Rental The car-rental scene on the Southern Cape is more competitive than elsewhere on the peninsula, and some good deals with unlimited mileage are available. Agencies include:
Dollar
    Transpeninsular just north of the intersection with Valerio González (☎ (114) 2-01-00, (114) 2-06-71 at the airport, fax (114) 2-10-98)
Hertz
    Aeropuerto Internacional Los Cabos (☎ (114) 2-09-19)
National
    Km 238 on the Transpeninsular (☎ (114) 2-24-24, fax (114) 2-01-60)
    Hotel Palmilla, Km 27 on the Transpeninsular (☎ (114) 2-17-07)
Thrifty
    Transpeninsular between Valerio González and Avenida Misiones (☎ (114) 2-16-71, fax (114) 2-38-61)
    Hotel Posada Real on the beach (☎ (114) 2-01-55)
    Blvd Mijares at the corner of Doblado

Bicycle Brisa del Mar Trailer Park (see Places to Stay in this entry) rents mountain bikes for US$15 per day.

AROUND SAN JOSÉ DEL CABO
East of Pueblo La Playa, a dirt road leads east-northeast toward Bahía Los Frailes and Los Barriles, but southeast of the junction with the Palo Escopeta road from San José's international airport, it becomes badly gullied and suitable only for narrow vehicles with short wheelbases. The road may be impassable for all vehicles after any sort of rain.

At Km 90, 10 miles (16 km) east of San José, **Santa Cruz de los Zacatitos** is the site of the first developers' assaults on the Eastern Cape area. Another 2 miles (3 km) east is the nearly identical **Playa Tortuga**, beyond which is **Shipwreck Beach**, a popular surf spot in summer swells. For more information on the Eastern Cape road toward Cabo Pulmo, see the Eastern Cape section in this chapter.

LOS CABOS CORRIDOR
West of San José is a succession of cookie-cutter luxury resorts along the four-lane, divided segment of the Transpeninsular to Cabo San Lucas. Completed in July 1993, large parts of the highway washed away only a few months later during torrential chubasco rains. The bridge across Arroyo El Tulé, built with culverts that clogged with flood debris rather than on pilings that would have let floodwaters pass beneath it, formed a dam that ultimately burst. The two westbound lanes of the bridge were rebuilt, but the eastbound lanes now drop down into the arroyo.

At Km 27 of the Transpeninsular, 3 miles (5 km) southwest of San José, **Playa Palmilla** features a small water-sports and dive shop that rents snorkels, masks, fins and other beach supplies, and also has a compressor for filling air tanks.

Near Hotel Palmilla (see below) are exceptional surfing beaches at Punta Mirador and at Km 28 of the Transpeninsular. Experienced surfers swear that summer reef and point breaks at the latter beach,

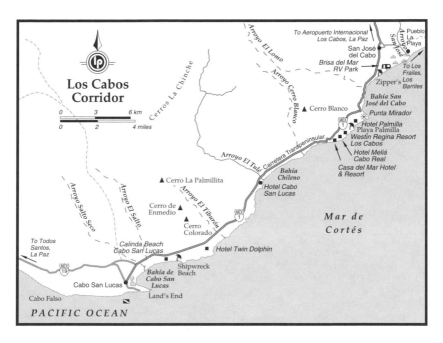

Los Cabos Corridor

popularly known as Zipper's, match the finest in Hawaii. In June and July championship events bring surfers from around the world.

Places to Stay & Eat

Hotel Palmilla (☎ (114) 2-05-82; (714) 833-3033, (800) 637-2226, fax (714) 851-2498 in the USA), at the western end of its namesake beach at Km 27, caters to royalty and movie celebrities, but its daily happy hour offers reasonably priced margaritas and appetizers. Room rates vary according to season and the quality of the room. In-season rates (November 1 to May 31) range from US$290 for a standard room to US$800 for a suite; off-season rates are US$210 to US$600. Rates do not include 12% taxes nor a 15% service charge in lieu of tipping. On weekends a three-day minimum stay is required.

Its *La Paloma* restaurant prepares grilled fish from the catch of the day; a full meal for two including wine averages about US$60, while the 18-hole golf course charges US$99 in summer, US$129 in winter. Hotel guests get a discount, but the course is open to the public. The US mailing address is 4343 Von Karman Ave, Newport Beach, CA 92660-2083.

Almost alongside Hotel Palmilla is the popular *Pepe's* (☎ (114) 4-50-40), specializing in Mexican seafood. The Italian restaurant *Da Giorgio* (☎ (114) 2-19-88), west of the Palmilla at Km 25.5, offers various Italian-style seafood dishes, pizza and pasta at top-end prices. More modest and agreeable, *Zipper's Bar & Grill*, which caters to surfers, specializes in mesquite-grilled beef and has live music Friday nights.

At Km 22.5, the *Westin Regina Resort Los Cabos* (☎ (114) 2-90-00, fax (114) 2-90-10; (800) 228-3000 in the USA and Canada) is yet another megaresort (243 rooms); oxygen aficionados will want to make a special effort to avoid the monthly cigar night at its restaurant, *Arrecifes*. Rates range from US$215 to US$315 single or double; the mailing address is Apdo Postal 145, San José del Cabo, Baja California Sur 23400, México.

At a prime waterfront location at Km 19.5, the five-star *Hotel Meliá Cabo Real* (☎ (114) 3-09-99, fax (114) 3-10-03; (800) 336-3542, fax (305) 530-1626 in the USA) is sister to the Hotel Meliá San Lucas in Cabo San Lucas. This self-contained complex has two restaurants, three bars, a coffee shop, tennis and squash courts, a water-sports center, deep-sea fishing, horseback riding and a golf course (in summer, US$60 for nine holes, US$88 for 18; in winter, US$88 for nine holes, US$143 for 18). In September the hotel sponsors a triathlon.

There are 292 double rooms and seven suites; singles/doubles range from US$202/ $247 in off-season to US$287/332 in peak season (plus 10% tax and service charges), depending on whether the room has an ocean view.

Almost alongside the Meliá, *Casa del Mar Hotel & Resort* (☎ (114) 4-00-30; (800) 221-8808 in the USA) charges US$275 to US$350 in off-season, US$325 to US$385 in peak season, depending on the room. Meals, taxes and service charges are additional.

At Km 14, about 11 miles (18 km) from San José on Bahía Chileno, *Hotel Cabo San Lucas* (☎ (114) 4-00-14) claims to be Mexico's most elegant resort. It is certainly one of the most pretentious, with 2500 acres (1000 hectares) of luxuriant tropical gardens, bogus Aztec fountains, trilevel swimming pools and an Oriental art boutique stuffed with museum-quality pieces. Along with a beachfront water-sports center (operated by Cabo Acuadeportes – see the activities entries for Cabo San Lucas) and cliffside tennis courts, the hotel offers a long list of activities and outings on land and sea. Snorkeling and diving are possible around the offshore reef.

Rates for rooms, studios, suites, townhouses and 'luxurious' villas start around US$155 per night and top out at US$1350 (no typo!) per night for a seven-bedroom

villa. For information, contact Hotel Services in the USA (☎ (213) 655-2323, (800) 733-2226, fax (213) 655-3243), 6523 Wilshire Blvd, Los Angeles, CA 90048.

On secluded Playa Santa María at Km 11.5, *Hotel Twin Dolphin* (☎ (114) 3-02-56, fax (114) 3-04-96 to contact guests only; (213) 386-3940, (800) 421-8925, fax (213) 380-1302 in the USA for reservations) has 44 luxurious rooms and suites overlooking the ocean; facilities include tennis courts, a swimming pool, a water-guzzling golf course, horseback riding and its own sportfishing fleet. In-season (November 1 to May 31) singles/doubles cost US$265 per day plus 10% tax; off-season rates are about one-third cheaper. Its US reservations office can be contacted at the numbers above or at 1625 W Olympic Blvd, Suite 1005, Los Angeles, CA 90015.

Beach access requires walking through the hotel, but as it's on federal land the hotel cannot exclude nonguests (who may not use the hotel's parking lot, however). The Twin Dolphin also arranges fishing charters through Juanita's Fleet (☎ (114) 3-05-22), starting around US$250 per day for up to four people.

At Km 9, people still camp at *Playa Barco Varado*, known to English-speakers as Shipwreck Beach. Shipwreck is accessible via an unmarked dirt road – watch carefully for the turnoff.

At Km 4.5, the *Calinda Beach Cabo San Lucas* (☎ (114) 3-00-44, fax (114) 3-00-77; (800) 228-5151 in the USA) is a cliffside hotel about 3 miles (5 km) east of Cabo San Lucas. It has 125 deluxe air-conditioned rooms, most overlooking the ocean; there are also tennis courts, a restaurant, swimming pools and jacuzzis. The rate structure is a little unusual for the area – singles/ doubles start at US$90 in winter but are unaccountably higher at US$110 the rest of the year.

CABO SAN LUCAS
By reputation, Cabo San Lucas is a world-class resort, but for numerous visitors its quintessential experience might be to stagger out of a bar at 3 am and pass out on

the beach, to be crushed or smothered at daybreak by a developer's rampaging bulldozer. In the past, survivors could call upon the Hacienda Beach Resort's handy therapist 'to help you strengthen, empower and revitalize your life,' but at present they have to settle for the same resort's Michelangelo Plastic Surgery Clinic.

Now a sister city to the equally pretentious Los Angeles suburb of Newport Beach, Cabo's status as a claustrophobic tourist enclave and North American retirement mecca has engendered considerable resentment among Mexicans. On seeing the

onetime fishing village entombed beneath the onslaught of Planet Hollywood, the Hard Rock Café and other vulgar, neon-studded foreign cultural monuments, one might well respond as ill-fated British explorer Robert Falcon Scott did to the South Pole: 'Great God! This is an awful place!'

To all appearances a permanent construction site rather than a part of Mexico or even Baja California, Cabo San Lucas often seems a prison whose inmates are too stunned to realize it has neither walls nor guards to pursue the few who escape to the

I'd Love a Cabo Time-Share, But . . .

Cabo's most sinister bottom feeders are not offshore sharks but real-estate agents and time-share sellers who have metamorphosed a placid, scenic coastal village into a claustrophobic, hedonistic jumble of exorbitant five-star hotels, pretentious restaurants, rowdy bars and tacky souvenir stands – an achievement comparable to turning Cinderella into her stepsisters. No visitor can completely avoid these predators, who may be either gringos or Mexicans, but the following phrases may discourage them:

WAYNE BERNHARDSON

No hablo inglés ni español.	I don't speak English or Spanish.
¿Habla Ud albanés/swahili/tibetano?	Do you speak Albanian/Swahili/Tibetan?
Lo siento, pero el doctor dice que me quedan solo dos meses de vida.	I'm sorry, but the doctor says I have only two months to live.
Lo siento, pero acabo de declarar bancarrota.	I'm sorry, but I've just declared bankruptcy.
Lo siento, pero la DEA confiscó todos mis bienes.	I'm sorry, but the DEA confiscated all my assets.
¿El contrato permite mi víbora cascabel?	Does the contract allow my pet rattlesnake?
Mi abogado dice que no puedo hacer inversiones hasta no cumplir mi libertad condicional.	My lawyer says no more investments until my parole is over.
Si Ud piensa que soy tan estúpido para comprar un tiempo compartido, me gustaría venderle un puente que tengo en Brooklyn.	If you think I'm dumb enough to buy a time-share, I have a bridge in Brooklyn I'd like to sell you.

CAPE REGION

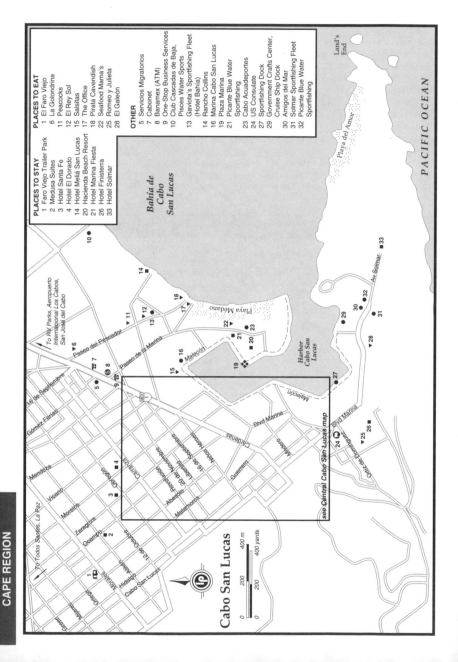

Cabo San Lucas

PACIFIC OCEAN

Land's End

Playa del Amor

Bahía de Cabo San Lucas

Playa Médano

Harbor Cabo San Lucas

Malecón

Blvd Marina

Av. Solmar

see Central Cabo San Lucas map

To RV Parks, Aeropuerto Internacional Los Cabos, San José del Cabo

To Todos Santos, La Paz

16 de Septiembre
Gómez Farias
Mendoza
Vicente
Morelos
Zaragoza
Ocampo
Abasolo
Arriel
12 de Octubre
Hidalgo
Morelos
Guerrero
Ortega
Niños Héroes
Narciso Mendoza
20 de Septiembre
16 de Septiembre
Revolución
Cárdenas
Madero
Matamoros
Guerrero
Blvd Marina
Obregón / Camino

Paseo del Pescador
Paseo de la Marina

PLACES TO STAY
1 Faro Viejo Trailer Park
2 Medusa Suites
3 Hotel Santa Fe
4 Hotel El Dorado
14 Hotel Meliá San Lucas
20 Hacienda Beach Resort
21 Hotel Marina Fiesta
26 Hotel Finisterra
33 Hotel Solmar

PLACES TO EAT
1 El Faro Viejo
6 La Golondrina
11 Peacocks
12 El Rey Sol
15 Salsitas
17 The Office
18 Pirata Cavendish
22 Seafood Mama's
25 Romeo y Julieta
28 El Galeón

OTHER
5 Servicios Migratorios
8 Cabonet
8 Banamex (ATM)
9 One-Stop Business Services
10 Club Cascadas de Baja, Pisces Water Sports
13 Gaviota's Sportfishing Fleet (Hotel Bahía)
14 Rancho Collins
16 Marina Cabo San Lucas
19 Plaza Marina
21 Picante Blue Water Sportfishing
23 Cabo Acuadeportes
24 US Consulate
27 Sportfishing Dock
29 Government Crafts Center, Cruise Ship Dock
30 Amigos del Mar
31 Solmar Sportfishing Fleet
32 Picante Blue Water Sportfishing

0   200   400 m
0   200   400 yards

Cabo San Lucas

delights of the surrounding Cape Region. Only a few blocks inland, away from the harbor, souvenir shops, restaurants, hotels and eternal construction, local people inhabit a different Cabo San Lucas, where burros and swine roam through shantytown gardens and dusty potholed streets punctuated by the occasional government-built prefab.

Even so, the standard of living is higher and unemployment is lower than in most mainland Mexican cities, thanks partly to the fact that, in the year ending November 1996, 452,000 frenzied tourists (versus a permanent population of 28,483) spent US$300 million in a town lacking any semblance of integrity.

Orientation

At the southernmost tip of the Baja Peninsula, Cabo San Lucas is 1059 miles (1694 km) from Tijuana and 137 miles (219 km) from La Paz. After splitting south of La Paz, the paved routes of the Transpeninsular and the Southern Cape Highway (México 19) rejoin at Cabo San Lucas, making a potentially fine bicycle circuit.

North of Lázaro Cárdenas, which leads out of town to the highway junction, Cabo San Lucas has a fairly regular grid pattern. South of Cárdenas, Blvd Marina curves along the harbor's western side toward Land's End.

Very few hotels, restaurants or any other locales have street addresses, and street names are primarily for the benefit of visiting gringos, so it's easiest to locate places by referring to the city map. The densely built-up center has almost no open space except Parque Amelia Wilkes, a plaza honoring a longtime local schoolteacher, on Hidalgo between Madero and Cárdenas.

Information

Several publicity rags, wholly or partly in English, are available free in restaurants and hotel lobbies. Generally more useful for discount coupons than for hard information, they include:

Los Cabos News – a fortnightly bilingual newspaper covering general and tourism-related news in the Los Cabos area

Cabo Life – probably the best of the bunch, a magazine-format monthly for residents and visitors, loaded with the usual tourist-trap and real estate ads but also containing a number of surprisingly well-written and substantive articles on the Los Cabos area. There are exceptions, though, such as an ill-informed attack on critics of the Laguna San Ignacio salt evaporator.

Tourist Office It's hard to walk a block without seeing a sign that says 'Tourist Information,' but don't be deceived – these are people who expect you to sit through four hours of time-share torture in exchange for a round of golf. Cabo does, however, have a new tourist office, the Fondo Mixto de Promoción Turística (☎ (114) 3-41-80) on Madero between Hidalgo and Guerrero, open 9 am to 2 pm and 4 to 7 pm weekdays, 9 am to 1 pm Saturday.

Foreign Consulate The US Consulate (☎ (114) 3-35-66) is on the western side of Blvd Marina, south of Plaza Las Glorias.

Immigration The Servicios Migratorios (☎ (114) 3-01-35) is at the corner of Cárdenas and Gómez Farías.

Money Banca Serfin is at Plaza Aramburo (at the corner of Zaragoza and Cárdenas), Banamex is at the corner of Cárdenas and Paseo de la Marina, and Banco Santander is at the corner of Cárdenas and Calle Cabo San Lucas. Bancomer is on the northern side of Cárdenas between Hidalgo and Guerrero, and Banco Unión is directly across the street from Bancomer. All cash traveler's checks and have ATMs.

Baja Money Exchange, whose most central office is on Plaza Náutica on Blvd Marina next to Café Europa, changes US dollars or traveler's checks at slightly lower rates than the banks and gives cash advances (with very high commissions) on Visa and MasterCard. It keeps much longer hours than the banks, however.

CAPE REGION

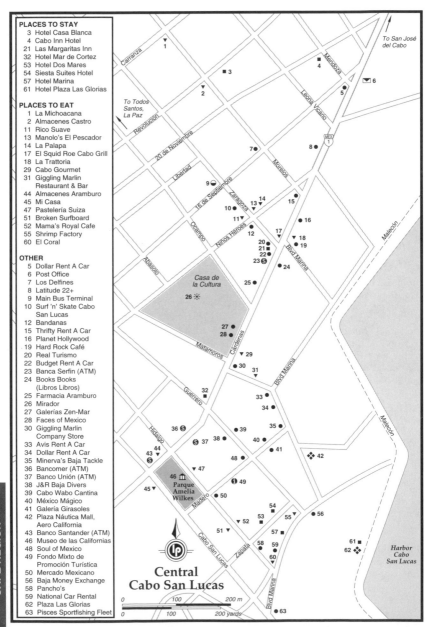

PLACES TO STAY
- 3 Hotel Casa Blanca
- 4 Cabo Inn Hotel
- 21 Las Margaritas Inn
- 32 Hotel Mar de Cortez
- 53 Hotel Dos Mares
- 54 Siesta Suites Hotel
- 57 Hotel Marina
- 61 Hotel Plaza Las Glorias

PLACES TO EAT
- 1 La Michoacana
- 2 Almacenes Castro
- 11 Rico Suave
- 13 Manolo's El Pescador
- 14 La Palapa
- 17 El Squid Roe Cabo Grill
- 18 La Trattoria
- 29 Cabo Gourmet
- 31 Giggling Marlin
  Restaurant & Bar
- 44 Almacenes Aramburo
- 45 Mi Casa
- 47 Pastelería Suiza
- 51 Broken Surfboard
- 52 Mama's Royal Cafe
- 55 Shrimp Factory
- 60 El Coral

OTHER
- 5 Dollar Rent A Car
- 6 Post Office
- 7 Los Delfines
- 8 Latitude 22+
- 9 Main Bus Terminal
- 10 Surf 'n' Skate Cabo
  San Lucas
- 12 Bandanas
- 15 Thrifty Rent A Car
- 16 Planet Hollywood
- 19 Hard Rock Café
- 20 Real Turismo
- 22 Budget Rent A Car
- 23 Banca Serfin (ATM)
- 24 Books Books
  (Libros Libros)
- 25 Farmacia Aramburo
- 26 Mirador
- 27 Galerías Zen-Mar
- 28 Faces of Mexico
- 30 Giggling Marlin
  Company Store
- 33 Avis Rent A Car
- 34 Dollar Rent A Car
- 35 Minerva's Baja Tackle
- 36 Bancomer (ATM)
- 37 Banco Unión (ATM)
- 38 J&R Baja Divers
- 39 Cabo Wabo Cantina
- 40 México Mágico
- 41 Galería Girasoles
- 42 Plaza Náutica Mall,
  Aero California
- 43 Banco Santander (ATM)
- 46 Museo de las Californias
- 48 Soul of Mexico
- 49 Fondo Mixto de
  Promoción Turística
- 50 Mercado Mexicano
- 56 Baja Money Exchange
- 58 Pancho's
- 59 National Car Rental
- 62 Plaza Las Glorias
- 63 Pisces Sportfishing Fleet

CAPE REGION

Central
Cabo San Lucas

To San José
del Cabo

To Todos
Santos,
La Paz

Casa de
la Cultura

Parque
Amelia
Wilkes

Harbor
Cabo
San Lucas

Malecón

Blvd Marina

0   100   200 m
0   100   200 yards

Post & Communications The post office is on the southern side of Cárdenas near the intersection with 16 de Septiembre, on the northeastern approach to downtown. The postal code is 23410.

Numerous long-distance offices have sprung up in stores and pharmacies, but Ladatel long-distance phones are abundant and convenient. One-Stop Business Services (☎ (114) 3-14-74, fax (114) 3-51-47), at the corner of Cárdenas and Paseo de la Marina, has phone, fax and email services, as does Cabonet (☎ (114) 3-01-20), half a block northeast.

Travel Agencies Real Turismo (☎ (114) 3-16-96) is in the Plaza Aramburo mall at the corner of Cárdenas and Zaragoza. Los Delfines (☎ (114) 3-30-96, fax (114) 3-13-97), at Morelos and 16 de Septiembre, publishes current flight schedules in *Los Cabos News*.

Bookstore Books Books (☎ (114) 3-31-71), known in Spanish as Libros Libros, in the Plaza Bonita mall at the junction of Blvd Marina and Cárdenas, carries a selection of coffee-table books on Baja California, potboiler novels and popular magazines in English, as well as the odd Lonely Planet guide.

Medical Services Cabo's IMSS hospital (☎ (114) 3-14-44) is at Km 3 of México 19, the highway to Todos Santos. A decent pharmacy, Farmacia Aramburo, is on Cárdenas near Ocampo.

If before going you need to contact the Hacienda Beach Resort's Michelangelo Plastic Surgery Clinic (☎ (114) 3-43-03, fax (114) 3-43-91), its US number is (seriously!) ☎ (800) FUNCABO.

Things to See
The INAH-sponsored **Museo de las Californias** is, at this point, an inadequate effort at providing the city a sorely needed sense of history, but it bears watching. It's in the former Aero California offices in Parque Amelia Wilkes.

The local **Casa de la Cultura** has little to interest foreign visitors, but its hilltop **mirador** offers outstanding panoramas of the town. The main entrance is on Niños Héroes between Matamoros and Ocampo; admission is free.

West of town, the **Faro Viejo** is Cabo San Lucas' abandoned historic lighthouse. The best ways to reach the lighthouse are by foot or by horseback tour (see the activities entries, below); visitors should consciously avoid ATV tours, which tear up the delicate dune ecology and, according to INAH research, also damage possible archaeological sites.

Beaches
Several good beaches are within walking distance of central Cabo San Lucas, but the best are outside town. For sunbathing and calm waters, **Playa Médano**, in front of the Hacienda Beach Resort, is ideal. **Playa Solmar**, on the Pacific side, has a reputation for unpredictable, dangerous breakers that drown several unsuspecting tourists every year. Nearly unspoiled **Playa del Amor** (Lover's Beach), near Land's End, is accessible by boat or a class 3 scramble over the rocks (at least at high tide) from Hotel Solmar.

For beaches between Cabo San Lucas and San José del Cabo, see the Los Cabos Corridor entry in this chapter.

Boat Trips
Most hotels and travel agencies can book trips to El Arco (the natural arch at Land's End), the local sea lion colony and Playa del Amor on the yacht *Trinidad* (☎ (114) 3-14-17) and other boats for about US$15 to US$30 per hour. Dos Mares (☎ (114) 3-32-66) sails glass-bottomed boats every 20 minutes from 9 am to 4 pm from the Plaza Las Glorias dock, and will drop off and pick up passengers on Playa del Amor (US$6).

From the dock at Plaza Las Glorias, the catamarans *Pez Gato I* and *Pez Gato II* (☎ (114) 3-24-58, (114) 3-37-97) offer two-hour sunset sails that, faithful to Cabo's schizophrenic ethos, are segregated into 'booze cruises' and 'romantic cruises.'

Both feature open bars and cost about US$30 for adults, US$15 for children. Pez Gato also runs four-hour snorkeling tours for US$50, departing from the Hacienda Beach Resort. Amigos del Mar (see the Diving entry, below) offers similar cruises for US$25, plus snorkeling and whale-watching (in season).

The semisubmersible *Nautilus VII* (☎ (114) 3-22-00) offers one-hour tours of the offshore marine sanctuary, with a chance to view whales, dolphins and sea turtles, for US$25 for adults, US$15 for children. Make reservations at Plaza Las Glorias, Local A-5.

Diving

Among the best diving areas are Roca Pelícano (where Jacques Cousteau filmed a documentary on the spectacular underwater sand falls), the sea lion colony off the tip of Land's End, the reef off Playa Chileno and the more distant Gordo Banks. Some divers have complained of poor underwater visibility near Land's End and claim that tourist hotels have dumped raw sewage into the bay. Local residents report that this situation has abated, but ask dive shops about water conditions and sewage.

Cabo's numerous dive shops are clustered mostly in and around the Blvd Marina malls, but some have additional offices in or near major hotels. Two-tank dives cost around US$75, introductory courses around US$100 and full-certification courses from US$350 to US$400. Rental equipment is readily available at reasonable prices.

Amigos del Mar (☎ (114) 3-05-05, fax (114) 3-08-07; (800) 447-8999 in the USA) is near the sportfishing dock at the southern end of Blvd Marina. Amigos' mailing address is Apdo Postal 43, Cabo San Lucas, Baja California Sur 23410, México.

Cabo Acuadeportes (☎ (114) 3-01-17), next to the Hotel Cabo San Lucas on Playa Chileno and in front of the Hacienda Beach Resort in town, is open 9 am to 5 pm daily. Its postal address is

Apdo Postal 136, Cabo San Lucas, Baja California Sur 23410, México.

Cabo Diving Services (☎ (114) 3-16-58), in Plaza Las Glorias on Blvd Marina, is open 9 am to 7 pm daily. Other services in Plaza Las Glorias include Neptune Divers (☎ (114) 3-34-00), Land's End Divers (☎ (114) 3-22-00) at Local A-6, Pacific Coast Adventures (☎ (114) 3-10-70, fax (114) 3-39-22) and Baja Dive Expeditions.

Underwater Diversions (☎ (114) 3-40-04, (114) 3-24-84; (714) 728-1026 in mainland California) is in the Plaza Marina, Local F-5. J&R Baja Divers (☎ /fax (114) 3-15-45) is on Guerrero opposite Cabo Wabo Cantina. Andromeda Divers (☎ (114) 3-27-65) is at Playa Médano alongside The Office restaurant.

Fishing

For a summary of local game-fish species and their seasons, see the San José del Cabo entry. The various fleets' prices for fishing excursions are similar, though short-term visitors sometimes find good-value packages through places like Hotel Solmar, which has its own sportfishing fleet (see Places to Stay, below).

Minerva's Baja Tackle (☎ (114) 3-12-82, fax (114) 3-04-40), at the corner of Madero and Blvd Marina, charters fishing boats and rents gear. Rates start around US$25 to US$30 per hour for pangas, with a four- to six-hour minimum for three people; 28-foot cruisers that can take four passengers cost US$275 to US$350 per day. Sportfisher 31-footers can take five or six for US$400 to US$500 per day.

Near the southern end of Blvd Marina, Solmar Sportfishing Fleet (☎ (114) 3-35-35, fax (114) 3-04-10; (310) 459-9861, (800) 344-3349 in the USA) has a 12-boat fleet and will arrange special charters as well; its mailing address is Apdo Postal 8, Cabo San Lucas, Baja California Sur 23410, México.

Pisces Sportfishing Fleet (☎ (114) 3-12-88, fax (114) 3-05-88) is on Blvd Marina at the corner of Calle Cabo San Lucas. Its mailing address is Apdo Postal

137, Cabo San Lucas, Baja California Sur 23410, México.

Picante Blue Water Sportfishing (☎ (114) 3-24-74; (909) 931-2511, fax (909) 931-2513 in mainland California) is in the Hotel Marina Fiesta (see Places to Stay, below) and on Avenida Solmar. Its US mailing address is 1589 W 9th St, Suite H, Upland, CA 91786.

Gaviota's Sportfishing Fleet (☎ (114) 3-04-30, fax (114) 3-04-97) is at the Hotel Bahía, Suite 526. Its local mailing address is Apdo Postal 144, Cabo San Lucas, Baja California Sur 23410, México; the US mailing address is 9245 Jamacha Blvd, Spring Valley, CA 91977.

Horseback Riding
Rancho Collins (☎ (114) 3-36-52), at the Hotel Meliá San Lucas (see Places to Stay, below), offers one- to 1½-hour beach rides for US$20 to US$25 and longer sunset tours to the Faro Viejo (the old lighthouse) for US$45. Hours are 8 am to noon and 2 to 6 pm.

Surfing
For suggestions on surf spots on the western coast, visit Surf 'n' Skate Cabo San Lucas (☎ (114) 3-04-65) on Zaragoza between 16 de Septiembre and Niños Héroes.

Water Sports
Equipment for kayaking, windsurfing, snorkeling and the like is available from Pisces Water Sports (☎ (114) 8-75-30) alongside Club Cascadas de Baja. Its mailing address is Apdo Postal 508, Cabo San Lucas, Baja California Sur 23410, México. One-person kayaks cost US$10 per hour, two-person kayaks US$15; windsurfing equipment costs US$20 per hour, while snorkel gear runs US$12 daily. Three-hour snorkel trips cost US$20.

Whale-Watching
Aero Calafia (☎ (114) 3-43-02, (114) 3-42-55), in Plaza Las Glorias, operates charter tours to whale-watching destinations at Puerto San Carlos. Its trips are expensive at US$290 per person, but its occasional half-price and two-for-one discounts are worth considering.

Cabo Yacht Charters (☎ (114) 3-05-41), at the Plaza Las Glorias Beach Club in front of the Hacienda Beach Resort, runs two-hour whale-watching trips on the 45-foot *Jade* for US$30. Don't expect too much – in the Los Cabos area you'll usually see whales only from a distance, though the humpbacks in the area can make the experience worthwhile. Other possibilities are Sunrider (☎ (114) 3-22-52) at the Plaza Las Glorias dock and Pez Gato (see the Boat Trips entry, above).

Special Events
Cabo San Lucas has several popular annual events, including many fishing tournaments. The town celebrates **Día de San Lucas** on October 18; one of few truly local celebrations, this is the festival of the town's patron saint. The **Cabo San Lucas Gold Cup**, held in late October, is a less serious event than other Cabo fishing tournaments. In October or November **Bisbee's Black & Blue Marlin Jackpot Tournament** is held, and proceeds from it go to Cabo's Escuela El Camino, a local school; entry fees are US$2000 per four-person team. Proceeds from the **Pete Lopiccola Memorial Marlin Tournament**, held in October or early November, go to leukemia research.

Places to Stay
Except for campgrounds and RV parks, budget and even midrange accommodations are scarce in Cabo San Lucas. Visitors unsure about staying here might prefer San José del Cabo, where lodging is cheaper and day trips to Cabo San Lucas are still convenient.

Places to Stay – budget
Camping In theory, local officials have banned free camping at sites like *Playa Arroyo Salto Seco* just east of the exclusive Club Cascadas de Baja; people still camp here, but the site has no services and is very dirty.

The most congenial camping, with dependable services, is at Dutch-operated *Surf Camp Club Cabo* (☎ (114) 3-33-48), about 1 mile (1.6 km) east of Club Cascadas de Baja by a narrow dirt road. Full hookups are available, but tent campers are equally welcome. It charges US$10 per site; a cabaña and two kitchenette apartments are available for US$39 single or double.

El Arco Trailer Park (☎ (114) 3-16-86), overlooking Cabo San Lucas from a mesa 3 miles (5 km) west of town, has 85 spaces with full hookups and hot showers for US$10 per vehicle site or tent. Its restaurant serves standard antojitos and more elaborate dishes like steak and scampi.

Inconspicuous *Faro Viejo Trailer Park* (☎ (114) 3-05-61, fax (114) 3-42-11), difficult to find on Morales between Matamoros and Abasolo, about 1 mile (1.6 km) northeast of downtown, has RV sites with full hookups for US$12. Given its limited shade and messy bathrooms, the park is overpriced despite having one of Cabo's best restaurants (see Places to Eat, below).

About 2 miles (3 km) east of town on the Transpeninsular, *Vagabundos del Mar RV Park* (☎ (114) 3-02-90, fax (114) 3-05-11) has occasional openings for about US$15; facilities include full hookups, a swimming pool, drinking water and an ice machine. Just east of Vagabundos, *Cabo Cielo* (☎ (114) 3-07-21, fax (114) 3-25-27) is a mostly barren, graded area; the sites along its eastern edge, however, are shady and have full hookups, and the spotless bathrooms have excellent hot showers. Fees are US$10 per site.

Hotels For US$17/20 single/double, the lowest rates in town, rundown but passable *Hotel Casa Blanca* (☎ (114) 3-02-60), on Revolución near Morelos, provides clean but dark rooms with concrete floors, lukewarm showers and ceiling fans. Up the block, on Morelos between Carranza and Obregón, *Hotel El Dorado* (☎ (114) 3-28-10, fax (114) 3-00-25) is probably the best value in town for US$22 double.

Places to Stay – middle
The water pressure is problematical at *Hotel Marina* (☎ (114) 3-14-99, fax (114) 3-24-84), on Blvd Marina near Guerrero, which has modest, motel-style, air-conditioned rooms clustered around a small swimming pool. Rates are US$30/50. The *Hotel Dos Mares* (☎ /fax (114) 3-03-30), on Zapata between Hidalgo and Guerrero, charges US$35/40 but is mediocre for the price.

Rooms in the older part of pseudo-colonial *Hotel Mar de Cortez* (☎ (114) 3-00-32, fax (114) 3-02-32; (408) 663-5803, (800) 347-8821, fax (408) 663-1904 in the USA), at Cárdenas and Guerrero, are a good value for US$33/37 plus taxes in peak season; rooms in the newer section go for US$43/47, while suites cost US$47/54. Off-season rates (June to mid-October) are about 25% less. There's also a swimming pool and an outdoor bar/restaurant. Make reservations at the hotel's US representative at the numbers above or by writing 17561 Vierra Canyon Rd, Suite 99, Salinas, CA 93907.

A new entry in the hotel scene is the *Cabo Inn Hotel* (☎ /fax (114) 3-08-19) on 20 de Noviembre between Mendoza and Leona Vicario; it charges US$39 double plus taxes, and US$10 more in peak season. Monthly and weekly rates are also available. The US mailing address is 9051-C Siempre Viva Rd, Suite 40-143, San Diego, CA 92173-3628.

The sparkling *Siesta Suites Hotel* (☎ /fax (114) 3-27-73; (909) 945-5940 in mainland California), on Zapata between Hidalgo and Guerrero, has one-bedroom apartments with fully equipped kitchenette for US$50 double plus tax; each additional person pays US$10. The local mailing address is Apdo Postal 310, Cabo San Lucas, Baja California Sur 23410, México.

Away from the madness of central Cabo, the *Medusa Suites* (☎ (114) 3-34-92, fax (114) 3-08-80), at the corner of Ocampo and Alikán, advertises junior suites with air-con, color TV, telephone and full kitchen for US$50 per night. *Las Margaritas Inn* (☎ (114) 3-22-50, fax

(114) 3-04-50), in the Plaza Aramburo mall at Zaragoza and Cárdenas, is comparable in price and amenities.

At *Hotel Santa Fe* (☎ (114) 3-44-01, fax (114) 3-25-52), a newer place at the corner of Zaragoza and Obregón, double rooms cost US$75. All 46 rooms have kitchenette, air-con, satellite TV and other amenities.

Places to Stay – top end

Just off Blvd Marina, cliffside *Hotel Finisterra* (☎ (114) 3-33-33, fax (114) 3-05-90) is a luxury hotel with both ocean and harbor views. Doubles start around US$120 plus service charges and taxes in the off-season; at the winter peak, prices are about 25% higher. All rooms are air-conditioned and a few have a fireplace; facilities include three swimming pools, tennis courts, a restaurant/bar and a travel desk. Its Whale-Watcher Bar, on the Pacific side, is ideal for viewing sunsets and, from January to March, spotting the occasional passing cetacean. For reservations, contact Baja Hotels in the USA (☎ (714) 450-9000, (800) 347-2252, fax (714) 450-9010), 6 Jenner, Suite 120, Irvine, CA 92618.

Hotel Solmar (☎ (114) 3-00-22; (310) 459-9861, (800) 344-3349 in the USA), on the Pacific side of Cabo San Lucas, is a secluded, stone-walled beachfront resort whose air-conditioned rooms face the ocean. Amenities include tennis courts, horseback riding and a swimming pool. Singles/doubles start at US$130 off-season (June 1 to October 1) plus 10% room tax and 10% service (for the room, meals and other gratuities). Various package deals include fishing trips and outside restaurant meals. For more information, contact Hotel Solmar at the numbers above or at PO Box 383, Pacific Palisades, CA 90272.

Alongside the harbor, the *Hotel Marina Fiesta* (☎ (114) 3-26-89, fax (114) 3-26-88) is yet another overpriced resort, with rates starting around US$152 double for a junior suite. *Hotel Plaza Las Glorias* (☎ (114) 3-12-20, fax (114) 3-12-38), on the harbor, is comparable for US$181.

The *Hacienda Beach Resort* (☎ (114) 3-01-22) is a resplendent, five-star luxury hotel in a Spanish-hacienda style with fountains and tropical gardens. Cabo Acuadeportes operates a water-sports center on the beach in front of the hotel; other facilities include tennis and paddle-tennis courts, a swimming pool and a putting green. Garden patio rooms start around US$125, but rise rapidly for oceanview rooms (US$185), beach cabañas (US$210), deluxe suites (US$235) and townhouses (US$255 to US$335 for up to four people). Taxes, service and meals are additional. The US contact is Hotel Services Corporation (☎ (213) 655-2323, (800) 733-2226, fax (213) 655-3243), PO Box 48872, Los Angeles, CA 90048.

At Playa Médano, *Hotel Meliá San Lucas* (☎ (114) 3-44-44, fax (114) 3-04-22; (800) 336-3542, fax (305) 530-1626 in the USA), run by the Madrid-based Compañía Meliá, is a huge, quasi-Spanish, orange stucco edifice. Spacious, well-decorated rooms have air-con, minirefrigerator, safe and TV, and most also have a balcony or patio. This five-star complex has five-star rates – depending on the season, rooms start around US$190/200 to US$265/275 plus 20% in tax and service.

Places to Eat

Cabo's countless restaurants, with prices much higher than elsewhere in Baja, cater to tourists. One of downtown's few genuine budget choices, the *Broken Surfboard* on the western side of Hidalgo between Madero and Zapata, prepares burritos, hamburgers, fish with rice, salads, tortillas and beans and a few other items. It has sidewalk seating. *Cabo Gourmet* (☎ (114) 3-45-55), on Cárdenas between Matamoros and Ocampo, provides takeout meals of exceptional quality, including outstanding sandwiches, cold cuts and cheeses.

An excellent breakfast choice, *Pastelería Suiza* (☎ (114) 3-34-94), on Hidalgo opposite Parque Amelia Wilkes, sells bread, bagels, pastries and pies. Well-established *Mama's Royal Cafe*, on Hidalgo between Madero and Zapata, is another outstanding breakfast choice. Highly regarded *Salsitas* (☎ (114) 3-17-40), in the Plaza Bonita mall on Blvd Marina just south of Cárdenas, serves very fine breakfasts and Mexican specialties.

For fine but reasonably priced seafood, try modest but friendly *Manolo's El Pescador* at the corner of Zaragoza and Niños Héroes; two doors east, *La Palapa* draws big crowds for more expensive seafood dinners that are still a good value. The Italian favorite *La Trattoria* (☎ (114) 3-00-68) is on Cárdenas near Blvd Marina, wedged between Planet Hollywood and the Hard Rock Cafe.

El Coral (☎ (114) 3-01-50), at the corner of Blvd Marina and Hidalgo, proclaims its 'authentic Mexican food,' but its cheap double margaritas and similar drinks are a better value than its rather ordinary meals. Breakfast is available any time, day or night, but Coral adds a 6% surcharge to credit-card purchases. The *Shrimp Factory* (☎ (114) 3-11-47), on Blvd Marina near Guerrero, specializes in seafood.

The moderately priced *Giggling Marlin Restaurant & Bar* (☎ (114) 3-06-06), on Matamoros just southeast of Cárdenas, is popular for partying, but the food, except for the appetizers, is mediocre. After imbibing enough alcohol, particularly during the 2 to 6 pm happy hour, patrons appear to enjoy being hoisted like trophy marlins and photographed in the act! *El Squid Roe Cabo Grill* (☎ (114) 3-06-55), on Cárdenas between Morelos and Zaragoza, is one of countless Carlos 'n' Charlie's restaurants; with casual decor, it's better known as a gringo watering hole than for its fairly ordinary food.

El Faro Viejo (☎ (114) 3-19-27), inside its namesake trailer park at Matamoros and Morales, lures gringos from their beachfront hotels for barbecued ribs, steaks and seafood. Prices are upscale, but some go out of their way to dine here. Now under the same management, *La Golondrina* (☎ (114) 3-05-42), one of Cabo's prettiest restaurants, was one of few buildings left standing after a flood devastated most of the town in 1906. Meals are expensive, but portions are large. It's on Paseo del Pescador just south of Cárdenas, across from the Pemex station near the northeastern approach to town.

El Rey Sol (☎ (114) 3-11-17), two blocks south of La Golondrina, serves appealing Mexican food and seafood from breakfast (try machaca and eggs) to dinner (fish cooked to order and garlic shrimp); prices are moderate by Cabo standards. Other restaurants in the vicinity include *Peacocks* (☎ (114) 3-15-58), *Pirata Cavendish* (☎ (114) 3-09-41) for seafood, and *The Office* (☎ (114) 3-34-64), with tables right on the beach, as well as *Seafood Mama's* (☎ (114) 3-12-20), known for seafood and salads.

Rotunda-shaped *El Galeón* (☎ (114) 3-04-43), on Blvd Marina near Avenida Solmar, specializes in mesquite-grilled lobster and beef. *Mi Casa* (☎ (114) 3-19-33), on Calle Cabo San Lucas just across from Parque Amelia Wilkes, features a pleasant, homelike environment and excellent Mexican and seafood specialties. *Romeo y Julieta* (☎ (114) 3-02-05), just west of the point where Blvd Marina turns east toward Land's End, is a local institution for its pizza and pasta; it's open 4 to 11 pm only.

Almacenes Castro (☎ (114) 3-05-66), a supermarket at the corner of Revolución and Morelos, is a junk-food paradise with shelf upon shelf of sterile pretzels, potato chips and peanuts, as well as produce, canned goods and pastas. Campers and boaters can stock up on staples here, but *Almacenes Aramburo* (☎ (114) 3-00-16), at the corner of Hidalgo and Cárdenas, has a larger selection.

La Michoacana, at the corner of Morelos and Carranza, serves the usual superb aguas and paletas. *Rico Suave*, on Zaragoza just north of Niños Héroes, features outstanding juices.

Entertainment

Bars Gold records and rock 'n' roll photos line the walls of *Cabo Wabo Cantina* (☎ (114) 3-11-88) on Guerrero between Madero and Cárdenas, which features live music from late at night to early in the morning, serves palatable if undistinguished food and occasionally sponsors special events like a blues festival.

Barhoppers will reportedly find Mexico's largest selection of tequilas at *Pancho's* (☎ (114) 3-09-73) on Hidalgo between Zapata and Blvd Marina, whose dinner menu is also extensive. At the corner of Zaragoza and Niños Héroes, *Bandanas* is another popular tequila spot.

The mega-transnational bar scene has clobbered Cabo hard with the arrival of *Planet Hollywood* (☎ (114) 3-39-19) and the *Hard Rock Café* (☎ (114) 3-37-79), both in the Plaza Bonita mall. *Latitude 22+* (☎ (114) 3-15-16), on Cárdenas between Morelos and Leona Vicario, fits here as well because it admits to the worst food in town.

Betting At the Plaza Náutica shopping center and at the Hotel Plaza Las Glorias, *LF Caliente* (☎ (114) 3-28-66) accepts bets for horse and greyhound racetracks as well as football, basketball, baseball, boxing and hockey in the USA. Several big-screen TVs are available for watching these events.

Things to Buy

Cabo's most comprehensive shopping area is the sprawling Mercado Mexicano at the corner of Madero and Hidalgo, containing dozens of stalls with crafts from all around the country. Other nearby places worth exploring are México Mágico on Madero between Guerrero and Blvd Marina, Soul of Mexico at the corner of Madero and Guerrero, and Galería Girasoles (a clothes and crafts outlet) on Madero between Guerrero and Blvd Marina.

Faces of Mexico, on Cárdenas between Matamoros and Ocampo, has a good selection of artisanal goods, including spectacular masks. Galerías Zen-Mar (☎ (114) 3-06-61), almost next door, offers Zapotec Indian weavings, bracelets and masks, as well as traditional crafts from other mainland Indian peoples. At the corner of Matamoros and Cárdenas, the Giggling Marlin Company Store offers souvenirs whose main purpose is to promote the overrated bar/restaurant.

One local specialty is handcrafted black-coral jewelry, available at a state-owned store at Cabo's cruise ship dock, but tourists should avoid buying this product, which will be confiscated at US ports of entry without the appropriate export permit from Mexico City. For information on export permits, see the Things to Buy entry in the Facts for the Visitor chapter.

Getting There & Away

Air The nearest commercial airport is north of San José del Cabo; see the San José Getting There & Away entry for detailed information on airlines and flight schedules.

Aero California's main office (☎ (114) 3-37-00, fax (114) 3-08-27) has moved to the Plaza Náutica mall on Blvd Marina near Madero. Hours are 8:30 am to 6:30 pm Monday to Saturday, 9 am to 3 pm Sunday. All other airlines have their offices in San José or at the airport proper.

Bus The main bus terminal (☎ (114) 3-04-00, (114) 3-50-20) is at the corner of Zaragoza and 16 de Septiembre. Autotransportes Aguila buses leave the terminal for San José del Cabo (US$2) 11 times daily between 7 am and 10:15 pm, for La Paz via Todos Santos (US$6) eight times daily between 6 am and 6 pm and for La Paz via San José del Cabo (US$8) six times daily between 7 am and 6:30 pm.

Autotransportes de La Paz has a separate terminal at the junction of México 19 and the Cabo bypass, as does Enlaces Terrestres. These buses, with fares similar to Aguila's, only go to La Paz.

Getting Around

To/From the Airport The government-regulated airport minibus (☎ (114) 3-12-20) leaves Plaza Las Glorias at 9 and 11 am, noon and 1 and 3 pm. The fare is US$10 per person, but shared taxis (☎ (114) 3-00-90) for US$20 can be a cheaper alternative for groups larger than two people.

Car Rental Car-rental agencies in town include:

Avis
    Matamoros at the corner of Blvd Marina
    (☎ (114) 3-46-07)
Budget
    Plaza Aramburo at the corner of Cárdenas
    and Zaragoza (☎ (114) 3-02-41)
    Hacienda Beach Resort (☎ (114) 3-02-51);
    both offices open 7 am to 7 pm daily
Dollar
    Cárdenas and Mendoza (☎ (114) 3-12-60)
    Hotel Plaza Las Glorias
    Blvd Marina between Matamoros
    and Madero
National
    Blvd Marina at the corner of Hidalgo,
    alongside the El Coral restaurant
    (☎ (114) 3-14-14, fax (114) 3-14-16)
Thrifty
    Cárdenas and Morelos (☎ (114) 3-16-66)
    Hacienda Beach Resort (☎ (114) 3-16-67)
    Hotel Cabo San Lucas, Km 14 on the
    Transpeninsular

Taxi Taxis are plentiful but lack meters and are not cheap; fares for destinations within town should average about US$3 to US$5.

Western Cape

The Western Cape, from Todos Santos south along the Southern Cape Highway (México 19), has so far been spared the grotesque overdevelopment of Cabo San Lucas, but subdivision signs continue to sprout along its sandy Pacific beaches. The near absence of potable water may yet save the area.

TODOS SANTOS
In recent years the placid historical village of Todos Santos has seen a major influx of North American expatriates, including artists for whom Santa Fe and Taos have grown too large and impersonal. In 1985 the completion of the paved Southern Cape Highway (México 19) through Todos Santos created a straighter and quicker western alternative to Cabo San Lucas than the serpentine Transpeninsular, improving

access to beaches south of town. Nevertheless, Todos Santos proper remains a charming destination unlikely to follow the example of overdeveloped Cabo.

It's not all utopia for resident gringos, though, as a new La Paz immigration officer has begun to clamp down on those she feels are taking advantage of Mexican immigration laws; the controversy even led to cancellation of Todos Santos' trademark art festival in 1997. The word is that, rather than struggling artists, officials may prefer retired folks with lots of money – perhaps like metal screamer Iggy Pop who, though not retired, owns property in the area (if Iggy stays true to his roots, expect a Michigan-style trailer park any day now).

History
Founded in 1724 as a Jesuit *visita* (outstation) dependent on La Paz, Misión Santa Rosa de Todos Los Santos became a full-fledged mission a decade later, but a two-year Pericú rebellion nearly destroyed it. When the La Paz mission was abandoned in 1749, it became Misión Nuestra Señora del Pilar de Todos Santos. Epidemics killed Indians relocated from San Luis Gonzaga and La Pasión, and Todos Santos then limped along until its abandonment in 1840.

In the late 19th century, the former colonial village became a prosperous cane-milling town with four red-brick *trapiches* (mills) producing the dark sugar known as *panocha*. The first mill was shipped from San Francisco to Cabo San Lucas and then overland to Todos Santos. Depleted aquifers eliminated most of the thirsty sugar industry, though mills still operate in nearby Pescadero and San Jacinto. Some farmers have instituted multicropping methods to grow fruits and vegetables with less reliance on chemical fertilizers.

Despite its small size, Todos Santos has given many notable historical figures to the peninsula and Mexico at large. Among them are General Manuel Márquez de León (who fought against the French intervention of 1861 and later, less heroically, led a Sinaloa rebellion against Porfirio Díaz

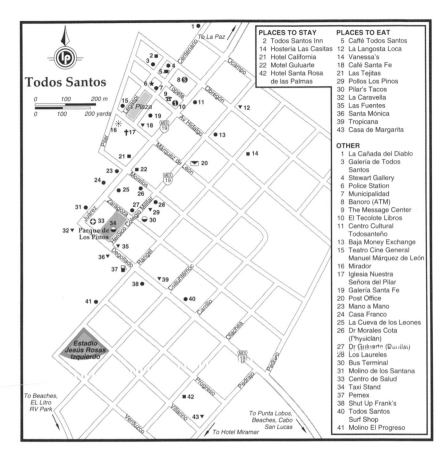

Todos Santos

PLACES TO STAY	PLACES TO EAT
2 Todos Santos Inn	5 Caffé Todos Santos
14 Hostería Las Casitas	12 La Langosta Loca
21 Hotel California	14 Vanessa's
22 Motel Guluarte	18 Café Santa Fe
42 Hotel Santa Rosa	21 Las Tejitas
de las Palmas	29 Pollos Los Pinos
	30 Pilar's Tacos
	32 La Caravella
	35 Las Fuentes
	36 Santa Mónica
	39 Tropicana
	43 Casa de Margarita

OTHER
1 La Cañada del Diablo
3 Galería de Todos
     Santos
4 Stewart Gallery
6 Police Station
7 Municipalidad
8 Banoro (ATM)
9 The Message Center
10 El Tecolote Libros
11 Centro Cultural
     Todosanteño
13 Baja Money Exchange
15 Teatro Cine General
     Manuel Márquez de León
16 Mirador
17 Iglesia Nuestra
     Señora del Pilar
19 Galería Santa Fe
20 Post Office
23 Mano a Mano
24 Casa Franco
25 La Cueva de los Leones
26 Dr Morales Cota
     (Physician)
27 Dr Guluarte (Dentist)
28 Los Laureles
30 Bus Terminal
31 Molino de los Santana
33 Centro de Salud
34 Taxi Stand
37 Pemex
38 Shut Up Frank's
40 Todos Santos
     Surf Shop
41 Molino El Progreso

when he felt insufficiently rewarded for his support of Díaz), Colonel Clodomiro Cota Márquez (also active against the French intervention), General Agustín Olachea Avilés and General Melitón Albañez (notable participants in the Mexican Revolution) and Dionisia Villarino Espinoza (a heroine of the Revolution).

Orientation
Like many Mexican towns, Todos Santos has a fairly regular grid plan, but local residents rely more on landmarks than street names for directions (though street names do exist).

Information
On sale at El Tecolote Libros, Todos Santos' de facto tourist office (see below), is Lee Moore's thorough *The Todos Santos Book*, with up-to-date local information on everything from the best restaurants and art galleries to how to contact a local *curandero* (Mexican folk healer).

Tourist Office El Tecolote Libros, an English-language bookstore, distributes a very detailed (some might say cluttered) town map and a sketched map of nearby beach areas. It's in a cluster of stores at the corner of Juárez and Avenida Hidalgo.

CAPE REGION

Money Banoro, at the corner of Juárez and Obregón, changes US dollars (but not traveler's checks) weekday mornings. At the time of this writing, the bank appeared to be installing an ATM. Los Laureles, at the corner of Heróico Colegio Militar and Morelos, also changes money, as does Baja Money Exchange at the corner of Heróico Colegio Militar and Avenida Hidalgo.

Post & Communications The post office is on Heróico Colegio Militar between Avenida Hidalgo and Márquez de León. The postal code is 23300.

The Message Center (☎ (114) 5-02-88, fax (114) 5-00-03), adjacent to El Tecolote Libros at the corner of Juárez and Avenida Hidalgo, provides phone, fax and message services.

Bookstore El Tecolote Libros maintains an outstanding selection of English-language books and magazines, specializing in Baja California; it also carries a selection of Lonely Planet guides. A two-for-one paperback book exchange is available.

Medical Services Todos Santos' Centro de Salud (☎ (114) 5-00-95) is at the corner of Juárez and Degollado. There is a private physician, Dr José Ramón Morales Cota, on Morelos between Juárez and Heróico Colegio Militar, and a good dentist, Dr Antonio Guluarte (☎ (114) 5-00-51), at the corner of Heróico Colegio Militar and Zaragoza.

Things to See
The restored **Teatro Cine General Manuel Márquez de León** (☎ (114) 5-01-22), on the northern side of the plaza, no longer shows films, but occasional live concerts and other performances still take place.

Murals at the **Centro Cultural Todosanteño**, Todos Santos' former schoolhouse (Escuela General Melitón Albañez) and current cultural center, on Juárez near Topete, date from 1933; their nationalist and revolutionary motifs depict missionaries and Indians, the Spanish conquistadores, Emiliano Zapata, cooperativism, rural laborers, industry, athletics ('vigor in mind and muscle') and 'emancipation of the rural spirit.' Scenes of the Revolution along the northern colonnade have faded, but restoration appears to be underway.

Scattered around Todos Santos are the remains of former mills, including **Molino El Progreso** alongside El Molino Trailer Park and **Molino de los Santana** on Juárez opposite the clinic. **Molino Cerro Verde** and **Molino Jesús Amador** are on the northern outskirts of town.

Beaches
Only about 1 mile (1.6 km) from Todos Santos, through the fields behind Hotel California (see Places to Stay, below), lie pleasant but rarely visited beaches. These spots are also accessible via the dirt road that leads west from the Pemex station (follow Rangel to reach the road); passing the ballpark, it becomes steep, rutted and gullied. The shoreline lagoons are good spots for bird-watching, and camping is possible, but bring water (local expatriates report that Todos Santos' tap water is potable).

More accessible but more populous beaches are south of town and 6½ miles (10 km) northwest of town; see the Around Todos Santos entry in this chapter for details.

For surfing information, contact Pat Baum at the Todos Santos Surf Shop (☎ (114) 5-03-99) on Degollado just south of Cuauhtémoc.

Special Events
Todos Santos' annual **Festival de Artes** (art festival), in late January, lasts two days; the 1997 event was canceled due to an immigration controversy, but the festival is likely to resume in the near future. Local artists, such as Charles Stewart, can be visited in their homes/studios, where their works are for sale.

In late February, Todos Santos holds a **tour of local historic homes**.

Places to Stay

Camping *El Litro RV Park*, still under development in the area southwest of the baseball park, offers spacious camping sites for US$4 and RV sites with hookups for US$10. The toilets are spotless but, as of this writing, the showers had no hot water.

Hotels & Motels In recent years Todos Santos' accommodations have improved in quality and increased in quantity, but they are still limited in all categories. Rather misnamed *Hotel Miramar* (☎ (114) 5-03-41), at the corner of Verduzco and Pedrajo southwest of the town center, has only limited ocean views from the 2nd-floor balconies, but it's clean and reasonably priced at US$8/11 single/double.

Motel Guluarte (☎ (114) 5-00-06), at the corner of Juárez and Morelos, has a swimming pool; if no one is on duty at the desk, check the grocery across the street. Rooms are about US$18 double. *Hostería Las Casitas* (☎ (114) 5-02-55), a Canadian-run B&B on Rangel between Obregón and Avenida Hidalgo, also offers moderately priced tent sites (US$5/7 single/double). Its rolled palapa roof edges, rarely seen nowadays, add authentic detail to the remodeled, five-room building. Prices run from about US$30 to US$50 double with a superb breakfast; the restaurant is open to the public. Las Casitas' mailing address is Apdo Postal 73, Todos Santos, Baja California Sur 23300, México.

Set among pleasant gardens on Olachea between Villarino and Progreso, *Hotel Santa Rosa de las Palmas* (☎ (114) 5-03-94) has 15 rooms with kitchenette for US$35 single or double. It lacks air-conditioning but has fans and a swimming pool.

Gringos line up to take photos of each other in front of longtime favorite *Hotel California* (☎ (114) 5-00-02), on Juárez between Márquez de León and Morelos, which plays on its supposed status as the inspiration for the Eagles' hit record (the evidence for this is ambiguous). The original owner bought gold from farmers in the Sierra de la Laguna and traded the gold for lumber from Mazatlán; its zigzag corridors and creaky floorboards give it a distinct personality. Clean singles/doubles, each with private bath and some with lumpy beds, cost about US$35/42; it lacks air-conditioning, but all rooms have ceiling fans. It also has a good restaurant and a clean, well-maintained pool.

The most genteel accommodations are at the US-owned *Todos Santos Inn* (☎ /fax (114) 5-00-40), a B&B in a restored 19th-century building at Legaspi 33. Rates range from US$85 to US$120 double, depending on the room.

Places to Eat

For fine food at bargain prices, try any or all of the *taco stands* along Heróico Colegio Militar between Márquez de León and Degollado; each has its own specialty, be it fish, chicken, shrimp or beef. Family-run *Casa de Margarita* (☎ (114) 5-01-84), on Pedrajo between Progreso and Villarino, has attracted a devoted following for fine, reasonably priced antojitos and seafood; it has also taken over the Sunday champagne brunch from the now defunct El Molino Trailer Park restaurant.

Caffeine junkies can down their cappuccinos at *Caffé Todos Santos* (☎ (114) 5-03-00), in new and expanded quarters on Centenario between Topete and Obregón. It has savory pastries and visually enticing fruit salads, and the deli-style sandwiches are also outstanding. *Vanessa's* (☎ (114) 5-02-55), at Hostería Las Casitas, serves very fine breakfasts and lunches to both guests and the public in the peak winter season, with dinners available by reservation; the rest of the year, it serves guests only. It's a tossup with Caffé Todos Santos for the best cinnamon rolls.

La Langosta Loca, on Heróico Colegio Militar at Obregón, serves various seafood dishes, such as tuna salad, shrimp salad and local grilled fish, under a big, palm-thatched roof. Hotel California's *Las Tejitas* has respectable breakfasts and other meals, but never seems to draw the

crowds that other local restaurants do. *Pollos Los Pinos*, on Heróico Colegio Militar between Zaragoza and Morelos, specializes in grilled chicken.

Las Fuentes (☎ (114) 5-02-57), at the corner of Degollado and Heróico Colegio Militar, serves very fine antojitos (the chicken with mole sauce is exceptional) and seafood specialties in a shady patio among colorful bougainvilleas and three refreshing fountains. Prices are moderate. Well-regarded *Santa Mónica* (☎ (114) 4-00-79), Todos Santos' oldest restaurant, is just across the street. Down the block, between Rangel and Cuauhtémoc, *Tropicana* is a shady site for steak, seafood and tacos.

La Caravella (☎ (114) 5-02-20), at the western end of Juárez, is a very fine Italian restaurant in attractive surroundings. In a class by itself, *Café Santa Fe* (☎ (114) 5-03-40) entices patrons from as far away as La Paz and Cabo San Lucas to its plaza location at the corner of Centenario and Márquez de León. The grub is Italian and prices are high, but service is excellent and it's well worth a holiday splurge; reservations are a good idea during holiday periods.

Entertainment

Proud of its tranquillity, Todos Santos is no party town, but *La Cueva de los Leones*, on Juárez between Morelos and Zaragoza, features live norteña and banda music on weekends. *La Langosta Loca* (see Places to Eat, above) offers dancing some evenings.

Most visitors will find walking around town entertaining enough, but the cheap, powerful margaritas at *La Cañada del Diablo*, a low-key palapa bar at the eastern end of Centenario, may leave you incapable of doing so under your own power. Snacks are available, but not full meals.

Shut Up Frank's – colloquially known as 'Callate Pancho' – is a sports bar and grill that keeps erratic hours; it's on Degollado between Rangel and Cuauhtémoc.

For live action, enthusiastic amateur baseball teams from Todos Santos and nearby communities play several nights weekly, as well as daytime games on weekends, at Estadio Jesús Rosas Izquierdo at the corner of Rangel and Villarino.

Things to Buy

As an artists' colony, Todos Santos has numerous stores and galleries open to the public, displaying samples of local crafts and artwork. Try Casa Franco on Juárez between Morelos and Zaragoza or Mano a Mano at the corner of Juárez and Morelos, which sells very attractive furniture and, almost as an afterthought, excellent juices.

Galería de Todos Santos, at the corner of Topete and Legaspi, features imaginative artwork by Mexican and North American artists, with regular openings. Galería Santa Fe, alongside its namesake restaurant on the southern side of the plaza, is well worth a visit, as is the Stewart Gallery on Obregón between Legaspi and Centenario.

Getting There & Away

Todos Santos has no bus terminal as such, but buses between La Paz and Cabo San Lucas stop at Pilar's Tacos at the corner of Heróico Colegio Militar and Zaragoza. At least six buses daily go to La Paz (US$2) between 6 am and 6 pm and to Cabo San Lucas (US$3) between 8 am and 7 pm.

Getting Around
Visitors not wishing to hike the roundabout route to the beaches west of Todos Santos can hire a taxi at Parque de Los Pinos, diagonally across from the bus stop.

AROUND TODOS SANTOS
Punta Lobos
At Punta Lobos' beach, about 1½ miles (2.5 km) south of Todos Santos, *pangueros* (skiff operators) sell their catch in the late afternoon, offering a cheaper, better selection than local markets. Shark fins bring nearly US$70 per kilogram in La Paz.

Campo Experimental Forestal Todos Santos
Four miles (6.5 km) south of Todos Santos, around Km 56, Mexico's Servicio Agrícola y de Recursos Hidráulicos operates this desert botanical garden, which is a good place to become acquainted with the peninsula's native plants (there are also areas planted with nonnatives). Separate sections emphasize food plants, medicinal plants and forage plants. The weekday staff will show visitors around, but on weekends there is only a watchman.

Playa San Pedrito
Across from the botanical garden, a 2½-mile (4-km) dirt road leads to this sandy crescent beach with surfable breaks. Spacious *San Pedrito RV Park* (☎ (114) 5-01-47) charges US$3 per person for camping without hookups, US$15 for RV sites with all hookups and US$35 double for modest

cabañas. Amenities include a restaurant and a swimming pool.

Playa Los Cerritos
In a northern swell, Los Cerritos' crescent beach has a good right break with only a few surfers. There is also good fishing from the rocky headland to the north.

At Km 64, *Los Cerritos RV Park* operates on a shoestring budget, but the toilets flush and the cold showers work (water is expensive because it's trucked in – consider a 'sea shower' to conserve this precious commodity). There is some shade but no electricity. Ejido Pescadero keeps the area weed-free, charging US$4 to park outside the fence, US$5 to park inside; there have been reports of thefts, so secure your possessions at night.

Playa Las Cabrillas
South of Playa Los Cerritos, livestock are common along the Southern Cape Highway (México 19); drive with care. Beyond Km 81, Playa Las Cabrillas features a long but steep sandy beach not really suitable for surfing. However, there are many good rustic campsites just off the highway.

Playa Migriño
Between Km 97 and Km 98, a dirt road leads half a mile (1 km) west among mangroves to **Estero Migriño**, a good birdwatching site that also has a right break in the winter months. Cow patties and insects are both abundant, so watch your step and bring bug repellent.

Internet Directory

Mexico in general and Baja California in particular are the subjects of a large and growing number of Internet resources, but their quality varies considerably.

Aeroméxico
http://www.wotw.com/aeromexico/
Schedules and reservations for one of Mexico's (and Baja's) major airlines.

Amigos de Baja's BajaNet Fishing & Information Resource
http://www.geocities.com/TheTropics/4888/
Fishing-oriented website with particularly good information on Baja backroads.

Baja California Resource Guide
http://users.aol.com/bajanomad/guide.htm
Text-only website with considerable details and opinions on Baja by a frequent traveler there, but recent updates are sketchy and sporadic.

Baja Life Online
http://www.bajalife.com
Online version of slick quarterly with a few substantive articles, extensive services listings and impressive advertising revenue; it's the Baja counterpart of *Condé Nast Traveler* but also the only place to read about Alice Cooper's surf-fishing experiences at Cabo San Lucas.

Baja Sun
http://www.bajasun.com
Web version of Ensenada's glibly promotional English-language monthly; has an occasional interesting article, but it's more useful for discount coupons.

Baja Travel Guidebook
http://www.bajatravel.com/guidebook/index.html
Misleadingly titled website focusing on a handful of destinations in Baja California Sur, with reliable but very incomplete information; bears watching for improvement.

Borderlink 1994
http://www.sdsu.edu/ciber/borderlink-1994.html
Report on economy, demographics, political institutions, transportation, tourism and environment in the San Diego/Tijuana border region.

Center of Languages and Latin American Studies
http://www.tnl-online.com/cllas/cllas.html
Home page for the highly regarded Ensenada language school.

Colegio de Idiomas de Ensenada/ International Spanish Institute
http://www.mexonline.com/intspan1.htm
Language school website; also provides travel information on Ensenada and surrounding area.

Conservation and Development in the Gray Whale Lagoons of Baja California Sur, Mexico
http://scilib.ucsd.edu/sio/guide/z-serge.html
Detailed Nature Conservancy report on current state of the California gray whale and potential threats to its conservation.

Don Pato's Gay Tijuana
http://donpato.simplenet.com/tijuana/
Website of interest to gay visitors to northern Baja, primarily covering Tijuana but also addressing Ensenada.

El Heraldo de Baja California
http://www.cincos.net/heraldo/heraldo.html
Web version of Tijuana's oldest daily; website under construction as of this writing.

Hotel Bahía Los Frailes
http://www.losfrailes.com/
Home page for one of the Eastern Cape's most secluded, distinctive and best hotels, which also has outstanding food.

Hotel Buena Vista Beach Resort
http://www.hotelbuenavista.com/
Home page for major Eastern Cape fishing resort, with irritating musical accompaniment.

Hotel, Motel, Tour & Business Guide to Loreto, Baja California Sur
http://members.aol.com/MulegeBaja/baja/loreto.htm
A work-in-progress, but has good information on Loreto, Mulegé and Santa Rosalía.

Information Pages on Baja California, Mexico
http://math.ucr.edu/%7Eftm/bajainfopage.html

Well-organized website that includes recent travelers' experiences, mostly but not exclusively from the Desierto Central south to La Paz; includes some good cultural material.

Latin America on the Net – Mexico: Government & Politics
http://www.latinworld.com/norte/mexico/government/
Useful online index to official Mexican government websites (including consular information) and unofficial websites on politics and current events in Mexico; some sites are bilingual or in English.

Mexicana
http://www.mexicana.com/index.html
Schedules and reservations for one of the major Mexican airlines serving the Baja Peninsula.

Picante Bluewater Sportfishing
http://www.PicanteSportfishing.com
Home page for one of the Cape Region's largest sportfishing outfits; includes details on the fleet and package trips.

Rancho La Puerta
http://www.rancholapuerta.com
Home page for Baja's most famous fat farm and pioneering New Age spiritual retreat.

Sanborn's
http://www.hiline.net/sanborns/index.html
Famous US-Mexican institution's website provides information on travelers' services, including vehicle insurance, highway travelogs and publications.

San Diego Union-Tribune
http://www.uniontrib.com/aboutut/
Perhaps the best coverage of Mexico (and undoubtedly of Baja California and Tijuana) of any English-language daily, with articles on topics ranging from government and politics to travel and tourism; includes an indexed archive, presently open to the public without charge but requiring a password.

Secretaría de Medio Ambiente, Recursos Naturales y Pesca
http://www.semarnap.gob.mx/
Home page of the Mexican government's primary conservation agency.

Secretaría de Turismo de Baja California
http://www.cincos.net/turismo/prueba.html
Official government tourism website with limited information in Spanish and English on Tijuana, Tecate, Mexicali and Ensenada; bears watching for improvement.

Secretaría de Turismo de México
http://mexico-travel.com/mex_eng.html
Official federal government website with information in English and Spanish; more useful for mainland Mexico information than for its very limited Baja California material.

Turtle Happenings – Sea Turtle News & Information
http://www.turtles.org/happen.htm#logger
Tracks progress of the loggerhead turtle 'Adelita' across the Pacific from Santa Rosalillita.

TOUR COMPANY WEBSITES
Many Baja tour operators maintain websites describing their specialties and offerings. The list below is as current as possible:

Specialty Travel Index, Baja California
http://www.spectrav.com/baja.html
Index listing Baja California tour companies' specialties, ranging from 'Archaeology' to 'Zoology.'

American Cetacean Society
http://www.acsonline.org

Backroads Bicycle Touring
http://www.backroads.com

Baja Discovery
http://www.bajalife.com/discover/index.htm

Baja Expeditions
http://www.bajaex.com

Baja Outdoor Activities
http://www.kayactivities.com

Baja Tropicales/Mulegé Kayaks
http://www.electriciti.com/~bajatrop

Forum Travel International
http://www.ten-io.com/forumtravel

Global Exchange
http://www.globalexchange.org

Green Tortoise Adventure Travel
http://www.greentortoise.com/home.html

Horizon Charters
http://www.earthwindow.com/horizon

Kayak Port Townsend
http://www.olympus.net/kayakpt/

Mountain Travel Sobek
http://www.mtsobek.com

**Mr Bill's Boardsailing Adventures/
Baja Dive Adventures**
http://www.jtr.com/baja/

National Outdoor Leadership School
http://www.nols.edu/

Natural Habitat Adventures
http://www.nathab.com

Outdoor Adventure River Specialists
http://www.oars.com

REI Adventures
http://www.rei.com/travel

**San Diego Natural
History Museum**
http://www.sdnhm.org

Southwest Sea Kayaks
http://www.swkayak.com/sw_hp.html

The Touring Exchange
http://www.bajatravel.com/tourex/index.html

Vela Windsurf Resorts
http://www.velawindsurf.com

Spanish for Travelers

Every Baja visitor should make an effort to speak Spanish, whose basic elements are easily acquired. Mexicans normally will be flattered by such attempts, so there is no need to feel self-conscious about vocabulary or pronunciation. There are many common cognates, so if you're stuck, try Hispanicizing an English word – it is unlikely that you'll make a truly embarrassing error. Do not, however, admit to being *embarazada* unless you are in fact pregnant!

When asking information, avoid leading questions that may invite incorrect responses. Instead of asking, for example, 'Is this the road to San Borja?' (a question that begs a positive answer, whether or not it is the correct road), ask 'Which road goes to San Borja?' (a form that gives the respondent an option). Though it's unlikely that a respondent would purposely lead you astray, a willingness to please can have the same results.

Phrasebooks & Dictionaries
Lonely Planet's *Latin American Spanish phrasebook*, by Anna Cody, is a worthwhile addition to your backpack. Another useful book is the *University of Chicago Spanish-English, English-Spanish Dictionary*, whose small size, light weight and thorough entries make it very convenient for foreign travel.

Pronunciation
Spanish pronunciation is, in general, consistently phonetic. Once you are aware of the basic rules, they should cause little difficulty. Speak slowly to avoid getting tongue-tied until you become confident of your ability.

Letters Pronunciation of the letters **f**, **k**, **l**, **n**, **p**, **q**, **s**, and **t** is virtually identical to their English pronunciation. **Ch**, **ll** (virtually identical to 'y') and **ñ** are separate letters with separate dictionary entries.

Vowels Spanish vowels are very consistent and have easy English equivalents:

a is like 'a' in 'ma.'
e is like 'ay' in 'say.'
i is like 'ee' in 'feet.'
o is like 'o' in 'go.'
u is like 'oo' in 'food.' After consonants other than 'q,' it is more like the English 'w.'
y is a consonant, except when standing alone or appearing at the end of a word, when it is identical to the Spanish 'i.'

Consonants Spanish consonants generally resemble their English equivalents, but there are some major exceptions:

b resembles its English equivalent but is undistinguished from the Spanish 'v.' For clarification, refer to the former as *b larga*, the latter as *b corta* (the word for the letter itself is pronounced like the English 'bay').
c is like the 's' in 'see' before 'e' and 'i'; otherwise, it is like the English 'k.'
d closely resembles 'th' in 'feather.'
g is like a guttural English 'h' before the Spanish 'e' and 'i'; otherwise it is like 'g' in 'go.'
h is invariably silent.
j most closely resembles the English 'h' but is slightly more guttural.
ñ is like 'ni' in 'onion.'
r is nearly identical to English, except at the beginning of a word, when it is often rolled.
rr is very strongly rolled.
v resembles English, but see 'b,' above.
x is normally like 'x' in 'taxi,' except for some words in which it resembles the Spanish 'j.'
z is like 's' in 'sun.'

Diphthongs Diphthongs are combinations of two vowels that form a single syllable. In Spanish, the formation of a diphthong depends on combinations of 'weak' vowels ('i' and 'u') or strong ones ('a,' 'e' and 'o'). Two weak vowels or a strong and a weak vowel make a diphthong, but two strong ones are separate syllables. Two weak vowels form a diphthong in the word *diurno* (during the day). The final syllable of *obligatorio* (obligatory) is a combination of weak and strong vowels.

Stress Stress, often indicated by visible accents, is very important, since it can change the meaning of words. In general, words ending in vowels or the letters 'n' or 's' have stress on the next-to-last syllable, while those with other endings have stress on the last syllable. Thus *vaca* (cow) and *caballos* (horses) both have accents on their next-to-last syllables.

Visible accents, which can occur anywhere in a word, dictate stress over these general rules. Thus *zócalo* (plaza or town square), *América* and *porción* (portion) have stress on different syllables. When words are written in capital letters, the written accent is often omitted but is still pronounced.

Useful Phrases

Below are English phrases with useful Mexican Spanish equivalents, most of which will be understood in other Spanish-speaking countries. Words relating to food and restaurants are covered in the Food entry in the Facts for the Visitor chapter.

At the Border

tourist card	*tarjeta de turista*
visa	*visado*
passport	*pasaporte*
identification	*identificación*
birth certificate	*certificado de nacimiento*
driver's license	*licencia de manejar*
car title	*título de propiedad*
car registration	*registración*
customs	*aduana*
immigration	*migración*
the border (frontier)	*la frontera*

Civilities

Like other Latin Americans, Mexicans are very conscious of civilities in their public behavior. Never, for example, approach a stranger for information without extending a greeting like *'Buenos días'* or *'Buenas tardes.'*

Sir/Mr	*Señor*
Madam/Mrs	*Señora*
Miss	*Señorita*
yes	*sí*
no	*no*
please	*por favor*
Thank you.	*Gracias.*
You're welcome.	*De nada.*
Excuse me.	*Perdóneme.*
Hello.	*Hola.*
Goodbye.	*Adiós.*
Good morning.	*Buenos días.*
Good afternoon.	*Buenas tardes.*
Good evening.	*Buenas noches.*
Good night.	*Buenas noches.*
I understand.	*Entiendo.*
I don't understand.	*No entiendo.*
Please repeat that.	
	Repítelo, por favor.
I don't speak much Spanish.	
	Hablo poco castellano or *español.*

Questions

Where?	*¿Dónde?*
Where is . . . ?	*¿Dónde está . . . ?*
Where are . . . ?	*¿Dónde están . . . ?*
When?	*¿Cuando?*
How? *¿Cómo?*	
How much?	*¿Cuanto?*
How many?	*¿Cuantos?*
I want . . .	*Quiero . . .*
I do not want . . .	*No quiero . . .*
I would like . . .	*Me gustaría . . .*
Give me . . .	*Déme . . .*
What do you want?	
	¿Que quiere usted?
Do you have . . . ?	
	¿Tiene usted . . . ?
Is/are there . . . ?	
	¿Hay . . . ?
How much does it cost?	
	¿Cuánto cuesta?

Some Useful Words

and	*y*
to/at	*a*
for	*por, para*
of/from	*de, desde*
in	*en*
with	*con*
without	*sin*
before	*antes*
after	*después*
soon	*pronto*
already	*ya*
now	*ahora*
right away	*ahorita*
here	*aquí*
there	*allí*
bad	*malo*
better	*mejor*
best	*el mejor*
more	*más*
less	*menos*

Family & Friends

I	*yo*
you (familiar)	*tú*
you (formal)	*usted*
you (plural)	*ustedes*
he/him	*él*
she/her	*ella*
we/us	*nosotros*
they/them (masculine and mixed groups)	*ellos*
they/them (feminine)	*ellas*
my wife	*mi esposa*
my husband	*mi esposo*
my sister	*mi hermana*
my brother	*mi hermano*
I am . . .	*Soy . . .*
a student	*estudiante*
American	*americano(a)*
a citizen of the USA	*estadounidense*
Australian	*australiano(a)*
British	*británico(a)*
Canadian	*canadiense*
German	*alemán (alemana)*
French	*francés (francesa)*

Transportation

car	*auto*
airplane	*avión*
train	*tren*
bus	*autobus*
ship	*barco, buque*
taxi	*taxi*
truck	*camión*
pickup	*camioneta*
motorcycle	*motocicleta, moto*
bicycle	*bicicleta*
airport	*aeropuerto*
train station	*estación del ferrocarril*
bus station	*estación del autobús, central camionera*

I would like a ticket to . . .
  Quiero un boleto a . . .
What's the fare to . . . ?
  ¿Cuánto cuesta hasta . . . ?
When does the next plane/train/bus leave for . . . ?
  ¿Cuándo sale el próximo avión/ tren/autobus para . . . ?

first/last/next	*primero/último/ próximo*
1st/2nd class	*primera/segunda clase*
one-way/roundtrip	*ida/ida y vuelta*
luggage storage	*guardería, equipaje*

Around Town

tourist information	*oficina de turismo*
bathing resort	*balneario*
street	*calle*
boulevard	*bulevar*
avenue	*avenida*
road	*camino*
highway	*carretera*
corner (of)	*esquina (de)*
block	*cuadra*
to the left	*a la izquierda*
to the right	*a la derecha*
on the left side	*al lado izquierdo*
on the right side	*al lado derecho*
straight ahead	*adelante*

north	*norte*
south	*sur*
east	*este*
west	*oeste*

Post & Communications

post office	*correo*
letter	*carta*
parcel	*paquete*
postcard	*postal*
airmail	*correo aéreo*
registered mail	*certificado*
stamps	*estampillas, timbres*
telephone office	*caseta de teléfono*
telephone booth	*cabina de teléfono*
local call	*llamada local*
long distance	*larga distancia*
person to person	*persona a persona*
collect call	*por cobrar*
busy	*ocupado*

At the Hotel

guesthouse	*casa de huéspedes*
room	*cuarto, habitación*
single room	*cuarto solo, cuarto sencillo*
double room	*cuarto para dos, cuarto doble*
double bed	*cama de matrimonio*
with twin beds	*con camas gemelas*
with private bath	*con baño*
shower	*ducha*
hot water	*agua caliente*
air-conditioning	*aire acondicionado*
blanket	*frasada*
towel	*toalla*
soap	*jabón*
toilet paper	*papel higiénico*
toothpaste	*pasta dentífrica*
dental floss	*hilo dental*

What is the price?
> *¿Cuál es el precio?*

Does that include taxes?
> *¿Están incluídos los impuestos?*

Does that include service?
> *¿Está incluído el servicio?*

the bill	*la cuenta*
too expensive	*demasiado caro*
cheaper	*mas económico*
May I see it?	*¿Puedo verla?*
I don't like it.	*No me gusta.*

Money

money	*dinero*
bank	*banco*
currency exchange house	*casa de cambio*
traveler's checks	*cheques de viajero*

I want to change money.
> *Quiero cambiar dinero.*

What is the exchange rate?
> *¿Que es el tipo de cambio?*

Is there a commission?
> *¿Hay comisión?*

Driving

gasoline	*gasolina*
unleaded	*sin plomo*
leaded	*con plomo*

Fill the tank, please.
> *Llene el tanque, por favor.*

How much is gasoline per liter?
> *¿Cuánto cuesta el litro de gasolina?*

tire	*llanta*
spare tire	*llanta de repuesto*
puncture	*agujero*
flat tire	*llanta desinflada*

My car has broken down.
> *Se me ha descompuesto el carro.*

I need a tow truck.
> *Necesito un remolque.*

Is there a garage near here?
> *¿Hay garage cerca?*

Time

Telling time is fairly straightforward. Eight o'clock is *las ocho*, while 8:30 is *las ocho y treinta* (literally, 'eight and thirty') or *las ocho y media* (eight and a half). However, 7:45 is *las ocho menos quince* (literally, 'eight minus fifteen') or *las ocho menos cuarto* (eight minus one-quarter). Times are modified by morning *(de la mañana)* or afternoon *(de la tarde)* instead of 'am' or 'pm.' It is also common to use the 24-hour clock, especially with transportation schedules. Midnight is *medianoche*, and noon is *mediodía*.

While Mexicans are flexible about time with respect to social occasions like meals and parties, schedules for public events (like bullfights and movies) and transportation (like airplanes and buses) should be taken very literally.

Days of the Week

Monday	*lunes*
Tuesday	*martes*
Wednesday	*miércoles*
Thursday	*jueves*
Friday	*viernes*
Saturday	*sábado*
Sunday	*domingo*

Toilets

The most common word for 'toilet' is *baño*, but *servicios sanitarios* (services)

is a frequent alternative. Men's toilets will usually bear a descriptive term like *hombres*, *caballeros* or *varones*. Women's restrooms will be marked *señoras* or *damas*.

Geographical Terms

The expressions below are among the most common in this book and in Spanish-language maps and guides:

bay	*bahía*
bridge	*puente*
cape	*cabo*
farm	*rancho*
hill	*cerro*
island	*isla*
lake	*lago, laguna*
marsh	*estero*
mountain	*cerro*
mountain range	*sierra, cordillera*
national park	*parque nacional*
pass	*paso*
point	*punta*
river	*río*
waterfall	*cascada, cataratа, salto*

Numbers

1	*uno*	17	*diecisiete*	70	*setenta*	1000 *mil*
2	*dos*	18	*dieciocho*	80	*ochenta*	1100
3	*tres*	19	*diecinueve*	90	*noventa*	*mil cien*
4	*cuatro*	20	*veinte*	100	*cien*	1200
5	*cinco*	21	*veintiuno*	101	*ciento uno*	*mil doscientos*
6	*seis*	22	*veintidós*	102	*ciento dos*	2000
7	*siete*	23	*veintitrés*	110	*ciento diez*	*dos mil*
8	*ocho*	24	*veinticuatro*	120	*ciento veinte*	5000
9	*nueve*	30	*treinta*	130	*ciento treinta*	*cinco mil*
10	*diez*	31	*treinta y uno*	200	*doscientos*	10,000
11	*once*	32	*treinta y dos*	300	*trescientos*	*diez mil*
12	*doce*	33	*treinta y tres*	400	*cuatrocientos*	50,000
13	*trece*	40	*cuarenta*	500	*quinientos*	*cincuenta mil*
14	*catorce*	41	*cuarenta y uno*	600	*seiscientos*	100,000
15	*quince*	50	*cincuenta*	700	*setecientos*	*cien mil*
16	*dieciséis*	60	*sesenta*	800	*ochocientos*	1,000,000
				900	*novecientos*	*un millón*

Glossary

For general information on the Spanish language, see the Spanish for Travelers section; for a list of food and drink terms, see the Food entry in the Facts for the Visitor chapter.

acequia – irrigation canal, often stone-lined, in Baja California missions

agave – century plant

agua purificada – purified water

albergue juvenil – youth hostel, a relatively inexpensive but uncommon form of accommodations in Baja

alto – stop; also means 'high'

Apdo – abbreviation of *Apartado* (Box); in addresses, stands for 'Post Office Box'

asentamientos irregulares – shantytowns of Tijuana, Mexicali and other border towns

asistencia – in colonial times, a way station between missions

bajacaliforniano – resident of Baja California

ballena – whale; also a colloquial term for a liter-sized bottle of Pacífico beer

banda – style of dance music

béisbol – baseball

biznaga – barrel cactus

borrego – bighorn sheep, a rarely seen species in the sierras of Baja California that is frequently represented in the pre-Columbian rock art of the peninsula

bracero – literally, 'farmhand'; used to describe work program established by the US and Mexican governments during WWII that allowed Mexicans to work north of the border to alleviate wartime labor shortages in the US

cabaña – cabin

cabecera – the administrative seat of a *municipio* (see below)

cabina – phone booth

caguama – any species of sea turtle, but most commonly the Pacific green turtle, *Chelonia mydas*, also known as the *caguama negra* or *caguama prieta* (literally, 'black turtle'); also a colloquial term for a liter-sized bottle of Tecate beer

Canaco – Cámara Nacional de Comercio (National Chamber of Commerce)

cardón – either of two species of *Pachycereus* cactus, a common genus in Baja

carga negra – hazardous cargo

casa de cambio – currency exchange house

casa de huéspedes – guesthouse, a relatively inexpensive but uncommon form of accommodations in Baja

cascabel – rattlesnake

casita – cottage

charreada – rodeo, frequently held during fiestas and other special occasions; particularly popular in northern Mexico

charro – Mexican cowboy or horseman; mariachi bands often dress in gaudy charro clothing

chilango – native or resident of Mexico City; depending on context, the term can be very pejorative

cholismo – rebellious youth movement, akin to punk, that has had some influence on the visual arts in Baja California

choza – hut

chubasco – in the Cape Region of southern Baja, a violent storm approaching hurricane force, associated with summer low-pressure areas in the tropical Pacific

científicos – a group of largely Eurocentric advisers who controlled the direction of Mexico's economy under dictator Porfirio Díaz

cirio – a 'boojum' tree *(Idria columnaris)*, a slow-growing species resembling an inverted carrot, common only within a limited range of the Sierra La Asamblea in north-central Baja

CITES – Convention on International Trade in Endangered Species of Wild Fauna and Flora, which regulates trade in such species

colonia – neighborhood in Tijuana or other large city; literally, 'colony'

corrida de toros – bullfight

corrido – folk ballad of the US-Mexico border region; corridos often have strong but subtle political content

Cotuco – Comité de Turismo y Convenciones, or the Committee on Tourism & Conventions

coyote – smuggler who charges up to US$500 or more to spirit illegal immigrants across the US-Mexican border

Cruz Roja – Red Cross

curandero – folk healer

datilillo – yucca

delegación – administrative subdivision of a municipio (see below)

ejidatario – a member of an *ejido*

ejido – cooperative enterprise, usually of peasant agriculturalists, created under the land reform program of President Lázaro Cárdenas (1934 – 40); ejidos also participate in economic activities such as mining, ranching and tourism

encomienda – system of forced labor and tribute which the Spanish crown instituted in mainland New Spain and other densely populated parts of its empire

fianza – bond posted against the return of a motor vehicle to the USA

fideicomiso – 30-year bank trust that has fostered the construction and acquisition of real estate by non-Mexicans in Baja California

Fonatur – Mexican federal government tourist agency

fraccionamiento – synonym for *colonia* (see above)

fronterizo – an inhabitant of the US-Mexico border region

frontón – venue for jai alai (see below)

glorieta – city traffic circle; most numerous in Mexicali and Tijuana

gotas – water purification drops

gringo – term describing any light-skinned person, but most often a resident of the USA; often but not always pejorative

güero – 'blond,' a descriptive term often used to describe any fair-skinned person in Mexico

hacienda – local treasury department

hielo – ice

hipódromo – horseracing track

huerivo – aspen tree

INAH – Instituto Nacional de Historia y Antropología (National Institute of Anthropology & History), which administers museums and archeological monuments such as the cave paintings in the Desierto Central of Baja California

indígena – indigenous person

internado – rural boarding school

IVA – *impuesto de valor agregado*, or value-added tax

jai alai – game of Basque origin resembling squash, played for bettors in Tijuana

Judiciales – Mexican state and federal police

Ladatel – *Larga Distancia Automática*, or Automatic Long Distance phones

La Frontera – the area where Dominican priests built their missions in colonial times (from 1774); it extends from immediately south of present-day San Diego (mainland California) as far as El Rosario, at about the 30th parallel

librería – bookstore

libro foráneo – foreign book for bettors; most often abbreviated 'LF'

licorería – liquor store; also called *vinos y licores*

llantera – tire repair shop, common even in Baja's most out-of-the-way places

machismo – an exaggerated masculinity intended to impress other men more than women; usually innocuous if rather unpleasant

Magonistas – followers of the exiled Mexican intellectual Ricardo Flores Magón, who attempted to establish a regional power base in the towns of northern Baja California during the Mexican Revolution

maguey – any of several species of a common Mexico fiber plant *(Agave* spp), also used for producing alcoholic drinks like tequila, mescal and pulque

malecón – waterfront promenade, as in La Paz

maquiladora – industrial plant in Tijuana, Mexicali or another border town that takes advantage of cheap Mexican labor to assemble US components for re-exportation to the north

matador – bullfighter

mestizo – person of mixed Indian and European heritage

moneda nacional – national money, meaning the Mexican peso as distinguished from the US dollar (both use the symbol '$'); often abbreviated as 'm/n'

mono – human figure, as represented in the pre-Columbian rock art of the Desierto Central

mordida – bribe; literally, 'the bite'

municipio – administrative subdivision of Mexican states, roughly akin to a US county; the states of Baja California and Baja California Sur each consist of four municipios

NAFTA – North American Free Trade Agreement, a pact between the USA, Canada and Mexico that reduces or eliminates customs duties and other trade barriers

nao – in colonial times, a Spanish galleon on the Acapulco-Manila trade route; such galleons frequently took shelter in Baja ports on their return voyages

nopal – any cactus of the genus *Opuntia* that produces edible fruit *(tuna),* which was common in the diet of pre-Columbian Baja and is still widely consumed today

noria – water- or animal-driven mill

ofrenda – offering to a saint in exchange for a wish or wishes granted

ola – wave

palafito – walled *palapa* (see below)

palapa – palm-leaf shelter

PAN – Partido de Acción Nacional, a free-market-oriented populist party that is strong in Mexican states along the US border, including Baja California; its acronym, more than coincidentally, reproduces the Spanish word for 'bread'

panga – fiberglass skiff used for fishing or whale-watching

panguero – one who owns or pilots a skiff; in practice, the word is synonymous with 'fisherman'

parque nacional – national park

pastillas para purificar agua – water purification tablets

peatonal – pedestrian walk

peligro – danger

Pemex – Petróleos Mexicanos, the Mexican government oil monopoly

piñata – papier-mâché animal full of candy, broken open by children at celebrations like Christmas and birthdays

pitahaya dulce – organ pipe cactus, a key element of the traditional diet of Baja's native peoples

plaza de toros – bullring

pollero – synonymous with 'coyote'; a smuggler of undocumented immigrants *(pollos* or 'chickens') into the USA

Porfiriato – de facto dictatorship of Porfirio Díaz, who held Mexico's presidency from 1876 until the Revolution of 1910; under his rule, much of Baja California was granted to foreign companies for ambitious colonization projects, most of which soon failed

posada – at Christmas, a parade of costumed children re-enacting the journey of Mary and Joseph to Bethlehem

presidio – during colonial times, a military outpost

PRI – Partido Institucional Revolucionario, the official party of government in Mexico since 1946 and a direct descendant of the Partido Nacional Revolucionario of the late 1920s

propina – tip, at a restaurant or elsewhere

pueblo – town

ranchería – subsistence unit of hunter-gatherers in the contact period with Europeans, or, later, units associated with missions; implies a group of people rather than a place

rancho – tiny rural settlement, ranging from about 20 to 50 people
rebozo – shawl
recinto fiscal – official vehicle-impound lot
registro – local records office
reglamento de tránsito – the Mexican drivers' manual

Secture – Secretaría de Turismo del Estado (State Tourism Office)
SEDUE – Secretaría de Desarrollo Urbano y Ecología, a Mexican government agency that regulates foreign hunting activity in Baja California and elsewhere in Mexico
Semarnap – Secretaría de Medio Ambiente, Recursos Naturales y Pesca, the Mexican government's primary conservation agency
Servicio Postal Mexicano – the Mexican national postal service
Servicios Migratorios – Immigration Office
SIDA – AIDS (Acquired Immune Deficiency Syndrome)
s/n (sin número) – street address without a specific number

todo terreno – mountain bike
tombolo – sandspit beach
tope – speed bump
torote – elephant tree

tortillería – tortilla factory or shop
tortuga carey – hawksbill turtle
tortuga laúd – leatherback turtle
trapiche – sugar mill
turista – tourist; also a colloquial name for diarrhea contracted by tourists

ultramarino – small grocery store
UNESCO – United Nations Educational, Scientific and Cultural Organization

vado – ford, as of a river; can also refer to a dip in a road
vaquero – Mexican cowboy
veda – seasonal or permanent prohibition against hunting or fishing of a given species
villa deportiva juvenil – youth hostel
visita – during colonial times, a mission's outstation

yodo – iodine, sold in pharmacies for water purification

zócalo – central plaza, a term more common in mainland Mexico than in Baja California
zona de tolerancia – in border cities like Tijuana and Mexicali, an area in which prostitution and related activities are concentrated
zona hotelera – hotel zone

Index

MAPS

Around Bahía de los
  Angeles 203
Around Guerrero Negro 207
Baja (regional map)
  between pgs 16-17
Baja locator map 9
Cabo San Lucas 288
  Central Cabo San
  Lucas 290
Cape Region 252
Ciudad Constitución 246
Desierto Central & Llano
  de Magdalena 199
Desierto del Colorado 172
Ensenada 140-141
Isla Cedros & Islas San
  Benito 214
La Frontera 103

La Paz 254-255
  Central La Paz 258
Loreto 237
Los Cabos Corridor 285
Map index 8
Mexicali 174-175
  Central Mexicali 178
Mission Development in
  Baja California 14
Mulegé 228
  Around Mulegé 233
Northern Desierto
  Central 200
Parque Nacional
  Constitución de 1857 156
Parque Nacional Sierra
  San Pedro Mártir 160
Playas de Rosarito 133

Rails across the
  Border 187
Regions of Baja California 20
San Felipe 191
San José del Cabo 278-279
San Quintín 164
Santa Rosalía 224
Southern Desierto Central &
  Llano de Magdalena 222
Tecate 125
Tijuana 106
  Central Tijuana 110-111
Tijuana-Ensenada
  Corridor 130
Todos Santos 299

TEXT

Map references are in **bold** type.

accommodations 69
  costs of 46
Agua Caliente 274
air travel
  airports & airlines 87
  departure taxes 93
  disabled travelers 87
  to/from Australia &
  New Zealand 89
  to/from mainland
  Mexico 90
  to/from the UK &
  Europe 89-90
  to/from the USA 87-89
  within Baja 94
Ajantequedo 162
Alamo Canal 171-173, 188
alcohol 65, 72-73
  customs regulations on 46
  See also breweries; drinks;
  wineries
Algodones Dunes 171
Andrade 173, 188
Arroyo El Tulé 284
Arroyo San José 277
Arroyo Santa Rosalía 228
arts 34-36, 104-105.
  See also dance; literature;
  music; theater; visual arts

Asalto a las Tierras 18, 173
ATMs 47

Bahía Asunción 215-216
Bahía Concepción 78, 233-234
Bahía de Calamajué 201
Bahía de La Paz 251
Bahía de la Ventana 80
Bahía de los Angeles 202-
  205, **203**
Bahía de Palmas 268
Bahía de Sebastián
  Vizcaíno 206
Bahía de Todos Santos 142
Bahía Los Frailes 272-273
Bahía Magdalena 22, 80,
  208, 244-245, 276
Bahía San Felipe 188, 189
Bahía San Francisquito 212-213
Bahía San Juanico 235
Bahía San Luis Gonzaga 197,
  201-202
Bahía Tortugas 215
Baja Beach Resort 153
Bajamar 138-139
bargaining 47
baseball 74, 182-183
bicycling 80, 100
boat permits 95-96

boat travel
  to/from mainland
  Mexico 93, 227, 265
  to/from the USA 92-93
boat trips 259, 291-292
Boca de la Sierra 274
Boca de Soledad 245
books
  activity guidebooks 50-51
  bookstores 53
  guidebooks & general
  interest 50
  history 52-53
  travel health guidebooks 55
  travel literature 51-52
border crossings 90, 108, 126,
  175-176. See also car travel;
  customs
boxing 74
breweries 127
bribes 66
Buena Vista 268-271
bullfights 75, 119, 183
bus travel
  to/from mainland Mexico 92
  to/from the USA 90-91
  within Baja 95
  within Baja cities 101
business hours 67

Cabo Pulmo 31, 272
Cabo San Lucas 40, 276,
    286-298, **288**, **290**
    accommodations 293-295
    beaches 291
    getting around 297-298
    getting there & away 297
    information 289-291
    Land's End 291
    orientation 289
    restaurants 295-296
    things to see 291
Caduaño 274
California Development
    Company 171-173, 188
Campo Experimental Forestal
    Todos Santos 303
Canal de Dewey 213
Canal de Kellet 213
Cañón del Diablo 161
Cañón Guadalupe 156, 186-187
Cañón La Trinidad 232
Cañón San Bernardo 274
Cañón San Dionisio 274
Cañón San Pablo
    (Cape Region) 274
Cañón San Pablo (Sierra de San
    Francisco) 218-219
Cantamar 137
Cantú Grade 130
Cape Region 19, 21, 22,
    251-303, **252**
    Central 273-274
    Eastern 267-273
    La Paz & vicinity 251-267
    Southern 275-298
    Western 298-303
car travel 91-92, 95-100
    emergencies 98-99
    gasoline 97
    insurance 91-92, 96-97
    off-highway driving 99
    permits 42, 43, 91, 95-96,
    144, 175
    rental 99-100
    road conditions 97-98
    See also border crossings;
    driver's license
Cárdenas, Lázaro 17, 18,
    105, 185
Casilepe 162
Cataviña 200-201
Catholicism 37-38. See also
    missions, history of
Cavendish, Thomas 12, 253, 275
Cedros. See Isla Cedros
Cerro El Chinero 186

Cerro Prieto 185
changing money 47
children, travel with 43-44, 55, 87
cinema 74
Ciudad Constitución 245-248,
    246
clamming 190
climate 21-22, 39
clothing 39-40
Cochimí people 12-13, 25, 34,
    213, 218
Coco's Corner 201
Colonet 159
Colonia Purísima 242
Colonia Vicente Guerrero
    162-163
Colorado River Land Company
    18, 173
Compañía del Boleo 16, 221
consulates 44-45
    foreign consulates in Baja
    45, 109, 289
    Mexican consulates abroad
    44-45
Cortés, Hernán 11-12, 251
costs 46
credit cards 47
crime 64, 112, 166, 202, 266
Cucapá El Mayor 185
Cucupah people 12, 34
Cuesta de la Ley 212
Cuesta de los Muertos 267, 271
Cuesta El Mechudo 267
Cuesta Palmarito 219-220
Cueva de las Flechas 218-219
Cueva del Ratón 217-218
Cueva Pintada 218-219
currency 46
currency exchange 47
customs 45-46

dance 34
Desierto Central 19, 21,
    198-244, **199**, **200**, **222**
Desierto de Vizcaíno 19-21,
    198, 215
Desierto del Colorado
    21, 171-197, **172**
Díaz, Porfirio 15, 33, 245
disabled travelers 87
discounts, student 47
diving 78, 146, 153, 230, 239,
    259, 272, 292
drinks 72-73. See also
    alcohol
driver's license 43
Dutch, role in early Baja 253

ecology & environment 23, 220
economy 32-33, 104
    borderlands 18-19, 32-33, 104
    See also maquiladoras; North
    American Free Trade
    Agreement
education 19, 34
Eiffel, Alexandre Gustave
    41, 221, 223, 225
Ejido Alfredo Bonfil 219-220
Ejido Conquista 250
Ejido Eréndira 158
Ejido Francisco Villa 235
Ejido José Saldaña No 2 187
Ejido Lázaro Cárdenas 165
Ejido Revolución 199
Ejido San Simón 165
Ejido Santa María 165
Ejido Uruapán 157
ejidos 17, 18, 185
El Alamo 156
El Arco 211-212
El Bosque 267
El Camino Real 104, 212
El Cardonal 271
El Cien 250
El Mármol 199-200
El Mirador 139
El Oasis 131
El Pescadero 274
El Pilón 234
El Rosario 169-170
El Sauzal 139
El Triunfo 268
electricity 55
email 50
endangered species 24-25, 26,
    28-29, 76, 208, 220
Ensenada 139-152, 276,
    140-141
    accommodations 147-149
    getting around 152
    getting there & away 151-152
    history 142-143
    information 143-144
    orientation 143
    restaurants 149-150
    Riviera del Pacífico 145
    things to see 144-146
Ensenada de los Muertos 267
entertainment 73-74
Estero Beach Resort 152-153

fauna 23-30. See also
    endangered species
fax 49
ferry travel. See boat travel

film 35
fishing 146, 166-167, 190-192,
    196, 202, 204, 220, 230, 239,
    259-260, 279, 292-293
    fish names in Spanish 79
    fishing license 44, 78
    general information on 78-79
    See also boat permits
flora 23-26. See also
    endangered species
Flores Magón, Ricardo
    17, 104-105, 124, 142
food 69-72
    health problems from 57

Gardner's Cave.
    See Cueva Pintada
geography 19-21
    regions of Baja **20**
golf 80, 279
government & politics 31
greyhound racing 119
Guadalupe 154-155
Guerrero Negro 65, 207-211,
    207

Hacienda Santa Verónica 129
Hanlon Headgate 173, 188
health 55-64
    eating & drinking 57
    health & travel insurance
        55-56
    heat-related problems 59
    medical kit 56
    medical problems &
        treatment 58-63
    predeparture preparations
        55-57
    travel health guidebooks 55
    women's health 64
highlights 40-41
hiking 80, 155, 161, 232, 273, 274
history 11-19, 253, 276
    contemporary era 18-19
    European exploration 11-12
    foreign investment 15-17,
        244-245
    Mexican-American War
        15, 244, 251
    Mexican Revolution 17, 18,
        104, 143, 173
    Mexican War of
        Independence 15
    missions 13-15
    pre-Columbian era 11, 12-13
    statehood 17
hitchhiking 100-101

horseback & muleback travel 101
horseback riding 80, 101, 134, 293
horseracing 74
hostels. See accommodations
hot springs 186-187, 274

Iglesia Santa Bárbara 223, 225
illegal border-crossing 19, 32,
    105, 124
Imperial Valley 171, 188
indigenous peoples 11, 12-13, 34.
    See also specific tribe
insurance
    car & other vehicle 67, 91-92,
        96-97
    health & travel 55-56
    legal 67
International Company of
    Mexico 15-16, 142, 165
Internet resources on Baja
    304-306
Isla Angel de la Guarda 21, 205
Isla Cedros 213-215, **214**
Isla Cerralvo 259, 267
Isla Coronado 204, 239, 242
Isla de las Focas 259
Isla del Carmen 239
Isla Espíritu Santo 266
Isla Magdalena 245, 248
Isla Natividad 79, 213
Isla Pelícanos 221
Isla San José 266
Isla San Marcos 227
Isla San Martín 163
Islas de Todos Santos 79, 152
Islas San Benito 40, 215, **214**

jai alai 74, 112, 120
Juárez, Benito 15, 244

kayaking 78-79, 153, 204-205,
    233-234, 239, 260, 280
Kino, Eusebio 13

La Base 221
La Bufadora 40, 153 154
La Costilla 197
La Fonda 138
La Fridera 221
La Frontera 15, 102-170, **103**
La Grulla 162
La Laguna 221
La Misión 138
La Paz 251-266, 276,
    254-255, 258
    accommodations 260-262
    beaches 266

getting around 265-266
getting there & away 264-265
history 15, 251, 276
information 253-257
orientation 251-253
restaurants 262-263
things to see 257-259
La Purísima 234-235
La Rivera 271-272
La Rumorosa 130
La Ventana 267
Laguna Chapala 201
Laguna Diablo 162
Laguna Hanson 30, 155
Laguna Ojo de Liebre 207, 208,
    211, 220
Laguna Salada 185-186
Laguna San Ignacio 208,
    220-221
language 38, 69-73, 79, 307-311
language courses 68, 146, 260
Las Paredes 197
laundry 55
legal matters 67
literature 35
Llano de Magdalena 244-250,
    199, 222
Llano de San Quintín 163
Loreto 31, 236-242, **237**
Los Algodones 187-188
Los Barriles 80, 268-271
Los Cabos corridor 284-286, **285**
Los Islotes 259
Lower California Company
    15, 244

machismo 37
Magonistas 17, 104, 142-143, 173
mail 48
Maneadero 157
maps 39
maquiladoras 19, 32-33, 102,
    104, 126
Mexicali 104, 171-185,
    174-175, 178
    accommodations 180
    border crossings 175-176
    Centro Cívico-Comercial 179
    getting around 185
    getting there & away 183-185
    historic buildings 179
    history 16-17, 171-173
    information 175-177
    La Chinesca 177
    orientation 173-175
    restaurants 181-182
    things to see 177-179

Mexican-American War
15, 244, 251
Mexican Land & Colonization
Company 165
Mexican Revolution 17, 18, 104,
143, 173
Mexican War of Independence 15
Midriff Islands 78, 223
Mike's Sky Rancho 162
military 19, 65-66
military checkpoints 65-66,
157, 206
minors. See children, travel with
Miraflores 274
Misión Calamajué 201
Misión del Descanso 137
Misión Dolores del Sur 250
Misión Guadalupe 232
Misión La Pasión 250, 267
Misión La Purísima
Concepción 234
Misión Nuestra Señora de
Guadalupe 142, 154
Misión Nuestra Señora de
Loreto 13, 236, 238-239
Misión Nuestra Señora del
Rosario 169
Misión San Borja 202, 206
Misión San Diego 102
Misión San Fernando 198-199
Misión San Francisco Javier 242
Misión San Ignacio 13, 213, 216
Misión San José de Comondú.
See Templo Misional de San
José de Comondú
Misión San Luis Gonzaga 244,
249, 267
Misión San Miguel 137
Misión San Miguel de la
Frontera 138
Misión San Pedro Mártir
162, 189
Misión San Vicente 158
Misión Santa Catalina 156-157
Misión Santa Gertrudis 212
Misión Santa María 201
Misión Santa Rosa de Todos Los
Santos 298
Misión Santa Rosalía 229
Misión Santo Domingo 162-163
Misión Santo Tomás 142,
157-158
missions, history of 13-15, 104,
142, **14**
Mitlán 205
money. See ATMs;
bargaining;

changing money; costs; credit
cards; currency; currency
exchange; discounts, student;
taxes; tipping; traveler's
checks
motorcycle travel 100
mountain biking. See bicycling
Mt Cuchumá 129
Mulegé 227-232, **228**, **233**
music 34-35

national parks & reserves 30-31.
See also individual park/
reserve listings
nationalism 37
natural hazards 66-67, 78
newspapers & magazines 53-54
nightclubs 74
Nopoló 40, 236, 242-243
North American Free Trade
Agreement 18, 28, 32-33, 104

Observatorio Astronómico
Nacional 161
Ojos Negros 156
Olachea Avilés, Agustín 246, 299
outdoor activities 78-86.
See also individual activity
listings

Palo Escopeta 273
Paralelo 28 206-207
Parque Marino Nacional Bahía
de Loreto 31, 236, 242
Parque Marino Nacional Cabo
Pulmo 31, 268, 272
Parque Nacional Constitución de
1857 30, 155-156, 186, **156**
Parque Nacional Sierra San
Pedro Mártir 30, 160-162,
189, **160**
Parque Natural de la
Ballena Gris. See Reserva
de la Biosfera
El Vizcaíno
Partido de Acción Nacional 31
Partido Institucional
Revolucionario 18, 31, 65
Paso Hondo 235
Península Pichilingue 266
Península Vizcaíno 21, 215-216
Pescadero 298
pet permit 44-45
photography 54
Picacho del Diablo 21, 30,
161, 189
Pichilingue 251

pirates 12, 251, 253, 275
planning 39-40
plants. See flora
Playa El Faro 152
Playa Las Cabrillas 303
Playa Los Cerritos 303
Playa Migriño 303
Playa Palmilla 284
Playa San Pedrito 303
Playa Tortuga 284
Playas de Rosarito 131-137, **133**
police 65-66
police checkpoints 238
population & people 33-34
Porfiriato 15
Pozo Alemán 212
Prohibition era 17, 105, 143
Protestantism 38
public holidays 67-68
Pueblo La Playa 277
Puertecitos 196-197, 201
Puertecitos-Laguna Chapala
Road 40
Puerto Chale 250
Puerto Escondido 243-244
Puerto López Mateos 245
Puerto Nuevo 137
Puerto San Carlos 248-249
Puerto San Isidro 158
Punta Abreojos 220
Punta Baja 170
Punta Banda 153
Punta Bufeo 197
Punta Chivato 227
Punta Colorada 272
Punta Concepción 230, 233
Punta Conejo 250
Punta La Gringa 204
Punta Lobos 303
Punta Márquez 250
Punta Mesquite 138
Punta Minitas 11
Punta Pequeña 235
Punta Pescadero 271
Punta Prieta 230
Punta Remedios 205
Punta Rosarito 206
Punta Salsipuedes 138
Punta San Carlos 170
Punta Santa Rosalillita 206

radio 54
railroads, history of 186-187,
187
Rancho Boca del Alamo 271
Rancho El Caporal 249
Rancho El Güerigo 274

Rancho El Progreso 198
Rancho Grande 197, 201
Rancho Iraquí 249
Rancho La Palmilla 249
Rancho La Puerta 129
Rancho La Trinidad 232
Rancho La Vinorama 273
Rancho Las Animas 250, 267
Rancho Las Arrastras de
    Arriola 201
Rancho Las Parras 242
Rancho Las Tinajitas 249
Rancho Los Ciruelos 250
Rancho Meling 159-160
Rancho Pozo de Iritú 249
Rancho Santa Clara 162
Rancho Santa Cruz 162
Rancho Santa Martha 220
Rancho Santo Domingo 274
Rancho Soledad 250, 267
Rancho Tecate Resort &
    Country Club 129
Rancho Viejo 242
Real del Castillo 189
religion. See Catholicism;
    missions, history of;
    Protestantism
Reserva de la Biosfera Alto
    Golfo y Delta del Río
    Colorado 30
Reserva de la Biosfera
    El Vizcaíno 30, 208, 211,
    218, 220
Reserva de la Biosfera Islas
    del Golfo 30
Reserva de la Biosfera Sierra
    de la Laguna 31
Río Colorado 171-173
Río Nuevo 173
rock art 11, 40, 198-199,
    217-220, 232, 235
rock climbing 155, 161, 234, 272
rodeos 74-76, 119-120
Rosarito 206. See also Playas de
    Rosarito

safety 64-67. See also crime;
    natural hazards
sailing. See boat travel; boat
    trips
Salinas de Gortari, Carlos 18,
    33, 47
Salton Sea 173, 188
saltworks 209, 220
Salvatierra, Juan María 13, 236
San Antonio 268

San Antonio del Mar 159
San Borja 40, 206
San Bruno 227
San Estanislao 232
San Evaristo 41, 250, 266-267
San Felipe 40, 188-196, **191**
    accommodations 193-195
    getting around 196
    getting there & away 196
    history 189
    information 189-190
    orientation 189
    restaurants 195
San Francisco de la Sierra
    40, 217-219
San Ignacio 21, 216-217
San Isidro 234-235
San Jacinto 298
San Javier 242
San José de Comondú 235
San José del Cabo 22, 275-284,
    278-279
    accommodations 280-281
    getting around 284
    getting there & away 283-284
    history 275
    information 277
    orientation 275-277
    restaurants 281-282
    things to see 277
San Juan de la Costa 266
San Juan de los Planes 267
San Juan del Aserradero 274
San Juanico 221, 235-236
San Miguel 139
San Miguel de Comondú 235
San Quintín 163-169, **164**
San Simón 165
San Telmo 159
San Vicente 158-159
Santa Catalina 157
Santa Cruz de los Zacatitos 284
Santa Inés Islands 230
Santa María 165
Santa María Toris 250
Santa Rita 250
Santa Rosalía 22, 41, 221,
    223-227, **224**
Santa Rosalillita 206
Santiago 273
Santo Tomás 157-158
Scammon, Charles Melville 208
Scammon's Lagoon.
    See Laguna Ojo de Liebre
scuba diving. See diving
seals 215

Serra, Junípero 13, 198, 236
Shipwreck Beach 284
shopping 76-77
Sierra Azteca 227
Sierra de Juárez 21, 30, 155-156
Sierra de la Giganta 21, 198,
    227, 234, 242, 267
Sierra de la Laguna 21, 31, 41,
    273-274
Sierra de San Francisco 18, 40,
    217-219
Sierra La Asamblea 21
Sierra San Pedro Mártir 21, 30,
    160-162
Sierra Santa María 215
snorkeling 239, 242, 259
soccer 76
society & conduct 36-37
Spanglish 38
special events 68
sportfishing. See fishing
sports. See individual sports and
    activity listings
study programs & expeditions
    80-81
surfing 79-80, 152, 167, 206,
    235, 280, 284-285

taxes
    departure 93
    hotel 47
taxis 92, 101
Tecate 40, 124-129, **125**
telegraph 49
telephones 48-49
Templo Misional de San José de
    Comondú 235
tennis 80, 279
theater 35-36
Tijuana 22, 102-124, **106**,
    110-111
    accommodations 115-117
    border crossings 108
    Centro Cultural Tijuana 114
    city monuments 114
    Frontón Palacio Jai Alai 112
    getting around 123-124
    getting there & away 121-123
    history 17, 102-107
    information 108-112
    La Revo 112
    orientation 107-108
    restaurants 117-118
    things to see 112-114
    toll road to Ensenada
    130-131

Tijuana-Ensenada corridor
    130-131, **130**
time 55, 206
time-shares 287
tipping 47
Todos Santos 41, 298-303,
    299
toll roads 130-131
tour companies 82-86
    specialties 81-82
    website addresses 305-306
tourist cards 42-43, 91, 132, 144,
    175, 256
tourist offices 41-42
    local tourist offices 41
    tourist offices abroad 41-42
tourist publications 42
tourist traps 40
tours, organized 81-86

train travel
    to/from mainland Mexico 92
    to/from the USA 91
traveler's checks 46-47
trolley travel 90-91
tropic of Cancer 273
turtles 28-30, 203-204
TV 54

Valle de los Médanos 137
Valle de Mexicali 171, 185
Valle de Trinidad 156-157
Villa Jesús María 200
Virgin of Guadalupe 38
visas 42
visual arts 36
Vizcaíno 215
Vizcaíno, Sebastián 12, 142,
    244, 251

Walker, William 15, 251, 276
walking 101
weights & measures 55
whales 27, 80, 208, 211,
    220-221, 245
whale-watching 80, 146, 209,
    211, 220-221, 245, 248, 260,
    293. *See also* tours,
    organized
windsurfing 80, 170,
    268-269
wineries 113, 145, 155
women travelers 64
    machismo 37
    women's health 64
work 69

Yuma 188

Zedillo, Ernesto 31, 46, 65

SIDEBARS

Angler's Glossary 79
Border Spanish 38
Corridas de Toros 75
The Dutch in the Pacific 253
Eiffel beyond the
    Tower 223
The Ejido & Its Future 18
Endangered Species 24-25

I'd Love a Cabo Time-Share,
    But . . . 287
Jai Alai 120
La Frontera 104-105
The Militarization of Mexico 65
Pass the Salt, Please 220
Phone Home or Fly Home? 49
Rails across the Border 186-187

Rock Art of the
    Desierto Central 218
Scammon & the Whales 208
Tourist Traps 40
Tracking the Turtle 28-29
Travelers with Special Needs 87
William Walker &
    the Cape 276

LONELY PLANET JOURNEYS

JOURNEYS is a unique collection of travel writing – published by the company that understands travel better than anyone else. It is a series for anyone who has ever experienced – or dreamed of – the magical moment when they encountered a strange culture or saw a place for the first time. They are tales to read while you're planning a trip, while you're on the road or while you're in an armchair, in front of a fire.

JOURNEYS books catch the spirit of a place, illuminate a culture, recount a crazy adventure, or introduce a fascinating way of life. They will always entertain, and always enrich the experience of travel.

'Idiosyncratic, entertainingly diverse and unexpected . . . from an international writership'

– The Australian

'Books which offer a closer look at the people and culture of a destination, and enrich travel experiences'
– American Bookseller

FULL CIRCLE
A South American Journey
Luis Sepúlveda

(translated by Chris Andrews)

Full Circle invites us to accompany Chilean writer Luis Sepúlveda on 'a journey without a fixed itinerary'. Whatever his subject - brutalities suffered under Pinochet's dictatorship, sleepy tropical towns visited in exile, or the landscapes of legendary Patagonia - Sepúlveda is an unflinchingly honest yet lyrical storyteller. Extravagant characters and extraordinary situations are memorably evoked: gauchos organizing a tournament of lies, a scheming heiress on the lookout for a husband, a pilot with a corpse on board his plane . . . Part autobiography, part travel memoir, *Full Circle* brings us the distinctive voice of one of South America's most compelling writers.

Luis Sepúlveda was born in Chile in 1949. Imprisoned by the Pinochet dictatorship for his socialist beliefs, he was for many years a political exile. He has written novels, short stories, plays and essays. His work has attracted many awards and has been translated into numerous languages.

'Detachment, humor and vibrant prose' **– El País**

'an absolute cracker' **– The Bookseller**

This project has been assisted by the Commonwealth Government through the Australian Council, its arts funding and advisory body.

LONELY PLANET PHRASEBOOKS

Building bridges,
Breaking barriers,
Beyond babble-on

Listen for the gems

Speak your own words

Ask your own questions

Master of your own image

- handy pocket-sized books
- easy to understand Pronunciation chapter
- clear and comprehensive Grammar chapter
- romanisation alongside script to allow ease of pronunciation
- script throughout so users can point to phrases
- extensive vocabulary sections, words and phrases for every situation
- full of cultural information and tips for the traveller

'...*vital for a real DIY spirit and attitude in language learning*' – **Backpacker**

'*the phrasebooks have good cultural backgrounders and offer solid advice for challenging situations in remote locations*' – San Francisco Examiner

'...*they are unbeatable for their coverage of the world's more obscure languages*' – The Geographical Magazine

---

Arabic (Egyptian)
Arabic (Moroccan)
Australia
  *Australian English, Aboriginal and
  Torres Strait languages*
Baltic States
  Estonian, Latvian, Lithuanian
Bengali
Brazilian
Burmese
Cantonese
Central Asia
Central Europe
  *Czech, French, German, Hungarian,
  Italian and Slovak*
Eastern Europe
  *Bulgarian, Czech, Hungarian, Polish,
  Romanian and Slovak*
Ethiopian (Amharic)
Fijian
French
German
Greek

Hindi/Urdu
Indonesian
Italian
Japanese
Korean
Lao
Latin American Spanish
Malay
Mandarin
Mediterranean Europe
  *Albanian, Croatian, Greek,
  Italian, Macedonian, Maltese,
  Serbian and Slovene*
Mongolian
Nepali
Papua New Guinea
Pilipino (Tagalog)
Quechua
Russian
Scandinavian Europe
  *Danish, Finnish, Icelandic, Norwegian
  and Swedish*

South-East Asia
  *Burmese, Indonesian, Khmer, Lao,
  Malay, Tagalog (Pilipino), Thai and
  Vietnamese*
Spanish (Castilian)
  Basque, Catalan and Galician
Sri Lanka
Swahili
Thai
Thai Hill Tribes
Tibetan
Turkish
Ukrainian
USA
  *US English, Vernacular,
  Native American languages and
  Hawaiian*
Vietnamese
Western Europe
  *Basque, Catalan, Dutch, French,
  German, Irish, Italian, Portuguese,
  Scottish Gaelic, Spanish (Castilian)
  and Welsh*

LONELY PLANET TRAVEL ATLASES

Lonely Planet has long been famous for the number and quality of its guidebook maps. Now we've gone one step further and produced a handy companion series: Lonely Planet travel atlases – maps of a country produced in book form.

Unlike other maps, which look good but lead travellers astray, our travel atlases have been researched on the road by Lonely Planet's experienced team of writers. All details are carefully checked to ensure the atlas corresponds with the equivalent Lonely Planet guidebook.

The handy atlas format means no holes, wrinkles, torn sections or constant folding and unfolding. These atlases can survive long periods on the road, unlike cumbersome fold-out maps. The comprehensive index ensures easy reference.

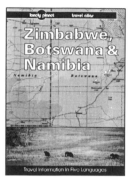

- full-colour throughout
- maps researched and checked by Lonely Planet authors
- place names correspond with Lonely Planet guidebooks
  – no confusing spelling differences
- legend and travelling information in English, French, German, Japanese and Spanish
- size: 230 x 160 mm

Available now:
Chile & Easter Island • Egypt • India & Bangladesh • Israel & the Palestinian Territories •Jordan, Syria & Lebanon • Kenya • Laos • Portugal • South Africa, Lesotho & Swaziland • Thailand • Turkey • Vietnam • Zimbabwe, Botswana & Namibia

---

LONELY PLANET TV SERIES & VIDEOS

Lonely Planet travel guides have been brought to life on television screens around the world. Like our guides, the programmes are based on the joy of independent travel, and look honestly at some of the most exciting, picturesque and frustrating places in the world. Each show is presented by one of three travellers from Australia, England or the USA and combines an innovative mixture of video, Super-8 film, atmospheric soundscapes and original music.

Videos of each episode – containing additional footage not shown on television – are available from good book and video shops, but the availability of individual videos varies with regional screening schedules.

Video destinations include: Alaska • American Rockies • Australia – The South-East • Baja California & the Copper Canyon • Brazil • Central Asia • Chile & Easter Island • Corsica, Sicily & Sardinia – The Mediterranean Islands • East Africa (Tanzania & Zanzibar) • Ecuador & the Galapagos Islands • Greenland & Iceland • Indonesia • Israel & the Sinai Desert • Jamaica • Japan • La Ruta Maya • Morocco • New York • North India • Pacific Islands (Fiji, Solomon Islands & Vanuatu) • South India • South West China • Turkey • Vietnam • West Africa • Zimbabwe, Botswana & Namibia

The Lonely Planet TV series is produced by:
Pilot Productions
The Old Studio
18 Middle Row
London W10 5AT UK

For video availability and ordering information contact your nearest Lonely Planet office.

Music from the TV series is available on CD & cassette.

PLANET TALK

Lonely Planet's FREE quarterly newsletter

We love hearing from you and think you'd like to hear from us.
When... is the right time to see reindeer in Finland?
Where... can you hear the best palm-wine music in Ghana?
How... do you get from Asunción to Areguá by steam train?
What... is the best way to see India?

For the answer to these and many other questions read PLANET TALK.

Every issue is packed with up-to-date travel news and advice including:

* a letter from Lonely Planet founders Tony and Maureen Wheeler
* travel diary from a Lonely Planet author–find out what it's really like out on the road
* feature article on an important and topical travel issue
* a selection of recent letters from our readers
* the latest travel news from all over the world
* details on Lonely Planet's new and forthcoming releases

To join our mailing list contact any Lonely Planet office .

Also available: Lonely Planet T-shirts. 100% heavyweight cotton (S, M, L, XL)

LONELY PLANET ONLINE

Get the latest travel information before you leave or while you're on the road

Whether you've just begun planning your next trip, or you're chasing down specific info on currency regulations or visa requirements, check out Lonely Planet Online for up-to-the-minute travel information.

As well as travel profiles of your favorite destinations (including maps and photos), you'll find current reports from our researchers and other travelers, updates on health and visas, travel advisories, and discussion of the ecological and political issues you need to be aware of as you travel.

There's also an online travelers' forum where you can share your experience of life on the road, meet travel companions and ask other travelers for their recommendations and advice. We also have plenty of links to other online sites useful to independent travelers.

And of course we have a complete and up-to-date list of all Lonely Planet travel products including guides, phrasebooks, atlases, Journeys and videos and a simple online ordering facility if you can't find the book you want elsewhere.

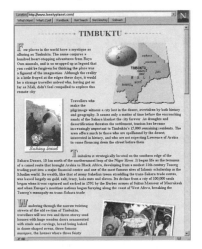

www.lonelyplanet.com or AOL keyword: lp

LONELY PLANET PRODUCTS

Lonely Planet is known worldwide for publishing practical, reliable and no-nonsense travel information in our guides and on our web site. The Lonely Planet list covers just about every accessible part of the world. Currently there are nine series: *travel guides, shoestring guides, walking guides, city guides, phrasebooks, audio packs, travel atlases, Journeys – a unique collection of travel writing and Pisces Books - diving and snorkeling guides.*

EUROPE

Amsterdam • Andalucia • Austria • Baltic States phrasebook • Berlin • Britain • Canary Islands• Central Europe on a shoestring • Central Europe phrasebook • Czech & Slovak Republics • Denmark • Dublin • Eastern Europe on a shoestring • Eastern Europe phrasebook • Estonia, Latvia & Lithuania • Finland • France • French phrasebook • Germany • German phrasebook • Greece • Greek phrasebook • Hungary • Iceland, Greenland & the Faroe Islands • Ireland • Italian phrasebook • Italy • Lisbon • London • Mediterranean Europe on a shoestring • Mediterranean Europe phrasebook • Paris • Poland • Portugal • Portugal travel atlas • Prague • Romania & Moldova • Russia, Ukraine & Belarus • Russian phrasebook • Scandinavian & Baltic Europe on a shoestring • Scandinavian Europe phrasebook • Slovenia • Spain • Spanish phrasebook • St Petersburg • Switzerland •Trekking in Spain • Ukrainian phrasebook • Vienna • Walking in Britain • Walking in Italy • Walking in Switzerland • Western Europe on a shoestring • Western Europe phrasebook

Travel Literature: The Olive Grove: Travels in Greece

NORTH AMERICA

Alaska • Backpacking in Alaska • Baja California • California & Nevada • Canada • Chicago • Deep South• Florida • Hawaii • Honolulu • Los Angeles • Mexico • Mexico City • Miami • New England • New Orleans • New York City • New York, New Jersey & Pennsylvania • Pacific Northwest USA • Rocky Mountain States • San Francisco • Seattle • Southwest USA • USA phrasebook • Washington, DC & the Capital Region

Travel Literature: Drive thru America

CENTRAL AMERICA & THE CARIBBEAN

• Bahamas and Turks & Caicos • Bermuda • Central America on a shoestring • Costa Rica • Cuba • Eastern Caribbean • Guatemala, Belize & Yucatán: La Ruta Maya • Jamaica

Travel Literature Green Dreams: Travels in Central America

SOUTH AMERICA

Argentina, Uruguay & Paraguay • Bolivia • Brazil • Brazilian phrasebook • Buenos Aires • Chile & Easter Island • Chile & Easter Island travel atlas • Colombia Ecuador & the Galápagos Islands • Latin American Spanish phrasebook • Peru • Quechua phrasebook • Rio de Janeiro • South America on a shoestring • Trekking in the Patagonian Andes • Venezuela

Travel Literature: Full Circle: A South American Journey

ISLANDS OF THE INDIAN OCEAN

Madagascar & Comoros • Maldives • Mauritius, Réunion & Seychelles

AFRICA

Africa - the South • Africa on a shoestring • Arabic (Moroccan) phrasebook • Cairo • Cape Town • Central Africa • East Africa • Egypt • Egypt travel atlas• Ethiopian (Amharic) phrasebook • The Gambia & Senegal • Kenya • Kenya travel atlas • Malawi, Mozambique & Zambia • Morocco • North Africa • South Africa, Lesotho & Swaziland • South Africa, Lesotho & Swaziland travel atlas • Swahili phrasebook • Tunisia • Trekking in East Africa • West Africa • Zimbabwe, Botswana & Namibia • Zimbabwe, Botswana & Namibia travel atlas

Travel Literature: Mali Blues • The Rainbird: A Central African Journey • Songs to an African Sunset: A Zimbabwean Story

MAIL ORDER

Lonely Planet products are distributed worldwide. They are also available by mail order from Lonely Planet, so if you have difficulty finding a title please write to us. North American and South American residents should write to 150 Linden St, Oakland CA 94607, USA; European and African residents should write to 10a Spring Place, London NW5 3BH; and residents of other countries to PO Box 617, Hawthorn, Victoria 3122, Australia.

NORTH-EAST ASIA

Beijing • Cantonese phrasebook • China • Hong Kong • Hong Kong, Macau & Guangzhou • Japan • Japanese phrasebook • Japanese audio pack • Korea • Korean phrasebook • Kyoto • Mandarin phrasebook • Mongolia • Mongolian phrasebook • North-East Asia on a shoestring • Seoul • Taiwan • Tibet • Tibet phrasebook • Tokyo
Travel Literature: Lost Japan

MIDDLE EAST & CENTRAL ASIA

Arab Gulf States • Arabic (Egyptian) phrasebook • Central Asia • Central Asia phrasebook • Iran • Israel & the Palestinian Territories • Israel & the Palestinian Territories travel atlas • Istanbul • Jerusalem • Jordan & Syria • Jordan, Syria & Lebanon travel atlas • Lebanon • Middle East • Turkey • Turkish phrasebook • Turkey travel atlas • Yemen
Travel Literature: The Gates of Damascus • Kingdom of the Film Stars: Journey into Jordan

ALSO AVAILABLE:

Brief Encounters • Travel with Children • Traveller's Tales• Not the Only Planet

INDIAN SUBCONTINENT

Bangladesh • Bengali phrasebook • Bhutan • Delhi • Goa • Hindi/Urdu phrasebook • India • India & Bangladesh travel atlas • Indian Himalaya • Karakoram Highway • Nepal • Nepali phrasebook • Pakistan • Rajasthan • South India • Sri Lanka • Sri Lanka phrasebook • Trekking in the Indian Himalaya • Trekking in the Karakoram & Hindukush • Trekking in the Nepal Himalaya
Travel Literature: In Rajasthan • Shopping for Buddhas

SOUTH-EAST ASIA

Bali & Lombok • Bangkok • Burmese phrasebook • Cambodia • Ho Chi Minh City • Indonesia • Indonesian phrasebook • Indonesian audio pack • Indonesia's Eastern Islands • Jakarta • Java • Laos • Lao phrasebook • Laos travel atlas • Malay phrasebook • Malaysia, Singapore & Brunei • Myanmar (Burma) • Philippines • Pilipino phrasebook • Singapore • South-East Asia on a shoestring • South-East Asia phrasebook • South-West China • Thailand • Thailand's Islands & Beaches • Thailand travel atlas • Thai phrasebook • Thai audio pack • Thai Hill Tribes phrasebook • Vietnam • Vietnamese phrasebook • Vietnam travel atlas

AUSTRALIA & THE PACIFIC

Australia • Australian phrasebook • Bushwalking in Australia • Bushwalking in Papua New Guinea • Fiji • Fijian phrasebook • Islands of Australia's Great Barrier Reef • Melbourne • Micronesia • New Caledonia • New South Wales • New Zealand • Northern Territory • Outback Australia • Papua New Guinea • Papua New Guinea phrasebook • Queensland • Rarotonga & the Cook Islands • Samoa • Solomon Islands • South Australia • Sydney • Tahiti & French Polynesia • Tasmania • Tonga • Tramping in New Zealand • Vanuatu • Victoria • Western Australia
Travel Literature: Islands in the Clouds • Sean & David's Long Drive

ANTARCTICA

Antarctica

THE LONELY PLANET STORY

Lonely Planet published its first book in 1973 in response to the numerous 'How did you do it?' questions Maureen and Tony Wheeler were asked after driving, busing, hitching, sailing and railing their way from England to Australia.

Written at a kitchen table and hand collated, trimmed and stapled, *Across Asia on the Cheap* became an instant local bestseller, inspiring thoughts of another book.

Eighteen months in South-East Asia resulted in their second guide, *South-East Asia on a shoestring*, which they put together in a backstreet Chinese hotel in Singapore in 1975. The 'yellow bible', as it quickly became known to backpackers around the world, soon became *the* guide to the region. It has sold well over half a million copies and is now in its 9th edition, still retaining its familiar yellow cover.

Today there are over 350 titles, including travel guides, walking guides, language kits & phrasebooks, travel atlases and travel literature. The company is the largest independent travel publisher in the world. Although Lonely Planet initially specialised in guides to Asia, today there are few corners of the globe that have not been covered.

The emphasis continues to be on travel for independent travellers. Tony and Maureen still travel for several months of each year and play an active part in the writing, updating and quality control of Lonely Planet's guides.

They have been joined by over 80 authors and 200 staff at our offices in Melbourne (Australia), Oakland (USA), London (UK) and Paris (France). Travellers themselves also make a valuable contribution to the guides through the feedback we receive in thousands of letters each year and on our web site.

The people at Lonely Planet strongly believe that travellers can make a positive contribution to the countries they visit, both through their appreciation of the countries' culture, wildlife and natural features, and through the money they spend. In addition, the company makes a direct contribution to the countries and regions it covers. Since 1986 a percentage of the income from each book has been donated to ventures such as famine relief in Africa; aid projects in India; agricultural projects in Central America; Greenpeace's efforts to halt French nuclear testing in the Pacific; and Amnesty International.

'I hope we send people out with the right attitude about travel. You realise when you travel that there are so many different perspectives about the world, so we hope these books will make people more interested in what they see. Guidebooks can't really guide people. All you can do is point them in the right direction.'

– **Tony Wheeler**

LONELY PLANET PUBLICATIONS

Australia
PO Box 617, Hawthorn 3122, Victoria
tel: (03) 9819 1877 fax: (03) 9819 6459
e-mail: talk2us@lonelyplanet.com.au

USA
150 Linden St
Oakland, CA 94607
tel: (510) 893 8555 TOLL FREE: 800 275-8555
fax: (510) 893 8572
e-mail: info@lonelyplanet.com

UK
10a Spring Place,
London NW5 3BH
tel: (0171) 428 4800 fax: (0171) 428 4828
e-mail: go@lonelyplanet.co.uk

France:
1 rue du Dahomey, 75011 Paris
tel: 01 55 25 33 00 fax: 01 55 25 33 01
e-mail: bip@lonelyplanet.fr

World Wide Web: http://www.lonelyplanet.com
or *AOL keyword: lp*